The Epistles
to the COLOSSIANS,
to PHILEMON,
and to the EPHESIANS

by

F. F. BRUCE

WILLIAM B. EERDMANS PUBLISHING COMPANY
GRAND RAPIDS, MICHIGAN

© 1984 Wm. B. Eerdmans Publishing Co.
2140 Oak Industrial Drive N.E., Grand Rapids, Michigan 49505 /
P.O. Box 163, Cambridge CB3 9PU U.K.

Printed in the United States of America

12 11 10 09 08   17 16 15 14 13

Library of Congress Cataloging-in-Publication Data

Bruce, F. F. (Frederick Fyvie), 1910-1990
The epistles to the Colossians, to Philemon, and to the Ephesians.
(The New International Commentary on the New Testament)
Bibliography: p. xix
Includes indexes.
1. Bible. N.T. Colossians — Commentaries. 2. Bible. N.T. Philemon — Commentaries.
3. Bible. N.T. Ephesians — Commentaries. I. Title. II. Series.
BS2650.3.B78   1984   227   84-13785
ISBN 978-0-8028-2510-0

www.eerdmans.com

TO
ROBBIE and JEAN ORR

CONTENTS

EDITOR'S PREFACE

In carrying out their policy of keeping the volumes of the New International Commentary up to date, the publishers and editor realize that, without such a policy, the adjective "new" as a description of the series would soon become absurdly irrelevant. As far as possible, they have preferred to entrust the revision of the earlier volumes to their original writers. Sadly, however, the death of some of those writers has made it necessary for others to undertake the revision or replacement of their contributions.

The commentary on Philippians and Philemon, which was published in 1955, was written by Professor Jacobus J. Müller of Stellenbosch, who died in 1977. When another scholar was invited to write a new commentary on Philippians, taking up a full volume by itself, it was decided to detach Philemon from Philippians and include it along with Colossians and Ephesians. There was indeed a notable precedent for presenting commentaries on Philippians and Philemon in one volume, by one author: that was Marvin R. Vincent's work on these two epistles in the International Critical Commentary (1897). But there are even better precedents for linking Philemon with Colossians: one need look no farther than Lightfoot's volume (1875).

The exposition of Ephesians by the veteran scholar E. K. Simpson (who died at an advanced age in 1961) was a work of literary distinction, well worthy of preservation in its own right; but it never fitted easily into the general pattern of the New International Commentary. It appeared in 1957, sharing one volume with a commentary on Colossians by the present general editor. When the time came to revise the commentary on Colossians, the writer of that commentary arranged, after completing the revision, to write new companion commentaries on Philemon and Ephesians. All three commentaries are now presented to the reader in this volume.

F. F. BRUCE

ix

AUTHOR'S PREFACE

When, in 1954, my volume on Acts in the New International Commentary on the New Testament was published, the general editor of the series, the late Professor Ned B. Stonehouse, invited me to follow it up with a commentary on Colossians. Several years before, he had received from Mr. E. K. Simpson the manuscript of his commentary on Ephesians. The plan of the series called for Ephesians and Colossians to be treated within the limits of one volume. Mainly because of his failing eyesight, Mr. Simpson was unable to accept an invitation to add a commentary on Colossians to what he had written on Ephesians; therefore, when I had completed my assignment on Acts, Dr. Stonehouse persuaded me to begin work on Colossians.

Colossians was the first Pauline epistle on which I ever wrote a commentary. Without an intensive study of the earlier Pauline epistles, I was singularly unequipped to tackle Colossians—much more unequipped than I could realize at that time. Today, when I have written commentaries on all the Pauline epistles except the Pastorals, I hope I understand better what is involved in the interpretation of Colossians. The revision of my commentary on this epistle ought to show a more adequate appreciation of the place of Colossians in relation to the main emphases of Paul's teaching.

On the appropriateness of attaching the commentary on Philemon in this (or any) series closely to that on Colossians nothing need be added to what has been said in the editorial preface. But I have welcomed the opportunity to expound Ephesians along with Colossians. The study of the two documents together has confirmed me in the belief that Ephesians continues the line of thought followed in Colossians—in particular because it draws out the implications of Christ's cosmic role (set forth in Colossians) for the church, which is his body. At the same time it constitutes the crown of Paulinism, gathering up the main themes of the apostle's teaching into a unified presentation *sub specie aeternitatis*.

In the first edition of the New International Commentary the English text on which the exposition was based was the American Standard Version of 1901. For this edition I have offered a translation of my own. If it is found to have much in common with the older versions principally in use, I shall not be surprised.

In the course of the exposition and notes I have acknowledged those works which I have found most useful in this study. I have sometimes learned most from scholars with whom I have agreed least: they compel one to think, and rethink.

One last thing I should say: in 1961 I produced a verse-by-verse exposition of *The Epistle to the Ephesians* (published by Pickering & Inglis of London and Glasgow). The commentary on Ephesians in this volume is in no way a revision of that earlier work: that remains an independent exposition in its own right, organized on a different pattern from the present commentary and designed for a different reading public.

December 1983   F. F. BRUCE

ABBREVIATIONS

AB	Anchor Bible
ad loc.	*ad locum*, at the place or text mentioned
AnBib	Analecta Biblica
ANS	Auslegung Neutestamentlicher Schriften
Ant.	*Antiquities* (Josephus)
ARSHLL	Acta Regiae Societatis Humaniorum Litterarum Lundensis
ARV/ASV	American Revised Version/American Standard Version (1901)
Asc. Isa.	*Ascension of Isaiah*
ASNU	Acta seminarii neotestamentici Upsaliensis
ATANT	Abhandlungen zur Theologie des Alten und Neuen Testaments
ATR	*Anglican Theological Review*
Att.	*Letters to Atticus* (Cicero)
AUL	Acta Universitatis Lundensis
BAG	W. Bauer–W. F. Arndt–F. W. Gingrich, *Greek-English Lexicon of the New Testament*...(Chicago: University of Chicago Press, 1957).
BBC	*Broadman Bible Commentary*
BGBE	Beiträge zur Geschichte der biblischen Exegese
BGU	Aegyptische Urkunden aus den Museen zu Berlin: Griechische Urkunden
BHT	Beiträge zur historischen Theologie
BJ	Bible de Jérusalem
BJ	*De Bello Judaico (Jewish War*, Josephus)
BJRL	*Bulletin of the John Rylands (University) Library*
BST	The Bible Speaks Today
BZ	*Biblische Zeitschrift*
BZAW	Beiheft zur *Zeitschrift für die alttestamentliche Wissenschaft*

ABBREVIATIONS

CB	Coniectanea Biblica
CBC	Cambridge Bible Commentary (on New English Bible)
CBQ	*Catholic Biblical Quarterly*
CD	(Book of) Covenant of Damascus
CGTC	Cambridge Greek Testament Commentary
C.H.	*Corpus Hermeticum*
CIG	*Corpus Inscriptionum Graecarum*
CIJ	*Corpus Inscriptionum Judaicarum*
CIL	*Corpus Inscriptionum Latinarum*
Clem. Hom.	*Clementine Homilies*
CNT	Commentaire du Nouveau Testament
DBSupp	*Dictionnaire de la Bible: Supplément*
Dial.	*Dialogue with Trypho* (Justin)
Diss.	*Dissertationes* (Epictetus)
EGT	*Expositor's Greek Testament*
EKKNT	Evangelisch-Katholischer Kommentar zum Neuen Testament
Enc. Bib.	*Encylopaedia Biblica*
EPC	Epworth Preachers' Commentaries
Ep. Barn.	*Epistle of Barnabas*
Ep. Clem.	*Epistle of Clement*
Ep. Diog.	*Epistle to Diognetus*
Ep. Polyc.	*Epistle of Polycarp*
Eph.	*To the Ephesians* (Ignatius)
EQ	*Evangelical Quarterly*
ERE	*Encyclopaedia of Religion and Ethics*
E.T.	English translation
Ev. Th.	*Evangelische Theologie*
EVV	English Versions (of the Bible)
ExR	*Exodus Rabba* (rabbinical commentary)
ExT	*Expository Times*
Fam.	*Letters to Family and Friends* (Cicero)
FRLANT	Forschungen zur Religion und Literatur des Alten und Neuen Testaments
FTS	Frankfurter Theologische Studien
GenR	*Genesis Rabba* (rabbinical commentary)
GNBC	Good News Bible Commentary (Harper & Row)
Haer.	*Against Heresies* (Irenaeus)
HCNT	Handcommentar zum Neuen Testament
HE	*Historia Ecclesiastica* (Eusebius; Socrates; Bede)
HNT	Handbuch zum Neuen Testament

Hom.	*Homilies*
HSNT	Die heiligen Schriften des Neuen Testaments
HTR	*Harvard Theological Review*
IB	*Interpreter's Bible*
ibid.	*ibidem* (in the same place)
IBNTG	*An Idiom Book of New Testament Greek* (C. F. D. Moule)
ICC	International Critical Commentary
IDB	*Interpreter's Dictionary of the Bible*
IG	*Inscriptiones Graecae*
Ign.	Ignatius
ILNT	*Introduction to the Literature of the New Testament* (J. Moffatt)
Int.	*Interpretation*
Iren.	Irenaeus
JAAR	*Journal of the American Academy of Religion*
JBL	*Journal of Biblical Literature*
JHS	*Journal of Hellenic Studies*
JÖAI	*Jahreshefte des österreichischen archäologischen Instituts*
JQR	*Jewish Quarterly Review*
JSNT	*Journal for the Study of the New Testament*
JSS	*Journal of Semitic Studies*
JTS	*Journal of Theological Studies*
KEK	Kritisch-Exegetischer Kommentar (Meyer Kommentar)
KJV	King James (Authorized) Version (1611)
Leg. Alleg.	*On the Allegorical Interpretation of the Laws* (Philo)
LSJ	Liddell and Scott's *Greek-English Lexicon*, revised by H. S. Jones
LUÅ	Lunds Universitets Årsskrift
LXX	Septuagint
MAMA	*Monumenta Asiae Minoris Antiqua*
Mart. Pol.	*Martyrdom of Polycarp*
MHT	J. H. Moulton–W. F. Howard–N. Turner, *Grammar of New Testament Greek*, I-IV (Edinburgh: T. & T. Clark, 1906-76)
MM	J. H. Moulton–G. Milligan, *The Vocabulary of the Greek Testament* (London: Hodder & Stoughton, 1930)
MNTC	Moffatt New Testament Commentary
MT	Masoretic Text (of the Hebrew Bible)
MTL	Marshall's Theological Library
NA[26]	E. Nestle–K. Aland, *Novum Testamentum Graece*, 26th edition

Nat. Hist.	*Natural History* (Pliny the elder)
NCB	New Century Bible
NClB	New Clarendon Bible
NEB	New English Bible
NF	Neue Folge
NGG	*Nachrichten von der (königlichen) Gesellschaft der Wissenschaften zu Göttingen*
NICNT	New International Commentary on the New Testament
NIDNTT	*New International Dictionary of New Testament Theology*
NIGTC	New International Greek Testament Commentary
NIV	New International Version
NovT	*Novum Testamentum*
NPNF	Nicene and Post-Nicene Fathers
n.s.	new series
NT	New Testament
NTC	New Testament Commentary
NTD	Das Neue Testament Deutsch
NTS	*New Testament Studies*
NTSR	New Testament for Spiritual Reading
Or. Sib.	*Sibylline Oracles*
OT	Old Testament
OTS	*Oudtestamentische Studiën*
P. Amh.	*Amherst Papyri*
Pan.	*Panarion* (Epiphanius)
PC	*Peake's Commentary on the Bible*
PEQ	*Palestine Exploration Quarterly*
P. Fay.	*Fayum Papyri*
PG	*Patrologia Graeca* (Migne)
PL	*Patrologia Latina* (Migne)
PNTC	Pelican New Testament Commentaries
Polyc.	Polycarp
P. Oxy.	*Oxyrhynchus Papyri*
P. Par.	*Paris Papyri*
Q	Qumran
1QH	*Hôdāyôṭ* (Hymns) from Qumran Cave 1
1QIs[a]	Complete Isaiah scroll from Qumran Cave 1
1QM	*Milḥāmāh* (War) scroll from Qumran Cave 1
1QpHab	*Pēšer* (commentary) on Habakkuk from Qumran Cave 1
1QS	*Seḍer* (rule) from Qumran Cave 1
QDAP	*Quarterly of the Department of Antiquities of Palestine*
RA	*Revue Archéologique*

ABBREVIATIONS

RB	*Revue Biblique*
Ref.	*Refutation of Heresies* (Hippolytus)
RGG	*Religion in Geschichte und Gegenwart*
RNT	Regensburger Neues Testament
Rom.	*To the Romans* (Ignatius)
RSV	Revised Standard Version
RTR	*Reformed Theological Review*
RV	Revised Version (1881)
RVV	Religionsgeschichtliche Versuche und Vorarbeiten
SAB	*Sitzungsberichte der preussischen Akademie der Wissenschaften zu Berlin*
SANT	Studien zum Alten und Neuen Testament
Sat.	*Satires* (Horace; Juvenal)
SBS	Sources for Biblical Study
SBT	Studies in Biblical Theology
SE	*Studia Evangelica*
SIG	*Sylloge Inscriptionum Graecarum* (W. Dittenberger)
SJT	*Scottish Journal of Theology*
SNT	Studien zum Neuen Testament
SNovT	Supplements to *Novum Testamentum*
SNTSM	Society for New Testament Studies Monograph Series
SR	*Studies in Religion/Sciences Religieuses*
SSR	*Song of Songs Rabba* (rabbinical commentary)
ST	*Studia Theologica*
STK	*Svensk Teologisk Kvartalskrift*
Strom.	*Stromateis* (Clement of Alexandria)
SUNT	Studien zur Umwelt des Neuen Testaments
SVT	Supplements to *Vetus Testamentum*
Targ. Ps. Jon.	Targum of Pseudo-Jonathan (on the Pentateuch)
TB	Babylonian Targum
TC	Torch Commentaries
TDNT	*Theological Dictionary of the New Testament*, E.T. (G. Kittel–G. Friedrich)
Test. Levi	*Testament of Levi*
Test. Sol.	*Testament of Solomon*
Theod.	Theodotion
TJ	Jerusalem (Palestinian) Talmud
TKNT	Theologischer Kommentar zum Neuen Testament (Herder)
TLZ	*Theologische Literaturzeitung*
TNTC	Tyndale New Testament Commentaries
Tos.	Tosefta

TQ	*Theologische Quartalschrift*
TR	Textus Receptus
Trall.	*To the Trallians* (Ignatius)
TTS	Trierer Theologische Studien
TU	*Texte und Untersuchungen*
TZ	*Theologische Zeitschrift*
UBS[3]	The United Bible Societies' *Greek New Testament*, 3rd edition
UCL	Catholic University of Louvain publications
VE	*Vox Evangelica*
Vig. Chr.	*Vigiliae Christianae*
VT	*Vetus Testamentum*
WBC	Word Biblical Commentary
WC	Westminster Commentaries
WH	B. F. Westcott–F. J. A. Hort, *The New Testament in Greek* (1881)
WMANT	Wissenschaftliche Monographien zum Alten und Neuen Testament
WSB	Wuppertaler Studienbibel
WTJ	*Westminster Theological Journal*
WUNT	Wissenschaftliche Untersuchungen zum Neuen Testament
ZBK	Zürcher Bibelkommentar
ZK	Zahn-Kommentar
ZNW	*Zeitschrift für die neutestamentliche Wissenschaft*

The abbreviations (*sigla*) for manuscripts, versions, and citations in notes on variant readings in the text are those used in the chief critical editions of the New Testament.

SELECT BIBLIOGRAPHY

I. COMMENTARIES

Abbott, T. K., *The Epistles to the Ephesians and to the Colossians*, ICC (Edinburgh: T. & T. Clark, 1897).

Allan, J. A., *The Epistle to the Ephesians*, TC (London: SCM, 1959).

Barth, M., *Ephesians*, AB (2 vols.; Garden City, NY: Doubleday, 1974).

Beare, F. W., "The Epistle to the Ephesians," *IB* 9 (New York/Nashville: Abingdon-Cokesbury, 1953), 595-749.

Beare, F. W., "The Epistle to the Colossians," *IB* 10 (New York/Nashville: Abingdon-Cokesbury, 1955), 131-241.

Beet, J. A., *A Commentary on St. Paul's Epistles to the Ephesians, Philippians and Colossians* (London: Hodder & Stoughton, ³1902).

Bengel, J. A., *Gnomon Novi Testamenti* [Tübingen, 1773] (London/Edinburgh: Williams & Norgate, ³1862), pp. 695-718 ("In Epistolam ad Ephesios"), 733-46 ("In Epistolam ad Colossenses"), 800-02 ("In Epistolam ad Philemonem").

Benoit, P., *Les Épîtres de Saint Paul aux Philippiens, a Philémon, aux Colossiens, aux Éphésiens*, BJ (Paris: du Cerf, 1959).

Bieder, W., *Brief an die Kolosser*, ZBK (Zürich: Zwingli, 1943).

Caird, G. B., *Paul's Letters from Prison*, NC1B (Oxford: University Press, 1976).

Calvin, J., *The Epistles of Paul the Apostle to the Galatians, Ephesians, Philippians and Colossians* [Geneva, 1548], E.T. (Edinburgh: Oliver & Boyd, 1965), pp. 121-226 ("Ephesians"), 297-362 ("Colossians").

Calvin, J., *The Second Epistle of Paul the Apostle to the Corinthians and the Epistles to Timothy, Titus and Philemon* [Geneva, 1549], E.T. (Edinburgh: Oliver & Boyd, 1964), pp. 393-401 ("Philemon").

Cambier, J., *Vie chretienne en Église: L'Épître aux Éphésiens lue aux chrétiens d'aujourd'hui* (Tournai: Desclée, 1966).

Carson, H. M., *The Epistles of Paul to the Colossians and Philemon*, TNTC (London: Inter-Varsity, ²1963).

Chadwick, H., "Ephesians," *PC* (London: Nelson, ²1962), pp. 980-84.

Conzelmann, H., "Der Brief an die Epheser" (pp. 56-91) and "Der Brief an die Kolosser" (pp. 130-54), in *Die kleineren Briefe des Apostels Paulus*, NTD 8 (Göttingen: Vandenhoeck & Ruprecht, ⁹1962).

Dibelius, M., and Greeven, H., *An die Kolosser, Epheser an Philemon*, HNT 12 (Tübingen: Mohr, ³1953).

Dodd, C. H., "Ephesians" (pp. 1222-37), "Colossians" (pp. 1250-62), "Philemon" (pp. 1292-94), in *Abingdon Bible Commentary* (New York: Abingdon, 1929).

Eadie, J., *A Commentary on the Greek Text of the Epistle of Paul to the Ephesians* (Edinburgh: T. & T. Clark, ³1883).

Eadie, J., *A Commentary on the Greek Text of the Epistle of Paul to the Colossians* (Edinburgh: T. & T. Clark, 1856).

Ernst, J., *Die Briefe an die Philipper, an Philemon, an die Kolosser, an die Epheser*, RNT (Regensburg: Pustet, 1974).

Ewald, P., *Die Briefe des Paulus an die Epheser, Kolosser und Philemon*, ZK (Leipzig: Deichert, ²1910).

Fitzmyer, J. A., "Philemon," in *Jerome Bible Commentary* (Englewood Cliffs: Prentice Hall, 1968), II, 332-33.

Foulkes, F., *The Epistle of Paul to the Ephesians*, TNTC (London: Inter-Varsity, 1963).

Friedrich, G., "Der Brief an Philemon," in *Die kleineren Briefe des Apostels Paulus*, NTD 8 (Göttingen: Vandenhoeck & Ruprecht, ⁹1962).

Gaugler, E., *Der Epheserbrief*, ANS 6 (Zürich: EVZ, 1966).

Gnilka, J., *Der Epheserbrief*, TKNT 10/2 (Freiburg: Herder, ²1977).

Grassi, J. A., "Ephesians" (II, 341-49) and "Colossians" (II, 334-40), in *Jerome Bible Commentary* (Englewood Cliffs: Prentice Hall, 1968).

Haupt, E., *Die Gefangenschaftsbriefe*, KEK 8-9 (Göttingen: Vandenhoeck & Ruprecht, ⁸1902).

Hendriksen, W., *The Epistle to the Ephesians*, NTC (Grand Rapids: Baker, 1967).

Hendriksen, W., *The Epistles to the Colossians and Philemon*, NTC (Grand Rapids: Baker, 1965).

Hodge, C., *A Commentary on the Epistle to the Ephesians* (London: Nisbet, 1856; repr. Grand Rapids: Eerdmans, 1950).

Houlden, J. L., *Paul's Letters from P. ison*, PNTC (Harmondsworth: Penguin Books, 1970).

Hugedé, N., *Commentaire de l'Épître aux Colossiens* (Geneva: Labor et Fides, 1968).

Hugedé, N., *L'Épître aux Éphésiens* (Geneva: Labor et Fides, 1974).

Johnston, G., *Ephesians, Philippians, Colossians and Philemon*, NCB (London: Nelson, 1967).

Kelly, W., *Lectures on the Epistle of Paul the Apostle to the Ephesians* (London: Morrish, 1870).

Kelly, W., *Lectures on the Epistle of Paul the Apostle to the Colossians* (London: Morrish, 1869).

Knox, J., "The Epistle to Philemon," *IB* 10 (New York/Nashville: Abingdon-Cokesbury, 1955), 553-73.

Leaney, A. R. C., *The Epistles to Timothy, Titus and Philemon*, TC (London: SCM, 1960).

Lehmann, R., *L'Épître à Philémon: Le christianisme primitif et l'esclavage*, Commentaires bibliques (Geneva: Labor et Fides, 1977).

Lightfoot, J. B., *Saint Paul's Epistles to the Colossians and to Philemon* (London: Macmillan, 1875).

Lindemann, A., *Der Kolosserbrief*, ZBK (Zürich: Zwingli, 1983).

Lock, W., *The Epistle to the Ephesians*, WC (London: Methuen, 1929).

Lohmeyer, E., *Die Briefe an die Philipper, Kolosser und an Philemon*, KEK 9 (Göttingen: Vandenhoeck & Ruprecht, ^{9}1953).

Lohse, E., *Colossians and Philemon*, E.T., Hermeneia (Philadelphia: Fortress, 1971).

MacPhail, S. R., *Colossians: With Introduction and Notes* (Edinburgh: T. & T. Clark, 1911).

Martin, R. P., "Ephesians," *BBC* 11 (Nashville: Broadman, 1972), 125-77.

Martin, R. P., *Colossians: The Church's Lord and the Christian's Liberty* (Exeter: Paternoster, 1972).

Martin, R. P., *Colossians and Philemon*, NCB (London: Oliphants, 1974).

Masson, C., *L'épître aux Éphésiens*, CNT 9 (Paris/Neuchâtel: Delachaux et Niestlé, 1953), 133-228.

Masson, C., *L'épître aux Colossiens*, CNT 10 (Paris/Neuchâtel: Delachaux et Niestlé, 1950), 85-159.

Meinertz, M., and Tillmann, F., *Die Gefangenschaftsbriefe*, HSNT 7 (Bonn: Hanstein, 1931).

Mitton, C. L., *Ephesians*, NCB (London: Oliphants, 1976).

Moule, C. F. D., *The Epistles of Paul the Apostle to the Colossians and to Philemon*, CGTC (Cambridge: University Press, 1957).

Moule, C. F. D., "Colossians and Philemon," *PC* (London: Nelson, ^{2}1962), pp. 990-95.

Moulton, H. K., *Colossians, Philemon and Ephesians*, EPC (London: Epworth, 1963).

Müller, J. J., *The Epistles of Paul to the Philippians and to Philemon*, NICNT (Grand Rapids: Eerdmans, 1955).

Mussner, F., "The Epistle to the Colossians," in J. Gnilka and F. Mussner, *Philippians and Colossians*, E.T., NTSR (London: Sheed & Ward, 1971).

O'Brien, P. T., *Colossians, Philemon*, WBC (Waco, TX: Word, 1982).

Oesterley, W. O. E., "The Epistle of Paul to Philemon," *EGT* IV (London: Hodder & Stoughton, 1910), 203-17.

Peake, A. S., "The Epistle of Paul to the Colossians," *EGT* III (London: Hodder & Stoughton, 1903), 475-547.

Radford, L. B., *The Epistle to the Colossians and the Epistle to Philemon*, WC (London: Methuen, ²1946).

Rienecker, F., *Der Brief an die Epheser*, WSB (Wuppertal: Brockhaus, ⁴1975).

Robbins, R. F., "Philemon," *BBC* 11 (Nashville: Broadman, 1972), 377-88.

Robinson, J. A., *St. Paul's Epistle to the Ephesians* (London: Macmillan, ²1914).

Salmond, S. D. F., "The Epistle of Paul to the Ephesians," *EGT* III (London: Hodder & Stoughton, 1903), 201-395.

Schlatter, A., "Die Briefe an die Galater, Epheser, Kolosser und Philemon," in *Erläuterungen zum Neuen Testament*, 7 (Stuttgart: Calwer Verlag, ⁶1963), 152-352.

Schlier, H., *Der Brief an die Epheser: Ein Kommentar* (Düsseldorf: Patmos, 1957).

Schnackenburg, R., *Der Brief an die Epheser*, EKKNT (Neukirchen-Vluyn: Benziger, 1982).

Schweizer, E., *The Letter to the Colossians*, E.T. (Minneapolis: Augsburg, 1982).

Scott, E. F., *The Epistles to the Colossians, to Philemon and to the Ephesians*, MNTC (London: Hodder & Stoughton, 1930).

Simpson, E. K., "The Epistle to the Ephesians," in E. K. Simpson and F. F. Bruce, *The Epistles of Paul to the Ephesians and to the Colossians*, NICNT (Grand Rapids: Eerdmans, 1957).

Soden, H. von, "Die Briefe an die Kolosser, Epheser, Philemon," HCNT 3.1 (Freiburg/Leipzig: Mohr, ²1893)

Staab, K., *Die Gefangenschaftsbriefe*, RNT 7 (Regensburg: Pustet, ³1959).

Strack, H. L., and Billerbeck, P., *Kommentar zum Neuen Testament aus Talmud und Midrasch*, III (München: Beck, 1926).

Stuhlmacher, P., *Der Brief an Philemon*, EKKNT (Neukirchen-Vluyn: Benziger, 1975).

Synge, F. C., *St. Paul's Epistle to the Ephesians* (London: SPCK, 1941).

Synge, F. C., *Philippians and Colossians*, TC (London: SCM, 1951).

Thomas, W. H. G., *Studies in Colossians and Philemon* (Grand Rapids: Eerdmans, ²1973).

Thompson, G. H. P., *The Letters of Paul to the Ephesians, to the Colossians and to Philemon*, CBC (Cambridge: University Press, 1967).

Vincent, M. R., *The Epistles to the Philippians and to Philemon*, ICC (Edinburgh: T. & T. Clark, ³1922).

Vine, W. E., *The Epistles to the Philippians and Colossians* (London: Oliphants, 1955).

Westcott, B. F., *St. Paul's Epistle to the Ephesians*, ed. J. M. Schulhof (London: Macmillan, 1906).

White, R. E. O., "Colossians," *BBC* 11 (Nashville: Broadman, 1971), 217-56.

Williams, A. L., *The Epistles . . . to the Colossians and to Philemon*, Cambridge Greek Testament (Cambridge: University Press, 1907).

Zerwick, M., *The Epistle to the Ephesians*, E.T., NTSR (London: Burns & Oates, 1969).

II. OTHER WORKS

Baggott, L. J., *A New Approach to Colossians* (London: Mowbray, 1961).

Bandstra, A. J., *The Law and the Elements of the World* (Kampen: Kok, 1964).

Banks, R. J., *Paul's Idea of Community* (Exeter: Paternoster, 1980).

Barth, M., *The Broken Wall* (London: Collins, 1960).

Barth, M., *Israel und die Kirche im Brief des Paulus an die Epheser* (München: Kaiser, 1959).

Bell, G. K. A., and Deissmann, A. (ed.), *Mysterium Christi* (London: Longmans, 1930).

Benoit, P., "Body, Head and *Pleroma* in the Epistles of the Captivity" (1956), E.T. in *Jesus and the Gospel*, II (London: Darton, Longman & Todd, 1974), 51-92.

Best, E., *One Body in Christ* (London: SPCK, 1955).

Bornkamm, G., "The Heresy of Colossians" (1948), E.T. in *Conflict at Colossae*, ed. Francis and Meeks (see below), pp. 123-45.

Bornkamm, G., "Die Hoffnung im Kolosserbrief—Zugleich ein Beitrag zur Frage der Echtheit des Briefes," in *Studien zum Neuen Testament und zur Patristik, Festschrift für Erich Klostermann = TU* 77 (Berlin, 1961), 56-64.

Bujard, W., *Stilanalytische Untersuchungen zum Kolosserbrief,* SUNT 11 (Göttingen: Vandenhoeck & Ruprecht, 1973).

Burger, C., *Schöpfung und Versöhnung: Studien zum liturgischen Gut im Kolosser- und Epheserbrief,* WMANT 46 (Neukirchen-Vluyn: Neukirchener, 1975).

Cadbury, H. J., "The Dilemma of Ephesians," *NTS* 5 (1958-59), 91-102.

Caird, G. B., *Principalities and Powers: A Study in Pauline Theology* (Oxford: Clarendon, 1956).

Caragounis, C. C., *The Ephesian Mysterion: Meaning and Content,* CB: NT 8 (Lund: Gleerup, 1977).

Carr, W., *Angels and Principalities,* SNTSM 42 (Cambridge: University Press, 1981).

Cerfaux, L., *Christ in the Theology of St. Paul,* E.T. (London: Nelson, 1959).

Cerfaux, L., *The Christian in the Theology of St. Paul,* E.T. (London: Nelson, 1967).

Cerfaux, L., *The Church in the Theology of St. Paul,* E.T. (London: Nelson, 1959).

Chadwick, H., "Die Absicht des Epheserbriefes," *ZNW* 51 (1960), 145-53.

Chavasse, C., *The Bride of Christ* (London: Faber, 1941).

Coutts, J., "The Relationship of Ephesians and Colossians," *NTS* 4 (1957-58), 201-07.

Cross, F. L. (ed.), *Studies in Ephesians* (London: Mowbray, 1956)

Crouch, J. E., *The Origin and Intention of the Colossian Haustafel,* FRLANT 109 (Göttingen: Vandenhoeck & Ruprecht, 1972).

DeBoer, W. P., *The Imitation of Paul* (Kampen: Kok, 1962).

Dibelius, M., *Die Geisterwelt im Glauben des Paulus* (Göttingen: Vandenhoeck & Ruprecht, 1909).

Dodd, C. H., *New Testament Studies* (Manchester: University Press, 1953).

Duncan, G. S., *St. Paul's Ephesian Ministry* (London: Hodder & Stoughton, 1929).

DuPlessis, I. J., *Christus as Hoof van Kerk en Kosmos* (Groningen: V. R. B. Kleine der A 3-4, 1962).

Dupont, J., *Gnosis: La connaissance religieuse dans les épîtres de Saint Paul,* UCL II.40 (Louvain: Nauwelaerts/Paris: Gabalda, 1949).

Dupont, J., *La réconciliation dans la théologie de Saint Paul* (Bruges: Desclée, 1953).

Ellis, E. E., *Prophecy and Hermeneutic in Early Christianity,* WUNT 18 (Tübingen: Mohr/Grand Rapids: Eerdmans, 1978).

Ernst, J., *Pleroma und Pleroma Christi* (Regensburg: Pustet, 1970).

Fischer, K. M., *Tendenz und Absicht des Epheserbriefes*, FRLANT 111 (Göttingen: Vandenhoeck & Ruprecht, 1973).

Foerster, W., "Die Irrlehrer des Kolosserbriefes," in *Studia Biblica et Semitica T. C. Vriezen dedicata*, ed. W. C. van Unnik and A. S. van der Woude (Wageningen: Veenman, 1966), pp. 71-80.

Foulkes, F., *Study Guide to Ephesians* (London: Inter-Varsity, 1968).

Francis, F. O., and Meeks, W. A. (ed.), *Conflict at Colossae*, SBS 4 (Missoula, MT: Scholars Press, 1975).

Gabathuler, H. J., *Jesus Christus: Haupt der Kirche—Haupt der Welt*, ATANT 45 (Zurich: Zwingli Verlag, 1965).

Goodenough, E. R., "Paul and Onesimus," *HTR* 22 (1929), 181-83.

Goodspeed, E. J., *The Formation of the New Testament* (Chicago: University Press, 1926).

Goodspeed, E. J., *The Key to Ephesians* (Chicago: University Press, 1956).

Goodspeed, E. J., *The Meaning of Ephesians* (Chicago: University Press, 1933).

Gundry, R. H., *"Sōma" in Biblical Theology*, SNTSM 29 (Cambridge: University Press, 1976).

Hanson, S., *The Unity of the Church in the New Testament: Colossians and Ephesians*, ASNU 14 (Uppsala: Almquist & Wiksells, 1946).

Harrison, P. N., "Onesimus and Philemon," *ATR* 32 (1950), 268-94.

Harrison, P. N., *Paulines and Pastorals* (London: Villiers, 1964).

Hengel, M., *Between Jesus and Paul*, E.T. (London: SCM, 1983).

Holtzmann, H. J., *Kritik der Epheser- und Kolosserbriefe* (Leipzig: Engelmann, 1872).

Hort, F. J. A., *Prolegomena to St. Paul's Epistles to the Romans and the Ephesians* (London: Macmillan, 1895).

Käsemann, E., "Epheserbrief," *RGG* II (Tübingen: Mohr, ³1958), cols. 517-20; "Kolosserbrief," *RGG* III (³1959), cols. 1727-28.

Käsemann, E., "Ephesians and Acts," in *Studies in Luke-Acts*, ed. L. E. Keck and J. L. Martyn (Nashville, TN: Abingdon, 1966), pp. 288-97.

Käsemann, E., "Das Interpretationsproblem des Epheserbriefes," *TLZ* 86 (1961), cols. 1-8.

Käsemann, E., *Leib und Leib Christi*, BHT 9 (Tübingen: Mohr, 1933).

Kirby, J. C., *Ephesians, Baptism and Pentecost* (London: SPCK, 1968).

Knox, J., *Philemon among the Letters of Paul* (Chicago: University Press, 1935; Nashville, TN: Abingdon/London: Collins, ²1959).

Knox, W. L., *St. Paul and the Church of the Gentiles* (Cambridge: University Press, 1939).

Knox, W. L., *Some Hellenistic Elements in Primitive Christianity* (London: Milford, 1944).

Lähnemann, J., *Der Kolosserbrief: Komposition, Situation und Argumentation*, SNT (Gütersloh: Mohn, 1971).

Lähnemann, J., and Böhm, G., *Der Philemonbrief: Zur didaktischen Erschliessung eines Paulus-Briefes* (Gütersloh: Mohn, 1973).

Lampe, G. W. H., *The Seal of the Spirit* (London: SPCK, 1951).

Lincoln, A. T., *Paradise Now and Not Yet*, SNTSM 43 (Cambridge: University Press, 1981).

Lucas, R. C., *Fullness and Freedom: The Message of Colossians and Philemon*, BST (Leicester: Inter-Varsity, 1980).

Mackay, J. A., *God's Order: The Ephesian Letter and This Present Time* (New York: Macmillan/London: Nisbet, 1953).

Manson, T. W., *Studies in the Gospels and Epistles* (Manchester: University Press, 1962).

Martin, R. P., "An Epistle in Search of a Life-Setting," *ExT* 79 (1967-68), 296-302.

Martin, R. P., *Reconciliation: A Study of Paul's Theology*, MTL (London: Marshall, 1981).

Meinertz, M., *Der Philemonbrief und die Persönlichkeit des Apostels Paulus* (Düsseldorf: Schwann, 1921).

Merklein, H., *Das kirchliche Amt nach dem Epheserbrief*, SANT 33 (München: Kösel, 1973).

Michaelis, W., *Versöhnung des Alls* (Bern: Siloah, 1950).

Minear, P. S., *Images of the Church in the New Testament* (London: Lutterworth, 1960).

Mitton, C. L., *The Epistle to the Ephesians: Its Authorship, Origin and Purpose* (Oxford: Clarendon, 1951).

Mitton, C. L., *The Formation of the Pauline Corpus of Letters* (London: Epworth, 1955).

Moule, H. C. G., *Colossian Studies* (London: Hodder & Stoughton, 1898).

Moule, H. C. G., *Ephesian Studies* (London: Hodder & Stoughton, 1900).

Munck, J., *Paul and the Salvation of Mankind*, E.T. (London: SCM, 1959).

Munro, W., *Authority in Paul and Peter*, SNTSM 45 (Cambridge: University Press, 1983).

Murphy-O'Connor, J. (ed.), *Paul and Qumran* (London: Chapman, 1968).

Mussner, F., *Christus, das All und die Kirche*, TTS 5 (Trier: Paulinus, 1968).

O'Brien, P. T., *Introductory Thanksgivings in the Letters of Paul*, SNovT 49 (Leiden: Brill, 1977).

Odeberg, H., *The View of the Universe in the Epistle to the Ephesians*, AUL NF 1.29.6 (Lund: Gleerup, 1934).

Ollrog, W.-H., *Paulus und seine Mitarbeiter*, WMANT 50 (Neukirchen-Vluyn: Neukirchener, 1979).

Percy, E., *Der Leib Christi in den paulinischen Homologoumena und Antilegomena*, LUÅ 1.38.1 (Lund: Gleerup, 1942).

Percy, E., *Die Probleme der Kolosser- und Epheserbriefe*, ARSHLL 39 (Lund: Gleerup, 1946).

Pokorný, P., *Der Epheserbrief und die Gnosis* (Berlin: Evangelische Verlagsanstalt, 1965).

Preiss, T., *Life in Christ*, E.T., SBT 13 (London: SCM, 1954).

Ramsay, W. M., *Cities and Bishoprics of Phrygia*, I-II (Oxford: University Press, 1895-1897).

Ramsay, W. M., *The Church in the Roman Empire before A.D. 170* (London: Hodder & Stoughton, ⁵1897).

Robertson, A. T., *Paul and the Intellectuals* (Garden City, NY: Doubleday, 1928).

Robinson, J. A. T., *The Body: A Study in Pauline Theology*, SBT 5 (London: SCM, 1952).

Roon, A. van, *The Authenticity of Ephesians*, SNovT 39 (Leiden: Brill, 1974).

Rowland, C., *The Open Heaven* (London: SPCK, 1982).

Rutherfurd, J., *St. Paul's Epistles to Colossae and Laodicea* (Edinburgh: T. & T. Clark, 1908).

Schille, G., *Frühchristliche Hymnen* (Berlin: Evangelische Verlagsanstalt, 1965).

Schlier, H., *Christus und die Kirche im Epheserbrief*, BHT 6 (Tübingen: Mohr, 1930).

Schlier, H., *Principalities and Powers in the New Testament*, E.T. (New York: Herder, 1961).

Schweizer, E., "Die Elemente der Welt," in *Verborum Veritas*, ed. O. Böcher and K. Haacker (Wuppertal: Brockhaus, 1970), pp. 245-59.

Schweizer, E., "Zur Frage der Echtheit des Kolosser- und des Epheserbriefes," *ZNW* 47 (1956), 287.

Steinmetz, F.-J., *Protologische Heilszuversicht: Die Strukturen des soteriologischen und christologischen Denkens im Kolosser- und Epheserbrief*, FTS 2 (Frankfurt: Knecht, 1969).

Stendahl, K. (ed.), *The Scrolls and the New Testament* (London: SCM, 1958).

Stott, J. R. W., *God's New Society: The Message of Ephesians*, BST (Leicester: Inter-Varsity, 1979).

Vielhauer, P., *Oikodome: Das Bild vom Bau in der christlichen Literatur vom Neuen Testament bis Clemens Alexandrinus* (Karlsruhe-Durloch: Tron, 1939).

Wickert, U., "Der Philemonbrief—Privatbrief oder Apostolisches Schreiben?" *ZNW* 52 (1961), 230-38.

Wiles, G. P., *Paul's Intercessory Prayers*, SNTSM 24 (Cambridge: University Press, 1974).

Zeilinger, F., *Der Erstgeborene der Schöpfung: Untersuchungen zur Formalstruktur und Theologie des Kolosserbriefes* (Wien: Herder, 1974).

The Epistle
to the
COLOSSIANS

INTRODUCTION TO COLOSSIANS

I. CITIES OF THE LYCUS VALLEY

Colossae, the home of the church to which Paul's letter to the Colossians was addressed, was a city in the Lycus valley of Western Anatolia (Asia Minor). Two neighboring cities, also in the Lycus valley, are mentioned in the letter—Laodicea and Hierapolis (Col. 2:1; 4:13, 15-16).

The river Lycus[1] (modern Çürük-su) is a tributary of the Maeander (modern Büyük Menderes). In antiquity the territory through which the Lycus ran was the southwestern part of the kingdom of Phrygia. Phrygia became the dominant power in Anatolia with the decline of the Hittite Empire after 1200 B.C., but was weakened by the Cimmerian invasion about 700 B.C., and had to yield to the hegemony of Lydia. When Cyrus the Great conquered Croesus, the Lydian king, in 547 B.C. and captured his capital, Sardis, Phrygia was incorporated into the Persian Empire and remained so until the conquest of Alexander the Great in 334 B.C. and the following years. In the division of Alexander's empire after his death southwestern Phrygia fell ultimately to the Seleucid monarchy.

A new, expansionist power, the kingdom of Pergamum, arose to the north of this territory after 283 B.C., when Philetaerus, governor of Pergamum under Lysimachus (ruler for a time of Macedonia and part of Anatolia), made a unilateral declaration of independence. His successors from 241 B.C. onward assumed the title of king. Between 277 and 230 B.C. Northern Phrygia was taken over by the Galatians, immigrant Celts from Europe, who were first invited into Anatolia as mercenary soldiers by the king of Bithynia.

---

[1]To be distinguished from the Lycus in Lydia (modern Kum Çayi), a tributary of the Hermus (modern Gediz Nehri), and from that in Pontus, Northern Anatolia (modern Kelkit Çayi).

When Antiochus III succeeded to the Seleucid throne in 221 B.C., he had to win back large areas of his kingdom in Anatolia which had been annexed by the king of Pergamum. In this he was aided by his mother's brother Achaeus, an able military commander. But when Achaeus recovered those areas, he proclaimed himself independent ruler over them and had himself crowned king at Laodicea in 220 B.C. Antiochus had to enter into a temporary alliance with Pergamum in order to put down Achaeus, who was captured and killed at Sardis in 214 B.C.[2] For the next quarter of a century the Lycus valley remained part of the Seleucid realm.

In 192 B.C., by crossing the Aegean and intervening in the affairs of the Greek city-states, Antiochus III clashed with Rome, which had lately proclaimed itself liberator and protector of those states. So began the long-drawn-out decline of his kingdom. The Romans drove him out of Greece, pursued him into Asia, and defeated him at the battle of Magnesia in 190 B.C. Two years later they imposed on him the Peace of Apamea (a Phrygian city near the source of the Maeander), by the terms of which he had to surrender most of his Anatolian possessions, many of which (including southwestern Phrygia) were handed over to the king of Pergamum, Rome's faithful ally.[3]

The last king of Pergamum, Attalus III, died without heirs in 133 B.C. and bequeathed his kingdom to the Roman state. When the Romans agreed to accept the legacy, they reconstituted the kingdom of Pergamum as the province of Asia. The cities of the Lycus valley were thenceforth subject to the authority of the Roman proconsul of Asia (apart from the three years following 88 B.C. when the Romans were forced to abandon the province by Mithridates VI, king of Pontus, and the brief overrunning of Anatolia by the Parthians in 40 B.C.).

Colossae was situated on the south bank of the Lycus. The spelling *Kolassai*, found in some NT manuscripts, may represent an earlier, possibly Phrygian, pronunciation. (If so, then the spelling *Kolossai* could represent an attempt to provide the place-name with an artificial etymology.)[4]

Colossae first appears in extant history in Herodotus, who tells how Xerxes, in his westward march against mainland Greece in 480 B.C., "came to Colossae, a great city of Phrygia, situated at a spot where the river Lycus plunges into a chasm and disappears. The river, after flowing underground for about five furlongs, reappears once more and . . . empties

---

[2]Polybius, *History* 5.48.12; 8.15-21.
[3]Polybius, *History* 21.45.
[4]As though it were related to κολοσσός, "statue."

itself into the Maeander."[5] This statement rests on a misunderstanding or a distorted report. Colossae stood at the beginning of a steep gorge, two and a half miles long, into which the Lycus descends rapidly from the upper to the lower valley. At some points in the upper part of the gorge the water penetrates the limestone bed and disappears, and this may account for the tale of an underground flow.

Eighty years later Cyrus the Younger, marching east from Sardis with an army of mercenaries in his bid for the Persian throne, crossed the Maeander and, after a day's march through Phrygia, arrived at Colossae, "an inhabited city, large and prosperous," where he stayed for seven days.[6]

The autonomous civic status which Colossae enjoyed under the Seleucid and Pergamene kings was retained under the Romans. It has sometimes been inferred from Strabo that, by the beginning of the Christian era, Colossae had dwindled in importance and become one of several unimportant small towns, but the inference is invalid because of a lacuna in Strabo's text at this point.[7] There is inscriptional evidence that Colossae retained its importance into the second and third centuries A.D.[8] The elder Pliny (died A.D. 79) includes it in a list of famous towns of Phrygia (although this list is extracted from an older source).[9]

The site of Colossae was discovered by W. J. Hamilton in 1835. He identified its ruins and acropolis south of the river and its necropolis on the north bank. Later the Byzantine Church of St. Michael the *Archistratēgos*, fated to be destroyed by Turkish raiders in 1189, was erected on the north bank. According to W. M. Ramsay, its ruins were still "plainly visible in 1881."[10] It remained the religious center of the district after the population of Colossae moved to Chonai (modern Honaz), three miles to the south, at the foot of Mount Cadmus (Honaz Dağ). Since the site of Colossae remains unoccupied, it presents an inviting prospect to archaeologists.

[5]Herodotus, *History* 7.30.
[6]Xenophon, *Anabasis* 1.2.6.
[7]Strabo, *Geography* 12.576. Colossae is not one of the πολίσματα which Strabo passes over with a bare mention.
[8]See *MAMA* VI (Manchester, 1939), xi, 15-18; W. M. Ramsay, *Cities and Bishoprics of Phrygia*, I (Oxford, 1895), 208-34; D. Magie, *Roman Rule in Asia Minor*, I (Princeton, 1950), 126-27; II (Princeton, 1950), 985-86.
[9]Pliny, *Nat. Hist.* 5.145.
[10]*Cities and Bishoprics of Phrygia*, I, 215. Michael is called the ἀρχιστράτηγος ("chief captain") in the Greek versions of Dan. 8:11 (cf. for the sense, though not for the word, Dan. 10:21; 12:1) and in several Greek apocrypha (e.g., *Testament of Abraham* 1; 9).

Laodicea (near modern Eskihisar, five miles northeast of Denizli)[11] was founded by the Seleucid king Antiochus II and named in honor of his wife Laodice—plainly at some point between his ascending the throne in 261 B.C. and his divorcing her eight years later. Like Colossae, it was situated on the south bank of the Lycus, ten or eleven miles downstream. According to the elder Pliny, it was founded on the site of an older settlement called first Diospolis and then Rhoas.[12] It makes one of its first appearances in history when Achaeus, rebelling against his nephew Antiochus III, had himself crowned king there in 220 B.C.

Laodicea rapidly gained in importance, to the point where it rivalled Colossae. Like Colossae, it retained its civic status under the Romans. From Cicero, to whose jurisdiction this part of Phrygia and other territories were added during his proconsulship of Cilicia (51-50 B.C.), we know that it was the center of a *conventus* or judicial circuit[13] (to which Hierapolis and, later, Cibyra belonged), and that it was also a center of financial and banking operations.[14] Its economic prosperity is attested at the beginning of the first century A.D. by Strabo.[15] It suffered repeatedly from earthquakes. One is recorded in the principate of Augustus: the case for relieving its citizens, together with those of Thyatira and Chios (who suffered in the same earthquake), was presented before the Roman senate by the emperor's stepson Tiberius.[16] A later one devastated the area under Nero, about the time when the letter to the Colossians was written (A.D. 60); Laodicea was destroyed, but was rebuilt from its own resources with no assistance from Rome.[17] In addition to its natural wealth, Laodicea benefited from the munificence of some of its grateful sons.[18] It appears also to have been the chief medical center of Phrygia.[19]

[11]See *MAMA* VI, x-xi, 1-14; W. M. Ramsay, *Cities and Bishoprics of Phrygia*, I, 32-83; D. Magie, *Roman Rule in Asia Minor*, I, 127; II, 986-87.
[12]Pliny, *Nat. Hist.* 5.105.
[13]Cicero, *Att.* 5.15.
[14]Cicero, *Fam.* 3.5.
[15]Strabo, *Geography* 12.578.
[16]Suetonius, *Tiberius* 5.
[17]Tacitus, *Annals* 14.27.1.
[18]Strabo especially mentions Hieron and the family of the orator Zenon in this regard.
[19]The "eye salve" (κολλύριον) of Rev. 3:18 was probably a preparation made from Phrygian stone (Galen, *On the Preservation of Health* 6.12). The medical school at or near Laodicea was perhaps sponsored by the temple of Mēn Karou some thirteen miles west of the city, but there is no evidence for the theory that Mēn Karou was hellenized as Asklēpios (W. M. Ramsay, *Cities and Bishoprics of Phrygia*, I, 52).

When the provincial system of the Roman Empire was reorganized toward the end of the fourth century, Laodicea became the seat of government of the newly constituted province of Phrygia Pacatiana.[20]

Hierapolis self-evidently means "the holy city."[21] It may have originated as a settlement attached to the temple of the Great Mother. It has been thought to have first received the status of a city (*polis*) from Eumenes II of Pergamum (197-160 B.C.), but was more probably a Seleucid foundation, going back to the time of Antiochus I (281-261 B.C.).[22] It stood on a road which left the main highway from Iconium to Ephesus at Laodicea and which led northwest across the mountains to Philadelphia, Sardis, and the Hermus valley—the road which Xerxes took to Sardis after leaving Colossae.[23] It looked across toward Laodicea from a terrace three hundred feet high on the north bank of the Lycus. In the plain below the terrace the Lycus flows into the Maeander. Behind the site a hot mineral spring wells up, covering the rocks beneath with white deposits of lime, producing stalactite formations which have given the place its Turkish name Pamukkale ("Cotton Castle").

The cave from which the spring emerges was believed to be an entrance to the lower world; the eunuch priests of the Great Mother were said to be the only living beings not to be asphyxiated by the carbon dioxide generated in the cave.[24] At a more practical level, visitors came to bathe in the hot water and their presence added to the prosperity of the city.

In the history of human thought the city's principal claim to fame lies in its having been the birthplace (*c.* A.D. 50) of the Stoic philosopher Epictetus.

The chief industry carried on in those cities was the manufacture and preparation of woolen fabrics. This was in fact the chief industry of all the cities in the Maeander and Hermus basins, for they had excellent

[20]Hence the footnote appended to 1 Timothy in later manuscripts and translated in the KJV: "The first to Timothy was written from Laodicea, which is the chiefest city of Phrygia Pacatiana."

[21]To be distinguished from Hieropolis near Synnada, in Phrygia Salutaris, about seventy miles to the northeast (where Avircius Marcellus was bishop late in the 2nd cent.).

[22]See W. M. Ramsay, *Cities and Bishoprics of Phrygia*, I, 84-121; D. Magie, *Roman Rule in Asia Minor*, I, 127-28; II, 987-88; F. Kolb, "Zur Geschichte der Stadt Hierapolis in Phrygien: Die Phyleninschriften im Theater," *Zeitschrift für Papyrologie und Epigraphik* 15 (1974), 255-70.

[23]Herodotus, *History* 7.31.

[24]Strabo, *Geography* 12.579. See W. C. Brice, "A Note on the Descent into the Plutonium of Hierapolis of Phrygia," *JSS* 23 (1978), 226-27.

communications with the Aegean ports through which their wares were exported. Although the cities of the Lycus valley began their production of those wares later than the older cities of Ionia and Lydia, they soon became famous for the high quality of their products. The glossy black wool of Laodicea was esteemed as finer even than that of Miletus, which was renowned for its excellence throughout the Near East from the sixth century B.C. until well into the Christian era.[25] Hierapolis in particular was famed for its superior dyeing processes. The color of the Colossian product was known as *colossinus*, a word used by Pliny the elder to describe the color of the cyclamen bloom.[26]

The Phrygian inhabitants of the Lycus valley were only gradually hellenized, except for those who lived in the cities. The new cities of Laodicea and Hierapolis were Greek cities from their foundation. When they came under Roman authority after 133 B.C., the cities were in some smaller degree romanized, but none of them was reconstituted as a Roman colony, as several cities farther east were.[27]

II. JEWISH SETTLEMENT IN THE LYCUS VALLEY

Some Jewish settlement in Western Anatolia can be traced back to quite an early date: apparently there were Jewish exiles in the Lydian city of Sardis in the time of the prophet Obadiah.[28] According to Josephus, Seleucus I (312-281 B.C.), founder of the Seleucid dynasty, granted Jews full civic rights in all cities which he founded[29] (it is wise to consider carefully what Josephus and other Jewish writers mean when they mention the enjoyment of full civic rights by Jews in a Hellenistic city). Antiochus II (261-248 B.C.) is said to have planted Jewish colonies in the cities of Ionia.[30] But Jewish settlement in Phrygia, on any substantial scale, is to be dated late in the third century B.C., when Antiochus III, having

---

[25]Strabo, *Geography* 12.578.

[26]Pliny, *Nat. Hist.* 21.51.

[27]By the time of Augustus, proconsular Asia was sufficiently peaceful not to require the stabilizing presence of new Roman colonies; in South Galatia, on the other hand, the threat of trouble from the Homonadensian tribes in the Taurus area and from other directions led to the creation of the colonies of Pisidian Antioch and Lystra in A.D. 6.

[28]Sepharad in Ob. 20, like Akkadian *Sapardu* and Old Persian *Sfarda*, probably approximates the Lydian pronunciation.

[29]Josephus, *Ant.* 12.119.

[30]Josephus, *Ant.* 12.125.

recovered Phrygia and Lydia from the Pergamenes and from his rebellious uncle Achaeus, ordered his satrap Zeuxis to send two thousand Jewish families, with their property, from Babylonia as military settlers in the garrisons and other vital spots of those two Anatolian regions. Houses and cultivable lands were to be provided for them, they were to be exempt from taxation for ten years, and they should have the right to live under their own laws.[31]

There is no reason to doubt the essential credibility of this report by Josephus, or of the royal decree which it embodies. The king's letter to Zeuxis, says M. Rostovtzeff, "undoubtedly gives us exactly the normal procedure when the Seleucids founded a colony."[32] The settlement should be dated shortly after 213 B.C., when Phrygia and Lydia were reincorporated in Antiochus's empire. One Zeuxis was satrap of Babylonia about 220 B.C.; he may be identical with the Zeuxis who was satrap of Lydia between 201 and 190 B.C.[33]

If it be asked why Babylonian Jews should have commended themselves to Antiochus as the kind of settlers who would help to stabilize disaffected areas of his empire, an enigmatic reference in 2 Maccabees may point to an answer. Judas Maccabaeus is said to have encouraged his troops on one occasion, when they were threatened by a much superior Seleucid army, by reminding them of "the battle with the Galatians that took place in Babylonia, when 8,000 Jews in all went into the affair, with 4,000 Macedonians; and when the Macedonians were hard pressed, the 8,000, by the help that came to them from heaven, destroyed 120,000 and took much booty" (2 Macc. 8:20).[34] This tradition, which has evidently lost nothing in the telling (especially as regards the numbers involved), probably relates to the earlier part of the reign of Antiochus III. The Galatians habitually hired out their services as mercenaries; presumably on this occasion Galatian mercenaries were engaged on the side of one of Antiochus's enemies. The help then given him by Babylonian Jews could well have moved Antiochus to settle a number of them in Phrygia and Lydia as guarantors of the peace of those territories.

The political changes by which the Lycus valley passed successively

---

[31]Josephus, *Ant.* 12.149.
[32]M. Rostovtzeff, *Social and Economic History of the Hellenistic World*, I (Oxford, 1951), 492. See also, to the same effect, A. Schalit, "The Letter of Antiochus III to Zeuxis regarding the Establishment of Jewish Military Colonies in Phrygia and Lydia," *JQR* 50 (1959-60), 289-318 (he dates the letter between 212 and 205 B.C.).
[33]Polybius, *History* 5.45ff.; 12.1, 24; 21.16, 24.
[34]See J. A. Goldstein, *II Maccabees*, AB (Garden City, N.Y., 1983), pp. 331-34.

under the rule of Pergamum and Rome made little difference to the Jews who resided there. Even Mithridates's conquest of proconsular Asia in 88 B.C., and the ensuing twenty-five years' war, did not seriously disturb them.[35] Almost immediately after the end of the Mithridatic wars we have evidence which points to a large and thriving Jewish population in the Lycus valley and elsewhere in Phrygia.

In 62 B.C. Lucius Valerius Flaccus, proconsul of Asia, impounded the proceeds of the annual half-shekel tax which the Jews of his province, in common with male Jews twenty years old and upward throughout the world, contributed for the maintenance of the temple in Jerusalem. His action was in line with the official ban on the exporting of gold and silver from the empire to foreign countries. It is likely indeed that by use and wont, if not by senatorial decree, an exception had been made in respect of the Jewish temple tax, and in any case it could be argued that from 63 B.C. Judaea itself was part of the empire and no longer a foreign country. Flaccus was brought to court in 59 B.C. on a charge of acting illegally in the matter; he was defended by Cicero, whose speech for the defense has been preserved.[36] Cicero argued that the province was being impoverished by the export of so much wealth year by year; one should therefore be prepared for some exaggeration in the estimate of the sums of money involved.

At Apamea, Cicero states, gold amounting to just under one hundred Roman pounds (*librae*) had been impounded; at Laodicea just over twenty pounds.[37] Since at this time the Pompeian standard of thirty-six *aurei* (gold denarii) to the gold *libra* was in force, and the *aureus* was reckoned to be equivalent to twenty-five drachmae or denarii, it has been calculated that nearly forty-five thousand half-shekels *(didrachma)* were collected at Apamea, and over nine thousand at Laodicea. These figures do not mean that there were respectively forty-five thousand and nine thousand male Jews of the appropriate age resident at Apamea and Laodicea, since these

[35]In 88 B.C. Mithridates raided the island of Cos and seized eight hundred talents which the Jews of proconsular Asia had deposited there for safety (together with money which Cleopatra III of Egypt had deposited there in 102 B.C.). Josephus, to whom we owe this information (*Ant.* 14.112-13), derives it from Strabo, but Strabo speaks generally of "the Jews." Josephus infers (probably rightly) that it was the Jews of Asia, and adds that the money was "God's"—i.e., that it was the yearly Jerusalem temple tax. But eight hundred talents would be the equivalent of nearly five million half-shekels: if the figure is accurate, it must have included much more than the proceeds of the half-shekel tax for one year.
[36]Cicero, *Pro Flacco.* Flaccus appears to have been acquitted.
[37]*Pro Flacco* 68. See A. J. Marshall, "Flaccus and the Jews of Asia (Cicero, *Pro Flacco* 28.67-69)," *Phoenix* 29 (1975), 139-54.

cities were centers to which the money collected in the surrounding districts was brought for conversion into more manageable form and eventual dispatch to Jerusalem. But even when allowance is made for some exaggeration, the Jewish population of Phrygia was considerable.

Later in the same century the collection and export of the half-shekel were expressly safeguarded by successive decrees of Julius Caesar[38] and Augustus.[39] Augustus's right-hand man Marcus Vipsanius Agrippa took specific measures in 14 B.C. (at Herod's request) to protect the Jews of Asia Minor against interference with this privilege (and also against compulsory appearance in law-courts on the sabbath).[40]

Josephus quotes a letter sent by the magistrates of Laodicea about 45 B.C. to a high Roman official, probably the proconsul of Asia, confirming that, in accordance with his directions, they would not impede the liberty of Jewish residents to observe the sabbath and other practices of their religion.[41] In A.D. 2/3 Augustus issued a full statement of Jewish rights in that part of the empire: it was posted in Ancyra, capital of the province of Galatia.[42]

After A.D. 70 the half-shekel payment was diverted to the upkeep of the temple of Jupiter Capitolinus in Rome;[43] otherwise the Jews of the dispersion continued to enjoy their privileges. There is documentary evidence for this in Alexandria[44] and Syrian Antioch;[45] the situation would not be different elsewhere in the eastern provinces. W. M. Ramsay discerned evidence for a specific provision safeguarding Jewish privileges at Apamea, in a tomb inscription of the third century A.D. directing that no one was to be buried in the tomb except its owner, Aurelius Rufus, and his wife Aurelia Tatiana. "If anyone acts [contrary to this direction]," the inscription concludes, "he knows the law of the Jews."[46] Ramsay thought at one time that "the law of the Jews" here could not be the Mosaic law, but a local regulation registered with the city authorities, protecting the

---

[38]Josephus, *Ant.* 16.162-63, where Augustus, confirming this right, cites the precedent set by Caesar, his adoptive father.
[39]Philo, *Legation to Gaius* 155-57.
[40]Josephus, *Ant.* 16.27-65.
[41]Josephus, *Ant.* 14.241-43.
[42]Josephus, *Ant.* 16.162-65. On this whole matter see E. M. Smallwood, *The Jews under Roman Rule* (Leiden, 1976), pp. 120-43.
[43]Cf. I. A. F. Bruce, "Nerva and the *Fiscus Iudaicus,*" *PEQ* 96 (1964), 34-45; E. M. Smallwood, *The Jews under Roman Rule*, pp. 371-85.
[44]Josephus, *Ant.* 12.121.
[45]Josephus, *BJ* 7.100-11. See E. M. Smallwood, *The Jews under Roman Rule,* pp. 358-68.
[46]*CIJ* 774.

burial privileges of the Jewish community.[47] This might be so, but two Jewish tomb-inscriptions of the mid-third century, from Blaundos and Akmonia in West-central Phrygia, invoke on the violator "the curses written in Deuteronomy" (presumably in Deut. 28:15-68);[48] thus the "law of the Jews" in the inscription from Apamea could very well be the Mosaic law. (A similar inscription from Hierapolis, of around A.D. 200, stipulates that for any unauthorized burial in the tomb a fine shall be paid to the Jewish community in that city.)[49]

Ramsay deduced from a comparative study of Greek inscriptions in Phrygia that the local Jewish communities were marked by a degree of religious laxity exceptional in the diaspora—that members of Jewish families could combine the office (or at least the title) of ruler of the synagogue[50] with responsible participation in pagan cults. The evidence is not so clear. For example, he quoted from an inscription from Akmonia a reference to one Julia Severa who was honored by the local synagogue[51] and who is mentioned on local coins of Nero, Agrippina, and Poppaea as having held municipal office together with her husband Servenius Capito (say, between A.D. 54 and 65).[52] It was difficult to hold such a magistracy without at least some involvement in local cults, or even in the imperial cult. But Julia Severa appears to have been a descendant of Herod,[53] and members of the Herod family were not typical Jews.

The inscription which mentions Julia Severa refers to Gaius Tyrronius Cladus as a lifelong ruler of the synagogue. Ramsay judged that "the strange name Tyrronius . . . may in all cases be taken as Jewish,"[54] and went on to draw inferences of doubtful cogency from its other inscriptional occurrences—a course which he himself admitted to be one "of speculation and uncertainty, where each step is more slippery than the preceding one."[55] Some outward conformity with pagan rituals on the part

[47]Ramsay, *Cities and Bishoprics of Phrygia*, II (Oxford, 1897), 538, 669.
[48]*CIJ* 760; *MAMA* VI, §§ 335, 335a (p. 116).
[49]*CIJ* 775.
[50]There is evidence, however, that the title of ἀρχισυνάγωγος could be held by a Gentile, the president of a non-Jewish assembly; see G. H. R. Horsley (ed.), *New Documents illustrating Early Christianity* (Macquarie University, North Ryde, New South Wales, 1981), § 5, pp. 26-27.
[51]*CIJ* 766.
[52]*Cities and Bishoprics of Phrygia*, II, 649-50.
[53]Cf. E. M. Smallwood, *The Jews under Roman Rule*, p. 479. In *CIG* 4033 one member of the family, Tiberius Severus, is called the "descendant of kings and tetrarchs" (βασιλέων καὶ τετραρχῶν ἀπόγονον).
[54]*Cities and Bishoprics of Phrygia*, II, 650.
[55]*Ibid.*

of influential Jews in Phrygia may be taken as established; but it would be precarious to draw conclusions from this about forms of syncretism which might be reflected in the beliefs and practices deprecated in the letter to the Colossians.

The influence of the Jewish settlements on the folklore of Phrygia is well illustrated by the way in which the story of Noah was taken over at Apamea[56] as a local cult-legend. Probably a local flood legend was there already, before Jewish settlement in the area began, but under Jewish influence it was merged with the flood narrative of Genesis. On Apamean coins of the third century A.D. there appears an ark with the inscription *NŌE* (the Greek form of Noah's name given in the Septuagint), floating on water; in it are two human figures, and two others, a male and a female, stand beside it; on top is a raven, and above it is a dove with an olive branch in its beak. Two phases of the story are thus represented—in one, Noah and his wife are in the ark; in the other, they are on dry land, returning thanks for their preservation.[57]

This Phrygian setting for the story of Noah is recorded in the *Sibylline Oracles*:

> In the land of Phrygia is the steep tapering mountain of Kelainē, called Ararat, whence the springs of the great Marsyas have their origin. The ark remained on the peak of that height when the waters abated.[58]

The Marsyas or Catarrhactes (modern Dinar-su) rises in a recess under the acropolis of ancient Celaenae; it flows through Apamea (modern Dinar), on the outskirts of which it falls into the Maeander. Evidently the Sibylline author identifies the acropolis of Celaenae with Ararat.

III. CHRISTIANITY IN THE LYCUS VALLEY

The inclusion of Phrygia among the places from which Jewish pilgrims came to Jerusalem for the feast of Pentecost following the death and

[56]The LXX word for ark (Κιβωτός) appears as an additional name of Apamea on coins and in Strabo, *Geography* 12.8.13, 576 (᾽Απάμεια ἡ Κιβωτὸς λεγομένη).
[57]See W. M. Ramsay, *Cities and Bishoprics of Phrygia*, II, 669-72.
[58]*Or. Sib.* 1.261-65:

ἔστι δέ τι Φρυγίης ἐπὶ ἠπείροιο Κελαινῆς
ἠλίβατον τανύηκες ὄρος, ᾽Αραρὰτ δὲ καλεῖται,
Μαρσύου ἔνθα φλέβες μεγάλου ποταμοῖο πέφυκαν,
τοῦ δὲ κιβωτὸς ἔμεινεν ἐν ὑψηλοῖο καρηνῷ
ληξάντων ὑδάτων.

resurrection of Jesus (Acts 2:10) may be designed to prepare the reader for the eventual evangelization of that region.[59] Whether that is so or not, Phrygia was evangelized within a quarter of a century from that date. In Phrygia Galatica ("the Phrygian and Galatian region" of Acts 16:6) the cities of Pisidian Antioch and Iconium—"the last [i.e., easternmost] city of Phrygia," as Xenophon calls it[60]—were evangelized by Barnabas and Paul in A.D. 47 or 48 (Acts 13:14–14:4). As for Phrygia Asiana farther west, including the Lycus valley, it was evangelized a few years later, during Paul's Ephesian ministry (A.D. 52-55), when "all the residents of Asia heard the word of the Lord, both Jews and Greeks" (Acts 19:10).

The Lycus valley was not evangelized by Paul himself: it is plain from Col. 2:1 that he was not personally acquainted with the churches there. He had certainly met individual members of those churches like Philemon of Colossae, who indeed appears to have been one of his converts (that is the natural sense of his reminder to him in Philem. 19b: "you owe me your very self"). The preaching of the gospel and planting of churches in the Lycus valley were evidently the work of Epaphras, whom Paul calls his "fellow-slave"[61] and "fellow-prisoner."[62]

It is possible that when Paul journeyed overland from the east to Ephesus to take up his ministry there in A.D. 52, he went by way of the Lycus valley. When Luke says that he arrived in Ephesus after passing through "the upper parts" (Acts 19:1), it may be the Lycus route that is indicated. Any district up-country could be called "the upper parts" from the standpoint of Ephesus and the coastal region. But it is more probable that he did not take the Lycus route but a higher road farther north, which left the road leading to the Lycus valley at Apamea and approached Ephesus on the north of Mount Messogis (Aydin Dağlari), not on the south of it, as the Lycus route did.[63]

It is a reasonable inference from Luke's account that, while Paul's personal headquarters were in Ephesus during the years of evangelization

---

[59]Luke's list of places deviates sufficiently from similar lists which have been compared to his to suggest that he did not take it over as such from some literary source (astrological or otherwise) but was himself responsible for the selection of place-names (cf. B. M. Metzger, "Ancient Astrological Geography and Acts 2:9-11," *New Testament Studies* [Leiden, 1980], pp. 46-56).

[60]Xenophon, *Anabasis* 1.2.19.

[61]Col. 1:7 (see pp. 43-44).

[62]Philem. 23 (see p. 224).

[63]See W. M. Ramsay, *The Church in the Roman Empire before A.D. 170* (London, [5]1897), p. 94. It is less likely that "the upper parts" (τὰ ἀνωτερικὰ μέρη) should be taken as resumptive of "the Galatian region and Phrygia" through which Paul is said to have passed on his westward journey in Acts 18:23.

of proconsular Asia, his fellow-workers (such as Epaphras in the Lycus valley) were active in other parts of the province. Probably all seven of the "churches of Asia" to which the Johannine Apocalypse was later addressed, and other Asian churches, were planted during that fertile period.[64]

The only direct information the NT supplies about Christianity in the Lycus valley is contained in the letters to the Colossians and to Philemon, and in the letter to the Laodicean church in Rev. 3:14-22. The last-named document shows how the churches of the Lycus valley shared the general prosperity of their environment; the cutting edge of their distinctive witness was accordingly blunted. Among various touches of local color in the letter is the lukewarmness for which the church is rebuked: in contrast to Hierapolis with its medicinal hot springs or Colossae with its refreshing supply of cold water, Laodicea had to fetch its water through high-pressure stone pipes from hot springs at Denizli, some five miles away, and by the time it reached Laodicea the water was lukewarm. Probably, like the water which the villagers of Eçirli are reported as drawing today from the hot springs of Pamukkale, it had to be left standing in stone jars until it was cool.[65]

Excavations took place on the site of Laodicea between 1961 and 1963. The most impressive discovery was of a nymphaeum with public fountains. After its destruction by an earthquake late in the fifth century the building was repaired for use as a Christian meeting-place.[66]

Sometime after the writing of the letter to the Colossians a large-scale departure from Paul's teaching is implied by the statement: "you are aware that all who are in Asia turned away from me" (2 Tim. 1:15). Something to the same effect may be gathered from the warning to the leaders of the church at Ephesus in Acts 20:29-30 that from within their

[64]It has sometimes been inferred from Polycarp's letter to the Philippian church (11:3) that the gospel first came to Smyrna after Paul had written Phil. 4:15; but more probably when Polycarp says, "we [the Smyrnaeans] had not yet known God," he refers not to the time when Paul's letter to the Philippians was written but to the time when the gospel first came to Philippi. "We need have no hesitation in dating the origin of the Christian church in Smyrna at some point within the period 53-56" (C. J. Cadoux, *Ancient Smyrna* [Oxford, 1938], p. 310).

[65]Cf. G. Weber, "Die Hochdruck-Wasserleitung von Laodicea ad Lycum," *Jahrbuch des kaiserlich-deutschen archäologischen Instituts* 13 (1898), 1-13; 19 (1904), 95-96; M. J. S. Rudwick and E. M. B. Green, "The Laodicean Lukewarmness," *ExT* 69 (1957-58), 176-78.

[66]Cf. J. des Gagniers, etc., *Laodicée du Lycos, Le nymphée, Campagnes 1961-1963*, Université Laval Recherches Archéologiques, Série I (Québec, 1969).

own ranks "will arise men speaking perverse things, to draw away the disciples after them."

As far as the churches of the Lycus valley are concerned, their faith received fresh stimulus in the latter part of the first century from the immigration of some Palestinian believers whose association with the Christian movement went back to early days. Among these were Philip and some at least of his four prophesying daughters, whose tombs were pointed out at Hierapolis toward the end of the second century.[67] There is some confusion in Eusebius or his sources between Philip the apostle and Philip the evangelist, but there is little doubt that we are to think of Philip the evangelist, with whom Paul and his companions spent several days at Caesarea in A.D. 57 before completing their fateful journey to Jerusalem (Acts 21:8-14). It is not surprising that Philip in due course had a church dedicated in his honor at Hierapolis.[68]

When Ignatius, bishop of Antioch, was taken to Rome about A.D. 110 to be exposed to the wild beasts in the Colosseum, he passed through Asia Minor.[69] It is not clear whether his military escort took the road through the Lycus valley or the higher road which forked right at Apamea and ran north of Mount Messogis. If they went through the Lycus valley, they would have turned north at Laodicea, passing through Hierapolis and going on by Xerxes' route to Philadelphia and Smyrna. Ignatius makes no mention in his letters of any city through which he passed before his arrival at Philadelphia.

In the first half of the second century the bishop of Hierapolis was Papias,[70] contemporary of Polycarp, bishop of Smyrna, and probably, like Polycarp, a hearer of John, "the disciple of the Lord."[71] Even if Papias's

---

[67]Eusebius, *HE* 3.31.2-5; 3.39.9; 5.24.2, quoting Polycrates of Ephesus and Proclus the Montanist. See P. Corssen, "Die Töchter des Philippus," *ZNW* 2 (1901), 289-99.

[68]The existence of this church is attested by a local inscription commemorating "Eugenius the little, archdeacon and president of the holy and glorious apostle and divine, Philip" (E. A. Gardner, "Inscriptions copied by [C. R.] Cockerell in Greece, II," *JHS* 6 [1885], § 71, p. 346; W. M. Ramsay, *Cities and Bishoprics of Phrygia*, II, § 419, p. 552). Above the city, outside the walls, stand the substantial remains of the *Martyrion* of Philip, a fifth-century octagonal structure. M. Hengel would not exclude the possibility that Philip the apostle and Philip the evangelist were the same person (*Between Jesus and Paul*, E.T. [London, 1983], p. 14).

[69]See p. 201.

[70]Eusebius, *HE* 2.15.2; 3.36.2; 3.39.1-17.

[71]In the so-called anti-Marcionite prologue to the Gospel of John Papias appears to be called "John's dear disciple." See J. Regul, *Die antimarcionitischen Evangelienprologe* (Freiburg, 1969), pp. 99-197. Irenaeus affirms that he was a disciple of John (*Haer.* 5.33.4); Eusebius virtually denies it (*HE* 3.39.2).

16

intelligence was as small as Eusebius reckoned it to be (and it probably was not),[72] the loss of his five volumes of *Exegesis of the Dominical Oracles* is to be greatly regretted. Whatever might be the historical value of the remnants of oral tradition which he gathered together in these volumes, it would be useful to know what they were.

Another bishop of Hierapolis, in the second half of the same century, was Claudius Apollinaris, who about A.D. 172 presented a work in defense of the Christian faith to the Emperor Marcus Aurelius. This work is lost, as are other works of his, including five volumes *Against the Greeks*, two volumes *Against the Jews*, two volumes *On the Truth*, and one or more treatises against the Montanists.[73]

The Montanists arose in Phrygia soon after the middle of the second century.[74] Their leader, Montanus, prophesied that the new Jerusalem would soon descend from heaven and take up its location near Pepouza, a city about thirty miles north of the Lycus valley, between the Maeander and the Senaros (Banaz Çayi). From its place of origin Montanism was known in other parts of the Christian world as the Phrygian heresy.

But orthodoxy remained vigorous in the Lycus valley, especially at Laodicea. A synod held at Laodicea around A.D. 363 promulgated sixty rules, the "Canons of Laodicea," which were acknowledged by later church councils as a basis of canon law.[75]

IV. THE "COLOSSIAN HERESY"

The recipients of the letter to the Colossians are warned against a "human tradition" which is characterized as "philosophy and empty illusion" (Col. 2:8). In the following words of ch. 2 more detailed indications are given of this "tradition." From this warning it has usually been inferred that there was a particular form of teaching current in the Lycus valley, to which the church of Colossae and the neighboring churches were exposed. This teaching was superficially attractive, but in fact its tendency was to undermine the gospel. Hence a warning was deemed necessary.

This reading of the situation was challenged in 1973 in a study by

---

[72] "He was a man of very little intelligence, as is attested by his own words" (*HE* 3.39.13), but "his own words" may be his own depreciatory self-estimate (cf. J. R. Harris, *Testimonies*, I [Cambridge, 1916], 119-20).

[73] Eusebius, *HE* 4.26.1; 4.27.1; 5.5.4; 5.16.1; 5.19.1-2.

[74] Eusebius, *HE* 5.3.4; 5.16.1–18.13.

[75] They are translated and annotated by H. R. Percival in *NPNF* 14, pp. 123-60. (See p. 120 below with n. 125.)

M. D. Hooker entitled "Were There False Teachers in Colossae?"[76] Professor Hooker did not answer her own question with a dogmatic "No," but she suggested that the data could be accounted for if Paul was arming his readers against the pressures of contemporary society with its prevalent superstitions, just as "a Christian pastor in twentieth-century Britain might well feel it necessary to remind those in his care that Christ was greater than any astrological forces."[77] The language, however, points to a specific line of teaching against which the readers are put on their guard, and the most natural reason for putting them on their guard against it would be that they were in some danger of being persuaded by it. It will be referred to henceforth for convenience as the "Colossian heresy."

The "human tradition" against which the Colossian Christians are warned is not a tradition "according to Christ" but a tradition "according to the 'elements *(stoicheia)* of the world.' " They themselves had evidently been subject to those "elements" at one time but, through faith-union with Christ, they had "died" in relation to them and so were no longer bound to obey them (Col. 2:20). The "elements" or "elemental forces" play the same part here as in the argument of Gal. 4:3, 9, where for Christians to submit to circumcision and similar requirements of the Jewish law is said to be reversion to slavery under the "elemental forces." So in the present argument, to submit to the prohibitions "Do not handle, do not taste, do not touch!" would be to reenter the state of bondage under the elemental forces from which those addressed had been delivered by their new life in Christ.

It is plain from the context that the prohibitions imply a degree of asceticism not usually associated with Jewish tradition. They refer to things that are ethically neutral, not to things that are sinful in themselves. Food, according to Paul, is ethically neutral, and "Do not handle, do not taste, do not touch!" is a vivid way of denoting various kinds of food restriction. Voluntary self-denial in matters of food can be a helpful spiritual exercise, and may on occasion be dictated by considerations of Christian charity,[78] but what is deprecated here is a form of asceticism for asceticism's sake, cultivated as a religious duty. Its association with angel worship (Col. 2:18) and "would-be religion" (Col. 2:23) could provide further help in identifying its nature and purpose.

[76]In *Christ and Spirit in the New Testament,* ed. B. Lindars and S. S. Smalley (Cambridge, 1973), pp. 315-31.
[77]*Ibid.,* p. 323.
[78]Cf. Rom. 14:20-21; 1 Cor. 8:13.

But the most help seems to be provided by the Jewish reference in "festival or new moon or sabbath" (Col. 2:16). Festivals and new moons were observed by non-Jews as well as Jews, but the sabbath was distinctively Jewish. As the Galatians' observance of "days and months and seasons and years" was a sign of their renewed and untimely subjection to the "weak and beggarly elemental forces" (Gal. 4:9-10), the same could be said of the Christians in Colossae or elsewhere if they allowed themselves to be dictated to with regard to the observance of "festival or new moon or sabbath."

Another Jewish reference may be recognized in Col. 2:11, where the inward purification symbolized in Christian baptism is called "a circumcision not made with hands"—probably in deliberate contrast to Jewish circumcision.

When an attempt is made by such indications to reconstruct the outlines of the Colossian heresy, the question naturally arises whether the reconstruction bears any resemblance to systems of thought of which something is already known.

John Calvin's acute and well-informed mind led him to identify the proponents of the heresy as Jews—but Jews of a speculative tendency, who "invented an access to God through the angels, and put forth many speculations of that nature, such as are contained in the books of Dionysius on the *Celestial Hierarchy*, drawn from the school of the Platonists."[79] The "celestial hierarchy" of Pseudo-Dionysius comprised nine orders of angels, by whose mediation God ordained that human beings should be raised to closer communion with himself.[80] His presentation of this scheme reflects a much later outlook than that of the first century, but the idea of a gradation of intermediaries which he elaborated certainly seems to have been present in the Colossian heresy.

In more recent times there has been a tendency to discern Pythagorean rather than Platonic influence. In 1970 Eduard Schweizer found analogies to the Colossian heresy in a Neopythagorean document of the first century B.C., in which he recognized the concentration of all the themes of the heresy with the exception of sabbath observance. The presence of sabbath observance in the teaching at Colossae suggested to him that it was a Jewish brand of Neopythagoreanism in which a central place

---

[79]J. Calvin, *The Epistles of Paul the Apostle to the Galatians, Ephesians, Philippians and Colossians* (1548), E.T. (Edinburgh, 1965), pp. 297-98.
[80]Pseudo-Dionysius, *Celestial Hierarchy* 1.1 (*PG* 3, cols. 119-22).

19

was given to the purification of the soul from everything earthly and its ascent to the upper ether, the dwelling place of Christ.[81]

Two generations ago the origin of the heresy was sought in an Iranian redemption myth, the outlines of which were reconstructed by Richard Reitzenstein in 1921.[82] Reitzenstein adduced various passages from Colossians to illustrate his reconstruction, but with the passage of time it has become increasingly evident that the Iranian "mystery of redemption" was more his invention than his reconstruction.

In a careful study published in 1917 Martin Dibelius traced detailed resemblances to the heresy in the record of initiation into the Isis mysteries preserved in the *Metamorphoses* of the second-century Latin writer Apuleius of Madaura.[83] It was not, of course, the Isis mysteries that attracted the Colossian Christians, but Dibelius brought out a number of striking analogies. These analogies remind us that there is a generic likeness between the actions or technical terms of many forms of initiation, no matter into what mystic cult or secret society people are initiated.

If it is asked how far initiation played a part in the Colossian heresy, the answer is presented in Col. 2:18, where it appears that the false teacher lays special weight on "the things which he has seen at his initiation."[84]

Initiation was involved in some of the gnostic movements of the second century—the Naassenes come to mind[85]—and it is easy to categorize the Colossian heresy as a first-century form of incipient gnosticism. It is not so easy, however, to relate it to any of the particular forms of

[81]E. Schweizer, "Die 'Elemente der Welt' Gal 4, 3.9; Col 2, 8.20," in *Verborum Veritas*, ed. O. Böcher and K. Haacker (Wuppertal, 1970), pp. 245-59, reprinted in his *Beiträge zur Theologie des Neuen Testaments* (Zürich, 1970), pp. 83-95; cf. *TDNT* 9, p. 850, n. 208 (*s.v.* ψυχή), and his *Colossians*, pp. 131-33. For the Neopythagorean text (preserved by Alexander Polyhistor) see H. Diels–W. Kranz, *Fragmente der Vorsokratiker*, I (Berlin, ³1952), p. 448, line 33-451 and line 19. (One theme of the Neopythagorean text, sexual abstinence, is not explicitly present in the data of Colossians, not even in Col. 2:21, μὴ ἄψῃ [despite the sense of ἅπτεσθαι in 1 Cor. 7:1], as proposed by A. R. C. Leaney, "Colossians ii.21-23," *ExT* 64 [1952-53], p. 92; the context of Col. 2:21 points to food restrictions.)

[82]R. Reitzenstein, *Das iranische Erlösungsmysterium* (Bonn, 1921); cf. his *Hellenistic Mystery Religions*, E.T. (Pittsburgh/Edinburgh, 1978).

[83]M. Dibelius, "The Isis Initiation in Apuleius and Related Initiatory Rites" (1917), E.T. in *Conflict at Colossae*, ed. F. O. Francis and W. A. Meeks (Missoula, MT, 1975), pp. 65-121. Cf. Apuleius, *Metamorphoses* 11.20-23.

[84]See exposition *ad loc.* (pp. 121-22 with nn. 131-35).

[85]See Hippolytus, *Ref.* 5.8.4 (cf. R. M. Grant, *Gnosticism: An Anthology* [London, 1961], pp. 106-07; W. Foerster, *Gnosis: A Selection of Gnostic Texts*, I [Oxford, 1972], 270-71).

developed gnosticism known from Irenaeus or Hippolytus or (more recently) from the Nag Hammadi texts. It may be that the christological use of the term *plērōma* in Colossians was designed to refute gnostic ideas associated with that term;[86] but it is impossible to be sure whether the term was used technically in the Colossian heresy or, if so, in what precise sense it was used.

There would be nothing extraordinary in the expansion of a system of incipient gnosticism in such a way as to make room within it for elements of Christianity. An instance of just such an expansion has been detected in the relation of two of the Nag Hammadi texts—*Eugnostos the Blessed* and *The Sophia of Jesus Christ. Eugnostos* takes the form of a didactic letter addressed by a teacher to his disciples; the *Sophia* takes the form of a revelatory discourse delivered by the risen Christ to his followers. While *Eugnostos* has no explicit Christian content, its substance is incorporated in the *Sophia* and christianized by means of expansions.[87]

But gnosticism, and even "incipient gnosticism," must be defined before they can be used intelligently in such a study as this. A suitable definition of gnosticism is that proposed by Gershom Scholem—it is the more suitable for our present purpose in that he had in mind especially what he called "Jewish gnosticism." He defined gnosticism as a "religious movement that proclaimed a mystical esotericism for the elect based on illumination and the acquisition of a higher knowledge of things heavenly and divine"—the higher knowledge being "soteric" as well as "esoteric."[88]

Some circles in Paul's mission field plainly set much store by knowledge *(gnōsis)* in the sense of intellectual achievement. It was to discourage such an attitude that he told the Corinthians that, by contrast with the upbuilding power of love, knowledge merely inflates the mind: "if anyone imagines that he knows something, he does not yet know as he ought to know" (1 Cor. 8:1-2). This is reminiscent of Socrates' comment that the Delphic oracle, in calling him the wisest of men, must have meant

---

[86]In Valentinianism the πλήρωμα meant the totality of aeons, the entire divine sphere, from which Sophia fell (Irenaeus, *Haer.* 1.1.3).

[87]The two treatises are set out conveniently in parallel columns in D. M. Parrott's translation, in *The Nag Hammadi Library in English*, ed. J. M. Robinson (Leiden, 1977), pp. 206-28; the Christian expansions in the *Sophia* are thus readily recognized. Cf. M. Krause, "The Christianization of Gnostic Texts," in *The New Testament and Gnosis*, ed. A. J. M. Wedderburn and A. H. B. Logan (Edinburgh, 1983), pp. 187-94.

[88]G. G. Scholem, *Jewish Gnosticism, Merkabah Mysticism, and Talmudic Tradition* (New York, 1960), p. 1.

that he knew that he did not know, whereas others equally did not know, but thought they did.[89] But when knowledge was cultivated for its own sake, as it was in some sections of the church of Corinth, it can be appreciated "into how congenial a soil the seeds of Gnosticism were about to fall."[90]

While the Colossian heresy was basically Jewish, it is not the straightforward Judaizing legalism of Galatians that is envisaged in Colossians, but a form of mysticism which tempted its adepts to look on themselves as a spiritual elite.

There were certainly movements within Judaism in which a higher knowledge was cultivated. Those who were caught up into such movements were unlikely to be uninfluenced by contemporary trends like incipient gnosticism and Neopythagoreanism. One body of Jews which laid claim to higher knowledge and special revelation was the Essene order. Bishop Lightfoot, with characteristic acumen, discerned elements of Essenism in the Colossian heresy: indeed, his three dissertations on the Essenes, included over a hundred years ago in his commentary on Colossians,[91] provided one of the most reliable accounts of the Essenes until the discovery of the Qumran texts in 1947 and the following years brought to light a wealth of literature emanating from one important branch of the Essene order.[92]

The members of the Qumran community repeatedly thank God for granting them knowledge of his "wonderful mysteries" which remain concealed from the uninitiated majority.[93] In doing so they have in mind the insight which they enjoyed into God's secret purpose and the epoch of its fulfilment. His purpose had been communicated to the prophets of earlier days, but many of its details, and especially the time of its fulfilment, had remained unrevealed. The time of its fulfilment was now approaching: this had been disclosed to the Teacher of Righteousness, together with other details of the interpretation of the prophetic oracles, and what was disclosed to him he imparted to his followers.[94] With regard to these mysteries Daniel had been told, "None of the wicked shall understand, but the wise (maśkîlîm) shall understand" (Dan. 12:10). The men of Qumran, regarding

[89]Plato Apology of Socrates 21A-23B.
[90]R. Law, The Tests of Life (Edinburgh, [3]1914), p. 28.
[91]J. B. Lightfoot, Colossians and Philemon, pp. 349-419.
[92]Cf. E. M. Yamauchi, "Qumran and Colosse," Bibliotheca Sacra 121 (1964), 141-52.
[93]E.g., 1QH 2.13: "thou hast made me an interpreter of knowledge in the wonderful mysteries" (rāzê pele').
[94]Cf. 1QpHab. 7.1-5 (on Hab. 2:3); CD 1.11-12.

themselves as the elect of the end-time, believed that this promise had been made good to them.[95]

It is unlikely that the Qumran community had members, even associate members, among the Jews of Phrygia; to follow anything like the Qumran way of life in such an environment as that would have been difficult indeed. But the Qumran community, and the wider Essene order, represented a far-flung tendency sometimes called Jewish nonconformity. This tendency is attested as far west as Rome; some features of Jewish practice there were markedly "nonconformist" in character, and persisted in later generations in Roman Christianity.[96]

To look to movements within Judaism for the sources of the Colossian heresy is a wiser procedure than to postulate direct influences from Iranian or Greek culture. There was no doubt a measure of religious syncretism in the Jewish communities of Phrygia, but some of the features of the Colossian heresy that have been thought to point to syncretism are in fact features that tend to recur in mystical experiences belonging to a wide variety of religious traditions. And not only in Jewish nonconformity but in what was destined to establish itself as normative Judaism there was present, as early as the first century B.C., a form of religious mysticism which was to endure for centuries.

This is the form known as *merkabah* mysticism, because of the place which it gave to exercises designed to facilitate entry into the vision of the heavenly chariot *(merkābāh)*, with God visibly enthroned above it— the vision granted to Ezekiel when he was called to his prophetic ministry (Ezek. 1:15-26).[97] For the gaining of such a vision punctilious observance of the *minutiae* of the law, not least the law of purification, was essential.

[95]Cf. 1QH 12.11-12: "as for me, as an instructor *(maśkîl)* I have come to know thee, my God, by the Spirit, which thou hast given to be within me, and I have heard what is trustworthy regarding thy wonderful secret counsel *(sôd)* by thy holy spirit."
[96]Cf. M. Black, *The Scrolls and Christian Origins* (London, 1961), pp. 75-88, 164-72; also pp. 99-101, 113-15, where the evidence of Hippolytus's *Apostolic Tradition* 21.5 (the order of baptism) is adduced to show that features of nonconformity survived from Roman Judaism into Roman Christianity; see further R. J. Zwi Werblowsky, "On the Baptismal Rite according to St. Hippolytus," *Studia Patristica* 2 = *TU* 64 (Berlin, 1957), 93-105.
[97]Cf. G. G. Scholem, *Major Trends in Jewish Mysticism* (Jerusalem, 1941, [3]1955/New York, [5]1971), pp. 39-78; *Jewish Gnosticism, Merkabah Mysticism, and Talmudic Tradition* (New York, [2]1965); "Merkabah Mysticism," *Encyclopaedia Judaica*, 11 (Jerusalem, 1971), cols. 1386-89. The importance of this element in the thought-world of early Christianity is examined by C. Rowland in "The Influence of the First Chapter of Ezekiel on Jewish and Early Christian Literature" (diss. Cambridge, 1974); *The Open Heaven* (London, 1982). See p. 33, note.

Moreover, in addition to what the law required of every pious Jew, a period of asceticism, variously estimated at twelve or forty days, was a necessary preparation. Then, when the heavenly ascent was attempted, the mediatorial role of angels was indispensable; it was important, therefore, not to incur their hostility, for the ascent was attended by great perils.

There is a well-known account in rabbinical tradition of the privilege of entering Paradise once granted to Rabbi Aqiba and three of his colleagues.[98] Aqiba was the only one of the four to return unscathed. Of the others, one died, one went mad, and one committed apostasy. The apostasy of Elisha ben Abuyah perhaps illustrates the dangers of the mystical ascent even better than what befell his two unfortunate companions: even for one who came through physically unharmed there was the risk of being so unbalanced by the experience that it was no longer possible to distinguish truth from error.

It is inevitable that one should recall how Paul himself once had (involuntarily, as it appears) a mystical experience of this kind, the details of which he could not or dared not divulge. As a memento of it he had to endure for the rest of his life a humiliating "thorn" in his flesh (2 Cor. 12:2-9). Whatever this physical affliction was, Paul learned to accept it as a prophylactic against the spiritual pride which was prone to beset those who had made the heavenly ascent. Such spiritual pride was evidently a strong temptation for those who had shared the mystical experience associated with the Colossian heresy: Paul describes one of those who boasted in the visions he had seen during such an experience as "inflated to no purpose by his carnal mind" (Col. 2:18).[99]

According to Gershom Scholem, the leading twentieth-century authority on *merkabah* mysticism, it was originally "a Jewish variation on one of the chief preoccupations of the second and third century gnostics and hermetics: the ascent of the soul from the earth, through the spheres of the hostile planet-angels and rulers of the cosmos, and its return to its divine home in the 'fullness' of God's light, a return which, to the Gnostic's mind, signified Redemption."[100] In terms of Scholem's definition of gnosticism (quoted above), *merkabah* mysticism may well be described, in his words, as "Jewish gnosticism."[101] The throne-world into which the *merkabah* mystic endeavored to penetrate was to him "what the *pleroma*, the 'fullness', the bright sphere of divinity with its potencies, aeons, archons

[98]Tos. *Ḥagigah* 2.3-4; TB *Ḥagigah* 14b; TJ *Ḥagigah* 77b; *SSR* 1.4.
[99]See p. 122 with nn. 136-37.
[100]G. G. Scholem, *Major Trends*, p. 48.
[101]Cf. the title of Scholem's work cited in n. 88 above; also the title of chapter 2 in *Major Trends* ("Merkabah Mysticism and Jewish Gnosticism," pp. 39-78).

and dominions is to the Hellenistic and early Christian mystics of the period who appear in the history of religion under the names of Gnostics and Hermetics."[102]

Perhaps the earliest description of the heavenly ascent in the literature of this mystical tradition is found in 1 Enoch 14:8-23, belonging probably to the early first century B.C. Here Enoch describes his upward flight to the dwelling-place of God, the "Great Glory" seated on the chariot-throne, attended by the cherubim. The description is based partly on Ezekiel's account of his inaugural vision and partly on Daniel's vision of the Ancient of Days (Dan. 7:9-10).

As time went on, the details were elaborated. Enoch speaks of two celestial houses, the throne room of God being situated in the second and higher of the two; but later descriptions of the ascent speak of the seven heavens which have to be passed through,[103] each controlled by its archon,[104] while within the seventh heaven itself the mystic must pass through seven halls or palaces (hêḵālôṯ),[105] each guarded by its angelic gatekeeper.[106] Only after all these had been safely negotiated could he behold the throne of glory. Before the throne of glory stood the angels of the divine presence, singing the praise of God; to participate in their worship and repeat their hymns was a prize highly valued by those who had completed the ascent. This is part at least of what is involved in the "angel worship" of Col. 2:18, but there is nothing reprehensible in the action of the people of God when, "with Angels and Archangels, and with all the company of heaven," they "laud and magnify" his "glorious Name; . . . saying, Holy,

---

[102]*Major Trends*, p. 43.

[103]Paul locates Paradise in the third heaven (2 Cor. 12:2-3). In *Test. Levi* 2.7-9 there appears to be an amalgamation of an earlier recension which spoke of three heavens with a later one which spoke of seven. For seven heavens cf. *Asc. Isa.* 6:13; 7:13–9:42; TB *Ḥagigah* 12b; *Pesiqta Rabbati* 98b. In 3 Baruch 2-11 there are five heavens (cf. *Apocalypse of Zephaniah* in Clement of Alexandria, *Stromateis* 5.11.77.2); in 2 Enoch 9-22 there are ten.

[104]K. Preisendanz, *Papyri Magicae Graecae*, II (Leipzig, 1931), 160, reproduces an amulet inscription of the fifth century A.D. giving the names of six of the heavens and their respective archons.

[105]From these "palaces" some of the principal treatises receive their names: the *Lesser Hekhaloth*, the *Greater Hekhaloth*, the *Book of the Hekhaloth* (edited with an English translation by H. Odeberg: *3 Enoch or the Hebrew Book of Enoch* [Cambridge, 1928]); the *Treatise of the Hekhaloth* (German translation by A. Wünsche in *Aus Israels Lehrhallen*, III [Leipzig, 1909], 33-47).

[106]From Origen, *Against Celsus* 7.40, it may be inferred that as early as Celsus (*c*. A.D. 180) the names of the heavenly gatekeepers featured in the ritual of the gnostic sect of Ophites.

holy, holy, Lord God of hosts, heaven and earth are full of thy glory."[107] However, the necessity of placating angelic powers in the course of the mystic ascent may have involved the offering of worship *to* angels over and above sharing in the worship offered *by* angels.[108] Moreover, where there was the slightest tendency to syncretism, it was almost inevitable that the seven heavens under their respective archons, or the seven palaces guarded by their respective gatekeepers, should be correlated with the seven planetary spheres ruled by their respective lords. Those who passed through the realms where such powers held sway would be careful not to offend them; otherwise, even if they succeeded in completing the upward journey, they might be impeded or injured on the way back.

It cannot be proved that the Colossian heresy involved an early form of *merkabah* mysticism, but the heavenly ascent implied in Col. 2:18 appears to have been of the same character as the experience which the *merkabah* mystics sought. The Colossian heresy evidently encouraged the claim that the fullness of God could be appreciated only by mystical experiences for which ascetic preparation was necessary. Paul's answer to such a claim is that the fullness of God is embodied in Christ, so that those who are united to him by faith have direct access in him to that fullness and have no need to submit to the ascetic rigor which the Colossian Christians were being recommended to practice, with its attendant spiritual dangers.[109]

V. THE TEACHING OF COLOSSIANS

The teaching of the letter to the Colossians is concerned with those aspects of the gospel which were chiefly threatened by the Colossian heresy—the

---

[107] "The Order of . . . Holy Communion," *Book of Common Prayer*. The Trisagion is voiced by heavenly beings in Isa. 6:3; Rev. 4:8 (it is presupposed in Revelation that the praise of the church on earth echoes that of the holy ones on high). In the *Apocalypse of Abraham* 17 Abraham recites a hymn of praise taught him by an angel. The Jewish liturgy has taken over some hymns which first figure as angelic hymns in mystical tradition, like the alphabetical acrostic composition beginning *Hā' adderet wᵉhā'ĕmûnāh lᵉḥay 'ôlāmîm* (called "the song of the angels" *par excellence*), sung on the high holy days. See also p. 119, n. 123.

[108] For the view that θρησκεία τῶν ἀγγέλων (Col. 2:18) means "participation in the angelic liturgy" (the genitive being subjective, not objective), see F. O. Francis, "Humility and Angel Worship in Col. 2:18," *Conflict at Colossae*, pp. 176-81; A. J. Bandstra, "Did the Colossian Errorists need a Mediator?" in *New Dimensions in New Testament Study*, ed. R. N. Longenecker and M. C. Tenney (Grand Rapids, 1974); also C. Rowland, "Apocalyptic Visions and the Exaltation of Christ in the Letter to the Colossians," *JSNT* 19 (October 1983), 73-83.

[109] Cf. C. A. Evans, "The Colossian Mystics," *Biblica* 63 (1982), 195-205.

uniqueness of the person of Christ, in whom the plenitude of deity was embodied; the perfection of the redeeming and reconciling work which he accomplished by his death on the cross, and the spiritual liberty enjoyed by all who by faith were united to him.

The letter was evidently called forth by the news which Epaphras had brought from the Lycus valley to Paul's place of imprisonment; Tychicus, a member of Paul's circle, was about to set out for proconsular Asia and the letter was entrusted to him for delivery.[110]

The antidote to the "human tradition" which, according to Epaphras, the Colossian Christians were disposed to accept (Col. 2:8), was a statement of the one trustworthy tradition, the true doctrine of Christ. This doctrine is presented in the words of what appears to have been an early Christian hymn (Col. 1:15-20). In two parallel strophes this hymn celebrates Christ as the image of God, the one through whom the universe was created, and also the one through whom the universe has been, or will ultimately be, reconciled to God.[111] This implies that the universe which God created has become alienated from him, so that a good relationship needs to be restored. In this regard special attention seems to be attached to "principalities and powers," forces in the spiritual world, which are evidently included among the objects of Christ's creative and reconciling agency alike.[112]

In Col. 2:8 a warning is uttered against the "human tradition" which, it is said, is in line with "the elemental forces of the world."[113] It is difficult not to associate these "elemental forces" (stoicheia) with the "principalities and powers," if not to identify them outright, and the protest against "angel worship" in Col. 2:18 probably refers to these same forces. In a vivid picture in Col. 2:14-15 Christ on the cross is portrayed as cancelling his people's indebtedness, incurred through their violation of the law, and at the same time as overcoming the "principalities and powers" and exposing their impotence.[114] This implies that his "reconciliation" of the principalities and powers amounted to their pacification through conquest, and also that their cult imposed a strict code of practice on its devotees. Emphasis is laid on the superiority of Christ to those forces, as their creator and conqueror, in order to point up the preposterousness of his people's being in bondage to them, disabled and discredited as they now are. His people have died with him and been raised to new life with him: his life is theirs—indeed, he is their life. Therefore his victory over

[110]Col. 4:7-8 (see pp. 176-77).
[111]See pp. 54-76.
[112]Col. 1:16, 20 (see pp. 63, 75).
[113]See pp. 95-100.
[114]See pp. 110-13.

the powers is theirs: let them enjoy the freedom which he has won for them!

A firm grounding in Christology, then, and in its practical implications for the daily life of believers was the best defense against the illusory attractiveness of the Colossian heresy. This appears also to be the most acceptable explanation of the almost entire absence of any reference to the Holy Spirit in this letter,[115] in contrast to most of the Pauline letters, including Ephesians. The role assigned to the Spirit in other letters is in Colossians assigned to the risen Christ. Thus, if elsewhere the indwelling Spirit is the pledge of coming glory (Rom. 8:11, 14-16, 23; 2 Cor. 5:5; Eph. 1:13-14), in this letter the indwelling Christ is his people's "hope of glory" (Col. 1:27). But time and again in Paul one comes upon parallel affirmations in which now the risen Christ and now the Spirit are said to communicate to believers the blessings of salvation. "The Spirit conveys what Christ bestows."[116] Theoretically and in principle the indwelling Christ and the indwelling Spirit are distinguishable, but practically and in experience they cannot be separated. Paul spoke of what he knew to be true in his own life and in the lives of his converts; and one of the most important things that he knew to be true was that the exalted Christ imparted his life and power to them through the Spirit. Dynamically, therefore, the exalted Christ and the indwelling Spirit were one, even if they were otherwise distinct.[117] If, in writing to the Colossians, Paul emphasized the present ministry of Christ rather than that of the Spirit, it was because he knew which emphasis was better calculated to help those particular readers in their current situation.[118]

VI. SOME CRITICAL QUESTIONS

It is not to be urged against the Pauline authorship of Colossians that such a heresy as is rebutted in the letter cannot have arisen before the second

[115]The one exception is the mention of the Colossian Christians' "love in the Spirit," reported by Epaphras (Col. 1:8).
[116]C. H. Pinnock, "The Concept of Spirit in the Epistles of Paul" (diss. Manchester, 1963), p. 105.
[117]Cf. F. F. Bruce, "Christ and Spirit in Paul," *BJRL* 59 (1976-77), 259-85 (especially 274-76).
[118]As is pointed out by E. Schweizer (*TDNT* 9, p. 650, *s.v.* ψυχή), commenting on the absence of a doctrine of the soul from Colossians and Ephesians, "the author is plainly conducting the controversy wholly in terms of christology and not anthropology"—nor yet, it may be added, pneumatology.

century A.D. If the "Colossian heresy" exhibited the features of fully developed Valentinianism or another of the gnostic systems expounded in some of the Nag Hammadi papyri or attacked by Irenaeus and Hippolytus, then the letter could scarcely be dated in the first century. But, insofar as the heresy can be characterized as gnostic, its gnosticism is but incipient and (as has been argued) predominantly Jewish in its affinities.

Another argument that has been brought against the Pauline authorship boils down to the feeling that the author of the letters to the Galatians, Corinthians, and Romans could not have adapted himself as the author of Colossians does to the situation with which this letter deals. But this imposes an unwarranted limitation on Paul's intelligence, versatility, and originality.[119] The apostle whose settled policy was to be "all things to all men" for the gospel's sake was not incapable of confronting the false *gnōsis* and worldly *askēsis* taught at Colossae with the true *gnōsis* and spiritual *askēsis* of Christ. While he opposes an uncompromising negative to the teaching which he attacks, he takes up some of its distinctive terms and shows how the truth which they vainly try to convey is embodied in Christ, the perfect revelation of God.

It has been said that Paul in this letter is doing two things at once: he is acting as the apologist for Christianity to the intellectual world of paganism at the same time as he is defending gospel truth within the church. As apologist to the Gentiles, he may have been the first to meet his pagan opponents on their own ground and use their language in a Christian sense, in order to show that the problems to which they unsuccessfully sought an answer elsewhere found their solution in the gospel.[120]

This employment of the distinctive vocabulary of the false teaching in what has been called a "disinfected" sense[121] goes some way to account for the difference in terminology which has been discerned between this letter (and Ephesians) on the one hand and the "capital" letters on the other. It may also have been partly in reaction to the false teaching that Paul developed his earlier picture of Christian fellowship in terms of the relation borne to one another by the various limbs or organs of one body to the point (reached in Colossians and Ephesians) where the church is

---

[119]While justification by faith is fundamental to Paul's outlook, it does not exhaust his message. Paulinism should not be equated so exclusively with the emphasis of Galatians and Romans that the corporate and cosmic insights of Colossians and Ephesians are felt to be non-Pauline. There is room in true Paulinism for both, and a gospel which does not make room for both will be lopsided and defective. See O. A. Dilschneider, *Das christliche Weltbild* (Gütersloh, 1951).

[120]See H. Chadwick, "All Things to All Men," *NTS* 1 (1954-55), 261-75.

[121]H. Chadwick, "All Things to All Men," p. 272.

viewed as the body of which Christ is the head. In this way not only the living fellowship among the members but the dependence of all the members on Christ for life and power is vividly brought out, and the supremacy of Christ is vindicated against a system of thought which threatened to cast him down from his excellency. That, in consequence, "body" is used in Colossians and Ephesians in correlation with "head," rather than (as in the earlier letters) with "spirit,"[122] is granted; but this provides no compelling reason for denying that the writer of the earlier letters could also have been the author of these two.

Again, some of the stylistic distinctiveness of this letter is bound up with its sustained notes of thanksgiving and credal affirmation, which probably echo the language of primitive Christian worship and confession.[123] For the rest, there is evidence within the letter that Timothy's name is not attached to Paul's in the prescript merely as a courtesy, but that he was in some degree joint-author (more so in Colossians than in any other letter which includes his name in the prescript).[124] Eduard Schweizer, who finds that this letter is neither Pauline nor post-Pauline, finds in the mention of Timothy a clue to its possible authorship. Paul, he concedes, was happy to endorse it with his signature at the end and made some personal contributions (as at Col. 1:23). According to Schweizer, the treatment of the law in Colossians is more positive than in Paul: to describe the law as a "shadow" of the reality which was embodied in Christ (Col. 2:17) is to give it a higher status than Paul would allow.[125] But if Paul and Timothy were in any degree joint-authors of a letter, the probability is that, while the literary style might be Timothy's, the ultimate authorship would be Paul's.

Some scholars, represented mainly by H. J. Holtzmann in the nineteenth century[126] and Charles Masson in the twentieth,[127] recognizing indubitable Pauline elements in Colossians, have tried to account for the

---

[122]But note the collocation of "one body" and "one Spirit" in Eph. 4:4 (p. 336).

[123]Outstandingly in the hymn of Col. 1:15-20 (pp. 54-76).

[124]See comment on Col. 1:3 (pp. 40-41).

[125]E. Schweizer, *The Letter to the Colossians*, E.T. (Minneapolis/London, 1982), pp. 15-24.

[126]H. J. Holtzmann, *Kritik der Epheser- und Kolosserbriefe* (Leipzig, 1872). The genuine nucleus discerned by Holtzmann consisted of Col. 1:1-5, 6a, 7, 8, 9a, 10 (in part), 13, 19-20 (in part), 21-23 (in part), 25, 29; 2:1, 2a, 4, 5, 6, 7b, 8, 9 (in part), 11 (in part), 12-14, 16, 18b, 20, 21, 22a, 23b; 3:3, 12, 13, 17; 4:2-5 (for the most part), 6-8, 10-11, 12 (in considerable part), 13-15.

[127]C. Masson, *L'Épître de Saint Paul aux Colossiens*, CNT 10 (Neuchâtel/Paris, 1950), 86 *et passim*. Masson's argument is independent of Holtzmann's, although his conclusions are generally similar.

presence of elements felt to be un-Pauline by supposing that the letter which Paul sent to the Colossians was shorter than the letter now in our hands. The shorter letter was drawn upon by the Paulinist who is supposed to have written the letter to the Ephesians. Then this Paulinist, not content with composing such a masterpiece as Ephesians, interpolated passages from Ephesians into the genuine Colossians, together with warnings against gnosticism, and thus produced the expanded document which has come down to us as the letter to the Colossians. Holtzmann attempted by this hypothesis to explain the curious phenomenon that, in passages substantially common to the two letters, sometimes Colossians and sometimes Ephesians appears to be the earlier. But A. S. Peake's comment on Holtzmann's formulation, "the complexity of the hypothesis tells fatally against it,"[128] is equally applicable to its formulation by Masson and more recent writers.

Yet the hypothesis continues to be resurrected in one form or another. Johannes Weiss thought that such a hypothesis would solve not only this particular problem but also further difficulties in NT criticism.[129] John Knox thought Holtzmann's formulation had been dismissed too quickly.[130] P. N. Harrison identified three passages in Colossians (1:9b-25; 2:8-23; 3:14-16) which, with one or two minor pieces, he believed to be inserted into the original text of Colossians by the author of Ephesians. Following John Knox and E. J. Goodspeed, he held the author of Ephesians to be Onesimus.[131] The interpolated passages (especially Col. 2:8-23) he found to be un-Pauline in style and vocabulary but quite similar in these respects to Ephesians. After writing Ephesians, he suggested, Onesimus "felt moved to add to this letter [Colossians], which meant so much to him, what he sincerely believed the Apostle would have added had he known what the future had in store for Christ's people."[132]

Without becoming involved in such complex hypotheses, others have found evidence for the influence of Ephesians on Colossians. F. C. Synge has found few followers in his theory that Ephesians was a genuine letter of Paul and Colossians a feeble imitation of it.[133] A more careful comparative study by J. Coutts argues for the priority of Ephesians on the

---

[128]A. S. Peake, *Critical Introduction to the New Testament* (London, 1909), p. 52.

[129]J. Weiss, *Earliest Christianity* (1937), E.T., I (New York, 1959), 150.

[130]J. Knox, *Christ the Lord* (Chicago, 1945), p. 102, n. 20.

[131]See pp. 202, 242.

[132]P. N. Harrison, *Paulines and Pastorals* (London, 1964), pp. 65-78 (the words quoted are from p. 77).

[133]F. C. Synge, *St. Paul's Epistle to the Ephesians* (London, 1941); *Philippians and Colossians* (London, 1951), pp. 51-57.

ground that, where literary dependence of one letter on the other is argued for, a Colossians passage (e.g., 2:19) can be derived in its entirety from one passage in Ephesians (e.g., 4:15b-16), whereas the Ephesians passage (4:15b-16) would, if dependent, have to be derived from three passages in Colossians (not only 2:19, but also 2:7 and 2:2). The repeated occurrence of this situation, together with evidence (as he saw it) that Colossians makes passing and even abrupt allusion to doctrinal statements which are carefully worked out in Ephesians, ruled out the view "that Ephesians is directly dependent on Colossians," although the possibility was left open that the relation between the two letters "is more complicated than that of simple dependence of either on the other."[134]

A more complicated relation is defended by Winsome Munro so far as the household codes in the two letters (Col. 3:18–4:1; Eph. 5:21–6:9) are concerned.[135] She goes along for the most part with C. L. Mitton's argument that Ephesians is predominantly dependent on Colossians, but maintains that "Col. 3:18–4:1 is dependent on, and therefore subsequent to, Eph. 5:21–6:9" (Eph. 5:21–6:9 being, as she further argues, a later interpolation into the text of Ephesians).[136]

In fact, the household code of Col. 3:18–4:1 belongs to the paraenetic tradition of the Pauline circle, as the hymn of Col. 1:15-20 belongs to the liturgical tradition. When we find arguments for the dependence of Ephesians on Colossians balanced by arguments for the dependence of Colossians on Ephesians, we may conclude that the relation between the two letters is not a purely literary one, but rather that both letters took shape at the same time in the circle of Paul and his co-workers. The one person to be recognized as the author is Paul, whatever part may have been played by Timothy or any other of his companions who were with him at the time.

As for the date and place of writing, dogmatism is to be avoided. Paul's Roman confinement at the beginning of the 60s is the life-setting preferred here—largely because it allows adequate time for the development of Paul's thought from the stage represented by his Corinthian correspondence. To date Colossians to the same period as the Corinthian correspondence, which would be required if it were assigned to an Ephesian imprisonment, is extremely difficult. To assign the letter to Paul's Caesarean imprisonment is much less difficult, but no argument in its favor

[134]J. Coutts, "The Relationship of Ephesians and Colossians," *NTS* 4 (1957-58), 201-07 (the words quoted are from p. 201).
[135]See p. 397, n. 4.
[136]W. Munro, *Authority in Paul and Peter* (Cambridge, 1983), pp. 27-37 (the words quoted are from p. 31).

can be produced either from internal evidence or from tradition; and one cannot readily envisage Onesimus as making his way from the Lycus valley to Caesarea.[137]

---

[137]See pp. 194-96 with nn. 11-16. The ablest case known to me in favor of the Caesarean provenance of Colossians, Ephesians, and Philemon is that presented by B. Reicke, "Caesarea, Rome and the Captivity Epistles," in *Apostolic History and the Gospel*, ed. W. W. Gasque and R. P. Martin (Exeter/Grand Rapids, 1970), pp. 277-86 (especially pp. 278-82).

Addition to n. 97 (p. 23). See also P. S. Alexander, Introduction to 3 Enoch in *The Old Testament Pseudepigrapha*, ed. J. H. Charlesworth, I (Garden City, N.Y., 1983), 223-54; "Comparing Merkavah Mysticism and Gnosticism," *Journal of Jewish Studies* 35 (1984), 1-18; P. Schäfer, "New Testament and Hekhalot Literature," *Journal of Jewish Studies* 35 (1984), 19-25.

ANALYSIS OF COLOSSIANS

I. PRESCRIPT (1:1-2)
II. THE PERSON AND WORK OF CHRIST (1:3-23)
    1. THANKSGIVING FOR NEWS OF THE COLOSSIANS' FAITH (1:3-8)
    2. PRAYER FOR THE COLOSSIANS' SPIRITUAL WELFARE (1:9-14)
    3. HYMN IN HONOR OF CHRIST (1:15-20)
        (1) Christ the Agent in Creation (1:15-16)
        (2) Lord of the Universe and Head of the Church (1:17-18a)
        (3) Christ the Agent in Reconciliation (1:18b-20)
    4. SINNERS RECONCILED TO GOD (1:21-23)
III. PAUL'S MINISTRY (1:24 – 2:7)
    1. STEWARDSHIP OF THE DIVINE MYSTERY (1:24-29)
    2. CONCERN FOR THE CHRISTIANS OF THE LYCUS VALLEY (2:1-5)
        (1) Reassurance of Paul's Prayers for Them (2:1-3)
        (2) His Anxiety Lest They Be Misled (2:4-5)
    3. MAINTAINING THE TRADITION OF CHRIST (2:6-7)
IV. FALSE TEACHING AND ITS ANTIDOTE (2:8 – 3:4)
    1. THE ALL-SUFFICIENCY OF CHRIST (2:8-15)
        (1) The Fullness of Christ (2:8-10)
        (2) The New Circumcision (2:11-12)
        (3) The Triumph of Christ (2:13-15)
    2. GUARD YOUR FREEDOM! (2:16-19)
        (1) Freedom in Respect of Food and Festivals (2:16-17)
        (2) Freedom in Respect of Asceticism and Angel Worship (2:18-19)
    3. YOU DIED WITH CHRIST; THEREFORE . . . (2:20-23)
    4. YOU WERE RAISED WITH CHRIST; THEREFORE . . . (3:1-4)
V. THE CHRISTIAN LIFE (3:5 – 4:6)

Text, Exposition, and Notes

COLOSSIANS 1

I. PRESCRIPT (1:1-2)

1 *Paul, an apostle of Christ Jesus through God's will, and our brother Timothy,*
2 *to the saints and faithful brothers in Christ at Colossae: grace and peace be yours from God our Father.*[1]

1 As in the companion letter to Philemon, by contrast with that to the Ephesians, Paul associates Timothy with himself in saluting the Christians of Colossae. Timothy's name is similarly linked with Paul's in the prescripts of 2 Corinthians, Philippians, Philemon, and (together with that of Silvanus) 1 and 2 Thessalonians. Timothy may have served Paul as amanuensis in the writing of these letters, but that would not be a sufficient reason for naming him in the prescript. (Tertius finds no place in the prescript of the letter to the Romans.) It is plain from Col. 4:7-14 that Paul had several other associates with him when this letter was written: that Timothy alone is named along with him in the prescript is due to Timothy's sharing his ministry on a permanent basis.

Timothy was a native of Lystra in Lycaonia (modern Zoldera, near Hatunsaray), the son of a Jewish mother and a Greek father. He became a Christian during Barnabas and Paul's first visit to his hometown (Acts 14:8-20). When Paul passed that way again a year or two later he was impressed by Timothy's spiritual development and enlisted him as a junior associate in his apostolic service, circumcising him first to regularize his anomalous religious status (Acts 16:1-3). Timothy willingly joined Paul and served him thereafter as his devoted adjutant (the quality of his de-

---

[1]The words "and the Lord Jesus Christ" (cf. KJV) appear in ℵ A C F G and the majority of cursives (exhibiting the Byzantine text); they are omitted by B D K L Ψ with the oldest Latin codices, the Syriac Peshitta, and Ambrosiaster. See p. 39, n. 6.

votion can be gathered from Paul's appreciative tribute to him in Phil. 2:20-22).

The designation "apostle" is reserved for Paul; it is not shared with Timothy—nor yet with Epaphras, who (as appears from v. 7) first brought the gospel to Colossae. Paul alone was the Colossians' apostle, even if he had never visited them in person. For, whereas he had been independently and directly commissioned by the risen Lord, Timothy and Epaphras and others, however much he loved and honored them as "fellow-servants," were his lieutenants, called to aid him in the twofold task of preaching the gospel and planting churches. Where, as in 1 Thess. 2:6, others (such as Silvanus and Timothy) are linked with Paul as "apostles of Christ," the term is used in a wider sense, in which apostleship, instead of being based on an immediate commissioning by Christ, is "grounded in the preaching of the genuine gospel, under the guidance of the Holy Spirit, whether in association with Paul or independently of Paul's mission."[2]

Paul identifies himself as Christ's "apostle" in the prescripts of all his extant letters except those to Philemon, the Thessalonians, and the Philippians. The noun "apostle" is qualified by the phrase "through God's will" in the prescripts of 1 Corinthians, 2 Corinthians, Ephesians, Colossians, and 2 Timothy. The phrase applies not only to his commissioning on the Damascus road (cf. Gal. 1:15-16) but to the entire discharge of his commission.

2 The people to whom the letter is sent are described as "saints

[2]D. W. B. Robinson, "Apostleship and Apostolic Succession," *RTR* 13 (1954), 38. On apostleship in the early church see also J. B. Lightfoot, *Galatians* (London, 1865), pp. 92-101; E. D. Burton, *Galatians*, ICC (Edinburgh, 1921), pp. 363-84; K. H. Rengstorf, *TDNT* 1, pp. 407-77 (*s.v.* ἀπόστολος); H. Riesenfeld, *RGG*[3] 1, pp. 497-99 (*s.v.* "Apostel"); D. Müller and C. Brown, *NIDNTT* 1, pp. 126-37 (*s.v.* "Apostle"); E. Käsemann, "Die Legitimität des Apostels," *ZNW* 41 (1942), 33-71; T. W. Manson, *The Church's Ministry* (London, 1948), pp. 31-52; A. Fridrichsen, *The Apostle and his Message* (Uppsala, 1947); H. von Campenhausen, "Der urchristliche Apostelbegriff," *ST* 1 (1948-49), 96-130; H. Mosbech, "Apostolos in the New Testament," *ST* 2 (1949-50), 166-200; J. Munck, "Paul, the Apostles and the Twelve," *ST* 3 (1950-51), 96-110; E. Lohse, "Ursprung und Prägung des christlichen Apostolats," *TZ* 9 (1953), 259-75; G. Klein, *Die zwölf Apostel* (Göttingen, 1961); R. Schnackenburg, "Apostles before and during Paul's Time," in *Apostolic History and the Gospel*, ed. W. W. Gasque and R. P. Martin (Exeter/Grand Rapids, 1970), pp. 287-303; C. K. Barrett, *The Signs of an Apostle* (London, 1970), and "*Shaliaḥ* and Apostle," in *Donum Gentilicium*, ed. C. K. Barrett, E. Bammel, and W. D. Davies (Cambridge, 1978), pp. 88-102; W. Schmithals, *The Office of Apostle in the Early Church*, E.T. (London, 1971); J. H. Schütz, *Paul and the Anatomy of Apostolic Authority* (Cambridge, 1975); R. W. Herron, "The Origin of the New Testament Apostolate," *WTJ* 45 (1983), 101-31.

and faithful brothers in Christ." The word "saints" marks them out as God's holy people, chosen and set apart by him for himself.[3] The phrase "faithful brothers" might be rendered "believing brothers," but if the adjective meant "believing," it would add nothing to the sense, whereas it clearly bears the fuller meaning "faithful" when qualifying "brother" or a similar noun in Col. 1:7; 4:7, 9.

The prescript of an ancient letter regularly consisted of three elements: the name of the sender or senders, the name of the addressee or addressees, and a message of greeting. The greeting used habitually by Jews was "Peace!" (Heb. *shālôm*) or, more fully, "Mercy and peace!" (cf. 2 Bar. 78:2). The form "grace and peace"[4] is characteristically Pauline: both terms have their full Christian force. Grace is God's unconditioned goodwill toward men and women which is decisively expressed in the saving work of Christ (cf. v. 6); peace is the state of life—peace with God (cf. v. 20) and peace with one another (cf. Eph. 2:14-18)—enjoyed by those who have effectively experienced the divine grace.

The Christian force of "grace and peace" is confirmed by the following words. Only in 1 Thess. 1:1 does the salutation "grace and peace be yours" stand alone, without any such amplification. The amplification usually takes the form: "from God our Father and the Lord Jesus Christ" (perhaps the whole salutation, including these words, was first employed in Christian worship and then taken over from a liturgical context to serve as an epistolary greeting).[5] It is difficult to say why the words "and the Lord Jesus Christ" are absent from the salutation in Colossians.[6] In any case, all that these words could convey is set forth in detail in the celebration of the person and work of Christ later in the letter (cf. vv. 13-20).

II. THE PERSON AND WORK OF CHRIST (1:3-23)

1. THANKSGIVING FOR NEWS OF THE COLOSSIANS' FAITH (1:3-8)

3 We thank God, the Father of our Lord Jesus Christ, as we pray for you at all times,

---

[3]See Eph. 2:19, with exposition and notes (pp. 302-03).

[4]Gk. χάρις καὶ εἰρήνη, as in Rom. 1:7; 1 Cor. 1:3; 2 Cor. 1:2; Gal. 1:3; Eph. 1:2; Phil. 1:2; 1 Thess. 1:2; 2 Thess. 1:2; Tit. 1:4 (amplified to χάρις ἔλεος εἰρήνη in 1 Tim. 1:2; 2 Tim. 1:2); Philem. 3.

[5]Cf. E. Lohmeyer, "Probleme paulinischer Theologie, I. Briefliche Grussüberschriften," *ZNW* 26 (1927), 158-73; also G. Friedrich, "Lohmeyers These über 'das paulinische Briefpräskript' kritisch beleuchtet," *ZNW* 46 (1955), 272-74.

[6]See n. 1 above. The very uniqueness of this reading speaks in its favor; there would be a very strong tendency to assimilate the wording to Paul's usual practice.

4 *because we have heard of your faith in Christ Jesus and the love which you have for all the saints,*

5 *on account of the hope which is laid up for you in heaven. You have already heard of this hope in the true message of the gospel*

6 *which has come to you, as indeed it is bearing fruit and increasing in all the world, just as it has been doing among you ever since the day you heard it and came to know the grace of God in truth.*

7 *This is how you learned it from our dear fellow-servant Epaphras, who is a faithful minister of Christ on your[7] behalf;*

8 *it was he indeed who informed us of your love in the Spirit.*

3 In Greek letters an expression of thanks occasionally follows the prescript.[8] Such an introductory thanksgiving is a special feature of Paul's epistolary style (it is significantly absent from Galatians).[9] The note of thanksgiving is particularly conspicuous in this letter. In the present passage the thanksgiving is interwoven (like other introductory thanksgivings in the Pauline letters) with an intercessory prayer-report.[10]

Even when someone else's name is conjoined with Paul's in the prescript of a letter, the thanksgiving which follows is normally expressed in the singular: "*I* thank God." This implies that the other person's name is conjoined with Paul's by way of courtesy; Paul is the real author of the letter. But in this letter, as in the two to the Thessalonians, the thanksgiving is expressed in the plural. In 1 and 2 Thessalonians this is because Silvanus

---

[7]The reading "our" (ἡμῶν) has in its favor the formidable combination of P^{46} and the Alexandrian and Western authorities; the Byzantine reading "your" (ὑμῶν) is attested in C Ψ and the Latin, Syriac, and other versions. In a context where either reading gives good sense, the weight of the textual evidence should be decisive. Yet UBS³ and NA²⁶ prefer ὑμῶν. There is constant confusion in Greek MSS between the various forms of ἡμεῖς ("we") and the corresponding forms of ὑμεῖς ("you"), partly because of the identity of pronunciation of the two pronouns in later Hellenistic Greek and partly because of the rhetorical preference for the inclusive "we" over "you." In a case like the present one the confusion may well go back beyond our earliest textual evidence—even (conceivably) to the author's dictating the one form and the copyist's writing down the other.

[8]Cf. P. Schubert, *Form and Function of the Pauline Thanksgivings* (Berlin, 1939); P. T. O'Brien, *Introductory Thanksgivings in the Letters of Paul* (Leiden, 1977), pp. 62-104. For epistolary thanksgiving to a deity immediately after the opening salutation cf. BGU II.423, as quoted by A. Deissmann, *Light from the Ancient East*, E.T. (London, ²1927), pp. 179-83 (thanksgiving to "the Lord Serapis").

[9]Cf. Rom. 1:8-9; 1 Cor. 1:4; Eph. 1:16; Phil. 1:3-4; 1 Thess. 1:2; 2 Thess. 1:3; Philem. 4.

[10]Cf. G. P. Wiles, *Paul's Intercessory Prayers* (Cambridge, 1974). For the assurance of unceasing prayer in such contexts cf. Rom. 1:9; 1 Cor. 1:4; Eph. 1:15; Phil. 1:3-4; 1 Thess. 1:2; 3:10 (νυκτὸς καὶ ἡμέρας); 2 Thess. 1:3, 11; Philem. 4.

is joint-author; it is a reasonable inference from the wording here ("we thank God") that Timothy to some extent shares the responsibility of authorship with Paul.

4 It is from Epaphras (as appears from v. 8) that the news of the Colossian Christians' spiritual progress has been received.

As the reasons for thanksgiving are enumerated, we recognize the familiar triad of Christian graces—faith, love, hope—similarly grouped together elsewhere in the Pauline writings (cf. 1 Cor. 13:13; also Rom. 5:1-5; Gal. 5:5-6; 1 Thess. 1:3; 5:8) and in other parts of the NT (cf. Heb. 10:22-24; 1 Pet. 1:21-22).[11] Here the three are not exactly coordinated: the Colossians' faith in Christ and love to their fellow-believers are here based on the hope which is laid up for them in heaven. The phrase "faith in Christ Jesus" indicates not so much that Christ Jesus is the object of their faith as that he is the living environment within which their faith is exercised. That is to say, the faith referred to is the faith which they have as men and women who are "in Christ" (cf. v. 2) or "in Christ Jesus," incorporated in him (cf. Col. 2:19).[12]

5 The emphasis on hope reminds us that the salvation which believers already enjoy in Christ has a future aspect. The hope is theirs here and now; its fulfilment lies ahead, in the resurrection age. Paul encourages his readers elsewhere to expect that fulfilment on the day of Christ's *parousia*; in this sense he speaks of salvation as being "nearer to us now than when we first believed" (Rom. 13:11). A proper appreciation of "realized eschatology" should not be allowed to eclipse the prospect of that "revealing of the sons of God" for which "the creation waits with eager longing" (Rom. 8:19). This Christian hope formed part of the subject-matter of the gospel as it was originally proclaimed at Colossae: "laid up in heaven" as it is, it cannot well be anything other than Christ himself,

---

[11]Cf. also *Ep. Barn.* 1:4; 11:8; *Ep. Polyc.* 3:2-3. "The triad of faith, hope and love is the quintessence of the God-given life in Christ" (G. Bornkamm, *Paul*, E.T. [London/New York, 1971], p. 219). A. M. Hunter (*Paul and his Predecessors* [London, ²1961], pp. 33-35) and others have maintained that the triad belongs to the vocabulary of pre-Pauline Christianity. See also R. Reitzenstein, *Die Formel Glaube, Liebe, Hoffnung bei Paulus*, NGG, philologische-historische Klasse (1916), p. 393.

[12]The preposition here is ἐν, not εἰς (as it is in Col. 2:5, τῆς εἰς Χριστὸν πίστεως ὑμῶν, where Christ is the object of their faith). For such a use of ἐν after πίστις cf. Eph. 1:15 (closely parallel to the present passage); also Gal. 3:26; 5:6; 1 Tim. 1:14; 3:13; 2 Tim. 1:13; 3:15. In most, perhaps all, of these passages the sphere of faith rather than the object of faith seems to be in view (cf. C. F. D. Moule, *IBNTG*, p. 81).

41

who lives there at God's right hand and at the same time indwells his people as their "hope of glory" (Col. 1:27; 3:1-4).[13]

The description of the Christian proclamation as "the true message of the gospel" (lit., "the word of the truth of the gospel") is echoed and amplified in Eph. 1:13, "the message of truth, the gospel of your salvation." In Christian idiom, indeed, "the truth" and "the gospel" are interchangeable terms: obeying the truth (Rom. 2:8; Gal. 5:7) and obeying the gospel (Rom. 10:16) are identical. (Compare also "the truth of the gospel" in Gal. 2:5, 14.)

6 When the gospel is described as "bearing fruit and increasing," there may be an echo of our Lord's parable of the sower (Mark 4:8 par.)— not that any of the canonical Gospels was available when this letter was composed, but outlines of the teaching of Jesus were in circulation, orally if not in some written form. It is unnecessary to suppose that the language about fruit-bearing presupposes a gnosticizing interpretation of the parable in the teaching which was being offered to the Colossians.[14] It has been pointed out that the same verb is found at the end of the thirteenth tractate of the *Corpus Hermeticum,* where there is a reference to "reaping the good fruits of truth, an immortal harvest"; but if there is any borrowing here (which is doubtful), it is on the Hermetic side.[15] (Paul's choice of words does not support those interpretations which exclude the thought of development from the parable and kindred parables.)

The message of the gospel, which was producing the vigorous and ever multiplying fruit of Christian life and testimony at Colossae, was doing the same, it is said, throughout the world. The letter was written (probably) in Rome, but in addition to Paul's own propagation of the gospel from Jerusalem to Illyricum, and now in the imperial city itself, the same gospel was being blazed abroad by other heralds too. "The whole gospel for the whole world" might well have been Paul's motto, and if at times the language which he uses to express this idea seems to outstrip what had actually been accomplished, it was with the eye of a prophet that he

---

[13]Cf. v. 23, "the hope of the gospel." See also C. F. D. Moule, *The Meaning of Hope* (London, 1954); J. E. Fison, *The Christian Hope* (London, 1954); J. Moltmann, *The Theology of Hope,* E.T. (London, 1967). See further on v. 27 below.

[14]Cf. W. L. Knox, *St. Paul and the Church of the Gentiles* (Cambridge, 1939), p. 149 n.

[15]*C.H.* 13.22a (καρποφορήσαντος ἐκ τῆς ἀληθείας τὰ ἀγαθά, τὰ ἀθάνατα γενήματα); cf. W. L. Knox, *Some Hellenistic Elements in Primitive Christianity* (London, 1944), p. 94.

descried the all-pervading course of the message of life rivaling that of the heavenly bodies of which the psalmist spoke: "Their voice has gone out to all the earth, and their words to the ends of the world" (Rom. 10:18, quoting Ps. 19:4).[16]

When the Colossians are reminded how they "came to know the grace of God in truth," the meaning may be that they came to know it truly; but it is more probable that "in truth" is equivalent to "with truth": the divine grace which they experienced was accompanied by truth.[17] In attaining the personal knowledge of Christ, they came to know the grace and truth which, as the prologue to the Fourth Gospel affirms, "came through Jesus Christ" (John 1:17).[18]

7 What was true of the progress of the gospel elsewhere was true at Colossae as well: the Christians of that city had continued to grow in spiritual character and in actual numbers since the day they first heard and believed the gospel. The gospel told them of the grace of God, brought near to them in Christ, and when they yielded their allegiance to Christ as Lord and Savior they came to know in personal and united experience the reality of that grace. The preacher from whom they first heard the saving message bore the name Epaphras. Paul refers to him in terms of affection and commendation, as a dear colleague in the service of God,[19] who had gone to Colossae and the neighboring cities as his own representative and as a trusty minister of Christ.

Epaphras is mentioned again in Col. 4:12 and in Philem. 23. The name is a shortened form of Epaphroditus. Elsewhere in the Pauline corpus we meet a Philippian Christian named Epaphroditus (Phil. 2:25; 4:18), but

[16]Cf. v. 23; Rom. 1:8; 1 Thess. 1:8. J. Munck interprets the universal terminology of such passages (especially Rom. 10:18) as reflecting Paul's conviction of the eschatological significance of his ministry (*Paul and the Salvation of Mankind*, E.T. [London, 1959], pp. 43-55, 275-79, etc.).

[17]That is to say, ἐν has comitative force; cf. Col. 4:2 (ἐν εὐχαριστίᾳ); Eph. 4:19 (ἐν πλεονεξίᾳ), etc. See K. G. Kuhn, "The Epistle to the Ephesians in the Light of the Qumran Texts," E.T. in J. Murphy-O'Connor (ed.), *Paul and Qumran* (London, 1968), pp. 119-20.

[18]Cf. John 1:14, where πλήρης χάριτος καὶ ἀληθείας is probably a rendering of *rab ḥeseḏ weʾĕmeṯ* in the revelation of the divine name in Exod. 34:6.

[19]He uses the term σύνδουλος ("fellow-slave"), used also of Tychicus in Col. 4:7. T. R. Glover regards Paul's fondness for compounds with σύν as a mannerism which discloses something of his character: "The dearest of all ties for Paul is to find men sharing things with him. The work, the 'athletic' life, the yoke, the slavery, the imitation,—these are all expressions of his relation with Jesus Christ, the very essence of life; how much more it is to him when he finds his friends standing with him in that great loyalty!" (*Paul of Tarsus* [London, 1925], p. 180).

there is no reason to identify the two.[20] In Philem. 23 Epaphras is described as Paul's fellow-captive,[21] but we know nothing of the circumstances in which he earned this description. Probably he shared one of Paul's more abundant imprisonments, possibly in Ephesus. At any rate he had discharged his responsibility well as the evangelist of the Lycus valley, for there were flourishing churches in that area—in Hierapolis and Laodicea as well as in Colossae—to testify to the enduring quality of his work.

8 More recently Epaphras had visited Paul and Timothy and told them how these churches were faring. Much of his news was good and encouraging, but some aspects of church life at Colossae were disquieting, and it was this that stimulated Paul and Timothy to write particularly to the Christians of that city. First of all, however, they dwell on the good report which Epaphras had brought: he "informed us," they say, "of your love in the Spirit." This is "God's love" which, according to Rom. 5:5, "has been poured into our hearts through the Holy Spirit"; it is the mutual love implanted and fostered within them by the indwelling Spirit and uniting them in a living bond.

This is the only explicit reference to the Spirit of God in the letter. The absence of reference to him elsewhere is the more striking since there are several points at which his activity might have been naturally introduced. Where other letters of Paul speak of the Spirit's presence with believers as the guarantee of their resurrection and eternal inheritance (Rom. 8:11, 15-17; Eph. 1:13-14), this letter speaks of the indwelling Christ as their hope of glory (v. 27). But the presence and ministry of the Spirit are implied here and there in Colossians—for example, in opposition to the "flesh" as the source of true knowledge.[22]

2. PRAYER FOR THE COLOSSIANS' SPIRITUAL WELFARE (1:9-14)

9 Therefore, since the day we heard this news, we for our part offer up unceasing prayers and requests on your behalf, that you may be

---

[20]As Glover does (*Paul of Tarsus*, p. 179), adding the two compounds with which Paul describes Epaphroditus (συνεργός, συνστρατιώτης, both in Phil. 2:25) to the two with which he describes Epaphras (σύνδουλος and συναιχμάλωτος, Philem. 23) to give him four in all.

[21]Like Aristarchus, similarly called συναιχμάλωτος in Col. 4:10.

[22]As in Col. 2:18. Cf. the adjective πνευματικός in v. 9.

filled with the knowledge of God's will together with all wisdom and spiritual understanding.[23]

10 *We pray that you may conduct yourselves in a manner worthy of the Lord, to please him in everything. May you bear fruit in every good work and increase in the knowledge of God;*

11 *may you be empowered with all power in accordance with his glorious might, and so attain all patience and perseverance.*

12 *May you give thanks with joy[24] to the Father, who has qualified you[25] for your share in the inheritance of the saints in the realm of light.*

13 *It is he who has rescued us from the dominion of darkness and transferred us into the kingdom of the Son whom he loves,*

14 *the Son in whom we have our redemption,[26] the forgiveness of our sins.*

9 Paul and Timothy repeat the assurance of their constant prayers on the Colossian Christians' behalf—prayers which have been redoubled since Epaphras came with news of their progress. The brief prayer-report of v. 3 is now amplified.

Their prayer for the Colossians, then, is that they may gain the full knowledge of God's will[27] through the insight that his Spirit imparts, and thus be able to please him in everything and live in a way that befits his

---

[23]Gk. ἐν πάσῃ σοφίᾳ καὶ συνέσει πνευματικῇ, where ἐν may be taken as comitative (cf. n. 17 above) or as instrumental ("by means of all wisdom . . ."). It is possible that πνευματικῇ qualifies σοφίᾳ as well as συνέσει, but σοφία unqualified is used in the Pauline writings in the sense of divine wisdom (cf. v. 28 below). See p. 260, n. 68.

[24]Gk. μετὰ χαρᾶς εὐχαριστοῦντες, but μετὰ χαρᾶς could well go closely with the preceding ὑπομονὴν καὶ μακροθυμίαν, replacing καὶ χαρὰν "in order to achieve variety of expression" (K. G. Kuhn, "The Epistle to the Ephesians in the Light of the Qumran Texts," p. 119). Like καρποφοροῦντες, etc. (vv. 10-11), εὐχαριστοῦντες refers to the Colossians.

[25]Gk. ἱκανώσαντι, for which a few authorities (mainly Western, but including the Sahidic, Armenian, and Ethiopic versions) have καλέσαντι ("called"). B conflates the two readings, καλέσαντι καὶ ἱκανώσαντι ("called and qualified"). ℵ and B, with a few other authorities, make the object ὑμᾶς ("you"), preferred by NA[26] and UBS[3] on the ground that the majority reading ἡμᾶς ("us") is probably an assimilation to v. 13. The preference for ὑμᾶς could be defended if the clause is to be read in the same sense as Eph. 2:19 (συμπολῖται τῶν ἁγίων); if it is so read, those addressed would be Gentile Christians as distinct from Jewish Christians (see p. 302).

[26]Many cursives add διὰ τοῦ αἵματος αὐτοῦ ("through his blood"), a borrowing from Eph. 1:7, which has been perpetuated by the TR and the KJV.

[27]For the knowledge of God's will cf. Rom. 12:2 (also Acts 22:14). From Rom. 2:18 it might be inferred that to "know the will" (namely, of God) was a current expression in Hellenistic-Jewish terminology.

children. Although there is only one explicit mention of the Holy Spirit in this letter (v. 8), there is an allusion to his operation here in the phrase "spiritual understanding." The wisdom and understanding which Paul and Timothy desire to see in the Colossian Christians are inseparable from the knowledge of God and of his will—a knowledge which, as the prophets of Israel insisted, is of the essence of true heart-religion.[28] Both this letter and the companion letter to the Ephesians have much to say about this knowledge as a means of promoting spiritual life.[29] This knowledge is no merely intellectual exercise, no theosophical *gnōsis* such as was affected by the teachers who threatened to lead the Colossian church astray. The Colossians must be impressed with the nature and importance of true knowledge before being warned against that "knowledge falsely so called" which was being pressed upon them.[30] True knowledge is founded in practical religion; it is that knowledge which, as the OT wisdom writers affirmed, starts with a proper attitude toward God: "The fear of the LORD is the beginning of knowledge" (Prov. 1:7).[31] Right knowledge leads to right behavior:[32] it was because the pagan world, according to Paul, "did not see fit to retain God in their knowledge" that they were abandoned "to a base mind and to improper conduct" (Rom. 1:28).

10 If the Colossian Christians are filled with this right knowledge, they will live and act in a manner worthy of the holiness of him whom

---

[28]Cf. Hos. 2:20; 6:3, 6.

[29]Cf. Col. 1:28; 2:1-3; 3:10.

[30]Perhaps one reason for Paul's preference for ἐπίγνωσις (cf. Rom. 1:28; 3:20; 10:2; Phil. 1:9, in addition to instances in Colossians, Ephesians, and the Pastorals) is his desire to point a contrast with the much canvassed γνῶσις. This is more likely than the view that he takes over a catchword of his opponents, by which they emphasized the more advanced knowledge they taught as against the ordinary γνῶσις (so W. L. Knox, *Some Hellenistic Elements in Primitive Christianity*, p. 150; cf. MM, p. 237). Whether the force of the prefix ἐπί here is intensive (J. B. Lightfoot, *Colossians and Philemon*, pp. 137-38), directive (J. A. Robinson, *St. Paul's Epistle to the Ephesians* [London, 1904], pp. 248-54), or "*ingressive* or—still better—*decisive*" (R. E. Picirelli, "The Meaning of 'Epignosis'," *EQ* 47 [1975], 85-93), or whether in fact it has any special force, is uncertain: no rule can be laid down covering all instances. In many, but not all, NT occurrences ἐπίγνωσις, like the verb ἐπιγινώσκω, "has become almost a technical term for the decisive knowledge of God which is involved in conversion to the Christian faith" (R. Bultmann, *TDNT* 1, p. 707 [*s.v.* γινώσκω, etc.]). See J. Dupont, *Gnosis: La connaissance religieuse dans les épîtres de saint Paul* (Louvain/Paris, 1949).

[31]Cf. Ps. 111:10; Prov. 9:10.

[32]Cf. Phil. 1:9-10; also Rom. 12:2; 15:14; 1 Cor. 1:6; 2:6-16; 3:2; 2 Cor. 8:7; 11:6; Phil. 3:10; Philem. 6.

they confess as their Lord.[33] The phrase "in a manner worthy of the Lord" or "worthy of God" (cf. 1 Thess. 2:12; 3 John 6; also Matt. 10:37; Wisdom 3:5) is a formula of a type appearing on inscriptions in the province of Asia; according to Deissmann, it seems to have been popular at Pergamum.[34] If pagans appreciated the importance of rendering worship which was worthy of the deities whose votaries they were, much more should Christians render the spiritual service of obedient lives to the living and true God and to his Son Jesus Christ.[35] Thus the fair fruit of good works would spring in greater abundance from the divine seed which had been sown in their hearts,[36] and at the same time they would make ever increasing progress in the knowledge of God. For obedience to the knowledge of God which has already been received is a necessary and certain condition for the reception of further knowledge.

11 The writers go on to pray that the Colossians may be endowed not only with knowledge but also with power, according to the measure of God's "glorious might" (lit., "the might of his glory").[37] The power which they long to see manifested in their readers' lives is the power of God himself—nothing less. In Ephesians this idea is made even more explicit: there Paul describes the "immeasurable greatness" of God's power which he imparts to believers in terms of the power which he exerted when he raised Christ from the dead and exalted him to the place of universal supremacy at his right hand (Eph. 1:20). Never was the divine power more signally manifested: with its present description as the "might of God's glory" we may compare Paul's statement elsewhere that "Christ was raised from the dead by the glory of the Father" (Rom. 6:4).

Such an endowment with divine power will enable them to stand firm in the face of trial and opposition and everything else that may come

---

[33]Gk. περιπατῆσαι ἀξίως τοῦ κυρίου. The ethical use of περιπατέω is a Hebraism (cf. Heb. *hālak̲*) common in the Pauline and Johannine letters, equivalent to the more idiomatic Hellenistic ἀναστρέφομαι (cf. Eph. 2:3). But ethical περιπατέω itself is used by some Hellenistic writers (e.g., Menander, Philodemus, Epictetus) where there is no question of Semitic influence.

[34]A. Deissmann, *Bible Studies*, E.T. (Edinburgh, ²1909), p. 248.

[35]Cf. Rom. 12:1. In the phrase εἰς πᾶσαν ἀρεσκείαν ("for all pleasing") ἀρεσκεία has a higher sense than "obsequiousness," which it frequently means. Parallels to this higher sense are found in Philo. Deissmann (*Bible Studies*, p. 224) quotes an example from a Bosporan inscription of uncertain date; MM (p. 75) give one from *P. Oxy.* 729 (2nd cent. A.D.). We might render: "so as to satisfy him in all respects."

[36]Cf. v. 6 above (p. 42 with n. 15).

[37]For this adjectival force of the genitive τῆς δόξης (a Hebraism) cf. v. 27; Rom. 8:21; 2 Cor. 4:4, 6; Eph. 1:18; 3:16.

to test the quality of their faith. Patient endurance belongs to the fruit of the Spirit (Gal. 5:22).[38] It was a quality highly esteemed by the Stoics, but in the NT it is associated with another quality not so characteristic of Stoicism—joyfulness.[39] Paul himself had long since learned to combine joyfulness with patient endurance. A Stoic in the stocks would have borne the discomfort calmly and uncomplainingly, but would he at the same time have been heard "singing hymns to God," as Paul and Silas did in the Philippian town jail (Acts 16:25)? Epictetus, indeed, commends the example of Socrates, who composed a paean in prison;[40] but such an example was more admired than followed. Early Christianity and Stoicism show a resemblance with respect to several ethical features, but the power which Christians received from God gave them something over and above what Stoicism could impart. The Stoic virtue of self-sufficiency[41] falls short of that habit of mind to which Paul gives expression when he says that he has learned to be content in all the circumstances of life, for Paul's contentment was attended by a joyful exuberance which overflowed to others.

12 In our translation above we have followed the punctuation which attaches the phrase "with joy" to the verb "give thanks"; it would be equally permissible, however, to attach it to the words which precede, regarding "joy" as a third quality listed along with "patience and perseverance."

---

[38]Patience (ὑπομονή) and perseverance (μακροθυμία) are closely akin: in the latter the note of steadfastness and staying power is stressed. In the *Testament of Joseph* 2:7 Joseph tells how he was steadfast (ἐμακροθύμησα) in all his trials, and adds that "μακροθυμία is a great medicine and ὑπομονή yields many good things." "A merciful man perseveres (μακροθυμεῖ)," according to Prov. 19:11 (i.e., he defers his anger). "With great patience" (ἐν πολλῇ μακροθυμίᾳ) toward the impenitent God postpones the day of reckoning (Rom. 9:22; cf. 2:4); and this, like his other ethical qualities, is to be reproduced in his children: "love (whether in him or in them) μακροθυμεῖ, is patient" (1 Cor. 13:4). Cf. Col. 3:12.

[39]Joy (χαρά), like μακροθυμία, is also an element in the fruit of the Spirit (Gal. 5:22).

[40]*Diss.* 2.6.26.

[41]Gk. αὐτάρκεια. The ideal Stoic, according to Horace, is *in se ipso totus teres atque rotundus* (*Sat.* 2.7.86); Paul's αὐτάρκεια (2 Cor. 9:8) was Christ-sufficiency rather than self-sufficiency; he expresses it in terms of his power to cope (αὐτάρκης εἶναι) with all the conditions of mortal existence through his divine enabler (Phil. 4:11-13). On Stoicism and early Christianity see R. Bultmann, "Das religiöse Moment in der ethischen Unterweisung des Epiktet und das Neue Testament," *ZNW* 13 (1912), 97-110, 177-91; A. Bonhöffer, *Epiktet und das Neue Testament* (Giessen, 1911); E. Bevan, *Stoics and Sceptics* (Oxford, 1913); D. S. Sharp, *Epictetus and the New Testament* (London, 1914); M. Pohlenz, *Paulus und die Stoa* (Darmstadt, 1964); also H. D. Betz, *Der Apostel Paulus und die sokratische Tradition* (Tübingen, 1972).

Patience, perseverance, and joy should continually be accompanied by a thankful spirit. In Christianity, it has been well said, theology is grace, and ethics is gratitude.[42] If God's action and attitude toward his people have been characterized by grace, their response to him, in life and conduct as well as in thought and word, should be characterized by gratitude.[43] Nothing less is fitting, considering how he has qualified them to share the inheritance of his holy people.[44]

Who are these "holy people" of God whose inheritance the Colossian believers now share? The older view is that they are human beings— either the people of God in the OT era, who are now being joined by their brethren and sisters of the Christian age, apart from whom "they should not be made perfect" (Heb. 11:40), or the first (Jewish) followers of Christ, who are now joined by Gentile Christians, like those to whom the letter is sent (cf. Eph. 1:12-13, "we who first hoped in Christ . . . you also . . ."). But an alternative view is that they are angels, God's "holy ones" in the realm of light.[45] There may be parallels to this use of the term elsewhere in the Pauline writings—for example, in the reference to "the coming of our Lord Jesus with all his saints" (1 Thess. 3:13), where it is difficult to miss the echo of Zech. 14:5, "the LORD your God will come, and all the holy ones with him."[46]

This alternative view has received an impetus from the Qumran texts. In the "Hymn of the Initiants" which concludes the *Rule of the Community* it is said that to God's chosen people "he has given a portion in the lot of the holy ones and has united their assembly with the sons of heaven" (where the "holy ones" and "sons of heaven" are manifestly angels).[47] This boon appears to have been granted to them already; it is not simply something to which they can look forward after death, like the

---

[42]Cf. T. Erskine, *Letters* (Edinburgh, 1877), p. 16.

[43]Cf. Col. 3:15.

[44]Gk. τῷ ἱκανώσαντι ὑμᾶς εἰς τὴν μερίδα . . . τῶν ἁγίων. C. H. Dodd compares Job 31:2 LXX, ἐμέρισεν ὁ θεὸς ἀπάνωθεν καὶ κληρονομία ἱκανοῦ ἐξ ὑψίστων ("God has made distribution from above, and the inheritance of the All-Sufficient is from the highest ones"). There, as in some other LXX passages, ἱκανός is a divine name, representing Heb. *Shaddai* (usually rendered "Almighty" in EVV). Dodd further suggests that Paul's use of the verb ἱκανόω ("qualify") here and in 2 Cor. 3:5-6 reflects this Septuagintalism (*The Bible and the Greeks* [London, 1935], pp. 15-16).

[45]Cf. E. Lohse, *Colossians and Philemon*, pp. 35-36.

[46]A. R. C. Leaney takes the "sons (children) of God" in Rom. 8:19-21 as angels ("The Righteous Community in St. Paul," *SE* 2 = *TU* 87 [Berlin, 1963], pp. 441-46).

[47]1QS 11.7-8.

righteous man in the book of Wisdom, whose persecutors are forced to ask in dismay, "Why has he been numbered among the sons of God? And why is his lot among the holy ones?" (Wisdom 5:5).[48]

These two alternatives have an exegetical parallel in Dan. 7:18, 22, where the "saints of the Most High" who are to receive the eternal kingdom after the collapse of pagan world-empires are usually (and rightly) taken to be the Jewish people, or the faithful remnant of the Jewish people, but have been identified with angelic beings by some more recent interpreters (Dan. 7:27 being rendered "the *host* of the holy ones . . .").[49]

Here, however, the sense in which "saints" or "holy ones" is used elsewhere in the letter (cf. v. 2 above) should probably decide its present meaning.[50] There is also the consideration that, where a similar expression occurs in two Pauline speeches in Acts, the reference is plainly to human beings who "have been sanctified" (Acts 20:32; 26:18, "sanctified by faith in me").[51]

For his holy people, the people of his choice, God in earlier days provided an earthly inheritance, a land which they might enter and possess. But the inheritance in view here belongs to a higher plane and a more enduring order than any terrestrial Canaan.[52] Like the recipients of the letter to the Ephesians, these Colossian Christians are no longer "strangers and sojourners," although they were Gentiles by birth; they have been reborn into the family of God, thanks to their all-enabling Father (cf. Eph. 2:19).

13 This inheritance is established in the realm of light;[53] it is ir-

---

[48]Cf. Luke 20:36, where those who attain the resurrection age are "equal to angels (ἰσάγγελοι) and are sons of God."

[49]Cf. M. Noth, "The Holy Ones of the Most High" (1955), E.T. in *The Laws in the Pentateuch and Other Studies* (Edinburgh, 1966), pp. 215-28; L. Dequeker, " 'The Saints of the Most High' in Qumran and Daniel," *OTS* 18 (1973), 108-87.

[50]Cf. E. Schweizer, *Colossians*, p. 51; P. T. O'Brien, *Colossians, Philemon*, pp. 26-27. See also on v. 26 below.

[51]Acts 26:18 (from the report of Paul's Damascus-road commission) presents especially close affinities with our present passage, referring as it does to turning "from darkness to light and from the power (ἐξουσία) of Satan to God" and to receiving "forgiveness of sins" (ἄφεσις ἁμαρτιῶν) as well as an "inheritance (κλῆρος, as here) among those who have been sanctified by faith" in Christ. If, as is generally agreed, Luke's sources did not include the Pauline letters, an interesting question arises about the source of this accurate reproduction of Pauline language.

[52]For non-Pauline accounts of this heavenly inheritance cf. Heb. 11:8-16; 1 Pet. 1:4.

[53]The phrase ἐν τῷ φωτί at the end of v. 12 does not qualify τῶν ἁγίων (as though "saints in light" were a special category of saints); it denotes the environment of the inheritance.

radiated by the brightness of the Sun of righteousness, shining in his people's hearts. It is contrasted with the realm to which they formerly belonged, the "dominion of darkness." There is no need to see here a reflection of Zoroastrian dualism.[54] Nor should we think in terms of Qumran influence, although parallels to this kind of language abound in the Qumran texts.[55] The statement of an ethical antithesis in terms of light and darkness (light being the correlate of goodness and truth, darkness of evil and falsehood) is too widespread for us to assume in such a reference as this the influence of any one system of thought in which these terms played a prominent part. It may indeed be that the teaching to which the Colossian Christians were being exposed made play with "light" and "darkness" as it apparently did with "wisdom" and "knowledge"; but there is good biblical precedent for their use, going back to the separation of light and darkness in the creation story of Gen. 1:4. Other Pauline instances are 2 Cor. 6:14; 1 Thess. 5:5; Eph. 5:8-14.

The phrase "the dominion of darkness," which is used here, appears in Luke's account of our Lord's arrest in Gethsemane, where he says to the men who have come to apprehend him, "When I was with you day after day in the temple, you did not lay hands on me. But this is your hour, and the dominion of darkness"[56] (Luke 22:53). These words refer to the sinister forces marshalled against him for a decisive combat in the spiritual realm.[57] The dark power did indeed have its brief hour of opportunity against the Son of Man, but it was only a brief hour, and it ended in the defeat of the dark power. By virtue of his conquest then, Christ vindicated his authority to raid the domain of darkness and rescue those who had hitherto been fast bound under the control of its guardians.[58] Those guardians, "the world rulers of this darkness," as they are called in Eph. 6:10, are probably the principalities and powers to which the Christians of Colossae were tempted to pay some meed of homage. But why should they do any such thing? They had already been rescued from the sphere dominated by those principalities, and translated into the domain of the victorious Son of God. No longer was there any need for them to live in fear of those forces which were believed to control the destinies of men and

---

[54]Cf. C. A. A. Scott, "The Dualistic Element in the Thinking of St. Paul," *ExT* 23 (1911-12), 488-92, 560-64.

[55]The principal Qumran text is 1QS 3.17–4.26, where human beings are apportioned between the two realms of the prince of light and the angel of darkness (these terms being ethically understood). Cf. 1QM, where the war of the end-time is waged between the sons of light and the sons of darkness.

[56]Gk. ἡ ἐξουσία τοῦ σκότους, as here.

[57]Cf. the references to "the ruler of this world" in John 12:31; 14:30; 16:11.

[58]Cf. Mark 3:27 (par. Matt. 12:29).

women: their transference to the realm of light had been accomplished once for all.

In the affirmation that believers have already been brought into the kingdom of God's beloved Son[59] we have an example of truly realized eschatology. That which in its fullness lies ahead of them has already become effective in them. "Those whom he justified he also glorified" (Rom. 8:30). The fact that God has begun a good work in them is the guarantee that it will be brought to fruition on the day of Jesus Christ (cf. Phil. 1:6). By an anticipation which is a genuine experience and not a legal fiction they have received here and now a foretaste of the glory that is yet to be revealed. The "inheritance of the saints in light" has not yet been received in its coming fullness, but the divine act by which believers have been fitted for it has already taken place. The divine kingdom has this twofold aspect throughout the NT. It has already broken into the world through the work of Christ (cf. Matt. 12:28 par. Luke 11:20); it will break in on a coming day in the plenitude of glory which invests Christ's *parousia*. Those who look forward to an abundant entrance in resurrection into that heavenly order which the present mortal body of flesh and blood cannot inherit[60] are assured at the same time that this order is already theirs. This assurance they derive (as Paul says elsewhere) from the indwelling Spirit or (as it is said in v. 27 below) from the indwelling Christ.

It appears that Paul tends to distinguish those two aspects of the heavenly kingdom by reserving the commoner expression "the kingdom of God" for its future consummation,[61] while designating its present phase by some such term as "the kingdom of Christ." Thus, in 1 Cor. 15:24 Christ, after reigning until all things are put under his feet, delivers up the kingdom to God the Father; his mediatorial sovereignty is then merged in the eternal dominion of God.[62]

14 Those who have been introduced into this new realm enjoy forthwith the principal benefits won for them by its ruler. In him they receive their redemption, with the forgiveness of their sins—in him, be-

---

[59]Lit., "the son of his love" (τοῦ υἱοῦ τῆς ἀγάπης αὐτοῦ), an adjectival genitive, a semitism like τὸ κράτος τῆς δόξης αὐτοῦ in v. 11 (cf. p. 47, n. 37).

[60]1 Cor. 15:50.

[61]So, at any rate, 1 Cor. 6:9-10; 15:50; Gal. 5:21. Other Pauline instances of ἡ βασιλεία τοῦ θεοῦ are Rom. 14:17; 1 Cor. 4:20; Col. 4:11 (see p. 180 below); 1 Thess. 2:12; 2 Thess. 1:5; these are more general in their reference. Eph. 5:5 speaks of "the kingdom which is Christ's and God's" (τῇ βασιλείᾳ τοῦ Χριστοῦ καὶ θεοῦ); here the two aspects appear to be conjoined (cf. 2 Tim. 4:1).

[62]Cf. G. Vos, *The Pauline Eschatology* (Grand Rapids, 1952), pp. 236-60; also W. D. Davies, *Paul and Rabbinic Judaism* (London, 1948), p. 296.

cause it is only as those who share the risen life of Christ that they have made effective *in* them what he has done *for* them.[63]

The "redemption" which is theirs in Christ is something that he has secured for them; it implies that their former existence was one of bondage from which they required to be ransomed.[64] The ransom-price is not explicitly mentioned here; what it was is evident not only from the parallel passage in Eph. 1:7 ("in him we have our redemption, through his blood") but from other Pauline texts where the same thought is expressed, notably in Rom. 3:24-25, where believers are said to be justified freely by the grace of God "through the redemption which is in Christ Jesus, whom God put forward as an agent of atonement by his blood, to be received by faith."[65] It is made clear that the emancipation which the people of Christ enjoy in him was purchased for them at the price of his life, freely offered up by him on the cross.

Adolf Deissmann asks whether this "manumission" is "merely a single summary act performed once for all in the past" or also (as he thinks probable) "an act of liberation experienced anew, in each single case of conversion, by every person newly incorporated in Christ."[66] The answer is that it is both: the redemption was procured by Christ for his people once for all, but it is appropriated by them individually as they become united with him by faith.

The companion blessing, "the forgiveness of sins," though frequent in the NT, is less characteristic of Paul: it appears in the Pauline corpus only here and in Eph. 1:7.[67] Normally Paul prefers to speak in terms of justification, which embraces all that is meant by forgiveness or remission

[63]Cf. J. A. T. Robinson, *The Body* (London, 1952), pp. 45-46.

[64]On "redemption" (ἀπολύτρωσις) cf. F. Büchsel, *TDNT* 4, pp. 351-56 (*s.v.* λύω, λύτρον, etc.); J. Schneider and C. Brown, *NIDNTT* 3, pp. 177-223 (*s.v.* "Redemption"); B. B. Warfield, *The Person and Work of Christ* (Philadelphia, 1950), pp. 429-75; E. K. Simpson, *Words Worth Weighing in the Greek New Testament* (London, 1944), pp. 8-9; L. Morris, *The Apostolic Preaching of the Cross* (London, [3]1965), pp. 11-64; S. Lyonnet and L. Sabourin, *Sin, Redemption and Sacrifice* (Rome, 1970), pp. 61-296.

[65]Cf. C. E. B. Cranfield, *The Epistle to the Romans*, ICC, I (Edinburgh, 1975), 205-11; E. Käsemann, *Commentary on Romans*, E.T. (Grand Rapids, 1980), pp. 95-101.

[66]A. Deissmann, *Light from the Ancient East* (London, [2]1927), p. 330.

[67]Gk. τὴν ἄφεσιν τῶν ἁμαρτιῶν (in Eph. 1:7, τὴν ἄφεσιν τῶν παραπτωμάτων). Cf. Matt. 26:28; Mark 1:4; Luke 1:77; 3:3; 24:27; Acts 2:38; 5:31; 10:43; 13:38; 26:18. The corresponding verb ἀφίημι is used by Paul in this sense only in the quotation from Ps. 32:1 (LXX 31:1) in Rom. 4:7. With ἄφεσις may be compared his use of πάρεσις in Rom. 3:25, of the "passing over" of sins committed in the past. Cf. the use of χαρίζομαι in Col. 2:13; 3:13.

of sins but includes much besides. It is probable that here and in Eph. 1:7 we have the reproduction of what had already become standard Christian language for acknowledging the blessings bestowed in Christ, possibly in the form of a primitive confession of faith.[68]

3. HYMN IN HONOR OF CHRIST (1:15-20)

(1) Christ the Agent in Creation (1:15-16)

> 15 *He is the image of the invisible God,*
> *firstborn before all creation,*
> 16 *because in him all things were created—*
> *things in heaven and things on earth,*
> *things visible and invisible,*
> *whether thrones or dominions,*
> *whether principalities or powers—*
> *they have all been created through him and for him.*

(2) Lord of the Universe and Head of the Church (1:17-18a)

> 17 *He indeed is before all things,*
> *and they all cohere in him;*
> 18 *He is also the head of the body, the church.*

(3) Christ the Agent in Reconciliation (1:18b-20)

> *He is the beginning,*[69]
> *firstborn from the dead,*[70]
> *that he might be preeminent in all things,*
> 19 *because in him it was decreed that all the fullness should take up*
> *residence*

[68]E. Percy observes that none of the distinctively Pauline terms, such as justification or the nonreckoning of trespasses, would suit the solemn liturgical diction of this passage so well as ἄφεσις τῶν ἁμαρτιῶν (*Die Probleme der Kolosser- und Epheserbriefe* [Lund, 1946], pp. 85-86). Besides, there may have been a special reason for bringing redemption and forgiveness of sins so closely together here if the Colossian theorists anticipated others who, according to Irenaeus (*Haer.* 1.21.2), distinguished "forgiveness of sins" as a preliminary stage and "redemption" as the perfect stage, the former being received in the baptism instituted by the "human" Jesus, the latter coming from the "divine" Christ that descended on him.

[69]Gk. ἀρχή, to which P^{46} B and a few other witnesses prefix the article ἡ.

[70]Gk. πρωτότοκος ἐκ τῶν νεκρῶν. P^{46} ℵ* and one or two other witnesses omit ἐκ (cf. Rev. 1:5, ὁ πρωτότοκος τῶν νεκρῶν).

20 *and that through him [God] should reconcile all things to himself,*[71]
having made peace through the blood of his cross—
[through him],[72] *whether those on earth or those in heaven.*

The prayer for the Colossians' spiritual well-being passes into one of the great christological passages of the NT, the transition being marked by the reminder in vv. 13 and 14 of their redemption, forgiveness, and translation into the kingdom of God's beloved Son. This mention of the Son of God leads on to a statement of his role in creation and reconciliation. This statement, we may be sure, was not introduced merely for rhetorical effect. It occupies this position because an intelligent appreciation of the doctrine of Christ is the best safeguard against most forms of heretical teaching, and certainly against that which was currently threatening the peace of the Colossian Christians.

These six verses are cast in a form of rhythmical prose which is found in much early Christian hymnody.[73] The repetition of key words or

[71]This presupposes the spelling εἰς αὐτόν (with Griesbach) instead of εἰς αὐτόν (see p. 74 below, with n. 165).

[72]δι' αὐτοῦ, repeated from the beginning of the verse, omitted by B D* F G etc., with the Latin and Sahidic versions, but present in P^{46} ℵ A C D¹ and the majority of witnesses, with the Syriac and Bohairic versions.

[73]The pioneers in recognizing a structured hymn in these verses were E. Norden, *Agnostos Theos* (Berlin/Leipzig, 1913), pp. 250-54, and E. Lohmeyer, *Die Briefe an die Philipper, an die Kolosser und an Philemon* (Göttingen, 1930), pp. 40-68. Out of the vast and constantly increasing literature which has subsequently appeared (in addition to commentaries *ad loc.*) may be mentioned G. Harder, *Paulus und das Gebet* (Gütersloh, 1936), pp. 46-51; E. Käsemann, "A Primitive Christian Baptismal Liturgy" (1949), E.T. in *Essays on New Testament Themes* (London, 1964), pp. 149-68; C. Maurer, "Die Begründung der Herrschaft Christi über die Mächte nach Col 1, 15-20," in *Wort und Dienst, Jahrbuch der Theologischen Schule Bethel,* NF 4 (1955), 79-93; J. M. Robinson, "A Formal Analysis of Colossians 1:15-20," *JBL* 76 (1957), 270-87; E. Bammel, "Versuch zu Col 1, 15-20," *ZNW* 52 (1961), 88-95; H. Hegermann, "Der Hymnus in Col 1," in *Die Vorstellung vom Schöpfungsmittler im hellenistischen Judentum und Urchristentum, TU* 82 (Berlin, 1961), 88-157; E. Larsson, *Christus als Vorbild* (Uppsala, 1962), pp. 188-96; R. P. Martin, "An Early Christian Hymn (Col. 1:15-20)," *EQ* 36 (1964), 195-205; "Reconciliation and Forgiveness in the Letter to the Colossians," in *Reconciliation and Hope,* ed. R. J. Banks (Exeter, 1974), pp. 104-24 (especially 108-16); "Some Reflections on New Testament Hymns," in *Christ the Lord,* ed. H. H. Rowdon (Leicester, 1982), pp. 37-49; H. J. Gabathuler, *Jesus Christus: Haupt der Kirche—Haupt der Welt* (Zürich, 1965); R. Deichgräber, *Gotteshymnus und Christushymnus in der frühen Christenheit* (Göttingen, 1967), pp. 143-55; N. Kehl, *Der Christushymnus im Kolosserbrief* (Stuttgart, 1967); J. T. Sanders, *The New Testament Christological Hymns* (Cambridge, 1971), pp. 12-14, 75-87;

phrases indicates the strophic arrangement. There appear to be two main strophes, *(1)* vv. 15-16, and *(3)* vv. 18b-20, with the transition between them supplied by *(2)* vv. 17-18a.[74] Each strophe begins with "He is" (lit., "who is")[75] and exhibits the key words "firstborn,"[76] "because in him,"[77] "through him,"[78] and "all things."[79] The transitional lines begin and end with "He indeed is" or "He is also" (identical in Greek),[80] the former summing up the preceding strophe, the latter introducing the following strophe.

The first strophe celebrates the role of Christ in creation, most probably in his character as the Wisdom of God. This early Christian theme, which exercised a major influence on the church's christological thought, was not restricted to the Pauline circle, and probably did not originate there. It comes to expression in the proem of Hebrews (Heb. 1:2b-3a), in the prologue to the Fourth Gospel (John 1:1-5), and even in the Apocalypse (Rev. 3:14). The second strophe celebrates the role of Christ in the new creation, especially as regards his work of reconciliation. In respect of the old and the new creation alike he enjoys the status of the "firstborn" (vv. 15, 18). If the first strophe, celebrating his role as the creative Wisdom, circulated independently before it was incorporated in this letter, it may be that it provided the model on which the second strophe was constructed.[81] Whether either strophe existed or not as an independent composition can, in the nature of the case, be only a matter of speculation.

P. Benoit, "L'hymne christologique de Col 1,15-20," in *Christianity, Judaism and Other Greco-Roman Cults,* ed. J. Neusner, I (Leiden, 1975), 226-63; W. McCown, "The Hymnic Structure of Colossians 1:15-20," *EQ* 51 (1979), 156-62; P. Beasley-Murray, "Colossians 1:15-20: An Early Christian Hymn Celebrating the Lordship of Christ," in *Pauline Studies,* ed. D. A. Hagner and M. J. Harris (Exeter/Grand Rapids, 1980), pp. 169-83; M. Hengel, "Hymns and Christology," E.T. in *Between Jesus and Paul* (London, 1983), pp. 78-96.

[74]For this arrangement see P. Benoit, "L'hymne christologique . . . ," p. 229; P. Beasley-Murray, "Colossians 1:15-20 . . . ," p. 170.

[75]Gk. ὅς ἐστιν (vv. 15a, 18b).

[76]Gk. πρωτότοκος (vv. 15b, 18b).

[77]Gk. ὅτι ἐν αὐτῷ (vv. 16a, 19).

[78]Gk. δι' αὐτοῦ (vv. 16 fin., 20a). One might add εἰς αὐτόν (vv. 16 fin., 20a), but see p. 55, n. 71, and p. 74, n. 165.

[79]Gk. τὰ πάντα (vv. 16 bis, 20a). Note also the chiastic repetition of ἐν τοῖς οὐρανοῖς καὶ ἐπὶ τῆς γῆς (v. 16)/ εἴτε τὰ ἐπὶ τῆς γῆς εἴτε τὰ ἐν τοῖς οὐρανοῖς (v. 20).

[80]Gk. καὶ αὐτός ἐστιν (vv. 17, 18).

[81]Cf. P. Benoit, "L'hymne christologique . . . ," pp. 248-50. In NA[26] vv. 15-18a are printed in lines of verse; not so vv. 18b-20, which run on as though they were ordinary prose.

If one or both of them did have an earlier existence, then one or both may have been expanded to suit the argument of the letter.[82] The presence and identity of such expansions must be even more speculative. Our concern, in any case, is with the text as it lies before us, in the only context in which it has come down to us.[83]

Here, then, Christ is presented as the agent of God in the whole range of his gracious purpose toward the human race, from the primeval work of creation, through the redemption accomplished at history's mid-point, on to the new creation in which the divine purpose will be consummated.

(1) First Main Strophe (1:15-16)

15 Christ, then, is said to be "the image of the invisible God." Paul has already said that he is "the image of God" in 2 Cor. 4:4,[84] in a context which appears to reflect Paul's conversion experience. Paul recognized the one who was revealed to him on the Damascus road as Jesus Christ, the Son of God; what if, in that same moment, he recognized him also as the *image* of God?[85] When Ezekiel, at an earlier date, received his vision of God, he saw enthroned at the heart of the rainbow-like brightness "a likeness as it were of a human form" (Ezek. 1:26). Paul had a similar experience when he recognized "the glory of God in the face of Christ" (2 Cor. 4:6). If so, he is not simply echoing someone else's form of words here; he is expressing what his own experience confirmed to be the truth.

To say that Christ is the image of God is to say that in him the nature and being of God have been perfectly revealed—that in him the

---

[82]The indented lines in the translation above are thought by many (e.g., P. Benoit) to be additions to an existing composition.

[83]R. P. Martin states what has become a majority view—that vv. 15-20 "form a compact, self-contained hymn written in praise of the cosmic Christ, the Lord of creation and redemption" (*Colossians: The Church's Lord and the Christian's Liberty* [Exeter, 1974], p. 39). M. D. Hooker is not convinced that there was a previously existing "hymn," but suggests that the passage "may . . . have been developed and formulated . . . in order to demonstrate that both creation and redemption are completed in Christ because he has replaced the Jewish Law" ("Were there False Teachers in Colossae?" in *Christ and Spirit in the New Testament*, ed. B. Lindars and S. S. Smalley [Cambridge, 1973], pp. 316-17, 329).

[84]Gk εἰκὼν τοῦ θεοῦ (cf. here, εἰκὼν τοῦ θεοῦ τοῦ ἀοράτου).

[85]Cf. S. Kim, *The Origin of Paul's Gospel* (Tübingen, 1981), pp. 137-62. Against J. Jervell, *Imago Dei* (Göttingen, 1960), pp. 171-336, and others, Kim denies that Paul borrows the εἰκών conception from the Hellenistic church; he further maintains the Pauline authorship of Col. 1:15-20 and argues that Paul's Adam christology and Wisdom christology were derived from his εἰκών christology, not *vice versa*.

invisible has become visible. "No one has ever seen God," says the Fourth Evangelist; "the only-begotten one, himself God, who has his being in the Father's bosom, it is he who has declared him" (John 1:18). Later, the same evangelist reports Christ himself as saying, "He who has seen me has seen the Father" (John 14:9). In another letter Paul affirms that, since the creation of the world, the everlasting power and divinity of the unseen Creator may be "clearly perceived in the things that have been made" (Rom. 1:20). But now an all-surpassing manifestation of his everlasting power and divinity has been granted: "the light of the gospel of the glory of Christ" has shone into his people's hearts through the same creative word as in the beginning called light to shine forth out of darkness (2 Cor. 4:4-6). The writer to the Hebrews expresses the same truth when he describes Christ, the Son of God, as the "effulgence[86] of his glory and the very impress of his being" (Heb. 1:3).

No reader of the OT scriptures, on reading the words now before us, could fail to be reminded of the statement in Gen. 1:26-27 that God created man, as male and female, "in his own image." Defaced as the divine image in humanity may be by reason of sin, yet in the order of creation it remains true that humanity is "the image and glory of God" (1 Cor. 11:7).[87] This image of God in humanity, moreover, is a copy or reflection of the archetypal image—that is to say, of God's beloved Son.[88] And so, as we are told later, when the havoc of sin is removed and the new man appears, the latter is renewed after the image of his Creator (Col. 3:10).

It may be observed in passing that there is a close association between the doctrine of man's creation in the divine image and the doctrine of our Lord's incarnation. It is because man in the creative order bears the image of his Creator that the Son of God could become incarnate as man and in his humanity display the glory of the invisible God.

Christ, in addition to being the image of God, is the "firstborn of

---

[86]Gk. ἀπαύγασμα, used of Wisdom in Wisdom 7:26, where she is described as "an effulgence from everlasting light, an unspotted mirror of the working of God, and an image (εἰκών) of his goodness."

[87]Gk. ἀνὴρ . . . εἰκὼν καὶ δόξα θεοῦ ὑπάρχων, where, because of the context, Paul uses ἀνήρ (man as distinct from woman) and not ἄνθρωπος (man as male and female), which is the word in Gen. 1:26-27 (LXX) on which his statement is based.

[88]J. B. Lightfoot (*Colossians, ad loc.*) points out Philo's repeated use of εἰκών as a description of the λόγος (see further on Col. 3:10, p. 147, n. 83). "Beyond the very obvious notion of likeness," Lightfoot adds, "the word εἰκών involves two other ideas: (1) *Representation* . . . (2) *Manifestation* . . ." (*Colossians,* p. 145). See also F. W. Eltester, *Eikōn im Neuen Testament* (Berlin, 1958), pp. 130-52.

all creation"—or, as it is rendered above, "firstborn before all creation."[89] The latter rendering is designed to clarify the force of the genitive phrase, "of all creation." This cannot be construed as though he himself were the first of all beings to be created. On the contrary, it is emphasized immediately that he is the one by whom the whole creation came into being.[90] What is meant is that the Son of God, existing as he did "before all things" (v. 17), exercises the privilege of primogeniture as Lord of creation, the divinely appointed "heir of all things" (Heb. 1:2). He was there when creation's work began, and it was for him as well as through him that it was completed.[91]

The title "firstborn" echoes the wording of Ps. 89:27, where God says of the Davidic king, "I will make him the firstborn, the highest of the kings of the earth."[92] But it belongs to Christ not only as the Son of David, but also as the Wisdom of God.[93] Whereas, in the wisdom literature of the OT, wisdom is at best the personification of a divine attribute or of the holy law,[94] the NT writers know that, when they speak of Wisdom in personal terms, they are referring to one who is truly alive, one whose

[89]Cf. A. Hockel, *Christus der Erstgeborene: Zur Geschichte der Exegese von Kol 1, 15* (Düsseldorf, 1965).

[90]A rabbinical parallel is the designation *qaḏmônô šel 'ôlām* ("first of the world") used of God by the mid-second-century Rabbi Eleazar ben Rabbi Simeon (*GenR* 38.7 on Gen. 11:2).

[91]A frequently cited parallel in English literature to this "exclusive" use of a superlative is the couplet from Milton's *Paradise Lost* IV.323-24:

    Adam, the goodliest man of men since born

    His sons; the fairest of her daughters Eve.

A. W. Argyle, remarking that most commentators are content to quote as a biblical Greek parallel πρῶτός μου ἦν (John 1:15), adduces a closer one from 2 Kingdoms 19:43 LXX (not found in the corresponding MT, 2 Sam. 19:43), πρωτότοκος ἐγὼ ἢ σύ "I was born before you" ("πρωτότοκος πάσης κτίσεως [Colossians i.15]," *ExT* 66 [1954-55], 61-62).

[92]This OT passage is echoed also in Rev. 1:5 (see p. 54, n. 70), where "highest" (Heb. *'elyôn*, LXX ὑψηλός) is rendered ἄρχων.

[93]C. F. Burney, "Christ as the ΑΡΧΗ of Creation," *JTS* 27 (1925-26), 160-77, finds in πρωτότοκος πάσης κτίσεως an allusion to the words with which Wisdom introduces herself in Prov. 8:22, *YHWH qānānî rē'šît darkô*, "The LORD begat me as (at) the beginning of his way." Then, in view of the third-century rabbinic use of *rē'šît* ("beginning") in Prov. 8:22 to explain *bᵉrē'šît* ("in the beginning") in Gen. 1:1 (see p. 62 below with n. 112), Burney goes on to treat Col. 1:15-18 as an elaborate exposition of Gen. 1:1, in which Paul aims to show that Christ exhausts every meaning that could be extracted from *rē'šît* (or from its cognate *rō'š*, "head")—"that he might be preeminent in all things." See also W. D. Davies, *Paul and Rabbinic Judaism* (London, 1948), pp. 147-76.

[94]This is true even of Philo's λόγος, even if it receives the epithet πρωτόγονος (*Confusion of Tongues* 146); Philo's λόγος, unlike John's, would never have become flesh and tabernacled among men.

ministry as a man resident in the Holy Land was still remembered by many. To all those writers, as to Paul, Christ was the personal (not personified) and incarnate Wisdom of God.[95]

As with all the other direct or indirect OT adumbrations of our Lord (including the messianic concept itself), this one is interpreted by the NT writers in terms of the historic and personal fact of Christ, and not *vice versa*. Thus, the well-known passage in Prov. 8:22-31, where personified Wisdom speaks of her presence at the creation of the world, is not regarded by the NT writers as a prophecy whose details may be pressed to yield christological conclusions, however much they may draw on its phraseology in depicting Christ as the Wisdom of God. Later Christian writers involved themselves in unnecessary embarrassment by trying to extract a christological exegesis from the passage.[96] What Paul and his contemporaries imply is not so much that the personified Wisdom of the OT books is really Christ, as that Christ—the Christ who lived on earth as man, who died and rose again, "whom God made our wisdom" (1 Cor. 1:30)—is the one who was before all creation, the preexistent, cosmic Christ.[97]

The idea of preexistence is not unknown in Jewish thought.[98] We meet it, for example, in later discussions about the Messiah[99] and in the

---

[95]As in 1 Cor. 1:24; cf. C. A. A. Scott, *Christianity according to St. Paul* (Cambridge, 1927), pp. 264-65. The question how such early Christian thinkers pictured Christ in the role of heavenly Wisdom is best answered by reference to his occasionally speaking in that role himself. Cf. J. R. Harris, *The Origin of the Prologue to St. John's Gospel* (Cambridge, 1917); *The Origin of the Doctrine of the Trinity* (Manchester, 1919).

[96]Followers of Athanasius were particularly embarrassed by the LXX wording, Κύριος ἔκτισέ με ("The LORD *created* me"), which seemed to play right into the hands of Arians and other heretics.

[97]On the primitive-Christian character of this affirmation see F. V. Filson, *The New Testament against its Environment* (London, 1950), pp. 61-62. More recently, J. D. G. Dunn has argued that the doctrine of the preexistence of Christ (as the Word of God) does not emerge in the NT before the Fourth Gospel, that Paul's presentation of him as the Wisdom of God does indeed imply a doctrine of incarnation, but one which views him as embodying God's creative and saving activity rather than as actually preexisting (*Christology in the Making* [London, 1980], pp. 176-96, 258-68). See also A. T. Hanson, *The Image of the Invisible God* (London, 1982).

[98]Cf. R. G. Hamerton-Kelly, *Pre-existence, Wisdom and the Son of Man* (Cambridge, 1973).

[99]One example will suffice: Messiah's preexistence was inferred from Ps. 72:17, "May his name continue as long as the sun" (lit., ". . . before the sun"), where the verb *yinnôn* ("may it continue") was treated as a proper noun and the clause taken to mean: "Before the sun his name was Yinnon" (TB *Sanhedrin* 98b, citing the school of R. Yannai).

preexistent Son of Man of the Enoch literature.[100] But such preexistent beings were, to the minds of those who discussed them, largely ideal; here preexistence is predicated of a man who had lived and died in Palestine within the preceding half-century.[101] This is not the only place in the Pauline letters where the preexistence of Christ is asserted or implied.[102] Nor is Paul the only NT writer to teach such a thing. The same teaching is found in Hebrews (Heb. 1:2; 10:5-9) and in the Fourth Gospel (John 1:1-2; 8:58), while in the Apocalypse Jesus is the Alpha and Omega, the first and the last, David's root as well as David's offspring (Rev. 1:17; 2:8; 22:13, 16).

But Paul speaks not only of a preexistent Christ, but of a cosmic Christ: that is to say, he finds in Christ "the key to creation, declaring that it is all there with Christ in view."[103] Whatever figures in Jewish literature, canonical or otherwise, may have preexistence predicated of them, to none of them are such cosmic activity and significance ascribed as are here ascribed to the preexistent Christ.[104] Nor is this the only place where Paul makes this ascription: he has already stated in 1 Cor. 8:6 that Christians have "one Lord, Jesus Christ, through whom are all things, and we through him," while in Rom. 8:19-21 he shows how the redemption secured by Christ works not only to the advantage of its immediate beneficiaries, "the sons of God," but through them to the whole creation.[105]

16 Christ, then, is prior to all creation and, as the Father's first-born, he is heir to it all. But more: it was "in him" that all things were created. If it be asked why the preposition "in" is used here instead of the more usual "through," the answer seems to be that Christ is the beginning "in" which, according to Gen. 1:1, "God created the heaven and the earth." This is not mere surmise: he is expressly called "the beginning" in v. 18. The phrase "in him" seems to mark Christ out as the "sphere" within which the work of creation takes place; one might compare Eph.

---

[100]Cf. T. W. Manson, "The Son of Man in Daniel, Enoch and the Gospels" (1950), in *Studies in the Gospels and Epistles,* ed. M. Black (Manchester, 1962), pp. 123-45; M. D. Hooker, *The Son of Man in Mark* (London, 1967), pp. 33-48; P. M. Casey, *The Son of Man* (London, 1979), pp. 99-112.

[101]"The heavenly Messiah of the apocalypses is a lifeless figure, clothed in unapproachable light. The risen Christ of Paul, on the other hand, is a person whom a man can love; indeed He is a person whom as a matter of fact Paul did love" (J. G. Machen, *The Origin of Paul's Religion* [New York, 1921], pp. 194-95).

[102]Cf. 2 Cor. 8:9; Phil. 2:6-7.

[103]A. M. Hunter, *Interpreting Paul's Gospel* (London, 1954), p. 60.

[104]"The Messiah of the apocalypses . . . is not thought of as being associated with God in the creation of the world" (Machen, *Origin,* p. 194).

[105]But see p. 49, n. 46.

1:4, where the people of God are said to have been chosen "in him" before time began. God's creation, like his election, takes place "in Christ" and not apart from him.[106]

When creation is said to have taken place "through him," as it is at the end of v. 16, he is denoted as the agent by whom God brought the universe into being.[107] This is corroborated by the writer to the Hebrews, who affirms that it was through the Son that God made the worlds (Heb. 1:2), and by the Fourth Evangelist, who declares in his own uncompromising way, "All things came into being through him, and apart from him none of the things that exist came into being" (John 1:3).[108]

This is not the same thing as Philo's doctrine of the function of the *logos* in creation. Philo's *logos* is practically identified with the "intelligible world" conceived in the mind of God as a blueprint for the material world;[109] its designation as God's first-begotten son is purely metaphorical.[110] And while it is easy to see affinities between Paul's language here and Stoic terminology, Paul's thought is derived not from Stoicism but from Genesis[111] and the OT wisdom literature, where Wisdom is personified as the Creator's assessor and "master workman"[112] (although, for Paul, "master workman" is no longer a figure of speech, but a description of the actual role of the personal, preexistent Christ).

So then, the one through whom the divine work of redemption has been accomplished is the one through whom the divine act of creation took place in the beginning. His mediatorial relation to the created universe provides a setting to the gospel of salvation which helps his people to

---

[106]Cf. E. Haupt, *Der Brief an die Kolosser* (Göttingen, 1897), pp. 30-31 on ἐν αὐτῷ in Col. 1:16 and Eph. 1:4.

[107]Gk. διά, as in 1 Cor. 8:6; Heb. 1:2; John 1:3, cited in the exposition above.

[108]On the punctuation of John 1:3-4 see B. M. Metzger, *A Textual Commentary on the Greek New Testament* (London/New York, 1971), pp. 195-96.

[109]Philo, *On the Making of the World* 20-23.

[110]Cf. p. 59, n. 94.

[111]Where God speaks and creation springs into existence; cf. Ps. 33:6, "By the word of the LORD the heavens were made. . . ."

[112]Heb. 'āmôn (Prov. 8:30). The rendering "master workman" ('ōmēn; cf. Num. 11:12, where it means "nursing father") was suggested by Rabbi Hoshaiah (in the first half of the 3rd cent.); he revocalized 'āmôn accordingly (*GenR* 1.1 on Gen. 1:1; see p. 59, n. 93). The ἀμήν of Rev. 3:14 (where the risen Christ calls himself "the Amen, . . . the beginning of the creation of God") perhaps echoes the 'āmôn of Prov. 8:30. By Hoshaiah, as in normative Judaism generally, wisdom was identified with the *tôrāh*, "the desirable instrument with which the world was created" (R. Aqiba in *Pirqê 'Abôt* 3.18). See also p. 65, n. 125.

appreciate that gospel the more.[113] For those who have been redeemed by Christ, the universe has no ultimate terrors; they know that their Redeemer is also creator, ruler, and goal of all.

Probably with special reference to the "Colossian heresy" it is now emphasized that, if all things were created by Christ, then those spiritual powers which received such prominence in that heresy must have been created by him. The denizens of the upper realms as well as the inhabitants of earth owe their being to his creative power—the invisible forces of the spirit world as well as the visible and material order.[114] Whether invisible or visible, all had Christ as their original creator, and all have him as their final disposer.

The early Christians had their Lord's authority for believing in angels good and bad. It is stressed here that, whether good or bad, all are alike subject to Christ. Perhaps, in view of the situation at Colossae, it is hostile rather than friendly powers that Paul has primarily in mind; but the first argument by which he tries to reduce them to their proper dimensions in the eyes of Christians is the fact that they owe their very existence to the Christians' Savior.[115]

In all, five classes of angel-princes seem to be distinguished in the NT—thrones, principalities, authorities, powers, and dominions.[116] These

---

[113]I. Henderson, *Myth in the New Testament* (London, 1952), pp. 31-32, points out that the doctrine of creation cannot be "demythologized" into existential terms; any attempt to do so simply removes it altogether. The consequence would be that Christianity would have nothing to say about God's relation to the material world, "which includes, it must be remembered, God's relation to man in so far as the latter, having a body, is himself in some sense part of the material world."

[114]W. Michaelis takes the ὁρατά to comprise the whole of the earthly sphere, with the stars and other heavenly phenomena, while the ἀόρατα are exclusively the "powers" (*TDNT* 5, p. 369, *s.v.* ὁράω, etc.).

[115]A further argument, presented in Col. 2:15, is that these powers were vanquished by that same Savior. "Paul emphasizes again and again that Christ has brought the All, i.e. these very cosmic powers, under his power and has rendered them harmless" (M. Dibelius, "The Isis Initiation in Apuleius and Related Initiatory Rites" (1917), E.T. in *Conflict at Colossae*, ed. F. O. Francis and W. A. Meeks [Missoula, MT, 1975], p. 82).

[116]Gk. θρόνοι, ἀρχαί, ἐξουσίαι, δυνάμεις, κυριότητες. Cf. Milton, *Paradise Lost* 5.601: "Thrones, dominations, princedoms, virtues, powers." The four orders listed here are θρόνοι, κυριότητες, ἀρχαί, and ἐξουσίαι. The "thrones" may bear some relation to the twenty-four enthroned elders of Rev. 4:4. See further G. B. Caird, *Principalities and Powers* (London, 1956); H. Schlier, *Principalities and Powers in the New Testament*, E.T. (Freiburg/London, 1961); W. Carr, *Angels and Principalities* (Cambridge, 1981), especially pp. 47-85.

probably represent the highest orders of the angelic realm, but the variety of ways in which the terms are combined in the NT warns us against any attempt to reconstruct a fixed hierarchy from them.[117] Here the point is that the highest angel-princes, like the rest of creation, are subject to Christ as the one in whom, through whom, and for whom they were created.[118] They were created *in* him, because all the Father's counsels and activities (including those of creation) are centered in the Son; they were created *through* him, because he is the divine agent in creation; they were created *for* him, because he is the goal to which they all tend.[119]

The conception of Christ as the goal of creation plays an essential part in Pauline christology and, indeed, soteriology. This is the more impressive when it is borne in mind that the person thus presented as creation's goal was Jesus of Nazareth, but lately crucified in Jerusalem, whose appearance as the risen Lord to Paul on the Damascus road called forth that overmastering faith and love which completely reoriented his thought and action and remained thereafter the all-dominating motive of his life. Any attempt to understand the christology of this letter without taking into consideration this personal commitment of Paul to Christ would be the kind of understanding that Paul himself dismisses as being "according to the elemental forces of the world, and not according to Christ" (Col. 2:8).[120]

This distinguishes Paul's teaching about Christ as the goal of creation from all the Jewish parallels which have been adduced to it.[121] Whatever was previously revealed about God has now received fresh illumination from the fact of Christ and from faith in Christ—not only with regard to God's saving activity but also with regard to his role as Creator of the

---

[117]In Col. 2:10, 15 (as in Eph. 3:10; 6:12), they are summed up more concisely as "principalities and powers" (ἀρχαὶ καὶ ἐξουσίαι).

[118]The tense of "were created" (ἐκτίσθη) at the beginning of v. 16 is aorist, referring to the act of creation as such; the tense of "have been created" (ἔκτισται) at the end of the verse is perfect, referring to the enduring result of the creative act.

[119]For the bringing together of various prepositional phrases to express the relationship of God or Christ to the universe cf. Rom. 11:36; 1 Cor. 8:6; Eph. 4:6. To relate such constructions to Stoic formulations—comparing them, for example, with Marcus Aurelius's apostrophe to nature: ἐκ σοῦ πάντα, ἐν σοὶ πάντα, εἰς σὲ πάντα (*Meditations* 4.23)—is to pay more attention to the form of words than to their substance. Paul's intention is as different from that of the Stoic philosophers as the God of whom Paul speaks is different from the pantheistically conceived world-soul of Stoicism.

[120]Cf. E. Percy, *Die Probleme*, p. 72.

[121]For example, TB *Sanhedrin* 98b records the opinion of R. Yohanan (d. A.D. 279) that the world was created with a view to Messiah.

universe and Lord of history. That God overrules the course of history for the accomplishment of his purpose is a major emphasis throughout the OT, but here it is shown how vitally the accomplishment of his purpose is bound up with the person and work of Christ. So, too, in Eph. 1:10 it is stated that God's purpose, conceived by him in Christ before time began, to be put into effect when the appointed epoch had fully come, is that all things, in heaven and on earth, should be summed up in Christ. Or, as Paul had put it at an earlier date, it is by means of the mediatorial world-rule of Christ that God's eternal kingdom is finally to be established (1 Cor. 15:24-28).[122]

(2) Transitional Link (1:17-18a)

17 The teaching of vv. 15 and 16 is now recapitulated in a twofold reaffirmation of the preexistence and cosmic significance of Christ: "he is indeed before all things, and they all cohere in him." "In the beginning God created the heaven and the earth," says Genesis; but in that beginning, says John, which was the beginning of all created things, the divine Word already existed (John 1:1). No matter how far back our imagination may press, we can never reach a point of which we may say, with Arius, "there was once when he was not."[123] For he is "before all things"[124]—a phrase which not only declares his temporal priority to the universe but also suggests his superiority over it (as the title "firstborn" has already implied).

As for the statement that all things cohere or hold together[125] in him, this adds something to what has been said about his agency in creation. What has been brought into being through him is maintained in being by him. Similarly, in Heb. 1:2-3 the Son of God is not only the one through whom the worlds were made but also the one who upholds them by his almighty and enabling word. The Greek verb translated "cohere" is found as a Platonic and Stoic term: according to Philo, the material of the human body "coheres and is quickened as into flame by the providence of God."[126] Ben Sira affirms that by the word of God "all things hold

---

[122]See above, p. 52 with n. 62.

[123]Gk. ἦν ποτε ὅτε οὐκ ἦν, a proposition explicitly anathematized in the Creed of Nicaea (A.D. 325).

[124]Gk. πρὸ πάντων, a phrase which denotes priority in importance in Jas. 5:12; 1 Pet. 4:8 (cf. C. F. D. Moule, *IBNTG*, p. 74).

[125]Gk. συνέστηκεν. This might also hark back to Prov. 8:30, if R. B. Y. Scott is right in interpreting 'āmôn in that verse as "a living link" or "vital bond" ("Wisdom in Creation: The 'Āmôn of Proverbs viii.30," *VT* 10 [1960], 213-23). In LXX 'āmôn is rendered ἁρμόζουσα ("one who fits together"), feminine in agreement with σοφία.

[126]Philo, *Who is Heir of Divine Things?* 58.

together" (Sir. 43:26).[127] But for Paul the living Christ, who died to redeem his people, is the sustainer of the universe and the unifying principle of its life.

18 Thus far Paul has set forth the doctrine of Christ in terms which he shares with other NT writers—terms which, in fact, may have belonged to a widespread Christian catechesis or confession, even if he stamps them with the imprint of his own experience and mind. But now he goes on to make a contribution to apostolic christology which is distinctively his own. This Christ, he says, "is also the head of the body, the church."

Those who recognize vv. 15-20 as a pre-Pauline hymn incorporated into the argument of this letter believe, for the most part, that "the church" is a gloss added by the writer of the letter to make plain the sense in which "the body" is to be understood (which may be so), and many think that in the original form of the hymn the body was the *kosmos*.[128] This letter certainly presents Christ as head of the *kosmos* in the sense that he is its creator and ruler—head, in particular, "of every principality and power" (Col. 2:10). But when head and body are used as correlative terms, the physiological relation is in the foreground, and it is not established that the *kosmos* was ever envisaged as the body of Christ in *this* sense.

The use of the body as a figure for the common life and interdependence of a political or social group was not unknown in antiquity. It finds classical expression in the fable of Menenius Agrippa, who persuaded the seceding plebeians of Rome to return and live among the patricians on the ground that, if the other parts of the body conspired to starve the belly because it did no work, they would soon find themselves suffering in

---

[127]Gk. ἐν λόγῳ αὐτοῦ σύγκειται πάντα (Heb. ûḇid̠eḇārâw yippāʿēl rāṣôn, "and by his words [his] will is done").

[128]For this view see E. Schweizer, "Die Kirche als Leib Christi in den paulinischen Antilegomena," in *Neotestamentica* (Zürich, 1963), pp. 293-316. E. Käsemann, who regards the original composition as being not only pre-Pauline but pre-Christian, thinks its subject was the gnostic Redeemer, identified with the Archetypal Man, and that "the church" and other additions were part of its adaptation as a Christian baptismal liturgy ("A Primitive Christian Baptismal Liturgy"). H. A. Wagenführer, *Die Bedeutung Christi für Welt und Kirche* (Leipzig, 1941), p. 62, takes τῆς ἐκκλησίας as an editorial gloss intruded into the text of Colossians—for this there is no textual evidence. N. Kehl, *Der Christushymnus*, p. 41, rejects the idea that the body is the *kosmos* (refusing to treat τῆς ἐκκλησίας as an addition to the original composition) on the ground that, if the universe is already related to Christ as its head, it should not need to be reconciled to God. (But in Col. 2:10 he is "the head of every principality and power," and some at least of these are hostile.) See also I. J. DuPlessis, *Christus as Hoof van Kerk en Kosmos* (Groningen, 1962).

consequence.[129] Again, Stoicism viewed the divine power as the world-soul, informing the material universe as the individual soul informs the body[130]—a view succinctly summed up in Alexander Pope's couplet:

All are but parts of one stupendous whole,
Whose body Nature is, and God the soul.[131]

But we should look elsewhere for the source of Paul's presentation of the church as not merely a body corporate but as the body of Christ—"one body in Christ" (Rom. 12:5).

The first place (in chronological order) where Paul speaks of the church in this way is 1 Cor. 12:12-27.[132] This section opens with the words: "For just as the body is one and has many members, and all the members of the body, though many, are one body, so it is with Christ. For in one Spirit we were all baptized into one body—Jews or Greeks, slaves or free—and we were all watered with one Spirit." And it is summed up at the end (in v. 27) by the statement: "Now you are Christ's body, and individually members of it." In these words Paul is concerned to impress on the Corinthian Christians the fact that, as fellow-members of the body of Christ, they have mutual duties and common interests which must not be neglected.

A year or two later, in Rom. 12:4-5, he declares that "as in one body we have many members, and all the members do not have the same function, so we, though many, are one body in Christ, and individually members one of another." Paul is here thinking of the variety of services rendered by the diverse members of the church, in accordance with their respective abilities, all together helping to build up the community to which they all belong.

---

[129]Livy, *History* 2.32.9-12.

[130]The analogy of the body was also applied by the Stoics to the state, in which each citizen had his part to play as has each member of a body. According to W. L. Knox (*St. Paul and the Church of the Gentiles*, p. 161), the political developments of the Hellenistic age modified the form of this analogy so that the emphasis was transferred from the mutual duties of the members to the superior importance of the head: "it is likely enough that the transition was accomplished in Alexandria in favour of the Ptolemies before it became a convenient method of flattering the Roman Emperors." He derives Paul's conception of the church as the body of Christ from this Stoic commonplace.

[131]Pope, *Essay on Man*, i.267-68.

[132]In 1 Cor. 6:15 the bodies of believers are said to be "members of Christ"; but the idea of the body corporate is not explicit there. Indeed, whoever "is united to the Lord becomes one spirit with him" (1 Cor. 6:17), not "one body" (but for the close association of "one spirit" and "one body" see 1 Cor. 12:13; Eph. 4:4).

In those earlier letters, where the terminology of the body and its constituent parts is used to express the mutual relations and obligations of church members,[133] Christ is not said to be head of the body: the head is mentioned incidentally as one among many members of the body (1 Cor. 12:21). But in this letter (and also in Ephesians)[134] Christ as head bears a unique relation to the church as his body.

The word "head" is used in a variety of figurative senses. Where it is used in relation to "body," one naturally thinks of the organic connection of head and body, but even here it is relevant to bear in mind special senses given to "head" in Paul's writings. Outstanding among these special senses is that found in 1 Cor. 11:3, where Paul teaches that "the head of every man is Christ, woman's head is man, and Christ's head is God." In these three clauses "head" is best understood as "source" or "origin" (the statement that "woman's head is man" being a reference to the formation of Eve from Adam's side in Gen. 2:21-22).[135] In our present text, where Christ is said to be "the head of the body, the church," there is, over and above the obvious organic relationship of body and head, the thought that Christ is the source of the church's life, and probably also (in accordance with another figurative sense of "head") the thought that he is the church's lord.

So far as the organic relationship is concerned, Christ and his people are viewed together as a living entity: Christ is the head, supplying life and exercising control and direction; his people are his body, individually his limbs and organs, under his control, obeying his direction, performing his work. And the life which animates the whole is his risen life, which he shares with his people.

When attention is paid to the way in which Paul develops the concept of the church as the body of Christ, it is improbable that he was indebted for the concept to Stoic thought,[136] and still more improbable that he was influenced by gnostic ideas.[137] He would have been acquainted with rabbinical speculation which pictured all humanity as members of

[133]Cf. also 1 Cor. 10:16-17; 11:29 (and, in more general terms, 1 Cor. 8:12; 2 Cor. 5:14; Gal. 3:27-28; 4:14).
[134]Cf. Eph. 1:23; 2:16; 4:4, 12, 16; 5:23, 30.
[135]Cf. S. Bedale, "The Meaning of κεφαλή in the Pauline Epistles," *JTS* n.s. 5 (1954), 211-15.
[136]Cf., in addition to W. L. Knox (n. 130 above), T. Schmidt, *Der Leib Christi* (Leipzig, 1919); G. Johnston, *The Doctrine of the Church in the New Testament* (Cambridge, 1943), p. 87. Even if Paul's language is influenced by Stoic terminology, the concepts expressed by his language are not Stoic ones.
[137]Cf. H. Schlier, *Christus und die Kirche im Epheserbrief* (Tübingen, 1930), pp. 37-60; E. Käsemann, *Leib und Leib Christi* (Tübingen, 1933), pp. 138-59; R. Bultmann, *Theology of the New Testament*, E.T., I (London, 1951), 178-79.

Adam,[138] and we know how he points the antithesis between being "in Adam" and being "in Christ."[139] But we need not think that his portrayal of all believers as members of one body, and that the body of Christ, was formed on the analogy of this kind of speculation. Rather, the rabbinical speculation and Paul's portrayal are both rooted in the older Hebrew way of thinking which has commonly been called "corporate personality."[140] Men and women, by natural birth, share the life of Adam (whose name means "mankind") and thus may be described as "in Adam"; heirs of the new creation, by spiritual rebirth, share the risen life of Christ (the "second man") and so are "in Christ." It is this existence "in Christ" that is given vivid expression in Paul's presentation of the church as the body of Christ.[141] The germ of this conception in Paul's mind may indeed be found in the words of Christ which he heard on the Damascus road—words in which the risen Christ identified himself with his followers: "why do you persecute me?" (Acts 9:4; 22:7; 26:14).[142]

The source of the conception, however, is less important than Paul's

[138]Cf. W. D. Davies, *Paul and Rabbinic Judaism*, pp. 53-55.

[139]Cf. Rom. 5:12-19; 1 Cor. 15:21-22, 45-49.

[140]Cf. A. Schweitzer, *The Mysticism of Paul the Apostle*, E.T. (London, 1931), *passim* (the particular aspect of corporate personality on which Schweitzer bases his argument is the predestined solidarity of Messiah with the messianic or elect people, a conception which he derives from apocalyptic literature); E. Best, *One Body in Christ* (London, 1955), pp. 93-95, 203-07. The expression "corporate personality" seems to have originated with H. W. Robinson, "The Hebrew Conception of Corporate Personality," in *Werden und Wesen des Alten Testaments*, BZAW 66, ed. P. Volz, etc. (Giessen, 1936), pp. 49-62, reprinted as *Corporate Personality in Ancient Israel*, ed. J. Reumann (Edinburgh, 1982); cf. J. W. Rogerson, "The Hebrew Concept of Corporate Personality: A Re-examination," *JTS* n.s. 21 (1970), 1-16.

[141]Cf. E. Percy, *Der Leib Christi* (Lund, 1942), pp. 18-43. Among other attempts to find the source of Paul's use of the term "body of Christ" for the church may be noted those of A. E. J. Rawlinson ("Corpus Christi," in *Mysterium Christi*, ed. G. K. A. Bell and A. Deissmann [London, 1930], pp. 225-44), who locates it in the eucharistic presentation of the body of Christ, and of C. Chavasse (*The Bride of Christ* [London, 1940], pp. 70-72), who locates it in the nuptial union of bridegroom and bride in "one flesh." But both the eucharistic (1 Cor. 10:16b-17) and the nuptial (Eph. 5:28-31) applications of Paul's thought on this subject are derived from his conception of the church as the body of Christ rather than *vice versa*.

[142]Cf. J. A. T. Robinson, *The Body* (London, 1952), p. 58. At this early stage the implication would simply have been that of the solidarity between Christ and his people, with no specific idea yet of Christ as the head crying out on behalf of the members (cf. Augustine, *Sermon* 279.1: "while the members were still on earth, the head cried out in heaven"). See also D. E. H. Whiteley, *The Theology of St. Paul* (Oxford, 1964), pp. 193-94; R. H. Gundry, *"Sōma" in Biblical Theology* (Cambridge, 1976), p. 240.

intention in using it. He uses it when he wishes to bring out certain aspects of the relation between church members, or between the church and Christ; when he wishes to bring out certain other aspects, he uses other terminology. From other points of view, for example, the church is thought of as the bride of Christ,[143] or as the building of which he is either the foundation or the chief cornerstone,[144] and so on. Some theologians, indeed, treat the conception of the church as the body of Christ differently from those other conceptions, admitting that they are metaphorical while insisting that the term "body of Christ" is to be taken "ontologically and realistically."[145]

But if they were right, one could go on to make assertions about the church's relation to Christ, on the analogy of the relation which the human body, with its parts and their functions, bears to the head, beyond what Paul has to say. It is better to recognize that Paul speaks of the church as the body of Christ for certain well-defined purposes, and to follow his example in using such language for these same purposes. It can be appreciated that those presentations which bring out the vital relation between Christ and the church are more adequate than others (there is no organic relation between a building and its foundation-stone or coping stone); for this reason the head/body and husband/wife analogies have an especially firm grasp on reality.[146]

Thus, in speaking of the church as the body of Christ, one thinks of it as vitalized by his abiding presence with it and his risen life in it; one thinks of it as energized by his power; one may even (without transgressing legitimate bounds) think of it as the instrument through which he carries on his work on earth.[147] But to think of it as an extension of his incarnation

[143]Cf. 2 Cor. 11:2; Eph. 5:22-32.

[144]Cf. 1 Cor. 3:11; Eph. 2:20.

[145]E. L. Mascall, *Christ, the Christian and the Church* (London, 1946), p. 112; see the critique by E. Best, *One Body in Christ*, pp. 98-101.

[146]T. F. Torrance, while acknowledging that all the terms in which the NT speaks of the church "must be used to correct and modify each other in our understanding and in any full discussion," argues that the body is to be regarded as "the central and all-important conception" (*Royal Priesthood* [Edinburgh, 1955], p. 29).

[147]Cf. E. Schweizer, *Das Leben des Herrn in der Gemeinde und ihren Diensten* (Zürich, 1946); T. W. Manson, *The Church's Ministry* (London, 1948); T. F. Torrance, *Royal Priesthood*, pp. 23-42. E. Best, however, demurs to this on the ground that the body-metaphor in the NT "looks inward and not outward" (*One Body in Christ*, pp. 113, 137, 157-58, 188). D. Cairns goes so far as to say "that probably it would be wrong even to claim that the Church continues Christ's mission" (*SJT* 8 [1955], 422, in a review of Best, *One Body in Christ*).

is to exceed the limits which the Pauline exposition of the body permits. There is substance in the argument that his incarnation cannot be dissociated from his atoning sacrifice, and that the sacrifice offered once for all can have no "extension" in the life of the church. Moreover, the view of the church as the extension of his incarnation takes insufficient account of the contrast between his sinlessness and the church's sinfulness.[148]

The conception of the church as the body of Christ helps us to understand how Paul can not only speak of believers as being "in Christ" but also of Christ as being in them. They are "in Christ" as members of his body, "baptized into Christ" (Gal. 3:27; cf. Rom. 6:3); he is in them because it is his risen life that animates them. Similarly, in the organic analogy of John 15:1-8, the branches are in the vine and the vine at the same time is in the branches.[149]

(3) Second Main Strophe (1:18b-20)

It is the *risen* Christ who is head of the body which is the church. In resurrection as well as in creation he receives the titles "the beginning"[150] and "the firstborn."[151] His resurrection marked his triumph over all the forces that held men and women in bondage.[152] That first Easter morning saw the dawn of a new hope for humanity.[153] Now Christ is "the firstborn among many brethren";[154] he is "the "firstfruits of those who have fallen asleep";[155] his own resurrection is the harbinger of the great resurrection-harvest of his people. But the coming resurrection is anticipated here and now by those who know him as the resurrection and the life and enjoy eternal life through their participation in him.[156] He who has been "designated Son of God in power . . . by his resurrection from the dead" (Rom. 1:4) exercises primacy in the new creation as well as in the old;

---

[148]Cf. A. M. Hunter, *Interpreting Paul's Gospel* (London, 1954), p. 43.

[149]Cf. L. S. Thornton, *The Common Life in the Body of Christ* (London, 1944), p. 144; also his essay "The Body of Christ in the New Testament," in *The Apostolic Ministry*, ed. K. E. Kirk (London, 1946), pp. 53-111.

[150]Gk. ἀρχή, as in Prov. 8:22 (see p. 59, n. 93). On the Hellenistic background see A. Ehrhardt, *The Beginning* (Manchester, 1968).

[151]Gk. πρωτότοκος (as in v. 15); cf. Rev. 1:5 (p. 54, n. 70).

[152]Cf. Heb. 2:14-15; 1 John 3:8b.

[153]Cf. 1 Pet. 1:3.

[154]Rom. 8:29 (πρωτότοκος ἐν πολλοῖς ἀδελφοῖς); cf. Rom. 8:11.

[155]1 Cor. 15:20 (ἀπαρχὴ τῶν κεκοιμημένων), 23 (ἀπαρχὴ Χριστός).

[156]Cf. John 3:15-16, 36; 6:51; 10:27-28; 11:25-26.

the divine purpose is thus fulfilled "that he might be preeminent[157] in all things."[158]

19 The statement that God decreed the preeminence of Christ over every order of being is now repeated in different terms—terms which may have been calculated to appeal with peculiar force to the Colossian Christians in their present situation. "In him it was decreed that all the fullness should take up residence." The impersonal "it was decreed" has been adopted as a provisional rendering. But the Greek verb is not impersonal: it means "decreed," "was well pleased" and implies a subject. Then who or what was well pleased? When the good pleasure or will is God's, there is precedent for the omission of the explicit name of God: "he was well pleased" would mean "God was well pleased" (cf. KJV: "it pleased *the Father* that in him should all fulness dwell"). On the other hand, the clause as it stands offers an explicit subject for the verb: "the fullness was well pleased to take up residence in him" (cf. RSV: "in him all the fulness of God was pleased to dwell").[159] One cannot decide certainly whether "God" or "the fullness" is the more probable subject: P. Benoit, for example, prefers to take "God" as the subject;[160] E. Käsemann declares this construction "not permissible" (on exegetical and theological, not on grammatical, grounds).[161] Before it can even be considered which of the two constructions is the more probable, the meaning of "fullness" in this clause must be considered. So far as the letter-writer's intention is concerned, its meaning is not in doubt: the sense is repeated more fully in Col. 2:9: "it is in him [i.e., in Christ] that all the fullness of deity dwells in bodily form." If then Col. 1:19 is construed to mean that "in him all the fullness of deity was well pleased to take up residence" (that is, presumably, at his exaltation), this is tantamount to saying that God himself (RSV "all the

---

[157]Gk. πρωτεύων. In Rev. 1:17; 2:8; 22:13 the Christ who died and lives again speaks as ὁ πρῶτος καὶ ὁ ἔσχατος. According to TB P⁽ᵉ⁾sahim 5a, the school of R. Ishmael (making a deduction from Isa. 41:27) taught that rī'šôn ("the first") is the name of Messiah.

[158]M. Dibelius finds an allusion to the two creations in v. 18a: he who is head of the body, the *kosmos* (as is implied in vv. 15-17), is now also head of the body, the church (but in that case καί would have been expected before τοῦ σώματος).

[159]Gk. ὅτι ἐν αὐτῷ εὐδόκησεν πᾶν τὸ πλήρωμα κατοικῆσαι (the aorist infinitive may be ingressive). Perhaps a desire to smooth the construction which understands ὁ θεός or ὁ πατήρ as subject of εὐδόκησεν was responsible for H. Venema's conjecture κατοικίσαι (for κατοικῆσαι): "God was well pleased to cause all the fulness to dwell in him."

[160]P. Benoit, "L'hymne christologique," p. 256.

[161]E. Käsemann, "A Primitive Christian Baptismal Liturgy," p. 158.

fulness of God") was pleased to dwell in him. There is then no substantial difference in meaning between the two constructions.

The Greek word translated "fullness" *(plērōma)* is one that Paul and other NT writers use in a variety of senses.[162] The peculiar force of its use here has been thought to lie in its probable employment in a technical sense by the heretical teachers at Colossae. In the mid-second century the word was used by Gnostics of the Valentinian school to denote the totality of aeons (divine entities or emanations),[163] and it is conceivable that it bore some such meaning in incipient forms of gnosticism in the mid-first century. We must constantly remind ourselves that we have no knowledge of the Colossian heresy apart from inferences drawn as cautiously as possible from the argument and wording of this letter, but it would make sense in the present context if the heresy envisaged powers intermediate between the supreme God and the world of humanity, so that any communication between God and the world, in either direction, had to pass through the spheres in which those powers exercised control. Those who thought in this way would be careful to treat those powers with becoming respect. But the whole of this theosophical apparatus is undermined here in one simple, direct affirmation: the totality of divine essence and power is resident in Christ. He is the one, all-sufficient intermediary

---

[162]In the Synoptic Gospels πλήρωμα is used of the patch put on to "fill up" the rent in an old garment (Matt. 9:16 par. Mark 2:21) and of the leftover fragments which "filled" several baskets after the miraculous feedings (Mark 6:43; 8:20). In Rom. 11:12, 25 it is used of the final sum-total of believing Jews and Gentiles respectively. In Rom. 13:10 it is used of love as the "fulfilling" of the law; in Rom. 15:29 of the "fullness" of Christ's blessing with which Paul hopes to visit Rome. In 1 Cor. 10:26 it appears in a quotation from Ps. 24:1 (LXX 23:1) of that which fills the earth. In Gal. 4:4 and Eph. 1:10 it denotes the completion of an appointed period of time (and consequently the arrival of an epoch; cf. Acts 2:1, συμπληροῦσθαι). There remain those occurrences which have theological or christological significance. In John 1:16 it is used of the "fullness" of Christ (his inexhaustible resources of grace) from which his people receive supplies to meet their spiritual need. In addition to the "fullness" of deity mentioned in our present text and in Col. 2:9, Eph. 3:19 speaks of the "fullness" of God and Eph. 4:13 of the "fullness" of Christ (in the sense of the Christian maturity which believers are to attain as members of his body). On the disputed force of the word in Eph. 1:23 (where it seems to refer to the church in its relation to Christ) see comment and notes *ad loc.* (pp. 275-77). Cf. J. Ernst, *Pleroma und Pleroma Christi* (Regensburg, 1970).

[163]Cf. Irenaeus, *Haer.* 1.1.1, etc.; translation in R. M. Grant, *Gnosticism: An Anthology* (London, 1961), pp. 163-81. E. Percy doubts whether πλήρωμα was a technical term in the Colossian heresy as is commonly supposed; he suggests that Paul may have chosen the word independently, to emphasize the supremacy of Christ in face of the false teaching (*Die Probleme*, pp. 76-77).

between God and the world of humanity, and all the attributes of God—his spirit, word, wisdom, and glory—are disclosed in him.

20 It was God's good pleasure, moreover, to reconcile[164] all things to himself[165] through Christ. The fullness of the divine energy is manifested in Christ in the work of reconciliation as well as in that of creation. In the words that follow (vv. 21-22) this reconciling activity is applied particularly to redeemed humanity, but here its universal reference comes first into view. In reconciliation as in creation the work of Christ has a cosmic significance:[166] it is God's eternal purpose (as it is put in Eph. 1:10) that all things should be summed up in him.[167]

If "all things," in heaven and on earth, were created through him (v. 16), and yet "all things"—"whether the things on earth or those in heaven"—have to be reconciled to God through him, it follows that all things have been estranged from their Creator. In Rom. 8:19-23 Paul speaks of the creation as involuntarily "subjected to futility" but as destined to "be set free from its bondage to decay and obtain the glorious liberty of the children of God." Since the liberty of the children of God is procured by the redemptive work of Christ, the release of creation from its bondage to decay is assured by that same redemptive work. That earlier argument is akin to the present one, but here it is not simply subjection to futility but positive hostility that is implied on the part of the created universe. The universe has been involved in conflict with its Creator, and needs to be reconciled to him: the conflict must be replaced by peace. This

---

[164]Here and in v. 22 the verb rendered "reconcile" is ἀποκαταλλάσσω, found also in Eph. 2:16 (see comment *ad loc.*) and nowhere else in the NT. It has been thought to be a Pauline coinage (cf. F. Büchsel, *TDNT* 1, p. 258, *s.v.* ἀλλάσσω); this is doubtful. It is evidently an intensified form of καταλλάσσω, which appears in Rom. 5:10 (twice); 2 Cor. 5:18, 19, 20 (also in 1 Cor. 7:11, but not there in a theological sense); the corresponding noun καταλλαγή is used in Rom. 5:11; 11:15; 2 Cor. 5:18-19. See J. Dupont, *La réconciliation dans la théologie de saint Paul* (Bruges/Paris, 1953); R. P. Martin, *Reconciliation: A Study of Paul's Theology* (London, 1981), especially pp. 111-26.

[165]The rough breathing (αὑτόν = ἑαυτόν) is required by the context, although in most editions the smooth breathing (αὐτόν) is printed. "In Col. i.20, δι' αὑτοῦ ἀποκαταλλάξαι τὰ πάντα εἰς αὑτόν, it is surprising that there appears to be no variant ἑαυτόν and that editors do not print αὑτόν, which seems to be required by the sense in order to distinguish *Christ*, referred to in δι' αὑτοῦ, from *God*, to whom (probably) the reconciliation is made" (C. F. D. Moule, *IBNTG*, p. 119).

[166]Cf. 2 Cor. 5:19 (κόσμον καταλλάσσων ἑαυτῷ); Rev. 5:13 (πᾶν κτίσμα).

[167]Eph. 1:10 is thus a commentary on Col. 1:16 (εἰς αὐτόν): everything was created with a view to Christ.

peace has been made through Christ, by the shedding of his life-blood on the cross.[168]

This note of universal reconciliation has been taken to imply the ultimate reconciliation to God not only of all mankind but of hostile spiritual powers as well—to imply, in fact, that Paul anticipated Origen in the view that fallen angels benefit from the redemption which Christ accomplished.[169] If the present argument is accepted as Paul's, however, it has to be understood in relation to his general teaching on the subject, and it is very difficult to press his language to yield anything like universal reconciliation in the sense in which the phrase is commonly used nowadays. It is contrary to the analogy of Scripture to apply the idea of reconciliation in the ordinary sense to fallen angels; and as for Paul, he thinks rather of hostile spiritual powers as emptied of all vitality by the work of Christ and the faith of his people.[170] And even with regard to the human race, to deduce from such words as these that every last man or woman, irrespective of moral record or attitude to God, will at last enjoy eternal bliss would be (to say no more) putting on them a burden of meaning heavier than they can bear.[171]

[168]Cf. Eph. 2:13, 16, where the reconciliation of Gentiles and Jews in one new humanity is effected ἐν τῷ αἵματι τοῦ Χριστοῦ . . . διὰ τοῦ σταυροῦ. It is God who makes peace through Christ: the nominative participle εἰρηνοποιήσας agrees in sense if not in form with the subject of εὐδόκησεν, and if the subject is πᾶν τὸ πλήρωμα that (being the fullness of deity, as explained in Col. 2:9) is equivalent in meaning to ὁ θεός. The compound verb εἰρηνοποιέω (cf. the adjective εἰρηνοποιός in Matt. 5:9) occurs here only in the NT; the similar passage in Eph. 2:15 has the two separate words ποιῶν εἰρήνην (where Christ is the subject). The "blood of his cross" (the literal rendering of τοῦ αἵματος τοῦ σταυροῦ) means his death by crucifixion, with some emphasis on the sacrificial character of his death. Cf. J. Behm, *TDNT* 1, pp. 174-75 (*s.v.* αἷμα); L. Morris, *The Apostolic Preaching of the Cross*, pp. 112-28.

[169]Origen, *Commentary on John* 1.35.

[170]Cf. J. Denney, *The Death of Christ* (London, [6]1907), pp. 194-200. E. Percy (*Die Probleme,* p. 95) holds that Col. 1:21 must be understood in the light of Col. 2:15. Both passages presume a certain hostility on the part of these powers toward God and Christ; they are reduced through subjugation (cf. 1 Cor. 15:28), and Christ's victory has reduced them to the status of ἀσθενῆ καὶ πτωχὰ στοιχεῖα (cf. Gal. 4:9). Cf. also J. Michl, "Die Versöhnung Kol 1, 21," *TQ* 128 (1948), 442-62; B. N. Wambacq, "Per eum reconciliare . . . ," *RB* 55 (1948), 35-42; P. T. O'Brien, "Col. 1:20 and the Reconciliation of All Things," *RTR* 35 (1974), 45-53.

[171]Cf. A. M. Hunter, *Interpreting Paul's Gospel,* p. 54; for the contrary view, that

The peace effected by the death of Christ may be freely accepted, or it may be imposed willy-nilly. This reconciliation of the universe includes what would otherwise be distinguished as pacification. The principalities and powers whose conquest is described in Col. 2:15 are certainly not depicted as gladly surrendering to divine grace but as being compelled to submit to a power which they are unable to resist. Everything in the universe has been subjected to Christ even as everything was created for him. By his reconciling work "the host of the high ones on high"[172] and sinful human beings on earth have been decisively subdued to the will of God and ultimately they can but subserve his purpose, whether they please or not. It is the Father's good pleasure that all "in heaven and on earth and under the earth" shall unite to bow the knee at Jesus' name and to acknowledge him as Lord (Phil. 2:10-11).

4. SINNERS RECONCILED TO GOD (1:21-23)

21 *You also, who formerly were estranged and hostile in mind, as was shown by[173] your wicked works,*

22 *he has now nevertheless reconciled[174] in the body of his flesh, through death, to present you holy, blameless, and irreproachable in his presence*

23 *— provided you remain firmly founded and stable in your faith and are not shifted from the hope of the gospel which you heard. This gospel has been preached in all creation under heaven; of this gospel I, Paul, have been made a minister.*

21 The central purpose of Christ's peacemaking work,[175] however,

---

universal reconciliation in the full sense of the restoration of friendly relations is meant, see W. Michaelis, *Versöhnung des Alls: Die frohe Botschaft von der Gnade Gottes* (Bern, 1950), pp. 25-30.

[172]Isa. 24:21.

[173]Gk. ἐν τοῖς ἔργοις τοῖς πονηροῖς, the ἔργα being πονηρά because they are the outworking of an inner enmity toward God (cf. G. Harder, *TDNT* 6, p. 557, n. 73, *s.v.* πονηρός). Hence ἐν, the "maid of all work" among the Greek prepositions, is rendered "as was shown by" above; this excludes any suggestion that the enmity was the consequence of the wicked works.

[174]For the majority reading ἀποκατήλλαξεν, the aorist passive ἀποκατηλλάγητε ("you were reconciled") is read by P^{46} B and Hilary. The passive reading involves an anacoluthon after the accusative ὑμᾶς at the beginning of v. 21, but for that reason might be regarded as original. The variants ἀποκαταλλαγέντες (D* F G b Iren.lat Ambst) and ἀποκατήλλακται (33) may be attempts to mend the anacoluthon; if so, the majority reading could represent a more successful attempt.

[175]If ἀποκατήλλαξεν be read, the following words show that Christ, not God, is now the subject.

is seen most clearly in those men and women who have heard the message of reconciliation and willingly rendered their submission, gratefully accepting the amnesty which the message holds out.[176] This indeed is the prior aspect of reconciliation in Paul's thinking. The introduction of the Christ-hymn before this point means that here personal reconciliation must be mentioned after cosmic reconciliation, which is celebrated in the final strophe of the hymn; but it is more likely that, for Paul, cosmic reconciliation was a corollary of personal reconciliation. In Rom. 5:1-11 it is those who have been justified by faith that have peace with God, having with justification received also reconciliation.

Paul has been criticized for analyzing the divine forgiveness into justification and reconciliation,[177] especially by those who deprecate the expression of this forgiveness in judicial categories at all. Paul had little choice in the matter: not only had he inherited the conception of God as Judge of all the earth, but in his own experience he had consciously entered through Christ into a right relationship with God and a state of peace with him which had eluded him in the days of his zeal for the law. Nor is this conception absent from the teaching of Jesus: he speaks of the day of judgment and tells his hearers what will secure their acquittal on that day and what will procure their condemnation. The distinction between justification and reconciliation, in which logical priority is given to justification, is rooted in the insight that peace, to be worthy of the name, must be founded on righteousness. If human beings are to be reconciled to God, to enjoy peace with him, they must have the assurance that he who will by no means clear the guilty has nevertheless accepted them, sinful as they are. Those who were offenders have been set right with him through the merit of another; those who were hostile have become his friends; his love, revealed in Christ, is poured out and wells up in their hearts.

It is people in whose lives this had come to pass that are addressed in these words. Once they had been estranged[178] from God, in rebellion against him. Sin is not only disobedience to the will of God; it effectually severs men and women's fellowship with him and forces them to live "without God in the world" (Eph. 2:12). Those who are estranged from

---

[176]Cf. 2 Cor. 5:18-20.

[177]Cf. J. Knox, *Chapters in a Life of Paul* (London, 1954), pp. 146-55.

[178]But not in the sense that they, as individuals, had ever been in another relation to God than one of estrangement. Here, as in Eph. 2:12 and 4:18, the perfect participle passive ἀπηλλοτριωμένος is equivalent to the adjective ἀλλότριος. As for their being hostile in mind (τῇ διανοίᾳ), it is to be observed that in the NT, as in the LXX, this word corresponds to Heb. *lēb, lēbāb,* "heart." See C. Masson, *L'Épître aux Éphésiens* (Neuchâtel/Paris, 1953), p. 159, n. 3.

the one in whom alone true peace is to be found are estranged also from one another, and lead lonely lives in a universe which is felt to be unfriendly. The barrier which sin sets up between them and God is also a barrier set up between them and their fellows. If this letter declares that their alienation from God has been abolished by the redemptive work of Christ, the companion letter to the Ephesians declares that their alienation from one another is similarly abolished by that redemptive work.[179]

22 But now the great change has been effected: those who were once far away from God have been brought close to him; those who used to be at war with him are at peace with him. For Christ has reconciled them to God "in the body of his flesh, through his death."[180] The historic act accomplished on their behalf once for all by the death of Christ is brought into close relation with what takes place in their own experience when they enter into peace with God, when the work done *for* them is made effective *in* them. If in v. 20 reconciliation is said to have been won by the blood of Christ, here it is said to have been procured for men and women "in the body of his flesh." Both expressions denote his self-oblation in death (as they do together in the Eucharist); but here the emphasis is on the fact that Christ endured death in his physical body[181] ("the body of his flesh" being evidently a Hebraism with that meaning).[182] It is highly probable that some such insistence on the real incarnation of Christ was a necessary corrective to a tendency in the Colossian heresy; more particularly, these words emphasize that there is a necessary bond between his incarnation and his atoning death. So, in Rom. 8:3, Paul tells how God achieved "what the law, weakened by the flesh, could not do" when, "sending his own Son in the likeness of sinful flesh and as a sin offering,

---

[179]See especially Eph. 2:13-22, with exposition and notes (pp. 295-307).

[180]The possessive pronoun brings out the force of the article (διὰ τοῦ θανάτου).

[181]The preposition ἐν probably has instrumental force: Jesus' body of flesh was the means by which he brought about reconciliation through his death. In Eph. 2:16 he has reconciled Jew and Gentile "to God in one body through the cross," ἐν ἑνὶ σώματι denoting the new unity into which they have been incorporated. There may be an oscillation of thought between the two meanings of σῶμα. "The thought which finds clear expression in Eph. 2:16, that the human beings to be reconciled are included in the body of Christ, and that at the very time when Christ died for them on the cross, also lies plainly behind ἐν τῷ σώματι τῆς σαρκὸς αὐτοῦ in Col. 1:22" (E. Percy, *Die Probleme*, p. 382).

[182]Heb. *bigᵉwiyyat bᵉśārô* in 1QpHab 9.3 (on Hab. 2:7) is the exact verbal equivalent of ἐν τῷ σώματι τῆς σαρκὸς αὐτοῦ here. See also 4Q 169.2.6; Sir. 23:17; 1 Enoch 102:5. See K. G. Kuhn, "New Light on Temptation, Sin and Flesh in the New Testament" (1952), E.T. in *The Scrolls and the New Testament*, ed. K. Stendahl (London, 1958), p. 107. See further on Col. 2:11.

he condemned sin *in the flesh.*" The incarnation of the Son of God was real and necessary for the demonstration of God's righteousness in the bestowal of his peace on sinners. Those who have received his peace have direct access to him already[183] and will have it in fullness when at length they are introduced[184] into his presence holy, blameless, and free from every charge against them. "In Christ this accused person becomes un-accused; he is awarded not condemnation but liberty."[185] The pronounce-ment of justification made in the believer's favor here and now anticipates the pronouncement of the judgment day: the holiness of life which is progressively wrought by the Spirit here and now is to issue in perfection of glory at Christ's *parousia.*

23 This, then, is the prospect which lies before the Colossian Christians, provided they remain firmly on the one foundation for faith.[186] If the gospel teaches the final perseverance of the saints, it teaches at the same time that the saints are those who finally persevere—in Christ. Con-tinuance is the test of reality. The language used may suggest that the readers' first enthusiasm was being dimmed, that they were in danger of shifting from the fixed ground of Christian hope. Indeed, to hold fast to hope is throughout the NT an indispensable condition for attaining the goal of full salvation to be revealed at the *parousia* of Christ.[187] It is difficult to distinguish between hope as an inward attitude and the object of hope: now the one idea, now the other, is uppermost.[188] The one implies the other. Hope in both senses forms an essential element of the gospel[189]—that gospel which (as has been emphasized already) is spreading and bear-ing fruit in all the world, having been proclaimed (as it is stated here in what may be a prophetic prolepsis) "in all creation under heaven."[190] The

---

[183]Compare the sequence of blessings which flow from justification by faith in Rom. 5:1-11.

[184]Gk. παραστῆσαι. The time referred to is the *parousia* of Christ; the same verb bears this eschatological sense in v. 28; cf. Rom. 14:10; 2 Cor. 4:14; 11:2; Eph. 5:27.

[185]A. Deissmann, *Paul,* E.T. (London, 1926), p. 168.

[186]For the foundation see 1 Cor. 3:11.

[187]Cf. I. H. Marshall, *Kept by the Power of God* (London, 1969).

[188]Cf. G. Bornkamm, "Die Hoffnung im Kolosserbrief—Zugleich ein Beitrag zur Frage der Echtheit des Briefes," in *Studien zum Neuen Testament und zur Patristik* (Berlin, 1961), pp. 56-64; he finds that the latter idea is uppermost in Colossians, whereas the former is characteristic of Paul.

[189]Especially in view of the *parousia*; cf. Eph. 1:18; Heb. 3:6; 6:11; 10:23; 1 Pet. 1:13; 1 John 3:3.

[190]See on v. 6 above; cf. Rom. 10:18.

catholicity of the gospel is a token of its divine origin and power.[191] That Paul, the former persecutor, should have been appointed a minister of this gospel was in his eyes a miracle of heavenly grace.[192] In a letter of joint authorship the locution "I Paul" indicates that at this point the apostle himself takes direct responsibility for what is said.[193] Paul sees his personal ministry as closely bound up with God's saving plan for the world.[194]

III. PAUL'S MINISTRY (1:24 – 2:7)

1. PAUL'S STEWARDSHIP OF THE DIVINE MYSTERY (1:24-29)

24 *Now I rejoice in my sufferings[195] for you, and fill up in my flesh whatever is lacking of the sufferings of Christ for the sake of his body, which is the church.*

25 *I have become a minister of the church according to the stewardship of God given to me with you in view, to make the word of God fully known.*

26 *This is the mystery which has been concealed for ages and generations,[196] but has now been manifested to his saints.*

27 *To them God chose to make known the glorious wealth of this mystery[197] among the Gentiles—it[198] is Christ in you, the hope of glory.*

---

[191]Cf. A. S. Peake, *Colossians*, p. 513.

[192]Cf. 1 Cor. 15:9-10; Eph. 3:7-8; 1 Tim. 1:12-14.

[193]Cf. 1 Thess. 2:18.

[194]Cf. Rom. 11:13; Eph. 3:2-6; see also J. Munck, *Paul and the Salvation of Mankind*, pp. 25-68.

[195]The implied pronoun μου ("my") is made explicit after τοῖς παθήμασιν in ℵ² 81 and several cursives.

[196]Lit., "from the ages and from the generations" (ἀπὸ τῶν αἰώνων καὶ ἀπὸ τῶν γενεῶν), where ἀπό has the temporal sense of "since"; it is not suggested that the ages and the generations were entities from which the mystery was concealed, as it was from the "rulers of this age" in 1 Cor. 2:8. Cf. Eph. 3:9, ἀπὸ τῶν αἰώνων (p. 319).

[197]Gk. τὸ πλοῦτος τῆς δόξης τοῦ μυστηρίου τούτου (τῆς δόξης is omitted in P⁴⁶). For the genitive τῆς δόξης used with qualifying force ("glorious") cf. v. 11 above, τὸ κράτος τῆς δόξης αὐτοῦ (see p. 47, n. 37). Paul is particularly given to the use of πλοῦτος with a dependent genitive (cf. Col. 2:2; Rom. 2:4; 9:23; 2 Cor. 8:2; Eph. 1:7; 2:7; 3:8). For "this mystery" several Western witnesses (D* F G b vg.codd Ambst) read "the mystery of God" (τοῦ θεοῦ for τούτου), perhaps under the influence of Col. 2:2. For τούτου ℵ* reads τοῦ ("the mystery which is among the Gentiles").

[198]For ὅ ("which"), in agreement with the antecedent μυστηρίου, ℵ C D H I Ψ and the majority of cursives read ὅς ("who"), attracted into the gender of Χριστός.

28 *It is he whom we preach, as we instruct everyone and teach every-one*[199] *in all wisdom, so as to present everyone perfect in Christ.*[200]

29 *This indeed is the end for which I labor, contending according to his power which operates mightily within me.*

24 Paul's introductory thanksgiving now passes into an account of his own pastoral care for the people whom he addresses.[201]

The hardships which he endures in the course of his apostolic service are endured for their sake. He can even rejoice in these hardships[202] because of the advantage that accrued through them to his converts—whether their conversion was due to his direct witness or, as with the Colossians, to the witness of one of his colleagues. For he realized that, by bearing hardships on behalf of the people of Christ, he was entering into the fellowship of Christ's sufferings—a fellowship which, as he told his friends at Philippi, he desired to know more fully (Phil. 3:10). "For," as he said to the Christians at Corinth, "as we share abundantly in Christ's sufferings, so through Christ we share abundantly in comfort too" (2 Cor. 1:5). The sufferings which he endured in his ministry enabled him to sympathize with his fellow-believers when they suffered, and he was able also to share with them the comfort which he himself constantly experienced at the hand of God. From his Damascus-road encounter he learned not only that Christ suffered in his people but also that he himself, who had made others suffer for Christ's sake, would henceforth have much to suffer for the name of Christ (Acts 9:16).

Here, however, he seems to go further. "In my own person,"[203] he says, "I am filling up[204] those afflictions of Christ which have yet to be

---

[199]Some Western witnesses (D* F G) and others (33 614 629 etc.) omit "everyone" (πάντα ἄνθρωπον) after "teach" (διδάσκοντες).

[200]Χριστῷ is amplified to Χριστῷ Ἰησοῦ in ℵ² D² H Ψ with the majority of cursives.

[201]Cf. Rom. 1:8-10 for a similar transition.

[202]Cf. Rom. 5:3, καυχώμεθα ἐν ταῖς θλίψεσιν.

[203]Gk. ἐν τῇ σαρκί μου, "in my flesh."

[204]Gk. ἀνταναπληρῶ. The force of ἀντί in this compound is disputed. J. B. Lightfoot (*ad loc.*) renders it "I fill up on my part," "I supplement," and argues, on the basis of classical and Hellenistic occurrences of the verb, that "it signifies that the supply comes *from an opposite quarter* to the deficiency." T. K. Abbott (*ad loc.*) points out, on the other hand, that in the two places in the NT where ἀναπληρόω is used with ὑστέρημα as its object (1 Cor. 16:17; Phil. 2:30), the supply equally comes from another quarter than the deficiency; the prefix ἀντί is

endured—filling them up for the sake of his body, the church."[205]

This remarkable statement can best be understood if we bear in mind the oscillation in Hebrew thought between individual and corporate personality.[206] The portrayal of the Isaianic Servant of Yahweh presents a relevant instance. In one place at least the Servant is a corporate entity, the Israel of God (Isa. 49:3):

> "You are my servant,
> Israel, in whom I will be glorified."

But Israel as a whole proved to be a disobedient servant, and the prophecy of the Servant's triumph through suffering was destined to find its fulfilment in one person, in whom the ideally obedient Israel is realized. In the NT this person is identified with Jesus,[207] who by his obedience, passion, and victory over death fulfilled what was written regarding the Servant, and is henceforth proclaimed as a light to the nations, as the agent of God's delivering grace throughout the world. But the Servant's identity, which narrowed in scope until it was concentrated in our Lord alone, has since his exaltation broadened out again and become corporate in his people. So, to take the most notable NT example, Paul and Barnabas at Pisidian Antioch announce to the members of the Jewish synagogue there that, in view of their opposition to the gospel, they will from now on turn to the Gentiles. And they find their authority for this course of action in the Servant Song just quoted (Isa. 49:6): "For so the Lord has commanded us, saying,

---

not required to indicate this. Cf. also 2 Cor. 9:12; 11:9, where a different prefix is used ($\pi\rho\sigma\sigma\alpha\nu\alpha\pi\lambda\eta\rho\dot{\omega}$ $\dot{\upsilon}\sigma\tau\dot{\epsilon}\rho\eta\mu\alpha/\dot{\upsilon}\sigma\tau\epsilon\rho\dot{\eta}\mu\alpha\tau\alpha$). For $\dot{\alpha}\nu\alpha\pi\lambda\eta\rho\dot{\omega}$ see also *C.H.* 13.1, $\tau\dot{\alpha}$ $\dot{\upsilon}\sigma\tau\epsilon\rho\dot{\eta}\mu\alpha\tau\alpha$ $\dot{\alpha}\nu\alpha\pi\lambda\dot{\eta}\rho\omega\sigma\sigma\nu$, "fill up what is lacking (in my knowledge)." It is simplest to regard the prefix $\dot{\alpha}\nu\tau\dot{\iota}$ here as suggesting correspondence: to the deficiency corresponds the supply. See also p. 83, n. 210. On the history of the interpretation of Col. 1:24b see J. Kremer, *Was an den Leiden Christi noch mangelt* (Bonn, 1956).

[205]Gk. $\dot{\upsilon}\pi\dot{\epsilon}\rho$ $\tau\sigma\tilde{\upsilon}$ $\sigma\dot{\omega}\mu\alpha\tau\sigma\varsigma$ $\alpha\dot{\upsilon}\tau\sigma\tilde{\upsilon}$, $\ddot{\sigma}$ $\dot{\epsilon}\sigma\tau\iota\nu$ $\dot{\eta}$ $\dot{\epsilon}\varkappa\varkappa\lambda\eta\sigma\dot{\iota}\alpha$. The preposition $\dot{\upsilon}\pi\dot{\epsilon}\rho$ ("on behalf of") may have the fuller sense "instead of" when the context so indicates, as it probably does here. Cf. E. K. Simpson, "Note on the Meaning of ΥΠΕΡ in Certain Contexts," *The Pastoral Epistles* (London, 1954), pp. 110-12; L. Morris, "Additional Note on $\dot{\upsilon}\pi\dot{\epsilon}\rho$ in Galatians 3:13," in *The Apostolic Preaching of the Cross*, pp. 62-64; M. J. Harris, "Prepositions and Theology in the Greek New Testament," *NIDNTT* 3, pp. 1196-97. P. Benoit sees in the explanatory clause $\ddot{\sigma}$ $\dot{\epsilon}\sigma\tau\iota\nu$ $\dot{\eta}$ $\dot{\epsilon}\varkappa\varkappa\lambda\eta\sigma\dot{\iota}\alpha$ the editorial hand of the redactor of Ephesians or of some other disciple of Paul's ("L'hymne christologique," p. 254 with n. 44).

[206]Cf. C. F. D. Moule, *Colossians and Philemon*, p. 76, for the view that the corporate Christ is intended here; R. Yates, "A Note on Colossians 1:24," *EQ* 42 (1970), 88-92. See also p. 69, n. 140.

[207]Cf. Acts 3:13; Rom. 4:25; Heb. 9:28; 1 Pet. 2:22-25.

'I have set you to be a light for the Gentiles,
that you may bring salvation to the uttermost parts of the earth' "
(Acts 13:47).

That is to say, the Servant's mission of enlightenment to the nations is to be carried on by the representatives of Christ.

The present context rules out any suggestion that the reconciliation effected by the death of Christ needs to be supplemented. Paul and his fellow-preachers, having themselves received the peace which was made "through the blood of his cross," now fulfil their ministry by presenting that peace for acceptance by others. But in the fulfilment of that ministry they are exposed to sufferings for Christ's sake, and these sufferings are their share in the afflictions of Christ.[208] There may be a hint in Paul's words that he is eager to receive more than his due share of those afflictions in order that there may be the less for his converts and other fellow-Christians to bear. So conscious was he of the special significance of his vocation to service and suffering.

At the back of Paul's mind there may be the rabbinical concept of the messianic birth pangs which were to be endured in the last days—from Paul's new Christian perspective, in the period leading up to the *parousia*.[209] Jesus, the Messiah, had suffered on the cross; now his people, the members of his body, had their quota of affliction to bear, and Paul was eager to absorb as much as possible of this in his own "flesh."[210] The suffering of affliction now was, for the followers of Christ, the prelude to glory at his advent, and such was the incomparable and "eternal weight

---

[208]The θλίψεις τοῦ Χριστοῦ are identical here with Paul's παθήματα ὑπὲρ ὑμῶν ("for you Gentiles," not only "for you Colossians"). Nowhere in the NT is the θλίβω word-group used of the personal passion of Christ. W. Michaelis takes θλίψεις τοῦ Χριστοῦ here to mean "afflictions *for* Christ" (*TDNT* 5, p. 933 with n. 20, *s.v.* πάθημα). Cf. E. Best, *One Body in Christ*, p. 132 ("the sufferings of the Messiah . . . are sufferings which his disciples are enduring, persecutions direct or indirect"); L. P. Trudinger, "A Further Brief Note on Colossians 1:24," *EQ* 45 (1973), 36-38.

[209]Cf. E. Best, *One Body in Christ*, p. 136; R. J. Bauckham, "Colossians 1:24 Again: The Apocalyptic Motif," *EQ* 47 (1975), 168-70.

[210]Cf. J. A. T. Robinson, *The Body*, p. 70, where the prefix ἀντί is taken to indicate Paul's willingness "to fill up in *their* stead . . . the tax of suffering still outstanding to them." C. F. D. Moule (*IBNTG*, p. 71) allows his interpretation (ἀντί "may anticipate the force of the ὑπέρ which follows"), but he admits the view preferred in n. 204 above, that ἀντί "may merely imply that fullness *replaces* lack." Ignatius (*Eph.* 8.1; *Trall.* 13.3) speaks of his imminent martyrdom as an offering on behalf of his Christian friends, but does not describe it as part of the suffering of Christ. On the other hand, the *Letter from the Churches of Vienne and Lyon* (Eusebius, *HE* 5.1) expressly speaks of Christ as suffering in the martyrs.

of glory" to which they could look forward that the hardships of the present were described, in relation to it, as "this slight momentary affliction" (2 Cor. 4:17).

25 This, at any rate, was Paul's estimate. He knew that he had been called to be a servant of the church for the discharge of a unique stewardship.[211] This stewardship, entrusted to him by Christ, was (as he puts it) the "fulfilment" of the word or message of God. The word of God is fulfilled in this sense when it is freely proclaimed in the world and accepted in faith; thus it achieves its purpose.[212] It was Paul's responsibility to discharge this stewardship by exercising his special apostleship to the Gentiles, among whom the Colossians were included. In the words of the parallel passage in Ephesians, "to me . . . this grace has been given, to bring to the Gentiles the good news of God's unfathomable wealth" (Eph. 3:8); and the Colossians were among the beneficiaries of Paul's apostolic commission, even if he had never visited them in person.

26 He now enlarges on the message with which he has been entrusted. It is a "mystery"—that is to say, something hitherto concealed but now revealed,[213] and especially (in biblical usage) some aspect of the divine purpose. Throughout ages and generations past this particular mystery remained unknown, but it has now been disclosed to the people of God, not least through Paul himself. This need not imply that no reference at all was made to it in the OT scriptures. The word "mystery," as used by Paul and other NT writers, has an OT background in the Aramaic part of the book of Daniel.[214] There the divine purpose is communicated in two stages: first as a mystery (as when Nebuchadnezzar sees the great

---

[211]Gk. οἰκονομία, used to denote Paul's special service also in 1 Cor. 9:17 and, more particularly, in Eph. 3:2, 9, where (as here) he speaks of himself as a steward of the divine mystery, that is, the divine purpose of bringing Gentile believers into one community with Jewish believers, as fellow-heirs of the promises of God and fellow-members of the body of Christ.

[212]Cf. Rom. 15:19, where Paul, early in A.D. 57, claims that he has "fully preached (Gk. πεπληρωκέναι, 'fulfilled') the gospel of Christ" from Jerusalem to Illyricum. J. Munck (*Paul and the Salvation of Mankind*, p. 48) compares our present passage and Rom. 15:19 (with 2 Tim. 4:17, "that through me the message might be fully declared [πληροφορηθῇ], and that all the Gentiles might hear") with the bringing in of the πλήρωμα τῶν ἐθνῶν in Rom. 11:25.

[213]Cf. Rom. 16:25; 1 Cor. 2:7-10.

[214]Aram. *rāz*, a word of Iranian derivation (rendered μυστήριον in Gk.); the interpretation is Aram. *pᵉšar* (Heb. *pēšer*, as in Eccl. 8:1), rendered σύγκρισις in Greek. Cf. F. F. Bruce, *Biblical Exegesis in the Qumran Texts* (Grand Rapids/London, 1960), pp. 7-11.

image in his dream, described in Dan. 2:31-35) and then by way of interpretation (as when Daniel in Dan. 2:37-45 gives the king the explanation of the dream—an explanation which he himself has received by direct revelation from God). This mystery-interpretation pattern gives its character to the exegetical principle found in the biblical commentaries of the Qumran community. According to this principle, God made known his purpose to the prophets of old, but withheld from the prophets one vital piece of information (without which the prophetic word remained a "mystery")—namely, the *time* when his purpose would be fulfilled (together with the identity of the persons who would be involved, on the one side or the other, in its fulfilment). What was withheld from the prophets, the Qumran community believed, was disclosed to the Teacher of Righteousness, who imparted it to his disciples: they therefore knew, and were humbly grateful for knowing, things that had been hidden from the wise and understanding.

27 For Paul the moment of revelation came on the Damascus road. He did not instantly grasp the full significance of what was revealed to him then: it had to be worked out and appreciated in the course of his apostolic experience. It was Christ in person that was revealed to him, with special reference to his role in Paul's Gentile mission. "God," as he says, "was pleased to reveal his Son in me, in order that I might preach him among the Gentiles" (Gal. 1:15-16).

The saving purpose of God was a major theme of the OT prophets, and that Gentiles as well as Israelites were embraced within its scope was also foreseen.[215] But the manner in which that purpose would come to fruition—by the incorporation of Gentile and Jewish believers alike in the common life of the body of Christ—was not made known. That remained a secret, a mystery, until the time of fulfilment, and now Paul, as steward of this mystery, unfolds its wonder to his readers, that the glory of God's rich grace thus lavishly dispensed may move them to grateful adoration. Had this grace been shown to believing Jews alone, it might not have excited such wonder; they, after all, were the messianic people. But non-Jews are included as well, and included on an equal footing with Jews;

---

[215]See Paul's catena of OT quotations to this effect in Rom. 15:9-12; cf. also Isa. 49:6, quoted in Luke 2:32 and Acts 13:47 (see pp. 82-83 above). The prophets spoke of Christ and his salvation (1 Pet. 1:10; Eph. 2:17) and the gospel was proclaimed to Abraham (Gal. 3:8), but how their words would come to pass was not understood before the appearance of Christ. "The apostles are the first to *know* what the prophets *said*" (H. J. Holtzmann, *Kritik der Epheser- und Kolosserbriefe* [Leipzig, 1872], p. 212).

and it is Paul's supreme joy, as it is his divinely imposed obligation, to "make known the glorious wealth of this mystery among the *Gentiles*."[216]

Christ is himself "the mystery of God" (Col. 2:2); in him the *deus absconditus* has become the *deus revelatus*. But Paul's special stewardship of this mystery involves its disclosure to Gentiles. "Christ is in *you*," he assures his Colossian readers, "Christ is in you (even in you Gentiles) as your hope of glory." The phrase "in you" might mean "in your midst" (as a community) or "within you" (as individuals). Neither sense should be excluded, but the thought of Christ as indwelling individual believers is completely in line with Pauline thought. The indwelling Christ and the indwelling Spirit are practically interchangeable thoughts for Paul (cf. Rom. 8:10-11), although elsewhere it is the indwelling Spirit that he presents as the hope or guarantee of coming glory. In this letter, however, he expresses himself in christological terms, and the readers are assured of the hope which is bound up with the indwelling Christ. The fact that here and now, as members of his body, they have his risen life within them, affords them a stable basis for confidence that they will share in the fullness of glory yet to be displayed, on the day of "the revealing of the sons of God" (Rom. 8:19).[217]

28 This Christ, whose life flows in all his people, is the one whom the apostle and his associates proclaim. He is the sum and substance of their message, whether in the saving news which they announce in the world to bring men and women to faith, or in the teaching which they impart to those who have believed. They have not learned all there is to know when once they have come to Christ; that is only the beginning. He is indeed the embodiment of divine wisdom, but the exploration of the wisdom that resides in him is the task of a lifetime, and even so the most

---

[216]Cf. the expansion of this thought in Eph. 3:2-12. The difference in the use of μυστήριον in the two letters is not so great as some exegetes have thought. According to M. Dibelius, the "mystery" in Col. 1:26-27 is "das eschatologisch-mystische Christusgeheimnis" (*An die Kolosser*, p. 84); according to C. L. Mitton, it is Christ's indwelling in his people (*The Epistle to the Ephesians* [Oxford, 1951], pp. 88-89). The "mystery" of Ephesians, on the other hand, is God's acceptance of the Gentiles which, says Dibelius, "is no μυστήριον for Paul." (Of course not, because it is being fulfilled in his ministry.) But the μυστήριον is not simply the acceptance of the Gentiles; it includes their incorporation together with Jewish believers in the community of the Messiah. And in Col. 1:26-27 the emphasis is not just on Christ's indwelling in his people but more specifically on his indwelling in *Gentile* believers. Cf. G. Bornkamm, *TDNT* 4, p. 820, n. 145 (*s.v.* μυστήριον); E. Percy, *Die Probleme*, pp. 379-82.

[217]Cf. Col. 3:4; also Rom. 5:2; 1 Cor. 2:7; 2 Cor. 4:17; 1 Thess. 2:12; 2 Thess. 1:10; 2:14.

enlightened of mortals can only "know in part" (1 Cor. 13:9). It is necessary, then, not only to preach the gospel but also, when people have believed the gospel, to "instruct everyone and teach everyone in all wisdom."

The repetition of "everyone" is emphatic. There is no part of Christian teaching that is to be reserved for a spiritual elite. All the truth of God is for all the people of God. A later NT writer, taking issue with a cult which professed a special grade of knowledge for a favored few, by contrast with the rank and file for whom elementary half-truths were good enough, assures even the "little children" among his Christian readers that, because they have been anointed by the Holy One, they all have access to the true knowledge.[218] And it may well be that at this earlier date a similar situation had developed in the Lycus valley, where certain teachers professed a form of "wisdom" higher than anything taught by Paul and his colleagues, a form of wisdom which not everyone could appreciate, and which therefore marked off those who accepted it and affected its jargon as intellectually superior to others. On the contrary, say Paul and Timothy, in the proclamation of Christ we bring all wisdom within the reach of all, and our purpose is to present each believer before the face of God in a state of complete spiritual maturity. There should be no exceptions; there are no heights in Christian attainment which are not within the reach of all, by the power of heavenly grace.[219]

The presentation of everyone "perfect" or fully grown in Christ is probably envisaged as taking place at his *parousia*.[220] The Christians of Thessalonica are assured that they are the hope and joy and crown of their fathers in the faith "before our Lord Jesus at his *parousia*" (1 Thess. 2:19-20), and prayer is offered that they may be entirely sanctified and kept sound and blameless, in spirit and soul and body, "at the *parousia* of our Lord Jesus Christ" (1 Thess. 5:23).[221] It is then that the work of grace in the believer's life is completed; it is then that perfect conformity to the likeness of Christ is attained. When "that which is perfect"[222] comes,

---

[218] 1 John 2:20, reading πάντες (with ℵ B P Ψ 398 and the Sahidic version) instead of πάντα.

[219] The accumulation of various parts and compounds of πᾶς ("all") is an effective rhetorical figure appearing repeatedly in the Pauline and other NT writings. Cf. Col. 3:11; Eph. 1:23; 2 Cor. 9:8, etc.

[220] The tense is aorist (παραστήσωμεν), as in v. 22 (see p. 79 with n. 184).

[221] In 1 Thess. 5:23 the verbs ἁγιάσαι and τηρηθείη are aorist, and the explicit mention of the *parousia* indicates the epoch referred to. Sanctification begins with the new birth, it progresses throughout the Christian life by the aid of the Holy Spirit, and is consummated at the *parousia*. Cf. 2 Cor. 3:18; 1 John 3:2.

[222] Gk. τὸ τέλειον (1 Cor. 13:10). Cf. Eph. 4:13, where the ἀνὴρ τέλειος seems to be the completed body of Christ.

the people of Christ will see "face to face" instead of obscurely, as in a metal mirror; they will know fully, as they themselves are known, instead of knowing in part as they do at present (1 Cor. 13:12). But this prospect of glory, which is the perfection of holiness, is held out to *all* his people.

29 For this blessed consummation, so devoutly to be wished, Paul himself expended all his strength.[223] His apostolic work did not rest with the conversion of his hearers. That was a beginning; the end would not be reached until the day of Christ, and the quality of his ministry would then be tested by the quality and maturity of those whom he could present as his spiritual children. What joy would be his if they were genuine and worthy believers; what shame if they were not! No wonder that he toiled and agonized for their growth in grace with this day of review and reward before him. But here he gladly acknowledges that the strength requisite for such unremitting labor is not his own; it is the strength powerfully wrought within him by his enabling Lord.[224]

---

[223]Gk. κοπιῶ, a strong word, denoting toil to the point of weariness or exhaustion (cf. 1 Cor. 4:12; 15:10; Gal. 4:11; Phil. 2:16, and the similar use of the substantive κόπος in 1 Cor. 15:58; 2 Cor. 6:5; 11:23, 27; 1 Thess. 2:9; 3:5; 2 Thess. 3:8). See J. Munck, *Paul and the Salvation of Mankind*, p. 108 with n. 4.

[224]Gk. κατὰ τὴν ἐνέργειαν αὐτοῦ τὴν ἐνεργουμένην ἐν ἐμοὶ ἐν δυνάμει. The present participle ἐνεργουμένην is probably to be construed in the middle voice rather than the passive, although here the sense is not affected one way or the other. It is the power of God that is at work within Paul, so that, if the form be taken as passive, God is the implied worker (as in Phil. 2:13, θεὸς . . . ὁ ἐνεργῶν). Cf. Eph. 3:20 (p. 331). For the general sense cf. Eph. 3:7, κατὰ τὴν ἐνέργειαν τῆς δυνάμεως αὐτοῦ. Paul uses ἐνέργεια of supernatural power.

COLOSSIANS 2

2. CONCERN FOR THE CHRISTIANS OF THE LYCUS VALLEY (2:1-5)

(1) Reassurance of Paul's Prayers for Them (2:1-3)

1 *For I want you to know how great is the contest in which I am engaged for you and those in Laodicea, and all who have not seen me face to face,[1]*

2 *that their hearts may be encouraged as they are united[2] in love, with a view to [their gaining] all the wealth of fullness of understanding—namely, the knowledge of the mystery of God, that is, Christ,[3]*

3 *in whom all the treasures of wisdom and knowledge are concealed.*

---

[1]Lit., "who have not seen my face in (the) flesh" (ὅσοι οὐχ ἑόρακαν τὸ πρόσωπόν μου ἐν σαρκί).

[2]Gk. συμβιβασθέντες, a "sense construction," the masculine form agreeing with the understood "they" (which is actually expressed by the periphrasis αἱ καρδίαι αὐτῶν, "their hearts"). ℵ² D² Ψ and the majority of cursives read the grammatically correct συμβιβασθέντων (in concord with αὐτῶν).

[3]Gk. εἰς ἐπίγνωσιν τοῦ μυστηρίου τοῦ θεοῦ, Χριστοῦ. This (the most satisfactory) reading appears in *P*⁴⁶ B, and is attested by Hilary, Pelagius, and Pseudo-Jerome. D* and a few other Western authorities give the same sense with the expanded reading ὅ ἐστιν Χριστός instead of Χριστοῦ. Other authorities omit Χριστοῦ or θεοῦ, or insert καί so as to yield the sense "the mystery of God and Christ," variously amplified to "the mystery of God the Father and of Christ" (441 1908) or even to "the mystery of God and the Father and of Christ" (D² K and the majority of cursives), or change Χριστοῦ to [τοῦ] ἐν Χριστῷ, "the mystery of God [which is] in Christ" (33). The reading of *P*⁴⁶ B is the point of departure for all the variants. We should take Χριστοῦ in apposition with μυστηρίου—Christ himself is the mystery of God. There is a helpful discusion of this passage, with

1 The toil and spiritual conflict in which Paul was engaged[4] on his converts' behalf embraced not only those whom he had personally met, and who had accepted the gospel as they heard it from his lips; but those also who, like the Colossian Christians, had been converted through the ministry of Paul's colleagues and assistants.[5] Into this category came the Christians of the neighboring city of Laodicea[6] and of other places in the Lycus valley,[7] who appear to have owed their souls to Epaphras.

The conflict is waged in the spiritual realm; the opposition is the false teaching to which the churches of the Lycus valley are exposed.

2 This spiritual conflict involved constant prayer that these young Christians might be strengthened[8] in heart and firmly bound together[9] in Christian love. For (no matter what some teachers might pretend) only so could they attain that wealth of spiritual experience which lay in a full

---

clear and detailed presentation of the evidence, in B. M. Metzger, *The Text of the New Testament* (Oxford, 1964), pp. 236-38. J. N. Darby, *The New Testament: A New Translation* (London, ²1871), *ad loc.*; W. Kelly, *Lectures on Colossians* (London, 1869), p. 40; and E. Lohmeyer, *ad loc.*, take Χριστοῦ as an early gloss and follow those texts which read simply "the mystery of God" (D¹ H P 31 424**); the following ἐν ᾧ (v. 3) then means "in which."

[4]Gk. ἡλίκον ἀγῶνα ἔχω. The noun ἀγών (cf. Phil. 1:30; 1 Thess. 2:2; 1 Tim. 6:12; 2 Tim. 4:7) and the derivative verb ἀγωνίζομαι (cf. 1 Cor. 9:25; Col. 1:29; 4:12; 1 Tim. 4:10; 6:12; 2 Tim. 4:7) are taken from the field of athletic contest and applied to missionary and pastoral activity. Cf. V. C. Pfitzner, *Paul and the Agon Motif* (Leiden, 1967), pp. 109-29. F. Field, *Notes on the Translation of the New Testament* (Cambridge, 1899), p. 195, suggests (unconvincingly) that the phrase here may be based on a reminiscence of Isa. 7:13 LXX: "Is it a small thing for you to cause conflict (ἀγῶνα παρέχειν) to human beings? How then do you cause conflict (ἀγῶνα παρέχετε) to the Lord?"

[5]A few of them may have met Paul elsewhere (e.g., in Ephesus); thus it appears from the letter to Philemon that Philemon and some members of his household (see further on Archippus, Col. 4:17) were personally known to Paul; but the majority of the Colossian Christians remained personally unknown to him.

[6]On Laodicea (cf. Col. 4:16; Rev. 1:11; 3:14-22) see Introduction, p. 6.

[7]Including, no doubt, Hierapolis (cf. Col. 4:14); indeed, καὶ τῶν ἐν Ἱεραπόλει is inserted here by 104 424 and a few other cursives.

[8]Gk. παρακαλέω, "encourage," "strengthen." For its use with καρδία as the object of the encouragement cf. Col. 4:8; Eph. 6:22; 2 Thess. 2:17.

[9]Gk. συμβιβάζω. M. Dibelius's view (*ad loc.*) that the passive participle συμβιβασθέντες means "instructed" here ("durch Belehrung in Liebe") finds some support from usage elsewhere, especially in the LXX (cf. the quotation from Isa. 40:13 in 1 Cor. 2:16); but the analogy of Col. 2:19 (with Eph. 4:16) is decisive for the present meaning "bound together" or "knit together."

discerning[10] of the divine revelation. Others might lead them astray with specious talk of mysteries; but there was one mystery above all others— the mystery of God's loving purpose, disclosed in Christ alone—and Paul's concern was that they should come to know this all-surpassing mystery, and know it as an indwelling presence.

Over against all those who tried to intellectualize the Christian faith, speaking of knowledge *(gnōsis)* as if it were an end in itself, Paul emphasizes that the revelation of God cannot be properly known apart from the cultivation of brotherly love within the community. The Corinthian church, which had special need to learn this lesson, was reminded that "knowledge *(gnōsis)* inflates, but love builds up" (1 Cor. 8:1), and it is later made clear in Eph. 3:17-18 that only as Christians are "rooted and well founded *in love*" can they "comprehend *with all the saints*" the fullness of the divine revelation.[11] And this revelation is personal: Christ himself is the mystery of God revealed—Christ, with whom they have now become one. "All the promises of God find their Yes in him" (2 Cor. 1:20). The personal knowledge of Christ is the royal road to the appreciation of the divine wisdom.

3 For it is in Christ that all the treasures of divine wisdom[12] and knowledge are stored up. Formerly they were stored up in concealment, but now that Christ has come they are unfolded to those who have believed in him. As once to the Corinthians, so now to the Colossians Paul insists that Christ is the Wisdom of God.[13] In him is enshrined the true knowledge, in contrast to the counterfeit *gnōsis* of the false teachers.

(2) His Anxiety Lest They Be Misled (2:4-5)

> 4 *What I mean is this: let no one lead you astray with persuasive talk;*
> 5 *for even if I am absent from you in the body, yet I am with with you*

---

[10]Gk. σύνεσις ("understanding"), as in Col. 1:9, implies the capacity to distinguish true from false. There as here σύνεσις is used in proximity to ἐπίγνωσις (see p. 46, n. 30).

[11]Eph. 3:17-18 is not documentarily dependent on Col. 2:2 (or 2:19); it is a fuller and independent expression of the same thought. For "in love" (ἐν ἀγάπῃ) cf. Eph. 4:15.

[12]The phrase "treasures of wisdom" (θησαυροὶ τῆς σοφίας) appears in Sir. 1:25; here Paul adds "and knowledge" (καὶ γνώσεως), "with a side-glance at the shibboleths of Gnosticism" (W. D. Davies, *Paul and Rabbinic Judaism* [London, 1948], p. 173). Despite the collocation of θησαυρός and ἀπόκρυφος, it is doubtful whether there is a conscious reminiscence here of Isa. 45:3 LXX, θησαυροὺς σκοτεινούς, ἀποκρύφους ἀοράτους ἀνοίξω σοι (cf. F. Hauck, *TDNT* 3, p. 138, *s.v.* θησαυρός).

[13]See p. 60 above (on Col. 1:15).

*in the spirit, rejoicing as I see your orderliness and the firmness of
your faith in Christ.*

4-5 "What I mean is this," says Paul, "don't let anyone talk you
round with plausible arguments.[14] Although I am personally absent from
you, I am with you in spirit, and I rejoice as I watch your orderly Christian
behavior and your firm Christian faith."[15]

Paul's sense of being spiritually present with his absent friends
could be extraordinarily strong and vivid. Perhaps the most remarkable
example is found in 1 Cor. 5:3-5, where he speaks of himself as present
in spirit at a church meeting in Corinth (at a time when he was resident
in Ephesus), in order to take a decisive part in a solemn act of discipline.
Here he speaks of himself as spiritually present with a distant church for
a much happier purpose. Whereas in the case of Corinth his spiritual
presence was promised to a church with which he was well acquainted,
here he gives the same assurance to a church in whose midst he had never
been present in body. The contemplation of the Colossians' faith and conduct gives him the utmost pleasure: so vivid, we may infer, was the picture
of their life and character which he had received from Epaphras.

3. MAINTAINING THE TRADITION OF CHRIST (2:6-7)

6 *So then, as you have received Christ Jesus the Lord, pursue your
way of life in him.*
7 *Be rooted and built up in him, firmly established in your faith, as
you have been taught, abounding in thanksgiving.[16]*

6 This short sentence introduces us to the concept of tradition in
apostolic Christianity. The idea of tradition, together with the terminology

---

[14]Gk. τοῦτο λέγω ἵνα μηδεὶς ὑμᾶς παραλογίζηται κτλ. C. F. D. Moule (*IBNTG*,
p. 145) points out that this is the imperatival use of ἵνα, not its final (telic) use,
in which case the meaning would be: "I am saying this *in order that* no one may
lead you astray."
[15]Gk. τὸ στερέωμα τῆς εἰς Χριστὸν πίστεως ὑμῶν, "the solidity of your faith
in Christ." LXX στερέωμα is the rendering of Heb. *rāqîa'*, "firmament," in Gen.
1:6-8. H. Chadwick suggests that the use of this word here, though possibly a
military metaphor, may echo the important part played in gnostic thought by the
στερέωμα or barrier between the upper realm and the lower ("All Things to All
Men," NTS 1 [1954-55], 272-73). See pp. 296-97 with nn. 113-14, on Eph. 2:14.
[16]Before ἐν εὐχαριστίᾳ B D² H and the majority of cursives insert ἐν αὐτῇ ("in
it"); ℵ² D* insert ἐν αὐτῷ ("in him"). P Ψ replace ἐν εὐχαριστίᾳ by ἐν αὐτῇ.

used to express it, is common in Judaism, where it especially designates the handing down of the oral law and its interpretation from one generation to another. The best-known summary of the Jewish handing down of tradition in the ages before A.D. 70 tells how "Moses received the Torah from Sinai, and he delivered it to Joshua, and Joshua to the elders,[17] and the elders to the prophets, and the prophets delivered it to the men of the great synagogue" (traditionally set up in the time of Ezra). From one of the last survivors of the "great synagogue," Simon the Just,[18] the Torah was received by Antigonus of Soko, and then it was delivered in turn to successive pairs of scholars, generation by generation, until Hillel and Shammai (c. 10 B.C.).[19] This was the "tradition of the elders" which Jesus denounced because in practice it nullified certain basic principles of the divine law which it was intended to safeguard and apply. "You leave the commandment of God," he said, "and hold fast the tradition of men" (Mark 7:8).

Paul uses this same phrase, "the tradition of men,"[20] of the teaching by which the Colossian Christians were in danger of being misled. By implication he opposes to it the tradition of Christ, which they had received when first they heard the gospel. When he says that they have "received" Christ Jesus as their Lord,[21] he uses the verb which was specifically employed to denote the receiving of something which was delivered by tradition.[22] In other words, the Colossians have received Christ himself as their "tradition," and this should prove a sufficient safeguard against following the "tradition of men" (v. 8). Emphasis is laid on the continuity of the transmission of Christian truth, relating to doctrine and practice

---

[17]That is, the elders of Josh. 24:31; Judg. 2:7.

[18]Probably the high priest Simon II (c. 200 B.C.).

[19]*Pirqê 'Abôt* 1.1.

[20]Gk. τὴν παράδοσιν τῶν ἀνθρώπων ("human tradition"), as in Mark 7:8.

[21]Gk. ὡς οὖν παρελάβετε τὸν Χριστὸν Ἰησοῦν τὸν κύριον. J. B. Lightfoot renders the last five words "the Christ, *even* Jesus the Lord," and suggests that this expression "might seem to be directed against the tendency to separate the heavenly Christ from the earthly Jesus, as though the connexion were only transient" (*Colossians and Philemon*, p. 112).

[22]Gk. παραλαμβάνω (equivalent to Heb. *qibbēl*, used in the first clause of the quotation from *Pirqê 'Abôt* above). It appears in this sense in Col. 4:17; 1 Cor. 11:23; 15:1, 3; Gal. 1:9, 12; Phil. 4:9; 1 Thess. 2:13; 4:1; 2 Thess. 3:6 (for the related noun παράδοσις in a Christian sense cf. 1 Cor. 11:2; 2 Thess. 2:15; 3:6). In 1 Cor. 11:23 and 15:3 παραλαμβάνω is accompanied by its correlative verb παραδίδωμι, "deliver" (the equivalent of Heb. *māsar*, so used in the above quotation from *Pirqê 'Abôt*); cf. Luke 1:2; Acts 6:14; 16:4; Rom. 6:17; 1 Cor. 11:2; 2 Pet. 2:21; Jude 3.

alike.[23] The teaching which has been delivered to the Colossians embodies the apostolic witness, derived from Christ, whose authority is supreme, and maintained in purity by his indwelling presence.[24]

7 Let them therefore see to it that their way of thought and life conforms continually to this teaching. Let them send their roots deep down into the truth as it is in Jesus, and their faith would not be quickly overturned.[25] Faith in Christ would give them a stability which nothing could subvert. Thus firmly based[26] on the revelation of the divine mystery (i.e., on Christ himself), they would not be exposed to uncertainty and doubt, but would have ample occasion to overflow with gratitude to God.[27] This gratitude is the spontaneous manifestation of the divine presence and power within them, as they enjoy daily fellowship with Christ; it is a sign that they are indeed living in the new age.

Protestants sometimes overlook that "tradition" in the NT has this better sense as well as a worse one; it is good to recognize and hold fast the true tradition, while rejecting all tradition which runs counter to the gospel.

IV. FALSE TEACHING AND ITS ANTIDOTE
(2:8 – 3:4)

1. THE ALL-SUFFICIENCY OF CHRIST (2:8-15)

What was this *gnōsis* which was being pressed on the Colossian Christians with such specious arguments? The answer to this question, insofar as it is attainable, must be gathered from this section of the letter. For here Paul deals more fully and expressly with the erroneous teaching which his readers were being invited to accept, and here, too, he prescribes the proper antidote. But we cannot be sure that we have grasped all the features

---

[23]Cf. O. Cullmann, "*Kyrios* as Designation for the Oral Tradition concerning Jesus," *SJT* 3 (1950), 180-97; "The Tradition," in *The Early Church*, E.T. (London, 1956), pp. 55-99; R. P. C. Hanson, *Tradition in the Early Church* (London, 1962); F. F. Bruce, *Tradition Old and New* (Exeter, 1970).

[24]Elsewhere than in this letter, the indwelling presence is usually that of the Holy Spirit.

[25]For ἐρριζωμένοι, "rooted," cf. Eph. 3:17 (ἐρριζωμένοι καὶ τεθεμελιωμένοι); in both places the botanical figure is accompanied by an architectural one (here ἐποικοδομούμενοι).

[26]Gk. βεβαιούμενοι (cf. the active voice of βεβαιόω with God as the subject in 1 Cor. 1:8; 2 Cor. 1:21).

[27]See on Col. 1:12 (εὐχαριστοῦντες), p. 49 with nn. 42, 43.

of the controverted teaching. This is because Paul could assume an acquaintance with it on the part of the Colossian church which his twentieth-century readers lack. It appears to have been basically Jewish, but to have included features of pagan affinity. Its Jewish features went beyond those principles which, at an earlier date, Judaizing Christians had endeavored to graft onto the faith of the young churches of Galatia. The teaching which Paul had to counter in Galatia was such as might have proceeded from Judaean "believers who belonged to the party of the Pharisees," who insisted that it was necessary to circumcise Gentile converts and "charge them to keep the law of Moses" (Acts 15:5); those who propagated it in Galatia probably aimed to bring the Pauline churches under the control of the leaders of the Jerusalem church.[28] Jerusalem plays no part in the Colossian debate. The Jewish law certainly figures in it, but it is associated with an asceticism which was not characteristic of the mainstream of Jewish life.

Those features which have pagan affinities are not necessarily of pagan origin. They are analogous to certain aspects of the mystery religions (if that term be used in a fairly comprehensive sense), in which security was sought from cosmic intimidation—from the terrors of existence in a world which was directed by hostile and implacable powers. Those powers are referred to in this letter as *stoicheia*—"elements" or "elemental forces."[29] In a universe governed by such forces, "man found two means by which to make his existence bearable: either he must worship the elements, in order not to be harmed by them, or he must entrust himself to a deity that governs the elements and secures his protégé against any threat by the *stoicheia*."[30] Of the two alternatives thus stated by Martin Dibelius, it appears that the Colossian Christians were disposed to embrace the former, while Paul commends the latter: faith in the heavenly Lord who is not only creator of the cosmic powers but has proved himself their master by his victory on the cross.

There were tendencies within rabbinical Judaism with features which were not dissimilar to aspects of mystery initiation among the pagans. Notable among these was *"merkabah* mysticism"—the practice of techniques for experiencing the vision of God, enthroned on his heavenly chariot *(merkābāh),* which was granted to Ezekiel when he was called to

---

[28]Cf. F. F. Bruce, *The Epistle to the Galatians* (Grand Rapids/Exeter, 1982), pp. 19-32 *et passim.*
[29]See on Col. 2:8, 20, where the στοιχεῖα are mentioned (pp. 98-99, nn. 40-41).
[30]M. Dibelius, "The Isis Initiation in Apuleius and Related Initiatory Rites," E.T. in *Conflict at Colossae,* ed. F. O. Francis and W. A. Meeks (Missoula, MT, 1975), p. 79.

the prophetic ministry (Ezek. 1:26-28).[31] That the meticulous observance of the sacred law was indispensable for such an experience went without saying, but a special regime of self-discipline was also a prerequisite. In the literature of *merkabah* mysticism angels are given a mediatorial role (as also, it seems, in the Colossian heresy). It was, moreover, almost inevitable that those who experienced the vision of God in this way should be considered, or should even consider themselves, to belong to a spiritual elite.[32]

When one recalls that features of incipient gnosticism have commonly (and no doubt rightly) been detected in the Colossian heresy, it is relevant to observe that the leading authority on *merkabah* mysticism has spoken of it as a form of "Jewish gnosticism."[33] In the syncretistic atmosphere of Phrygia, also, Jews and Christians would have been exposed to the assumption, lying behind many forms of gnostic thought, that spirit and matter were antithetical the one to the other, so that no direct contact was conceivable between the supreme God and the created universe. If this assumption lay behind the Colossian heresy, some emphases in Paul's refutation of it are more easily understood.

For a system of thought based on such an assumption was bound to undermine the gospel. If God and the material world cannot come into direct relation, the world cannot be the creation of God. Neither is it thinkable that the Wisdom of God should have been incarnated in a "body of flesh" (Col. 1:22), that the Son of God should have been "born of a woman" (Gal. 4:4). Communication between God and human beings on earth cannot be direct: it must be carried on through a series of intermediaries.[34] The Colossian heresy may not have drawn out all these logical conclusions of the gnostic presupposition, but it probably did envisage a

[31]Cf. G. Scholem, *Major Trends in Jewish Mysticism* (London, 1955); G. Quispel, "Ezekiel 1:26 in Jewish Mysticism and Gnosis," *Vig. Chr.* 34 (1980), 1-13.
[32]Hence the humiliating affliction by which Paul was kept from being "too elated" after his ascent and heavenly vision (2 Cor. 12:7).
[33]Cf. the title of G. Scholem's work, *Jewish Gnosticism, Merkabah Mysticism and Talmudic Tradition* (New York, 1965). Features of incipient gnosticism have also been detected in the Qumran texts; cf. B. Reicke, "Traces of Gnosticism in the Dead Sea Scrolls?" *NTS* 1 (1954-55), 137-41; O. Cullmann, "The Significance of the Qumran Texts for Research into the Beginnings of Christianity," in *The Scrolls and the New Testament,* ed. K. Stendahl (London, 1958), pp. 18-32; but also E. M. Yamauchi, *Pre-Christian Gnosticism* (Grand Rapids, 1973), pp. 143-62.
[34]These intermediaries might be rulers (ἄρχοντες) of the cosmic zones through which initiants had to pass to attain the vision of God (cf. M. Dibelius, "The Isis Initiation," p. 93; he compares the experience of the πνευματικοί among the Naassenes, as described by Hippolytus, *Ref.* 5.8-9).

series of intermediaries between God and the world of humanity, through whom communications in either direction had to pass.

Against the implied denial of the biblical doctrine of creation, Paul has already insisted that the universe was brought into being in, through, and for Christ. Against the enticing offer of a higher wisdom, he has emphasized that all the treasures of wisdom and knowledge are accessible in Christ. Against the belief in an indefinite series of intermediaries between God and our world, he sets forth Christ as the personal embodiment of the fullness of deity. Against the idea that these intermediaries should receive some meed of homage from those who have to approach God through them, he affirms that they have all been conquered by Christ and can no longer claim the allegiance of those whom Christ has redeemed. The whole body of teaching which the Colossian Christians were being urged to accept was a refurbishing of old patterns of thought and life which Christ had rendered obsolete; it should receive no countenance from men and women who had died with Christ and risen with him to newness of life.

(1) The Fullness of Christ (2:8-10)

8 *See to it that no one carries you away captive through philosophy and empty illusion, according to human tradition, according to the elemental forces of the world, and not according to Christ;*

9 *because it is in him that all the fullness of deity resides in bodily reality,*

10 *and you have found your fullness in him—in him, who is head of every principality and power.*

8 Having encouraged his readers to remain firmly anchored to Christ and the gospel, Paul now warns them not to be shifted from this impregnable position by any plausible form of persuasion. It is not necessary to infer from his language that he has one particular teacher in view;[35] he warns them against any attempt to lead them astray by imposing arguments. The verb rendered "carries . . . away captive" (a rare one)[36] has been variously translated "rob" or "kidnap": does the apostle mean "Don't let anyone plunder you" or "Don't let anyone carry you off as plunder"? On the whole, the latter and more forcible alternative is preferable: they are in danger of being carried off into captivity, and must be

---

[35]Cf. C. Masson, *ad loc.*

[36]Gk. συλαγωγέω. BAG quote two later occurrences, one from Heliodorus (3rd cent. A.D.) with the meaning "kidnap" and one from Aristaenetus (5th cent. A.D.) with the meaning "despoil." Cf. the similar use of αἰχμαλωτίζω in 2 Tim. 3:6.

put on the alert lest they become the prey of those who wish to take away their freedom. The spiritual confidence-tricksters against whom they are put on their guard did not inculcate a godless or immoral way of life: the error of such teaching would have been readily exposed. Their teaching was rather a blend of the highest elements of religion known to Judaism and paganism; it was, in fact, a philosophy. Paul does not condemn philosophy as such, but a philosophy of this kind—one which seduces believers from the simplicity of their faith in Christ. "Everything that had to do with theories about God and the world and the meaning of human life was called 'philosophy' at that time, not only in the pagan schools but also in the Jewish schools of the Greek cities."[37]

For all its attractiveness, this philosophy was but empty illusion.[38] If the Colossians embraced it, they would be the losers and not the gainers thereby. Those who knew what they were about when they "received Christ Jesus the Lord" could not find it acceptable; it was a human tradition[39] which overthrew the essential truths of Christian faith and life. It sounded good, it appealed to natural religious instincts, but there was nothing in it for Christians. It was not a teaching "according to Christ"— in line with the tradition handed down from him (v. 6)—but one which accorded with the "elements *(stoicheia)* of the world *(kosmos)*."[40]

---

[37]A. Schlatter, *Erläuterungen zum Neuen Testament,* Teil 7 (Stuttgart, [6]1963), p. 275. Compare Josephus's description of the various Jewish sects (including the Zealots) as φιλοσοφίαι (*BJ* 2.118-66; *Ant.* 18.9-25).

[38]In the Greek text κενῆς ἀπάτης comes under the same regimen as φιλοσοφίας. The "philosophy" and the "empty illusion" are identical.

[39]A "human tradition" might be Jewish or Gentile or both; cf. Mark 7:8, where it is Jewish (see p. 93 above); 1 Pet. 1:18, where the addressees' former pagan way of life is described as πατροπαράδοτος ("received by tradition from your fathers").

[40]Gk. τὰ στοιχεῖα τοῦ κόσμου (cf. Gal. 4:3). The noun στοιχεῖα means primarily things placed side by side in a row; it is used (*inter alia*) of the letters of the alphabet, the ABCs, and then, since learning one's ABCs is the first lesson in a literary education, it comes to mean "rudiments," "first principles" (cf. Heb. 5:12, the "rudiments" of the gospel). Again, since the letters of the alphabet were regarded as the "elements" of which words and sentences are made up, στοιχεῖα comes to denote the "elements" of the material world (as in 2 Pet. 3:10, 12); Philo uses the phrase τὰ στοιχεῖα τοῦ κόσμου in this sense (*Age of the World* 109). Elsewhere (*Contemplative Life* 3) Philo speaks of the Greeks who venerate the four στοιχεῖα (earth, water, air, fire) and give them divine names (Demeter, Poseidon, Hera, Hephaestus); in yet another place he says that "some have deified the four στοιχεῖα—earth, water, air and fire—while others have deified the sun and moon and the other planets and fixed stars; others again the heaven alone; others the whole world," and he mentions the names under which they are worshipped (*Decalogue* 53). In Wisdom 13:2 the various elements are said to receive

There are two Pauline letters which use this term *stoicheia* (rendered "rudiments" in the KJV and the ARV, "elemental spirits" in the RSV and the NEB, "basic principles" in the NIV). The other is the letter to the Galatians. In Gal. 4:3, 9, the *stoicheia* are the forces which regulated both Jewish life under the law and pagan life in the service of "beings that by nature are no gods." The Galatian converts' reversion to the domination of the *stoicheia* was shown in their observance of the Jewish sacred calendar: "You observe days, and months, and seasons, and years" (Gal. 4:10). Since those calendrical divisions are regulated by the heavenly bodies, some association of the *stoicheia* with the planets may be implied.[41] (It may be inferred from Col. 2:16 that similar calendrical observances were enjoined by the Colossian heresy.) Again, the argument of Galatians has suggested to many exegetes that the *stoicheia* in that letter are closely related to (if not identical with) the angels by whose agency the law is said to have been administered (Gal. 3:19).[42] The objection that some of

---

worship from those who do not know God, but are called not στοιχεῖα but πρυτάνεις κόσμου ("rulers of the world"). On the Pauline use of στοιχεῖα see, in addition to commentaries on Galatians and Colossians, G. Delling, *TDNT* 7, pp. 683-86 (*s.v.* στοιχεῖον); H. H. Esser, *NIDNTT* 2, pp. 452-53 (*s.v.* "Law"); E. Percy, *Die Probleme*, pp. 156-67; J. Blinzler, "Lexikalisches zu dem Terminus τὰ στοιχεῖα τοῦ κόσμου bei Paulus," in *Studiorum Paulinorum Congressus 1961* 17-18 (Rome, 1963), II, 429-43; A. J. Bandstra, *The Law and the Elements of the World* (Kampen, 1964); E. Schweizer, "Die Elemente der Welt Gal 4, 3.9; Col 2, 8.20," in *Beiträge zur Theologie des Neuen Testaments* (Zürich, 1970), pp. 147-63.

[41]A. D. Nock, *Early Gentile Christianity and its Hellenistic Background* (New York, 1964), p. 98, n. 4: "In the στοιχεῖα Jewish and planetary ideas meet." He points out an analogy (but not an identity) between bondage to the στοιχεῖα, against which the Galatian and Colossian churches are warned, and bondage to the planetary gods (i.e., to fate), from which, according to the first *Poimandres* tractate, human beings can escape by knowing the truth; in so escaping the soul leaves the body and passes upward through the celestial spheres (*C.H.* 1.15, 19-26). (This ascension, indeed, has probably more in common with the Colossian heresy than with the way of release presented by Paul.) Cf. also G. Bornkamm, "The Heresy of Colossians" (1948), E.T. in *Conflict at Colossae*, ed. Francis and Meeks, p. 139, n. 9 (among other things, he draws attention to the parallelism between the στοιχεῖα and the seven Avestan *Amesha Spentas*, a parallelism established by R. Reitzenstein and H. H. Schaeder and reflected in the Sogdian translation of στοιχεῖα in Gal. 4:3 by *amahraspands*, a term used in Manichaeism to denote the elements).

[42]Cf. the reference to angel worship in v. 18 below (p. 118-20 with nn. 116-27). Possibly the Colossian heresy contained features in common with the teaching of Cerinthus, according to whom, if we may believe Epiphanius (*Pan.* 28), not only the law but also the prophets were inspired by angelic beings, the angelic giver of the law being one of the angels who made the world (κόσμος).

these meanings are not attested for *stoicheia* until later[43] may be answered in part by the consideration that the phrase "the elements of the world" *in this sense* is an original Pauline contribution to religious vocabulary. In the divine providence there was a time when the *stoicheia* fulfilled a supervisory role in the lives of the people of God, as a slave-attendant[44] looked after a freeborn child until he came of age. The coming of age of the people of God coincided with the advent of faith in Christ: to remain under the control of the *stoicheia* after that was a sign of spiritual immaturity.

So, too, the form of teaching which was gaining currency at Colossae was something which belonged to a pre-Christian stage of experience; therefore, whatever its precise nature might be, to accept it now would be a mark of spiritual retrogression. As Paul goes on to assure them, they had said a long farewell to all such forces when they died with Christ to begin a new life in him.[45] Formerly, when they were "in the flesh,"[46] they were unable to throw off the domination of the powers which controlled the present world-order in opposition to God. But now one has come to conquer these powers and liberate human beings from their sway;[47] how foolish, then, it is for those who have enjoyed this liberation to go back and put themselves under the yoke of these discredited tyrants all over again! They have transferred their allegiance to the ruler of a new order, who has defeated the hostile powers; let his will and teaching be their rule of life henceforth.

9 The teachers of error may have talked of the fullness of divine being as distributed among a hierarchy of spirit-powers, through which it was filtered down to this world:[48] Christians had something better. They had Christ, the personal revelation of the Father, the one mediator between God and human beings, in whom (truly man as he was) the plenitude of

[43]For the meaning "heavenly bodies" cf. (probably) *Ep. Diog.* 7:2 (mid-2nd cent. A.D.); in Diogenes Laertius, *Lives of Philosophers* 6.102 (3rd cent. A.D.) τὰ δώδεκα στοιχεῖα are the signs of the zodiac. In *Test. Sol.* 8:1-2; 18:1-2 (4th cent. A.D.) στοιχεῖον is used alongside δαίμων and πνεῦμα in the sense of a spiritual being. See further M. Dibelius, *Die Geisterwelt im Glauben des Paulus* (Göttingen, 1909); E. Percy, *Die Probleme,* pp. 156-67; for a different conclusion from theirs see A. J. Bandstra, *The Law and the Elements of the World* (Kampen, 1964).
[44]Gk. παιδαγωγός (Gal. 3:24).
[45]See v. 20 below.
[46]Cf. Rom. 8:9, where ἐν σαρκί is contrasted with ἐν πνεύματι (see also v. 13 below).
[47]Cf. Mark 3:27; Luke 11:20.
[48]This would imply that they anticipated to some extent the second-century Valentinian doctrine of the πλήρωμα (see p. 73 with n. 163). M. Dibelius ("The Isis Initiation in Apuleius," pp. 63ff.) refers to Lucius's cultic/mystical journey *per omnia . . . elementa* (Apuleius, *Metamorphoses* 11.23).

deity was embodied.[49] Far from there being any inherent impossibility in the nature of things for God to communicate directly with this world, he who shared the divine nature had become flesh and made his dwelling with men and women. The adverb (meaning "corporeally") at the end of v. 9 no doubt implies his incarnation, but probably carries something of the sense which the noun "body" bears in v. 17—the substance as opposed to the shadow (hence the rendering above: "in bodily reality").[50]

10 Not only so, but Christians by their union with him participated in his life. If the fullness of deity resided in him, his fullness was imparted to them. There is an affinity in sense here with the language of the Johannine prologue: "from his fullness have we all received, grace upon grace" (John 1:16). Without him his people must remain forever *disiecta membra*—incomplete, unable to attain the true end of their existence. But united with him, incorporated in him, they are joined with him in a living bond in which he and they complement each other (although they are not essential to his fullness as he is to theirs).[51]

Moreover, the one with whom Christians are united, and in whom

---

[49]Gk. ὅτι ἐν αὐτῷ κατοικεῖ πᾶν τὸ πλήρωμα τῆς θεότητος σωματικῶς. The terms ἐν αὐτῷ, κατοικέω, and πᾶν τὸ πλήρωμα are repeated from the Christ-hymn (Col. 1:19). Indeed, the whole passage (vv. 9-15) has been described by J. M. Robinson (*Int.* 10 [1956], 349, in review of *IB* 11) as "clearly a baptismal homily on the anti-gnostic kerygmatic hymn in Col. 1:15-20." G. Bornkamm ("The Heresy of Colossians," p. 125) thinks that the heresy might have accepted the statement of Col. 2:9, "only with the difference that it did not put the ἐν αὐτῷ . . . *in opposition* to the indwelling of the divine πλήρωμα in the στοιχεῖα, but regarded the divine fulness in Christ as given *in his relationship* to the elements." Nowhere else in the NT does θεότης occur. J. B. Lightfoot (*ad loc.*) aptly quotes two passages from Plutarch to illustrate the difference between it and θειότης (also found once in the NT, in Rom. 1:20): *On the obsolescence of oracles* 415C (where a few δαίμονες are said after long probation to attain θεότης) and *On the malice of Herodotus* 857A (where θειότης is used of divine inspiration in human beings). Cf. also E. K. Simpson, *Words Worth Weighing in the Greek New Testament* (London, 1946), pp. 12-13, on the appropriateness of θειότης with reference to the *hand* of God in creation but θεότης with reference to the unveiling of his *face* in Christ.

[50]Gk. σωματικῶς. For the view preferred above cf. G. B. Caird, *ad loc.* ("in solid reality"). See also P. T. O'Brien, *ad loc.* According to L. Cerfaux, *Christ in the Theology of St. Paul*, E.T. (New York, 1959), p. 427, "The whole sanctifying power of the divinity in this world came to be concentrated in Christ and in his risen body"; he refers to J. Dupont, *Gnosis* (Louvain, 1949), pp. 420-93, for a study of "the whole complex of stoic ideas and formulas," including σῶμα and its derivatives, which Paul has taken over and modified.

[51]G. B. Caird (*ad loc.*) takes the meaning to be that the fullness of life exemplified in the risen Christ is possessed already by Christians "*in him,* i.e. in union with his representative and inclusive manhood."

they are filled, is the "head of every principality and power."[52] As in Col.
1:16 all principalities and powers are said to have been created through
him, he is their head in the sense of being the source of their being, and
therefore also their ruler. But the head/body relationship is probably not
implied here. Whatever the original intention of the Christ-hymn of Col.
1:15-20 may have been, it is quite unlikely that Paul or any of his associates
wished to suggest that the principalities and powers, or the world to which
they belonged, formed in any sense the body of which Christ is head.
What is emphasized here, as in the Christ-hymn to which the present
passage harks back, is Christ's primacy over all creation, including the
principalities and powers.[53]

It has been argued that all that is meant by this clause is that Christ
is superior to all rule and authority.[54] But that more than this is intended
may be gathered from the references to principalities and powers in the
Christ-hymn and more particularly in the celebration of Christ's victory
over them in v. 15. There is more point to the mention of "every principality and power" in v. 10 if in fact forces in the spiritual world, denoted
comprehensively as "principalities and powers," played some part in the
Colossians' thinking. Those who are united to Christ have no need to pay
their respects to those forces over which he has vindicated his preeminence.

(2) The New Circumcision (2:11-12)

11 *In him, too, you were circumcised with a circumcision not made
with hands, by the stripping off of the body of flesh[55]—that is to say,
with the circumcision of Christ—*

12 *when you were buried with him in baptism.[56] In baptism,[57] too, you*

[52]Gk. ὅς ἐστιν ἡ κεφαλὴ πάσης ἀρχῆς καὶ ἐξουσίας. For the view that "every
principality and power" should be understood here as the body of which Christ is
head see E. Lohmeyer, *ad loc.*; H. Lietzmann, *The Beginnings of the Christian
Church,* E.T. (London, 1949), p. 215.

[53]See pp. 63-64 above.

[54]See W. Carr, *Angels and Principalities* (Cambridge, 1981), p. 81.

[55]Gk. τοῦ σώματος τῆς σαρκός. After τοῦ σώματος א² D¹ Ψ with the majority
of cursives and the Syriac versions insert τῶν ἁμαρτιῶν (cf. KJV: "the body of
the sins of the flesh").

[56]Our witnesses vary between βαπτισμῷ (P⁴⁶ א² B D* F G etc.) and βαπτίσματι
(א* A C D² Ψ with the majority of cursives). For Christian baptism (as for John's
baptism) βάπτισμα is the form regularly used in the NT. In Mark 7:4 and Heb.
9:10 (certainly) and in Heb. 6:2 (probably) βαπτισμός is used of Jewish ceremonial washing. For this reason it is more likely that an original βαπτισμῷ here
would have been changed to βαπτίσματι than *vice versa.*

[57]Gk. ἐν αὐτῷ. It is possible that this might mean "in whom" (with antecedent
"Christ"), but this is less likely since αὐτῷ is clearly to be understood with
συνηγέρθητε ("you were raised with him") as it has already been expressed with
συνταφέντες, and to attach "in whom" to "you were raised" would overweight
the construction.

were raised with him through faith in the power of God who raised him from the dead.[58]

11 If only they called to mind their baptism, and all that was involved and implied in it, they would be delivered from such inconsistent syncretism.

Their baptism involved a spiritual circumcision—"a circumcision not made with hands." Even in the OT the symbolical character of the outward sign of circumcision was emphasized: what God really desired was not the external sign for its own sake, but the "circumcision of the heart" (Deut. 10:16; 30:6; Jer. 4:4), an inward purification, which to Paul was the true circumcision.[59] But the Israelite who appreciated the primary importance of "heart-circumcision" did not normally think himself exempt on that ground from the requirement of physical circumcision;[60] now, however, the work of Christ has so thoroughly exhausted the significance of the original ordinance (as of the whole ceremonial law) that it is henceforth superseded.[61] Paul's choice of language here would be especially apt if circumcision were one feature of the syncretism which was being inculcated in the church of Colossae. No longer is there any place for a circumcision performed by hands[62] (which, being restricted to males, was in

[58]Gk. ἐκ νεκρῶν (B D F G and many cursives read ἐκ τῶν νεκρῶν).
[59]Cf. Rom. 2:28-29; Phil. 3:3.
[60]Cf. Philo, *Migration of Abraham* 92; Josephus, *Ant.* 20.34-48. Some members of the school of Hillel maintained, in debate with the school of Shammai, that proselyte baptism was sufficient for Gentile converts apart from circumcision (TB Yᵉbāmôṯ 46a); but this was more a debating point than a matter of practical policy.
[61]Justin Martyr allegorizes the narrative of the Israelites' circumcision at Joshua's hands with knives of flint (Josh. 5:2-3) as denoting the spiritual circumcision which Christians receive at the hands of the true Joshua (Jesus), "from idolatry and all manner of wickedness, by sharp stones, that is, by the words of the apostles of him who is the corner-stone cut out without hands" (*Dial.* 114). Early Christian anti-Judaic apologetic grouped together circumcision, sacrifice, and sabbath as having been abolished by Christ (cf. V. Burch, "Circumcision of the Heart," *ExT* 29 [1917-18], 330-31; J. R. Harris, *Testimonies* II [Cambridge, 1920], 105-06). O. Cullmann holds that the understanding of Christian baptism as a repeal of Jewish circumcision "is not just a theological foundling, appearing only at a late date after the Apologist Justin"; it is explicit in our present text and implicit elsewhere in the NT (*Baptism in the New Testament*, E.T. [London, 1950], pp. 56-57).
[62]Cf. Eph. 2:11, περιτομῆς ἐν σαρκὶ χειροποιήτου. The negative ἀχειροποίητος was almost a technical term of primitive Christianity to denote the realities of the new order, used not only of the new circumcision (as here) but of the new temple (Mark 14:58) and the resurrection body (2 Cor. 5:1).

any case inappropriate for the new order in Christ)[63]; the death of Christ
has effected the inward cleansing which the prophets associated with the
new covenant,[64] and of this Christian baptism is the visible sign.

This spiritual circumcision is further called "the circumcision of
Christ." This phrase may mean either the circumcision undergone by Christ
or (preferably) the circumcision effected by Christ.[65] If it bears the former
meaning, the reference is not so much to his circumcision as a Jewish
infant of eight days old (Luke 2:21) as to his crucifixion, of which his
circumcision in infancy was at best a token anticipation. In that case the
"stripping off[66] of the body of flesh"[67] will denote what Christ did in his
death; baptism is viewed (as in Rom. 6:3-4) as a symbolical sharing in
Christ's death. "This circumcision of the Christ is reproduced sacramentally in the members of the community by baptism."[68]

If, on the other hand, the "circumcision of Christ" is the circumcision which he effects, the inward cleansing brought about by his death,
resurrection, and indwelling presence in those who are united to him by
faith, then the "stripping off of the body of flesh" refers to the believer's
baptismal experience (described in Rom. 6:6 as the crucifixion of "our old
self" and the destruction of "the sinful body"). It involves the reckoning
of one's former self with its desires and propensities to be dead, as a
necessary prelude to putting on the new nature—putting on Christ himself
in his resurrection life.[69] What the believer puts off is "the whole personality organized for, and geared into rebellion against God."[70]

---

[63]It is because in Christ there is neither circumcision nor uncircumcision (cf. Col.
3:11) that the distinction is abrogated not only between Jew and Gentile but also
between male and female, in the sense of Gal. 3:28.
[64]Cf. Jer. 31:31-34; Ezek. 36:25-27.
[65]"The circumcision of Christ is then the circumcision which belongs to Christ,
which is given by him, which brings forgiveness of sins and thus makes it possible
for people to live ethically in a new way" (E. Schweizer, *Colossians, ad loc.*,
p. 143). For the view that "it is better to regard the statement as denoting the
circumcision that Christ underwent, that is, his crucifixion," see P. T. O'Brien, *ad
loc.* (p. 117).
[66]Gk. ἀπέκδυσις. No independent instance of this compound is attested; it could
be a Pauline coinage. Cf. the verb ἀπεκδύομαι in v. 15 and Col. 3:9. The double
prefix gives special emphasis: "stripping right off."
[67]Cf. Col. 1:22 for τὸ σῶμα τῆς σαρκός (p. 78 with n. 182).
[68]E. Käsemann, "A Primitive Christian Baptismal Liturgy," p. 162.
[69]Cf. Col. 3:9-10; Eph. 4:22-24; Rom. 13:14. In Rom. 6:6; Gal. 2:20; 5:24 Paul
speaks of "crucifying" instead of "putting off."
[70]J. A. T. Robinson, *The Body*, p. 31.

12 Their baptism might, again, be viewed as their participation in Christ's burial.[71] The "stripping off of the body of flesh" and its burial out of sight alike emphasized that the old life was a thing of the past. They had shared in the death of Christ; they had also shared in his burial. Similarly, in Rom. 6:3-14 Paul argues that those who have been buried with Christ "by baptism into death" must henceforth lead new lives in him, no longer enslaved to sin.

For baptism not only proclaims that the old order is past and done with; it proclaims that a new order has been inaugurated. The convert did not remain in the baptismal water; he emerged from it to "walk in newness of life" (Rom. 6:4). Baptism, therefore, implies a sharing in Christ's resurrection as well as in his death and burial.[72]

The resurrection of Christ is held forth by Paul as the supreme demonstration of the power of God. Those who have been raised with Christ have been raised through faith in the divine power which brought him back from the dead, and from now on that power energizes them and maintains the new life within them—the new life which is nothing less than Christ's resurrection life flowing through all the members of his body.[73] In him they already enjoy eternal life, the life of the age to come.

This whole conception is thoroughly and characteristically Pauline. It may well be that in this place (together with Col. 3:1 and Eph. 2:6) the idea of the believer's participation in the risen life of Christ finds clearer expression than it does elsewhere in the Pauline letters, but to suppose that a Paulinist rather than Paul is responsible for this phraseology is to suppose that someone other than Paul could give clearer expression to a central thought of Paul's than Paul himself could give.[74]

---

[71]The burial of Christ might be viewed as setting the seal on his death and symbolizing his entry into the realm of the dead (found by some interpreters in Eph. 4:9-10). His own baptism in the Jordan was a symbolical anticipation of his descent into death and Sheol; cf. his references to his approaching passion in baptismal terms (Mark 10:38-39; Luke 12:50). On the imagery involved see A. R. Johnson, "Jonah 2:3-10," in *Studies in Old Testament Prophecy*, ed. H. H. Rowley (Edinburgh, 1950), pp. 82-102, especially p. 102.

[72]Cf. Col. 3:1; Eph. 2:6; Rom. 6:4-5. While Rom. 6:5 places the believer's full participation in Christ's resurrection in the future, the "newness of life" is already present and is expected to find ethical expression here and now.

[73]Cf. Eph. 1:19-23 for the elaboration of this thought of the divine ἐνέργεια, which is here the object of faith. (Cf. Col. 1:29 for the divine ἐνέργεια manifested in the apostle's ministry.)

[74]Cf. E. Percy, *Die Probleme*, p. 113.

And be it noted: it is through faith that the believer bids farewell to the old life and embarks upon the new. The sacrament of baptism derives its efficacy not from the water or from the convert's token burial in it, but from the saving act of Christ and the regenerating work of God, producing that faith-union with the risen Lord of which the sacrament is the sign and seal.[75]

(3) The Triumph of Christ (2:13-15)

13 Yes, when you[76] were dead in your trespasses, uncircumcised Gentiles as you were,[77] he brought you[78] to life together with him. He forgave us[79] all our trespasses;

14 he blotted out the bond which stood against us, ordinances and all,[80]

[75]Cf. J. S. Stewart, A Man in Christ (London, 1935), pp. 171, 192. On the subject-matter and interpretation of vv. 11-12 see also G. W. H. Lampe, The Seal of the Spirit (London, 1951), pp. 5, 56, 83, 85 et passim.

[76]Gk. καὶ ὑμᾶς . . . συνεζωοποίησεν, with which may be compared καὶ ὑμᾶς . . . ἀποκατήλλαξεν in Col. 1:21-22. As the Christ-hymn is followed by a personal application to the readers, so is this "baptismal homily" on the hymn (cf. p. 101, n. 49), and in a parallel construction.

[77]Lit., "in the trespasses and the uncircumcision of your flesh" ([ἐν] τοῖς παραπτώμασιν καὶ τῇ ἀκροβυστίᾳ τῆς σαρκὸς ὑμῶν). Before each of these instrumental datives ἐν is read by a variety of witnesses.

[78]Gk. ὑμᾶς, resumptive of ὑμᾶς in καὶ ὑμᾶς, but P[46] B and some other witnesses read ἡμᾶς, anticipating ἡμῖν in the following clause, while many (including א[2] D F G Ψ and the majority of cursives) omit the pronoun entirely.

[79]For ἡμῖν א[2] K* L P and some other witnesses read ὑμῖν.

[80]Gk. τὸ καθ᾽ ἡμῶν χειρόγραφον τοῖς δόγμασιν. The translation above treats τοῖς δόγμασιν as a dative of accompaniment ("ordinances and all"). E. Percy (Die Probleme, pp. 88-90) takes τοῖς δόγμασιν with the following clause ὃ ἦν ὑπεναντίον ἡμῖν, so that the meaning is "the handwriting that was against us, which by virtue of the ordinances testified against us." The ordinances are, in his view, the Mosaic commandments. It is, however, awkward to construe τοῖς δόγμασιν with the following adjective clause, in spite of the parallels which Percy adduces. He maintains that, on any other construction, the clause ὃ ἦν ὑπεναντίον ἡμῖν is a superfluous repetition of καθ᾽ ἡμῶν. J. A. T. Robinson (The Body, p. 43, n. 1) takes καθ᾽ ἡμῶν to mean "in our name," an attractive suggestion which would be accepted with greater alacrity if such a sense could be established for κατά with the genitive (the use of this construction with verbs of swearing and asseveration is not a sufficient parallel). The same writer (ibid.) construes τὸ . . . χειρόγραφον τοῖς δόγμασιν as "our subscription to the ordinances." C. F. D. Moule (IBNTG, p. 45) acknowledges the plausible and ingenious character of this interpretation, and appears to regard it as preferable to Percy's, which involves "too much violence to word-order"; but he himself renders the phrase "the document with its decrees (meaning, apparently, a document containing, or consisting of, decrees)." E. Lohse, who thinks that "a fragment of a confession formulated

the bond that was opposed to us; he has taken it out of the way, nailing it to the cross.[81]

15 *He stripped*[82] *the principalities and powers and made a public ex-*

---

in hymnic phrases underlies vss 14-15," suggests that τοῖς δόγμασιν might have been inserted by the author of Colossians in order "to emphasize that with the forgiveness of sins each and every claim of the 'elements of the universe' (στοιχεῖα τοῦ κόσμου) was nullified" (*ad loc.*, pp. 106-07). R. P. Martin similarly regards τοῖς δόγμασιν (and also ὃ ἦν ὑπεναντίον ἡμῖν) as inserted by Paul into a hymnic fragment in praise of the Redeemer "to clarify the special sense in which he wishes τὸ χειρόγραφον to be understood" ("Reconciliation and Forgiveness in the Letter to the Colossians," in *Reconciliation and Hope*, ed. R. Banks [Exeter, 1974], pp. 116-20). Cf. Eph. 2:15, ἐν δόγμασιν ("consisting of ordinances").

[81]The subject of συνεζωοποίησεν (v. 13) is God, and there is no formal indication of a change of subject before the end of v. 15. Hence some translations (e.g., RSV) and commentators (e.g., Lohse) take God as the subject throughout. But the description of what was accomplished on the cross (vv. 14-15) more naturally implies that Christ is the subject (J. B. Lightfoot, *ad loc.*, locates the change of subject at ἦρκεν ἐκ τοῦ μέσου [v. 14b]). Such a change of subject would naturally come about if we recognize in vv. 14 and 15 the quotation of a hymn celebrating in pictorial terms the redemptive work of Christ on the cross (so R. P. Martin, "Reconciliation and Forgiveness in . . . Colossians," pp. 116-23).

[82]Gk. ἀπεκδυσάμενος, the verb corresponding to ἀπέκδυσις (v. 11). The force of this aorist participle middle is much debated. In Col. 3:9 ἀπεκδυσάμενοι means "having put off," as of clothes. So some, taking τὰς ἀρχὰς καὶ τὰς ἐξουσίας to be the object of ἀπεκδυσάμενος here, have thought of Christ as stripping off the hostile powers from himself, as they clung to him on the cross like a shirt of Nessus. This was the general view of the Greek fathers, and is approved by J. B. Lightfoot (*ad loc.*). On the other hand, ἀπεκδυσάμενος could be used intransitively, in the sense "having stripped," "having undressed himself" (τὰς ἀρχὰς καὶ τὰς ἐξουσίας being then the object of ἐδειγμάτισεν only). In that case what Christ put off was his "body of flesh" (cf. v. 11); this was the general view of the Latin fathers and has been upheld more recently by C. A. A. Scott, *Christianity according to St. Paul* (Cambridge, 1927), pp. 34-37; E. Käsemann, *Leib und Leib Christi* (Tübingen, 1933), p. 139; W. L. Knox, *St. Paul and the Church of the Gentiles* (Cambridge, 1939), p. 169 n.; G. H. C. Macgregor, "Principalities and Powers: The Cosmic Background of St. Paul's Thought," *NTS* 1 (1954-55), 23; J. A. T. Robinson, *The Body*, pp. 41-42; R. P. Martin, "Reconciliation and Forgiveness in . . . Colossians," pp. 121-23. It may well be, however, that the middle voice here simply indicates the personal interest of the subject in the action of the verb; in fact, Hellenistic Greek does not lack examples of the middle voice of such verbs in an active sense (cf. A. Oepke, *TDNT* 2, p. 319, *s.v.* δύω, etc.; *BAG*, *s.v.* ἀπεκδύομαι). In that case the sense would be "having completely disarmed" (cf. E. Lohmeyer, *ad loc.*, "having divested of their dignity"; E. Schweizer, *ad loc.*). "These angel-powers have been deprived of all their previous power through the removal of the charges which the law brought against men and therewith also of the demands of the law itself" (E. Percy, *Die Probleme*, p. 98).

hibition of them, triumphing over them[83] *by it.*[84]

13 Yes, the apostle insists, this is what has happened to you.[85] You were spiritually and morally dead in your earlier pagan days. But now you have been brought to life again—brought to life in Christ, who was himself dead and came to life again.[86] Your new life, indeed, is a sharing in the new life which Christ received when God raised him from the dead. And in giving you this new life with Christ, God has broken you clean away from your past. He has freely forgiven[87] all your sins—and not yours only, but ours too.[88] Paul insisted that Jews, who had received the divine law by revelation, and pagans, who had not received it—not in the same form, at least—were alike morally bankrupt before God and equally in need of his pardoning grace.[89] Jews had disobeyed his will in the form in which

[83]Gk. θριαμβεύσας αὐτούς, where αὐτούς is a sense construction, referring to the ἀρχαί and ἐξουσίαι but treating them as personal beings, not as abstractions. For the figure of a triumphal procession cf. 2 Cor. 2:14, τῷ . . . θριαμβεύοντι ἡμᾶς where, however, "we" are not the defeated captives but the retinue of the conqueror, joyful witnesses to his victory. (The accusative after θριαμβεύω is attested in both senses.) W. Carr maintains that the accusative αὐτούς here has the same force as ἡμᾶς in 2 Cor. 2:14, the principalities and powers being Christ's army, the heavenly host of Col. 1:16, following him and crying "Io triumphe!" (*Angels and Principalities*, p. 63); this is improbable.

[84]Gk. ἐν αὐτῷ, "by it" (the cross) if Christ is the subject; "in him" (Christ) if God is the subject.

[85]Note the successive aorists: περιετμήθητε (v. 11), συνταφέντες (v. 12), συνηγέρθητε (v. 12; Col. 3:1), συνεζωοποίησεν (v. 13), ἐδειγμάτισεν (v. 15), ἀπεθάνετε (v. 20; Col. 3:3). Note, too, how many of them are compounded with συν-, indicating that what was accomplished for believers has also been accomplished in them, so that they are reckoned as having participated with Christ in his death, burial, and resurrection.

[86]Here we have a short paraphrase of Rom. 6:1-11, although now the "realized" aspect of believers' being raised with Christ is alone in view, without the counterbalancing ἐσόμεθα of Rom. 6:5.

[87]Gk. χαρισάμενος. The verb χαρίζομαι is used in Eph. 4:32 of God's forgiving human beings, as here (cf. χάρισμα in Rom. 6:23), and also of their forgiving one another (as in Col. 3:13; cf. 2 Cor. 2:10). For the similar use of ἀφίημι and ἄφεσις cf. p. 53, n. 67 (on Col. 1:14). See also n. 90 below.

[88]The sentence begins καὶ ὑμᾶς, with special reference to Gentile readers, but the second person quickly gives way to the comprehensive first person plural, because circumcised Jews as well as uncircumcised Gentiles have experienced the divine forgiveness. The change of pronoun could indeed be due to the incorporation of a hymn which spoke of "us" into a context which spoke of "you," but it is easily explained without that hypothesis. Cf. Eph. 2:1-8, with the transition from ὑμᾶς in v. 1 to ἡμᾶς in v. 5.

[89]Cf. Rom. 1:18–3:20 where the moral bankruptcy of first pagans and then Jews is established and their equal need of the justifying grace of God is made plain.

they knew it (the law); pagans had disobeyed it in the form in which they knew it (the inner voice of conscience). But, like the creditor in the parable faced with his two debtors, "when they had nothing to pay, he frankly forgave⁹⁰ them both" (Luke 7:42).

14 The sins which have now been forgiven represented, so to speak, a mountain of bankruptcy which those who had incurred it were bound to acknowledge but could never have any hope of discharging. They had violated the ordinances of the law, and nothing that they might do could afford redress. But Christ wiped the slate clean and gave them a fresh start. He took that signed acknowledgment of indebtedness⁹¹ which stood as a perpetual witness against them and cancelled it by his death.⁹²

⁹⁰Gk. ἐχαρίσατο. This use of χαρίζομαι to denote the free cancellation of a debt may influence its use in v. 13 (see n. 87 above) to denote the divine forgiveness. For παραπτώματα see p. 259 with n. 62 (on Eph. 1:7).

⁹¹Gk. χειρόγραφον, "handwriting," a term (found also in Plutarch and Artemidorus) very common in the papyri, among which many original χειρόγραφα have been preserved (cf. A. Deissmann, *Bible Studies*, E.T. [Edinburgh, 1909], p. 247; MM, p. 687). J. A. T. Robinson (*The Body*, p. 43, n. 1) describes this χειρόγραφον as "our written agreement to keep the law, our certificate of debt to it" (he compares the oral undertakings of Exod. 24:3; Deut. 27:14-26). But our failure to keep the law has turned this certificate into a bond held against us to prove our guilt; it is this bond, representing the power which the law has over us, rather than the law itself, which Paul views as cancelled by Christ. This is vastly preferable to Lohmeyer's view that the χειρόγραφον is an IOU (a *Schuldschein*) which Adam gave to the devil in Paradise at the time of the fall of man (*ad loc.*, pp. 116-17; cf. G. Megas, "Das χειρόγραφον Adams: Ein Beitrag zu Kol 2, 13-15," *ZNW* 27 [1928], 305-20). O. Blanchette, "Does the Cheirographon of Col. 2:14 represent Christ himself?" *CBQ* 23 (1961), 306-12 (followed in part by A. J. Bandstra, *The Law and the Elements of the World*, pp. 158-63), invokes a supposed early Christian identification of the χειρόγραφον with Christ's body, which was in fact nailed to the cross. J. A. T. Robinson seems to come nearer to the sense of the passage; cf. also C. F. D. Moule, *ad loc.*

⁹²He has removed it (ἦρκεν ἐκ τοῦ μέσου); this removal is elaborated in two stages: he blotted it out (ἐξαλείψας), and he nailed it to the cross (προσηλώσας αὐτὸ τῷ σταυρῷ). According to Deissmann (*Paul*, E.T. [London, 1926], p. 172), papyrus debt records illustrate the popular appeal of this double figure: the bond is first blotted out and then cancelled. Cf. two successive petitions in the Jewish prayer *'Abinu Malkenu*: "Our Father, our King! blot out our transgressions, and make them pass away from before thine eyes. Our Father, our King! erase in thy abundant mercies all the records of our debts" (S. Singer, *The Authorised Daily Prayer Book* [London, 1939], p. 56). As for the bold conception of the χειρόγραφον being nailed to the cross, Deissmann thinks of the cancellation of a bond or similar document when it is crossed out with the Greek letter X (*Light from the Ancient East*, E.T. [London, 1927], p. 333). The Greek verb for such crossing out is χιάζω (from *chi*, the name of the letter). But it is not clear that σταυρός would suggest the X shape. On the alleged " 'ancient custom' of can-

It might even be said that he took the document, ordinances and all, and nailed it to his cross as an act of triumphant defiance in the face of those blackmailing powers that were holding it over men and women in order to command their allegiance.

There is perhaps an allusion here to the fact that our Lord's own accusation was fixed to his cross. Jesus nails the accusation against his people to the cross, just as his own accusation had been nailed there. Thus his victorious passion liberates them from their bankruptcy and bondage. As Krishna Pal put it:

> *Jesus for thee a body takes,*
> *Thy guilt assumes, thy fetters breaks,*
> *Discharging all thy dreadful debt—*
> *And canst thou then such love forget?*

15 Christ by his cross releases his people not only from the guilt of sin but from its hold over them. "He breaks the power of cancelled sin." Not only has he blotted out the record of their indebtedness but he has subjugated those powers whose possession of that damning indictment was a means of controlling them. The very instrument of disgrace and death by which the hostile forces thought they had him in their grasp and had conquered him forever was turned by him into the instrument of their

---

celling a bond by driving a nail through it" (adduced by J. Pearson, *An Exposition of the Creed* [(1659) Oxford, 1890], p. 373) see F. Field, *Notes on Translation,* pp. 195-96; he finds no real authority for it, and thinks rather of the custom of hanging up spoils of war in temples (but it is unlikely that such an analogy was in Paul's mind here).

The Nag Hammadi *Gospel of Truth* (20:4-35), in what seems to be an early Valentinian interpretation of this passage (linked with Rev. 5:1-7), speaks of "the living book of the living" which recorded the Father's thought before the foundation of the universe, the book which "no one was able to take since it is reserved for the one who will take it and will be slain. No one could have appeared among those who believed in salvation unless that book had intervened. For this reason the merciful one, the faithful one, Jesus, was patient in accepting sufferings until he took that book, since he knows that his death is life for many. Just as there lies hidden in a will, before it is opened, the fortune of the deceased master of the house, so (it is) with the all, which lay hidden while the Father of the all was invisible. . . . For this reason Jesus appeared; he put on that book; he was nailed to a tree; he published the edict of the Father on the cross. O such great teaching! He draws himself down to death though life eternal clothes him. Having stripped himself of the perishable rags, he put on imperishability, which no one can possibly take away from him. Having entered the empty spaces of terrors, he passed through those who were stripped naked by oblivion, being knowledge and perfection, proclaiming the things that are in the heart of the [Father] . . ." (translated by G. W. MacRae, in *The Nag Hammadi Library in English,* ed. J. M. Robinson [Leiden, 1977], p. 39).

defeat and disablement. As he was suspended there, bound hand and foot to the wood in apparent weakness, they imagined they had him at their mercy, and flung themselves on him with hostile intent. But, far from suffering their attack without resistance, he grappled with them and mastered them, stripping them of the armor in which they trusted, and held them aloft in his outstretched hands, displaying to the universe their helplessness and his own unvanquished strength. Such seems to be the picture painted in these words.[93]

Had they but realized the truth, those "rulers of this age"—had they (as Paul puts it in another letter) known the hidden wisdom of God which decreed the glory of Christ and his people— "they would not have crucified the Lord of glory" (1 Cor. 2:8).[94] But now they are dethroned and incapacitated, and the shameful tree has become the victor's triumphal chariot, before which his captives are driven in humiliating procession, the involuntary and impotent confessors of his superior might.[95]

The cross of Christ, in short, is the answer to the theosophy which was beguiling the minds of the Lycus churches. How absurd it now appeared to pay tribute to those principalities and powers which, it was held, controlled the way from God to this world and back from this world to God! That way is controlled by one person—by him who has vindicated his sovereignty over the principalities and powers. Their envious enmity to human beings can no longer be indulged; they have been pacified[96] by a stronger than themselves.[97] Whatever power they once exercised, they

---

[93]On ἐδειγμάτισεν ("made a public exhibition") cf. H. Schlier, *TDNT* 2, pp. 31ff. (*s.v.* δείχνυμι, δειγματίζω). A. T. Hanson sees a typological relation between its occurrence here and the exemplary hanging (παραδειγματίζω) of the ringleaders of the Baal-peor apostasy (Num. 25:4 LXX): "Moses punished the rulers by hanging them . . . on a tree, whereas Christ overcame the powers by himself hanging on a tree" (*Studies in Paul's Technique and Theology* [London, 1974], p. 153 *et passim*).

[94]Against the view (adopted here) that the ἄρχοντες τοῦ αἰῶνος τούτου in 1 Cor. 2:8 are spirit powers see W. Carr, *Angels and Principalities*, pp. 118-20; he sees in them a reference to Pilate and Caiaphas.

[95]In Eph. 3:10 the principalities and powers are spectators of God's many-hued wisdom displayed in the church; but there is no emphasis on their hostility (see p. 321 with n. 68).

[96]For pacification see p. 75, n. 170 (on Col. 1:21).

[97]Cf. the overpowering of the "strong man armed" in Matt. 12:29 par. Luke 11:21-22; of the devil in John 12:31 (with 14:30 and 16:11); Heb. 2:14 (where the partaking of "blood and flesh" and the gaining of victory "through death" are especially significant); and of death itself in 1 Cor. 15:26. The conquest of Col. 2:15 might be regarded as the first stage in that victorious progress which ends with the destruction of the "last enemy."

are now the "weak and beggarly elemental forces" that Paul declares them to be in Gal. 4:9.

The principalities and powers which figured so largely in the Colossian heresy may play no part in the world outlook of most of our contemporaries—although the number of those who accept the invitation to "plan with the planets" in the columns of popular newspapers or watch astrological programs on television should warn us not to frame such a statement in absolute terms. The angelic beings through which the law was held to have been mediated may mean nothing to modern men and women. Angels and demons may be unknown to them by name. But many of them are unprecedentedly aware of powerful and malignant "demonic" forces operating against them, which they are quite unable to master, whether by individual strength or by united action. These forces may be Frankenstein monsters of their own creation; they may be subliminal horrors over which they have no conscious control. "We are still conscious that, apart from the victory of Christ, man is a helpless victim in a hostile cosmos. It is little comfort to us that the inexorable fate which was once expressed in terms of the influence of the stars, conceived as personal demons, is now expressed in terms of psychological, or physical or economic determinism. We still ask how a man is to triumph over an evil heredity, or how he can be free and victorious in a world of rigid law and scientific necessity. We still suffer from 'astronomical intimidation'—terror at the insignificance of man and the vastness of the material universe encompassing him."[98] Moreover, we are acutely conscious of our inevitable involvement in situations from which our moral sense recoils—but can anything effective be done about it?[99] But for the gospel, we might well think of ourselves as puppets in the hand of a blind and unfriendly fate. And what would it matter whether we resist and be crushed sooner, or acquiesce and be crushed a little later?

The message proclaimed by Paul to the Colossians remains the one message of hope to men and women in frustration and despair. Christ crucified and risen is Lord of all: all the forces of the universe are subject to him, not only the benign ones but the hostile ones as well. They are all subject to the one through whom they were created; the hostile forces are

---

[98]G. H. C. Macgregor, "Principalities and Powers," p. 27; he quotes to much the same effect from A. D. Galloway, *The Cosmic Christ* (London, 1951), p. 28. Cf. R. Bultmann, *Jesus Christ and Mythology*, E.T. (London, 1960), p. 21, on non-mythological modern language about "demonic powers which rule history, corrupting political and social life."

[99]Cf. J. S. Stewart, "On a Neglected Emphasis in New Testament Theology," *SJT* 4 (1951), 296-97.

also subject to the one by whom they were conquered. Therefore, to be united to him is to be liberated from their thraldom, to enjoy perfect freedom, to overcome the powers of evil through participation in his victory. The redemption that is in Christ Jesus is a cosmic redemption; its healing virtue streams out to the farthest bounds of creation. But it is a personal and particular redemption too: the conqueror who is enthroned at God's right hand, supreme above the universe and filling it with his presence, is at the same time enthroned as king in each believer's heart. Though "we do not yet see everything in subjection to him" (Heb. 2:8), we are nevertheless assured that, because of his redemptive act, all creation will ultimately "be set free from its bondage to decay and obtain the glorious liberty of the children of God" (Rom. 8:21). And here and now those who have already entered into that liberty may share Paul's persuasion "that neither death nor life, . . . nor principalities, . . . nor powers, . . . nor anything else in all creation, will be able to separate us from the love of God in Christ Jesus our Lord" (Rom. 8:38-39).

2. GUARD YOUR FREEDOM! (2:16-19)

Since the new teaching involved an ascetic discipline which combined food restrictions and calendar regulations with a form of angel worship, Paul goes on to warn the Colossian Christians of the necessity of guarding on those particular fronts the freedom which is theirs in Christ.

(1) Freedom in Respect of Food and Festivals (2:16-17)

16 *Let no one therefore sit in judgment on you in the matter of food and[100] drink, or with regard to a festival or new moon or sabbath.*

17 *These things[101] are a shadow of the things to come, but the substance is Christ's.*

16 Don't let anyone sit in judgment on you, he tells them, in matters of food or drink. He had said this sort of thing already when addressing a situation in which people of different practices and traditions in such matters shared one Christian fellowship: "let not him who abstains pass judgment on him who eats" (Rom. 14:3). But now he is not simply referring to an attempt to impose Jewish food laws on Gentile believers,

---

[100]καί is read here by P^{46} B 1739 1881 and a few other authorities; the majority reading is ἤ (א A C D F G I Ψ etc.).

[101]Gk. ἅ ("which things"), for which the singular ὅ is read by B F G 614 and a few other witnesses.

nor yet to a ban on eating the flesh of animals that had been sacrificed to pagan deities—a subject which had been discussed in his correspondence with the church of Corinth (1 Cor. 8:1-13; 10:19-30). The Jewish food laws did not extend to beverages, but here the reference is to more stringent regulations of an ascetic nature, perhaps involving the renunciation of animal flesh and of wine and strong drink[102] (after the Nazirite fashion). In any case, Paul lays down the principle of Christian liberty in all such matters, in the spirit of his Master who, by one comprehensive pronouncement, "declared all foods clean" (Mark 7:19).

Elsewhere, in dealing with these matters, the apostle introduces a further principle which might impose a voluntary limitation on one's Christian liberty—the principle of respect for the tender conscience of a "weaker brother" (Rom. 14:13-21; 1 Cor. 8:7-13). But this latter principle is invoked when Christians are asserting their liberty at all costs (even at the cost of Christian charity); at Colossae it is precisely Christian liberty that needs to be asserted in face of specious attempts to undermine it.

And don't let anyone sit in judgment on you, he goes on, in respect of holy days. The observance of the sacred calendar, like the observance of the levitical food laws, was obligatory on Jews. But Christians are free from obligations of this kind. If a Christian decides to abstain from certain kinds of food and drink, or to set aside certain days or seasons for special observance, commemoration, or meditation, good: these are questions to be settled between the individual conscience and God. Concerning such questions Paul writes in another letter: "Let everyone be fully convinced in his own mind. He who observes the day, observes it in honor of the Lord. He also who eats, eats in honor of the Lord, since he gives thanks to God; while he who abstains, abstains in honor of the Lord and gives thanks to God" (Rom. 14:5-6). But to regard them as matters of religious obligation is a retrograde step for Christians to take. When the churches of Galatia were minded to adopt the observance of special "days, and months, and seasons, and years," Paul told them that this was nothing less than placing themselves afresh under the yoke of the "weak and beggarly" elemental ordinances which regulated these time divisions (Gal. 4:9-10). He now uses a similar argument for the benefit of the Colossian church, which was being criticized by the innovators for not observing festivals and new moons and sabbaths.

Most cultures had their festivals, and many observed the appearance of the new moon (which was normally important for the ordering of the

---

[102]It would be in line with the thinking behind much religious asceticism if such renunciation were recommended as facilitating the vision of God.

calendar), but the sabbath was peculiarly Jewish. It is therefore probable that the festivals in question are those of the Jewish year, and that the reference to the new moon is to the Jewish celebration of the first of the month (Num. 10:10; 28:11-15).[103] Like the Galatians at an earlier date, the Colossians are now told that the observance of these occasions as obligatory is an acknowledgment of the continuing authority of the powers through which such regulations were mediated—the powers that were decisively subjugated by Christ. It would be preposterous indeed for those who had reaped the benefit of Christ's victory to put themselves voluntarily under the control of the powers which he had conquered.

Had this lesson been kept in mind in post-apostolic generations, there might have been less friction than there was in the church over the divergent calculations of the date of Easter (whether during the quarto-deciman controversy or later).[104] No doubt it was awkward (as it still is) for Christians to have differing procedures for fixing the anniversary of their Lord's passion and resurrection when they wished to commemorate the saving events year by year; but the adjustment of such discrepancies is a matter of expediency, not of principle. And sabbatarian controversies among Christians would be laid to rest if serious account were taken of the injunction: "Let no one sit in judgment on you with regard to a sabbath."[105]

17 Why must they refuse to be dictated to in these matters? Be-

---

[103]It is unlikely that the calendar recommended to the Colossians was that observed in the Qumran community (the calendar of the book of Jubilees), since the new moon played no part in it. The Jubilees/Qumran month was a calendar month of thirty days, which disregarded the phases of the moon. But even the Pharisees and Sadducees, who shared the lunisolar calendar of 354 days to a year (with appropriate intercalations to correct the rapidly accumulating discrepancy with the solar year), disagreed on several details, including the precise dating of certain festivals. Cf. L. Finkelstein, *The Pharisees* (Philadelphia, 1946), pp. 115-18, 601-02; A. Jaubert, "Le calendrier des Jubilés," *VT* 3 (1953), 250-64; 7 (1957), 35-61; J. Morgenstern, "The Calendar of the Book of Jubilees," *VT* 5 (1955), 34-76; R. T. Beckwith, "The Significance of the Calendar for Interpreting Essene Chronology and Eschatology," *Revue de Qumran* 10 (1980), 167-202.

[104]For the quartodeciman controversy see Eusebius, *HE* 5.23.1–24.18. For a later controversy over the Roman and Celtic computations of Easter see Bede, *HE* 3.25. The church historian Socrates shows a more Pauline attitude on such questions: "Since no one can produce a written command as an authority, it is evident that the apostles left each one to his own free will in the matter, in order that each might do what is good neither by fear nor by compulsion" (*HE* 5.22).

[105]The *onus probandi* lies on those who argue that the weekly sabbath is not included in this reference. When the sabbath is mentioned in the OT or the NT with no contextual qualification, the weekly sabbath is intended.

cause all such matters belonged to a transitory order. The legal prescriptions of yesteryear were but a shadow;[106] with the coming of Christ and the proclamation of the gospel they now have the substance. This analogy of the legal shadow and the gospel substance is elaborated in the letter to the Hebrews, with special reference to the sacrificial ritual.[107] Eduard Schweizer has argued that "Paul, in speaking of the law, could never use the relatively innocuous image of the shadow of that which is to come,"[108] since his assessment of the law in relation to the gospel was much more negative. But when Paul is not polemicizing against legalism, he can use language which is not so far removed from the shadow/substance antithesis. Thus, in 1 Cor. 5:7-8, the sacrifice of Christ is the reality which was foreshadowed by the passover in Egypt, and the festival of unleavened bread which followed the passover is used as a picture of the Christian life which the sacrifice of Christ makes possible.

In developing this argument, Paul could have been adapting principles which he had learned in the course of his rabbinical education. Many Jews looked on their festivals and sacred seasons as adumbrations of the messianic age. There are rabbinical texts which treat the sabbath as a foretaste of that coming time[109]—the time which, for Paul and other Christians, has come already in Christ.

Paul might have been expected to say "the substance is Christ" rather than "the substance is Christ's"; indeed, it has been suggested that "Christ's" might here be emended to "Christ."[110] But the word which is

---

[106]See S. Schulz, TDNT 7, p. 398 (s.v. σκιά, D2); H.-J. Schoeps, Aus frühchristlicher Zeit (Tübingen, 1950), p. 163.

[107]Cf. Heb. 8:5; 10:1, σκιὰν . . . ἔχων ὁ νόμος τῶν μελλόντων ἀγαθῶν.

[108]E. Schweizer, Colossians, p. 156.

[109]E. Lohmeyer (ad loc.) quotes from 'Abot de-Rabbi Nathan 2 ([?]3rd cent. A.D.) a comment on the title of Ps. 92 ("A psalm: a song for the sabbath") which interprets it of "that day which is all sabbath, on which there is no eating or drinking, . . . but the righteous sit with crowns on their heads and refresh themselves with the vision of the Shekhinah" (cf. Heb. 4:9). Other references in the same sense are listed by Strack-Billerbeck, Kommentar 4, pp. 839-40.

[110]Cf. E. Schweizer, ad loc. (pp. 157-58). J. B. Lightfoot (ad loc.) renders Gk. τὸ δὲ σῶμα τοῦ Χριστοῦ "but the substance belongs to Christ." Attempts to understand σῶμα τοῦ Χριστοῦ here as the "body of Christ" in the distinctive Pauline sense are unsatisfactory; such are the suggested translation "but (let) the body of Christ (judge such matters)," quoted as acceptable by G. Farmer, "Mr. Robson on the Lord's Supper," ExT 6 (1894-95), 137, and the punctuation found in an unidentified manuscript by H. Grotius: τὸ δὲ σῶμα τοῦ Χριστοῦ μηδεὶς ὑμᾶς καταβραβευέτω, "but let no one disqualify you, (you who are) the body of Christ" (G. Farmer, "Grotius," ExT 17 [1905-06], 430, where Grotius's quotation from Photius is also mentioned: "the body of Christ, that is, the truth").

used in the sense of "substance" is the ordinary Greek word for "body" *(sōma)*, and the use of this word in the context to denote the body of Christ may have influenced the choice of the genitive instead of the nominative: it is as members of the body of Christ that his people now possess the substance, so that they may cheerfully let the shadow go.

(2) Freedom in Respect of Asceticism and Angel Worship (2:18-19)

18 *Let no one disqualify you*[111] *through delight in "humility" and angel worship—the things which he has seen*[112] *at his initiation—inflated to no purpose by his carnal mind,*

19 *and not holding fast the head,*[113] *from which the whole body, supplied and fitted together through the joints and ligaments, grows with the growth that comes from God.*

18 Don't let anyone disqualify you, Paul goes on, by a show of superior humility. Some people love to make a parade of exceptional piety. They pretend to have found the way to a higher plane of spiritual experience, as though they had been initiated into sacred mysteries which give them an infinite advantage over the uninitiated. Others are overprone to be taken in by such people, for this kind of claim impresses those who always fall for the idea of an "inner ring."[114] But (says the apostle) don't be misled by such people. For all their lofty pretension, for all the delight which they take in self-abasement and angel worship, for all their boasting

---

[111]Gk. μηδεὶς ὑμᾶς καταβραβευέτω. The compound καταβραβεύω is very rare (see Col. 3:15 for the simple βραβεύω) and literally means "give an unfavorable ruling" on a competitor in some athletic contest, the ruling being given by the umpire (βραβεύς). In all passages quoted for the use of the compound it conveys the idea of depriving someone of something which he or she would otherwise have possessed, such as an opportunity to compete (hence RSV "disqualify") or a prize (βραβεῖον, as in 1 Cor. 9:24; Phil. 3:14) awarded for excelling in a competition (hence ARV "rob you of your prize"; so also J. B. Lightfoot, W. M. Ramsay, etc.). F. Field (*Notes on Translation,* p. 196) regards the thought of a "prize" as otiose; the verb, then, will mean "give an adverse decision against" and so "condemn" (a stronger synonym for κρίνω in v. 16). Cf. T. K. Abbott, *ad loc.,* pp. 265-66; H. N. Bate, *A Guide to the Epistles of St. Paul* (London, 1926), pp. 139-40, n. 1.

[112]Gk. ἃ ἑόρακεν (ἑώρακεν). ℵ² C D² Ψ and the majority of cursives put μή before the verb; F G have οὐκ. The negative is read also in lat syr. See p. 120, n. 130.

[113]Gk. οὐ κρατῶν τὴν κεφαλήν, after which D* and the Harclean Syriac add the epexegetic Χριστόν.

[114]Cf. C. S. Lewis, "The Inner Ring" (1944), in *Screwtape Proposes a Toast and Other Pieces* (London, 1965), pp. 28-40.

of the special insight which they have received into divine reality, they are simply inflated by the pride of their own unspiritual minds, having lost contact with him who is the true head and fount of life and knowledge.

Humility is a Christian virtue,[115] but the "humility" professed by the people here referred to is a counterfeit "humility." The truly humble person is unconscious of his or her humility, let alone taking delight or pride in it. We may recall Uriah Heep and others of his tribe who make a parade of "humility," though their "humility" does not always take the form of asceticism or "mortification" of the body, as was evidently so in the present case.

As for the angel worship, this seems to go beyond such speculation about angels as was common in several Jewish circles (such as the Essenes and apocalyptists), with the claim to participation in the worship offered by the heavenly host, and to denote an actual cult of angels. While Paul may have the elemental forces chiefly in mind, or those principalities and powers to which he has made earlier allusion, he seems to refer here more generally to angels as a class. Some indeed, like Ernst Percy, suggest that "angel worship" is but another way of designating subjection to legalism, since that involved subjection to the angels through whom the law was mediated. "By their legalism and asceticism the heretics are worshipping the angels instead of God."[116] But something more than this is required to satisfy Paul's strong language about an angel cult "figuring centrally in the plan of salvation."[117]

---

[115]On humility (ταπεινοφροσύνη) see Col. 3:12 (p. 154, n. 127). According to Hermas (Shepherd, Vision 3.10.6-7), humility (ταπεινοφροσύνη), almost in the sense of "mortification," including fasting, is necessary for receiving revelations in a vision. The rendering above, "through delight in humility," takes the Greek phrase θέλων ἐν ταπεινοφροσύνῃ to be a Septuagintalism (following the Hebrew use of the preposition b^e with the verb ḥāpēṣ, "to delight in"). C. F. D. Moule (IBNTG, p. 183) compares Ps. 112:1 (LXX 111:1), where ἐν ταῖς ἐντολαῖς αὐτοῦ θελήσει σφόδρα renders Heb. b^emiṣwôṭāyw ḥāpēṣ $m^{e'}$ōḏ ("he will greatly rejoice in his commandments"). E. Percy (Die Probleme, p. 145) also quotes Testament of Asher 1:6, ἐὰν οὖν ἡ ψυχὴ θέλει ἐν καλῷ ("if therefore the soul delight in good"). J. B. McClellan, "Colossians II.18: A Criticism of the Revised Version and an Exposition," Expositor, series 7, 9 (1910), 388, prefers to take θέλων closely with καταβραβευέτω, "let no one condemn you at will in the matter of . . ."; θέλων, he thinks, expresses the attitude hoc uolo, sic iubeo, stet pro ratione uoluntas (Juvenal, Sat. 6.223). There is certainly no need to emend the text, as Hort suggested, to ἐν ἐθελοταπεινοφροσύνῃ ("with voluntary humility"), this noun being a conjectural coinage of similar stamp to ἐθελοθρησκεία in v. 23 (see p. 128, n. 163).

[116]E. Percy, Die Probleme, p. 168.

[117]E. Percy, Die Probleme, p. 155; he has a full discussion of the θρησκεία τῶν ἀγγέλων on pp. 149-69.

In a number of OT theophanies the angel of Yahweh is an extension of Yahweh's personality; he speaks as Yahweh and is addressed as Yahweh.[118] Something of this order reappears in the concept of a superior angel in later phases of the *merkabah* tradition, where Metatron, "the prince of the countenance" (mentioned in the Babylonian Talmud as the angel of whom God says in Exod. 23:21, "my name is in him"),[119] is called "the lesser Yahweh" or "the lesser Lord."[120] It is the same angel who is called Yahoel in the second-century *Apocalypse of Abraham* (an appellation given to him, he says, by the supreme God "in virtue of the ineffable name that is dwelling in me").[121] Earlier still, in the *Melchizedek* fragment from Cave 11 at Qumran, Melchizedek figures as the "God" who holds judgment "in the midst of the gods" (Ps. 82:1) and who "judges the peoples" (Ps. 7:8), the God whose reign is announced in Isa. 52:7. Melchizedek here is the angel prince who, by passing sentence on the hosts of Belial, inaugurates the age of release for the righteous.[122] Also from Qumran (Cave 4) comes an angelic liturgy which takes up the theme, "Praise God, all ye angels," and exhorts the angels, under many names, to offer various forms of worship to God.[123] The exhortation formed part of the liturgy of the burnt offering sabbath by sabbath throughout the year (according to the Qumran calendar): the liturgy of the people of God on earth is designed to reproduce that presented by the angels before the heavenly throne. Such a liturgy might well be called "the worship of angels"—although there angels are not the objects of the worship but rather the initiators and exemplars of the worship.[124]

It has been suggested that this feature of the Colossian heresy reflected a local tendency which persisted for centuries. Thus W. M. Ram-

[118]E.g., Judg. 6:12-24.
[119]TB *Sanhedrin* 38b; cf. also *Ḥagigah* 15a; *'Abodah Zarah* 3b.
[120]3 Enoch 12:5 ("the lesser Yahweh").
[121]*Apocalypse of Abraham* 10.
[122]11QMelch.
[123]4Q ŠirŠabb (cf. J. Strugnell, "The angelic liturgy at Qumrân: 4Q Serek Šîrôt 'Ôlat Haššabbāt," *SVT* 7 [1960], 318-45). Three other manuscripts of this liturgy have been identified from Qumran Cave 4 and one from Masada.
[124]See Introduction, p. 26 with n. 108. J. B. McClellan, "Colossians II.18," pp. 385-98, argues that τῶν ἀγγέλων is neither objective genitive after θρησκεία ("worship offered to angels") nor subjective genitive ("worship offered by angels"); it indicates rather that the worship proceeds from (or is dictated by) angels: "ceremonial religion [*or* ordinances] of the angels." θρησκεία usually refers to religious practice (cf. Jas. 1:27 for the θρησκεία of Christianity). K. L. Schmidt, *TDNT* 3, p. 157 (*s.v.* θρησκεία), compares Eusebius, *HE* 6.41.2, where pagan persecutors behave as if the maltreatment of Christians were the θρησκεία τῶν δαιμονίων, "the worship of their divinities." See also A. L. Williams, "The Cult of the Angels at Colossae," *JTS* 10 (1909), 413-38.

say quotes from Canon 35 of the Synod of Laodicea (c. A.D. 363) and from the commentary of Theodoret on this letter (ad loc.) words which indicate that the practice of praying to angels was maintained by some Phrygian and Pisidian Christians in face of official ecclesiastical prohibition.[125] (In later centuries the practice which had once been condemned as idolatrous came to be reckoned as piety in the form of the veneration of Michael the archangel, who was credited from the ninth century onward with being the author of a natural phenomenon in the vicinity of Colossae—"the miracle at Khonai," as Ramsay calls it.)[126] It is most improbable, however, that the practices attested by the Canons of Laodicea and by Theodoretus have any direct connection with the situation to which Paul here addresses himself.[127]

The difficulty of translating v. 18 as it stands gave rise to a variety of conjectural emendation. The main difficulty was posed by the participle which has been translated above "at his initiation."[128] No such meaning was attested for the verb before 1912, although it was known in Greek literature in the sense "investigate."[129] (It was no doubt the attempt to give it this sense in the present context that led to the early insertion of a negative into the preceding adjective clause, which yielded the sense "investigating things that he has not seen.")[130] But in 1912 and 1913 Martin

[125]W. M. Ramsay, The Church in the Roman Empire before A.D. 170 (London, [5]1897), p. 477.

[126]The Church in the Roman Empire, p. 490. Khonai (Χῶναι) is the Greek name of the place called Honaz by the Turks, three miles south of the site of Colossae. Such legends, involving a Christian saint or angel, often go back to pagan times, the saint or angel having displaced an earlier divinity or genius loci.

[127]It is noteworthy that Colossians concerns itself with the angels' relation to Christ more than any other Pauline letter does. Cf. Heb. 1:4-14; 2:2, 5, 9, 16, and T. W. Manson's suggestion that Hebrews deals with a rather later development of the same situation as is treated in Colossians (Studies in the Gospels and Epistles (Manchester, 1962), pp. 242-58. (Cf. p. 185, n. 73.)

[128]Gk. ἐμβατεύων.

[129]Cf. 2 Macc. 2:30, "It is the duty of the original historian to explore the ground (ἐμβατεύειν)."

[130]Cf. p. 117, n. 112. This reading and interpretation were defended by F. Field, Notes on Translation, pp. 197-98, and J. B. McClellan, "Colossians II.18," pp. 393-98. It is easier to explain the editorial insertion of the negative (where ἐμβατεύων was not properly understood) than its deletion. Several scholars have been attracted by the simple device (first propounded by Alexander More and Étienne de Courcelles) of detaching -κεν from ἑώρακεν and making it a prefix to ἐμβατεύων, so that the phrase reads ἃ ἑώρα (imperfect instead of perfect) κενεμβατεύων ("talking emptily of what he saw"). J. B. Lightfoot carried the process of emendation a little farther, suggesting as the original text ἑώρα (or αἰώρα) κενεμβατεύων, "treading the void while suspended in air" (i.e., "indulging airily

Dibelius and W. M. Ramsay,[131] almost simultaneously, recognized that the verb was used here in a sense which it bore in recently published inscriptions from the sanctuary of Apollo at Claros, a few miles northwest of Ephesus.[132] The effect of the verb as used here by Paul, says Ramsay, "depends on the fact that it was a religious term familiar to his Phrygian readers."[133] Strictly speaking, it does not denote the initiation itself but the next stage, entering the sacred area in order to see the mysteries.[134] These

---

in vain speculations"). E. Percy (*Die Probleme*, pp. 173-74) is inclined to follow Lightfoot. A similar emendation to Lightfoot's, ἀέρα κενεμβατεύων, "emptily treading on air" (i.e., "treading on empty air") was suggested by C. Taylor, "A Conjectural Emendation of Colossians II.18," *Journal of Philology* 7 (1877), 130-33. "Taylor's brilliant conjecture," as H. N. Bate calls it (*Guide to Epistles of Paul*, p. 142, n. 1), was approved by F. J. A. Hort (*Notes on Select Readings* [Cambridge and London, 1882], p. 127), but J. W. Burgon satirized it as something "which (if it means anything at all) may as well mean 'proceeding on an airy foundation to offer an empty conjecture' " (*The Revision Revised* [London, 1883], p. 356). "That was witty, but not very wise," said J. R. Harris, who found Taylor's "charming simplification" a "very simple and convincing solution" (*Sidelights on New Testament Research* [London, 1908], p. 200). Harris later suggested that Paul had Aristophanes' *Clouds* in his mind, more particularly line 225, where Socrates (pictured by the poet as an ascetic) says ἀεροβατῶ καὶ περιφρονῶ τὸν ἥλιον, "I tread on air and overlook the sun" ("St. Paul and Aristophanes," *ExT* 34 [1922-23], 151-56). This led him on to imagine that περιφροσύνη might have been the original reading in this verse and v. 23 (see p. 118, n. 115), rather than ταπεινοφροσύνη of all our texts. All emendations based on the conjecture κενεμβατεύων have to surmount the obstacle that this word is unknown, although κενεμβατέω is quite classical in the sense "indulge in empty speculation" (it is for this word that Plutarch, Lucian, etc. should have been cited in BAG, *s.v.* κενεμβατεύω, not for κενεμβατεύω). While Lightfoot defends κενεμβατεύω as an "unobjectionable" formation, Field (*loc. cit.*) dismisses it as a ghost-word, a *vox nulla*, "the inviolable laws regulating this class of compound verbs stamping κενεμβατεῖν as the only legitimate, as it is the only existing, form."

[131]Dibelius, *An die Kolosser* (Tübingen, 1912), *ad loc.*; W. M. Ramsay, "Ancient Mysteries and their Relation to St. Paul," *Athenaeum*, January 25, 1913, pp. 106-07; *The Teaching of Paul in Terms of the Present Day* (London, 1913), pp. 286-304.

[132]See the account given by M. Dibelius, "The Isis Initiation in Apuleius," pp. 83-88; on pp. 85-86 he cites six Claros inscriptions containing ἐμβατεύω or related terms from T. Macridy's reports: "Altertümer von Notion," *JÖAI* 8 (1905), 155-73; "Antiquités de Notion, II," *JÖAI* 15 (1912), 36-67.

[133]W. M. Ramsay, *The Teaching of Paul*, p. 300.

[134]Similarly F. O. Francis, "Humility and Angel Worship in Col. 2:18," in *Conflict at Colossae*, pp. 166-67. On the other hand, A. D. Nock takes ἃ ἑόρακεν as object to ἐμβατεύων, "entering at length upon the tale of what he has seen" ("The Vocabulary of the New Testament," *JBL* 52 [1933], 132), "expatiating on what he has seen" ("Hellenistic Mysteries and Christian Sacraments," *Mnemosyne*, series 4, 5 [1952], 200).

mysteries could well be described, however (as in our translation), as "the things which he has seen at his initiation."[135] The readers would catch the suggestion that the person alluded to had formally "entered upon" his higher experience like someone being admitted to secret rites from which the vulgar mob was excluded, and was now appealing to that superior enlightenment in support of his teaching.

Whatever may have been the precise nature of the mystical experience which this teacher had undergone, his exploitation of it forms a striking contrast to Paul's apologetic reticence when he refers to the strange thing that once happened to him when he was "caught up into Paradise" and "heard things that cannot be told, which man may not utter" (2 Cor. 12:3-4). In the sequel Paul incurred a humiliating disability to keep him, as he says, "from being too elated by the abundance of revelations" (2 Cor. 12:7); but the person who is now in view, in the absence of such a visitation, could not resist being "inflated . . . by his carnal mind"[136] as he contemplated his extraordinary visions—and all to no purpose.

His "carnal mind" is literally "the mind of his flesh"[137]—a remarkable locution, quite out of keeping with the general Greek concept of the relation between body and mind. The "sensuous mind" (as the RSV renders it) is the mind that is taken up with sense perceptions (including those received in a state of ecstasy). Paul's distinctive use of the term "flesh" points to the attitude and outlook characteristic of the old nature, before the regenerating grace of the Holy Spirit has taken effect. Even in believers this antiquated tendency may linger on: so to the Christians of Corinth Paul could write that, despite their conversion to faith in Christ, they were "still of the flesh" in their thoughts and actions, "babes in Christ," "behaving like ordinary men," unfit as yet to be treated as spiritual (1 Cor. 3:1-3).

---

[135]Two inscriptions from the 1905 report (see n. 132 above) contain the words μυηθέντες καὶ ἐνβατεύσαντες (II 2); μυηθέντες ἐνεβάτευσαν (IV 4), "having been initiated they made their entrance." The persons referred to were delegates (θεοπρόποι) from various places who came to Claros to obtain an oracular response from Apollo.

[136]εἰκῇ before φυσιούμενος intensifies the idea of futility expressed by the verb; self-inflation is a fruitless exercise.

[137]Gk. ὑπὸ τοῦ νοὸς τῆς σαρκὸς αὐτοῦ (cf. Rom. 8:6-7, τὸ φρόνημα τῆς σαρκός). The νοῦς is that part of the human mentality which can distinguish good from evil, can recognize and respond to the claims of God (cf. Rom. 7:21-26; 12:2), but may remain subservient to the old unregenerate outlook so long as one goes on living κατὰ σάρκα. See J. Behm, TDNT 4, pp. 958-59 (s.v. νοῦς); BAG (s.v. νοῦς); J. Goetzmann, NIDNTT 3, pp. 122-30 (s.v. "Reason"); J. A. T. Robinson, The Body, p. 25, n. 2. Cf. Eph. 4:17, 23 (pp. 355, 358).

19 This self-inflation and pride in private religious experiences come of not maintaining contact with the head. Here at any rate it is best to understand "head" and "body" in their physiological relation to each other. Each part of the body functions properly so long as it is under the control of the head: if it escapes from this control and begins to act independently, the consequences can be very distressing. It is under the direction of Christ, then, that the various parts of his body function harmoniously together, since they share his common life and grow to maturity under the fostering care of God,[138] supplied with nutriment and fitted to each other by means of the "joints and ligaments."[139]

In spite of Dibelius's argument, developed in agreement with his exposition of Col. 1:18 and 2:10, that the body here is the cosmos,[140] it is preferable by far to take the present passage in the same sense as Eph. 4:16, the body being the church.[141] Dibelius's interpretation, according to which the false teachers hold fast to the members of the cosmos-body (that is, to the principalities and powers) instead of to Christ as the head of that body, introduces into the argument an element which is not only un-Pauline but not really consistent with its context. What is more probably meant here is that the false teachers, by failing to maintain contact with him who is head of his body the church, have no true part in that body, since it is from Christ as their head that all the members of the body acquire their capacity to function aright in harmony with one another.

3. YOU DIED WITH CHRIST; THEREFORE . . . (2:20-23)

20 If[142] you died with Christ from (subjection to) the elemental forces

---

[138]Gk. αὔξει τὴν αὔξησιν τοῦ θεοῦ, cognate or internal accusative. Cf. Eph. 4:15-16 (pp. 352-53).

[139]Gk. διὰ τῶν ἀφῶν καὶ συνδέσμων. Cf. Eph. 4:16, διὰ πάσης ἀφῆς. In both places Paul may be developing a conception of the interlinking of bodily joints and ligaments which had already begun to take shape in his mind as a figure of the mutual dependence and harmonious cooperation of believers as members of the body of Christ. For σύνδεσμος cf. Col. 3:14; Eph. 4:3.

[140]*An die Kolosser, ad loc.*, and on v. 10 above. Dibelius's view is cited with apparent approval by C. L. Mitton, *The Epistle to the Ephesians* (Oxford, 1951), p. 84.

[141]Cf. Col. 3:15, "in one body." See C. F. D. Moule, "A Note on Eph. 1:22, 23," *ExT* 60 (1948-49), 224: "I very much doubt whether there is any essential difference between the two uses" (i.e., of σῶμα in Eph. 4:16 and Col. 2:19 respectively).

[142]After εἰ ℵ² and a number of cursives insert οὖν (perhaps on the model of Col. 3:1).

of the world,[143] *why, as though living in the world, do you submit to regulations—*

21 *"Do not handle, do not taste, do not touch!"*

22 *in reference to things which are all destined to perish by the very use that is made of them—according to human commandments and teachings?*

23 *Those regulations have a reputation for wisdom with their would-be religion and asceticism*[144] *and*[145] *severity to the body, but they are not of any value against the indulgence of the flesh.*[146]

Paul has already told the Colossians that they were participators in the death of Christ (v. 11). Now he takes up this crucial fact again and applies it to them in a practical way. You died with Christ (he says): and in that death with him (which is what your baptism was all about), your former relation of bondage to the elemental forces of the world has been terminated. That former existence, which they dominated, has come to an end. From their point of view, you are dead. Why, then, do you go on serving them as though that former existence were still going on?[147] You submit to their restrictive regulations: "Hands off this! Don't eat that! Don't touch that other thing!"[148] And you imagine that asceticism of this kind is true holiness! But how wrong you are! Only consider: the things with which these prohibitions are concerned are all material things, belonging to this

---

[143]Gk. ἀπὸ τῶν στοιχείων τοῦ κόσμου, "out from under the elements of the world" (J. A. T. Robinson, *The Body*, p. 43).

[144]Gk. ταπεινοφροσύνη (as in v. 18). F G with some Old Latin witnesses add τοῦ νοός ("of the mind").

[145]καί is omitted by P^{46} B 1739 and a few other witnesses.

[146]Gk. οὐκ ἐν τιμῇ τινι πρὸς πλησμονὴν τῆς σαρκός. The difficulty of translating this phrase has given rise to attempts at emendation. The text of v. 23 has been described as "hopelessly corrupt" (W. Carr, *Angels and Principalities*, p. 81); indeed, J. Moffatt speaks of "the corrupt state of the text" of vv. 17-23 (*ILNT*, p. 156). The difficulty may in part be due to the quotation of technical terms: according to G. Bornkamm, "in Col. 2:23 five key words of the Colossian heresy occur"; he adds that in the last phrase of the verse Paul's irony has changed a concept of the heretics into its opposite ("The Heresy of Colossians," p. 134). See pp. 128-29, n. 167.

[147]The style of argument in v. 20 is similar to that of Paul's remonstrance with Peter in Gal. 2:14.

[148]It is amazing that some commentators, both in antiquity and more recently, have taken the prohibitions of v. 21 to be imposed by Paul himself. So Hilary, Ambrose, and Pelagius; Jerome and Augustine, on the other hand, grasped the true sense. These prohibitions are not the negative commandments of the Decalogue, nor yet their amplification in the oral law of rabbinical tradition, but the special restrictions laid down in the ascetic philosophy which is here opposed.

transitory order of time and sense. They are things which come to an end
in the very act of being used. Handling them, eating them, or the like
involves their destruction. Food, once eaten, ceases to be food. These are
not the things that matter most; these are not the ultimate realities. Yet
these things are the burning concern of those merely human commandments and teachings. The commandments and teachings of Christ provide
more important matters than these to engage your attention. O, I agree
that the acceptance of these prohibitions looks very good: it makes a favorable impression on many people and suggests that you have attained a
high plane of wisdom from which you can despise the material world.
There is something very specious about all this voluntary piety, this self-
abasement, this harsh treatment of the body. But does it really get you
anywhere? Let me assure you that it does not. The acceptance of all these
ascetic restrictions is of no account when it comes to a real struggle against
indulgence of the "flesh." In fact, the most rigorous asceticism can coexist
with insufferable spiritual pride, one of the subtlest and most intractable
of the "works of the flesh."[149] You are following the wrong road, one
which can never lead you to your true goal—a road, moreover, which is
barred to all believers in Christ who know what it means to have shared
in his death.

20 The idea of the believer's dying with Christ appears in earlier
Pauline letters. Paul puts it most emphatically when he says of himself,
"I have been crucified with Christ" (Gal. 2:19).[150] In Rom. 6:1-14 the
proposal that believers should continue in sin, to give God's grace further
opportunity of displaying itself in its superabundance, is refuted by the
argument that those who have died to sin can no longer live in sin. Baptism
proclaims the believer's death with Christ: "all of us who were baptized
into Christ Jesus were baptized into his death" (Rom. 6:3). The finality
of that death-with-Christ has been confirmed by their burial-with-Christ—
a burial from which they are now risen-with-Christ to begin a new life-in-
Christ.[151] As death severs the bond which binds a slave to his master, so
their death-with-Christ has severed the bond which bound them to sin.[152]
As death severs the bond which binds a wife to her husband, so their
death-with-Christ has severed the bond which bound them to legal ordinances.[153] Here the argument presented to the Colossian Christians is that,

[149]Compare the distasteful company in which the ὑπερήφανοι find themselves in
Rom. 1:30.
[150]Cf. also 2 Cor. 4:10-12; 2 Tim. 2:11.
[151]Cf. Col. 2:11-12.
[152]Rom. 6:16-23.
[153]Rom. 7:1-6; cf. Gal. 2:19.

as death severs the bond which binds a subject to his ruler, so their death-with-Christ has severed the bond which bound them to the service of the principalities and powers. Why then should they go on submitting to the rules[154] imposed by these powers? All these rules and regulations belong to the sphere of the "flesh"[155]—the old, pre-Christian life—and only in that sphere do they have any binding validity. Those who live "not according to the flesh, but according to the Spirit" (Rom. 8:4) are under no further obligation to obey them.

21 What sort of regulations are these which the elemental forces impose? Completely negative ones: "Don't, don't, don't." There may be a stage in children's development when they must be told not to do this and not to touch that, before they can understand the reasons for such prohibitions. But when they come to years of discretion and can appreciate their parents' point of view, they are able to look at life from a responsible angle and do what is proper without having to conform to a list of prohibitions such as are suitable and necessary for the years of infancy. These would-be guides were trying to keep the Colossian Christians in leading strings; Paul encourages them to enjoy the liberty with which Christ has set them free.[156] The imposition of prohibitions from without can do nothing to create or develop new life within. "Merely negative rules do not avail for the maintenance and growth of Christian life, for life is not offered merely to our acceptance, it is offered to our acquisition. Not abstinence, not indulgence, not mystic immersion into an external symbolism, as in the mysteries of Eastern Greece—not in these, but in the appropriation of Christ in His person and His work does the Christian life consist. The Christian must live over again the experience of the Christ; he must die with Him, rise with Him, live with Him in an endless, ever-growing life."[157]

22 Besides, all the things covered by these taboos are perishable objects of the material world, doomed to pass away by the very use that

---

[154]Gk. τί . . . δογματίζεσθε? Similarly the calendrical rules to which the Galatian churches were disposed to submit were part of the domain of the στοιχεῖα according to Gal. 4:8-10, where those forces are described as τοῖς φύσει μὴ οὖσιν θεοῖς (so-called gods that are really no gods at all).
[155]For this use of σάρξ see Rom. 7:5, 14-25; 8:3-4; Gal. 3:3; Eph. 2:11; cf. E. Schweizer, *TDNT* 7, pp. 125-38 (*s.v.* σάρξ); A. Sand, *Der Begriff "Fleisch" in den paulinischen Hauptbriefen* (Regensburg, 1967). See further on v. 23 below (pp. 128-29).
[156]Compare Paul's argument in Gal. 3:23–4:7.
[157]J. Iverach, "The Epistle to the Colossians and its Christology," *ExT* 25 (1913-14), 208.

is made of them.[158] This is plainly so where food is concerned: food ceases to exist as such by the very act of being digested. The Corinthians had a saying, "Food is meant for the stomach and the stomach for food"; but, Paul adds, "God will destroy both one and the other" (1 Cor. 6:13). But the Corinthians who summed up their outlook in these words were probably not thinking of food alone, but also of sexual relations: they too, it was implied, were bodily functions, as irrelevant ethically or religiously as food or drink. May it be, then, that the asceticism recommended at Colossae included abstention from sexual relations (even within marriage) as well as from various kinds of food or drink?[159] This may well have been so, but the reference to "things which are all destined to perish by the very use that is made of them" would not be applicable to sexual relations; what Paul thought about the lasting effect of these, even of the most casual kind, may be gathered from 1 Cor. 6:15-20.

Moreover, these taboos are not divinely ordained: they are imposed "according to human commandments and teaching." Behind this phrase lies the wording of Isa. 29:13, where the God of Israel says of his people, "their hearts are far from me, and their fear of me is a commandment of men learned by rote." These words were quoted by Jesus in reference to the "tradition of the elders" by which, he averred, the scribes of his day had nullified the word of God.[160] From his use of the text it passed into

[158]Gk. ἅ ἐστιν πάντα εἰς φθορὰν τῇ ἀποχρήσει. The noun ἀπόχρησις is used in this sense by Plutarch and Dionysius of Halicarnassus. The sense "abuse" which it sometimes bears is inappropriate in the present context. The transitory character of the things in question is emphasized by the consideration that they disappear simply by being used in the proper and ordinary manner. Therefore it shows a gross lack of any sense of proportion to make such transient and perishable matters so central in religious teaching. Lightfoot compares Seneca (*On the Blessed Life* 7), "in ipso usu sui periturum" ("doomed to perish by the very use that is made of it"), which is exactly Paul's point here. Cf. BAG (*s.v.* ἀπόχρησις) for a similar instance of the verb ἀποχράομαι in Polybius.
[159]The first of the three prohibitions (μὴ ἅψῃ μηδὲ γεύσῃ μηδὲ θίγῃς) has been thought to point to sexual relations because of the use of the same verb in 1 Cor. 7:1 (καλὸν ἀνθρώπῳ γυναικὸς μὴ ἅπτεσθαι); cf. A. R. C. Leaney, "Colossians ii.21-23 (The Use of Πρός)," *ExT* 64 (1952-53), 92 (he suggests that μηδὲ θίγῃς "refers to such taboos as Lev. 11:24 ff."). In the *uenerabilis continentia* prescribed for Lucius before his Isis initiation, which Dibelius ("The Isis Initiation in Apuleius," p. 89) adduces as an analogy to the Colossian asceticism, abstention from animal flesh and wine are specifically enjoined (Apuleius, *Metamorphoses* 11.23).
[160]Mark 7:6-7 (see on v. 6 above). The LXX version of Isa. 29:13, quoted by Mark, διδάσκοντες ἐντάλματα ἀνθρώπων καὶ διδασκαλίας, is plainly the source of Paul's κατὰ τὰ ἐντάλματα καὶ διδασκαλίας τῶν ἀνθρώπων.

the arsenal of "testimonies" by which early Christian apologists explained Jewish reluctance to accept the gospel.[161] When Paul echoes the prophet's words here, therefore, it is with the implication that these taboos frustrate the pure teaching of God with its emancipating emphasis.

23 These prohibitions carry with them a reputation for wisdom, it is true. They are associated in people's minds with schools of ascetic philosophy, like that of the Pythagoreans,[162] and win for those who inculcate and practice them a veneration which is, after all, cheaply acquired. But there is no necessary connection between such impressive asceticism and the true spirit of the gospel. By contrast with the spiritual service which true Christianity enjoins in harmony with the will of God, "good and acceptable and perfect" (Rom. 12:1-2), this "would-be religion"[163] is a "self-made cult," as Deissmann puts it,[164] or a "faked-religion," as Bate has it.[165] The term which Paul uses implies that these people thought they were offering God a voluntary addition to his basic requirements—a supererogatory devotion by which they hoped to acquire superior merit in his sight. Far from being of any avail[166] against the indulgence of the "flesh,"[167] as its proponents claimed, it could and often did coexist with

---

[161]Cf. Justin, *Dialogue with Trypho* 48, 140.

[162]E. Schweizer ("Versöhnung des Alls," in *Jesus Christus in Historie und Theologie,* ed. G. Strecker [Tübingen, 1975], pp. 494-99; *Colossians,* pp. 130-33) finds affinities to the Colossian heresy in a Jewish Pythagoreanism attested as early as the first century B.C. See Introduction, pp. 19-20.

[163]Gk. ἐθελοθρησκεία, the first of "five key words of the Colossian heresy" which G. Bornkamm ("The Heresy of Colossians," p. 134) discerns in this verse, the others being (*b*) ταπεινοφροσύνη, (*c*) ἀφειδία σώματος, (*d*) τιμή, (*e*) πλησμονή. The *hapax legomenon* ἐθελοθρησκεία has been thought to be a Pauline coinage on the analogy of ἐθελοδουλεία, used by Plato and others in the sense of "voluntary subjection" (cf. MM, *s.v.* ἐθελοθρησκεία). J. R. Harris ("St. Paul and Aristophanes," pp. 133-34) conjectured νεφελοθρησκεία ("cloud worship"), pointing out that in Aristophanes' *Clouds* 316, the clouds are acclaimed as divinities worthy of worship. This conjecture belongs to the Aristophanic region of Νεφελοκοκκυγία, "Cloud-cuckoo-land."

[164]Deissmann, *Paul,* E.T. (London, 1926), p. 118 (he contrasts it with the λογικὴ λατρεία of Rom. 12:1).

[165]H. N. Bate, *Guide to Epistles of Paul,* p. 143.

[166]Gk. οὐκ ἐν τιμῇ τινι, "not in any honor," "not of any value" (cf. J. Schneider, *TDNT* 8, p. 177, *s.v.* τιμή).

[167]Gk. πρὸς πλησμονὴν τῆς σαρκός. Bornkamm (see n. 163 above) sees in πλησμονή ("fullness," "filling") Paul's ironical dismissal of the heretics' claim to be filled (πληροῦσθαι) with the divine power through their initiation. See G. Delling, *TDNT* 6, pp. 133-34 (*s.v.* πίμπλημι etc.). The translation of πρός as "against" in this context (for which Lightfoot's precedent can be cited) has been questioned. It would be natural to understand the preposition in the sense "leading

overweening self-conceit, making it extremely difficult for those who accepted it to admit the truth that in God's sight they were sinners, desperately in need of his salvation. When they commended harsh usage of the body as a specific against fleshly indulgence, they thought in terms of the Greek antithesis between body and soul. But this is not Paul's thought. When he speaks of "severity to the *body*," he means the body in its ordinary sense; but when he speaks of "indulgence of the *flesh*," he means the old Adam-nature in its rebellion against God.[168] A chief ingredient in that rebellion is the proud spirit of self-sufficiency which has nothing to do with the body in the ordinary sense, but springs from the will. And the asceticism disparaged by Paul feeds this particular indulgence of the "flesh" instead of starving it.[169]

---

to," but this would involve supplying some additional words (in thought, if not in writing): the ἐθελοθρησκεία and so forth "have an appearance of wisdom but are not of any value; [they lead only] to indulgence of the flesh." See B. Reicke, "Zum sprachlichen Verständnis von Kol 2, 23," *ST* 6 (1953), 39-53; B. Hollenbach, "Col. ii.23: Which Things lead to the Fulfillment of the Flesh," *NTS* 25 (1978-79), 254-61. A. R. C. Leaney, "Colossians ii.21-23," takes πρός in the sense "in comparison with" (cf. Rom. 8:18): "but not of any value compared with actual indulgence of the flesh" (i.e., "this man-made asceticism . . . is no more service of God than living the life of the flesh"). See also P. L. Hedley, "Ad Colossenses 2,20–3,4," *ZNW* 27 (1928), 211-16. There is a helpful statement of the situation in C. F. D. Moule, *ad loc.* (pp. 108-10); of the various possibilities which he lists, he prefers Lightfoot's interpretation.

[168]Cf. E. Percy, *Die Probleme*, p. 262; J. A. T. Robinson, *The Body*, p. 27.
[169]Cf. E. Percy, *Die Probleme*, p. 139.

COLOSSIANS 3

4. YOU WERE RAISED WITH CHRIST; THEREFORE . . . (3:1-4)

1 *So then, if you were raised with Christ, seek those things that are above, where Christ is, seated at God's right hand.*
2 *Set your minds on the things above, not on the things on earth.*
3 *For you died; and your life is hidden with Christ in God.*
4 *When Christ, your[1] life, is manifested, then you also will be manifested in glory with him.*

The Colossians are reminded that they not only died with Christ; they were raised from the dead with him too—as indeed they have already been told (Col. 2:12). When Christ left the tomb, he was raised on high, and is now enthroned in glory, at God's right hand. What does this mean for those who by faith have been united with him in his death and resurrection? They continue to live on earth in their mortal bodies, but they have embarked on a new way of life. The motive power enabling them to follow this new way of life is imparted by him from the glory in which he now lives. Since his people share his risen life, their interests are now centered in him; his interests, in fact, have become theirs. They must therefore pursue those things which belong to the heavenly realm where he reigns; their mind, their attitude, their ambition, their whole outlook must be characterized by their living bond with the ascended Christ. The conclusion is inescapable. Having died with Christ, they now live with him and in him. Their life is bound up with his; it is, in other words, laid up in safekeeping with him, securely hidden in God. Because he lives, his people

---

[1]The weight of the evidence is slightly in favor of ὑμῶν ("your"), read by P^{46} א C D* F G P Ψ etc., over against ἡμῶν ("our"), read by B D¹ H and the majority of cursives.

live also: because he is their life, their life is as eternal as his. The world cannot see their real life at present, just as it cannot see the exalted Christ. A day is coming, however, when Christ will be revealed in glory, and those whose life is at present hidden with him will necessarily be revealed with him and share his glory.

1 The readers knew (in theory, at least) that, like their fellow-Christians throughout the world, they had been brought to new life with Christ when they were spiritually dead, that they had been "raised with him through faith in the power of God" (Col. 2:12). On every occasion when they recalled their baptism and its meaning, they ought to be impressed afresh with the reality of their participation in Christ's death and resurrection, and draw the logical and practical conclusions. If their death with Christ severed the links that bound them to the old world-order, which was trying to impose its dominion on them again, their resurrection with Christ established new links, binding them to a new and heavenly order, to that spiritual kingdom in which Christ their Lord was sovereign.

When Christ's present position of supremacy is described in the Pauline writings as being "at the right hand of God,"[2] the apostle is usually echoing the language of some primitive confession of faith, presumably familiar to his readers. Christ's ascension to the right hand of God was an essential and constant element in the earliest apostolic preaching.[3] It goes back to the messianic interpretation of Ps. 110:1, one of the most primitive of Christian *testimonia*.[4] There we find reproduced an oracle of Yahweh addressed to someone whom the psalmist calls "my Lord": "Sit at my right hand, till I make your enemies your footstool."

In the Synoptic Gospels Jesus refers to this oracle on two occasions. During his debates with the scribes of the Pharisaic party in the temple precincts he asked them why they should call the Messiah the son of David since in this psalm David speaks of him as "my lord" (Mark 12:35-37). It is presupposed that they would agree that the person addressed in the divine oracle was the Davidic Messiah. Again, during the inquiry before the high priest and his colleagues which followed his arrest in Gethsemane, he was asked if he was the Messiah, "the Son of the Blessed," and he replied: "I am; and you will see the Son of man sitting at the right hand

---

[2]Cf. Rom. 8:34; Eph. 1:20.
[3]Cf. Acts 2:33-35; 5:31; 7:55-56; Heb. 1:3, 13; 8:1; 10:12; 12:2; 1 Pet. 3:22; Rev. 3:21.
[4]Cf. D. M. Hay, *Glory at the Right Hand: Psalm 110 in Early Christianity* (Nashville/New York, 1973).

of the Almighty, and coming with the clouds of heaven" (Mark 14:61-62).[5] The form of his reply may suggest the sense: "If 'Messiah' is the term you insist on using, then I can only say 'Yes': but if I am to choose my own form of words, then let me say that you will have the answer to your question when you see the Son of Man sitting at the right hand of the Almighty, and coming with the clouds of heaven." It was his own chosen form of words—and perhaps in particular his apparent self-identification with the "one like a son of man" who, in Dan. 7:13-14, receives eternal and universal dominion from the Ancient of Days[6]—that enabled his judges to pronounce him guilty of blasphemy. He was claiming, they held, to be the peer of the Most High. But after his resurrection the apostles proclaimed that the enthronement to which he looked forward had actually taken place: Christ was now reigning as king from the right hand of the Almighty, and would continue so to reign until all opposing forces in the universe had submitted to him.[7]

The apostles knew very well that they were using figurative language when they spoke of Christ's exaltation in these terms: they no more thought of a location on a literal throne at God's literal right hand than their twentieth-century successors do. The static impression made by conventional artistic representations of the heavenly session of Christ obscures the dynamic NT picture of the exalted Christ going forth by his Spirit in all the world, conquering and to conquer.[8] What Paul understood by the heavenly session can be gathered from other terms used in his writings to convey the same idea: Christ has been given "the name which is above every name, that at the name of Jesus every knee should bow . . . and every tongue confess that Jesus Christ is Lord" (Phil. 2:10-11): he has "ascended high above all the heavens, in order to fill all things" (Eph. 4:10). Because he has been elevated to the position of highest sovereignty over the universe, he pervades the universe with his presence.

This reference to the exaltation of Christ, the seal of divine approval on his saving work, is not introduced here for an ornamental purpose. Paul is about to commence the paraenetic section of his letter, and his

---

[5]There are some significant features in the parallels in Matt. 26:64 and Luke 22:69, especially their insistence that the session will begin forthwith (ἀπ' ἄρτι, Matthew; ἀπὸ τοῦ νῦν, Luke).

[6]Cf. F. F. Bruce, *New Testament History* (London, ³1982), pp. 188-89; *The Hard Sayings of Jesus* (London, 1983), pp. 245-47.

[7]Cf. 1 Cor. 15:24-28.

[8]Martin Luther satirizes "that heaven of the fanatics *(Schwärmer)* with its golden chair and Christ seated at the Father's side, vested in a choir cope and a golden robe, as the painters love to portray him!" (*Werke*, Weimarer Ausgabe 23, p. 131).

paraenetic sections regularly presuppose the content of the apostolic preaching.[9] What God has done for his people in Christ is the grand argument and incentive for Christian living. The apostolic teaching or *didache* may be distinguished from the preaching or *kerygma*, but it is founded on the preaching—and in any case the distinction between the two should not be pressed too sharply. Whatever affinities may be traced between Paul's ethical exhortations and those of contemporary moralists, their whole emphasis in Paul's writings depends on their arising directly out of the work of Christ.[10] It is because believers have died with Christ and been raised to new life with him that their conduct is henceforth to be different.

What, then, are the practical implications of being raised with Christ? In the first place, believers have now no private life of their own. Their life is the life of Christ, maintained in being by him at God's right hand and shared by him with all his people.[11] Their interests must therefore be his interests. Instead of waiting until the last day to receive the resurrection life, those who have been raised with Christ possess it here and now. The new creation[12]—the "regeneration"[13]—has already begun in them. Spiritually—that is to say, "in Christ"—they belong already to the age to come and enjoy its life.

2 Aim then at what is above, says Paul; set your minds on that[14] and let it give character to your outlook on everything. The Gnostics also believed in aiming at what was above. They were seriously concerned with living on a higher plane than this mundane one. But Paul has in mind a higher plane than theirs. Go in for the higher things (he says)—higher things than the principalities and powers which dominate the planetary spheres, for Christ has ascended far above these.[15] Don't let your ambitions be earthbound, set on transitory and inferior objects. Don't look at life and the universe from the standpoint of these lower planes; look at them from Christ's exalted standpoint. Judge everything by the standards of that new creation to which you now belong, not by those of the old order to which you have said a final farewell.[16]

[9]Cf. Rom. 6:1-11; 1 Cor. 5:7-8, etc.
[10]Cf. W. D. Davies, *Paul and Rabbinic Judaism* (London, 1948), pp. 88, 112, 136.
[11]Cf. Rom. 8:10; Gal. 5:25.
[12]Cf. 2 Cor. 5:17; Gal. 6:15.
[13]Cf. Matt. 19:28
[14]Gk. τὰ ἄνω φρονεῖτε (a variation on τὰ ἄνω ζητεῖτε of v. 1) is practically synonymous with φρονεῖν τὰ τοῦ θεοῦ of Mark 8:33, as τὰ ἐπὶ τῆς γῆς (φρονεῖν) is with (φρονεῖν) τὰ τῶν ἀνθρώπων.
[15]Cf. Eph. 1:20-21.
[16]Cf. 2 Cor. 5:16.

3 For, you see, you *died* in relation to that old order.[17] The idea is so strange that it must be repeated and emphasized. You *died*, I say, and as for the new life on which you have entered, its true abode is where Christ himself is. "When our Forerunner triumphed, 'He bore up with Him into safety the spiritual life of all His people.' "[18]

There is a widespread belief in many cultures that a person's life is bound up with some external object, some "life-token."[19] This object, sometimes actually referred to as the person's "life," is safely hidden away in the belief that, so long as it is preserved intact, no harm can befall that person. There is no such idea in Paul's mind here; yet the belief could serve as a parable of the truth he expresses. The believer's life is safely "hidden away" with Christ. Its well-being depends on his. His people's true life is an extension of that indissoluble life which is his in the Father's presence.

Not only is their life hidden "with Christ" but "with Christ in God"—"a double rampart, all divine."[20] The expression "in God" is unusual in the Pauline corpus, in comparison with "in Christ" or "in the Lord." The Thessalonian church is said to have its being "in God the Father" as well as in "the Lord Jesus Christ" (1 Thess. 1:1; 2 Thess. 1:1). A closer parallel to the present wording appears in Eph. 3:9, where the "mystery" now received and proclaimed by Paul is said to have been "hidden from eternity in God." The divine purpose enshrined in that mystery is said to have been conceived eternally in Christ (Eph. 1:4, 9-10); it is, indeed, embodied in Christ (Col. 2:2). So the life of believers is hidden "with Christ" because they died with him and have been raised with him: it is hidden "in God" because Christ himself has his being in God[21] and therefore those who belong to him have their being there too.[22]

4 "You know your life to be safely hidden with Christ," says Paul, "although in the eyes of the world you are, spiritually speaking, without

[17]Cf. Rom. 6:6-11.
[18]E. K. Simpson, *The Pastoral Epistles* (London, 1954), p. 63, quoting from an unspecified source.
[19]E. S. Hartland in *ERE* 8 (Edinburgh, 1915), 44-57 (*s.v.* "Life-Token"); cf. C. M. Draper, " 'Your Life is Hid with Christ in God' (Colossians iii.3)," *ExT* 27 (1915-16), 427.
[20]H. C. G. Moule, *Colossian Studies* (London, 1898), p. 190.
[21]Cf. John 1:18, ὁ ὢν εἰς τὸν κόλπον τοῦ πατρός.
[22]Cf. J. S. Stewart, *A Man in Christ* (London, 1935), pp. 171-72. Deissmann says, "The faith of Paul is then the union with God which is established in fellowship with Christ," and he describes Christians as ἔνθεοι ἐν Χριστῷ Ἰησοῦ (*Paul*, E.T. [London, 1926], pp. 164-65). But his endeavor to illustrate this spiritual relationship by means of a geometrical diagram (p. 298) does not really help to understand Paul's thought.

visible means of support. But when Christ, the true life of all his people, is manifested in his *parousia*, then you who share his life will share his glorious epiphany."[23]

"Christ your life." The apostle who could say, "For to me to live is Christ" (Phil. 1:21), does not think of this as something which is true of himself alone. Christ is the life of all those who are united to him by faith, members of his body.

Nor is he their life only; because he is their life, he is also their hope. The indwelling Christ who is at present their hope of glory[24] is the Christ whose manifestation at his *parousia* will bring them the realization of that glory. The inward revelation of his saving glory which has come home to them already is the earnest of a fuller revelation yet to come, the grand consummation of the union between Christ and his people. "The same man whose daily thanksgiving was that 'it pleased God to reveal His Son' in him could also hope for a day 'when Christ, who is our life, shall appear.' "[25] That is the day for which, as Paul says in another letter, the whole creation looks with eager expectation.[26] Hitherto it is fast held in the bondage of frustration: as the Preacher saw, "Vanity" is written large over it.[27] But what the Preacher did not see was that creation would one day be liberated from the frustrating cycle of change and decay, and participate in the glorious liberty of the children of God.[28] That glorious liberty will be manifested on the day of their revelation, for the revelation of the Son of God in glory carries with it the revelation of the sons and daughters of God in that same glory[29]—the glory which is his by right and theirs by the grace which unites them with him.

A later NT writer voices the same thought in his own characteristic phraseology: "Beloved, we are God's children now; what we shall be has not yet been manifested, but we know that, when he is manifested, we shall be like him, because we shall see him as he is" (1 John 3:2). To share in the revealed glory of Christ is to attain his likeness, as indeed Paul

---

[23]Whereas παρουσία is used in the Pauline *homologoumena* (cf. 1 Cor. 15:23; 1 Thess. 2:19; 3:13; 4:15; 5:23; 2 Thess. 2:1), it is replaced by ἐπιφάνεια in the Pastorals (1 Tim. 6:14; 2 Tim. 1:10; 4:1, 8; Tit. 2:13); the two words are combined in 2 Thess. 2:8 (τῇ ἐπιφανείᾳ τῆς παρουσίας αὐτοῦ, "by the dawning of his *parousia*").
[24]Cf. Col. 1:27.
[25]J. S. Stewart, *A Man in Christ*, p. 202.
[26]Rom. 8:19.
[27]Eccl. 1:2, etc. Paul may have had Ecclesiastes (LXX) in mind when he describes the creation as subjected to ματαιότης (Rom. 8:20).
[28]Rom. 8:21.
[29]Rom. 8:19, τὴν ἀποκάλυψιν τῶν υἱῶν τοῦ θεοῦ.

indicates again when he tells the church in Philippi that its constitution is laid up in heaven, from which "we await a Savior, the Lord Jesus Christ, who will change our lowly body to be like his glorious body" (Phil. 3:20-21). And what is this but the fullness of Christian sanctification? Here and now, according to the teaching of other Pauline letters, it is the province of the Holy Spirit within the people of Christ to reproduce his likeness increasingly in their lives,[30] but the consummation of this sanctifying work awaits the day of Christ.[31] Indeed, the presence and activity of the Spirit here and now is their guarantee of the heritage which is reserved for believers against that day.[32] In this letter, as we have seen, this function is discharged by the indwelling Christ, his people's "hope of glory." The day of revelation and glory will but bring to complete and public fruition something that is already true—that Christians have died with Christ and been raised with him, and in him are partakers of the age to come.[33]

When the day of revelation and glory will dawn Paul does not suggest. Its date is unknown; its advent is certain. This consummating act in the series of saving events is assured by those which have already been accomplished. Those whom God foreknew "he also predestined to be conformed to the image of his Son, in order that he might be the firstborn among many brethren; and those whom he predestined he also called; and those whom he called he also justified: and those whom he justified he also glorified" (Rom. 8:29-30). The day of glory may be future but (as the past tense of the verb "glorified" implies)[34] its arrival is as sure as if it were already here. For those whose faith is placed in him, Christ is already their glory, as certainly as he is their hope: the hope and the glory are comprehended in the life which all his people have in him.

With this reaffirmation of the Christian hope, the apostle concludes the more strictly theological section of the letter.

V. THE CHRISTIAN LIFE (3:5 – 4:6)

The teaching contained in the preceding sections of the letter is now applied

---

[30]Cf. 2 Cor. 3:18.
[31]Cf. 1 Thess. 5:23.
[32]Cf. Eph. 1:14, where the Spirit is the ἀρραβὼν τῆς κληρονομίας ἡμῶν.
[33]Cf. C. H. Dodd, *The Apostolic Preaching and its Developments* (London, 1936), pp. 147-48; W. D. Davies, *Paul and Rabbinic Judaism*, pp. 318-19; O. Cullmann, *Salvation in History*, E.T. (London, 1967), pp. 255-68.
[34]The aorist ἐδόξασεν may be an imitation of the Hebrew prophetic perfect (cf. Jude 14, quoting 1 Enoch 1:9, ἰδοὺ ἦλθεν κύριος).

in detailed practice. As in other Pauline letters, the transition is marked by the conjunction "therefore."[35]

Paul's ethical teaching is evidently cast in forms which were in widespread use among early Christians. These forms may be traced back to the ethical teaching of Jesus himself. But Paul emphasizes the logical connection between theology and practice. He does not inculcate Christian doctrine simply in order that his readers may have a firm intellectual grasp of it; he insists that it must find expression in Christian living.[36] On the other hand, his ethical teaching is never left suspended in air: it is firmly founded on the saving revelation of God in Christ. If his theology is a theology of grace, the practical response to that grace is gratitude—gratitude in action as well as in word.[37]

Here, then, he enunciates general Christian maxims: there are old practices to be abandoned; there is a new way of life to be adopted. The old must be "put off"; the new must be "put on"—a figure of speech which has been associated with the wearing of new garments at one's baptism.[38]

It appears that the church began at an early date to classify its ethical teaching in categories which would be easily taught and remembered, each being introduced by a sort of catchword. The steady increase in the number of believing Gentiles made it desirable that they should receive the elements of Christian ethics in a form which could be readily assimilated.[39] These catechetical forms are recognizable in several NT letters, and their recurrence is not to be accounted for by the dependence of one letter on another but by the indebtedness of all to a common *par-*

---

[35] With νεκρώσατε οὖν here cf. Rom. 12:1 (παρακαλῶ οὖν ὑμᾶς); Eph. 4:1 (παρακαλῶ οὖν ὑμᾶς). Col. 3:5–4:6 sets out the implications for earthly life of the heavenly-mindedness inculcated in Col. 3:1-4; cf. A. T. Lincoln, *Paradise Now and Not Yet* (Cambridge, 1981), pp. 130-31.

[36] Cf. John 13:17, "If you know these things, blessed are you if you do them."

[37] "In the New Testament religion is grace, and ethics is gratitude" (T. Erskine, *Letters* [Edinburgh, 1877], p. 16).

[38] According to Clement of Alexandria, the βαπτιζόμενοι put off their old garments and put on new ones (*Pedagogue* 2.6.23.4).

[39] Cf. A. Seeberg, *Der Katechismus der Urchristenheit* (Leipzig, 1903); G. Klein, *Der älteste christliche Katechismus* (Berlin, 1909); P. Carrington, *The Primitive Christian Catechism* (Cambridge, 1940); A. M. Hunter, *Paul and his Predecessors* (London, ²1961), pp. 52-57; E. G. Selwyn, *The First Epistle of St. Peter* (London, 1946), Essay II (pp. 363-466); C. H. Dodd, *Gospel and Law* (Cambridge, 1951); G. B. Caird, *The Apostolic Age* (London, 1955), pp. 109-13; R. Schnackenburg, *The Moral Teaching of the New Testament,* E.T. (New York, 1965); L. Nieder, *Die Motive der religiös-sittlichen Paränese in den paulinischen Gemeindebriefen* (München, 1956).

adosis of practical teaching.[40] Of these forms with their distinctive catch-words four are discernible here: they consist of the paragraphs which expand the injunctions to "put off" (Col. 3:5-11); "put on" (Col. 3:12-17); "be subject" (Col. 3:18–4:1); and "watch and pray" (Col. 4:2-6).

1. "PUT OFF" (3:5-11)

5 *Therefore, treat your[41] earthly members as dead—fornication, impurity, passion, evil desire,[42] and covetousness, which is idolatry.*
6 *It is because of these things[43] that the wrath of God is coming [on the disobedient].[44]*
7 *Formerly you also behaved in that way, when you lived in such practices;*
8 *but now you also must put them all off—wrath, anger, malice. Get slander and foul language right out of your mouths.[45]*
9 *Tell no lies one to another, since you have put off the "old man" with his actions*
10 *and have put on the "new man," who is being renewed after his Creator's image so as to attain true knowledge.*
11 *Here there is no[46] Greek and Jew, circumcision and uncircumcision, barbarian, Scythian, slave or[47] free; but Christ is all[48] and in all.*

Now that you are new men and women in Christ, says the apostle, live like new men and women. You have said good-bye to your old life; therefore have done with all those things that were characteristic of it. You have died with Christ; act and speak and think therefore so as to make it plain that this "death" is no mere figure of speech, but a real event which

[40]Cf. Rom. 12:1–13:14; Gal. 5:13-26; Eph. 4:17–6:18; 1 Thess. 4:1-12; Heb. 13:1-17; Jas. 1:2–4:12; 1 Pet. 1:13–4:11.
[41]ὑμῶν is inserted after τὰ μέλη by ℵ² A C³ D F G H and the majority of cursives; it is omitted by P⁴⁶ ℵ* B C* Ψ and a number of cursives (either way, "your members" is meant).
[42]Gk. ἐπιθυμίαν κακήν (κακήν is omitted by P⁴⁶ F G).
[43]Gk. δι᾽ ἅ (δι᾽ ὅ is read by C* *vid* D* F G; διὰ ταῦτα γάρ by P⁴⁶).
[44]Lit., "on the sons of disobedience," ἐπὶ τοὺς υἱοὺς τῆς ἀπειθείας, which is omitted by P⁴⁶ B D* *vid* lat^b co^sa Clem Cypr Ambst. The clause was probably added at an early stage in the transmission under the influence of Eph. 5:6.
[45]F G lat^vet vg.codd co Ambst add μὴ ἐκπορευέσθω (from Eph. 4:29).
[46]D* F G 629 lat^vet vg.codd Hil Ambr insert ἄρσεν καὶ θῆλυ (from Gal. 3:28).
[47]The asyndeton βάρβαρος, Σκύθης, δοῦλος, ἐλεύθερος is broken by the insertion of καί before ἐλεύθερος in A D* F G 629.
[48]Gk. τὰ πάντα (τά is omitted in ℵ* A C and a few cursives).

has severed the links which bound you to the dominion of sin. In short, be (in actual practice) what you now are (by a divine act).

There is a true Christian *askēsis,* which is quite different from the *askēsis* which the Colossians were being urged to undertake. The Christian *askēsis* consists in the renunciation of all sinful propensities and pursuits, so that the new nature, divinely implanted within, may find outward expression in the fair fruit of a holy life.

5 While the first of the four ethical paragraphs contains the catchword "put off" (v. 8), the paragraph is introduced by the equivalent injunction "put to death" or, as it might be rendered, "reckon as dead."[49] "Reckon as dead those 'members' of yours which partake of the nature of the old earthly life." Paul is not talking here of the actual members of the human body, nor is he expressing himself in quite the sense intended by Jesus when he said that the offending hand or foot should be cut off or the offending eye plucked out, if entrance into life could not otherwise be gained. This seems plain from the apposition of the noun "members" with the following list of vices.[50] Yet this apposition is so abrupt that attempts have been made to ease the difficulty of the construction by expedients which nevertheless are unconvincing. Thus Lightfoot puts a heavy stop after "treat your earthly members as dead" and regards the following nouns ("fornication, impurity, . . .") as "prospective accusatives" governed by some such verb as "put off" in v. 8.[51] On this showing, Paul intended to make the accusatives directly dependent on the verb "put off," but before he reached the verb he introduced intervening clauses which led to a change in the structure of the sentence. To be sure, such breaches of construction (*anacolutha*) are by no means uncommon in Paul's epistolary style; but in

---

[49]Gk. νεκρώσατε. This is the only NT instance of νεκρόω in this sense (it is used in the perfect participle passive νενεκρωμένος in Rom. 4:19 and Heb. 11:12 to describe Abraham's body in old age, "as good as dead"). In Rom. 6:11 λογίζεσθε . . . νεκρούς ("reckon as dead") is synonymous with νεκρώσατε here, except that νεκρώσατε is aorist and λογίζεσθε is present (there must be a decisive initial act introducing a settled attitude). Cf. the similar sense of θάνατον in Rom. 7:4; 8:13; elsewhere in the NT this verb has the literal sense "put to death."

[50]G. Bornkamm, following W. Bousset (*Hauptprobleme der Gnosis* [Göttingen, 1907], p. 229, and R. Reitzenstein, *Das iranische Erlösungsmysterium* [Bonn, 1921], p. 161, n. 2), takes the five vices listed here to be the "members" of the old man, making up his essence, in accordance with the Iranian-Gnostic "pentad scheme," as the five virtues of v. 12 are the "members" which make up the essence of the new man ("The Heresy of Colossians," in *Conflict at Colossae,* ed. Francis and Meeks [Missoula, MT, 1975], p. 133).

[51]J. B. Lightfoot, *ad loc.* (p. 211). On this A. S. Peake justly says, "It is true that the apposition of μέλη and the list of sins that follows is strange, but not so strange as to make this very forced construction preferable" (*ad loc.*).

this place, if he had meant to make the accusatives directly dependent on the verb "put off," he would almost certainly have put that verb in front of them.[52] Even less convincing is Charles Masson's expedient: he takes "members" as vocative and interprets the passage thus: "You members [of the body of Christ] are therefore to reckon as dead the things which are on the earth—fornication, impurity, etc."[53]

What we have here is rather an extension of the ordinary sense of "members." Since these people's bodily members had been used as instruments of sin in their former life (cf. Rom. 6:19), they are viewed here as comprehending the various kinds of sin which were committed by their means. In Rom. 7:23 Paul speaks of "the law of sin which dwells in my members"; here he goes farther and practically identifies the members with the sins of which they had once been the instruments.[54] But what he really has in mind is the practices and attitudes to which his readers' bodily activity and strength had been devoted in the old life. Of these he mentions first of all fornication, impurity, passion, evil desire, and covetousness, proceeding from the more overt to the less overt. These things had to be regarded as dead. Since believers have died with Christ, the domination of the old habits and instincts has been broken. But this severance of the old relation by reason of death can equally well be expressed the other way around: if, from one point of view, believers have died to these things, then, from another point of view, these things are dead so far as believers are concerned: they are no longer able to enforce their claims as they once did. So, in Rom. 6:11, Paul exhorts his readers to reckon *themselves* as dead to sin but alive to righteousness, while in Rom. 8:13 he says, "if by the Spirit you put to death the deeds of the body you will live" (the "deeds of the body" being such things as are listed here in Col. 3:5).[55]

It has been said that, in his oscillation between the idea of the Christian's having died with Christ and the idea of his still having to "put

[52]As in Rom. 13:12; Eph. 4:22, 25; cf. Jas. 1:21; 1 Pet. 2:1.
[53]CNT, *ad loc.* Such an absolute use of μέλη in this sense would be tolerable only if their membership in the body of Christ were stressed in the immediate context.
[54]This transition of thought "is easily explained on psychological grounds by the inrush of various associations when a picture-word is being used" (M. Dibelius, *ad loc.*). With this extended use of the word "members" may be compared the use of the word "body" in Rom. 6:6 ("the body of sin"); 7:24 ("this body of death"). According to N. A. Dahl ("Der Epheserbrief und der erste Korintherbrief," in *Abraham unser Vater,* ed. O. Betz, M. Hengel, and P. Schmidt [Leiden/Köln, 1963], p. 72), the vices listed are the members of the "body of flesh" which has been laid aside in baptism. Cf. Col. 2:11, with exposition (pp. 103-04 above).
[55]Cf. Gal. 5:16.

to death" the old bad habits, or to reckon himself as dead, Paul can be charged with inconsistency. "He is working with an abstract theological idea which does not fit in with the facts of life, and in his effort to assert it he is involved in constant trouble."[56] This criticism does less than justice to the reality of the believer's union with Christ and reception of new life in him, which is much more than an "abstract theological idea." The difficulty arises rather from the circumstance that believers, in fact and in conscious experience, exist on two planes so long as mortal life endures: spiritually they already belong to the age to come, while temporally they are involved in this present age; spiritually they are united to Christ at God's right hand, while temporally they live on earth. The impartation of the new nature by Christ does not effect the immediate annihilation of the old hereditary nature; so long as they live in this world, the old nature persists like a dormant force which may spring into activity at any time. Hence the tension, which arises not from any inconsistency between Paul's premises and his recognition of the facts of human life, but from well-known conditions of Christian existence.

The believer is dead to the world with Christ (Col. 2:20; 3:3), having put off the old nature in him (Col. 2:11; 3:9) and been liberated from sin (Rom. 6:6-7, 11, 18, 22); on the other hand, the believer is still in the world in a mortal body and exposed to sinful temptations. Hence this antinomy in the apostle's thought; hence his transition back and forth between the indicative and the imperative:[57] "Be what you are!"[58]

In moving from the outward manifestations of sin to the cravings of the heart—from improper acts to their inner springs—Paul proceeds in the manner of our Lord, who in the Sermon on the Mount traces murder back to the angry thought, and adultery to the lustful glance (Matt. 5:21-22, 27-29). Catalogues of vices were common form among pagan moralists and in the antipagan polemic of Jewish propagandists.[59] Such lists appear repeatedly in Paul's letters (cf. Rom. 1:29-31: 1 Cor. 5:11; 6:9-10; Gal. 5:19-21; Eph. 5:3-4), receiving a special significance from the Christian context in which they are set.

---

[56]E. F. Scott, *ad loc.* (pp. 65-66). In a later work, *Paul's Epistle to the Romans* (London, 1947), Scott showed a truer appreciation of Paul's thought.

[57]In the Johannine literature the indicative predominates.

[58]E.g., in 1 Cor. 5:7-8, Christians are exhorted to be "unleavened" because they *are* "unleavened." Cf. pp. 357-59 (on Eph. 4:22-24).

[59]On such catalogues of vices (and of virtues, as in v. 12) see A. Vögtle, *Die Tugend- und Lasterkataloge im Neuen Testament* (München, 1936); S. Wibbing, *Die Tugend- und Lasterkataloge im Neuen Testament und ihre Traditionsgeschichte* (Berlin, 1959).

Fornication,[60] which appears first in the list of sins, receives the same preeminence among the "works of the flesh" enumerated in Gal. 5:19-21. It means primarily traffic with harlots; it is found also as a near-technical term for sexual relations within prohibited degrees[61] and, more widely, of sexual irregularity in general. In its primary sense it was so common in Graeco-Roman antiquity that, except when carried to excess, it was not regarded as especially reprehensible. Some of Paul's churches had difficulty in abandoning their former pagan tolerance of it; hence his specific warnings against it: "Shun fornication" (1 Cor. 6:18); "abstain from fornication" (1 Thess. 4:3).

Impurity[62] has a wider range of meaning than fornication. It includes the misuse of sex, but is applicable to various forms of moral evil: Demosthenes, for example, uses it of one who, pretending to be a man's friend, commits perjury to do him an injury.[63]

The word translated "passion" covers a variety of emotion and affection, but when it appears in this kind of context it denotes "dishonorable passions,"[64] as it is put explicitly in Rom. 1:26. So also the word translated "desire" denotes strong desire whether good or bad, but here it is expressly qualified as "evil." (Even if the adjective be omitted, as it is in some textual witnesses, the context would be sufficient to indicate that evil desire is meant, which indeed is the usual significance of the word in Paul's writings.)[65]

The climax of the present list is covetousness, which is equated with idolatry, as in Eph. 5:5.[66] Covetousness is idolatry because it involves

---

[60]Gk. πορνεία, from πόρνη ("harlot").

[61]As perhaps in the Matthaean exceptive clauses (Matt. 5:32; 19:9); in the apostolic decree (Acts 15:20, 29; 21:25); and in 1 Cor. 5:1.

[62]Gk. ἀκαθαρσία, which comes second among the "works of the flesh" in Gal. 5:19. Cf. Rom. 1:24; 6:19; Eph. 4:19; 5:2; 1 Thess. 4:17.

[63]Demosthenes, *Against Midias* 119. Cf. 1 Thess. 2:3, where ἀκαθαρσία has been thought by some to denote more general lack of integrity.

[64]Gk. πάθη ἀτιμίας. Cf. Rom. 7:5, τὰ παθήματα τῶν ἁμαρτιῶν.

[65]See p. 139, n. 42. For a better sense of ἐπιθυμία see Phil. 1:23 (of Paul's desire to depart this life and be with Christ); 1 Thess. 2:17 (of the writers' longing to see their friends again). The word is closely associated with πάθος (as here) in 1 Thess. 4:5, μὴ ἐν πάθει ἐπιθυμίας.

[66]The word (πλεονεξία) denotes not merely the desire to possess more than one has, but more than one ought to have, especially that which belongs to someone else. This inordinate desire can become the ruling passion of a person's life, to the point where it does indeed become εἰδωλολατρεία. In Mark 7:22 it is included, along with fornication, adultery, murder, and the like, among the "evil things"

the setting of one's affections on earthly things and not on things above, and therefore the putting of some other object of desire in the place which God should occupy in his people's hearts. So, in Phil. 3:19-20, the contrast is pointed between those whose minds are "set on earthly things" and those whose citizenship is in heaven. The exceeding sinfulness of covetousness was revealed to Paul, according to Rom. 7:7-13, when he became aware of the commandment "Thou shalt not covet" (and even if that passage is not truly autobiographical, the validity of his argument is not affected). The sins which precede covetousness in the catalogue appear regularly in such lists, and certainly they were sins against which converts from paganism needed to be put on their guard; but covetousness is the more dangerous because it may assume so many respectable forms.

6 As Paul emphasizes elsewhere, and above all in the great arraignment of the pagan world in Rom. 1:18-32, these vices incur divine retribution.[67] God has written his decree against them not only in the law as Israel received it, but in the conscience and constitution of men and women, so that it cannot be violated with impunity. The retribution manifests itself in the inevitable consequences incurred by those who freely choose a course of life that sets the Creator's law at nought. The textually doubtful phrase "on the disobedient" (lit., "on the sons of disobedience"),[68] which may have been imported from Eph. 5:6, denotes those whose lives are characterized by defiance of the law of God and consequent liability to his wrath; the opposite idea is conveyed by the phrase "obedient children" (lit., "children of obedience") in 1 Pet. 1:14.[69]

7 You yourselves used to practice these vices,[70] Paul reminds the

---

which come from within the human heart and convey real defilement. It is closely associated with πορνεία in 1 Cor. 5:10-11; 6:9-10, and with ἀκαθαρσία in Eph. 4:19; 5:3. In 1 Thess. 4:6 πλεονεκτέω apparently denotes illicit designs on the womenfolk of someone else's household.

[67] Gk. ὀργή. On the divine ὀργή in the NT see G. Stählin, *TDNT* 5, pp. 422-47 (s.v. ὀργή); cf. also commentaries on Romans by C. E. B. Cranfield (pp. 108-12) and E. Käsemann (pp. 37-38).

[68] The locution υἱοὶ τῆς ἀπειθείας (cf. Eph. 2:2; 5:6) is probably a Hebraism (like τέκνα . . . ὀργῆς in Eph. 2:3). Deissmann (*Bible Studies,* E.T. [Edinburgh, ²1909], pp. 163-66) is unwilling to call such expressions Hebraisms pure and simple, preferring to regard them as "analogical formations" to similar Hebrew phrases which are rendered literally in the LXX (the distinction does not amount to much).

[69] Gk. τέκνα ὑπακοῆς.

[70] Gk. ἐν οἷς καὶ ὑμεῖς περιεπατήσατέ ποτε. If the phrase ἐπὶ τοὺς υἱοὺς τῆς ἀπειθείας be retained, ἐν οἷς means "among whom" (masculine); if it be omitted, ἐν οἷς means "in which" (neuter, referring, like δι' ἅ at the beginning of the preceding clause, to the vices listed in v. 5).

Colossians; you too were numbered among "the disobedient." This is not the only place in the NT where a catalogue of pagan vices is immediately followed by a reminder to the readers that not so long ago their own lives were marked by these things.[71] It was largely for this reason that Paul's critics thought him so foolishly impractical in stressing gospel liberty where such people were concerned. Gospel liberty, they thought, might be all very good for Jews and God-fearers who had learned to acknowledge the law of God in their lives, but people so lately weaned from pagan immorality ought to be subjected first to a period of probation before they could be properly recognized as full members of the church. Paul's policy was different: pagans though these people had once been, they had now received a new nature; they were in Christ and Christ lived in them. If they accepted the logic of this new situation, if they looked on themselves as dead to their former desires and alive to God in Christ, then the Christ-life now coming to maturity within them would manifest itself in a new pattern of behavior.

8 So, he tells them, put off[72] all those old habits, just as you would discard an outworn suit of clothes which no longer fitted you. And a repulsive collection of habits they are, to be sure—anger, quick temper,[73] malice,[74] and the language which accompanies these things, slander and

[71]Cf. 1 Cor. 6:9-11; also Rom. 6:19-21; Tit. 3:3; 1 Pet. 4:1-5.
[72]Gk. ἀπόθεσθε (cf. Rom. 13:12; Eph. 4:22, 25; Heb. 12:1; Jas. 1:21; 1 Pet. 2:1 for this ethical use; the literal use in reference to clothes is found in Acts 7:58). For the representation of behavior or character as a garment cf. Job 29:14; Ps. 35:26; 109:29; 132:9; Isa. 11:5; 59:17; Rom. 13:12, 14; 1 Thess. 5:8. The idea is extended to the putting off of the old (terrestrial) body and the putting on of a new (celestial) one in 1 Cor. 15:53-54; 2 Cor. 5:2-4.
[73]Gk. ὀργή, θυμός. The two terms overlap in meaning, and both can be used in a nobler and a less noble sense. For ὀργή in the sense of divine retribution see v. 6 above, but human beings are urged to be "slow to anger, because human anger does not produce divine righteousness" (Jas. 1:19-20). In Rom. 2:8 θυμός is used along with ὀργή of divine retribution against those who "obey wickedness"; but elsewhere Paul mentions it as something which Christians should avoid. For Plato θυμός is the "spirited" element in the human soul, which needs to be controlled by the rational element, much as a sheepdog needs to be controlled by the shepherd (*Republic* 4.440D). Aristotle says that uncontrolled θυμός "does indeed seem to hear the voice of reason, but to hear it wrongly, like impetuous servants who rush off before hearing all that is said, or like dogs which start barking before waiting to see if one is a friend or not" (*Nicomachean Ethics* 7.6.1.1149a3). To θυμός as to ὀργή the injunction of Eph. 4:26 applies: "Be angry (ὀργίζεσθε) without sinning" (see p. 361 below). On the Stoic definition of ὀργή see H. Kleinknecht, *TDNT* 5, p. 384, n. 6 (*s.v.* ὀργή).
[74]Gk. κακία, the attitude that wishes or does harm to another.

foul talk.[75] Get rid of them all; do not let your mouths be polluted with the scurrilous and filthy language that used to flow readily from them.

9 Another thing that polluted your mouths was lying: you used to tell lies as though it were the natural thing to do; have done with such conduct.[76] Your tongues were given you to speak the truth; be known as men and women of your word.

You see, he goes on, you have stripped off[77] the "old man" that you used to be, together with the practices in which he loved to indulge.[78] This was emphasized in Col. 2:11-22, where their baptism was said to be, in effect, not the removal of an insignificant scrap of bodily tissue, as the old circumcision was, but the stripping off of the whole "body of flesh"— the renunciation of the sinful nature in its entirety. This they had already done, in principle at least, and by the same token they had put on a new nature.[79] But what was that new nature? It was the "new man" who was being continually renewed[80] with a view to their progressive increase in true knowledge[81]—renewed in conformity with the Creator's image.

10 When Paul speaks of the renewal of the new man, his intention is much the same as when he says in 2 Cor. 4:16, "though our outer nature is wasting away, our inner nature is being renewed every day." The life and power of Christ within is thus being constantly renewed, as the Christlikeness is being reproduced more and more in the believer's life.[82]

---

[75]Gk. βλασφημία, αἰσχρολογία (the latter, meaning obscene or abusive speech, occurs here only in the NT).

[76]The present imperative (μὴ ψεύδεσθε) implies "Don't go on telling lies." On the construction of prohibitions cf. C. F. D. Moule, *IBNTG*, pp. 20-21.

[77]Gk. ἀπεκδυσάμενοι (cf. Col. 2:15 and, for the noun ἀπέκδυσις, Col. 2:11). This verb is more forceful than ἀποτίθεμαι (v. 8); its sense is conveyed in different metaphors in Rom. 6:6 (ὁ παλαιὸς ἡμῶν ἄνθρωπος συνεσταυρώθη); 8:12 (ὀφειλέται ἐσμὲν οὐ τῇ σαρκί, τοῦ κατὰ σάρκα ζῆν). Cf. Eph. 4:23 (p. 358).

[78]It was this passage that suggested to John Bunyan his picture of the sinister character of "Adam the First," who "dwelt in the town of Deceit," whose invitation to go with him and be his servant and son-in-law Faithful was "somewhat inclinable" to accept, until he noticed the words inscribed on his forehead: "Put off the old man with his deeds" (*The Pilgrim's Progress*, Part 1).

[79]Perhaps the Colossian heresy made some play with the concept of the new man. With the use of ἐνδύομαι ("put on") W. L. Knox compares GenR 50.2 (on Gen. 19:1), where the *men* of Gen. 18:16 are said to "put on" *angels* (*St. Paul and the Church of the Gentiles* [Cambridge, 1939], p. 173 n.).

[80]The participle (ἀνακαινούμενον) is in the present tense. Cf. Eph. 4:23, "be renewed (ἀνανεοῦσθαι) in the spirit of your mind"; Rom. 12:2, "be transformed (μεταμορφοῦσθε) by the renewal (ἀνακαίνωσις) of your mind."

[81]Gk. εἰς ἐπίγνωσιν. Cf. Col. 1:9 (p. 46, n. 30).

[82]Cf. 2 Cor. 3:18.

146

In the phrase "after his Creator's image" it is impossible to miss the allusion to Gen. 1:27, where the first Adam is said to have been created by God "in his own image."[83] But the first Adam is now seen as the "old man" who must be discarded, in order that the believer may put on the new man, the "last Adam." Nor is there any doubt about the identity of the new man. Paul had already told the Corinthians that, as "the first man Adam became a living being" (Gen. 2:7), so "the last Adam became a life-giving spirit . . . the first man was from the earth, a man of dust; the second man is from heaven" . . . and "just as we have borne the image of the man of dust, we shall also bear the image of the man of heaven" (1 Cor. 15:45-49).[84] The "last Adam" or "new man," that is to say, is effectively Christ. So, in Gal. 3:27, instead of telling his readers (as here) that they have put on the "new man," Paul says directly, "as many of you as were baptized into Christ have put on Christ."[85] To "put on Christ" is the necessary corollary of being "in Christ."

The conception of Christ as the Second Man, the last Adam, head of a new creation as the first Adam was of the old creation, is thoroughly biblical, and there is no need to look for its sources outside the biblical tradition. The age to come is pictured as a new creation in the OT[86] and

---

[83]Cf. Col. 1:15 (pp. 57-58, nn. 84-88). Lightfoot (ad loc.) quotes from Philo (On the Formation of the World 6), where the word (λόγος) of God is said to be "the archetypal exemplar, the 'form' of 'forms' " (ἰδέα τῶν ἰδεῶν), and the first man is described as the "image of the image" (εἰκὼν εἰκόνος). The phrase "his Creator" (τοῦ κτίσαντος αὐτόν) does not imply that Christ personally is a created being, although he cannot be dissociated from the "new man" whom believers have "put on"; the new man who is created is the new personality that each believer becomes on being reborn as a member of the new humanity or new creation (2 Cor. 5:17; Gal. 6:15). Cf. Eph. 4:24, "put on the new man (καινός, not νέος as here), who has been created according to God in true righteousness and holiness." Cf. Ignatius, Eph. 20:1, for an explicit mention of "the new (καινός) man Jesus Christ"; also Ep. Barn. 16:8, where believers "have become new (καινοί), being created again from the beginning" (ἐξ ἀρχῆς), and Ep. Diog. 2:1, where Diognetus "has become as it were a new man from the beginning" (ὥσπερ ἐξ ἀρχῆς καινὸς ἄνθρωπος).

[84]For φορέσομεν ("we shall bear") P[46] and the majority of witnesses read φορέσωμεν ("let us bear"). C. H. Dodd suggests that Paul's "doctrine of the heavenly Man, or Second Adam, has behind it the primitive 'Son of Man' Christology. The heavenly Man is the 'new man' which the believer assumes in becoming a member of the Church, and the 'perfect man' into which the entire Church grows up" (According to the Scriptures [London, 1953], p. 121).

[85]With this indicative (ἐνεδύσασθε) compare the imperative of Rom. 13:14, "put on (ἐνδύσασθε) the Lord Jesus Christ."

[86]E.g., in Isa. 65:17.

147

postbiblical Judaism,[87] and in that new creation (as in the old) dominion is divinely bestowed on "one like a son of man" (Dan. 7:13). In the NT this "one like a son of man" is identified with Jesus.[88] While the presentation of Jesus as the second Adam in the NT is predominantly Pauline,[89] it is not exclusively so: it may be traced in the Gospels,[90] in Hebrews,[91] and in Revelation.[92] As the first Adam's posterity, by virtue of their solidarity with him in the old creation, are involved in his transgression, so the people of Christ, by virtue of their solidarity with him in the new creation, share the redemption and eternal life which he has procured.[93]

One result of the putting on of the new man is a new knowledge. The "knowledge" *(gnōsis)* that was held out to the Colossians was a distorted and imperfect thing in comparison with the true knowledge accessible to those who, through their union with Christ, had been transformed by the renewing of their minds. This true knowledge was, in short, nothing less than the knowledge of God in Christ, the highest knowledge to which human beings can aspire.

11 It is not only the old sinful habits and attitudes that are done away with in this new creation. The barriers that divided human beings from one another are done away with as well. There were racial barriers, like that between Gentile[94] and Jew; this was also a religious barrier, as the reference to circumcision and uncircumcision indicates. There were cultural barriers, which divided Greeks and barbarians—or, in the circumstances of the first century A.D., divided those outside the pale of Graeco-Roman civilization, like the Scythians, from those within. There were

---

[87]See the exhaustive discussion by W. D. Davies in *Paul and Rabbinic Judaism*, pp. 36-57.

[88]Cf. Mark 13:26; 14:62; Rev. 1:7, 13.

[89]Cf. M. Black, "The Pauline Doctrine of the Second Adam," *SJT* 7 (1954), 170-79.

[90]E.g., in the Synoptic temptation narratives, where a comparison and contrast are implied between the first Adam's failure in the garden and the second Adam's victory in the wilderness (note also the reference to the beasts in Mark 1:13).

[91]Especially in Heb. 2:5-9 where the world dominion promised to Adam in Gen. 1:26-30 is to be exercised by Christ, in terms of Ps. 8:4-6.

[92]E.g., Rev. 12:5; he grants a share in his dominion to faithful confessors (Rev. 2:26-28) and admits them to "the tree of life which is in the paradise of God" (Rev. 2:7).

[93]Cf. Rom. 5:12-19 with J. Murray, *The Imputation of Adam's Sin* (Grand Rapids, 1959). In *Ep. Barn.* 6:11-12 the "new type" of humanity which God has created by the remission of sins receives the fulfilment of the creative promise: "let them have dominion" (Gen. 1:26).

[94]Here, as elsewhere (e.g., Rom. 1:16; 2:9-10; 3:9; 1 Cor. 1:24; 10:32; 12:13; Gal. 3:28), Ἕλλην is used in the wider sense of Gentile as opposed to Jew.

social barriers, such as that between slaves and free persons. Outside the Christian fellowship those barriers stood as high as ever, and there were Christians on the one side and on the other. From the viewpoint of the old order these Christians were classified in terms of their position on this side or that of the barriers. But within the community of the new creation— "in Christ"—these barriers were irrelevant; indeed, they had no existence.

There is a close similarity between this passage and Gal. 3:28, where Paul affirms that for those who have been baptized into Christ and have put on Christ "there is neither Jew nor Greek, there is neither slave nor free, there is no 'male and female'; for you are all one in Christ Jesus." There the choice of antitheses is apparently made so as to assert the abolition of the religious privileges enjoyed in Judaism by a Jew over a Gentile, a slave over a free person, a man over a woman.[95] Here the wording is more general.

As for the obliteration in Christ of the old religious distinction between Jew and Gentile, this was one of the most remarkable achievements of the gospel within a few decades. The wonder of it is especially celebrated in the first three chapters of Ephesians. No iron curtain of the present day presents a more forbidding barrier than did the middle wall of partition which separated Jew from Gentile. As to the Galatians, so now to the Colossians Paul no doubt found it necessary to emphasize the abolition of this distinction in view of elements of the teaching which he was countering in the one situation as in the other. "There is no distinction between Jew and Greek" either in respect of their need of salvation or in respect of the grace of God, bestowed impartially on both; "for God has consigned all to disobedience, that he may have mercy on all" (Rom. 3:22; 10:12; 11:32). Natural and racial idiosyncrasies may survive, but in such a way as to contribute to the living variety of the people of Christ, not so as to create or perpetuate any difference in spiritual status.

Where cultural differences exist, the gospel ignores them. Paul reckoned himself to be debtor "both to Greeks and barbarians, both to the wise and to the foolish" (Rom. 1:14)—that is, to all sorts and conditions of men and women. Greeks divided the human race into two camps— Greeks and barbarians (those whose language was not Greek). As the area of Greek civilization spread, especially after the Roman conquest, when

[95]Cf. F. F. Bruce, *The Epistle to the Galatians* (Grand Rapids/Exeter, 1982), pp. 187-90. In both places W. A. Meeks recognizes a baptismal formula emphasizing the reunification of opposites in Christ ("The Image of the Androgyne: Some Uses of a Symbol in Earliest Christianity," *History of Religions* 13 [1973-74], 165-208, especially 180-83).

"captured Greece took her savage captor captive,"[96] so people like the Romans, who were not Greeks by nationality, came to be included in the wider Graeco-Roman civilization of the Mediterranean world. Outside this area of civilization were the barbarians, and among the barbarians the Scythians had for long been looked on as particularly outlandish. "Scythian" is not set here in antithesis to "barbarian"; it intensifies the concept expressed by "barbarian." Since the Scythian invasion of the Fertile Crescent toward the end of the seventh century B.C.,[97] "Scythian" had been a byword for uncultured barbarism. In the fifth and fourth centuries B.C. Scythian slaves did police duty in Athens, and Scythian policemen are figures of fun in Attic comedy because of their uncouth ways and speech.[98] But the gospel overrides cultural frontiers; they have no place in the Christian church.

The same is true of the distinction between slave and free. For Greeks and Romans alike, a slave in law was not a person but a piece of property. Aristotle could define a slave as "a living tool, as a tool is an inanimate slave."[99] But within the believing community slaves as much as free persons were brothers and sisters "for whom Christ died."[100] Paul did something revolutionary when he sent Onesimus back to his former owner Philemon "no longer as a slave, but better than a slave—a dear brother," since to the previous temporal bond between them there was now added the bond which united them "in the Lord" (Philem. 16).[101] Philemon might still receive obedience from Onesimus, but now it would be obedience gladly rendered by one Christian brother to another. The old relationship is transformed by the new. "We might say that the distinction of social function remains but the distinction of class is destroyed—because all are brothers in Christ. It is only when the latter is added to the former that snobbery is produced and ill-feeling is bred between those of different social function."[102] (Similarly, when Paul says in Gal. 3:28 that in Christ "there is no 'male and female,' " he does not mean that the distinctive roles and capacities of man and woman are abolished, but that any inequality between them in religious status or function has been removed.)

Perhaps in this way the gospel made its deepest impression on the pagan world. A slave might be a leader in a Christian church by virtue of

---

[96]*Graecia capta ferum cepit captorem* (Horace, *Epistles* 2.1.156).
[97]Cf. Zeph. 1:2-6; 2:4-6; Jer. 1:14-15; 4:5-31; Herodotus, *History* 1.103-06; E. M. Yamauchi, *Foes from the Northern Frontier* (Grand Rapids, 1982), pp. 63-129.
[98]Cf. Aristophanes, *Lysistrata* 451ff.; *Thesmophoriazusae* 1017ff.
[99]*Nicomachean Ethics* 8.11.6.1161b4.
[100]Cf. Rom. 14:15.
[101]See pp. 216-19.
[102]E. Best, *One Body in Christ,* p. 27.

his spiritual stature and ability, and freeborn members of the church would humbly and gratefully accept his direction.[103] In times of persecution slaves showed that they could face the trial and suffer for their faith as courageously as freeborn Romans. The slave-girl Blandina and her mistress both suffered in the persecution which broke out against the churches of the Rhone valley in A.D. 177, but it was the slave-girl who was the hero of the persecution, impressing friend and foe alike as a "noble athlete" in the contest of martyrdom.[104] In the arena of Carthage in A.D. 202 a profound impression was made on the spectators when the Roman matron Perpetua stood hand-in-hand with her slave Felicitas, as both women faced a common death for a common faith.[105] What real difference could there be for a Christian between bond and free?[106]

Nor has the time gone by when this note needed to be sounded. Our world is crossed and recrossed by barriers of one kind and another, and our life is scarred by the animosities cherished by one side against the other. But in Christ these barriers must come down—iron curtains, color bars, class distinctions, national and cultural divisions, political and sectarian partisanship. It is not difficult to rephrase, in terms of the divisions of modern life, Paul's declaration that "in one Spirit we were all baptized into one body—Jews or Greeks, slaves or free" (1 Cor. 12:13). In the unity of that body there is no room for old cleavages: Christ is all, and in all.[107] The Christ who lives in each of his people is the Christ who binds them together in one. This "restoration of the original image of creation"[108] will yet be universally displayed; but how good and pleasant it is when here and now that day of the revelation of the sons and daughters of God is anticipated and our divided world is confronted with a witness more eloquent than all our preaching and feels constrained to say, as in Tertullian's time, "See how they love one another!"[109]

---

[103]There is evidence that the Roman bishops Pius (c. A.D. 150) and Callistus (217-222) were of servile origin.

[104]Eusebius, *HE* 5.1.17-19, 37-42.

[105]*The Passion of S. Perpetua*, ed. J. A. Robinson (Cambridge, 1891).

[106]Stoic humanitarianism held up the ideal of universal brotherhood in which slaves had equal rights with free persons. And we remember Epictetus. But did even Stoicism produce a Blandina or a Felicitas?

[107]Cf. the "new man" of Eph. 2:15, with E. F. Scott's comment *ad loc.*: "Christ was the Adam of a new type of human beings, among whom nothing was to count but their common participation in his life (cf. Col. 3:11). In him as a centre the race was to be reunited" (*The Epistles of Paul to the Colossians, to Philemon and to the Ephesians* [London, 1930], p. 172).

[108]J. A. T. Robinson, *The Body*, p. 83.

[109]Tertullian, *Apology* 39.7.

2. "PUT ON" (3:12-17)

12 *Therefore, as God's chosen people, holy and dear to him, put on a compassionate heart, kindness, humility, gentleness, patience,*

13 *bearing with one another and forgiving whatever complaint[110] one may have against another. As the Lord[111] forgave you, so do you also forgive.*

14 *And above all these put on love, the perfect bond.[112]*

15 *Let the peace of Christ,[113] to which you were called in one[114] body, be arbiter in your hearts; and be thankful.*

16 *Let the word of Christ[115] dwell in you richly, as you teach and instruct one another in all wisdom, singing with thanksgiving in your hearts to God, in psalms, hymns, and Spirit-inspired songs.[116]*

17 *Whatever you do, in word or in action, do[117] it all in the name of the Lord Jesus,[118] giving thanks through him to God the Father.*

As those who have put on the "new man," the apostle continues, Christians should cultivate and manifest the qualities which are characteristic of him. Those qualities, as one considers them, are seen to be those which were preeminently displayed in the life of Jesus; no wonder, then, that when Paul in another place wishes to commend the whole body of Christian graces, he sums them up by saying, "put on the Lord Jesus Christ" (Rom. 13:14).

[110]Gk. μομφήν ("blame"), for which D* reads the cognate μέμψιν (F G read ὀργήν, "wrath").

[111]For κύριος ℵ² C D² Ψ and the majority of cursives read Χριστός, ℵ* lat^{vg.codd} read θεός, 33 reads θεὸς ἐν Χριστῷ (under the influence of Eph. 4:32). κύριος is attested by a wide spread of text types, represented by P^{46} A B D* F G lat.

[112]Gk. σύνδεσμος τῆς τελειότητος (for the last word Western witnesses, D* F G lat^{vet vg.codd} Ambst, read ἑνότητος, probably under the influence of Eph. 4:3; this reading was favored by Richard Bentley).

[113]For Χριστοῦ ℵ² C² D² Ψ and the majority of cursives read θεοῦ (probably under the influence of Phil. 4:7).

[114]P^{46} B and a few other witnesses omit ἑνί (probably by haplography after ἐν).

[115]For Χριστοῦ ℵ* I 1175 and a few other witnesses read κυρίου, A C* and several other witnesses read θεοῦ.

[116]Gk. ψαλμοῖς, ὕμνοις, ᾠδαῖς πνευματικαῖς, with asyndeton; C³ D² Ψ with the majority of cursives insert καί before both ὕμνοις and ᾠδαῖς (probably under the influence of Eph. 5:19).

[117]The imperative (ποιεῖτε, "do") is not expressed in the Greek text; it is plainly to be understood from the adjective clause ὅ τι ἐὰν ποιῆτε.

[118]Gk. κυρίου Ἰησοῦ, for which A C D* F G read Ἰησοῦ Χριστοῦ and ℵ^{(2)} D² and a few other witnesses read κυρίου Ἰησοῦ Χριστοῦ.

12 Believers in Christ are God's chosen people.[119] As the nation which God chose in OT times "to be a people for his own possession, out of all the peoples that are on the face of the earth," was enjoined to be "careful" to keep his commandments (Deut. 7:6-11) and to be holy, as he was holy (Lev. 11:44, etc.), so men and women of the new creation, his choice souls, whom he has set apart for himself and into whose hearts he has poured his love, should inevitably exhibit something of his nature. Jesus made this point in the Sermon on the Mount when he said that peacemakers would be known as the sons of God, and that members of God's family ought to be compassionate like their heavenly Father (Matt. 5:9; Luke 6:36).[120] So here, and probably by way of echoing the teaching of Jesus, Paul tells his readers to "put on" compassion, kindness, humility, gentleness, and patience—graces that were perfectly blended in their Master's character and conduct.

The "compassionate heart" is literally "bowels of compassion"[121] (because the tender emotions in biblical idiom have their seat in the bowels). From the Greek word for "bowels" is derived a verb which is repeatedly used of Jesus' compassionate reaction to people in need, as when he "had compassion" on the leaderless multitude of Mark 6:34.[122] As for the noun translated "compassion," Paul uses it when he appeals to the Roman Christians "by the mercies of God" (Rom. 12:1)[123] and when, writing to the Corinthians, he calls God "the Father of mercies" (2 Cor. 1:3).[124] Like Father, like children.

"Kindness"[125] (included in the ninefold "fruit of the Spirit" in Gal. 5:22) is also a quality of God. "Taste and see that the LORD is kind," says the psalmist (Ps. 34:8).[126] Jesus taught his hearers to be kind, because God is "kind to the ungrateful and ungenerous," and those who imitate him in this "will be sons of the Most High" (Luke 6:35). His "kindness and severity" are displayed in his dealings with human beings (Rom. 11:22); his kindness is designed to bring them to repentance (Rom. 2:4) and his children are urged to "continue in his kindness" (Rom. 11:22).

---

[119]Gk. ὡς ἐκλεκτοὶ τοῦ θεοῦ, ἅγιοι καὶ ἠγαπημένοι. For the association of election and holiness see Eph. 1:4 (p. 255); 1 Pet. 1:2; for the connection between being chosen by God and loved by God see 1 Thess. 1:4; 2 Thess. 2:13.

[120]Cf. Eph. 4:32; 5:1.

[121]Gk. σπλάγχνα οἰκτιρμοῦ. For the collocation of the two words (in parataxis) cf. Phil. 2:1, σπλάγχνα καὶ οἰκτιρμοί.

[122]Gk. σπλαγχνίζομαι (cf. Mark 8:1; 9:22; Luke 10:33; 15:20).

[123]Gk. διὰ τῶν οἰκτιρμῶν τοῦ θεοῦ.

[124]Gk. ὁ πατὴρ τῶν οἰκτιρμῶν.

[125]Gk. χρηστότης.

[126]Ps. 33:8 LXX, ὅτι χρηστὸς ὁ κύριος (quoted in 1 Pet. 2:3).

True humility (by contrast with the pride that apes humility of which the Colossian heresy made much) was not esteemed as a virtue in pagan antiquity; the word meant "mean-spiritedness."[127] The OT attitude is different: those who would walk with God must humble themselves to do so (Mic. 6:8), because he makes his dwelling by preference with those who are "of a humble and contrite spirit" (Isa. 57:15). Humility is especially fitting for the followers of Jesus, who was "gentle and lowly in heart" (Matt. 11:29),[128] and a community in which this grace is cultivated is likely to be free from the tensions which spring from pride and self-assertiveness.

Gentleness,[129] included (like kindness) in the fruit of the Spirit (Gal. 5:23), is the quality which has traditionally been rendered "meekness." Moses was "very gentle" (Num. 12:3)[130] in the sense that, faced with undeserved criticism, he did not give way to rage but interceded with God for the offenders. "The gentle shall inherit the land" (or "the earth"), according to Ps. 37:11[131]—a saying which is taken over in the Matthaean beatitudes (Matt. 5:5)—the implication being perhaps that the militants will wipe one another out and leave the gentle in possession. Jesus was "gentle" (Matt. 11:29), but was perfectly capable of indignation. Paul entreats his Corinthian friends "by the gentleness and forbearance of Christ" (2 Cor. 10:1),[132] but if the language which follows that entreaty is an expression of gentleness and forbearance, one wonders what he would have said had he been unrestrained by those graces. Yet those graces are evident in his affectionate concern for his converts—a concern matched by his indignation against those who were leading them astray.

Gentleness has much in common with patience,[133] the fifth of the virtues listed here. Patience, too, belongs to the fruit of the Spirit (Gal. 5:22); like compassion and kindness it is a quality of God which should be reproduced in those who bear his image. In the revelation of the divine

---

[127]Cf. Col. 2:18 (p. 118, n. 115). A good example of the pejorative sense of ταπεινοφροσύνη is provided by Josephus, *BJ* 4.494, where it is used of Galba's "meanness" in withholding from the praetorian guards a gift which had been promised them in his name.

[128]Gk. πραΰς εἰμι καὶ ταπεινὸς τῇ καρδίᾳ.

[129]Gk. πραΰτης.

[130]LXX πραΰς σφόδρα (Heb. 'ānāw m"'ōḏ).

[131]LXX Ps. 36:11, where οἱ πραεῖς renders Heb. '"nāwîm.

[132]Gk. διὰ τῆς πραΰτητος καὶ ἐπιεικείας τοῦ Χριστοῦ.

[133]Gk. μακροθυμία (cf. Col. 1:11, p. 48 with n. 38). In the older English versions it is usually rendered "longsuffering"; it implies perseverance under provocation.

name in Exod. 34:6 patience is included along with compassion and mercy. In the NT God shows patience not only toward his chosen people (Luke 18:7) but toward the impenitent also (Rom. 2:4); in his patience he postpones the day of retribution (Rom. 9:22). Love is patient, says Paul (1 Cor. 13:4), and he urges his Christian friends to show patience to one another and to all (Eph. 4:2; 1 Thess. 5:14).

13 Mutual forbearance, mutual tolerance, and mutual forgivingness should mark all their relations with one another.[134] Did not Jesus himself inculcate the principle of unwearying and unceasing forgiveness, until "seventy times seven" (Matt. 18:22)? More than that, had they not received his forgiveness, in far greater measure than they were ever likely to have to emulate in forgiving others? For he taught the lesson of unlimited forgiveness by example and not only by precept. In his teaching, too, he made it clear that those who seek the forgiveness of God must be ready to forgive others.[135] Not that human forgiveness is a work that earns the divine forgiveness—the initiative in forgiveness lies with God—but an unforgiving spirit is an effective barrier to the reception of his forgiveness. So, in the parallel passage in Eph. 4:32, the readers are directed to be kind and tenderhearted to one another, "forgiving one another, just as God in Christ forgave you." In fact, Paul reproduces Jesus' insistence on the close relation between God's forgiveness of us and our forgiveness of others in a way that suggests he may have known the Lord's Prayer.[136]

14 Above all else, Paul adds, put on the grace which binds all the

---

[134]The succession of present participles (ἀνεχόμενοι ἀλλήλων καὶ χαριζόμενοι ἑαυτοῖς . . .) is characteristic of extended ethical injunctions in the NT. The use of the participle in an imperative sense was a Hellenistic development; cf. J. H. Moulton, MHT, I (Edinburgh, 1906), 180-83; D. Daube, "Appended Note: Participle and Imperative in I Peter," in E. G. Selwyn, *The First Epistle of St. Peter* (London, 1946), pp. 467-88; H. G. Meecham, "The Use of the Participle for the Imperative in the New Testament," *ExT* 58 (1946-47), 207-08. Cf. Rom. 12:9-19; 13:11; Eph. 4:2-3; 1 Pet. 2:18; 3:1, 7-9. In ἀλλήλων . . . ἑαυτοῖς an instance of stylistic variation is to be seen. The encroachment of the reflexive on the reciprocal pronoun is a Hellenistic feature (cf. v. 16), as is the encroachment of the third person of the reflexive pronoun on the first and second persons (cf. C. F. D. Moule, *IBNTG*, pp. 119-20).

[135]Cf. Matt. 6:14-15; 18:23-35; Mark 11:25.

[136]Cf. Matt. 6:12 par. Luke 11:4. The Greek verb used there and in the texts cited in n. 135 is ἀφίημι, whereas here (and in Eph. 4:32) it is χαρίζομαι, as in Col. 2:11 (see p. 108-09, nn. 87, 90). For the argument that Paul was acquainted with the Lord's Prayer see E. F. Scott, *ad loc.* (pp. 72-73); A. M. Hunter, *Paul and his Predecessors* (London, ²1961), pp. 50-51; W. D. Davies, *Paul and Rabbinic Judaism* (London, 1948), p. 139.

other graces together, the crowning grace of love.[137] In Gal. 5:6 love is the active expression of justifying faith; in Gal. 5:22 it is the primary fruit of the Spirit; in 1 Cor. 13:13 it is the supreme Christian grace; in Rom. 13:9-10 all the commandments are summed up in one: "You shall love your neighbor as yourself."[138] Love is the fulfilment of the law of God because love does a neighbor nothing but good. In all these places Paul's ethic is directly dependent on the teaching of Jesus, according to whom the whole OT ethic hung on the twin commandments of love to God and love to one's neighbor. God's love in Christ to human beings and their answering love to him are presupposed here as the basis of that mutual love which the readers of the letter are called on to practice. It is by such love that the body of Christ is built up; "love," as Moffatt renders it, "is the link of the perfect life."[139]

15 From love the apostle moves to peace. It is noteworthy that in Eph. 4:3 peace itself is the bond in which the unity of the Spirit is maintained. This is one of the incidental indications that the two letters are the product of the same mind around the same time. If, in the author's mind, the general idea of love and peace was linked with the idea of a unifying bond uniting believers in one common life, manifesting itself in the Christian graces, this would sufficiently account for the similar, if divergent, modes of expression.

"Let the peace of Christ be arbiter[140] in your hearts," he says. When hostile forces have to be kept at bay, the peace of God *garrisons*[141] the believer's heart, as in Phil. 4:7. But here the common life of fellow-members of the body of Christ is in view; when differences threaten to

---

[137]Cf. Eph. 4:3, σύνδεσμος τῆς εἰρήνης. Simplicius (*Epictetus* 208a) says that the Pythagoreans regarded friendship (φιλία) as the σύνδεσμος πασῶν τῶν ἀρετῶν, "the bond of all the virtues." Philo, with a different emphasis, says that "to honor the one God is the most effectual love-charm (φίλτρον), the indissoluble bond (δεσμός) of unifying good will" (*Special Laws* 1.52).

[138]Cf. Gal. 5:14 (similarly quoting Lev. 19:18).

[139]"Love . . . holds Christians together in fellowship under the strain of all common life. Love checks the selfish, hard tempers which keep people apart and thus militate against the maturing of good fellowship. Here τελειότης is the full expression of the divine life in the Community, devoid of bitter words and angry feelings, and freed from the ugly defects of immorality and dishonesty. The argument is a parallel to that of Matthew 5:43-48" (J. Moffatt, *Love in the New Testament* [London, 1929], p. 191).

[140]Gk. βραβεύω (here only in the NT) is the simple verb from which is derived the compound καταβραβεύω, used in Col. 2:18 (see p. 117, n. 111).

[141]Gk. φρουρέω.

spring up among them, the peace of Christ[142] must be accepted as *arbitrator*. If the members are subject to Christ, the peace which he imparts must regulate their relations with one another. It was not to strife but to peace that God called them in the unity of the body of Christ.[143] Peace in this sense figures prominently in the fruit of the Spirit (Gal. 5:22). In a healthy body harmony prevails among the various parts. Christians, having been reconciled to God,[144] enjoying peace with him through Christ,[145] should naturally live at peace with one another.[146] Strife inevitably results when men and women are out of touch with him who is the one source of true peace; but there is no reason why those who have received the peace which Christ established by his death on the cross should have any other than peaceful relations among themselves.

"And be thankful," he adds, for Christian behavior (to repeat what has been said before) can be viewed as the response of gratitude to the grace of God. One of the counts in Paul's indictment of the pagan world in his letter to the Romans is that, "although they knew God, they did not honor him as God or give thanks[147] to him" (Rom. 1:21). If thanksgiving is God's due from all humanity for his gifts of creation and providence, how much more is it his due from those who have received the surpassing gift of his grace?

16 What is meant by the injunction: "Let the word of Christ dwell in you richly"? Does "in you" mean "within you" (as individual Christians) or "among you" (as a Christian community)? Perhaps it would be unwise to rule either alternative out completely, although the collective sense may be uppermost in view of the context. Let there be ample scope for the proclamation of the Christian message and the impartation of Christian teaching in their meetings. Christian teaching must be based on the teaching of Jesus himself; it must be unmistakably "the word of Christ."[148] It

---

[142]Deissmann describes ἡ εἰρήνη τοῦ Χριστοῦ as the "mystical genitive"— the sense of the phrase being "the peace which is yours in union with Christ" (*Paul*, p. 163).

[143]Cf. 1 Cor. 7:15. With the words "you were called in one body" cf. the fuller expression of Eph. 4:4. The church is the community of those whom God has called (cf. 1 Cor. 1:9; 1 Thess. 2:12).

[144]Cf. Col. 1:21-22.

[145]Cf. Rom. 5:1.

[146]Cf. Mark 9:50; 2 Cor. 13:11; 1 Thess. 5:13—and not only with one another but, as far as possible, with everybody (Rom. 12:18).

[147]Gk. εὐχαριστέω, with which cf. εὐχάριστοι γίνεσθε here.

[148]This takes the genitive in ὁ λόγος τοῦ Χριστοῦ to be subjective (the word proceeding from Christ); less probably it might be objective (the word concerning Christ), with which cf. Rom. 10:17, διὰ ῥήματος Χριστοῦ.

would "dwell richly" in their fellowship and in their hearts if they paid heed to what they heard, bowed to its authority, assimilated its lessons, and translated them into daily living.

The punctuation of this sentence is disputed, but it makes better sense if the phrase "in all wisdom" is attached to "teach and instruct" (not to "dwell richly") and the words "in psalms, hymns, and spiritual songs" modify the verb "singing" (and not "teach and instruct").[149]

The Colossian Christians, like those at Rome,[150] should be able to instruct one another;[151] but such instruction should be given wisely and tactfully. If wisdom or tact be absent, the instruction, however well intentioned, could provoke the opposite reaction to that which is designed.

Whatever view is taken of the punctuation or construction of the sentence, the collocation of the two participial clauses (as they are in the Greek text), "teaching and instructing . . ." and "singing . . . ,"[152] suggests that the singing might be a means of mutual edification as well as a vehicle of praise to God. In 1 Cor. 14:26 Paul insists that, when Christians come to their meetings prepared with a psalm or any other spiritual exercise, they must have regard to the essential requirements of general helpfulness and good order. In our present passage, as in the closely similar Eph. 5:19, antiphonal praise or solo singing at church meetings is probably recommended. We recall the younger Pliny's report to the Emperor Trajan (A.D. 111-112) of the way in which Christians in Bithynia met on a fixed day before dawn and "recited an antiphonal hymn to Christ as God";[153] or Tertullian's description eighty or ninety years later of the Christian lovefeast at which, "after water for the hands and lights have been brought in, each is invited to sing to God in the presence of the others from what he knows of the holy scriptures or from his own heart."[154]

It has been asked sometimes if a strict threefold classification of praise is signified in the mention of "psalms, hymns, and spiritual songs." It is unlikely that any sharply demarcated division is intended, although the "psalms" might be drawn from the OT Psalter (which has supplied a chief vehicle for Christian praise from primitive times),[155] the "hymns"

---

[149]So successive editions of Nestle's *Novum Testamentum Graecum* (also the RSV).
[150]Cf. Rom. 15:14 (also Heb. 5:12).
[151]Gk. ἑαυτούς, here in the sense of ἀλλήλους (cf. p. 155, n. 134), not, as in the ARV margin, "teaching and admonishing *yourselves*."
[152]The participles may have imperatival force, as in v. 13 (p. 155, n. 134).
[153]Pliny, *Epistles* 10.96; *quasi deo* should perhaps be rendered "as to a god."
[154]Tertullian, *Apology* 39:18. Cf. p. 381, n. 62.
[155]It is unlikely that the ψαλμοί and ὕμνοι and ᾠδαὶ πνευματικαί should be confined to three types of composition specified in the Hebrew titles to the OT

might be Christian canticles (some of which are reproduced, in whole or in part, in the NT text),[156] and the "spiritual songs" might be unpremeditated words sung "in the Spirit,"[157] voicing holy aspirations.

Plainly, when early Christians came together for worship, they not only realized the presence of Christ in the breaking of the bread but also addressed prayers and praises to him in a manner which tacitly, and at times expressly, acknowledged him to be no less than God. If here the Colossian Christians are encouraged to sing in their hearts *to God,* the parallel Ephesians passage speaks of "singing and making melody in your hearts *to the Lord"* (meaning, presumably, Christ). The voice must express the praise of the heart if the singing is to be really addressed to God. Again, the necessity of a thankful spirit is emphasized, although the phrase rendered "with thanksgiving" might mean "with grace" or "in a state of grace."[158]

Psalter—*mizmōrîm, tᵉhillîm,* and *šîrîm* respectively. Nor should the etymological force of the terms be pressed, as though ψαλμός inevitably meant a song sung to the accompaniment of a stringed instrument (psaltery or lute), the strings of which were plucked by the hand (so Gregory of Nyssa, *On the Titles of the Psalms, PG* 44.493B). While such plucking of the strings is the original sense of ψάλλω (for which cf. Eph. 5:19), the verb is used in the NT with the meaning "sing psalms" (1 Cor. 14:15; Jas. 5:13; also, probably, the quotation from Ps. 18:49 [LXX 17:50] par. 2 Sam. [LXX 2 Kingdoms] 22:50 in Rom. 15:9). Cf. pp. 380-81.

[156]Such as the *Magnificat* (Luke 1:46-55), *Benedictus* (Luke 1:68-79), and *Nunc Dimittis* (Luke 2:29-32), which have been used in Christian praise from the early centuries. Other canticles or portions of canticles have been recognized in the Christ-hymns of Col. 1:15-20; Phil. 2:6-11; and 1 Tim. 3:16, in the baptismal hymn of Eph. 5:14 (see p. 376, n. 43), and in the lyrics of Revelation (where the heavenly choir sings the hymns which are echoed by the church on earth). See R. P. Martin, *Carmen Christi: Philippians ii.5-11* (Cambridge, 1967); "Some Reflections on New Testament Hymns," in *Christ the Lord,* ed. H. H. Rowdon (Leicester, 1982), pp. 37-49; R. Deichgräber, *Gotteshymnus und Christushymnus in der frühen Christenheit* (Göttingen, 1967); J. T. Sanders, *The New Testament Christological Hymns* (Cambridge, 1971); M. Hengel, "Hymn and Christology," *Studia Biblica* 3 = *JSNT Sup.* 3 (Sheffield, 1980), pp. 173-97, reprinted in *Between Jesus and Paul* (London, 1983), pp. 78-96.

[157]"Spirit-inspired," as in the translation above. Cf. 1 Cor. 14:15, ψαλῶ τῷ πνεύματι. Spiritual songs continued to be sung after NT times; cf. the *Song of the Star* (Ignatius, *Eph.* 19:2-3) and the *Odes of Solomon*—not to mention such gnostic compositions as the *Hymn of the Pearl* (Acts of Thomas 108-13) and *Hymn of Christ* (Acts of John 94-96).

[158]In WH the punctuation comes after ἐν [τῇ] χάριτι, as though the meaning were "teaching and instructing one another in psalms and hymns and spiritual songs with grace" (followed by "singing in your hearts to God"). Dibelius (*ad loc.*) deduces from the article in ἐν [τῇ] χάριτι that the phrase means something like "in a state of grace" (in his second edition of 1927 he had opted for the meaning

17 Finally, these general injunctions are summed up in an exhortation of universal scope, covering every aspect of life.

The NT does not contain a detailed code of rules for the Christian. Codes of rules, as Paul explains elsewhere,[159] are suited to the period of immaturity when the children of God are still under guardians; but children who have come to years of responsibility know their father's will without having to be provided with a long list of "Do's" and "Don't's."[160] What the NT does provide is those basic principles of Christian living which may be applied to varying situations of life as they arise. So, after answering the Corinthian Christians' question about the eating of food that has been offered to idols, Paul sums up his advice in the words: "whether you eat or drink, or whatever you do, do all to the glory of God" (1 Cor. 10:31). Phrases current in worship, like "to the glory of God" or (as here) "in the name of the Lord Jesus," were given a practical relevance by being applied to the concerns of ordinary life.

The Christian (whether of the apostolic age or any other generation), when confronted by a moral issue, may not find any explicit word of Christ relating to its particular details. But the question may be asked: "What is the Christian thing to do here? Can I do this without compromising my Christian confession? Can I do it (that is to say) 'in the name of the Lord Jesus'—whose reputation is at stake in the conduct of his known followers? And can I thank God the Father through him[161] for the opportunity of doing this thing?" Even then, the right course of action may not be unambiguously clear, but such questions, honestly faced, will commonly provide surer ethical guidance than special regulations may do. It is often easy to get around special regulations; it is less easy to get around so comprehensive a statement of Christian duty as this verse supplies. In the NT and the OT alike it is insisted that our relation to God embraces and controls the whole of life, and not only those occasions which are sometimes described as "religious" in a narrow sense of the word.

3. "BE SUBJECT" (3:18–4:1)

The Christian duty of mutual deference is inculcated in several of the ethical sections of the NT letters.[162] Thus, in the section of Ephesians

---

"with thanks"). The RSV is probably right in rendering "with thankfulness" (linking εὐχάριστοι in v. 15 and εὐχαριστοῦντες in v. 17). Cf. Heb. 12:28, where χάρις ("thanks") is necessary for the acceptable worship of God "with reverence and awe."

[159] E.g., in Gal. 3:23–4:7.

[160] Like the prohibitions of Col. 2:21.

[161] For giving thanks to God through Christ cf. Rom. 1:8; 7:25; 16:27, and especially Eph. 5:20 (p. 381, n. 64).

[162] Cf. Rom. 12:9-16; Phil. 2:3-4.

which corresponds to Col. 3:18–4:1 the Christian wife's deference to her husband is enjoined as a particular expression of the general duty of submissiveness which all Christians are encouraged to show to one another: "Be subject one to another in the fear of Christ—wives [in particular] to your own husbands, as to the Lord" (Eph. 5:21-22).[163]

Here in Colossians, however, there is a more definite paragraph division between the preceding general instructions ("Put on") and the specific directions for the Christian household. Certainly in Col. 3:18–4:1 the general principles of Christian behavior laid down in the foregoing paragraph (Col. 3:12-17) are applied in the special setting of the Christian home, but the exposition of the theme "be subject" is confined to that setting.

The household *(familia)* was recognized as a stabilizing element in ancient society, and treatises on household administration were common.[164] The household was wider than the nuclear family of the Western world today: it included all who were under the authority of its head. In NT times the head of a household might be a woman, like Lydia of Philippi (Acts 16:15), Chloe of Corinth, who may or may not have been a Christian (1 Cor. 1:11), and Nympha of the Lycus valley (Col. 4:15). But usually the head of the household was a man, who exercised within it the authority of a husband, a father, and a master.[165]

As in society in general, so in the Christian community the household appears to have been the basic unit or cell. Where the family home was of a convenient size, the household could be expanded for certain purposes by the inclusion of fellow-believers who joined its members from time to time to form, with them, the "church" in So-and-so's house.[166] When the head of a household was converted to Christianity, the whole household appears normally to have joined in adhering to the new faith and receiving baptism, but it was not invariably so, and in 1 Cor. 7:12-16 provision was made for tensions which might arise from divided religious allegiance.

In the literary treatment of household administration, codes of domestic behavior were a regular feature. In these the mutual duties of husbands and wives, parents and children, masters and slaves, and so forth were prescribed. The Byzantine anthologist Stobaeus has some very in-

---

[163]See p. 382.
[164]Of such treatises περὶ οἰκονομίας the best known is Xenophon's *Oeconomicus* ("On the duties of domestic life").
[165]In Latin terms he was the *paterfamilias,* exercising *patria potestas.*
[166]Cf. R. J. Banks, *Paul's Idea of Community: The Early House Churches in their Historical Setting* (Exeter/Grand Rapids, 1980).

teresting quotations from ancient authors on these mutual duties.[167] Similar summaries of domestic duties are found here and there in the NT; that in Col. 3:18–4:1 is the earliest extant instance of such a Christian summary. Its relation to summaries given elsewhere in the NT letters suggests that such instruction formed part of a fairly well-defined body of catechesis imparted to converts from early times.[168]

While many of the ethical emphases in these Christian summaries can be paralleled from Jewish and Stoic sources,[169] to say that the addition of such a phrase as "in the Lord" (vv. 18, 20) "Christianizes them in the simplest possible way"[170] is to say everything, for such an addition introduces a difference in kind and not merely in degree. Here is a new and powerful dynamic:

> *This is the famous stone*
> *That turneth all to gold.*[171]

If the Stoic disciple asked why he should behave in a particular way, his teacher would no doubt tell him that it was "fitting" because it was in conformity with nature.[172] When a Christian convert asked the same question, he was told that such behavior was "fitting in the Lord";[173] members of the believing community should live thus for Christ's sake. The added words, simple as they are, transform the whole approach to ethics.

The inclusion of such summaries of domestic responsibilities here

---

[167]Stobaeus, *Anthologies* 4.19, 23-26.
[168]Cf. Eph. 5:22–6:9; 1 Tim. 6:1-2; Tit. 2:1-10; 1 Pet. 2:13–3:7. From the rich bibliography on the subject mention may be made of K. Weidinger, *Die Hausta-feln: Ein Stück urchristlicher Paränese* (Leipzig, 1928); E. G. Selwyn, *The First Epistle of St. Peter*, pp. 419-39; O. J. F. Seitz, "Lists, ethical," *IDB* 3, pp. 137-39; D. Schroeder, "Lists, ethical," *IDB* Sup. Vol., pp. 546-47; P. Stuhlmacher, "Christliche Verantwortung bei Paulus und seinen Schülern," *Ev. Th.* 28 (1968), 165-86; J. E. Crouch, *The Origin and Intention of the Colossian Haustafel* (Göttingen, 1972); W. Schrage, "Zur Ethik der neutestamentlichen Haustafeln," *NTS* 21 (1974-75), 1-22; W. Lillie, "The Pauline House-tables," *ExT* 86 (1974-75), 179-83; D. Lührmann, "Neutestamentliche Haustafeln und antike Ökonomie," *NTS* 27 (1980-81), 83-97; W. Munro, *Authority in Paul and Peter* (Cambridge, 1983).
[169]C. H. Dodd compares Paul's exposition of duties with the social ethics of Hierocles the Stoic (*New Testament Studies* [Manchester, 1953], pp. 116-17).
[170]W. K. L. Clarke, *New Testament Problems* (London, 1929), p. 159.
[171]George Herbert, *The Elixir* (the whole poem is a prayer-commentary on the words "for thy sake").
[172]The Stoic way of life could be summed up as ὁμολογουμένως ζῆν, "to live in harmony (with nature)." Conduct in accordance with nature was καθῆκον, "fitting" (cf. ἃ οὐκ ἀνῆκεν, Eph. 5:4).
[173]Cf. v. 18, ὡς ἀνῆκεν ἐν κυρίῳ.

and in Eph. 5:22–6:9, it has been said, shows "a sense of the values of ordinary family life."[174] That is an understatement. It is in the closest and most familiar relationships of daily living that the reality of one's Christian profession will normally be manifest, if at all.

Luther referred to these domestic codes as the *Haustafeln*, and it has become customary to refer to them in English, in a literal (or over-literal) translation of the German, as the "house tables" or "household tables." They are here divided into three correlative pairs.

(1) Wives and Husbands (3:18-19)

18 *Wives, be subject to your husbands,*[175] *as is fitting in the Lord.*
19 *Husbands, love your wives*[176] *and do not treat them harshly.*

The first of the three pairs deals with the mutual duties of wives and husbands.

18 The family was a long-established social unit, as the church was not. The church was God's new creation, and provided a setting in which the principles of the new creation could be put into practice. In the church, therefore, women had equal status with men and slaves with free persons, just as Gentiles had with Jews. But the structure of the family was already in being, and it was no part of the business of early Christianity to destabilize society, which would have been the effect of radically changing the family structure. That structure, hierarchical as it was, was left unaltered, apart from the introduction of the new principle, "as is fitting in the Lord"—which indeed was to be more revolutionary in its effect than was generally foreseen in the first Christian century. The authority of the husband, father, and master continued to be exercised, but only "as was fitting in the Lord," and it continued to be acknowledged by

---

[174]C. H. Dodd, *New Testament Studies,* p. 81. But there is not such a contrast between the attitude of these two passages and that of 1 Cor. 7:32-34 as Dodd suggests, nor is there any need to account for the change of tone in terms of Paul's "second conversion" or eschatological reorientation. The tone of 1 Cor. 7 is due in large part to the situation in Corinth, and less is said about subordination in 1 Cor. 7 than in the household codes. In 1 Cor. 7 interdependence is stressed (cf. 1 Cor. 11:11).

[175]Gk. τοῖς ἀνδράσιν without genitive of the pronoun; ὑμῶν is supplied after ἀνδράσιν in D* F G, while L and many cursives insert ἰδίοις ("[your] own") before ἀνδράσιν (cf. Eph. 5:22; Tit. 2:5; 1 Pet. 3:1).

[176]Gk. τὰς γυναῖκας without genitive of the pronoun, but ὑμῶν is inserted after γυναῖκας in C² D* F G, while ℵ reads τὰς ἑαυτῶν γυναῖκας and 1175 τὰς γυναῖκας ἑαυτῶν. Cf. Eph. 5:25 (p. 382, n. 71).

the wife, children, and household slaves—similarly, "as was fitting in the Lord."

It is not suggested here or anywhere else in the NT that the woman is naturally or spiritually inferior to the man, or the wife to the husband.[177] The phrase "as is fitting" has a thoroughly Stoic ring about it; but it ceases to be Stoic when it is baptized into Christ by the added words: "in the Lord."[178] When the relation between man and woman, husband and wife, is viewed in the context expressed by these words, the essential dignity of women in general and of wives in particular is placed on a firm foundation.

Paul believed that there was a hierarchical order in creation, and that in this order the man was the "head" of the woman (1 Cor. 11:3).[179] But when he speaks his own language instead of reproducing Christian household codes, he shows himself to be ahead of his time in the liberality with which he insists on equal rights between husbands and wives, especially where their marital relationship is concerned (1 Cor. 7:3-4).

19 The wife's subordination to her husband has as its counterpart the husband's obligation to love his wife. This is not simply a matter of affectionate feeling or sexual attraction; it involves his active and unceasing care for her well-being.[180] The accompanying clause, "and do not treat them harshly,"[181] indicates the meaning of the positive injunction more precisely by prohibiting the opposite attitude and treatment. A husband's

---

[177]Cf. J. Foster, "St. Paul and Women," *ExT* 62 (1950-51), 376-78; G. B. Caird, "Paul and Women's Liberty," *BJRL* 54 (1971-72), 268-81; R. Scroggs, "Paul and the Eschatological Woman," *JAAR* 40 (1972), 283-303; "Paul and the Eschatological Woman: Revisited," *JAAR* 42 (1974), 532-37; W. A. Meeks, "The Image of the Androgyne"; P. K. Jewett, *Man as Male and Female* (Grand Rapids, 1975); S. B. Clark, *Man and Woman in Christ* (Ann Arbor, 1980).

[178]The phrase ἐν κυρίῳ occurs four times in Colossians (cf. v. 20; 4:7, 17); it appears some forty times in the Pauline corpus. For its application to domestic relationships cf. 1 Cor. 7:22, 39; Eph. 6:1; Philem. 16. It sums up the relationship existing among fellow-members of Christ—a relationship which does not supersede earthly relationships but subsumes them and lifts them on to a higher plane. Cf. C. F. D. Moule, *The Origin of Christology* (Cambridge, 1977), pp. 54-63.

[179]The argument for the subordination (ὑποτάσσεσθαι) of wives to husbands is elaborated in Eph. 5:23-24 (see p. 384 with n. 82). Cf. p. 68 with n. 135.

[180]But this sense of "love" does not arise from the bare fact that ἀγαπάω is the verb used: ἀγαπάω can be used of an unworthy or self-regarding love (cf. John 3:19; 2 Tim. 4:10; 2 Pet. 2:15; 1 John 2:15). It is the context that gives fuller meaning to the verb.

[181]Gk. καὶ μὴ πικραίνεσθε πρὸς αὐτάς. Plutarch uses a compound of this verb in his essay *On the Control of Anger* (457a), where he condemns those who "behave harshly to women" (πρὸς γύναια διαπικραίνονται). For the general thought cf. TB *Baba Meṣi'a* 59a: "Rab said, 'One should always be on his guard against wronging his wife, for since her tears are frequent she is quickly hurt.' "

legal authority over his wife was such that she had little hope of redress at law for harsh or unfeeling conduct on his part. But such a situation should not arise in a Christian household: the forbearance and forgiveness which are enjoined in the preceding section of the letter, together with compassion, kindness, humility, gentleness, and patience, forbid a Christian man to be harsh in his treatment of anyone, especially of his own wife.

(2) Children and Parents (3:20-21)

20 *Children, obey your parents in all things, for this is well pleasing in the Lord.*[182]
21 *Fathers, do not irritate*[183] *your children, lest they be disheartened.*

20 Then come the mutual duties of children and parents. Children are enjoined to render complete obedience to their parents, as something which is acceptable or delightful "in the Lord." The RSV rendering, "for this pleases the Lord," is based on a slightly different Greek reading.[184] When obedience "in all things"[185] is laid down, it is a Christian family that is in view: the situation is not contemplated here in which parental orders might be contrary to the law of Christ. In such a situation the law of Christ would have to take precedence even over parental orders, but in a spirit of love, not of defiance, since the law of Christ is the law of love. In the household codes, however, children and parents are bound together "in the Lord" as well as by the ties of natural kinship.

21 If children are exhorted to render obedience, parents, and specifically fathers,[186] are urged not to irritate their children by being so unreasonable in their demands that the children lose heart and come to think that it is useless trying to please their parents. On this Sir Robert Anderson (head of the C.I.D. at Scotland Yard in his day) had some wise remarks to make in a little-known book:

The late Mr. Justice Wills, who combined the heart of a philan-

---

[182]Gk. ἐν κυρίῳ (as in v. 18); τῷ κυρίῳ (dative dependent on εὐάρεστον) is read by 0198 and a number of cursives, including 81.
[183]Gk. ἐρεθίζετε, for which A C D* F G L 0198 and some cursives read παροργίζετε (under the influence of Eph. 6:4).
[184]See n. 182 above.
[185]Gk. κατὰ πάντα (as in v. 22).
[186]Gk. πατέρες may mean "parents" (as in Heb. 11:23), but here the admonition is directed to the head of the household (in v. 20 "parents," translating γονεῖς, definitely includes the mother).

thropist with the brain of a lawyer, used to deplore the ill-advised legislation which so multiplies petty offences that high-spirited lads, without any criminal intention, are caught in the meshes of the criminal law. But the traps laid by modern bye-law legislation are few as compared with the "don'ts" which confront the children of many a home during all their waking hours. And against this it is that the Apostle's "Don't" is aimed: "You fathers, don't irritate your children."

For the children his only precept is "Obey your parents"; let parents see to it that they deserve obedience: and more than this, that they make obedience easy. The law, which for the Christian is summed up in the word "love," is formulated in "thou shalt not" for the lawless and disobedient. And the "thou-shalt-not's" of Sinai have their counterpart in the "don'ts" of the nursery. Grace teaches us to keep His commandments; law warns us not to break them. And it is on this latter principle that children are generally trained. "Don't be naughty" is the nursery version of it. . . .

William Carey . . . wrote to his son: "Remember, a gentleman is the next best character to a Christian, and the Christian includes the gentleman." And if a little of the effort used to teach the children not to be naughty were devoted to training them to be gentlemen and ladies, parents would come nearer to fulfilling the Apostolic precept![187]

Stobaeus follows up a consideration of the duty of children with a collection of passages from ancient authors under the general heading: "How fathers ought to behave to their children." He quotes many sayings to much the same effect as the present household code, including these two from Menander: "A father who is always threatening does not receive much reverence," and "One should correct a child not by hurting him but by persuading him."[188] In the setting of this letter, however, these ethical observations, good as they were in their pagan expression, are given a Christian significance and emphasis, which are made the more explicit in Eph. 6:4 with the appending of the positive injunction: "but bring them up in the nurture and instruction of the Lord."[189]

(3) Slaves and Masters (3:22–4:1)

22 *Slaves, obey your earthly*[190] *masters in all things,*[191] *not with eye-*

---

[187]R. Anderson, *The Entail of the Covenant* (London, 1914), pp. 20-22.
[188]*Anthologies* 4.26.7, 13: πατὴρ δ᾽ ἀπειλῶν οὐκ ἔχει μέγαν φόβον (7) and οὐ λυποῦντα δεῖ / παιδάριον ὀρθοῦν, ἀλλὰ καὶ πείθοντά τι (13).
[189]See pp. 398-99.
[190]Gk. τοῖς κατὰ σάρκα κυρίοις ("your masters according to the flesh").
[191]Gk. κατὰ πάντα (cf. v. 20) is omitted by P⁴⁶ 81 and a few other witnesses.

service,[192] as men-pleasers, but in sincerity of heart, fearing the Lord.[193]

23 *Whatever you do, do it heartily,[194] as for the Lord[195] and not for human beings.*

24 *You should know that it is from the Lord that you will receive the reward you have inherited;[196] for[197] the master whom you serve is Christ.*

25 *He who does wrong will be requited for his wrongdoing; there is no favoritism[198] (with your heavenly master).*

4:1 *Masters, treat your slaves justly and fairly, knowing that you also have a master in heaven.*

22-24 Christian slaves are next addressed. Within the context of a household code household slaves are primarily in view, and slaves in a Christian household at that. But the directions given would be applicable to slaves whose duties were not within the household (slaves employed in agriculture or industry, for example), and to slaves of pagan masters.

Both in this letter and in Ephesians the injunctions to slaves are more extended than those to masters, and are accompanied by special encouragement. This, it has been suggested, is "a reflection of the social structure of these churches"[199] (the implication being that they contained more slaves than masters). That may well be so. On the other hand, it has been pointed out that "the content of the admonitions would certainly be more readily approved by owners than by slaves."[200]

The companion letter to Philemon affords an illuminating com-

---

[192]Gk. ἐν ὀφθαλμοδουλίᾳ (א C Ψ with the majority of cursives read the plural ἐν ὀφθαλμοδουλίαις).

[193]For "the Lord" (τὸν κύριον) P[46] א[2] D[2] and the majority of cursives read "God" (τὸν θεόν).

[194]Gk. ἐκ ψυχῆς, as in Eph. 6:6.

[195]After τῷ κυρίῳ A and a few other witnesses insert δουλεύοντες (under the influence of Eph. 6:7); P[46] B 1739 omit καί before οὐκ ἀνθρώποις.

[196]Gk. τῆς κληρονομίας, after which F G and some other Western witnesses read τοῦ κυρίου ἡμῶν Ἰησοῦ Χριστοῦ, ᾧ, "(the inheritance) of our Lord Jesus Christ, whom (you serve)."

[197]"For" (γάρ) is omitted by the majority of earlier witnesses, but is read by D[2] Ψ and the majority of cursives.

[198]Gk. καὶ οὐκ ἔστιν προσωπολημψία, after which F G I 629 lat[vet] add παρὰ τῷ θεῷ to complete the sense (cf. παρ᾽ αὐτῷ in Eph. 6:9).

[199]A. Deissmann, *Paul,* p. 243. Cf. G. B. Caird, *The Apostolic Age* (London, 1955), p. 103. In the household codes of 1 Peter (2:18–3:8) the instructions to slaves (2:18-25) have no correlative instructions to masters (see W. Munro, *Authority in Paul and Peter,* p. 53).

[200]W. A. Meeks, *The First Urban Christians* (New Haven, 1983), p. 64.

mentary on the mutual responsibilities of slaves and masters within the Christian fellowship, and on the transforming effect of this fellowship on their relationship.[201] The relationship belongs to this present world-order; it is "earthly" (lit., "according to the flesh").[202] In the higher and abiding relationship which is theirs in Christ, believing slaves and masters are brothers. The slave/master relationship might persist in the home and business life: within the church it was swallowed up in the new relationship (cf. Col. 3:11). Paul treats the distinction in status between the slave and the free person as irrelevant in the new order (which perhaps was easier for him than it would have been for one who was enslaved to an earthly master). He sees the advantages of being free rather than enslaved, and the slave who has an opportunity of gaining freedom is encouraged to make use of the opportunity; but if there is no such opportunity, "never mind. . . . For he who was called in the Lord as a slave is a freedman of the Lord; likewise he who was free when called is a slave of Christ" (1 Cor. 7:21-22).[203] If a Christian slave came to be recognized as a leader in the church, he would be entitled to receive due deference from his Christian master.[204] But the Christian slave would not presume on this new relationship or make it an excuse for serving his master less assiduously; on the contrary, he would serve him more faithfully because of this new relationship.

If a Christian slave had an unbelieving master, he would serve him more faithfully now because the reputation of Christ and Christianity was bound up with the quality of his service.[205] Slaves in general might work hard when the master's eye or the foreman's eye was on them;[206] they would slack off as soon as they could get away with it. And why not? They owed their masters nothing. Far more culpable is the attitude of modern "clockwatchers," who have contracted to serve their employer and receive an agreed remuneration for their labor. But Christian slaves—or Christian employees today—have the highest of all motives for faithful

---

[201]See pp. 197-98. But there is no reason to suppose that Paul had Onesimus and Philemon especially in mind in the present passage.

[202]Gk. κατὰ σάρκα, as in Eph. 6:5 (cf. Philem. 16, ἐν σαρκί).

[203]Cf. S. S. Bartchy, ΜΑΛΛΟΝ ΧΡΗΣΑΙ: First-Century Christianity and the Interpretation of I Corinthians 7:21 (Missoula, 1973).

[204]Cf. Col. 3:11 (p. 151 with n. 103).

[205]Cf. 1 Tim. 6:1-2; Tit. 2:9-10; 1 Pet. 2:18-20.

[206]This is the usual interpretation of ὀφθαλμοδουλία ("eye-service"), found in the NT only here and in Eph. 6:6. C. F. D. Moule, however, suggests that the meaning is not "while the master's eye is on you" but "with reference to what the eye can see" (of service performed so as to attract attention), in contrast to ἐκ ψυχῆς ("A Note on ὀφθαλμοδουλία," ExT 59 [1947-48], 250).

and conscientious performance of duty; they are above all else servants of Christ, and will work first and foremost so as to please him.[207] Not fear of an earthly master, but reverence for their heavenly Lord,[208] should be the primary motive with them. This would encourage Christian servants to work eagerly and zestfully even for a master who was harsh, unconscionable, and ungrateful; for they would receive their thanks not from him but from Christ.[209] A rich recompense is the assured heritage of all who work for Christ;[210] and the Christian servant can work for Christ by serving an earthly master in such a way as to "adorn the doctrine of God our Savior in everything" (Tit. 2:10).

25 All believers, according to Paul, must "appear before the judgment seat of Christ, so that each one may receive good or evil, according to what he has done in the body" (2 Cor. 5:10).[211] In the household codes of Colossians and Ephesians these words are applied especially to slaves, with requital for evil emphasized in Colossians and requital for good in Ephesians. It is uncertain why the emphasis here should be on requital for the wrongdoer. It has been suggested that there was unrest at the time among the slaves of Colossae, so that a warning was thought necessary; but there is no substantial evidence for this.[212]

The judgment on disobedience is as certain as the reward for faithfulness. While salvation in the Bible is according to grace, judgment is according to works, whether good or bad, for believers as for unbelievers.

---

[207]Paul sets a contrast in Gal. 1:10 between being a slave of Christ (Χριστοῦ δοῦλος) and pleasing human beings (ἀνθρώποις ἀρέσκειν). With the compound ἀνθρωπάρεσκος (here and in Eph. 6:6; also in LXX Ps. 52 [MT 53]:5; Ps. Sol. 4:7-8, 19) cf. ἀνθρωπαρεσκῆσαι in Ignatius, *Rom.* 2:1.

[208]Gk. φοβούμενοι τὸν κύριον (cf. Eph. 6:5, μετὰ φόβου καὶ τρόμου).

[209]"You should know" (Gk. εἰδότες, participle) in v. 24 (as in the following injunction to masters in 4:1) has been thought to indicate that Paul is invoking a pattern of teaching well known to Christians (cf. J. Munck, *Paul and the Salvation of Mankind*, E.T. [London, 1959], pp. 126-27). Cf. Eph. 6:8-9.

[210]This "reward of the inheritance" (ἀνταπόδοσις τῆς κληρονομίας) is part of the total inheritance of glory laid up for all believers (cf. Gal. 3:18; 4:1-7; Eph. 1:14; 5:5, etc.); here it is brought into close association with the most practical issues of daily life.

[211]In 2 Cor. 5:10 as here the verb rendered "receive" is κομίζομαι (middle voice); here the wrongdoer will (literally) "receive the wrong he has done" (κομίσεται ὃ ἠδίκησεν), as in Eph. 6:8 "whatever good thing each has done, this he will receive (τοῦτο κομίσεται)."

[212]Cf. W. A. Meeks, *The First Urban Christians*, p. 219, n. 80, where he refers to an unpublished Yale dissertation by J. M. Bassler, "The Impartiality of God: Paul's Use of a Theological Axiom" (1979). See p. 219, n. 89 (on Philem. 18) for the suggestion that Onesimus is in view.

It is probably implied that, while the sowing is now, the reaping is here-after—before the tribunal of Christ (as in 2 Cor. 5:10).[213] It may be difficult to understand how one who by grace is blessed with God's salvation in Christ will nevertheless be requited for wrongdoing before the divine tribunal, but it is in accordance with biblical teaching that judgment should "begin with the household of God" (1 Pet. 4:17),[214] and even if the tribunal is a domestic one, for members of the family of God, it is by no means to be contemplated lightly.

Whereas here the statement that there is no favoritism[215] is attached to the admonition to slaves, in Eph. 6:9 it is attached to the admonition to masters. God arbitrates with impartial fairness toward both masters and servants. So in the OT legislation impartiality was prescribed in lawsuits between rich and poor: "you shall not be partial to the poor or defer to the great, but in righteousness shall you judge your neighbor" (Lev. 19:15).

---

[213]Cf. Rom. 14:10-12; 1 Cor. 3:12-17; 4:4-5.

[214]In 1 Pet. 4:17 there is probably an allusion to Ezek. 9:4. Cf. also 1 Cor. 11:29-32; Heb. 10:30-31.

[215]With προσωπολημψία (also in Rom. 2:11; Eph. 6:9; Jas. 2:1) cf. the *nomen agentis* προσωπολήμπτης (Acts 10:34) and the verb προσωπολημπτέω (Jas. 2:9). These compounds are not attested earlier than their NT occurrences; they reflect Heb. *nāśā' pānîm,* "lift (someone's) face," that is, show someone favor, and hence, in a pejorative sense, show favoritism. In the LXX this was literally rendered by πρόσωπον λαμβάνω or a similar phrase (e.g., Lev. 19:15; cf. NT Luke 20:21; Gal. 2:6). While no explanatory phrase accompanies οὐκ ἔστιν προσωπολημψία here, something like παρὰ τῷ θεῷ is implied, as in Rom. 2:11 (οὐ γάρ ἐστιν προσωπολημψία παρὰ τῷ θεῷ); cf. Eph. 6:9, παρ' αὐτῷ.

170

COLOSSIANS 4

1 If slaves like Onesimus have their duties, so do masters like Philemon; they must treat their slaves fairly and justly. They are masters on earth, but they themselves have a Master in heaven: let them treat their servants with the same consideration as they themselves hope to receive at the hands of their heavenly Master. Such consideration is the opposite of the threatening or overbearing attitude which is forbidden in Eph. 6:9. No command is given for the manumission of slaves. Paul does give Philemon a broad hint of what is expected of him with regard to Onesimus, but at the same time he makes it clear that the virtue of such an act lies in its being done voluntarily (Philem. 12-14).

The household codes do not give detailed advice for the complexities of modern industrialism. For that matter, they do not even give detailed advice for critical situations which might arise in the first century between master and slave, when one or both belonged to the Christian fellowship. Had such detailed advice been given, in place of the more general exhortations which are found in the codes, readers of other days would derive less help from them than they do. They embody basic and abiding Christian principles, which can be applied in changing social structures from time to time and from place to place.[1]

The household codes did not set out to abolish or reshape existing social structures, but to christianize them. As far as slavery was concerned, it took a long time for the essential incompatibility of the institution with the ethic of the gospel, or indeed with the biblical doctrine of creation, to be properly assimilated by the general Christian consciousness.[2]

[1]Cf. A. Richardson, *The Biblical Doctrine of Work* (London, 1952), p. 50.
[2]For comparison of the household codes of Colossians and Ephesians, and further observations, see pp. 160-63, 382-84.

4. "WATCH AND PRAY" (4:2-6)

2 *Persevere[3] in prayer; keep alert in it with thanksgiving.[4]*

3 *At the same time, pray also for us, that God may open to us a door for the message, so as to utter[5] the mystery of Christ,[6] on account of which[7] I am a prisoner,*

4 *in order that I may make it known, as I ought to utter it.*

5 *Conduct yourselves in wisdom toward those who are outside, buying up the present opportunity.*

6 *Let your speech be always with grace, seasoned with salt, that you may know how to answer each one.*

2 As was evident in the introductory prayer (Col. 1:3), prayer and thanksgiving can never be dissociated from each other in the Christian life. The remembrance of former mercies not only produces spontaneous praise and worship; it is also a powerful incentive to renewed believing prayer. Our Lord's words to his disciples, "Keep awake, and pray not to fail in the test" (Mark 14:38 par.), had special relevance to the trial of faith which faced them in the immediate future, but they have a message for his people at all times. He taught his hearers that they "ought always to pray and not lose heart" (Luke 18:1).[8] Men and women of persistent prayer are those who are constantly on the alert,[9] alive to the will of God and the need of the world, and ready to give an account of themselves and their stewardship.

3-4 As in the parallel passage in Eph. 6:18, the exhortation to general prayer leads into a specific request for prayer for Paul and his associates. The plural pronoun in "pray also for us" refers primarily to Paul and Timothy (cf. Col. 1:1), but no doubt it includes friends and companions who are mentioned later in this chapter. But Paul is conscious

---

[3]For the imperative προσκαρτερεῖτε a few witnesses (including I 33 1881) read the participle προσκαρτεροῦντες (cf. Rom. 12:12).

[4]ἐν εὐχαριστίᾳ is omitted by D* Ambst.

[5]Before λαλῆσαι A inserts ἐν παρρησίᾳ (cf. Eph. 6:19).

[6]For Χριστοῦ B* L 614 2495* (with some Latin and Coptic codices) read θεοῦ (cf. Col. 2:2).

[7]Gk. δι' ὅ, for which B F G read δι' ὅν ("on account of whom").

[8]For the use of προσκαρτερέω in relation to prayer cf. Acts 1:14; 2:42; 6:4; Rom. 12:12. In Eph. 6:18 the noun προσκαρτέρησις is used in a similar sense.

[9]For this catechetical use of γρηγορέω cf. Acts 20:31; 1 Cor. 16:13; 1 Thess. 5:6; 1 Pet. 5:8; Rev. 3:2-3 (see E. G. Selwyn, *The First Epistle of St. Peter*, pp. 439-61, where the relevance of this note to persecution as well as to eschatology is pointed out). In the parallel passage in Eph. 6:18 the synonymous ἀγρυπνέω is used (see p. 412, n. 90).

of his special need of spiritual strength and wisdom.[10] His commission to make known among the Gentiles the Lord who had been revealed to him on the Damascus road remained unfinished so long as earthly life lasted; and his present restrictions, far from hindering the prosecution of this commission, gave him unforeseen opportunities of discharging it. The "mystery of Christ" which he has to declare is identical with the gospel which he received at his conversion "through a revelation of Jesus Christ" (Gal. 1:12); indeed, in the light of Col. 2:2, we might treat "of Christ" as a genitive of definition and identify the mystery with Christ, the Son of God, whom the Father "was pleased to reveal" to him on that occasion (Gal. 1:16). For Paul, to preach the gospel was to preach Christ, and so to make known the "hidden wisdom" of God, which was "decreed before the ages" for his people's glory (1 Cor. 2:7).[11]

The Colossians are asked to pray, then, that a "door" may be opened for the message. The figure of a door being opened for the gospel message (and for the messenger) is found elsewhere in the NT; we may compare 1 Cor. 16:9 (where Paul says that at Ephesus "a wide door for effective work has opened") and 2 Cor. 2:12 (where at Troas, he says, "a door was opened for me in the Lord").[12] Deissmann thought that Paul might have found the expression current in general speech;[13] this may very well be so, as similar phrases are known from contemporary idiom. That an open door was indeed set before Paul in Rome is evident from the closing words of Acts and from his own account in Phil. 1:12-18 ("what has happened to me has really served to advance the gospel").[14] The opportunities were great, but the situation called for special wisdom, whether Paul was "preaching the kingdom of God and teaching about the Lord Jesus Christ" to those who frequented the lodgings where he lived under house arrest (Acts 28:30-31), or looking forward to his appearance before the imperial tribunal when his appeal came up for hearing. He would have to answer the charges brought against him, but he desired to do so in such a way that the content and nature of his apostolic preaching would be

[10]Cf. καὶ ὑπὲρ ἐμοῦ (Eph. 6:19); also Rom. 15:30-32; 1 Thess. 5:25; 2 Thess. 3:1-2.

[11]Cf. Col. 1:26-27 (pp. 84-86 with nn. 214-16).

[12]Cf. also Acts 14:27; Rev. 3:8. E. Lohmeyer (ad loc.) suggests that here θύρα τοῦ λόγου does not mean (as in 1 Cor. 16:9; 2 Cor. 2:12) an opportunity to preach the gospel but access to the right thing to say (cf. Eph. 6:19). This interpretation is criticized by E. Percy, Die Probleme, pp. 393-94.

[13]A. Deissmann, Light from the Ancient East, p. 301, n. 2.

[14]It has been denied that Phil. 1:12-18 refers to the situation in Rome; see, however, F. F. Bruce, Philippians, GNBC (San Francisco/New York, 1983), pp. 16-22.

made plain to all who heard. He was in Rome, under official custody,[15] on account of Christ and the gospel; it was of the highest importance that the interests of Christ and the gospel should be promoted by the way in which he made his defense before the supreme court. For this he prayed himself, and asked his friends to pray too.

5 Reverting from his personal circumstances to the general principles of Christian conduct, he bids his readers behave themselves wisely in their dealings with non-Christians.[16] Distorted accounts of Christian conduct and belief were in circulation; it was important that Christians should give no color to these calumnies, but should rather give the lie to them by their regular manner of life. It remains true that the reputation of the gospel is bound up with the behavior of those who claim to have experienced its saving power. People who do not read the Bible for themselves or listen to the preaching of the word of God can see the lives of those who do, and can form their judgment accordingly. Let Christians make full use, then, of the present season of opportunity. Here the injunction to "redeem the time"[17] (as the older English versions render the phrase) seems to have special application to their duty to unbelieving neighbors (its reference in Eph. 5:15-16 is more general). Paul wishes to emphasize that, while he has an exceptional opportunity of witness-bearing at the heart of the empire, each Christian has a special opportunity for witness and should make the most of it while it lasts.

6 The grace and wisdom that Paul desires for his own utterance are enjoined upon his readers too. They never know when they may be called on to give an answer with regard to their faith, whether in private conversation or more publicly. Jesus promised his disciples that, when occasion for such a defense arose in a court of law, he himself would give them "a mouth and wisdom" (Luke 21:15),[18] and the narrative of Acts

---

[15]Gk. δέδεμαι, "I am bound" (v. 3).

[16]For οἱ ἔξω ("the outsiders") cf. 1 Cor. 5:12-13; 1 Thess. 4:12. They were the proper targets for evangelistic activity, but they would be put off rather than encouraged to come inside by unworthy conduct on the part of Christians. Cf. also 1 Tim. 3:7, where a bishop "must be well thought of by outsiders" (ἀπὸ τῶν ἔξωθεν).

[17]On τὸν καιρὸν ἐξαγοραζόμενοι ("making the most of the time," RSV) here and in Eph. 5:15 see R. M. Pope, "Studies in Pauline Vocabulary," *ExT* 22 (1910-11), 552-54. In a context like the present, καιρός implies a critical epoch, a special opportunity, which may soon pass: "grasp it," says the apostle; "buy it up while it lasts." In Dan. 2:8 (LXX, Theod.) τὸν καιρὸν ἐξαγοράζετε means "you are trying to gain time."

[18]In the parallels Mark 13:11 and Matt. 10:11 (cf. Luke 12:12) it is the Spirit that speaks through them on such occasions.

repeatedly illustrates the fulfilment of this promise. Those who debated with Stephen, for example, "could not withstand the wisdom and the Spirit with which he spoke" (Acts 6:10).

If Christians practice grace of speech, it will not desert them when they find themselves suddenly confronted by the necessity of defending their belief. Nor will their speech be acceptable if it is insipid.[19] Those who are the salt of the earth[20] may reasonably be expected to have some savor about their language.[21] In pagan usage "salt" in such a context means "wit";[22] here perhaps it is rather the saving grace of common sense. The replies of some of the early martyrs to their interrogators may illustrate what is meant; there is no lack of this kind of "salt," for example, in the narrative of the trial of Justin Martyr and his companions. "No right-thinking person," says Justin, "turns away from true belief to false." "Do what you will," say his companions, "for we are Christians, and Christians do not sacrifice to idols."[23]

Moreover, the conversation of Christians must not only be "opportune as regards the time; it must also be appropriate as regards the person."[24] The importance attached in the primitive church to the proper answering of questions about the faith is attested by various passages in the Gospels,[25] as also by the exhortation in 1 Pet. 3:15, "Always be prepared to make a defense to anyone who calls you to account for the hope that is in you, yet do it with gentleness and reverence."

VI. PERSONAL NOTES (4:7-17)

1. PAUL'S MESSENGERS (4:7-9)

7 As for my affairs, you will learn everything from Tychicus, our dear brother and a trusty servant and fellow-slave in the Lord.

[19]Cf. J. B. Phillips: "Speak pleasantly to them, but never sentimentally" (The New Testament in Modern English [London, ²1972], p. 424).
[20]Cf. Matt. 5:13; Mark 9:49-50; Luke 14:34-35.
[21]Since salt prevents corruption, its presence would be a check on the "corrupt language" (λόγος σαπρός) forbidden in Eph. 4:29—where the ministration of grace (χάρις) to the hearers is also enjoined.
[22]Cf. Latin sales Attici, meaning "Attic wit" (e.g., in Cicero, Fam. 9.15.2).
[23]Acts of Justin 5.
[24]J. B. Lightfoot, ad loc., on ἑνὶ ἑκάστῳ.
[25]Cf. n. 18 above.

8 *I am sending him*[26] *to you for this very purpose, that you may learn our news*[27] *and that he may encourage your hearts.*

9 *He is accompanied by Onesimus, our trusty and dear brother, who is one of yourselves. They will tell you all that is going on here.*[28]

7 The reference to Tychicus is almost word for word identical with Eph. 6:21-22. He was evidently the bearer of the letter to the Ephesians as well as of this one, and possibly of a letter to Laodicea as well (see v. 16). He was himself a native of the province of Asia, as we learn from Acts 20:4, where he is named in the list of Paul's fellow-travelers on his last journey to Jerusalem. The evidence of Paul's letters indicates that those fellow-travelers were delegates from Gentile churches, bearing those churches' gifts for their brethren in Jerusalem; Tychicus was therefore, in all probability, commissioned on that occasion to carry the contributions from one or more of the churches of Asia. He is also mentioned on two occasions in the Pastoral Letters as a messenger of Paul (2 Tim. 4:12; Tit. 3:12). Paul speaks of him here as a faithful colleague of his and a trusty servant of Christ, in fact his own "fellow-slave" in the Lord, using the same term as was used of Epaphras earlier (Col. 1:7).[29]

8 Tychicus, it appears, had paid Paul and Timothy a visit in Rome, and was now on his way back to his native province. It was convenient, then, to entrust him with this and other letters intended for recipients in that province. He would be able to give the recipients further information about Paul and his companions. Moreover, if the variant reading were to be followed,[30] he would be able to find out the present state of affairs in the Colossian church, and no doubt find means of sending a message to Paul to give him the latest news. But more important than that: a visit

---

[26]Gk. ἔπεμψα, "I have sent" (epistolary aorist).

[27]Gk. ἵνα γνῶτε τὰ περὶ ἡμῶν (A B D* F G P 048 33 81 etc.), but the harder reading, ἵνα γνῷ τὰ περὶ ὑμῶν ("that he may learn your news"), has the strong attestation of P^{46} ℵ² C D¹ Ψ and the majority of cursives with the Latin, Syriac, and Bohairic versions (ℵ* has the mixed reading ἵνα γνῶτε τὰ περὶ ὑμῶν). One can no longer say of the reading of B etc., as Lightfoot did, that "the preponderance of ancient authority is decidedly in its favour" (*ad loc.*); the evidence is quite evenly balanced and it should be considered whether this is not a situation in which the precept *praestat lectio ardua* should be heeded.

[28]Gk. πάντα . . . τὰ ὧδε, to which F G add πραττόμενα (cf. Lat. *omnia quae hic aguntur*).

[29]Gk. πιστὸς διάκονος καὶ σύνδουλος ἐν κυρίῳ. Cf. Col. 1:7, ἀπὸ Ἐπαφρᾶ τοῦ ἀγαπητοῦ συνδούλου ἡμῶν, ὅς ἐστιν πιστὸς ὑπὲρ ὑμῶν διάκονος τοῦ Χριστοῦ. The analogy of Col. 1:7 suggests that, while Tychicus is Paul's ἀδελφός, he is not Paul's διάκονος but Christ's.

[30]See n. 27.

from Tychicus would be helpful to the church; he could impart stability and encouragement.

9 Onesimus, unlike Tychicus, is not mentioned in the letter to the Ephesians; he was bound for Colossae in circumstances of which further information is supplied in the letter to Philemon.[31] Onesimus was a member of the household of Philemon, a Colossian Christian, and therefore the Colossian church would feel some responsibility for him. During his absence from Colossae Onesimus came somehow into touch with Paul in his place of custody and through his ministry became a believer. He quickly proved himself a devoted attendant and friend to the apostle while he remained with him, but when Tychicus's journey to Asia provided a suitable opportunity, Paul sent Onesimus along with him so that he might return to Philemon on a new footing.[32] It was necessary that the difference which had parted two men who were now fellow-Christians should be resolved in reconciliation.

But Onesimus was now in good standing as a church member; he was probably attached to one of the house-churches in Rome. He would therefore naturally receive from the Colossian church the same welcome as would be given to any other visiting Christian, especially one armed with a letter of commendation from Paul. But his welcome would be the warmer since the Colossian church already knew him as Philemon's slave. Since Philemon had been wronged personally, it was necessary in addition that a personal letter should be sent to him, inviting him to forgive Onesimus and welcome him back home. But Onesimus's welcome by the whole church of Colossae, on Paul's commendation, would be a powerful lever for Philemon's acceptance of him too.

2. GREETINGS FROM PAUL'S COMPANIONS (4:10-14)

10 *Aristarchus my fellow-prisoner sends his greetings; so do Mark, Barnabas's cousin (you have received orders concerning him: if he comes to you, give him a welcome),*

11 *and Jesus called Justus. So far as members of the circumcision are concerned, these only are my fellow-workers for the kingdom of God; they have been a comfort to me.*

12 *Epaphras, who is one of yourselves, a slave of Christ Jesus,[33] sends*

---

[31]See pp. 196-98.
[32]See p. 150 (on Col. 3:11).
[33]Gk. Χριστοῦ Ἰησοῦ. Ἰησοῦ is omitted by P[46] D F G Ψ and the majority of cursives; P and a few other witnesses read Ἰησοῦ Χριστοῦ.

his greetings. He constantly strives for you in his prayers, that you may be established[34] mature and complete[35] in all God's will.

13 *I testify on his behalf that he toils hard[36] for you and for those in Laodicea and Hierapolis.*

14 *Luke, my dear physician,[37] sends you his greetings; so does Demas.*

10 Greetings are now sent to the Colossian church from six of Paul's friends who are in his company while this letter is being written: three of Jewish birth (Aristarchus, Mark, and Jesus Justus) and three of Gentile birth (Epaphras, Luke, and Demas).

Aristarchus sends his greetings simultaneously to Philemon (Philem. 24); otherwise he is not mentioned in the Pauline corpus. In the narrative of Acts he appears as a native of Thessalonica, who was with Paul at Ephesus and was exposed to personal danger during the riotous assembly in the Ephesian theater (Acts 19:29). Later he accompanied Paul on his last voyage to Judaea (Acts 20:4), presumably as one of two delegates from the Thessalonian church (the other being Secundus), and again when he set sail from Caesarea for Italy (Acts 27:2). It is not said explicitly that he went all the way to Rome with Paul, and some have thought that he accompanied him only as far as Myra, where they trans-shipped (Acts 27:5-6), and then went home to Thessalonica.[38] But we are more probably intended to understand that he accompanied him to Rome[39]—that he remained one of the company designated by the pronoun "we" as far as Acts 28:16 ("and when we came into Rome . . ."). At any rate, he was with Paul and Timothy when this letter was on the point of being dispatched, and is described by Paul as his "fellow-prisoner"—literally, his fellow-prisoner-of-war.[40] Ramsay suggested that Aristarchus shared Paul's

---

[34]Gk. ἵνα σταθῆτε. א² A C D F G Ψ and the majority of cursives read ἵνα στῆτε ("that you may stand").

[35]Gk. πεπληροφορημένοι, for which P⁴⁶ D¹ and the majority of cursives read πεπληρωμένοι.

[36]Gk. ἔχει πολὺν πόνον (א A B C P 81 etc.). For πόνον a variety of synonyms and near-synonyms is attested: κόπον (D* F G 629), πόθον (104 etc.), ἀγῶνα (6 1739 1881 etc.), ζῆλον (D² Ψ and the majority of cursives).

[37]Gk. ὁ ἰατρὸς ὁ ἀγαπητός. Cod. 33 and a few other cursives omit ὁ ἀγαπητός.

[38]So J. B. Lightfoot, *St. Paul's Epistle to the Philippians* (London, 1868), pp. 11, 35.

[39]So C. H. Dodd, *New Testament Studies* (Manchester, 1953), p. 92.

[40]Gk. συναιχμάλωτος. In Philem. 23, where Aristarchus and Epaphras are named together, it is Epaphras who is called συναιχμάλωτος. In Rom. 16:7 Andronicus and Junia are so styled; they may have won the right to this description during Paul's Ephesian ministry.

captivity voluntarily, perhaps passing as his servant.[41] One who looked on himself as a soldier of Jesus Christ, as Paul did,[42] would not unnaturally think of himself during his captivity as a prisoner-of-war.

Greetings are sent also from Mark, another of Paul's companions at the time. It is from this reference alone that we learn that Mark was Barnabas's cousin[43]—a piece of information which throws light on the special consideration which Barnabas gives to Mark in the narrative of Acts. Between twelve and fourteen years previously Mark had disgraced himself in Paul's eyes by deserting him and Barnabas at Perga instead of going up-country with them to evangelize the cities of South Galatia.[44] By this time, however (no doubt in great measure owing to the kindly tutelage of Barnabas, the "son of encouragement," as the Jerusalem apostles called him),[45] he had redeemed his reputation.[46] In what circumstances he had come to Rome we do not know. Possibly he had already begun to accompany Peter as that apostle's interpreter or aide-de-camp when he embarked on a more extended ministry, but it is unlikely that Peter himself was in Rome during Paul's captivity there; otherwise some reference to him, however oblique, might have been expected.[47]

The fact that Paul identifies Mark here in terms of his relationship to Barnabas implies that Barnabas was known to the Colossian Christians by name, even if they had never met him personally.[48] There is no record of any visit by Barnabas to proconsular Asia, but then there is no certain record of any of his movements after he went to Cyprus with Mark about A.D. 48 (Acts 15:39). The joint-founder of churches in Galatic Phrygia (those of Pisidian Antioch and Iconium) would be known by repute at least in the later-founded churches of Asian Phrygia.

---

[41]W. M. Ramsay, *St. Paul the Traveller and the Roman Citizen* (London, [14]1920), p. 316.

[42]Compare his application of the term συστρατιώτης to Archippus (Philem. 2) and Epaphroditus (Phil. 2:25).

[43]Gk. ἀνεψιός, "first cousin." In Num. 36:11 (LXX) the daughters of Zelophehad are married to their ἀνεψιοί (RSV "sons of their fathers' brothers"); in Tob. 7:2 Tobit and Raguel are ἀνεψιοί.

[44]Acts 13:13; 15:36-40.

[45]Acts 4:36.

[46]The restoration of Paul's confidence in Mark is reflected in 2 Tim. 4:11, where he is said to be εὔχρηστος εἰς διακονίαν.

[47]For tentative reconstructions of the movements of Peter (and Mark) around this time see G. Edmundson, *The Church in Rome in the First Century* (London, 1913), pp. 80, 84; T. W. Manson, *Studies in the Gospels and Epistles* (Manchester, 1962), pp. 38-45.

[48]He was evidently well known (at least by name) to the Corinthian Christians too, to judge from Paul's reference to him in 1 Cor. 9:6.

The Colossian Christians had already received some communication with regard to Mark. It is best, with Lightfoot, to suppose that the "orders" came from Paul himself, and that the words "if he comes to you, give him a welcome" sum up their substance. No one else was in a position to give "orders" to a church in Paul's mission field—no one, certainly, whose orders Paul would endorse as he does here. There is no way of knowing if Mark did make his way to Colossae; we have no further information, indeed, of a visit paid by him to the province of Asia (unless an uncertain inference may be drawn from 2 Tim. 4:11).[49]

11 Jesus, surnamed Justus, also sends his greetings. All that is known about him is that he was a Jewish Christian, who was with Paul as these words were being dictated. He is not mentioned elsewhere, not even in the letter to Philemon, where the five other companions of Paul mentioned here send their greetings again. Jesus is the Greek/Latin form of Joshua or Jeshua; Justus was a common Latin cognomen.[50]

These three men—Aristarchus, Mark, and Jesus Justus—were the only Christians of Jewish birth[51] who were actively cooperating with Paul in his gospel witness at this time: "my fellow-workers for the kingdom of God," he calls them. When Paul speaks of the kingdom of God, he usually

---

[49]A special interest on Peter's part in the Christians of Asia and the neighboring provinces may be inferred from 1 Pet. 1:1, and Mark's greetings are sent to them in 1 Pet. 5:13.

[50]Another Jewish believer with the additional name Justus is mentioned in Acts 1:23. Cf. J. Munck, *Paul and the Salvation of Mankind*, E.T. (London, 1959), p. 116, n. 2.

[51]For the construction οἱ ὄντες ἐκ περιτομῆς οὗτοι μόνοι . . . see C. F. D. Moule, *IBNTG*, p. 31; on its meaning see J. Munck, *Paul and the Salvation of Mankind*, pp. 106 with n. 3, 107 with n. 1. What Paul says here is taken by J. B. Lightfoot (*ad loc.*) as pointing to the "antagonism of the converts from the Circumcision in the metropolis"; he compares the reference in Phil. 1:17 to those who "proclaim Christ out of partisanship." But the statement is not necessarily to be taken as a "péssimistic remark," as Deissmann says, "thrown off in a mood comparable with that of the peevish lines in Phil. 2:20-21, which also need not be weighed too nicely" (*Light from the Ancient East*, p. 438). This judgment is quite unwarranted (with regard to Phil. 2:20-21 as well as to the present passage). Nor is there much to be said in favor of Deissmann's further note that "it is not certain whether Paul is describing all three men as Jews; Aristarchus might be a pagan convert to Christianity" (*ibid.*, n. 3). Even if Aristarchus belonged to a mainly Gentile church, his being ἐκ περιτομῆς was no bar to his being a member of it, and even a delegate on a suitable occasion. In the light of Acts 16:3, Timothy would also be included among οἱ ἐκ περιτομῆς who were with Paul at this time, but his inclusion as co-author of the letter (Col. 1:1) would render it less appropriate for him to be mentioned here.

has its future consummation in mind,[52] and this may be so here: his wording may mean "fellow-workers with a view to the kingdom of God." But a present reference is more probable, as in Rom. 14:17, where he says that "the kingdom of God is . . . righteousness and peace and joy in the Holy Spirit." We recall again how Paul is said in Acts 28:30-31 to have spent two years in Rome "preaching the kingdom of God"; in this work he had these men of Jewish birth to assist him at this particular point in the course of those years, and he found great comfort[53] in their presence and help.[54]

12-13 Paul had fellow-Christians of Gentile birth with him also, and they too sent their greetings. First among these comes Epaphras, the Colossians' own evangelist and friend, whose name has appeared earlier in this letter (Col. 1:7). Epaphras is described as a true bondman[55] of Christ, devoted to him and to his people, and especially solicitous for the welfare of his own beloved converts and friends in the Lycus valley. Now that he was far distant from them, they were never out of his mind: he was continuously engaged in intense intercession to God on their behalf, praying for their perfect establishment in all the will of God. Praying is working; and by such fervent prayer Epaphras toiled effectively on behalf of the churches of Colossae, Laodicea, and Hierapolis.[56]

14 The two other Gentile Christians who sent their greetings to Colossae were Luke and Demas. It is from the present reference to Luke that we know what his profession was: "my dear physician," Paul calls him. Since the second century at least he has been identified in tradition with the author of the Third Gospel and the Acts of the Apostles. At one time it was argued that the vocabulary of Luke–Acts showed the author to have been a physician.[57] The lexical evidence adduced lacks demon-

---

[52]See p. 52, n. 61 (on Col. 1:13).
[53]Gk. παρηγορία (not elsewhere in the NT). "The idea of consolation, comfort, is on the whole predominant in the word," perhaps because it and its derivates "were used especially as medical terms, in the sense of 'assuaging,' 'alleviating' " (Lightfoot, *ad loc.*).
[54]On these and other συνεργοί see E. E. Ellis, "Paul and his Co-Workers," *NTS* 17 (1970-71), 437-52, reprinted in *Prophecy and Hermeneutic in Early Christianity* (Grand Rapids/Tübingen, 1978), pp. 3-22; W.-H. Ollrog, *Paulus und seine Mitarbeiter* (Neukirchen, 1979).
[55]With δοῦλος here cf. σύνδουλος in Col. 1:7.
[56]For Laodicea cf. Col. 2:1; for all three cities see Introduction, pp. 3-8.
[57]Especially by W. K. Hobart, *The Medical Language of St. Luke* (Dublin, 1882); cf. also A. von Harnack, *Luke the Physician*, E.T. (London, 1907), pp. 175-98. But see for a critical assessment of the evidence H. J. Cadbury, *Style and Literary Method of Luke* (Cambridge, MA, 1920).

strative force, but it retains considerable illustrative value. That the author of Luke–Acts accompanied Paul to Rome is the most natural inference from the last of the "we" sections of Acts. It is from this reference, too, that we may most surely conclude that Luke was a Gentile by birth—as the author of Luke–Acts appears to have been, to judge by some internal evidence.[58]

Of Demas very little is known.[59] He is mentioned along with Luke as a sender of greetings in Philem. 24 and later in 2 Tim. 4:10-11. In the latter place he is said to have left Paul and gone to Thessalonica, out of love for "this present world"[60]—which may imply that some temporal interest took him off at a time when the imprisoned apostle would have valued his continued presence. Luke alone remained with him—inevitably serving him (inter alia) as his amanuensis.[61]

3. MESSAGES FOR VARIOUS FRIENDS (4:15-17)

15 Greet the brethren in Laodicea, and Nympha and the church in her[62] house.

16 When the letter has been read among you, see to it that it is read also in the church of the Laodiceans, and that you in your turn read the letter from Laodicea.

[58]Quite unconvincing is Deissmann's argument (Light from the Ancient East, p. 438) that this passage need not imply that Luke was a Gentile, as is also his suggestion that Luke might be Paul's kinsman (συγγενής) Lucius, mentioned in Rom. 16:21. Luke (Gk. Λουκᾶς, Lat. Lucas) may well be a shortened or familiar form of Lucius, but Lucius was a very common praenomen throughout the Roman world.
[59]Demas is an abridged form of some such name as Demetrius, Democritus, Demosthenes, etc.
[60]Gk. αἰών. It is implied that Demas found the interests of this age more pressing than those of the age to come. Compare the terms in which love of the κόσμος is deprecated in 1 John 2:15; Jas. 4:4.
[61]On Luke's relation to the Pastoral Letters see C. F. D. Moule, "The Problem of the Pastoral Epistles: A Reappraisal," BJRL 47 (1964-65), pp. 430-52; The Birth of the New Testament (London, ³1981), pp. 281-82; A. Strobel, "Schreiben des Lukas? Zum sprachlichen Problem der Pastoralbriefe," NTS 15 (1968-69), 191-210; N. Brox, "Lukas als Verfasser der Pastoralbriefe?" Jahrbuch für Antike und Christentum 13 (1970), 62-77; J. D. Quinn, "The Last Volume of Luke: The Relation of Luke-Acts to the Pastoral Epistles," in Perspectives on Luke-Acts, ed. C. H. Talbert (Edinburgh, 1978), pp. 62-75; S. G. Wilson, Luke and the Pastoral Epistles (London, 1979).
[62]Gk. αὐτῆς (B 6 1739 1881 etc. syr^hcl co^sa), for which αὐτοῦ is read by D (F G) Ψ with the majority of cursives and syr^pesh hcl.mg and αὐτῶν by ℵ A C P 33 81 etc. co^bo.

17 *Say to Archippus, "Look to the ministry which you have received in the Lord: see that you fulfil it."*

15 The Colossian Christians are now asked to convey greetings from Paul and Timothy to their fellow-Christians in the neighboring city of Laodicea, which lay about ten miles to the northwest and (like Colossae itself) on the south bank of the Lycus. One member of the Laodicean church is mentioned in particular—Nympha (for the name is most probably feminine)[63]—perhaps because it was in her house that the local church, or an important part of it, met.[64] Such house-churches are frequently referred to in the NT. Sometimes the whole church in one city might be small enough to be accommodated in the home of one of its members; but in other places the local church was quite large, and there was no building in which all the members could conveniently meet together. This was certainly true of the Jerusalem church. There we find one group meeting in the house of Mary, the mother of Mark (Acts 12:12); and although Luke does not specifically call that group the church in her house, it could very well have been described thus. Priscilla and Aquila were accustomed to extend the hospitality of their home to such groups in the successive cities where they lived—in Ephesus, for example (1 Cor. 16:19), and in Rome (Rom. 16:5). The presence of other house-churches in Rome is probably implied in the greetings of Rom. 16:3-16. At Colossae itself Philemon's house served such a purpose. We may compare Lydia's house in Philippi (Acts 16:15, 40) and Gaius's in Corinth (Rom. 16:23), as well, probably, as Phoebe's in Cenchreae, if that is what is meant by her being a "patroness"[65] to many (Rom. 16:1-2). Such house-churches were apparently smaller circles of fellowship within the larger fellowship of the city *ekklēsia.*[66]

---

[63]The name is variously accented Νύμφαν, accusative of the feminine Νύμφα, or Νυμφᾶν, accusative of the masculine Νυμφᾶς (an abridged form of Nymphodorus or the like). Lightfoot's argument (*ad loc.*) that the feminine is "in the highest degree improbable," because it would be an instance of the (by this time) unusual Doric form, was answered by J. H. Moulton, who saw here an Attic feminine form with short *alpha* (alongside the normal Attic Νύμφη), not the Doric form with long alpha ("Nympha," *ExT* 5 [1893-94], 66-67). The accents are not marked in the oldest codices, and would not have been marked in the original letter.

[64]Not only is the reading "her house" well attested; there would be every inclination to change it to "his house" or "their house" (no ancient scribe would have changed either of these readings to "her house," thus gratuitously giving a woman prominence in the church). That the house was in Laodicea is a reasonable inference from its juxtaposition to Laodicea in the text.

[65]Gk. προστάτις, the equivalent of Lat. *patrona.*

[66]Cf. A. Deissmann, *Paul,* p. 214; O. Cullmann, *Early Christian Worship,* E.T. (London, 1953), pp. 9-10.

16 The Colossians are then told to pass on this letter, when it has been read to them at a meeting of the church, to the Laodicean church, in order that it may be read there too. It is likely that the Laodicean Christians were exposed to the same disquieting influences as their brethren in Colossae, and the teaching given in this letter would be helpful to both churches. At the same time the Colossians are told to procure a certain letter from Laodicea and have it read in their own church. Much discussion has been devoted to this "letter from Laodicea," but to very little purpose. It was presumably a letter sent by Paul or one of his co-workers (possibly by the hand of Tychicus), but if so it may have been lost at an early date—too early for it to be salvaged and included in the Pauline corpus at the beginning of the second century.[67]

One view identifies it with the letter to the Ephesians[68] (perhaps rightly, if the Laodicean church was the nearest community to Colossae to receive a copy of Ephesians). In Marcion's canon the letter to the Ephesians was entitled "To the Laodiceans";[69] but Marcion probably knew Ephesians in a form which lacked the words "at Ephesus" in the prescript, and found what seemed to be a pointer to its destination in Col. 4:16.[70] This is more likely than the suggestion that he deliberately suppressed the reference to Ephesus in Eph. 1:1[71]—whether because the Ephesian church had refused his doctrine or for any other reason.

[67]P. N. Harrison suggested that it was lost in the earthquake of A.D. 60 (see p. 6 above). Then, he went on, thirty years later Onesimus composed the document which has come down to us as the letter to the Ephesians (a view which Harrison took over from E. J. Goodspeed and J. Knox) and, knowing that Paul's letter to the Laodiceans was lost beyond recall, transferred its title to this new document which was designed to replace it. The omission of the original reference to Laodicea in early manuscripts (without, at first, any attempt to substitute another place-name) "may well have been due to the waning reputation of Laodicea" to which witness is borne in Rev. 3:15-19 (*Paulines and Pastorals* [London, 1964], p. 55).
[68]The first scholar of comparatively modern times to make this identification was John Mill in his *Prolegomena* (1707); see A. Fox, *John Mill and Richard Bentley* (Oxford, 1954), p. 85. Cf. also J. B. Lightfoot, *ad loc.*; A. von Harnack, "Die Adresse des Epheserbriefes des Paulus," *SAB* (1910), pp. 696-709; J. Rutherfurd, *St. Paul's Epistles to Colossae and Laodicea* (Edinburgh, 1908); J. Knabenbauer, *Commentarius in S. Pauli Apostoli Epistolas*, 4 (Paris, 1912), 7-8; B. W. Bacon, "St. Paul to the Laodiceans," *Expositor*, series 8, 17 (1919), 19-35; G. B. Caird, *ad loc.* (see pp. 230-31 below).
[69]Cf. Tertullian, *Against Marcion* 5.17.
[70]Cf. A. Souter, *The Text and Canon of the New Testament* (London, ²1954), p. 152.
[71]Cf. T. W. Manson, *Studies in the Gospels and Epistles* (Manchester, 1962), pp. 229-30.

Yet another suggestion about the "letter from Laodicea" is Edgar J. Goodspeed's: he wished to identify it with the letter to Philemon.[72] But if Onesimus is commended to the Colossian Christians as "one of yourselves" (v. 9), it is more natural to think of Philemon, to whose household Onesimus belonged, as a member of the church at Colossae.

We must, in short, remain in doubt about this Laodicean letter. It may be that the Laodicean church required a letter on similar lines to the letter to the Colossians; yet the two were sufficiently different for directions to be given that either letter should be read in the other church.[73]

This reference to a letter not included (or not obviously included) in the NT canon gave rise at a later date to the fabrication of a spurious "Letter of Paul to the Laodiceans"[74] (just as the OT references to the book of Jashar and other "lost books" have stimulated the composition of works bearing their titles).

17 A special message is sent to one Archippus, who appears from Philem. 2 to have been a member of Philemon's household, perhaps his son. But why should a message to him be so closely linked with references to the Laodicean church? Lightfoot suggested that, while Archippus's parents were Colossians, he himself lived at Laodicea and had pastoral responsibility for the church there.[75] The precise nature of the ministry with which he had been entrusted cannot be determined. It is unlikely that it had to do with the reception or manumission of Onesimus.[76] Whatever it

---

[72]E. J. Goodspeed, *Introduction to the New Testament* (Chicago, 1937), p. 224.

[73]A. Deissmann, *Light from the Ancient East*, p. 238. C. P. Anderson, "Who wrote 'the Epistle from Laodicea'?" *JBL* 85 (1966), 436-40, suggested that this was a letter from Epaphras, dealing with problems in the church of Laodicea similar to those in the Colossian church; later, in "Hebrews among the Letters of Paul," *SR* 5 (1975-76), 258-66, he made the further suggestion that it was the letter known to us as Hebrews. (Cf. p. 120, n. 127.)

[74]Extant in Latin; for the reconstructed Greek text and discussion see J. B. Lightfoot, *Colossians and Philemon*, pp. 274-300; for introduction and translation see E. Hennecke, *New Testament Apocrypha*, ed. W. Schneemelcher and R. McL. Wilson, E.T., II (London, 1965), 128-32. In the fifteenth century two independent English translations were interpolated into manuscripts of the Wycliffite versions of the Bible. A. von Harnack ascribed a Marcionite origin to it in "Der apokryphe Brief des Apostels Paulus an die Laodicener, eine marcionitische Fälschung aus der zweiten Hälfte des zweiten Jahrhunderts," *SAB* (1923), pp. 235-45. (Whether the Muratorian canon's reference to "an alleged epistle to the Laodiceans" implies that the compiler knew this document, or merely knew that this title appeared in Marcion's ἀποστολικόν, is uncertain.)

[75]J. B. Lightfoot, *Colossians and Philemon*, pp. 244, 308-10.

[76]For this suggestion see J. Knox, *Philemon among the Letters of Paul* (Nashville/New York, ²1959), pp. 49-51. Cf. p. 199.

was, it had to be discharged in a spirit of Christian faithfulness. Presumably he would be present when the letter was read, either in the Colossian church or, later, when it had been sent on to Laodicea. This was perhaps calculated to impress him the more with the solemnity of his responsibility to carry out his service. Might it not have been an embarrassment to him to have this personal commission given such publicity? We may be sure that Paul took this into consideration, and knew very well how to make his charge most effective.

VII. FINAL GREETING AND BENEDICTION (4:18)

18 *The greeting of me Paul with my own hand. Remember my chains. Grace be with you.*[77]

18 Paul regularly dictated his letters, but wrote the last sentence or two with his own hand to confirm their genuineness.[78] It was his autograph rather than his signature that provided this confirmation. It was not usual in ancient letter-writing for the writer to sign his name at the end; it was sufficient that his name should appear in the prescript. But it was not uncommon, if the letter as a whole was dictated to an amanuensis, for the sender to write the last few sentences himself for the sake of authentication.[79] Paul appends his signature here, as in 1 Cor. 16:21 and 2 Thess. 3:17.[80] Where a colleague played some part in the composition of the letter, like Silvanus in 2 Thessalonians and Timothy in Colossians, Paul's signature would stamp the whole with his apostolic authority.

The plea, "Don't forget that I am in chains" or "Remember that

---

[77]$\aleph^2$ D Ψ and the majority of later witnesses add ἀμήν. See p. 224, n. 111.

[78]Cf. Gal. 6:11. O. Roller argues (quite unconvincingly) that when Paul statedly wrote the final greeting himself it is implied that he wrote the whole letter; otherwise the amanuensis composed the final greeting (*Das Formular der paulinischen Briefe* [Stuttgart, 1933], pp. 187-91).

[79]Cicero commonly wrote his letters himself, but when he used an amanuensis he indicated that the letter-closing was in his own hand (*"hoc manu mea," Att.* 13.28). In a letter to Atticus he quotes a sentence from a letter which he himself had received from Pompey and says that the sentence came *"in extremo, ipsius manu"* (*Att.* 8.1). Deissmann (*Light from the Ancient East*, pp. 171-72) quotes as a parallel BGU 37, where a different hand (presumably the author's) at the end of the letter adds ἔρρωσο ("Farewell") and the date. See also Deissmann's remarks in *Paul*, p. 13, on some practical implications of the fact that Paul's letters were usually dictated.

[80]See also his autograph and signature in the body of the letter to Philemon (v. 19).

the hand that writes this is a chained hand" (a fact of which Paul would be acutely aware as he took up the pen himself), is essentially a request for their continued prayers on his behalf.

The brief benediction "Grace be with you"[81] brings the letter to an end.

---

[81] This is the basic form of the Pauline benediction; so also in 1 Tim. 6:21; 2 Tim. 4:22. Elsewhere it is variously expanded.

The Epistle
to
PHILEMON

INTRODUCTION TO PHILEMON

I. AUTHORSHIP

The letter to Philemon is one of the two truly personal letters in the NT. The other is 3 John, sent to one Gaius by his friend "the elder" (otherwise unnamed). In both letters one man is addressed by one man. In the letter to Philemon the one man who addresses the other introduces himself as Paul. While Paul associates Timothy with himself in the prescript, and greetings are sent to members of Philemon's extended household, the body of the letter is a private communication from Paul to Philemon.

The Pauline authorship has been accepted by most critics. The letter is too short for the most efficient computer to yield a significant analysis of its style and vocabulary.[1] If its authenticity is questioned, it is questioned mainly on account of its close association with Colossians, which some exegetes are unable to accept as Pauline. For Colossians and Philemon were, to all appearances, written at the same time and place, sent to the same place, carried by the same messenger or messengers.[2] Of the six companions of Paul who send their greetings in Colossians, five send greetings to Philemon.[3] Apart from these, Archippus is mentioned in both, and Onesimus evidently reaches his destination at the same time as both letters.

Ernest Renan was so sure of the genuineness of Philemon that for its sake he was willing to admit the genuineness of Colossians. "The Epistle to the Colossians," he wrote, "though full of eccentricities, does not embrace any of those impossibilities which are to be found in the

---

[1]Cf. A. Q. Morton, *The Times* (London), April 24, 1963: "there seems no reason to exclude it from the works of Paul."
[2]Col. 4:7-9.
[3]Col. 4:10-14; Philem. 23-24.

Epistles to Titus and to Timothy. It furnishes even many of those details which reject the hypothesis [of its pseudonymity] as false. Assuredly of this number is its connection with the note to Philemon. If the epistle is apocryphal, the note is apocryphal also; yet few of the pages [of the Pauline corpus] have so pronounced a tone of sincerity; Paul alone, as it appears to us, could write that little masterpiece."[4]

But it might be argued that Renan's romantic nature was so responsive to the human appeal of the letter to Philemon that the edge of his critical faculty was blunted. Ferdinand Christian Baur also appreciated the human appeal of the letter, but his critical faculty retained its keenness. "What," he asked, "has criticism to do with this short, attractive, graceful and friendly letter, inspired as it is by the noblest Christian feeling, and which has never yet been touched by the breath of suspicion?"[5] Yet, he went on, even here apostolic authorship must not be taken for granted. Since the other "captivity epistles" to which Philemon is so clearly related are not authentically Pauline, the authenticity of this epistle too must be abandoned: it is in fact (said Baur) a Christian romance in embryo, comparable in this respect to the third-century *Clementine Homilies*. The *Clementine Homilies* show how "Christianity is the permanent reconciliation of those who were formerly separated by one cause or another, but who by a special arrangement of affairs brought about by Divine Providence for that very purpose, are again brought together; through their conversion to Christianity they know each other again, the one sees in the other his own flesh and blood."[6] So the letter to Philemon suggests that perhaps Onesimus and his master were temporarily separated in order that they might be reunited and belong to each other forever, no longer as slave and master but as loving brothers in Christ.

W. C. van Manen, who rejected the authenticity of all thirteen Pauline letters, including even the four "capital letters" which Baur accepted (those to the Romans, Corinthians, and Galatians), added to Baur's arguments against the genuineness of Philemon some considerations of his own. For one thing, the ambiguity of the direction speaks against Pauline authorship: the letter is addressed by Paul and Timothy to three named individuals and a household church, while the bulk of it is a personal letter from Paul to Philemon. "This double form . . . is not a style that is natural to any one who is writing freely and untrammelled, whether to one person

[4]E. Renan, *Saint Paul*, E.T. (London, 1889), p. x.
[5]F. C. Baur, *Paul: his Life and Works*, E.T., II (London, 1875), 80.
[6]Baur, *Paul*, II, 83.

or to many."[7] More probably the unknown writer has modeled his composition on a letter sent by the younger Pliny to his friend Sabinianus, interceding on behalf of a freedman of the latter who has offended his patron and has sought Pliny's good offices in bringing about a reconciliation.[8] The writer to Philemon makes the freedman into a slave, and rewrites the letter so as to portray the ideal "relations which, in his judgment, that is, according to the view of Pauline Christians, ought to subsist between Christian slaves and their masters, especially when slaves have in some respect misconducted themselves, as for example by secretly quitting their master's service."[9]

This reconstruction is hypercritical and naïve at the same time. There is no need to propound such a farfetched explanation of a document which bears a much more probable explanation on its face—namely, that it is a genuine letter of Paul, concerning a slave called Onesimus, who somehow needs the apostle's help in restoring good personal relations between himself and his master (one of Paul's friends), and that Paul quite naturally takes the opportunity at the beginning and end of the letter to send greetings and good wishes to other members of the household. Because of what they recognize as the transparent genuineness of this letter, several scholars who are unable to accept the whole of Colossians as Pauline feel constrained nevertheless to salvage some of it for the apostle— enough, at least, to keep Philemon company.[10]

II. DATE AND PROVENANCE

If, then, it was written by Paul, was it sent from Rome in the beginning of the 60s, or from some other place a few years earlier? Over and above the issues relating to this group of "captivity letters" in general, debate with regard to Philemon has fastened on two points: (1) the length of the journey that Onesimus must have made from his master's home to the

---

[7]W. C. van Manen, "Philemon, Epistle to," *Enc. Bib.*, III (London, 1902), col. 3695.

[8]Pliny, *Epistles* 9.21. For translations see J. B. Lightfoot, *Colossians and Philemon*, p. 318; J. Knox, *Philemon among the Letters of Paul* (London, ²1959), pp. 16-17; E. M. Blaiklock, *From Prison in Rome* (London, 1964), pp. 71-72.

[9]"One might add," van Manen continued, "that he has thus given us a practical commentary on such texts as Col. 3:22-25; Eph. 6:5-9; 1 Cor. 7:21-22" (*Enc. Bib.*, col. 3696).

[10]Cf. P. N. Harrison, "Onesimus and Philemon," *ATR* 32 (1950), 268-94; *Paulines and Pastorals* (London, 1964), pp. 74-78.

place of Paul's confinement, and (2) Paul's request for the preparation of a guestroom in view of his hope of an early release and a visit to the Lycus valley.

The case has been argued one way and the other, by none more ably than by G. S. Duncan and C. H. Dodd. Duncan's case for an Ephesian provenance, because Ephesus was so much nearer to Colossae than Rome was (100 miles over against more than 1,000), was answered by Dodd, who thought the remoter city more probable. Duncan replied to Dodd, but the question has remained unresolved.

With regard to Onesimus's choice of a place of refuge, "only in the most desperate circumstances," said Duncan, "such as the letter gives us no reason to assume, would a fugitive from justice have undertaken over unknown and dangerous roads a thousand miles by land, together with two sea voyages extending over some five days, especially when comparatively near at hand there was a city with which he was no doubt already familiar, and which was of sufficient size to afford him all the security that he was likely to require."[11]

With regard to the visit proposed by Paul in v. 22, Duncan went on to say:

> How natural such a visit would be at a time when his activities, temporarily interrupted by imprisonment, were directed towards the evangelisation of Asia: not far from him as he lay at Ephesus were those churches in the Lycus valley which in some indirect way no doubt owed their origin to his missionary-work in the province, but which he had never so far visited, and in at least one of which, Colossae, the conditions gave him grave cause for anxiety. On the other hand, how unlikely was he to contemplate such a visit, let alone give thought to the provision of a lodging there, when he lay a prisoner at Rome. . . . From Rome he meant, not to turn back to the Lycus valley, but to advance into Spain.[12]

To the argument that Onesimus was more likely to have fled to neighboring Ephesus than to distant Rome, Dodd says:

> This seems plausible. But a moment's reflection may convince us that we are here talking of things about which we know nothing. We cannot know either what was in Onesimus' mind or what his opportunities for travel may have been. If we are to *surmise*, then

---

[11]G. S. Duncan, *St. Paul's Ephesian Ministry* (London, 1929), pp. 72-73; cf. P. N. Harrison, "Onesimus and Philemon," p. 271.

[12]*St. Paul's Ephesian Ministry*, pp. 74-75; cf. P. N. Harrison, "Onesimus and Philemon," p. 281.

it is as likely that the fugitive slave, his pockets lined at his master's expense, made for Rome *because* it was distant, as that he went to Ephesus because it was near. But this meeting of the runaway slave with the imprisoned apostle is in any case an enigma. Did he mean to go to Paul? Or was it the long arm of coincidence that brought about such an improbable meeting? No secure argument can be based upon an incident which we cannot in any case explain.[13]

To the argument that Paul's request for a lodging at Colossae comes more naturally if he was at Ephesus at the time than if he was at Rome, he says:

> This is a real point in favour of the Ephesian hypothesis. At the same time we do not know that Paul would have held to his intention in the greatly changed circumstances. Like all practical men, he was open to change his mind, as in fact we know both from Acts and from the Epistles he not infrequently did. On the Roman hypothesis, the emergence of the Colossian heresy may well have led Paul to plan a visit to Asia before setting out on further travels, whether or not the plan was ever fulfilled.[14]

When Duncan replied to these points, he added little on the first score to what he had said before (apart from a footnote allusion to the suggestion of J. Pongrácz that the temple of Artemis could have provided a place of refuge for Onesimus at Ephesus); on the second score he conceded that Paul might have changed his plans during his Roman imprisonment and decided to visit Colossae.

> But long before he could have arrived at that remote and unimportant town in the Lycus valley, must we not allow of the eager news preceding him of his release, his journeyings eastwards, his subsequent arrival at Ephesus or some such centre in Asia? That one so situated should bespeak quarters at Colossae suggests the air-mindedness of the twentieth century rather than the rigorous conditions, which Paul himself knew so well (2 Cor. 11:25 ff.), of travel in the first.[15]

On this last point it might be said that long before the air-minded twentieth century most students of the letter to Philemon, including some who experienced travel conditions not notably less rigorous than those

---

[13]C. H. Dodd, "The Mind of Paul, II," *BJRL* 18 (1934), 80, reprinted in *New Testament Studies* (Manchester, 1953), p. 95.
[14]*Ibid.*
[15]G. S. Duncan, "The Epistles of the Imprisonment in Recent Discussion," *ExT* 46 (1934-35), 296.

which Paul endured in the first century, had no difficulty in believing that Paul did from Rome bespeak quarters at Colossae. And it was not only the Colossian heresy that caused Paul concern. The developing situation in the province of Asia as a whole, as he learned of it from Epaphras and other visitors, may well have seemed to him to demand his presence as soon as he regained his freedom (if indeed he did regain it). His opponents there were exploiting his absence to gain support for their policy and to undermine his authority. Even if things had not yet reached the pass described in 2 Tim. 1:15, where "all who are in Asia" are said to have turned away from him, the beginnings of this trend were already apparent.

As for a Caesarean provenance,[16] unless this can be established for the companion letters, nothing in the letter to Philemon supports it. Onesimus might make his way to Ephesus because it was near, or work his passage to Rome because it was distant, but what could take him to Caesarea?

If Philemon be considered by itself, the arguments for an Ephesian provenance are weighty. But when Philemon is considered along with Colossians, they are outweighed by the arguments for a Roman provenance.

III. PAUL AND ONESIMUS

The picture sometimes drawn of Paul's meeting Onesimus as a fellow-prisoner is misleading. One of G. S. Duncan's arguments against a Roman provenance for the letter is the radical change in the conditions of Paul's imprisonment which would have to be envisaged "if, following on two years spent in his own hired house (Acts 28:30), he was reduced to sharing the same prison-cell as a fugitive slave."[17]

But there is no need to conjure up any such picture in our minds. Nothing in the letter suggests that Onesimus was a prisoner: he was evidently free to set out on a journey, as Paul was not. We may think of Paul as still living under house-arrest in his lodgings, albeit handcuffed to his military guard (and therefore technically a prisoner), when Onesimus came to him.

E. R. Goodenough had recourse to Athenian law to illustrate the situation.[18] In Athenian law a slave in danger of his life was permitted to seek sanctuary at an altar. That altar might be the hearth of a private

---

[16]Cf. E. Lohmeyer, *Der Kolosser- und der Philemonbrief* (Göttingen, [11]1957), pp. 172-73.
[17]*St. Paul's Ephesian Ministry*, p. 73.
[18]E. R. Goodenough, "Paul and Onesimus," *HTR* 22 (1929), 181-83.

family. The head of the family would then be obliged to give the slave protection while he tried to persuade him to return to his master; he would no doubt use his good offices to mollify the master's anger. If the slave refused to go back, the householder's duty was to put him up for auction and hand over the price received for him to his former master. This provision operated in Egypt under the Ptolemies, and survived into Roman imperial times, since it influenced Ulpian's jurisprudence early in the third century A.D. Philo of Alexandria, who knew the Egyptian practice, modified the Deuteronomic law of the fugitive slave to conform with it.[19]

In explaining the case of Onesimus in terms of this Athenian provision, Goodenough found it necessary to suppose that Paul was free at the time, and that his reference to being in chains might be figurative.[20] But if the apostle was under house-arrest in his own lodgings, might not the place where he lived count as his "hearth" within the meaning of the act—always supposing that the provision was valid in that city, and that Onesimus availed himself of it?

There is no way of deciding how in fact Onesimus made his way to Paul. Perhaps Epaphras of Colossae, who was on a visit to Paul at the time, came across Onesimus in the city, recognized him, and brought him to Paul because he knew that Paul would help him in his predicament. One cannot be sure. It may even be outrunning the evidence to conclude that Onesimus was a runaway slave in the usual sense of the term. It could be argued that his master had sent him to fulfil some commission, and that he had overstayed his leave and required a note of excuse from Paul begging pardon for his unduly long absence. In view of our ignorance of so many details, the possibilities are numerous.

The letter throws little light on Paul's attitude to the institution of slavery. More formal teaching on the subject is given in the household codes of Colossians and Ephesians, but Paul's mind on the subject finds clearest expression in incidental remarks in 1 Cor. 7:20-24.[21] What the letter to Philemon does is to bring the institution into an atmosphere where

[19]Philo, *On the Virtues* 124 (see F. H. Colson's notes *ad loc.* in the Loeb edition of Philo, VIII [Cambridge, MA, 1960], 238-39, 447-48). The law of Deut. 23:15-16 forbade the surrender of a fugitive slave to his master: "he shall dwell with you, in your midst, . . . where it pleases him best; you shall not oppress him." The Israelites had good reason to know from experience that God cared for runaway slaves. To Paul this law, unparalleled in the ancient Near East, carried divine authority; even so, he would not invoke it without Philemon's consent, preferring Philemon to act spontaneously in its spirit.

[20]He also cast doubt on the identity of Philemon's slave with the Onesimus of Col. 4:9 ("Paul and Onesimus," p. 182, n. 7).

[21]See pp. 150-51, 168.

it could only wilt and die. Where master and slave were united in affection as brothers in Christ, formal emancipation would be but a matter of expediency, the legal confirmation of their new relationship. If the letter were a document on slavery, it could be copiously illustrated by accounts of conditions in the Roman Empire over several centuries. One might quote an advertisement of 156 B.C. requesting information about two runaway slaves and giving a description of the slaves themselves and of the goods which they had on them when they were last seen,[22] or one might refer to an inscribed bronze collar of the late fifth or early sixth century A.D., worn by the slave of a Christian archdeacon in Sardinia.[23]

Paul had no means of compelling Onesimus to go back to Philemon: if Onesimus had refused to go, or had changed his mind on the way back to Phrygia, Paul could have done nothing about it. (The idea of reporting Onesimus to the authorities, as a fugitive slave, was out of the question.) That Onesimus agreed to go back, and presumably did so, must be seen as evidence that the grace of Christ which worked so powerfully in Paul, and which (Paul hoped) would work in Philemon, was also at work in Onesimus. It would help Onesimus, no doubt, to have the congenial and encouraging companionship of Tychicus on his way back: it may well have been Tychicus's departure for the Lycus valley that provided Paul with a suitable opportunity for sending Onesimus back.

IV. THE SIGNIFICANCE OF THE LETTER

A clearer idea of the nature and purpose of the letter to Philemon may be gained if three questions are asked:

> *(1) What is Paul requesting?*
> *(2) Was his request granted?*
> *(3) Why was the letter preserved?*

Although formally these are three distinct questions, materially they are parts of one comprehensive question, covering the character of the document and its place in the New Testament.

---

[22]*P. Par.* 10; for text and translation see C. F. D. Moule, *Colossians and Philemon*, pp. 34-36.

[23]Reproduced in G. H. R. Horsley (ed.), *New Documents illustrating Early Christianity* (Macquarie University, North Ryde, New South Wales, 1981), pp. 140-41, § 91. The inscription runs: *s[ervus sum] Felicis ar(ch)idiac(oni): tene me ne fugiam,* "I am the slave of Felix the archdeacon: hold me lest I run away." He had probably run away before and been recaptured; before Roman law was christianized he might well have been branded in the face.

(1) What is Paul requesting? He is requesting his friend and convert, Philemon of Colossae, to receive back his slave Onesimus on a new footing—no longer as a slave but as a fellow-Christian and as a partner in the service of the gospel to which Philemon, like Paul himself, is dedicated. In addition, he is delicately letting Philemon know that what he would really like him to do is to send Onesimus back to him to continue the personal service that he has already begun to render Paul.

It has indeed been argued that the request is addressed not to Philemon but to Archippus, to whom Paul and Timothy also send their greetings in the prescript.[24] John Knox, who propounds this argument, finds it supported in the cryptic message to Archippus at the end of the letter to the Colossian church, where the church is directed to tell Archippus to make sure to fulfil the ministry that he has received "in the Lord" (Col. 4:17). Paul there enlists the aid of the Colossian church in persuading Onesimus's master to do what Paul wants him to do.

Who then was Philemon? Philemon, it is said, was overseer of the churches of the Lycus valley; he lived at Laodicea. Paul arranged that the letter about Onesimus should be delivered to Philemon first because he could use his influence with Archippus; this was the "letter from Laodicea" which Paul asked the church of Colossae to procure and read (Col. 4:16).

It is quite probable that the ministry which Archippus was to fulfil had something to do with Laodicea, since it is mentioned immediately after the reference to the "letter from Laodicea." But after the extraordinary delicacy with which Paul's plea for Onesimus is worded in the letter to Philemon, it would be incredibly maladroit to put pressure on Onesimus's owner by name in another letter which was to be read aloud at a church meeting where the owner would presumably be present. No one should be embarrassed by the unobtrusive commendation of Onesimus in Col. 4:9: "Onesimus, our trusty and dear brother, who is one of yourselves"—it would perhaps add just a little more weight to Paul's plea in the letter to Philemon, but would not put Onesimus's owner on the spot. Any attempt to put him on the spot would neutralize the confident—and confidential—diplomacy of the letter to Philemon.

That diplomacy would be even more effectively neutralized if the letter to Philemon were read aloud before an assembled church. Greetings are indeed sent in that letter to the church in the recipient's house as well

---

[24]J. Knox, *Philemon among the Letters of Paul* (Chicago, 1935; Nashville, TN/London, ²1959); cf. also his introduction and exegesis on Philemon in *IB* XI (New York, 1955), 555-73, with H. Greeven, "Prüfung der Thesen von J. Knox zum Philemonbrief," *TLZ* 79 (1954), cols. 373-78.

as to Philemon, Apphia, and Archippus; but that does not mean that the private contents of vv. 4-21 were to be divulged even to that household church, not to speak of the wider city church.

"It is evident that Philemon's house is meant":[25] Philemon's name comes first among those saluted in the prescript, and this in itself is "fatal to the theory that Archippus is primarily the one addressed."[26] Philemon is Onesimus's master, to whom Paul's very personal plea is directed. It is unlikely that Knox would have come to any other conclusion but for his desire to link the burden of the letter to Philemon with the ministry laid on Archippus in Col. 4:17.

(2) Was Paul's request granted? Yes; otherwise the letter to Philemon would not have survived. That it survived at all is a matter calling for comment, but if Philemon had hardened his heart and refused to pardon and welcome Onesimus, let alone send him back to Paul, he would certainly have suppressed the letter.

(3) Why was the letter preserved? Here we come to those features of John Knox's *Philemon among the Letters of Paul* which make it one of the most important and fascinating studies of this letter ever to have been published.

Knox's work took shape against the background of the Chicago school of NT studies led by Edgar J. Goodspeed. Goodspeed pioneered the view that the Pauline corpus of ten letters (that is, lacking the three Pastorals) was edited and published at Ephesus about the end of the first century A.D., and that the document which we know as the letter to the Ephesians was composed by the editor to serve as an introduction to the corpus.[27] Other members of the school undertook supporting studies, and Knox's book belongs to this category.

---

[25]E. J. Goodspeed, *Introduction to the New Testament* (Chicago, 1937), p. 111.
[26]C. F. D. Moule, *Colossians and Philemon*, pp. 16-17.
[27]E. J. Goodspeed, "The Place of Ephesians in the First Pauline Collection," *ATR* 12 (1929-30), 189-212; *Introduction to the New Testament*, pp. 210-19, 222-39; *The Meaning of Ephesians* (Chicago, 1933). Goodspeed also identified the letter to Philemon with the "letter from Laodicea" of Col. 4:16, but thought that Archippus and Onesimus, as well as Philemon, lived at Laodicea. Archippus would not be present when the letter to the Colossians with its message for him was read in the church to which it was addressed: "If he were in Colossae, why should the Colossians have to 'tell' him? He would be present at the meeting of the church and would hear the message without being told" (*Introduction*, pp. 109-12). Later, in *The Key to Ephesians* (Chicago, 1956), pp. xiv-xv, Goodspeed accepted Knox's conclusion that Onesimus was the author of Ephesians, as also did P. N. Harrison (*Paulines and Pastorals*, pp. 31-78).

Knox accepts the general Goodspeed position and goes on to suggest a reason for the inclusion of Philemon in the ten-letter corpus. It was included because it meant very much to a man who played a prominent part in the publication of the corpus—namely, Onesimus.

Here is his argument. When Ignatius, bishop of Antioch in Syria, was being taken to Rome for execution about A.D. 110, he was visited in Smyrna by the bishop of Ephesus, who was named Onesimus. But why should one connect this Onesimus with the Onesimus who figures in the letter to Philemon fifty years earlier?

Because, says Knox, Ignatius shows himself familiar with this letter when he writes a letter of thanks to the church of Ephesus. Ignatius's letter to the Ephesians is, indeed, one of the few places in patristic literature which clearly echoes the language of the letter to Philemon. Not only so, but the part of Ignatius's letter which echoes the language of the letter to Philemon is the part which mentions Bishop Onesimus—the first six chapters. In these six chapters the bishop is mentioned fourteen times;[28] in the remaining fifteen chapters he is not mentioned at all (apart from one more general reference to the bishop's office: "obey the bishop and the presbytery with an undisturbed mind").[29]

This consideration is impressive. One especially impressive point is that, just as Paul plays on the meaning of Onesimus's name ("profitable") when he says to Philemon, "may I have this 'profit' from you" (v. 20), so apparently does Ignatius when he writes to the Ephesian church, "may I always have 'profit' from you" (2:2).[30]

All this does not demonstrate the identity of the two Onesimi; it could simply be that the name of the bishop of Ephesus reminded Ignatius of the Onesimus whom Paul befriended.[31] As the earlier Onesimus, formerly unprofitable, was henceforth going to be as profitable as his name

[28]Including three times by name (Ignatius, *Eph.* 1:3; 2:1; 6:2).
[29]Ignatius, *Eph.* 20:2.
[30]See p. 221 with n. 94 (on Philem. 20).
[31]The name "Onesimus" was in widespread use throughout the Graeco-Roman world, and not exclusively as a slave-name. Two random instances may be mentioned: in a song from an Atellan farce performed before the Emperor Galba, "Onesimus has come from his country house" (Suetonius, *Galba* 13), and in an inscription from Eumeneia in Asian Phrygia, where the Jewish owner of a tomb (Aurelius Gaius Apella) says he prepared it "for himself and his wife and mother and his excellent friend Onesimus and his wife" (*CIJ* 761). It even appears as the name of a woman, ὀνήσιμος being an adjective of two terminations (Horsley, *New Documents*, p. 89, § 54).

promised,[32] so Onesimus of Ephesus was eminently worthy of that "well-loved name."[33] But the identification is not impossible; one might go farther and say that it is not improbable. We have no idea how old Paul's Onesimus was when he wrote about him; but a young man in his later teens or early twenties at that time would be about seventy by the time of Ignatius's martyrdom—not an incredible age for a bishop in those days.

Knox then ventures farther in his reconstruction of the situation. If (as the Goodspeed school held) Ephesus was the place where the Pauline corpus was first published, early in the second century, then the Onesimus of Ignatius's letter was bishop of Ephesus around that time and must have had some responsibility with regard to the editing of the corpus. Why should he not have been the editor himself? If so, we need look no farther for the reason for the careful preservation of the letter to Philemon and its inclusion in the published corpus of Paul's letters. But if Onesimus was editor of the corpus, then (according to the Goodspeed school) he would have been author of the canonical letter to the Ephesians. If that were so, Paul accomplished something more wonderful than he could have realized the day he won Onesimus to faith in Christ!

But the Goodspeed line has not found wide acceptance.[34] For those who are unable to follow it, Knox's reconstruction has more of fancy than of fact about it. Yet the preservation and canonization of this private letter must be explained. To Onesimus the letter was his charter of liberty. That Onesimus did become bishop of Ephesus is not improbable. If so, then, wherever and by whomsoever the Pauline corpus was first compiled and published, Onesimus could scarcely fail to get to know about it, and would make sure that *his* Pauline letter found a place in the collection.

[32]Paul does not imply, as Knox thinks, that Onesimus was the new Christian name which he himself gave to his convert; he would not introduce him in the letter by a name which his master would not recognize. (See p. 214 with n. 62.)
[33]Knox argues that Ignatius's reference to the Ephesian church's "well-loved name" (τὸ πολυαγάπητόν σου ὄνομα, *Eph.* 1:1) is to be understood as an allusion to the name of its bishop, who went to Smyrna to greet Ignatius as his church's representative: "I received in the name of God your whole community in Onesimus" (*Eph.* 1:3).
[34]See J. I. Cook, *Edgar Johnson Goodspeed: Articulate Scholar* (Chico, CA, 1981), pp. 9-21.

ANALYSIS OF PHILEMON

Texts, Exposition, and Notes

PHILEMON

I. PRESCRIPT (1-3)

1 *Paul, a prisoner[1] of Christ Jesus, and our brother Timothy, to Philemon, our dear friend[2] and fellow-worker,*
2 *and to our sister[3] Apphia and Archippus, our comrade-in-arms, and to the church in your house:*
3 *grace and peace be yours from God our Father and the Lord Jesus Christ.*

1 Like the letter to the Colossians, this one shows Timothy's name linked with Paul's in the prescript, but here there is no question of Timothy's sharing the authorship with Paul. Throughout the body of this letter one man (Paul) addresses one man (Philemon). Timothy is associated with Paul in the initial salutation, instead of being included among other friends whose greetings are sent in vv. 23 and 24, because he was Paul's permanent partner in his ministry.

Paul is asking Philemon for a favor; therefore he is careful not to assert his apostolic status, as he does in most of his prescripts. He designates himself rather as a prisoner, a man in chains; yet even this is an honorable designation, for he is not so much Caesar's prisoner (which in terms of Roman law he was) as a prisoner of Christ Jesus.[4] In chains or at liberty, he remained an ambassador, and if for the time being his sovereign directed him to exercise his ambassadorship under military custody,

---

[1]Gk. δέσμιος, for which D* reads ἀπόστολος, 629 ἀπόστολος δέσμιος, and 323 945 and a few other cursives δοῦλος.
[2]Gk. Φιλήμονι τῷ ἀγαπητῷ, after which D* and one or two Old Latin witnesses add ἀδελφῷ.
[3]Gk. τῇ ἀδελφῇ, for which D² Ψ and the majority of cursives read τῇ ἀγαπητῇ, and 629 with a few Latin witnesses and syr^hcl ἀδελφῇ τῇ ἀγαπητῇ.
[4]Cf. Eph. 3:1; 4:1.

his directive must be obeyed: as it is put below in v. 9, Paul was simultaneously "ambassador but now also a prisoner of Christ Jesus."

Of Philemon nothing is known beyond what can be gathered from this letter.[5] He was evidently residing in Colossae (so much may be inferred from the mention of Onesimus as "one of yourselves" in Col. 4:9). But this letter gives a strong impression that, unlike the other Christians in the Lycus valley, Philemon was personally known to Paul and reckoned by him among his "fellow-workers."[6] Indeed, it is evident from v. 19b that he was one of Paul's converts. But when and where Paul and he had met must be a matter of speculation.

2 Apphia and Archippus, who are also saluted by name, were presumably members of Philemon's household, probably his wife and his son. The name Apphia (not to be confused with the Roman Appia[7]) is well attested in Phrygia and elsewhere in Western Anatolia: one Apphia of Colossae is commemorated on a tombstone set up by her husband Hermas.[8] As for Archippus, he is the recipient of a cryptic message in Col. 4:17—cryptic to the modern reader, but no doubt well understood by him.[9] (The idea that the message had to do with the treatment of Onesimus, as though Paul's plea in this letter were addressed to Archippus rather than to Philemon, has nothing to be said in its favor.)[10] He is here referred to as "our comrade-in-arms" or fellow-soldier[11]—a designation given by Paul also to Epaphroditus of Philippi (Phil. 2:25). Some personal association with Archippus in the work of the gospel is implied, but what it was is unknown to us.

The inclusion of the church in Philemon's house among the recipients of these initial greetings suggests that some of the Christians in the city had their regular meeting-place there. While they are greeted thus in the prescript, they are in no sense included among the addressees of the letter: the letter is a private one, intended for Philemon alone (as is plain from the use of the singular pronoun of the second person).[12] The involve-

---

[5]The name is a common one in Greek history and literature.
[6]Cf. Col. 4:11 (p. 181 with n. 54).
[7]The Latin versions regularly transcribe her name as Appia.
[8]*CIG* 3, 4380.k.3: "Hermas to Apphia [or Apphias, dative Ἀπφιάδι from Ἀπφιάς], his own wife, the daughter of Tryphon, a Colossian by family: in memory." See commentaries by Dibelius-Greeven and Lohse (E.T.), *ad loc.*
[9]See p. 185.
[10]Cf. J. Knox, *Philemon among the Letters of Paul* (Nashville/New York, [2]1959), pp. 49-51.
[11]Gk. συστρατιώτης.
[12]The plural pronoun ὑμεῖς appears only in the prescript (v. 3), in a more general personal note (v. 22b), and in the benediction (v. 25).

ment of the church—even of Philemon's house-church—in what was Philemon's personal responsibility could well have been counterproductive. (The commendation of Onesimus in Col. 4:9 is on a different footing.)[13]

3 The prescript ends with Paul's habitual invocation of "grace and peace"—here, as is usual, "from God our Father and the Lord Jesus Christ."[14] Grace and peace are invoked on all those mentioned in the prescript along with Philemon, but with that the message to them is concluded, until the plural pronoun "you" reappears in the expressed hope of seeing them again (v. 22b) and in the final grace-benediction (v. 25).

II. THANKSGIVING FOR NEWS OF PHILEMON'S LIBERALITY (4-7)

4 *I thank my God as I mention you always in my prayers,*
5 *because I hear of the love and loyalty[15] which you show to the Lord Jesus[16] and to all the saints.*
6 *(I pray) that the liberality which is the expression of your faith may become effective in the experience of every good thing[17] which is ours[18] in Christ.[19]*
7 *I have received great joy[20] and encouragement at the news of your love,[21] because you have refreshed the hearts of the saints, my brother.*

4 The prescript is followed by the customary Pauline expression of thanks, interwoven (as usual) with an intercessory prayer-report.[22] Both

---

[13]See p. 177.

[14]See p. 39 with n. 5 (on Col. 1:2b).

[15]P^{61} (vid.) D and several cursives transpose the order: "loyalty and love" (τὴν πίστιν καὶ τὴν ἀγάπην for τὴν ἀγάπην καὶ τὴν πίστιν).

[16]Gk. πρὸς τὸν κύριον Ἰησοῦν. A C and a few cursives read εἰς for πρός, as does D*, with the addition of Χριστόν after Ἰησοῦν. 629 reads ἐν Χριστῷ Ἰησοῦ.

[17]For παντὸς ἀγαθοῦ F G and a few other witnesses read παντὸς ἔργου ἀγαθοῦ (cf. Col. 1:10; also 2 Cor. 9:8; 2 Thess. 2:17; and in the Pastorals *passim*).

[18]Gk. ἐν ἡμῖν, for which ἐν ὑμῖν is read by P^{61} ℵ F G P 33 1739 1881 etc. lat[a b vg] syr co.

[19]Τὸ εἰς Χριστόν, ℵ² D F G Ψ with the majority of cursives, lat syr[pesh] add Ἰησοῦν.

[20]Gk. χαράν, for which the majority of cursives read χάριν ("grace").

[21]Lit., "at your love" (ἐπὶ τῇ ἀγάπῃ σου).

[22]On this thanksgiving and prayer-report see P. T. O'Brien, *Introductory Thanksgivings in the Letters of Paul* (Leiden, 1977), pp. 47-61; G. P. Wiles, *Paul's Intercessory Prayers* (Cambridge, 1974), pp. 215-25.

the ground of the thanksgiving and the substance of the prayer are closely related to the purpose of the letter.[23] The qualities which called forth Paul's thanksgiving in the news he received about Philemon were the qualities which he wished him to show in the particular matter about which he was writing; the fulfilment of his prayer for Philemon would provide an atmosphere most congenial to Philemon's readiness to grant his personal request.

5 It was probably Epaphras who had given Paul the news about Philemon which caused the apostle so much joy, as it was he too who gave Paul the news about the Colossian church in general. Onesimus also could have given Paul news about Philemon and his household, but Epaphras's news would have been more objective. The love and loyalty which Philemon showed, according to this news, were the practical outcome of his Christian faith.[24] The same word (Gk. *pistis*) does duty for both "faith" and "loyalty"; but "loyalty" or "faithfulness" appears to be its meaning here, both because of its position after "love" and because it is directed not only toward "the Lord Jesus" (who is the proper object of "faith" in the sense of trust) but also toward his people—"all the saints." The difference in construction between these words and those in Col. 1:4 and Eph. 1:15 ("hearing of your faith in Christ Jesus[25] and your love for all the saints") involves a difference in meaning. Love and loyalty to the people of Christ[26] provide visible evidence of love and loyalty to the unseen Christ.[27]

6 This verse presents several problems in translation. A fairly literal rendering is provided in the ARV: "that the fellowship of thy faith may become effectual, in the knowledge of every good thing which is in you, unto Christ" (the phrase "which is in you" represents a variant reading from that presupposed in the translation above: "which is in us").[28] But such a literal rendering calls for detailed interpretation.

The "fellowship" is probably to be understood actively, of Philemon's "sharing" his resources with others in a spirit of liberality which

---

[23]Compare τῶν προσευχῶν μου (v. 4) with τῶν προσευχῶν ὑμῶν (v. 22), σου τὴν ἀγάπην (v. 5) with διὰ τὴν ἀγάπην (v. 9), ἡ κοινωνία (v. 6) with κοινωνόν (v. 17), παντὸς ἀγαθοῦ τοῦ ἐν ἡμῖν (v. 6) with τὸ ἀγαθόν σου (v. 14), τὰ σπλάγχνα τῶν ἁγίων ἀναπέπαυται (v. 7) with ἀνάπαυσόν μου τὰ σπλάγχνα (v. 20).

[24]Cf. Gal. 5:6, "faith (πίστις) working through love (ἀγάπη)."

[25]Eph. 1:15 reads "in the Lord Jesus"; as in Col. 1:4 the preposition is ἐν (see p. 41).

[26]On "saints" (ἅγιοι) as a designation of believers cf. Col. 1:2 (pp. 38-39).

[27]Cf. 1 John 4:20-21.

[28]See p. 207, n. 18.

springs from his faith in Christ.[29] In the context this is more probable than such other interpretations as "your communication of the faith (to others),"[30] "the fellowship which you enjoy (with others) by faith,"[31] "the fellowship which you enjoy (with Christ) by faith,"[32] "your share in the faith,"[33] or "the share (which others have) in your faith."[34] All these are possible meanings for the Greek phrase in itself.

If this is so, then the prayer that[35] Philemon's liberality may become "effective"[36] is a prayer that he may experience the truth of the principle: "he who sows bountifully[37] will also reap bountifully" (2 Cor. 9:6). What Philemon will reap, if the prayer is answered, is the knowledge[38] and enjoyment of every blessing that Christians have in Christ, in the spirit of 2 Cor. 9:8: "God is able to provide you with every blessing in abundance, so that you may always have enough of everything and may provide in abundance for every good work."[39] Paul has one particular good work in his mind for Philemon to perform, and the resources necessary for its performance are resources not of material affluence but of Christian grace. If "unto Christ"[40] (ARV) is the correct rendering of the last phrase in the verse, then it would mean, as Lightfoot interprets it, "leading to Him as the goal," and would be attached in sense not to "which is ours" but to "may become effective. . . ." The expression "which is ours" is literally "which (is) in us";[41] it might mean "implanted within each of us" or "which is among us (or 'at our disposal') as the people of Christ." In a context where sharing is emphasized the collective sense is more probable, and this sense is reinforced by the rendering "in Christ."[42]

---

[29]Gk. ἡ κοινωνία τῆς πίστεώς σου.

[30]Cf. M. R. Vincent, ad loc.

[31]Cf. E. Lohmeyer, ad loc.; he takes πίστεως as genitive of origin.

[32]Cf. M. Dibelius, ad loc.

[33]Cf. C. H. Dodd, ad loc.

[34]Cf. Moffatt's rendering: "their participation in your loyal faith."

[35]The conjunction ὅπως at the beginning of v. 6 introduces the content of Paul's prayer.

[36]Gk. ἐνεργής.

[37]The repeated "bountifully" renders the repeated ἐπ' εὐλογίαις ("with blessings").

[38]Gk. ἐπίγνωσις, for which see p. 46 with n. 30 (on Col. 1:9). G. B. Caird (ad loc.) takes the meaning here to be "deeper insight into good to be performed."

[39]Gk. εἰς πᾶν ἔργον ἀγαθόν, which invites comparison with παντὸς ἀγαθοῦ here.

[40]Gk. εἰς Χριστόν.

[41]Gk. τοῦ ἐν ἡμῖν.

[42]That is to give εἰς Χριστόν the sense normally expressed by ἐν Χριστῷ. The change of preposition might be put down to dissimilation from ἐν in the preceding ἐν ἡμῖν. "Paul's intercessory prayer report may thus be paraphrased: 'I pray that

7 The joy of which Paul speaks was his response to the good news he had received about Philemon's liberality.[43] It was natural for him to rejoice that one of his converts was showing the reality of his faith by the practice of Christian charity, but his joy was coupled with encouragement as he reflected that a man who gave evidence of such qualities was the more likely to grant the personal request which he was about to make. Verse 7 indeed forms a transition from the thanksgiving and intercession of vv. 4-6 to the appeal voiced in the following verses.

Philemon, it appears, was fairly well-to-do, and used his means to help his fellow-Christians. But he showed grace not only in the fact of his generosity but in the manner in which he practiced it: those who benefited by it were not made to feel embarrassed. Not only were their needs supplied; their hearts[44] were refreshed through him as they appreciated the love which prompted his giving.

III. PAUL'S REQUEST (8-14)

8 *Therefore, while in Christ I have full liberty to point out the path of duty to you,*

9 *yet I prefer to appeal to you for love's sake. I do so in my capacity as Paul, an ambassador—but now also a prisoner—of Christ Jesus.*

10 *I appeal to you, then, for my own child, whose father I have become in my place of imprisonment.[45] I mean Onesimus.*

11 *Once you found him unprofitable, but now he is profitable to you and me alike.[46]*

12 *I am sending him back to you, then, and in him I am sending you my very heart.[47]*

---

your generosity, which arises from your faith, may lead you effectively into a deeper understanding and experience of every blessing which belongs to us as fellow-members in the body of Christ' " (P. T. O'Brien, *Introductory Thanksgivings*, p. 58). It would be difficult to improve on this.

[43]The aorist ἔσχον in χαρὰν . . . πολλὴν ἔσχον may refer to Paul's reaction at the moment of receiving the news, but he continued to rejoice. Cf. 3 John 3, ἐχάρην . . . λίαν, of the elder's joy when brethren brought him news of Gaius's fidelity and hospitality. It is a pleasant coincidence that the two really personal letters in the NT should both be addressed to men so like-minded in their generosity.

[44]Gk. σπλάγχνα ("bowels"), as in vv. 12, 20. Cf. Col. 3:12 (p. 153 with n. 121).

[45]The personal note is emphasized by the insertion of ἐγώ before ἐγέννησα (A lat[a]) or of μου after δεσμοῖς (ℵ[2] C D[2] Ψ with the majority of cursives).

[46]Gk. καὶ σοὶ καὶ ἐμοί. The first καί is omitted in ℵ[2] A C D and the majority of cursives.

[47]Gk. ὃν ἀνέπεμψά σοι, αὐτόν, τοῦτ' ἔστιν τὰ ἐμὰ σπλάγχνα. The relative ὅν is virtually repeated in αὐτόν, which is thus emphatic ("Onesimus himself").

13 *I should have liked to keep him with myself, in order that he might*
serve me on your behalf, in chains as I am for the sake of the gospel.

14 *But I refused to do anything without your consent, so that your good*
deed to me might be done not, so to speak, compulsorily but on your
willing initiative.

8 Paul could, of course, have exercised his authority as an apostle
of Christ and directed Philemon to do what he wished—which was, moreover, the proper thing[48] for Philemon to do. But he has no mind to do any
such thing; that is not how one friend approaches another. Yet he cannot
forbear to point out that, if he had been minded to exercise his authority,
he had full liberty to do so. The word here translated "liberty" is the noun
which normally means "freedom of speech" or "boldness of action"[49]—
the Greek noun *parrhēsia*. In a study of the NT use of this word W. C.
van Unnik regards Paul's introduction of it here as a typical example of
"frankness" between Christians. "Paul, who according to worldly standards is far inferior to the wealthy Philemon, and is in prison, is bold
enough to give orders[50] to Philemon to do his duty, but he refrains from
that right; here again the 'freedom of speech' Paul enjoys is 'in Christ'."[51]

9 Orders are liable to be resented, from whomsoever they come,
but an appeal from a friend is difficult to resist, especially when it is made
expressly "for love's sake." The Lord whose ambassador Paul is can command obedience with supreme authority, but even he prefers to appeal to
his people "for love's sake," as being more congenial to his nature.[52] The
ambassador, vested with his Lord's authority, will follow his Lord's ex-

---

At varying positions, and with some modifications of the wording, a number of
witnesses (including $\aleph^2$ C D Ψ with the majority of cursives and the Latin versions)
add προσλαβοῦ, "receive" (from v. 17), to which αὐτόν, τοῦτ᾽ ἔστιν τὰ ἐμὰ
σπλάγχνα is then the object.

[48]Gk. τὸ ἀνῆκον. Cf. Col. 3:18 (p. 162, nn. 172, 173).

[49]Gk. παρρησία (cf. Col. 2:15; Eph. 3:12; 6:19, 20).

[50]Gk. ἐπιτάσσειν, rendered "point out" in the translation above (as in the NEB);
it is quite a forceful word, however. Cf. Paul's use of the corresponding noun
ἐπιταγή in 1 Cor. 7:6, "I say this by way of concession, not of command (κατ᾽
ἐπιταγήν)," and in 2 Cor. 8:8 (where the tone is not dissimilar to that of our
present passage), "I say this not as a command (κατ᾽ ἐπιταγήν), but to prove
. . . the genuineness of your love."

[51]W. C. van Unnik, "The Christian's Freedom of Speech in the New Testament,"
BJRL 44 (1961-62), 474.

[52]Cf. John 14:15, 23. For Paul, as for Jesus, "love is the fulfilling of the law"
(Rom. 13:10; Gal. 5:14; Mark 12:29-31, quoting Deut. 6:4-5 and Lev. 19:18);
where the law is fulfilled in the spirit of love, it is fulfilled "not compulsorily but
spontaneously."

ample. The older translations represent Paul as speaking of himself here not as an "ambassador" but as an old man (cf. ARV: "such a one as Paul the aged"). It is true that the Greek word here has the sense of "old man" in the classical language; it differs by one letter from the word meaning "ambassador" (which comes from the same root, for ambassadors were regularly elder statesmen).[53] If Paul did refer to himself here as an old man (which, around the age of sixty, he was indeed entitled to do), then his appeal would appear to be based on pity as well as love, and it might be thought that the reader's sense of pity would be deepened as he considered the appeal as coming not only from an old man but also from one who was in chains for the gospel's sake. But, whatever Philemon or others might think, Paul did not regard his being "a prisoner of Christ Jesus" as a disgrace, or as a situation calling for pity; to him it was a matter of pride. Therefore we should expect the term which he uses in such close conjunction with this to be also a designation of honor; and the more recent versions are probably right to prefer the rendering "ambassador" to "old man." There is no need to resort to a conjectural emendation of the Greek;[54] in this period the two words, or at least the two spellings, are practically interchangeable.[55] Paul, in fact, speaks here in the same twofold capacity as in Eph. 6:20, where he says that, for the gospel's sake, he is "an ambassador in chains."[56]

10 In appealing (as he says) "for my own child," Paul employs, probably deliberately, a phrase which can be understood in more than one way. The words can mean "my appeal is concerning my own child"; and that, of course, was true. Onesimus is the subject of his letter. But the words can also mean "my appeal is for my own child" in the sense: "I am appealing to you to give me my own child."[57] And the terms in which

[53]The word here is πρεσβύτης, whereas the word normally used for "ambassador" is πρεσβευτής (cf. the verb πρεσβεύω in 2 Cor. 5:20; Eph. 6:20).

[54]R. Bentley conjectured πρεσβευτής here.

[55]J. B. Lightfoot and E. Lohmeyer (*ad loc.*) adduce examples of the use of πρεσβύτης in the sense of "ambassador"—e.g., 1 Macc. 14:22 א, πρεσβῦται Ἰουδαίων ("ambassadors of the Jews"); *Clem. Hom.*, *Ep. Clem.* 6, ὁ τῆς ἀληθείας πρεσβύτης ("the ambassador of the truth").

[56]πρεσβεύω ἐν ἁλύσει (cf. p. 413).

[57]In classical usage παρακαλῶ σε περὶ τοῦ ἐμοῦ τέκνου would mean "I beseech you concerning my child"; but J. Knox points out that "study of the relatively infrequent cases in which παρακαλῶ was followed by this preposition [περί] in late Greek will show that περί often, if not usually, designated the content of the request" (*Philemon among the Letters*, p. 19). He quotes Appian's statement (*Punic Wars* 136) that the poor of Rome asked Caesar for land on his return to the capital (τῶν ἀπόρων . . . περὶ γῆς παρακαλούντων), and mentions similar instances from the papyri.

Paul amplifies his appeal make it clear that this is indeed his meaning, but he expresses himself tactfully, so that when Philemon accedes to his appeal he may feel that he is acting on his own initiative.

Paul was accustomed to speak of his converts as his "children": Timothy is "my beloved and faithful child in the Lord" (1 Cor. 4:17; cf. 1 Tim. 1:2; 2 Tim. 1:2); Titus is "my true child in a common faith" (Tit. 1:4); the Corinthian Christians are "my beloved children" to whom he is free to address a fatherly admonition (1 Cor. 4:14), and the Galatian Christians are "my little children,[58] with whom I am again in travail until Christ be formed in you" (Gal. 4:19). So here Onesimus is described as the child whom he has acquired—literally, "begotten"—in and despite his present detention. When Onesimus came to see him, or was brought to see him, in his place of custody, Paul helped him to receive the liberating grace of Christ and, in so doing, secured his grateful affection. But who (Philemon might wonder) is this child of whom Paul writes? Now at last comes the child's identity: it is Onesimus. J. B. Phillips brings out the paradox as he paraphrases Paul's announcement thus: "Yes, I have become a father though I have been under lock and key, and the child's name is—Onesimus!"

11 Onesimus bore a name which occurs as a common adjective meaning "useful" or "profitable."[59] It was quite customary to give slaves names like this[60]—not necessarily because they were in fact useful or profitable, but in the hope that, if they were called by such a name, their nature or conduct might come to match it. Paul, having named Onesimus, now plays on the meaning of his name, using a synonym and an antonym from another root.[61] "Profitable as he is by name," he says, "I know that you found him the reverse of that—quite unprofitable, indeed, if not a dead loss. But now there has been a change: he is in a position to be highly profitable to you, as he has already proved to be to me." Knowing what was in Paul's mind, one might ask how Onesimus would be profitable to Philemon if he were sent straight back to continue to be of service to Paul. The answer is simple: Onesimus would be useful to Philemon if he performed the services which Philemon himself would like to perform for Paul, but could not perform in person.

[58]Many witnesses here read the diminutive τεκνία μου (in the other texts quoted the word is τέκνον).
[59]Gk. ὀνήσιμος, from the root of the verb ὀνίνημι, "bring profit or advantage to someone" (cf. ὀναίμην in v. 20). Cf. the name Onesiphorus ("bearing profit") in 2 Tim. 1:16; 4:19.
[60]Cf. the name Chrestus (Gk. χρηστός, verbal adjective from χράω, χράομαι), confused with Christ (Christus, Χριστός) by Suetonius (Claudius 25.4) and others.
[61]He was formerly ἄχρηστος but is now εὔχρηστος (from χράω, χράομαι, "use"); the latter adjective is applied to Mark in 2 Tim. 4:11.

John Knox suggests that Onesimus was the new "Christian name" given him by Paul at his conversion. He bases this conclusion partly on the grammatical construction of Paul's language at this point.[62] But it is an unnatural reading of the language: Paul means rather that, with the new nature that Onesimus has received as a believer in Christ, he has for the first time become true to his name.

12 Well, says Paul, I am sending him back to you, and it is like tearing out my very heart. Paul's language emphasizes how strong was the bond of mutual affection which now bound Onesimus and himself to each other. The word rendered "heart," literally meaning "bowels" (as in v. 7), is occasionally attested in Greek literature with the figurative sense of "offspring";[63] but it would be a mistake to see this sense here. Paul has indeed used the language of parenthood to describe his relation to Onesimus, but the present word is repeatedly used by Paul to convey the sense of affection,[64] the bowels being regarded as the seat of the deep emotions. "In sending *him*,"[65] Paul means, "I am in truth sending part of myself."

13 Paul now makes it very clear what he is asking Philemon to do. When he says, "I should have liked[66] to keep him with myself,"[67] he uses a verbal form which could simply mean "I wished to keep him with myself," but is capable of the more tentative sense "I should like" or "I should have liked." But Paul would not keep Onesimus without Philemon's approval, not only because he would break the law if he did so, but much

---

[62]This would be the natural conclusion if Paul said ὃν Ὀνήσιμον ἐγέννησα. But he says ὃν ἐγέννησα ἐν τοῖς δεσμοῖς, Ὀνήσιμον. The masculine relative pronoun ὅν has been attracted into the gender of Ὀνήσιμον instead of the neuter gender of its antecedent τέκνου (ὅ). The postponement of "Onesimus" to the end of the adjective clause is rhetorically effective: "I am asking for my child, whom I have begotten while a prisoner; I am asking, in short, for—Onesimus!"

[63]LSJ cite Artemidorus, *Onirocriticus* 1.44: οἱ παῖδες σπλάγχνα λέγονται ("children are called 'bowels' "); cf. Sophocles, *Antigone* 1066: τῶν σῶν . . . ἐκ σπλάγχνων ἕνα ("one from your own loins").

[64]Cf. 2 Cor. 6:12; 7:15; Phil. 1:8; 2:1; Col. 3:12.

[65]The pronoun αὐτόν in ὃν ἀνέπεμψά σοι, αὐτόν is not necessary to complete the sense, but it adds emphasis (cf. p. 210, n. 47).

[66]Gk. ἐβουλόμην, as in Acts 25:22, ἐβουλόμην . . . ἀκοῦσαι, "I should like to hear" (cf. the similar imperfect ηὐχόμην in Rom. 9:3, ηὐχόμην . . . ἀνάθεμα εἶναι, "I could pray to be accursed"). C. F. D. Moule (*IBNTG*, p. 9) calls this the "desiderative imperfect"; he mentions, however, the possibility that the tense in the present instance might be epistolary (this, *me iudice*, is less likely). This usage of ἐβουλόμην without ἄν is classical as well as Hellenistic (cf. W. W. Goodwin, *Syntax of the Moods and Tenses of the Greek Verb* [London, 1929], § 425, pp. 157-58; E. D. Burton, *Syntax of the Moods and Tenses in New Testament Greek* [Edinburgh, 1898], § 33, pp. 15-16).

[67]For the sense of πρός in πρὸς ἐμαυτόν ("with myself") cf. Mark 6:3; 9:19; 14:49; John 1:1-2; 1 Thess. 3:4.

more because it would be a breach of his friendship and Christian fellowship with Philemon. Onesimus had probably begun to make himself useful to Paul, but he could hardly have been said to serve him on Philemon's behalf without Philemon's knowing anything about it. If, however, Philemon sent him back to continue his service to Paul, then the service would be rendered by Philemon as well as by Onesimus. Restricted in his movements as he was, Paul depended in great measure on the personal service of others. Timothy was with him, indeed, but Timothy was his agent in evangelistic and pastoral concerns which sometimes involved him in long absences (as when he was sent from Rome to Philippi with news of the outcome, or probable outcome, of Paul's appearance before the imperial tribunal).[68] But if Onesimus were sent back, he could be available all the time to attend to Paul's personal needs, and this would be no mean contribution to the service of the gospel.

A parallel to Onesimus's serving Paul on Philemon's behalf is provided by Epaphroditus of Philippi. Epaphroditus was sent to Rome by his fellow-members of the Philippian church to deliver a monetary gift to Paul and to stay on and minister to his need on their behalf. (Paul, however, sent him back rather soon to allay the anxiety with which the Philippian Christians had received the news of a nearly fatal illness which Epaphroditus had suffered in the course of his journey.)[69]

The letter to the Philippians also provides parallels to Paul's speaking of himself as being (literally) "in the chains of the gospel"[70]—in Phil. 1:7, where the Christians of Philippi, being partners of grace with him in his chains, are thereby partners with him "in the defense and confirmation of the gospel," and in Phil. 1:13, where he rejoices that to the whole praetorian guard and all the other officials who are in any way involved with his case it has been made manifest that his chains are "in Christ"— that is, that his imprisonment is for the gospel's sake. To wear "the chains of the gospel" was for Paul a badge of honor, a Distinguished Service Order awarded by his commander-in-chief.

14 Philemon, then, is given plainly to understand what is expected of him, but the favor which Paul asks must be granted spontaneously,[71] under the prompting of Christian grace. Only so would he be happy to receive it. Paul might have kept Onesimus with him and sent Philemon a letter by the hand of Tychicus, saying, "I have kept him here to serve me as your representative, because I know that is what you would wish"—

[68]Phil. 2:19-23; cf. 1 Cor. 4:17-18; Acts 19:22.
[69]Phil. 2:25-30; 4:18 (cf. F. F. Bruce, *Philippians*, GNBC, pp. 70-75).
[70]Gk. ἐν τοῖς δεσμοῖς τοῦ εὐαγγελίου.
[71]Gk. κατὰ ἑκούσιον.

but then Philemon would have had little option in the matter; he would be rendering Paul a service "as it were compulsorily."[72] Practically the same phrase is used in relation to the Jerusalem relief fund in 2 Cor. 9:7, where the Corinthians are encouraged to make their contributions "each one as he has chosen to do, not reluctantly or *compulsorily*,[73] for 'God loves a cheerful giver.' "[74] It would cheer Paul's heart if Philemon acceded to his request cheerfully; his free and genuine consent[75] indeed was essential.

IV. THE REQUEST REINFORCED (15-20)

15 *Perhaps the reason he was separated from you for a time was that you might have him to yourself[76] forever,*

16 *no longer as a slave, but more than a slave—a dear brother, dear especially to me, and how much more to you, both in your earthly relationship and in the Lord.*

17 *So then, if you regard me as a partner, receive him as you would me.*

18 *And if he has wronged you in any way, if he owes you anything, put it down to my account.*

19 *I write this with my own hand: "I will repay it. PAUL." (I need not mention that, for your part,[77] you owe me your very self.)[78]*

20 *Yes, my brother, may I for my part have this "profit" from you in the Lord; refresh my heart in Christ.[79]*

15 The "separation"[80] of Onesimus from Philemon was of Onesimus's making; Philemon's part in the matter was wholly involuntary and passive. But Paul refers to the separation as though it were God's act,[81] brought about, or at least overruled, by him for the lasting benefit of

[72]Gk. ὡς κατ᾽ ἀνάγκην.

[73]Gk. μὴ ἐκ λύπης ἢ ἐξ ἀνάγκης.

[74]A quotation from Prov. 22:8a LXX (ἄνδρα ἱλαρὸν καὶ δότην εὐλογεῖ ὁ θεός).

[75]χωρὶς δὲ τῆς σῆς γνώμης, "but without your consent," says Paul, "I would take no action" (οὐδὲν ἠθέλησα ποιῆσαι, possibly, but not necessarily, epistolary aorist); for γνώμη in the sense of "consent" or "approval" cf. Ignatius, *Polyc.* 5:2, "it is right for men and women who marry to be joined with the consent of the bishop (μετὰ γνώμης τοῦ ἐπισκόπου)."

[76]Gk. ἀπέχω, an emphatic compound of ἔχω, used (e.g.) of receiving payment in full (as in Phil. 4:18), hence rendered "have him to yourself," "keep him."

[77]Rendering the emphatic καί.

[78]D* adds ἐν κυρίῳ (as at the end of v. 16).

[79]D² and the majority of cursives read ἐν κυρίῳ.

[80]J. Knox (*Philemon among the Letters*, p. 22) sees (tentatively) a connection between ἐχωρίσθη here and χωρὶς . . . τῆς σῆς γνώμης in v. 14; this is quite improbable.

[81]The implied agent in the passive ἐχωρίσθη is God.

Philemon and Onesimus alike, and indeed for Paul's benefit too.[82] But for the separation, Onesimus would have remained with Philemon as his slave until their relationship was terminated in some way or other—by emancipation, redemption, resale, or death. Then the relationship would exist no more. But, thanks to the separation, Onesimus was now a member of Christ, as Philemon already was, and a new and deeper relationship was thus established which would never come to an end.

16 Whatever their earthly relationship might be from now on, henceforth Onesimus was Philemon's "forever" (and equally Philemon was Onesimus's). Was Onesimus still Philemon's slave (and Philemon, therefore, Onesimus's master)? In law, yes; unless Philemon took steps to end that relationship. But Paul commends Onesimus to Philemon "no longer as a slave." He writes as one who assumes that Philemon will do the decent thing—that he will take legal steps to change the master-slave relationship. He could exercise his apostolic authority and direct Philemon to free Onesimus, but he could not *compel* him to do so: the responsibility and initiative must lie with Philemon. Even if he directed him to free Onesimus and Philemon unwillingly obeyed, there would be no virtue in that, and it would not promote a feeling of brotherly friendship between Philemon and Onesimus. But if Philemon set Onesimus free as the spontaneous expression of the grace of God working in his heart, he would derive real joy from the act, and the joy would be shared by Onesimus. As Christian brothers, they would belong to each other for eternity as well as time.[83]

As for Paul himself, he had already begun to appreciate Onesimus as "a dear brother"—although he preferred to call him his dear "child." When he says, "dear especially to me," his meaning would naturally be taken to mean "even dearer to me than to you," but for the fact that he goes on immediately to say, "and how much more to you."[84] Since Ones-

---

[82] "For this reason (διὰ τοῦτο), perhaps, he was separated from you": in the NT (where the pronoun ὅδε is rarely used) διὰ τοῦτο may refer either backward or forward; here (*pace* J. Knox, *Philemon among the Letters*, p. 22, n. 11) it is most naturally understood as referring forward, anticipating the ἵνα clause. Paul's "perhaps" (τάχα) envisages at least the possibility that Philemon might keep Onesimus with himself and not send him back, as Paul hopes he will.

[83] The adjective αἰώνιος (in ἵνα αἰώνιον αὐτὸν ἀπέχῃς) might mean "lifelong"; but since brotherhood "in the Lord" is not terminated by death, there is no need so to restrict its meaning.

[84] Gk. μάλιστα ἐμοί, πόσῳ δὲ μᾶλλον σοί. C. F. D. Moule (*ad loc.*) takes μάλιστα as elative, but he mentions that Lightfoot treats Paul's wording as an enthusiastic illogicality: "most of all to me—*more* than most of all to thee." Less satisfactorily, J. Knox, taking μάλιστα as a real superlative, understands μᾶλλον to mean that Onesimus is to be dearer *than before* to his owner (*Philemon among the Letters*, pp. 23-24).

imus was a member of Philemon's household (and, if emancipated, would continue to be one as Philemon's freedman), an earthly relationship was already established between them. Now, however, to that earthly relationship was added their new relationship in the Lord.

The phrase "in your earthly relationship" has been chosen to translate the two Greek words which are rendered literally "in (the) flesh."[85] This has suggested to some readers that there was a blood-relationship between the two men. Such a state of affairs would be not at all unusual: if, for example, Onesimus were the son of Philemon's father by a slave-girl, then Onesimus and Philemon would be half-brothers, but Onesimus (unless emancipated) would still be a slave. But nothing in Paul's language implies that this in fact was the situation: his language means that, whereas the master-slave relationship was a relationship "in the flesh," the new brotherly relationship into which the two men had entered was a relationship "in the Lord." Relationships "in the flesh" are limited to earthly life; relationships "in the Lord" endure forever.

17 Paul has spoken of himself as sending back to Philemon his very heart, a part of himself (v. 12). Now he asks that Philemon should recognize this through his reception of Onesimus: Onesimus, he hopes, will be greeted with the kind of welcome that Paul himself would be given. Even the most forgiving of Christian masters would normally find it difficult to exclude a note of disapproval on finding the prodigal servant back again at his door: no, says Paul, give him the same warm welcome as you would give to me if you found me unexpectedly at your door. Paul and Philemon were "partners" in this at least, that they shared the same fellowship of grace and faith; and this fellowship had recently made room for Onesimus: he was now a member of Paul's circle of friendship. Apparently the partnership between Paul and Philemon was not simply a matter of their being fellow-Christians; if Philemon was Paul's "dear fellow-worker," he was probably involved with him in some aspect of his ministry.[86] On the strength of that partnership Paul asks Philemon to receive Onesimus.

---

[85]Gk. ἐν σαρκί, expressing the idea more commonly expressed by κατὰ σάρκα. Elsewhere in Paul ἐν σαρκί means "in an unregenerate state" (e.g., Rom. 8:8-9) or "in mortal body" (e.g., 2 Cor. 10:3). For κατὰ σάρκα expressing earthly relationships cf. Rom. 1:3; 9:3, 5, and especially (with regard to the master/slave relationship) Col. 3:22; Eph. 6:5.

[86]"If, then, you have me as a partner," says Paul (εἰ οὖν με ἔχεις κοινωνόν); for this sense of ἔχω cf. (e.g.) Matt. 14:5, ὡς προφήτην αὐτὸν εἶχον, "they regarded him as a prophet." The force of κοινωνός here seems to be more specific than that of κοινωνία in v. 6.

The receiving of fellow-believers was an elementary Christian duty: "receive one another," says Paul to the Romans, "as Christ also received you, to the glory of God" (Rom. 15:7). The verb used in his present request to Philemon is the same as that used in his exhortation to the Romans, and in an appropriate context it means "take on as a partner."[87] Here we undoubtedly have an appropriate context for this nuance. "If you regard me as a partner," says Paul, "take him on as a partner too, on the same footing as myself." Whatever share Philemon had taken in Paul's ministry entitled him to be called a "fellow-worker." Onesimus, who had begun to make a valued contribution to Paul's ministry, was also a "fellow-worker"; henceforth Philemon and Onesimus must look on each other as partners in the work of Christ.

18 But before someone could be taken on as a partner, some assurance of his financial solvency would be expected.[88] Philemon need have no misgivings on this score where Onesimus is concerned; Paul will be Onesimus's guarantor.

More than this is involved, however. It could be that Onesimus had done Philemon some injury in law, and not only by depriving him of his services.[89] Paul mentions this possibility tactfully, but he would not have raised the matter at all and risked sowing gratuitous suspicions in Philemon's mind if he had not had reason to know that Onesimus had indeed defrauded him in some way. When he left Philemon's service, did he take enough of his master's money to finance his journey? Since he himself was in law part of Philemon's property, a sophist might argue that, if he

---

[87]Gk. προσλαμβάνομαι (middle, as always in the NT); with προσλαβοῦ here cf. προσλαμβάνεσθε . . . προσελάβετο in Rom. 15:7 (as also in Rom. 14:1, 3). LSJ cite various instances of both active and middle in the sense "take on as a helper or partner," including Aristotle, *Politics* 5.8.19.1312b, προσλαβὼν τὸν δῆμον ("having got the populace on to his side") and papyrus instances of the middle, of which *P. Fay.* 12.10 (προσλαβόμενος συνεργόν), c. 103 B.C., and *P. Amh.* 100.4 (προσελάβετο . . . κοινωνόν), c. A.D. 200, are especially apposite to the present context.

[88]If Paul means this, he means it playfully; only if Onesimus were emancipated would he be either solvent or insolvent. J. Knox (*Philemon among the Letters*, p. 24, n. 13) refers to *P. Oxy.* 1209.19, where a slave is described in a contract of sale as "free from external claim" (ἐκτὸς ὄντα . . . ἐπαφῆς).

[89]Gk. εἰ δέ τι ἠδίκησέν σε. J. Knox (*Philemon among the Letters*, pp. 31-33) sees a link between this and ὁ γὰρ ἀδικῶν κτλ in Col. 3:25, which he takes to be inexplicable unless "it is . . . Onesimus who must pay for the wrong he has done, and no exception will be made. Paul has assumed his obligations, but that does not mean that he will not have to make them good." It is unlikely that the church of Colossae would read so minutely between the lines of the letter sent to it by Paul.

appropriated some of his master's money, he was but moving it from one part to another part of his master's estate. But even a sophist would find that argument less than persuasive if the slave at the same time did his best to remove himself from his master's effective jurisdiction. Sophistry apart, restitution must be made; this was integral to the reconciliation which Paul was endeavoring to bring about. But Onesimus was in no position to make, or even to guarantee, restitution. No matter, says Paul to Philemon, "whatever debt he owes you, put it down on my account."

19 Here is my undertaking, my IOU, he goes on, written and signed with my own hand: "I will make it good."[90] At this point, handcuffed though he was, Paul took the pen from the amanuensis and wrote out this promissory note, signing it with his name. He does not limit his liability; whatever be the scale of the indebtedness, let Philemon name it: it shall be repaid. It may be asked how Paul knew that he would have access to sufficient resources to honor his pledge; he had served the Lord long enough to be assured that he always supplied the resources necessary for carrying on his own work. That the reconciliation of two fellow-believers was the Lord's work Paul would not have doubted for a moment.

He adds—parenthetically, and not as an element in the promissory note—that he need hardly remind Philemon of the debt that he owes Paul.[91] That debt was his new existence as a man in Christ. As Philemon would no doubt have readily agreed, that was a debt far outweighing in kind and in value any debt that Onesimus might owe. Paul will underwrite Onesimus's debt, but how can Philemon's debt be repaid? Very simply, if one reads between the lines: by his sending Onesimus back to continue his usefulness to Paul in the service of the gospel.

---

[90]Gk. ἐγὼ ἀποτίσω (the one NT instance of ἀποτίνω), written as a χειρόγραφον (cf. Col. 2:14). The aorist ἔγραψα is epistolary.

[91]Of Onesimus he has said εἰ δέ τι . . . ὀφείλει ("if he owes anything"); to Philemon he says καὶ σεαυτόν μοι προσοφείλεις ("you owe me in addition even yourself"). The prefix προσ- in προσοφείλεις may imply: over and above the debt I have mentioned (owed by Onesimus), there is another debt to which I could refer if I had a mind to (ἵνα μὴ λέγω, "not to mention," involves the mention of the very thing which needs no mention). Or perhaps Paul means: you owe me your regaining of Onesimus; let me remind you of another debt you owe me. At any rate he reminds Philemon that he owes Paul his Christian life: Paul is his spiritual father. If Col. 2:1 is rightly taken to mean that Paul had not visited the Lycus valley (see p. 90), he and Philemon must have met elsewhere, perhaps while Philemon was on a visit to Ephesus. If Paul could say cheerfully with regard to Onesimus's debt τοῦτο ἐμοὶ ἐλλόγα ("put this on my account"; "charge it to me"), who would underwrite Philemon's debt to Paul? No one, of course; only Philemon could make some practical acknowledgment of it—by granting Paul the favor for which he does not ask outright.

20 That this is precisely what Paul is asking for is made clear by his play on words when he invites Philemon to grant him this "profit" in the Lord, using the verb from which Onesimus's name is derived—a verb found nowhere else in the NT.[92]

Fifty years later, Ignatius, bishop of Antioch, who in other ways betrays his acquaintance with the letter to Philemon,[93] perpetrates the same play on words. In his letter to the church of Ephesus, Ignatius finds much significance in the fact that the bishop of Ephesus bore the name Onesimus and, using the same verbal form as Paul uses here, says, "May I always have 'profit' from you, if I am worthy."[94]

If Paul were granted this "profit" in the Lord, then his heart[95] would truly be refreshed in Christ. There may be a slight difference in emphasis at times between "in the Lord" and "in Christ"; it is difficult to see any difference here.[96]

Philemon had won a good reputation for refreshing the hearts of the saints (v. 7). Here he is presented with a rare opportunity for enhancing that reputation by refreshing Paul's heart as he alone can refresh it—by sending Onesimus back to him. If Philemon is Paul's "dear fellow-worker," then, as Theophylactus of Achrida commented nine centuries ago, "if dear, he will grant the favor requested; if a fellow-worker, he will not retain the slave, but send him back for the ministry of preaching, in which he himself also is a worker."[97]

V. PROMISE OF A VISIT (21-22)

21 *I have confidence in your obedience as I write to you; I know that you will do more than I say.*

---

[92]Gk. ὀναίμην, optative of ὀνίνημι (cf. p. 213, n. 59).
[93]See p. 201.
[94]Ignatius, *Eph.* 2:2, ὀναίμην ὑμῶν διὰ παντός, ἐάνπερ ἄξιος ὦ (the construction is the same as Paul's ἐγώ σου ὀναίμην ἐν κυρίῳ).
[95]Gk. σπλάγχνα, as in v. 7 (cf. v. 12).
[96]Cf. p. 164, n. 178 (on Col. 3:18). "If one uses the familiar Christian cliché, 'Become what you are!', the one may say that what you are is 'in Christ', and what you are to become is 'in the Lord' " (C. F. D. Moule, *The Origin of Christology* [Cambridge, 1977], p. 59). Here the phrase "in the Lord" is tantamount to "in the Lord's service" (Moule, *op. cit.*, p. 54) or "for the service of the gospel" (E. Lohmeyer, *ad loc.*, quoted with approval by J. Knox, *Philemon among the Letters*, p. 25).
[97]Theophylactus, *Commentary on the Letter to Philemon* (*PG* 125.174B): εἰ ἀγαπητός, δώσει τὴν χάριν· εἰ συνεργός, οὐ καθέξει τὸν δοῦλον, ἀλλὰ πάλιν ἀποστελεῖ πρὸς ὑπηρεσίαν τοῦ κηρύγματος, οὗ καὶ αὐτὸς ἐργάτης ἐστίν.

THE EPISTLE TO PHILEMON

22 *At the same time, please prepare a guestroom for me; I hope that,
thanks to your prayers, I shall be granted to you.*

21 If Paul does not give orders to Philemon, he at least expects
"obedience" from him, even if the obedience be acquiescence in a request
rather than compliance with a demand.[98] He is sure, he says, that Philemon
will not only read what is written in his letter but read between the lines
and see what Paul would really like him to do—and do it.

In accordance with his custom, Paul writes the closing sentences
himself: so much may be inferred from his words "I write to you."[99] It is
indeed conceivable that he kept the pen in his hand after writing the promissory note of v. 19. It is unnecessary to infer, as Lightfoot does, that he
wrote the whole letter himself—a procedure which would have been "quite
exceptional," as Lightfoot admits (in his notes on v. 19). With chains on
his wrists, and with Timothy available as his amanuensis, it was much
more natural for Paul to dictate the greater part of the letter.

22 The request to Philemon to have a guestroom[100] ready in preparation for a visit by Paul if their prayers are answered and he is released
has been thought to be a further piece of gentle pressure on Philemon; but
it is not necessarily so. Proponents of an Ephesian or Caesarean provenance
for this letter and its companions have pointed to this request in support
of their case:[101] from Rome, they say, Paul intended (in the event of his
discharge) to go on to Spain. But there are indications that the situation
in Paul's Aegean mission field had changed in ways which called for a
brief personal visit from him (if this were possible) before he went to
Spain. In the letter to the Philippians (for which the internal evidence for

---

[98]Gk. ὑπακοή, used of the obedience which, by virtue of his apostolic authority,
he demands from his recalcitrant converts in Corinth (2 Cor. 7:15; 10:6); it is
ultimately obedience to Christ (2 Cor. 10:5).

[99]See p. 186, nn. 78, 79 (on Col. 4:18). The bare fact of his writing ἔγραψα
(epistolary aorist, as in v. 19) would not necessarily mean that his hand held the
pen (this inference is not naturally drawn from the repeated ἔγραψα of 1 Cor. 5:9,
11 and it would be wrong to draw it from Rom. 15:15): *qui facit per alium facit
per se.* But in the *clausula* of the letter the author's own handwriting would be
expected.

[100]Gk. ξενία, used in Acts 28:23 of Paul's lodgings in Rome. It is not expressly
said here that the guestroom would be in Philemon's house, but a house which
could accommodate a local church would no doubt have room for an apostle whose
requirements were very modest. Theodoret, bishop of Cyrrhus A.D. 423–c. 466,
says in the preface to his commentary on this letter that Philemon's house had
survived to his own day (*PG* 82.871A).

[101]Cf. M. Dibelius, *ad loc.*; see also pp. 194-95 above.

a Roman provenance is especially cogent) he expresses the hope of visiting Philippi soon (Phil. 2:24).

Despite his statement to the Roman Christians that, at the beginning of A.D. 57, he had "no longer . . . any room for work" in the Aegean world (Rom. 15:23), and Luke's report of his telling the elders of the Ephesian church a month or two later that they would never see him again (Acts 20:25), a change in his schedule cannot be ruled out. His travel plans were never inflexible; they were always subject to his conviction of divine guidance. Indeed, his readiness to change them sometimes proved disconcerting to his friends and gave his opponents ground for charging him with vacillation (cf. 2 Cor. 1:15–2:1). If a Roman provenance for Philemon is probable on other grounds, Paul's expressed hope of visiting the Lycus valley is not a decisive argument against it.

When he speaks of "*your* prayers" and of being "granted to *you*," Paul uses the plural of the second person pronoun:[102] in this matter (by contrast with the body of the letter) Philemon's associates are involved as well as himself.

Such a section as this in Paul's correspondence, including the mention of an impending visit, has been called the "travelogue" or the "apostolic *parousia*."[103]

VI. GREETINGS FROM PAUL'S COMPANIONS (23-24)

23 *Epaphras, my fellow-prisoner, sends you his greetings in Christ Jesus;*
24 *so do Mark, Aristarchus, Demas, and Luke, my fellow-workers.*

23 It is natural that Epaphras, out of Paul's present companions, should be mentioned first as sending personal greetings to Philemon.[104] As the evangelist of the Lycus valley, he would be personally known to Phi-

---

[102]Gk. διὰ τῶν προσευχῶν ὑμῶν χαρισθήσομαι ὑμῖν, "I shall be granted to you," not so much by Caesar's favorable judgment as by God's answer to their prayers.

[103]For the term "travelogue" see R. W. Funk, *Language, Hermeneutic and the Word of God* (New York, 1966), pp. 264-74; for "apostolic *parousia*" see R. W. Funk, "The Apostolic *Parousia*: Form and Significance," in *Christian History and Interpretation,* ed. W. R. Farmer, C. F. D. Moule, and R. R. Niebuhr (Cambridge, 1967), pp. 249-68.

[104]The pronoun of the second person is again singular: ἀσπάζεταί σε.

lemon, as probably the others were not.[105] Paul speaks of him here as his "fellow-prisoner";[106] this certainly means more than "fellow-Christian,"[107] but in what circumstances Epaphras had earned this title we can but speculate. He shares the title, among Paul's friends, with Aristarchus (Col. 4:10) and with Andronicus and Junia (Rom. 16:7). He may have shared Paul's imprisonment at the time when this letter was written, or at some earlier time. It may well have been he who brought Paul and Onesimus together.

"Greetings in Christ Jesus" are greetings sent to a fellow-believer, a fellow-member of the body of Christ.

24 Paul's four other fellow-workers who send their greetings to Philemon are similarly joined with Epaphras in sending greetings to the church of Colossae (Col. 4:10-14). Here they are not divided into those "of the circumcision" and others, as they are in Colossians; their names are arranged in no special order. The only one in the Colossians list whose name does not appear here is Jesus Justus; he had perhaps moved elsewhere by the time this letter was written.[108] If these men are Paul's fellow-workers,[109] and Philemon is also his fellow-worker (v. 1), Philemon and they are fellow-workers together.

VII. FINAL BENEDICTION (25)

25 The grace of the Lord[110] Jesus Christ be with your spirit.[111]

25 The grace-benediction is addressed to Philemon and his associates—all those greeted in the prescript, including the church in his house. The form of the benediction here is identical with that in Phil. 4:23 (and

---

[105]Cf. Col. 1:7; 4:12.

[106]Gk. συναιχμάλωτος, literally "fellow-prisoner-of-war" (cf. p. 178, on Col. 4:10).

[107]"Mitchrist," says M. Dibelius (*ad loc.*, and on Col. 4:10).

[108]E. Amling, "Eine Konjektur im Philemonbrief," *ZNW* 10 (1909), 261-62, argued that the name of Jesus Justus was omitted from the present list by a scribal mistake.

[109]Gk. συνεργοί, as in Col. 4:11.

[110]After κυρίου, A C D Ψ and the majority of cursives with lat syr^pesh co insert ἡμῶν ("our").

[111]A final ἀμήν is added in ℵ C D² Ψ and the majority of cursives with lat syr co^bo. As in Col. 4:18 and other letters where it was probably absent from the original text, the addition of "Amen" is due to its being the congregation's response when the letter was read aloud as part of the church's lectionary (cf. p. 331 with n. 115).

with that in Gal. 6:18, except that there the vocative "brothers" and a final "Amen" are added). "With your spirit" is a variant on "with you" (as in the well-known versicle and response: "The Lord be with you / And with thy spirit").[112]

[112]See L. G. Champion, *Benedictions and Doxologies in the Epistles of Paul* (Oxford, 1934).

The Epistle
to the
EPHESIANS

INTRODUCTION TO EPHESIANS

I. EPHESIANS AND THE PAULINE CORPUS

The letter to the Ephesians has been described, not unjustly, as "the quintessence of Paulinism."[1] It sums up in large measure the leading themes of the Pauline writings, together with the central motif of Paul's ministry as apostle to the Gentiles. But it does more than that: it carries the thought of the earlier letters forward to a new stage. An even better designation for it than "the quintessence of Paulinism" would be, in C. H. Dodd's words, "the crown of Paulinism."[2]

Ephesians is not an easy document for the NT student to come to terms with. "It is really a tract dressed up in epistolary form," says R. H. Fuller.[3] Markus Barth calls it "a stranger at the door" of the Pauline corpus.[4] E. J. Goodspeed spoke of it, ominously, as "the Waterloo of commentators."[5] More promisingly, he described it as "a great rhapsody of the Christian salvation."[6] It reads, he said further, "like a commentary on the Pauline letters"[7]—a rather strange way of referring to a document which, a few lines previously, was compared to "a mosaic of Pauline

[1]So F. F. Bruce, *Paul: Apostle of the Free Spirit* (Exeter/Grand Rapids, 1977), p. 424. The phrase "the quintessence of Paulinism" was the title of a lecture by A. S. Peake in *BJRL* 4 (1917-18), 285-311, reprinted in J. T. Wilkinson (ed.), *Arthur Samuel Peake* (London, 1958), pp. 116-42.
[2]C. H. Dodd, "Ephesians," in *The Abingdon Bible Commentary,* ed. F. C. Eiselen, E. Lewis, and D. G. Downey (New York, 1929), pp. 1224-25: "whether the Epistle is by Paul or not, certainly *its thought is the crown of Paulinism"* (and this Dodd regarded as the weightiest argument for its Pauline authorship).
[3]R. H. Fuller, *A Critical Introduction to the New Testament* (London, 1966), p. 66.
[4]M. Barth, *The Broken Wall* (London, 1960), p. 9.
[5]E. J. Goodspeed, *The Meaning of Ephesians* (Chicago, 1933), p. 15.
[6]*The Meaning of Ephesians,* p. 3.
[7]*The Meaning of Ephesians,* p. 9.

materials."[8] A mosaic made up of fragments of an author's writings is not best calculated to provide a commentary on them. But, if not a commentary, it is indeed an exposition of the Pauline mission and message.

Ephesians has a structural unity not unlike that of its own "building fitly framed together."[9] This structural unity is matched by an inner unity of conception and execution; the loftiness of the thought thus conceived and executed moved Coleridge to characterize the document as "the divinest composition of man."[10]

"In form," said Goodspeed, "it is an encyclical."[11] This is a widely held view, to which some support is given by the textual evidence of the prescript, which throws doubt on the mention of Ephesus as the place to which the letter was to be sent.[12] It might be called a general letter to Gentile Christians, more particularly in the province of Asia—Gentile Christians who (like the readers of 1 Peter) needed to be shown what was involved in their recent commitment to the way of Christ. But these Gentile Christians are not personally known to Paul: he has heard of their faith and love, and it is evidently by hearsay that they know of him and his commission to preach the gospel to the Gentiles. If, then, they live in the province of Asia, we shall not look for them in Ephesus or its neighborhood, but in some region of the province which Paul himself had not visited. The special affinities between Ephesians and Colossians might suggest that Ephesians, like Colossians, was destined for Christians in the Lycus valley. If so, it is natural to ask whether it could have been the "letter from Laodicea" mentioned in Col. 4:16.[13] We know that in Marcion's *apostolikon* Ephesians was listed as "the letter to the Laodiceans";[14] we do not know if he had any more substantial ground for so entitling it than an inference from Col. 4:16. It is conceivable that, when a special letter was sent to the church of Colossae, one in more general terms was sent by the same messenger to other churches in the district, including

[8]*The Meaning of Ephesians*, p. 8.
[9]Eph. 2:21 (KJV).
[10]S. T. Coleridge, *Table Talk*, May 25, 1830; see H. N. Coleridge (ed.), *Specimens of the Table Talk of the late Samuel Taylor Coleridge* (London, 1835), p. 88. "The Epistle to the Ephesians," said Coleridge on this occasion, "is evidently a catholic epistle, addressed to the whole of what might be called St. Paul's diocese. . . . It embraces every doctrine of Christianity;—first, those doctrines peculiar to Christianity, and then those precepts common to it with natural religion."
[11]*The Meaning of Ephesians*, p. 3.
[12]See pp. 249-50 with nn. 4, 6, 10.
[13]See p. 184-85 with nn. 67-73.
[14]Tertullian, *Against Marcion* 5.17.

those of Hierapolis and Laodicea, and that this might be our Ephesians. More than this cannot be said.

If in Colossians the role of Christ as Lord over the cosmos has been unfolded, Ephesians carries on the same train of thought by considering the implications of this for the church as the body of Christ. What is the church's relation to Christ's cosmic role, to the principalities and powers, to God's eternal purpose? This change of perspective from Christ to the church may go far to account for the different nuances which have been discerned in the use of such terms as "fullness" and "mystery" in Ephesians as compared with Colossians.[15]

While the affinities of Ephesians are closest with Colossians among the Pauline letters, its affinities with other letters in the collection are unmistakable. It has manifest affinities with 1 Corinthians: in particular, the teaching about the church which in the earlier epistle is applied to the life of one local congregation is universalized in Ephesians. Nor can its links with the teaching of Romans be overlooked. If Paul in Romans emphasizes that "there is no distinction" between Jew and Gentile, whether "in Adam" or "in Christ" (Rom. 3:22; 10:12), so in Ephesians all the spiritual blessings which are available to human beings "in the heavenly realm in Christ Jesus" are shown to be accessible on an equal footing to both Jews and Gentiles (Eph. 1:3; 2:6-7, 11-22; 3:6). If Paul in Romans magnifies his ministry as apostle to the Gentiles and tells how he has discharged this ministry, winning obedience from Gentiles, "from Jerusalem and as far around as Illyricum" (Rom. 11:13; 15:15-21), Ephesians presents him as "a prisoner of Christ Jesus" in the interests of the Gentiles and sees an astounding token of divine grace in the fact that he, of all people, has been chosen "to bring to the Gentiles the good news of Christ's unfathomable wealth" (Eph. 3:1, 8). In Rom. 5:11 it is through Christ that "we have now received our reconciliation"; in Ephesians it is made clear that this reconciliation has been effected through the cross so thoroughly

---

[15]In Col. 1:19; 2:9 the πλήρωμα (of deity) resides in Christ; in Eph. 1:23 it is commonly held that the church is the πλήρωμα of Christ. But see the exposition and notes on the latter passage (pp. 275-77); in any case, πλήρωμα has a wide range of meaning and need not be tied to one technical sense. As for μυστήριον, the μυστήριον of God is Christ (Col. 2:2), who is the substance of the gospel (Eph. 6:19). Distinct, but related, aspects of this μυστήριον are expounded in the two letters: in Col. 1:27 the truth that the indwelling Christ is the hope of glory for his people (Gentile as well as Jewish); in Eph. 3:2-12 the truth that in Christ Gentiles are fellow-heirs (of glory) with Jewish believers. See the discussions in E. Percy, *Die Probleme der Kolosser- und Epheserbriefe* (Lund, 1946), pp. 384-86 (on πλήρωμα), 379-80 (on μυστήριον); C. L. Mitton, *The Epistle to the Ephesians* (Oxford, 1951), pp. 94-97, 245 (on πλήρωμα), 86-91, 245 (on μυστήριον).

for Jews and Gentiles alike that both groups are reconciled not only to God but to each other, "in one body" (Eph. 2:16). In both letters Gentile believers, now incorporated in that one body with their fellow-believers of Jewish origin, have to be reminded that the Jewish believers were there first: in Rom. 11:18 Gentile Christians are told that it is the root that supports them, and not *vice versa,* while in Eph. 2:19 they are described as fellow-citizens with the (original) saints, with those who were the first to place their hope in Christ (Eph. 1:12). The Jews' standing in the divine purpose is not imperiled by the ingathering of Gentiles; rather, the grace of God is magnified in his dealings with both Jews and Gentiles. The climax of the argument of Romans is reached in the revelation of God's purpose as comprising the bringing in of "the full number of the Gentiles" and the salvation of "all Israel" (Rom. 11:25-26); Ephesians celebrates the accomplishment of this purpose and shows how the new, united community thus brought into being is the harbinger and instrument of the cosmic reconciliation yet to be realized (Eph. 1:9-10; 3:9-12).

In the eyes of many NT students, Galatians and Ephesians stand at opposite extremes of the Pauline spectrum. But both letters have in common some of the most distinctively Pauline emphases.[16] As in Gal. 1:11-16 Paul insists that he received the gospel which he was commissioned to preach among the Gentiles from no earthly teacher but through the "revelation of Jesus Christ" granted to him by God at his conversion, so in Eph. 3:3-10 he speaks of the "mystery" which was made known to him so that he might communicate it to the Gentiles. The terms "revelation" and "mystery" declare the divine origin of Paul's gospel and of his call to make that gospel known to the Gentiles in particular. The resultant incorporation of Gentile believers in the new community on an equal basis with Jewish believers was something for which Paul had to contend in Galatians, without much assurance that he would win the day. By the time Ephesians was written, some twelve years later, the presence—indeed, the predominance—of Gentiles within the community was a *fait accompli,* thanks in very large measure to Paul's own apostolic activity. The purpose of God to create a new humanity out of Jews and Gentiles (Eph. 2:15) was now being visibly realized. Tensions might remain, but they were not exclusively tensions between former Jews and former Gentiles. There is no good reason to doubt that the situation reflected in Ephesians was one which Paul could welcome within his own lifetime. When he paid his last visit to Jerusalem, the leaders of the mother-church conceded without

[16]See M. Barth, "Die Einheit des Galater- und Epheserbriefs," *TZ* 32 (1976), 78-91.

question the rightful inclusion of Gentiles within the church. The suspicions of the numerous "zealots for the law" within the Jerusalem church had not been allayed, but they were no longer in a position to imperil the status of Gentile believers (Acts 21:20-25).

Above all, one emphasis remains constant from Galatians to Ephesians—the emphasis that God's salvation is all of grace (to be received through faith) and not at all of works. "It is not by legal works that one is justified, but through faith in Jesus Christ," says Paul in Gal. 2:16, and so he still says in Eph. 2:8-9. In Galatians he says "one is justified," because the question of justification was integral to the Galatian crisis; in Ephesians he says, using a more general term, "you have been saved," perhaps because justification in the more specific sense was not a controversial issue for the readers of this letter.

Christ 2nd coming

II. THE PAROUSIA AND THE SPIRIT

One feature that Galatians and Ephesians have in common which sets them apart from the main Pauline letters is their limited reference to the *parousia*. Where the *parousia* does feature, however, it is associated in both Galatians and Ephesians with the Holy Spirit. In Gal. 5:5—the sole allusion to the *parousia* in that letter—"through the Spirit, by faith, we wait for the hope of righteousness." Twice in Ephesians the *parousia* is called the time of redemption, and on both occasions it is linked with the Spirit. In Eph. 1:14 the Spirit is "the guarantee of our inheritance, until the redemption of God's possession"; again in Eph. 4:30 it is by "the Holy Spirit of God" that believers "were sealed against the day of redemption."

The doctrine of the Spirit plays a prominent part in Ephesians, in keeping with its centrality in Paul's teaching. In view of this centrality, and especially in view of the close relation between Ephesians and Colossians, it is the more surprising that the doctrine is almost entirely absent from Colossians.[17]

In the NT in general the presence of the Spirit is a sign that the last days have come, in accordance with the prophecy of Joel 2:28-32 as quoted in Acts 2:16-21: "And in the last days it shall be, God declares, that I will pour out my Spirit upon all flesh. . . ." The presence of the Spirit, moreover, is the witness that Jesus is indeed the Messiah, the one who (in John the Baptist's words) would baptize with the Spirit (Mark 1:8; John 1:33). In other words, the new era which Jesus' passion and triumph

[17]See p. 28.

have inaugurated is the age of the Spirit to which the prophets pointed forward. This perspective pervades the NT writings, including those of Paul, in whose eyes the age of the Spirit has superseded the age of Torah.

But, in addition to the general Christian perspective on the Spirit which Paul received, he makes at least two distinctive contributions: (1) the Holy Spirit is the present guarantee of coming resurrection and glory; (2) in the Holy Spirit the people of Christ have been baptized into one corporate entity. Both these contributions, expounded in the "capital" letters, are given prominence in Ephesians.

The Spirit is called "the Holy Spirit of promise" in Eph. 1:13— not simply because he is the promised Spirit, but (as the context indicates) because to those whom he indwells he is himself the promise of resurrection life and all the heritage of glory associated with it. The *locus classicus* of this teaching is Rom. 8:9-28. There "the Spirit of him who raised Jesus from the dead" will "quicken" the mortal bodies of those who believe in Jesus; as "the Spirit of adoption" he enables them to realize their privileges and responsibilities as sons and daughters of God against the day when they will be publicly revealed as such. This "revelation" (for which, says Paul, all creation eagerly waits in order to share "the liberty of the glory of the children of God") coincides with "the redemption of our bodies"— that is, the resurrection. And of this consummation believers have already received the "first fruits" in the person of the Spirit. To the same effect Paul speaks in 2 Cor. 5:5, with reference to believers' coming investiture with their "heavenly dwelling": "He who has prepared us for this very thing is God, who has given us the Spirit as a guarantee."

This is precisely the doctrine of the Spirit in Ephesians. It is the distinctively Pauline doctrine, not merely the more general Christian doctrine. Believers, both Jewish and Gentile, have been "sealed" with the Spirit, who is the "guarantee" of their inheritance, pending God's redemption of his own possession (Eph. 1:13-14). This collocation of "seal" and "guarantee" has already appeared in 2 Cor. 1:22: "God has sealed us and set the guarantee of the Spirit in our hearts." The sealing is coincident with their believing; the occasion is that indicated in 1 Cor. 12:13, when "in one Spirit we were all baptized into one body—Jews or Greeks, slaves or free—and were all watered with one Spirit."

These words of 1 Cor. 12:13 sum up the other aspect of Paul's distinctive doctrine of the Spirit. Baptism in the Spirit (the baptizer being Christ himself) is not simply an individual experience; it is the divine act by which believers in Christ are incorporated into his body. Incorporation into Christ is implied by Paul elsewhere, when he speaks of being "baptized into Christ" (Gal. 3:27; Rom. 6:3) or "putting on Christ" (Gal. 3:27;

Rom. 13:14), but it is in 1 Cor. 12:13 that the Spirit's part in this experience finds clearest expression. This is the teaching that underlies the injunction of Eph. 4:3, to "preserve the unity of the Spirit in the bond of peace"; this "unity of the Spirit" is the unity of the body of Christ into which the people of Christ are baptized in his Spirit, for (in the words that follow immediately) "there is one body and one Spirit" (Eph. 4:4).

III. IMAGERY OF EPHESIANS

While the thought of the church as the body of Christ, animated by his Spirit, pervades Ephesians, other images are used. In Eph. 2:19-22 the church is portrayed rather as a building than as a body (although, just as architectural language is used of the body in Eph. 4:12-16, so biological language is used of the building in Eph. 2:21); but here too it is "in the Spirit" that the building takes shape, as the individual components are bonded together by Christ the "cornerstone." Here too it is in the "one Spirit" that Jewish and Gentile believers together have common access to the Father (cf. Rom. 5:2) or, by a change of figure, constitute a holy dwelling-place or temple for God (an idea anticipated in 1 Cor. 3:16-17).

These concepts of the body of Christ and the temple of God are interwoven with the concept of the "new man." In a mingling of the architectural and biological figures, the full-grown man, "the measure of the stature of Christ's fullness," is presented in Eph. 4:13-16 as the climax of the church's development. The body of Christ is "built up," growing up to match him who is its head. Christ as the second man, the last Adam, the head and embodiment of the new creation, meets us in Rom. 5:12-19 and 1 Cor. 15:20-28, 42-50. When believers' putting on Christ is mentioned in Rom. 13:14 and Gal. 3:27, this (as has been said) involves incorporation into Christ as well as the personal imitation of Christ. So, when the "new man" is said in Eph. 4:24 to be "created according to God in righteousness and true holiness" (cf. Col. 3:10, "renewed after his Creator's image so as to attain true knowledge"), the new man or new humanity is Christ himself—not Christ in isolation from his people but Christ *in* his people, the same Christ as Paul had in mind when he told his Galatian converts how he endured birth pangs over them until "Christ should be formed" in them (Gal. 4:19).

Even the analogy drawn between Christ's relation to the church and a husband's relation to his wife (Eph. 5:22-33) is adumbrated in 2 Cor. 11:2, where Paul speaks of himself as the *paranymphios* betrothing the Corinthian church to Christ "as a pure virgin to her one husband." (The

235

same analogy was developed in a completely non-Pauline stream of primitive Christianity, as may be seen from the vision in Rev. 21:2, where the beloved community is seen "coming down out of heaven from God, prepared as a bride adorned for her husband.")[18]

When we consider how the main themes and images of Ephesians are rooted in the earlier Pauline letters, there is little need to seek extraneous sources for them. In a monograph published in 1930, Heinrich Schlier argued that Ephesians was indebted for its dominant *motifs* only in a minor degree to the common stock of primitive Christianity and in much greater measure to early gnostic sources. To the common stock of primitive Christianity he traced the themes of Christ's self-devotion on his people's behalf (Eph. 5:2, 25) and God's raising him from the dead and putting all things beneath his feet (Eph. 1:20, 22). For the rest, he derived from the world of gnostic thought the motifs of the redeemer's ascent to heaven, the heavenly wall, the heavenly man, the church as the body of Christ, the body of Christ as a heavenly building, and the heavenly bridal union.[19] But when one considers how many of those motifs have their roots in Paul's thinking, as attested by his earlier letters, and how scanty, or even nonexistent, is the evidence for their presence in gnosticism at anything like a relevant date, Schlier's arguments lose some of their cogency. Twenty-seven years later, in fact, in his excellent commentary on the epistle, Schlier presented a much more balanced account (in which, among other things, he readily accepted the Pauline authorship).[20]

Quite a different origin for some of the distinctive features of the epistle was propounded in 1960 by K. G. Kuhn.[21] He found affinities between it and the Qumran literature in vocabulary (e.g., in the use of the word "mystery"), in style (e.g., a plerophoric manner of expression), and in paraenesis (including the light-darkness antithesis). The only area in Ephesians where no affinities were found in the Qumran texts was Christology, "which of course in Ephesians also includes ecclesiology" (expounded in the head-body imagery and the bridal union of Christ and the

---

[18]There are OT antecedents for both the Pauline and the Johannine presentations of this analogy (see p. 387, n. 95).

[19]H. Schlier, *Christus und die Kirche im Epheserbrief* (Tübingen, 1930); cf. K. L. Schmidt, *TDNT* 3, pp. 510-11 (*s.v.* ἐκκλησία).

[20]H. Schlier, *Der Brief an die Epheser* (Düsseldorf, 1957).

[21]K. G. Kuhn, "Der Epheserbrief im Lichte der Qumrantexte," *NTS* 7 (1960-61), 334-46 (based on a paper read to the Studiorum Novi Testamenti Societas at Aarhus, Denmark, in August 1960), E.T. "The Epistle to the Ephesians in the Light of the Qumran Texts," in *Paul and Qumran*, ed. J. Murphy-O'Connor (London, 1968), pp. 115-31.

church); one would not expect to find this in the literature of a Jewish community. As for the affinities to which Kuhn drew attention, the explanation has been offered that "either Paul or a disciple, who was entrusted under his direction with the final redaction of the epistle, had a first-hand knowledge of the writings of Qumran," and that Ephesus was a place where such knowledge could have been acquired.[22]

IV. INCIPIENT CATHOLICISM

It has been urged that Ephesians is most plainly seen to be post-Pauline in the incipient or emergent catholicism of its teaching about the church.[23] Chief among the elements of incipient catholicism, so far as Ephesians is concerned, is the conception of the church throughout the world as a unity.

We have seen that Ephesians universalizes the church doctrine of 1 Corinthians, but the universal principle which finds clear expression in Ephesians is latent in 1 Corinthians, which is addressed not only to "the church of God that is in Corinth" but also to "all those who in every place call on the name of our Lord Jesus Christ" (1 Cor. 1:1). It is emphasized in 1 Cor. 12:4-6 that the unity of the church follows from the fact that "the same Spirit, . . . the same Lord . . . and the same God" control all the diversities of ministry within it. But by the same token, wherever the church exists, it comprises one people of Christ, indwelt by the one Spirit, confessing the one Lord, and through him worshipping the one God. Thus the same argument as is presented in 1 Cor. 12:4-6 for the unity of the local church is applied in Eph. 4:4-6 to the unity of the universal church. And the church in which, according to 1 Cor. 12:28, God has appointed apostles, prophets, and other ministers cannot be restricted to the Christian community in Corinth.

We might *a priori* have expected Paul to think of the Christians throughout his mission field as forming a unity; indeed, he went farther and promoted a sense of practical unity between them and other churches,

---

[22]P. Benoit, "Qumran and the New Testament," E.T. in *Paul and Qumran*, ed. J. Murphy-O'Connor, p. 17. Cf. H. Koester, "Gnomai Diaphoroi: The Origin and Nature of Diversification in the History of Early Christianity," *HTR* 58 (1965), 279-318.

[23]See E. Käsemann, "Epheserbrief," *RGG*[3] 2, cols. 517-20; "Ephesians and Acts," in *Studies in Luke-Acts*, ed. L. E. Keck and J. L. Martyn (Nashville/New York, 1966), pp. 288-97 ("In the New Testament it is Ephesians that most clearly marks the transition from the Pauline tradition to the perspectives of the early Catholic era").

especially the church of Jerusalem. He knew that "Israel after the flesh" did not exist only in local synagogues; it was an ecumenical reality. The synagogue in any city was the local manifestation of the whole "congregation of Israel."[24] It was natural that Paul should think in the same way of the new community, embracing Jews and Gentiles indiscriminately.

Moreover, all Christians had been "baptized into *Christ*,"[25] not merely into a local fellowship. They therefore formed part of one spiritual entity, which Paul calls the body of Christ. In baptism they had been united with Christ in his death, to rise with him in the likeness of his resurrection and so "walk in newness of life" (Rom. 6:3-5). The Christians in Corinth are reminded that they are Christ's body, and individually members thereof (1 Cor. 12:27); similarly those in Rome are told that "we" (that is, not the Roman Christians alone but the Roman Christians in fellowship with Paul and others), "though many, are one body in Christ, and individually members one of another" (Rom. 12:5). To Paul's way of thinking Christ could no more be divided among the several congregations than he could be divided among the factions within the congregation at Corinth.[26] The explicit teaching about the church universal in Ephesians is a corollary of Paul's understanding of the phrase "in Christ" and all that it implies.

Language such as Paul uses to the Corinthian and Roman Christians about membership in the body of Christ could not be locally restricted, even if the occasions that called forth the letters to Corinth and Rome directed its application to the conditions of local fellowship. All believers—in Corinth and Rome, in Ephesus and Jerusalem, and everywhere else—had together died with Christ and been raised with him;[27] as participators in his life they could not but constitute one universal fellowship.

When incipient catholicism is discerned in NT documents, it is implied that those features are present which were to characterize the life and theology of the later church, the church itself being viewed as the

[24]On the analogy in this regard between the synagogue and the church see K. L. Schmidt, *TDNT* 3, pp. 524-26 (*s.v.* ἐκκλησία).

[25]Gal. 3:27; Rom. 6:3.

[26]The "one body" into which, as Paul tells the Corinthians, "we were all baptized in one Spirit" (1 Cor. 12:13) cannot be restricted to the church of Corinth. When members of the Corinthian church moved to another city and joined another congregation (as Priscilla and Aquila moved from Corinth to Ephesus and back from there to Rome), they remained members of the same body of Christ.

[27]Although in Rom. 6:5 those who have (baptismally) shared Christ's death will at some time in the future share his resurrection, yet in Rom. 6:11 they are exhorted to reckon themselves as being already "alive to God in Christ Jesus"; in that sense they have already shared his resurrection (cf. Col. 2:13; 3:1; Eph. 2:5-6).

locus of salvation.[28] But the universal church is far from being presented in Ephesians as a cultic institution, with a priesthood mediating the means of grace to the rank and file of the faithful. Not even in the latest NT documents has it come anywhere near that stage of development. The church's ministry in Ephesians is still mainly charismatic: it is not regulated as it is in the Pastorals. The apostles and the prophets of Eph. 4:11 constitute foundation ministries (as in Eph. 2:20); as for the evangelists, pastors, and teachers, they do not reserve the ministry to themselves but are given to the church by the ascended Lord that they may enable all its members to discharge their respective ministries, each member functioning for the health and growth of the whole body.[29]

In Paul's capital letters the one instance of interchurch organization is provided by the relief fund for the "saints" at Jerusalem. To promote the collection and conveyance of the money for this purpose he invited the contributing churches (all Gentile churches of his own planting) to appoint one or two delegates each.[30] In Ephesians there is naturally no reference to the relief fund (it was a thing of the past by the time this letter was written), but it contains no hint of any other interchurch organization. In Ephesians the universal church is an organism, not an organization, just as the local church is in 1 Corinthians. Even so, despite hints of a wider unity in 1 Corinthians, it remains true that the organism in view in that letter is predominantly the local church, as certainly as that the organism in view in Ephesians is the church universal.

Could this development from a local to a catholic ecclesiology, seen especially in the transition from 1 Corinthians to Ephesians, have taken place not merely in Paul's lifetime but in his own thinking? The confidence with which the answers "Yes" and "No" have been given to this question suggests that the issue is not to be decided on strictly objective criteria. On the one hand, W. G. Kümmel may be cited as representative of those who answer "No." The fact that "in Ephesians *ekklēsia* is used exclusively of the universal church (1:22; 3:10, 21; 5:23-25, 27, 29, 32), whereas in all the Pauline epistles, even in Colossians, *ekklēsia* indicates the individual congregations as well as the total church" is one among several arguments which lead him to the conclusion that "the theology of Ephesians makes the Pauline composition of the Epistle completely impossible."[31] On the other hand, Henry Chadwick reviews the main arguments propounded

[28]Cf. E. Käsemann, "Ephesians and Acts," pp. 289-90.
[29]This is denied by C. Masson, *L'Épître aux Éphésiens*, CNT (Neuchatêl/Paris, 1953), p. 199.
[30]1 Cor. 16:3; 2 Cor. 8:18-23; 9:3-5.
[31]W. G. Kümmel, *Introduction to the New Testament*, E.T. (London, 1966), p. 254.

against the Pauline authenticity of the document, and finds them inconclusive. There is, in his judgment, "no sufficient ground" for regarding Paul as incapable of producing Ephesians, and in his short commentary on the letter "the author is called Paul without either apology or question-begging."[32] The present commentary takes leave to follow his example.

If those who reject the Pauline authorship are more emphatic in their rejection than those who affirm it are in their affirmation, the reason may be that those who reject it are consciously going against tradition, whereas those who affirm it know that they have tradition behind them.[33]

No useful purpose would be served here by listing the champions on either side of the debate, but special mention may be made of one scholar whose studies led him to abandon one side for the other. This was the late Heinrich Schlier, a member of the Bultmann school who shared the general perspective of that school which rendered the Pauline authorship of Ephesians out of the question—both as regards the incipient catholicism of the document and also because of the gnostic derivation of its dominant imagery (the theme of his above-mentioned monograph, *Christus und die Kirche im Epheserbrief*).[34] His continuing study of the subject led him to the conviction that incipient catholicism and other features which he and his colleagues had identified as postapostolic accretions on the original message were in fact part and parcel of authentic primitive Christianity. His consequent publication of a commentary on Ephesians which accepted the Pauline authorship without question dismayed some of his friends almost as much as another consequence of his change of perspective—his moving over from Lutheranism into the Roman Catholic Church.[35]

V. NATURE AND PURPOSE OF EPHESIANS

Apart from the prescript (Eph. 1:1-2) and the personal notes and greeting at the end (Eph. 6:21-24), which give the document the form of a letter, Ephesians falls into two parts:

[32]H. Chadwick, "Ephesians," in *Peake's Commentary on the Bible*[2], ed. M. Black (London, 1962), p. 982.

[33]But "the argument against the tradition, strong as it may be, falls some distance short of the demonstration claimed for it by the over-enthusiastic" (H. Chadwick, "Ephesians," p. 982). H. J. Cadbury suggested that scholars sometimes "answer the question [of the authenticity of the letter] one way or the other, more because of their unwillingness to admit indecision than out of clear conviction" ("The Dilemma of Ephesians," *NTS* 5 [1958-59], 93).

[34]See p. 236 above, with nn. 19, 20.

[35]See E. Käsemann's appreciation of the commentary ([2]1958): "Das Interpretationsproblem des Epheserbriefes," *TLZ* 86 (1961), cols. 1-8.

(1) an extended benediction and prayer, constituting the framework for a celebration of God's accomplishment in Christ of his eternal purpose, which embraces the incorporation into one divine society of Gentiles and Jews on an equal footing, and leading into a final doxology (Eph. 1:3–3:21). The liturgical character of this part is no doubt responsible for the plerophoric style (notably the piling up of genitival phrases)[36] which is such a distinctive feature of Ephesians.

(2) a lengthy paraenesis (Eph. 4:1–6:20) of a kind which must have been current in the Gentile churches. It is interrupted by a psalm quotation and interpretation in which the OT is found to foretell the ascended Christ's bestowal of gifts on his church (Eph. 4:7-16, citing Ps. 68:18), and it includes a household code in which the temporal relationship between husband and wife is set forth as an analogy to the unending relationship between Christ and the church (Eph. 5:21-33).

Whatever be the literary relation between Ephesians and Colossians,[37] Ephesians provides the logical sequel to Colossians, expounding the cosmic role of the church, the body of Christ, as Colossians expounds the cosmic role of Christ, who is head of his body, the church, and at the same time "head of every principality and power" (Col. 1:18; 2:10).

The purpose of this exposition, and the constituency for which it was designed, have been matters of wide and deep speculation.

One of the best-known hypotheses is that first propounded by E. J. Goodspeed and elaborated in particular by John Knox and C. L. Mitton. Goodspeed faced a critical consensus which rejected the tradition of Pauline authorship but could find no adequate *raison d'être* for the composition of such a pseudepigraph. Of the supposed author Adolf Jülicher had written: "it is impossible to see what purpose he could have served or why he made such a particularly thorough use of Colossians, when he himself did not lack independent ideas and was also acquainted with other Pauline Epistles."[38] Goodspeed undertook to show the purpose which Jülicher was unable to see. He first stated his hypothesis briefly: "Ephesians was written in the latter part of the first century, not to any single church but as a general letter. It shows the influence of Colossians and must have been written in connection with the movement to collect Paul's letters, probably as an introduction to them."[39] In a succession of later works he elaborated

---

[36]For example, εἰς ἔπαινον δόξης τῆς χάριτος αὐτοῦ (Eph. 1:6); κατὰ τὴν ἐνέργειαν τοῦ κράτους τῆς ἰσχύος αὐτοῦ (Eph. 1:19); εἰς πάσας τὰς γενεὰς τοῦ αἰῶνος τῶν αἰώνων (Eph. 3:21).

[37]See pp. 29-32.

[38]A. Jülicher, *An Introduction to the New Testament*, E.T. (London, 1904), pp. 146-47.

[39]E. J. Goodspeed, *The Formation of the New Testament* (Chicago, 1926), p. 28.

this suggestion.[40] Late in the first century a Christian, resident probably in the Lycus valley, who had read and reread the letter to the Colossians until he knew it practically by heart, acquired a copy of Luke-Acts. The study of this work kindled in him a keen interest in Paul, which moved him to collect as many of the letters of the apostle as he could. He decided to make the collection of Paul's letters available to the church at large, and composed Ephesians as an introduction to the collection, setting forth the main emphases of Paul's teaching in a form relevant to the needs of that later day.

John Knox took over this hypothesis and argued that the collector was Paul's convert Onesimus; he identified him with that Onesimus who, as we know from Ignatius, was bishop of Ephesus at the beginning of the second century.[41] Goodspeed was persuaded that this refinement of his own hypothesis represented the truth.[42] Knox further explained how Ephesians came to lose its original place at the head of the collected letters of Paul: when Marcion promulgated his canon around A.D. 144, he put Galatians in the first place for reasons of dogmatic preference and put Ephesians in the place formerly occupied by Galatians.[43]

C. L. Mitton presented a detailed comparative study of the text of Ephesians with Colossians and the earlier letters of Paul, with the effect of placing the main elements of Goodspeed's hypothesis on a firmer basis than Goodspeed himself had laid.[44] He does not think that the reading of Luke-Acts necessarily stimulated the collector's interest in Paul, but finds it probable that the publication of Acts created a widespread interest in the apostle which provided the collector with a unique opportunity of publishing the collection of letters with his own introduction. Perhaps, Mitton suggests, when the collector read Paul's Miletus speech to the elders of the Ephesian church in Acts 20:18-35, he paid it special attention and allowed it to influence his composition of Ephesians.[45] The collector (whether he was Onesimus or not) may have submitted his work to the aged Tychicus, one of Paul's former co-workers, who agreed that it was "a worthy presentation of Paul's message" and whose encouragment was acknowledged by the inclusion of his name in Eph. 6:21-22.[46]

---

[40]Especially E. J. Goodspeed, *The Meaning of Ephesians* (Chicago, 1933); *The Key to Ephesians* (Chicago, 1956). See also p. 200, n. 27.
[41]J. Knox, *Philemon among the Letters of Paul* (London, ²1960), pp. 85-92. (The first edition appeared in 1935.) See pp. 201-02 above.
[42]E. J. Goodspeed, *The Key to Ephesians*, pp. 14-15.
[43]*Philemon among the Letters of Paul*, pp. 67-78.
[44]C. L. Mitton, *The Epistle to the Ephesians* (Oxford, 1951).
[45]*The Epistle to the Ephesians*, pp. 213, 217-20, 266-67.
[46]*The Epistle to the Ephesians*, p. 268.

Mitton went on in a later monograph to present an account of the formation of the Pauline corpus, built on the foundation of his major work on Ephesians.[47]

If Goodspeed's hypothesis, despite the skill and learning with which it has been stated by himself and others, has failed to win wide acceptance, it is not because another hypothesis has proved more persuasive, but simply because it falls well short of demonstration.

N. A. Dahl has argued that Ephesians was written (by Paul himself) to give members of newly planted Gentile churches instruction on the meaning of their baptism. The benediction beginning in Eph. 1:3 may be regarded as based on the blessing uttered before the baptismal act, a blessing which is in turn a Christian adaptation of the blessing said before a Jewish ritual bath. Gentile converts are reminded of the status which is now theirs through their incorporation into the community of the people of God, created by him as a new humanity; they are reminded at the same time of the obligation which henceforth lies on them to lead lives worthy of this high status to which God has called them. What more appropriate occasion than their baptism could be envisaged for such a reminder as this?[48] (A similar case has been made out for regarding 1 Peter, or at least the greater part of it, as a baptismal address in written form; the evidence in 1 Peter is more explicit than in Ephesians.)[49]

J. C. Kirby also recognizes the baptismal reference in Ephesians; however, he disagrees with Dahl in that he considers the readers' baptism to have taken place some indefinite time before the letter was sent to them. The readers are being recalled to an awareness of the meaning of their baptism: as at their baptism they had "put off the old man" and "put on the new man," so they must continue to put off the one and put on the other.[50] What is envisaged, in fact, is something like the covenant renewal ceremony attested for the Qumran community.[51] This letter would have provided suitable reading for such a ceremony which, if indeed it existed,

---

[47]C. L. Mitton, *The Formation of the Pauline Corpus of Letters* (London, 1955).
[48]N. A. Dahl, "Dopet i Efesierbrevet," *STK* 21 (1945), 85-103; "Adresse und Proömium des Epheserbriefes," *TZ* 7 (1951), 241-64.
[49]See R. Perdelwitz, *Die Mysterienreligionen und das Problem des I. Petrusbriefes*, RVV 11.3 (Giessen, 1911); W. Bornemann, "Der erste Petrusbrief, eine Taufrede des Silvanus?" *ZNW* 19 (1919-20), 143-65; H. Preisker, in H. Windisch-H. Preisker, *Die katholischen Briefe*, HNT 15 (Tübingen, ³1951), 156-62; F. L. Cross, *I Peter: A Paschal Liturgy* (London, 1954), with critiques by C. F. D. Moule, "The Nature and Purpose of I Peter," *NTS* 3 (1956-57), 1-11; T. C. G. Thornton, "I Peter, A Paschal Liturgy?" *JTS* n.s. 12 (1961), 14-26.
[50]J. C. Kirby, *Ephesians, Baptism and Pentecost* (London, 1968), pp. 145, 159.
[51]*Ephesians, Baptism and Pentecost*, pp. 144-45 (cf. 1QS 1.16–3.12).

"was probably held on the Feast of Pentecost."[52] There are other features in the letter which could have a pentecostal reference: Ps. 68, for example, which is quoted and given a Christian interpretation in Eph. 4:8-10, figures as a proper psalm for Pentecost in Jewish liturgical tradition.[53] While Kirby does not push the evidence beyond due limits, he justly claims "a high degree of probability" for his thesis "that Ephesians has close connections with Jewish liturgical forms and also with Jewish and Christian traditions of Pentecost."[54] He dates the letter "probably sometime in the seventies," and ascribes it to a leader of the Ephesian church who aimed at providing his readers with "a distillation of the thought of the apostle," which had been preserved in that church's memory and worship;[55] but his central thesis would be equally applicable if the letter were composed around A.D. 60, and by Paul, possibly with the collaboration of fellow-workers who were available to him at the time.

Henry Chadwick supposes that many people in Paul's environment were somewhat embarrassed by the idea that the true revelation of God, which the gospel claimed to disclose, should have been given so late in time. "In the ancient world it is a generally acknowledged truth that nothing new can be true."[56] In Ephesians, therefore, the continuity of the new community with the people of God in earlier times is stressed; not only so, but the new community is viewed *sub specie aeternitatis*. It was divinely chosen in Christ before the world's foundation (Eph. 1:4), it is the means by which God will accomplish his eternal purpose "in the fullness of the times" (Eph. 1:9-10), and at present it provides an object-lesson of "God's manifold wisdom" to "the principalities and powers in the heavenly realm" (Eph. 3:10).

If Gentile Christians could be brought to understand the place which they have, alongside Jewish Christians, in God's plan of the ages, and to recognize the way of life which befits those who have been given such a place, their embarrassment would be dissipated. Their ingathering was no saving afterthought on God's part, no device for filling up the vacancies in his community which had been left through the failure of so

---

[52]*Ephesians, Baptism and Pentecost*, p. 145. Kirby suggests further that the household code, the "code of subordination," which is unparalleled in Qumran literature, may have come "into the Church by way of the Synagogue" and "may have been added to the admonition on the 'Way of Light and of Darkness', because it probably formed part of the ethical teaching connected with baptism" (p. 145).
[53]See pp. 340-45.
[54]*Ephesians, Baptism and Pentecost*, p. 149.
[55]*Ephesians, Baptism and Pentecost*, p. 169.
[56]H. Chadwick, "Die Absicht des Epheserbriefes," *ZNW* 51 (1960), 148.

many Jews to confess Jesus as Lord and Christ. Their salvation was due to divine grace, true: but so was the salvation of their fellow-believers of Jewish stock.[57]

There is at least firm internal evidence that the letter was written to encourage Gentile Christians to appreciate the dignity of their calling, with its implication not only for their heavenly origin and destiny but also for their present conduct on earth, as those who were heirs of God, sealed with his Spirit. Let them learn afresh the practical commitment they made when they first called on the name of Jesus as their one Lord, confessed their one faith, and sealed their new allegiance in their one baptism. Thus they would fulfil God's purpose, leading lives worthy of the calling to which he had called them.

Tychicus, on his way to the Lycus valley (and possibly other parts of proconsular Asia) with copies of this letter for the various churches to which it was addressed, would probably have passed through Ephesus. If he showed the Ephesian Christians a copy of this letter, which was a general letter with no private message, some of them might well have wished to make a copy for themselves (although they, unlike the intended recipients, were well known to the apostle). This copy would have omitted any indication of addressee.[58] If, further, this was the copy eventually used in the compilation of the *corpus Paulinum,* the fact that it belonged to the archives of the Ephesian church would be a reason for inserting the words "at Ephesus" in the prescript or labeling it "To the Ephesians," to keep it in line with the other documents in the collection. But this can be nothing better than a guess.

Be that as it may. In 1 Cor. 2:6-10 Paul tells the Corinthian Christians that, for all their claims to wisdom, he has to feed them with milk and not with solid food, because they are still spiritually immature. Their

---

[57]Chadwick argues further that a subsidiary purpose in the writing of Ephesians was to persuade members of Gentile churches which had not been founded by Paul to recognize his authority nevertheless as the duly appointed apostle of Jesus Christ to the whole Gentile world. "There must have been many such Gentile churches, which owed their existence to missionaries who stood right outside the Pauline circle" ("Die Absicht des Epheserbriefes," p. 153). There is only one church, embracing both Jewish and Gentile believers; but within this one church the Gentile congregations, whether planted by Paul and his associates or by others, are called on to see Paul as their unique representative and to give him and his mission their personal loyalty. If this is so, then the destination of Ephesians should not be sought exclusively in the churches of the Lycus valley (which, owing their existence to Epaphras, fell within Paul's apostolic sphere) but in a wider range of Gentile churches.

[58]See N. A. Dahl, "Adresse und Proömium des Epheserbriefes," pp. 247-48.

immaturity was due to deficiency not in *gnōsis* (of which they had plenty of a kind) but in *agapē*. "Nevertheless," he assures them, "to those who are mature we do impart wisdom—not the wisdom of this age . . . but God's wisdom in a mystery, the hidden wisdom ordained before the ages for our glory, . . . as it is written:

> *What eye never saw, what ear never heard,*
> *What never entered the human heart,*
> *What God prepared for those who love him—*

this is what God has revealed to us through the Spirit." Should it be asked if this divine "wisdom in a mystery" is imparted to the "mature" anywhere in the Pauline corpus, Heinrich Schlier gives an affirmative answer: it is imparted in the letter to the Ephesians.[59] He is right.

[59]H. Schlier, *Der Brief an die Epheser*, pp. 21-22.

ANALYSIS OF EPHESIANS

I. PRESCRIPT (1:1-2)
II. THE NEW HUMANITY A DIVINE CREATION (1:3 – 3:21)
   1. INTRODUCTORY *EULOGIA* (1:3-14)
     (1) Praise for Election and Adoption (1:3-6)
     (2) Praise for Redemption and Final Reconciliation (1:7-10)
     (3) Praise for the Assurance of the Believers' Heritage (1:11-14)
   2. INTRODUCTORY THANKSGIVING AND INTERCESSORY PRAYER (1:15-23)
     (1) Thanks for the Readers' Faith and Love and Prayer for Their Increase in Knowledge (1:15-19)
     (2) God's Mighty Strength Shown in the Raising of Christ (1:20-23)
   3. THE SAVING GRACE OF GOD (2:1-10)
     (1) New Life in Christ (2:1-7)
     (2) God's New Creation (2:8-10)
   4. THE INCORPORATION OF THE GENTILES (2:11-22)
     (1) Their Former Plight (2:11-12)
     (2) Their Present Access (2:13-18)
     (3) Their Membership in the House of God (2:19-22)
   5. INTERCESSORY PRAYER RESUMED (3:1)
   6. THE MYSTERY OF CHRIST (3:2-13)
     (1) Paul's Stewardship (3:2-7)
     (2) The Eternal Purpose (3:8-13)
   7. INTERCESSORY PRAYER CONCLUDED (3:14-19)
   8. DOXOLOGY (3:20-21)
III. THE NEW HUMANITY IN EARTHLY LIFE (4:1 – 6:20)
   1. EXHORTATION TO UNITY (4:1-3)
   2. CONFESSION OF FAITH (4:4-6)
   3. PROVISION FOR SPIRITUAL HEALTH AND GROWTH (4:7-16)

Text, Exposition, and Notes

EPHESIANS 1

I. PRESCRIPT (1:1-2)

1 *Paul, an apostle of Christ Jesus[1] through God's will, to the saints[2] who are[3] [at Ephesus][4], believers in Christ Jesus:*
2 *grace and peace be yours from God our Father and the Lord Jesus Christ.*

1 The prescript follows the regular Pauline pattern. As in Romans (and the Pastorals) Paul's name appears unaccompanied: in his other letters one or more colleagues are associated with him.[5] As in the prescripts of most of his letters, he identifies himself as Christ's apostle; as in 1 and 2 Corinthians, Colossians, and 2 Timothy, his apostleship is "through God's will." In the receiving and in the discharge of his ministry he is under divine direction; he has received his orders and, as he says in 1 Cor. 9:16-17, it is not for him to choose whether or not he will obey them by preaching the gospel: necessity is laid upon him.

The identity of the addressees involves a well-known textual problem. The weight of documentary evidence indicates that the phrase "at

[1]For Χριστοῦ Ἰησοῦ ℵ A F G Ψ and the majority of cursives, with lat^vet vg.cl syr^pesh, read Ἰησοῦ Χριστοῦ.
[2]After τοῖς ἁγίοις ℵ² A P 81 etc. lat^b f vg co^bo add πᾶσιν.
[3]Gk. τοῖς οὖσιν (P^46 D omit τοῖς).
[4]ἐν Ἐφέσῳ is omitted by P^46 ℵ* B* 6 424^c 1739. It appears to have been lacking in the text known to Marcion and, possibly, Tertullian (although Tertullian read *Ad Ephesios* in the title and not "To the Laodiceans," as Marcion did), and also in the texts known to Origen and Basil.
[5]Usually by name; in Gal. 1:2 they are referred to anonymously as "all the brethren who are with me."

Ephesus" is not part of the original wording.[6] This is consistent with the internal evidence of the letter: there is nothing in the contents to suggest that it was written to the church in a city where Paul had spent the best part of three years. There are no references to individuals or groups among the people addressed; there are no allusions to features or problems in a local situation. Even the letter to the Colossians, sent to a church with which Paul was not personally acquainted, is more personal from this point of view than Ephesians.

Those manuscripts which omit "at Ephesus" put nothing in its place. In Marcion's canon the letter was listed as "To the Laodiceans," but this destination has not found its way into any extant witness for Eph. 1:1. The construction without "at Ephesus" or any similar phrase is awkward: "to the saints who are also believers in Christ Jesus"[7] is not a natural form of address. For Paul and his circle "saints" and "believers in Christ Jesus" are synonymous. There is no such awkwardness about the construction of "to the saints and faithful brothers in Christ" in Col. 1:2, where the "saints" and "faithful brothers" are self-evidently the same people.[8] In Eph. 1:1 some indication of place is required by the construction,[9] and if "at Ephesus" be omitted, the best translation is: "to the saints who are . . . , believers in Christ Jesus." A space is thus left for the insertion of an indication of place, which would be appropriate in a circular letter, except that such a device, familiar as it is today, is difficult to attest for the first century.[10]

The word "believers" might be rendered "faithful" (in the sense of "loyal") but, in contrast to Col. 1:2 (where it qualifies the substantive

---

[6]One may wonder, indeed, if the words "at Ephesus" were added in an early edition (not the first edition) of the *corpus Paulinum*, having been absent from the text before the letter was included with others in a public collection. When it was so included, a title became necessary to distinguish this letter from its companions, and from the title Πρὸς Ἐφεσίους the corresponding phrase ἐν Ἐφέσῳ found its way into the prescript. (See n. 4 above.)

[7]Gk. τοῖς ἁγίοις τοῖς οὖσιν καὶ πιστοῖς ἐν Χριστῷ Ἰησοῦ.

[8]See pp. 38-39.

[9]The participial phrase τοῖς οὖσιν prepares the reader for an indication of place (cf. Rom. 1:7; Phil. 1:1, and τῇ οὔσῃ agreeing with τῇ ἐκκλησίᾳ in 1 Cor. 1:2; 2 Cor. 1:1). The participle of εἰμί in the attributive position has almost the sense of "local" when used with ἐκκλησία—for example, of the church in Jerusalem (Acts 11:22), of the church in Antioch (Acts 13:1).

[10]But G. Zuntz, pointing out that multiple copies of royal letters, identical in wording, were sent out to various addresses in the Hellenistic period, concludes that they were based on a master-copy "with the address left blank, and it is most probable that the blank in the address of Ephesians goes back to such an original" (*The Text of the Epistles* [London, 1954], p. 228, n. 1).

"brothers"), "believers" is more probably the sense here. The phrase "in Christ Jesus" is incorporative—that is to say, it does not point to Christ Jesus as the object of belief but implies that the saints and believers are united with him, partakers together of his new life.[11]

2 The salutation "grace and peace be yours" probably originated in the language of public worship and was taken over by Paul and others as an epistolary greeting.[12] The Christian reference of the grace and peace is emphasized by the added words "from God our Father and the Lord Jesus Christ."[13] That true grace and true peace come from God Paul would readily have agreed before his conversion. Now the close association of the Lord Jesus Christ with God the Father (under the government of one preposition)[14] bespeaks the place which Paul the Christian accords to his Lord—a place which (he believes) is consistent with the status to which God the Father has exalted him, sharing with him "the name which is above every name" (Phil. 2:9). Divine grace and peace are bestowed supremely in the salvation which the gospel proclaims, and in providing this salvation God and Christ are at one. The grace which lies behind this salvation (cf. Eph. 2:5, 8) is indiscriminately called "the grace of God" (Eph. 3:2) and "the grace of Christ" (Gal. 1:6); the peace which this salvation produces (cf. Eph. 2:14-17; 6:15) is indiscriminately called "the peace of God" (Phil. 4:7) and "the peace of Christ" (Col. 3:15).

II. THE NEW HUMANITY A DIVINE CREATION (1:3 – 3:21)

1. INTRODUCTORY *EULOGIA* (1:3-14)

(1) Praise for Election and Adoption (1:3-6)

> 3 *Blessed be the God and Father*[15] *of our Lord Jesus Christ! He has blessed us with every spiritual blessing in the heavenly realm in Christ,*

[11]Cf. Col. 1:4 (p. 41 with n. 12).
[12]Cf. Col. 1:2 (p. 39 with nn. 4, 5).
[13]So (with minimal variations) in Rom. 1:7; 1 Cor. 1:3; 2 Cor. 1:2; Gal. 1:3; Phil. 1:2; 2 Thess. 1:2; cf. Tit. 1:4. In Col. 1:2 "and the Lord Jesus Christ" is absent; in 1 Thess. 1:1 "from God our Father and the Lord Jesus Christ" is absent. In 1 Tim. 1:2 and 2 Tim. 1:2 "grace and peace" is amplified to "grace, mercy, and peace."
[14]Gk. ἀπὸ θεοῦ πατρὸς καὶ κυρίου Ἰησοῦ Χριστοῦ.
[15]B omits "and Father" (καὶ πατήρ).

4 *as he chose us in him*[16] *before the world's foundation, that we should be holy and blameless before him in love.*

5 *He foreordained us to be instated as his sons through Jesus Christ, according to the good pleasure of his will,*

6 *for the glorious praise of his grace, which*[17] *he has freely bestowed on us in the Beloved One.*[18]

3 In most of the Pauline letters the prescript is immediately followed by an introductory thanksgiving ("I thank God" or, less often, "we thank God"). In 2 Corinthians, however, the place of the introductory thanksgiving is taken by a *eulogia*[19] or expression of praise in the third person: "Blessed be the God and Father of our Lord Jesus Christ . . ." (2 Cor. 1:3). The expression of praise introduced by these words presents a different construction from the introductory thanksgiving (for which see Col. 1:3-8 and Philem. 4-7, with accompanying exposition and notes); it is a form taken over from Jewish synagogue worship, and commonly called the *berakhah* (the Hebrew word for "blessing"). In Ephesians, however, the *berakhah* does not replace the introductory thanksgiving; it precedes it.[20] The introductory thanksgiving follows in vv. 15-23.

The original single-sentence *berakhah* form is familiar enough from the OT Psalter: "Blessed be God . . ." (Ps. 66:20); "Blessed be the LORD, the God of Israel . . ." (Ps. 41:13, etc.). Paul christianizes the wording, identifying the one to whom blessing is ascribed as "the God and Father of our Lord Jesus Christ." In a typical OT *berakhah* the name of God is followed by the relative pronoun and an adjective clause, setting forth the reasons for which God is to be blessed: "Blessed be God, who has not rejected my prayer . . ." (Ps. 66:20); "Blessed be the LORD, the God of

---

[16]In place of ἐν αὐτῷ F G read ἑαυτῷ ("for himself").

[17]Gk. ἧς, by Attic attraction to the case of the antecedent χάριτος, but ℵ² D (F) G Ψ and the majority of cursives read the unattracted form ἐν ᾗ ("in which" or "with which").

[18]Gk. ἐν τῷ ἠγαπημένῳ, after which D* F G 629 lat^vet vg.cl syr^hcl** co^sa add υἱῷ αὐτοῦ ("in his beloved Son").

[19]For Gk. εὐλογία ("thanksgiving," "benediction") cf. 1 Cor. 10:16 (τὸ ποτήριον τῆς εὐλογίας, because over the cup were spoken the words: "Blessed art thou, . . . who createst the fruit of the vine"); Rev. 5:12-13; 7:12. The present construction is called a *eulogia* because it opens with the verbal adjective εὐλογητός (corresponding to Heb. *bārûk*).

[20]See P. T. O'Brien, "Ephesians 1: An Unusual Introduction to a New Testament Letter," *NTS* 25 (1978-79), 504-15, who suggests that, since God's grace to Jewish believers is being celebrated in vv. 3-12 before his grace to Gentile believers, the introductory *berakhah* form is "ideal for this purpose."

Israel, who alone does wondrous things" (Ps. 72:18).[21] The same construction is reproduced in the NT: "Blessed be the God and Father of our Lord Jesus Christ, . . . who comforts us . . ." (2 Cor. 1:3-4); "Blessed be the God and Father of our Lord Jesus Christ, who . . . has begotten us anew . . ." (1 Pet. 1:3).[22] Here too the reason for blessing God is given in a similar clause: "who has blessed us. . . ."[23] The same verb is used for men and women's blessing God and for his blessing them, but not in the same sense. In the latter use it denotes God's conferring of benefits; in the former use it denotes the ascription of praise to God.

God is to be praised, then, because he has bestowed on his people "in Christ"[24] every spiritual blessing. Spiritual blessings are to be distinguished, probably, from material blessings, which are also bestowed by God—such blessings as are promised in Deut. 28:1-14, for example, to those who obey his commandments. The nature of the spiritual blessings here referred to is not in doubt: they are detailed in the following words of the *berakhah*. They include election to holiness, instatement as God's sons and daughters, redemption and forgiveness, the gift of the Spirit, and the hope of glory.

These blessings are enjoyed "in the heavenly realm." The adjective translated "heavenly" occurs several times in the NT, but in this letter it occurs five times, without an expressed noun, in a phrase which might be literally rendered "in the heavenlies."[25] Nothing in this form of the adjective indicates whether it is masculine or neuter. If it is masculine, then the phrase means "among the heavenly beings";[26] if it is neuter, the meaning

---

[21]Compare the Jewish grace before eating: "Blessed art thou, O LORD our God, King of the universe, who bringest forth bread from the earth" (Mishnah *Berakhoth* 6.1), and indeed all eighteen of the blessings in the *'Amidah* of the synagogue service.

[22]In these two NT texts (and others) the construction with the definite article and the participle (ὁ παρακαλῶν . . . , ὁ . . . ἀναγεννήσας) is equivalent to an adjective clause.

[23]Gk. ὁ εὐλογήσας (article with participle; cf. preceding note). God may be the subject of εὐλογέω (as here) or the object (as in 1 Cor. 14:16; cf. the passive force of εὐλογητός at the beginning of this sentence).

[24]The incorporative ἐν Χριστῷ (the blessings about to be listed cannot be enjoyed apart from Christ). For the argument that in Ephesians ἐν Χριστῷ "is no longer the formula of incorporation into Christ, but has become the formula of God's activity through Christ" see J. A. Allan, "The 'In Christ' Formula in Ephesians," *NTS* 5 (1958-59), 54-62.

[25]Gk. ἐν τοῖς ἐπουρανίοις (cf. Eph. 1:20; 2:6; 3:10; 6:12). See A. T. Lincoln, "A Re-examination of 'the Heavenlies' in Ephesians," *NTS* 19 (1972-73), 468-83.

[26]Cf. οἱ ἐπουράνιοι in 1 Cor. 15:48.

is "in the heavenly places" or "in the heavenly realm."[27] The latter suits the five contexts better. The "heavenly realm" is the realm to which Christ has been raised (v. 20) and to which his people, united to him by faith, have been raised with him (Eph. 2:6). Even if they live on earth in mortal bodies, they can enter into the good of their heavenly inheritance here and now through the ministry of the Spirit (vv. 13-14). Nor is it surprising that these blessings are bestowed and enjoyed "in Christ." Believers are not isolated entities; they share a common life through faith in Christ, and this common life is nothing other than his resurrection life. Elsewhere in the letter this is expressed in terms of their common membership in the body of Christ, as in v. 23. This is the setting in which God grants his people every spiritual blessing—from eternal election to eternal glory.

4 It was in Christ, then, that God chose his people[28] "before the world's foundation." This phrase (or a similar one) appears a number of times in the NT, but here only in the Pauline corpus.[29] It denotes the divine act of election as taking place in eternity. Time belongs to the created order: believers' present experience of the blessings bestowed by God is the fulfilment on the temporal plane of his purpose of grace toward them conceived in eternity. As the fulfilment is experienced "in Christ," so it is in him that the purpose is conceived. If, as Col. 1:16 affirms, it was "in him" that all things were created, so, we are here assured, earlier still it was "in him" that the people of God were chosen. He is the Chosen One of God *par excellence;*[30] it is by union with him, according to the divine purpose realized in time, that others are chosen. Less than justice is done to the present language when it is debated whether Christ is the foundation or origin, or merely the executor of election. He is foundation,

---

[27]A similar ambiguity attaches to the genitive plural ἐπουρανίων in Phil. 2:10 (cf. F. F. Bruce, *Philippians,* GNBC [San Francisco, 1983], p. 55).

[28]Gk. καθὼς ἐξελέξατο ἡμᾶς ("just as he chose us"). For καθώς in thanksgivings cf. 2 Cor. 1:5; Phil. 1:7; Col. 1:6-7; 1 Thess. 1:5; 2 Thess. 1:3. P. Schubert goes too far in stating that "a very definite formal and functional significance within the thanksgiving pattern attaches to" καθώς in such a setting; indeed, he himself modifies the statement by conceding that "these καθώς-clauses to some extent differ among themselves in formal as well as functional detail" (*Form and Function of the Pauline Thanksgivings* [Berlin, 1939], p. 31).

[29]Gk. πρὸ καταβολῆς κόσμου. The same phrase occurs in John 17:24; 1 Pet. 1:20 (and, with ἀπό instead of πρό, in Matt. 13:35; 25:34; Luke 11:50; Heb. 4:3; 9:26; Rev. 13:8; 17:8); καταβολή is the act of laying or putting down (καταβάλλω) a foundation (cf. Heb. 6:1).

[30]He is called ὁ ἐκλελεγμένος in Luke 9:35; the Messiah is God's ἐκλεκτός in Luke 23:35; John 1:34, and God introduces his Servant in Isa. 42:1 as ὁ ἐκλεκτός μου.

origin, and executor: all that is involved in election and its fruits depends on him.[31]

Calvin regards the phrase "in Christ" as a "second confirmation of the freedom of election" (the first being that it took place before the world's foundation). "For if we are chosen in Christ, it is outside ourselves. It is not from the sight of our deserving, but because our heavenly Father has engrafted us, through the blessing of adoption, into the Body of Christ. In short, the name of Christ excludes all merit, and everything which men have of themselves; for when he says that we are chosen in Christ, it follows that in ourselves we are unworthy."[32]

There is a dominant ethical quality about the divine election, as is inevitable in view of the character of the electing God. In 1 Peter 1:15-16, where the wording of our present text is echoed, this lesson is pointed with a quotation from the OT law of holiness: "as he who called you is holy, be holy yourselves in all your conduct; since it is written, 'You shall be holy, for I am holy.' "[33] No other way of life is fitting for those who are "chosen and destined by God the Father and sanctified by the Spirit for obedience to Jesus Christ" (1 Peter. 1:2). So here, the purpose of God's choosing his people in Christ is that they should be "holy and blameless"[34] in his presence, both here and now in earthly life and ultimately when they appear before him. The perspective is the same as in Col. 1:22, where the purpose of Christ's reconciling work is the presentation of his people "holy, blameless, and irreproachable in his presence." There they appear in the presence of Christ, while here they appear in the presence of God; but it is one and the same appearance: for Paul the tribunal of Christ (2 Cor. 5:10) and the tribunal of God (Rom. 14:10) are the same tribunal. The "holiness without which no one will see the Lord" (Heb. 12:14) is progressively wrought within the lives of believers on earth by the Spirit, and will be consummated in glory at the *parousia*, the time of the "redemption" anticipated in Eph. 1:14; 4:30. If "holiness" expresses the pos-

---

[31]Cf. J. Murray, *Collected Writings*, IV (Edinburgh, 1983), 325-26. See also T. F. Torrance, "Predestination in Christ," *EQ* 13 (1941), 108-41; H. H. Rowley, *The Biblical Doctrine of Election* (London, 1950); K. Barth, *Church Dogmatics*, E.T., II.2 (Edinburgh, 1957), pp. 3-506; G. C. Berkouwer, *Divine Election*, E.T. (Grand Rapids, 1960); E. H. Trenchard and J. M. Martínez, *Escogidos en Cristo* (Madrid, 1966).

[32]J. Calvin (*ad loc.*), *The Epistles of Paul the Apostle to the Galatians, Ephesians, Philippians and Colossians* (1548), E.T. (Edinburgh, 1965), p. 125.

[33]Cf. Lev. 11:44-45; 19:2; 20:7-8, 26.

[34]Gk. ἁγίους καὶ ἀμώμους (cf. Eph. 5:27 for the collocation of the same two adjectives in a similar perspective).

itive quality, "blamelessness" expresses its negative counterpart: freedom from blemish or fault.

If the phrase "in love" is attached to what precedes (as it is in the Greek text followed in this commentary), then it adds a specific quality to holiness and blamelessness: the consummation of holiness is perfect love. The preposition is best understood as having "comitative" force: the purpose of God is that his people should be marked by holiness and blamelessness, coupled with love.[35]

5 If, on the other hand, the phrase "in love" is attached to what follows (as it is in the RSV and the NIV), it expresses God's attitude to his people when he foreordained them for adoption into his family. "Those whom he foreknew," according to Rom. 8:29, "he also predestined to be conformed to the image of his Son, in order that he might be the firstborn among many brethren." The fulfilment of this purpose is the "adoption" confidently expected by those "who have the first fruits of the Spirit" (Rom. 8:23). It is that "revealing of the sons of God" for which "the creation waits with eager longing" (Rom. 8:19), their public instatement, investiture, and manifestation as members of that family in which Christ is the firstborn.[36] But, thanks to "the first fruits of the Spirit," the enjoyment of the new relationship as children of God is theirs already. The Spirit is "the Spirit of adoption"; so, "when we cry, 'Abba! Father!' it is the Spirit himself bearing witness with our spirit that we are children of God" (Rom. 8:15-16).[37]

The legal process of adoption was apparently unknown in Hebrew society. The levirate marriage, by which a dead man might acquire by proxy a posthumous son who would perpetuate his name and inheritance in Israel, is nowhere referred to in terms of adoption.[38] Adoption may have been practiced in patriarchal times, in a manner similar to that attested in the Nuzu texts—one might compare Eliezer's potential relation to Abraham (Gen. 15:2-3) or Jacob's to Laban (Gen. 29:14ff.)[39]—but it left no trace in post-settlement legislation or custom. Yet something analogous to the

---

[35]So NEB: "he chose us . . . to be dedicated, to be without blemish in his sight, to be full of love." Cf. Eph. 6:24; Col. 1:6 (p. 43 above with n. 17). See also K. G. Kuhn, "The Epistle to the Ephesians in the Light of the Qumran Texts" (1961), E.T. in *Paul and Qumran* (London, 1968), pp. 119-20.

[36]Cf. Col. 1:18, πρωτότοκος ἐκ τῶν νεκρῶν.

[37]Cf. Gal. 4:4-7. See pp. 266, 301 below.

[38]Cf. R. de Vaux, *Ancient Israel*, E.T. (London, ²1965), pp. 21-22, 37-38, 42, 51-52.

[39]See C. J. Mullo Weir, "Nuzi," in *Archaeology and Old Testament Study*, ed. D. W. Thomas (Oxford, 1967), pp. 73-86.

NT doctrine of adoption appears in Yahweh's relation to Israel: "When Israel was a child, I loved him, and out of Egypt I called my son" (Hos. 11:1). Commenting on the prophet's language G. A. Smith wrote: "God's eyes, passing the princes of the world, fell upon this slave boy, and He loved him and gave him a career."[40] D. J. Theron's conclusion, that "Paul's metaphor of adoption . . . might even have been derived from Israel's deliverance out of bondage in Egypt,"[41] is rendered the more probable by Paul's own reference to "Israelites, to whom belongs the adoption" (Rom. 9:4).

In some of his references to adoption Paul seems to trace an analogy between the divine act and current Roman legal procedure, with its requirement of seven witnesses to the transaction. There is little evidence of this here, unless a relation is discerned between the adoption and the inheritance of v. 14.[42]

Since incorporation into the family of God comes about "through Christ," that is, by union with the Son of God, God's foreordaining his people to adoption is another aspect of his electing them for holiness. To be conformed to the image of Christ is to reflect his character (cf. 2 Cor. 3:18). To be chosen in Christ involves both wearing his image and sharing his holiness.

God's election and foreordaining of his people are alike "according to the good pleasure of his will." Since God is God, his purpose and activity have no ultimate cause outside his own being. "God's will has no 'Why,' " said Luther.[43] But since God in his own person is "the love which moves the sun and the other stars,"[44] his purpose and activity express the divine love. Whatever be the syntactical relation of the phrase "in love" between vv. 4 and 5, it was in love that God chose his people before the world's foundation and foreordained them to be his sons and daughters through Christ.

6 There is little distinction between God's love and his grace, ex-

---

[40]G. A. Smith, *The Book of the Twelve Prophets*, II (London, ²1928), 317.

[41]D. J. Theron, " 'Adoption' in the Pauline Corpus," *EQ* 28 (1956), 14. See also F. Lyall, "Roman Law in the Writings of Paul—Adoption," *JBL* 88 (1969), 458-66; J. I. Cook, "The Concept of Adoption in the Theology of Paul," in *Saved by Hope: Essays in Honor of R. C. Oudersluys*, ed. J. I. Cook (Grand Rapids, 1978), pp. 133-44.

[42]See F. F. Bruce, *The Epistle to the Galatians*, NIGTC (Grand Rapids/Exeter, 1982), pp. 192-98.

[43]"Gottes Wille hat kein Warumbe" (quoted by G. S. Hendry, *God the Creator* [London, 1937], p. 141).

[44]Dante, *Paradiso* 33.145.

cept that the word "grace" emphasizes its free and sovereign character.[45] God's grace is his eternal and unconditioned good will which found decisive expression in time in the saving work of Christ. In this saving work, and in its becoming effective in the lives of believers, God is glorified: his grace is manifested as worthy of "glorious praise."[46] In Ps. 66:2 the whole earth is summoned to give God "glorious praise";[47] if this was the fitting response to his acts of deliverance in national and personal life which the psalmist celebrates, it is supremely fitting as a response to his delivering act in Christ. This note of glorious praise is repeatedly sounded throughout the *eulogia* of vv. 3-14.

God's grace has extended to his people and enfolded them: he has "be-graced" them, says Paul (using a verb derived from the Greek word for "grace").[48] But, like every other phase of God's dealings with them, this "be-gracing" is received by them not in their own right but in Christ: God's grace is freely bestowed on them "in the Beloved One." This designation marks Christ out as the supreme object of the Father's love— "the Son of his love," as he is called in Col. 1:13.[49] A slightly different form is used in the report of the heavenly voice which addressed Jesus at his baptism and on the mount of transfiguration (Mark 1:11; 9:7 and parallels), but the sense is the same: God acclaims him as "my Son, the beloved,"[50] or, as the words are regularly rendered in the Old Syriac version, "my Son and my Beloved" (indicating two distinct titles). J. A. Robinson, surveying the literary usage, concludes that "The Beloved (One)" may have been in use as a messianic title among Jews before it came to be used by Christians with reference to Jesus.[51]

---

[45]Cf. J. Moffatt, *Love in the New Testament* (London, 1929); *Grace in the New Testament* (London, 1931); N. P. Williams, *The Grace of God* (London, 1930); C. Spicq, *Agape in the New Testament*, E.T., I-II (St. Louis, 1963-66).

[46]Lit., "for praise of glory" (εἰς ἔπαινον δόξης), the genitive being construed as the Hebraic qualifying genitive, as in Col. 1:11, 27a (p. 47, n. 37; p. 80, n. 197).

[47]RSV "give to him glorious praise" apparently takes kāḇôḏ in śîmû kāḇôḏ tᵉhillāṯô (lit., "make glorious his praise") as kᵉḇôḏ, construct state.

[48]Gk. χαριτόω, from χάρις. The one other NT occurrence of the verb is in Luke 1:28, where Mary is acclaimed as κεχαριτωμένη (RSV "O favored one").

[49]See p. 52, n. 59.

[50]Gk. ὁ υἱός μου ὁ ἀγαπητός, where ὁ ἀγαπητός is probably an echo of Isa. 42:1 (ἀγαπητός being a variant rendering for ἐκλεκτός, for which see n. 30 above).

[51]J. A. Robinson, *Ephesians*, pp. 229-33; he suggests (with reason) that the designation ὁ ἠγαπημένος (LXX for *Jeshurun* in Deut. 32:15; 33:5, 26; Isa. 44:2) was transferred from Israel to the Messiah (compare the transference of "my firstborn son," used of Israel in Exod. 4:22, to the Davidic king in Ps. 2:7; 89:27). For ὁ ἠγαπημένος used of Christ see also *Ep. Barn.* 3:6; 4:3, 8; ὁ ἀγαπητός is similarly used in *Asc. Isa.* 3:13 *et passim*.

(2) Praise for Redemption and Final Reconciliation (1:7-10)

7 *In him[52] we have our redemption, through his blood, the forgiveness of our trespasses, according to the wealth of his grace,[53]*

8 *which he has multiplied toward us with all wisdom and understanding.*

9 *He has made known to us the mystery of his will, according to his[54] good pleasure which he planned in him,[55]*

10 *to be administered in the fullness of the times—namely, to bring everything together in Christ, the things in[56] heaven and the things on earth.*

7 Those who were chosen in Christ before the world's foundation have been redeemed in him in the course of time. The mention of redemption and forgiveness is paralleled in Col. 1:14, on which indeed it may depend, except that "sins" in Colossians is replaced by "trespasses" here[57] and the reference to redemption is amplified by the phrase "through his blood."[58] The blood of Christ, that is, his sacrificial death, is the means by which his people's redemption has been procured. A similar explanatory phrase occurs in Rom. 3:25,[59] and while there it is more closely attached to "atonement"[60] than to "redemption"[61] (in v. 24), in sense it is applicable to both.

"Trespasses" and "sins" are used as synonyms by Paul and other NT writers.[62] In Eph. 2:1 the two words are used together to express one idea. If "sins" is the word used in Col. 1:14, "trespasses" is used in Col. 2:13; in both places they are the object of God's pardoning act.

"Wealth" is a term found repeatedly in this letter with reference to the divine attributes: "the wealth of his grace"[63] is mentioned again in

---

[52]Several witnesses (including ℵ* D* Ψ 104 2495 and the Coptic versions) read the aorist ἐσχομεν ("we have received") for the present ἐχομεν ("we have").

[53]For χάριτος A 365 and a few other witnesses read χρηστότητος (under the influence of Rom. 2:4).

[54]αὐτοῦ is omitted by D F G lat^b ^vg.codd (probably because it seemed pleonastic with the following ἐν αὐτῷ).

[55]For ἐν αὐτῷ P reads ἐν ἑαυτῷ ("in himself").

[56]Our witnesses vary between ἐπί (P⁴⁶ ℵ* B D etc.) and ἐν (ℵ² A F G K Ψ etc.); the latter might arise from assimilation to Col. 1:20.

[57]τὴν ἄφεσιν τῶν παραπτωμάτων as against τὴν ἄφεσιν τῶν ἁμαρτιῶν (Col. 1:14); see p. 53, n. 67.

[58]Gk. διὰ τοῦ αἵματος αὐτοῦ (cf. Col. 1:20, διὰ τοῦ αἵματος τοῦ σταυροῦ αὐτοῦ).

[59]ἐν τῷ αὐτοῦ αἵματι (cf. Rom. 5:9, δικαιωθέντες νῦν ἐν τῷ αἵματι αὐτοῦ).

[60]Gk. ἱλαστήριον (Rom. 3:25).

[61]Gk. ἀπολύτρωσις (Rom. 3:24); on this word see p. 53 with n. 64.

[62]Cf. Rom. 5:20, . . . ἵνα πλεονάσῃ τὸ παράπτωμα· οὗ δὲ ἐπλεόνασεν ἡ ἁμαρτία κτλ.

[63]Gk. κατὰ τὸ πλοῦτος τῆς χάριτος αὐτοῦ.

Eph. 2:7, "the wealth of his glory" in Eph. 1:18 and 3:16 (cf. also Eph. 3:8). It is a Pauline usage: cf. "the wealth of his kindness" in Rom. 2:4; "the wealth of his glory" in Rom. 9:23; "the wealth of God's wisdom and knowledge"[64] in Rom. 11:33.

8 Grace is a quality which requires personal relationships for its exercise. To speak of the "wealth" of God's grace implies that he has shown it in abundance toward its recipients; similarly, when he is described as being "rich in mercy" (Eph. 2:4), the implication is that the beneficiaries of his mercy enjoy it in overflowing measure. So here, not only by implication but expressly, he is said to have "multiplied" his grace toward his people. The adjective clause "which he has multiplied"[65] is parallel to that in v. 6, "which he has freely bestowed"; the antecedent to both relatives is the grace of God. The superabundance of his grace has been emphasized by Paul in Rom. 5:20: "where sin abounded, grace was more exceedingly multiplied."[66]

The unstinting bestowal of God's grace is accompanied by other spiritual gifts: wisdom and understanding are mentioned here because of their relevance to what follows.[67] Wisdom and understanding are gifts of God, but they must be cultivated in order to become effective. Therefore it is not inconsistent for Paul to pray, as he does in the parallel passage in Col. 1:9, that believers may be filled "with all wisdom and spiritual understanding"[68] (using a different word for "understanding" from that which is used here). Indeed, a few sentences below in this very letter he prays that those who have received wisdom and understanding along with God's abundant grace may be given the "spirit of wisdom and revelation" (v. 17). At present, however, the "already" aspect of the heavenly gift is emphasized; elsewhere the "not yet" aspect finds expression. The Spirit whom believers have received is "the Spirit of wisdom and understanding" (as he is called in Isa. 11:2), and it is through his ministry that the wisdom and understanding which he imparts are to be increasingly appropriated.

9 The "already" aspect of God's ways with his people continues

---

[64]In ᾧ βάθος πλούτου καὶ σοφίας καὶ γνώσεως θεοῦ the genitives σοφίας and γνώσεως are probably dependent on πλούτου, not on βάθος.

[65]Gk. ἧς ἐπερίσσευσεν, where ἧς (as in v. 6) is an instance of Attic attraction.

[66]Gk. οὗ δὲ ἐπλεόνασεν ἡ ἁμαρτία, ὑπερεπερίσσευσεν ἡ χάρις (cf. Rom. 5:15, ἡ χάρις τοῦ θεοῦ . . . εἰς τοὺς πολλοὺς ἐπερίσσευσεν).

[67]Gk. ἐν πάσῃ σοφίᾳ καὶ φρονήσει, the ἐν being comitative (cf. ἐν ἀγάπῃ, v. 4). The only other NT occurrence of φρόνησις is in Luke 1:17.

[68]Gk. ἐν πάσῃ σοφίᾳ καὶ συνέσει πνευματικῇ (cf. Isa. 11:2, LXX, where the πνεῦμα σοφίας καὶ συνέσεως will rest on the promised prince of the house of David).

to be stressed in the statement that he "has made known to us the mystery of his will." In v. 18 below the apostle prays that his readers may know by experience (and enjoy by anticipation) things that belong to the mystery of God's will—the hope to which he has called them and the inexhaustible glory of the inheritance which he has in store for them.

As regularly in the NT, a "mystery" is something which has formerly been kept secret in the purpose of God but has now been disclosed. In Col. 1:27 the aspect of his purpose which has now been manifested to his people relates to their hope of glory, of which the indwelling Christ provides the guarantee here and now.[69] But elsewhere Paul makes it plain that the coming glory of the people of God is only part of his purpose of grace: all creation is to share in the fruits of Christ's redemptive work, even in "the glorious liberty of the children of God" (Rom. 8:21). So here, the universe has its place in God's secret purpose, now revealed. In Col. 1:20 God's good pleasure was "to reconcile all things to himself" through Christ. Nothing less than that is contemplated here in his "good pleasure," his eternal decree, which he "planned" in Christ. (In this context "in Christ" is much more suitable as a rendering than the KJV's "in himself.")[70]

10 It was "in Christ" (as we have been told in vv. 4 and 5) that God chose his people and foreordained them to be instated as full members of his family, "according to the good pleasure of his will"; it is equally "in Christ" that he has planned to "gather up"[71] the fragmented and alienated universe. The verb here used as an alternative to "reconcile" occurs in one other place in the Pauline writings, where the whole law is said to be "summed up" in the single commandment of love to one's neighbor (Rom. 13:9). All things, then, are to be "summed up" in Christ and presented as a coherent totality in him.

The reconciliation celebrated in Colossians is the reconciliation of "all things" to God (and more particularly the reconciliation of human beings to him).[72] The reconciliation celebrated in Ephesians is the reconciliation of human beings to one another, as a stage in the unification of a divided universe.[73] It is this unification that is presented here as the goal

[69]See pp. 84-86 with nn. 213-16.
[70]The KJV presupposes the reading ἐν ἑαυτῷ (see n. 55 above).
[71]Gk. ἀνακεφαλαιώσασθαι (the middle voice emphasizing the divine interest and initiative). See J. B. Lightfoot, *Notes on the Epistles of St. Paul* (London, 1895), pp. 321-23.
[72]See Col. 1:20-22 (pp. 74-78 with nn. 164-82).
[73]See Eph. 2:14-18 (pp. 295-301).

of God's determinant counsel. The "administering" of God's good pleasure is "the manner in which the purpose of God is being worked out in human history."[74] So says J. A. Robinson, adding that in the phrase "in the fullness of the times" (lit., "of the fullness of the times")[75] "fullness" is a genitive of further definition. As, according to Gal. 4:4, God sent his Son into the world "when the fullness of the time had come,"[76] that is, when the time was ripe for his coming, so, when the time is ripe for the consummation of his purpose, in his providential overruling of the course of the world, that consummation will be realized.

The "administering" of God's good pleasure here has much the same force as the "administering" of the long-hidden mystery in Eph. 3:9.[77] In Eph. 3:9, however, the thought is closely related to Paul's apostolic commission, there stated to be the bringing together into one body of Gentile believers on the same basis as Jewish believers. This uniting of Jews and Gentiles in Christ was, in Paul's eyes, God's masterpiece of reconciliation, and gave promise of a time when not Jews and Gentiles only, but all the mutually hostile elements in creation,[78] would be united in that same Christ. Paul was thus an instrument in God's hand for the accomplishment of his eternal purpose.[79]

(3) Praise for the Assurance of the Believers' Heritage (1:11-14)

11 *It was in Christ, too, that we were claimed by God as his portion,[80] having been foreordained according to the purpose[81] of him who works all things according to the counsel of his will,*

12 *in order that we, who first placed our hope in Christ, should be for his glorious praise.*

---

[74]J. A. Robinson, *Ephesians*, p. 145. See also S. S. Smalley, "The Eschatology of Ephesians," *EQ* 28 (1956), 152-57.

[75]Gk. εἰς οἰκονομίαν τοῦ πληρώματος τῶν καιρῶν.

[76]Gk. ὅτε δὲ ἦλθεν τὸ πλήρωμα τοῦ χρόνου. See F. F. Bruce, *The Epistle of Paul to the Galatians*, NIGTC, p. 194. There is no material difference between χρόνος there and καιρός (καιροί) here.

[77]Gk. ἡ οἰκονομία τοῦ μυστηρίου (see p. 319 below).

[78]As in Col. 1:16, 20, τὰ πάντα is further explained as comprising "things in heaven and things on earth." From Gen. 1:1 onward, "the heaven and the earth" is the OT expression for "the universe" or "all creation."

[79]Cf. J. Munck, *Paul and the Salvation of Mankind*, E.T. (London, 1959), p. 41.

[80]For ἐκληρώθημεν a few witnesses (A D F(*) G) read ἐκλήθημεν ("we were called").

[81]After κατὰ πρόθεσιν D F G 81 104 365 1175 and a few other witnesses insert τοῦ θεοῦ ("of God").

13 *In Christ you*[82] *also were sealed with the Holy Spirit of promise when you heard the message of truth, the gospel of your salvation, and believed—*

14 *(the Holy Spirit of promise, I say, for) he*[83] *is the guarantee of our inheritance, until the redemption of God's possession, for his glorious praise.*

11 The verb translated "we were claimed . . . as his portion"[84] has been rendered more freely in a number of recent versions. In the RSV it is taken together with the following participle[85] and rendered comprehensively "we . . . have been destined and appointed." The NEB, less freely, renders it "we have been given our share in the heritage." The NIV renders it "we were . . . chosen." But we are dealing with a passive form of the verb which means "appoint by lot," "allot," "assign," and the passive sense should be brought out unless there is good reason to the contrary. The reason for the rendering "we were claimed by God as his portion" (rather than "we were assigned our portion") is that it is in keeping with OT precedent.[86] In the Song of Moses (Deut. 32:8-9) the nations of the world are assigned to various angelic beings ("the sons of God"),[87] but Yahweh retains Israel as his personal possession:

> *"for the* LORD'S *portion is his people,*
> *Jacob his allotted heritage."*

So here, believers in Christ are God's chosen people, claimed by him as his portion or heritage. That this is the sense is confirmed by the reference in v. 18 to "the glorious wealth of his inheritance in the saints."

The idea of the divine foreordination is repeated from v. 5. There God is said to have foreordained his people "according to the good pleasure of his will"; here this is said to be part of his eternal governance of the universe, for he "works all things according to the counsel of his will." His will may be disobeyed, but his ultimate purpose cannot be frustrated,

[82]The tendency of scribes to confuse ἡμεῖς and ὑμεῖς, regardless of the sense, is shown by the number of witnesses (א¹ A K L Ψ and several cursives) that read the discordant ἡμεῖς for ὑμεῖς here (similarly K Ψ and several cursives read ἡμῶν for ὑμῶν in the following phrase "your salvation"). Cf. p. 279, n. 2.

[83]Gk. ὅ ἐστιν ἀρραβών, where א D Ψ and the majority of cursives replace ὅ by ὅς (a sense construction, having regard to the personality of the Spirit).

[84]Gk. ἐκληρώθημεν.

[85]Gk. προορισθέντες ("having been foreordained"); cf. the active προορίσας at the beginning of v. 5.

[86]Cf. J. A. Robinson's well-argued conclusion that "the meaning must be '*we have been chosen as God's portion*' " (*Ephesians*, p. 146).

[87]So LXX (κατὰ ἀριθμὸν ἀγγέλων θεοῦ) and 4QDeut^{q} (*bny 'lhym*) as against MT *bᵉnê yiśrā'ēl*.

for he overrules the disobedience of his creatures in such a way that it subserves his purpose. So in Acts 4:27-28 the apostles in their praise and prayer acknowledge before God that Herod and Pontius Pilate and the other enemies of Jesus conspired together, all unwittingly, "to do whatever thy hand and thy plan had predestined to take place."[88]

12 In v. 5 the instatement of believers as sons and daughters of God, the purpose of their foreordination, redounds to "the glorious praise of his grace"; here again "his glorious praise" is the object of their being foreordained. God is honored in the presence of human beings and angelic powers when men and women, redeemed from sin, live in accordance with his will and display the family likeness which stamps them as his children. "We who first placed our hope in Christ"[89] are Jewish believers, foundation members of the new community, the first fruits of the people of God in the age which Christ has inaugurated by his death and resurrection.

13 But God's portion is not confined to Jewish believers. "We who first placed our hope in Christ" have now been joined by "you also"[90]— that is to say, by Gentile believers. It is to Gentile believers that this letter is specifically addressed, assuring them that their share in God's heritage is as full and firm as that of their brothers and sisters of Jewish birth. Gentiles also heard the gospel, and realized that the salvation of which it spoke was for them as well as for Jews. The gospel is "the message of truth"—"the true message of the gospel," as it is called in Col. 1:5— because it has God for its author; it is "the gospel of God" (Rom. 1:1). The communication of the gospel to Gentiles was undertaken reluctantly by the first believers, who could scarcely entertain the thought that the fulfilment of God's promises to Israel should embrace outsiders within its saving scope. Apart from Peter, who required a special revelation from heaven before he could bring himself to accept Cornelius's invitation to visit him and tell him and his household the way of salvation,[91] Gentile evangelization began as the result of private enterprise, when unnamed Hellenists of Cyprus and Cyrene came to Antioch and told the story of Jesus to Gentiles as well as Jews.[92] From then on, throughout the provinces of the eastern Roman Empire, many more Gentiles than Jews believed the gospel, and the terms on which they might be admitted became a matter

[88]In a Christian interpretation of Ps. 2:1-2, where God's predestinating plan was read.
[89]Gk. τοὺς προηλπικότας ἐν τῷ Χριστῷ (the only NT occurrence of προελπίζω); for the simple ἐλπίζω used in the sense of placing one's hope in Christ cf. Rom. 15:12 (quoting Isa. 11:10); 1 Cor. 15:19.
[90]Gk. καὶ ὑμεῖς.
[91]Acts 10:9-20; 11:5-17.
[92]Acts 11:19-21.

of serious concern in the mother church at Jerusalem. When, as Luke records, "the apostles and the elders" at Jerusalem "were gathered together to consider this matter," Peter argued that it would be wise to follow the example of God, who gave proof of his acceptance of Gentile believers by "giving them the Holy Spirit just as he did to us; and he made no distinction between us and them, but cleansed their hearts by faith" (Acts 15:6-9).

There is a remarkable similarity between Peter's argument at the Council of Jerusalem and what is said here. The Gentiles, on believing the gospel, were "sealed[93] with the Holy Spirit of promise." The figure of sealing is used by Paul in relation to the Spirit in 2 Cor. 1:22 where, associating his Corinthian converts closely with himself and his colleagues, he says, "it is God who establishes us with you in Christ and has anointed us; he has also sealed us and given us the guarantee of the Spirit in our hearts." Of the three figures used there—the anointing, the seal, and the guarantee—two reappear here: the seal and the guarantee.

The seal of the Spirit was received by the Gentiles here addressed as it had been received earlier by Jewish Christians—when they believed. The verbal form used here is identical with that found in Acts 19:2, where Paul at Ephesus asks a group of "disciples" if they received the Holy Spirit when they believed; it is a participial form meaning "having believed" or "on believing."[94] By giving believers the Spirit, God "seals" or stamps them as his own possession. The Spirit is variously called "the Spirit of God" or "the Spirit of Christ"; "if anyone has not the Spirit of Christ, he does not belong to him" (Rom. 8:9). Here he is called "the Holy Spirit of promise."[95] This might mean "the promised Holy Spirit" (cf. Acts 2:33, "the promise of the Holy Spirit");[96] but more probably it indicates that the Holy Spirit brings with him when he is received the promise of glory yet to come. So, in Eph. 4:30, believers are said to have been sealed with the Spirit "for the day of redemption"—a statement which summarizes the words that follow in our present context.

---

[93]Gk. ἐσφραγίσθητε. See G. W. H. Lampe, *The Seal of the Spirit* (London, 1951).

[94]Gk. πιστεύσαντες, to be construed in both places as the "coincident" aorist participle (MHT I, p. 131, n. 1). Here πιστεύω has the same sense as ἐλπίζω in the compound προελπίζω in v. 12. The phrase ἐν ᾧ before καὶ πιστεύσαντες ἐσφραγίσθητε, resumed from the beginning of v. 13, relates to ἐσφραγίσθητε rather than to πιστεύσαντες.

[95]Gk. τῷ πνεύματι τῆς ἐπαγγελίας τῷ ἁγίῳ.

[96]Gk. τήν . . . ἐπαγγελίαν τοῦ πνεύματος τοῦ ἁγίου, where πνεύματος is a genitive of definition. In Acts 1:4 the same promise is called τὴν ἐπαγγελίαν τοῦ πατρός, where πατρός is subjective genitive.

14 The word rendered "guarantee"[97] is of Semitic origin; it was probably borrowed by the Greeks in the early days of trade with the Phoenicians. It was a commercial word denoting a pledge—some object handed over by a buyer to a seller until the purchase price was paid in full. The Hebrew word (identical with the Phoenician) is used in Gen. 38:17-18 of items of Judah's personal property which he handed over to Tamar for the time being, until he had opportunity to send her the agreed price.[98] In the NT it is used only in the Pauline writings, and only with reference to the Spirit. In 2 Cor. 5:5, where Paul looks forward to the "heavenly dwelling" which is to replace the present mortal tenement, he says, "he who has prepared us for this very thing is God, who has given us the Spirit as a guarantee." The gift of the Spirit, then, is the guarantee of coming immortality. This is Paul's distinctive contribution to the NT doctrine of the Holy Spirit. Another term which he uses to express the same thought is "first fruits":[99] in Rom. 8:23 the Spirit is the "first fruits" of the eagerly awaited "adoption,[100] the redemption of our bodies," where the resurrection of the people of Christ at his *parousia* is meant. The same word for "redemption" is used there as here,[101] and the same future hope is in view.

The Spirit consciously received is "the guarantee of our inheritance,"[102] the pledge given to believers by God to assure them that the glory of the life to come, promised in the gospel, is a well-founded hope, a reality and not an illusion. The word "inheritance"[103] is used in this chapter both of God's portion in his people (vv. 11, 18) and of the everlasting portion which he has reserved for them. They can enter into the enjoyment of this everlasting portion here and now by the ministry of the Spirit. Redemption is already theirs through the sacrifice and death of Christ (v. 7), but one aspect of that redemption remains to be realized. On the day of resurrection God will "redeem" his own possession, and the evidence of his commitment to do so is given in his "sealing" that possession with the Spirit.

The word translated "possession"[104] occurs in the same sense in 1 Peter 2:9, where believers (again, as it happens, Gentile believers) are called "a chosen race, a royal priesthood, a holy nation, a people for

---

[97]Gk. ἀρραβών (cf. its use in the Mod. Gk. form ἀρραβῶνα, in the sense of an engagement ring).
[98]Heb. 'ērābôn (cf. 'ărubbāh, from the same root, in 1 Sam. 17:18; Prov. 17:18).
[99]Gk. ἀπαρχή.
[100]Cf. v. 5 above (pp. 256-57).
[101]Gk. ἀπολύτρωσις, as in v. 7 above (p. 259).
[102]The ἀρραβών of the Spirit may be understood as the initial down payment as well as the guarantee.
[103]Gk. κληρονομία (used in the LXX of Deut. 32:8; cf. p. 263).
[104]Gk. περιποίησις (in 1 Pet. 2:9, λαὸς εἰς περιποίησιν).

266

[God's] possession." Language is there deliberately applied to Gentile believers which in the OT is used of God's people Israel—notably in Exod. 19:5, where Yahweh calls Israel "my own possession[105] among all peoples." The verb corresponding to the noun "possession" is used in a similar sense in Acts 20:28, where Paul directs the elders of the church of Ephesus to "feed the church of God, of which he obtained possession[106] through the blood of his own [Son]." These words also echo an OT passage—Ps. 74:2, where God is entreated: "Remember thy congregation, of which thou hast obtained possession long since."[107] That such language should now be applied to Gentile believers is a token of the security of their new standing within the community of God's own people, fully sharing present blessing and future hope with their fellow-believers of Jewish stock.

As those who first placed their hope in Christ are designed "for his glorious praise," so it is with "you also"—believers of Gentile origin. Here too there is perhaps an echo of OT language—more particularly of Isa. 43:20-21, where God speaks of "my chosen people, the people whom I formed for myself that they might declare my praise."[108]

The liturgical note on which this *eulogia* opened in v. 3 has been sustained throughout, not least by means of the recurring refrain of glorious praise. Such a liturgical passage does not lend itself well to comparative analysis in terms of epistolary usage, whether Paul's or anyone else's. But it strikes the keynote for the rest of the letter, with its emphasis on the inclusion of Gentiles together with Jews within the new society of the people of God.

2. INTRODUCTORY THANKSGIVING AND INTERCESSORY PRAYER (1:15-23)

(1) Thanks for the Readers' Faith and Love and Prayer for Their Increase in Knowledge (1:15-19)

15 *Therefore, having heard of your faith[109] in the Lord Jesus and your love[110] toward all the saints, I for my part*

---

[105]Heb. (*'am*) *se gullāh*, LXX λαὸς περιούσιος (cf. Exod. 23:22 LXX; Deut. 7:6; 14:2; 26:18; Tit. 2:14). In Mal. 3:17 *se gullāh* is rendered εἰς περιποίησιν.
[106]Gk. τὴν ἐκκλησίαν τοῦ θεοῦ, ἣν περιεποιήσατο.
[107]Ps. 73:2 LXX, τῆς συναγωγῆς σου, ἧς ἐκτήσω.
[108]LXX λαόν μου, ὃν περιεποιησάμην τὰς ἀρετάς μου διηγεῖσθαι (quoted in 1 Pet. 2:9b).
[109]Gk. τὴν καθ' ὑμᾶς πίστιν, differing little or not at all in sense from the usual τὴν πίστιν ὑμῶν. For the following ἐν τῷ κυρίῳ Ἰησοῦ cf. Col. 1:4 (p. 41 with n. 12).
[110]τὴν ἀγάπην *om* P[46] ℵ A B P 33 365 1739 1881 *pc*.

16 *do not cease giving thanks for you as I mention you[111] in my prayers.*

17 *May the God of our Lord Jesus Christ, the Father all-glorious, give you[112] a spirit of wisdom and revelation in the knowledge of him!*

18 *May your spiritual eyesight be enlightened,[113] so that you may know what is the hope of your calling,[114] what is the glorious wealth of his inheritance in the saints,.*

19 *and what is the surpassing greatness of his power in us[115] who believe, according to the operation of his mighty strength!*

15-16 The introductory thanksgiving which (contrary to custom) follows the *eulogia* is cast in the characteristic Pauline style.[116] Paul assures his readers of his unceasing gratitude to God for the good news he has received about them, and assures them of his constant intercession. Whereas the *eulogia* praises God for blessings received by the writer and his fellow-Christians, the thanksgiving is concerned rather with the work of God in the lives of those addressed.[117] The parallelism of this thanksgiving with that in Col. 1:3-4 in particular is unmistakable. In both places the readers' faith and love are tokens of the grace of God which they have received— unless indeed "your love" should be omitted here as an editorial addition to the text made under the influence of Col. 1:4 ("your faith in Christ Jesus and the love which you have for all the saints").[118] If "your love" is indeed to be omitted, then their "faith" (including the sense of fidelity) is exercised within the Christian fellowship ("in the Lord Jesus")[119] and thus shown toward all their fellow-believers.

[111]Gk. μνείαν ποιούμενος, implying ὑμῶν, which is however added by D[1] F G Ψ and the majority of cursives.

[112]Gk. ἵνα ὁ θεὸς . . . δώῃ (δῷ B 1739 1881 *pc*) ὑμῖν πνεῦμα κτλ, expressing the object of his prayers.

[113]Gk. πεφωτισμένους τοὺς ὀφθαλμοὺς τῆς καρδίας ὑμῶν (ὑμῶν, which is in any case implied, is omitted in P^{46} B 6 33 1175 1739 1881 *pc*), accusative in dependence on δώῃ. For καρδίας TR, following a few cursives, reads the less metaphorical διανοίας (whence KJV "the eyes of your understanding").

[114]ℵ[2] D[2] Ψ and the majority of cursives insert καί.

[115]For ἡμᾶς D* F G P 33 and a number of cursives read ὑμᾶς. Unlike ἡμᾶς in v. 12, ἡμᾶς is here inclusive (referring to all believers, whether Jewish or Gentile). The context suggests that εἰς ἡμᾶς means not merely "toward us" but "in us" (cf. ἐν ἡμῖν, Eph. 3:20).

[116]See P. Schubert, *Form and Function of the Pauline Thanksgivings* (Berlin, 1939); P. T. O'Brien, *Introductory Thanksgivings in the Letters of Paul* (Leiden, 1977); "Thanksgiving within the Structure of Pauline Theology," in *Pauline Studies*, ed. D. A. Hagner and M. J. Harris (Grand Rapids/Exeter, 1980), pp. 50-66. (See also p. 40, n. 8.)

[117]Cf. P. T. O'Brien, *Introductory Thanksgivings*, p. 3, n. 5.

[118]See n. 110 above.

[119]Cf. the force of ἐν Χριστῷ Ἰησοῦ in Col. 1:4 (p. 41, n. 12).

With the emphatic "I for my part" may be compared the emphatic "we for our part" with which the intercessory prayer is introduced in Col. 1:9.[120] Here the introductory thanksgiving is quite brief, with a rapid transition to the intercessory prayer—or, more strictly, prayer-report.[121]

17 As in Col. 1:9 the object of the intercessory prayer is that the readers "may be filled with the knowledge of God's will together with all wisdom and spiritual understanding," so here prayer is offered that the readers may be given "a spirit of wisdom and revelation in the knowledge of him" (i.e., of God). More particularly, prayer is offered that the ideal set forth in the *eulogia* may be realized in their experience—perfectly in the resurrection age but in measure at present through the ministry of the Spirit.[122]

Verses 17-19 state the substance of Paul's unremitting intercession on the readers' behalf, although the very fact of his reporting the intercession implies its repetition as he does so. His common designation of the Almighty, "the God and Father of our Lord Jesus Christ" (cf. v. 3), is here amplified to "the God of our Lord Jesus Christ, the Father all-glorious"—literally, "the Father of glory." This is the only place where he speaks of "the Father of glory." He frequently speaks of the glory of God, and once of "the glory of the Father" (Rom. 6:4). Since God is the source of all true glory, he may well be called "the Father of glory" or, as he is called in Ps. 29:3 (LXX Ps. 28:3) and Acts 7:2, "the God of glory." In 1 Cor. 2:8 Jesus is called "the Lord of glory." In this verse, as above (in vv. 6, 12, 14), the phrase "of glory" is treated as an adjectival genitive.

A "spirit of wisdom and revelation"[123] can be imparted only through him who is the personal Spirit of wisdom and revelation. God's abundant grace has already been described in v. 8 as bestowed by him "with all wisdom and understanding." Understanding in the sense of "spiritual understanding" (Col. 1:9) is the correlative of revelation; only as God reveals by his Spirit can his people understand by that same Spirit. The goal of this gift of wisdom and revelation is the personal knowledge of God. So, in Col. 1:10, Paul and Timothy pray that the Colossian Christians, bearing fruit in every good work, may "increase in the knowledge of God."[124] This is much more than the bare knowledge of God from his works which was available to the pagan world (Rom. 1:21); it is that

---

[120]Gk. κἀγώ (by crasis from καὶ ἐγώ); cf. Col. 1:9, καὶ ἡμεῖς.

[121]See G. P. Wiles, *Paul's Intercessory Prayers* (Cambridge, 1974).

[122]Cf. H. Chadwick, "Ephesians," *PC,* ed. M. Black and H. H. Rowley (London, ²1962), p. 983.

[123]Gk. πνεῦμα σοφίας καὶ ἀποκαλύψεως.

[124]In Col. 1:10, as here, "knowledge" is ἐπίγνωσις (cf. p. 46, n. 30). Cf. Eph. 4:13 for "the knowledge (ἐπίγνωσις) of the Son of God."

personal knowledge of him in experience which involves a two-way relation, entered into by those who "have come to know God, or rather to be known by God" (Gal. 4:9), for "if one loves God, one is known by him" (1 Cor. 8:3).

18 Paul goes on to pray that they may be given enlightened eyes— "the eyes of your heart" or, less literally, "spiritual eyesight." He has used similar language in 2 Cor. 4:6, where the light-creating God is said to have shone in his people's hearts so as to give "the illumination[125] of the knowledge of the glory of God (the glorious knowledge of God) in the face of Christ." Here, as a corollary to the knowledge of God himself, prayer is made that they may understand his ways and his purpose, with special reference to his dealings with his people: the hope to which he has called them, the rich inheritance which he possesses in them, and the mighty power with which he energizes them.[126]

The hope to which he has called them[127] is the hope of glory, confirmed to them here and now by the indwelling Christ (Col. 1:27) and the seal of the Spirit— "the first instalment which promises future payment in full."[128] The "hope of the glory of God" in which believers rejoice (Rom. 5:2) is the hope of sharing that glory—the hope of being manifested in glory with Christ at his appearing (Col. 3:4; cf. Rom. 8:17-30). This hope is expressed in different language later in the letter, where Christ at his *parousia* will "present to himself the church invested with glory, free from spot, wrinkle, or anything of the sort, but . . . holy and faultless" (Eph. 5:27).

"The glorious wealth of his inheritance[129] in the saints" has been alluded to in v. 11, according to which believers have been "claimed by God as his portion" in Christ, and v. 14, where God will redeem his possession on the day of consummation. That God should set such high value on a community of sinners, rescued from perdition and still bearing too many traces of their former state, might well seem incredible were it not made clear that he sees them in Christ,[130] as from the beginning he chose them in Christ. The supreme place in the love and purpose of God which Christ occupies is attested in Colossians and in this letter alike, as

---

[125]Gk. φωτισμός, formed from the verb φωτίζω (used here).

[126]For the construction εἰδέναι . . . τίς ἐστιν ἡ ἐλπίς, cf. Eph. 3:9 (φωτίσαι τίς ἡ οἰκονομία), 18 (καταλαβέσθαι . . . τί τὸ πλάτος).

[127]Gk. ἡ ἐλπὶς τῆς κλήσεως αὐτοῦ ("the hope of his calling").

[128]H. Chadwick, "Ephesians," *ibid.*

[129]For the κληρονομία of God cf. Deut. 32:9 LXX, σχοίνισμα κληρονομίας αὐτοῦ Ἰσραήλ (p. 263 above).

[130]Cf. Col. 2:1-10.

indeed in all the Pauline correspondence:[131] God's estimate of the people of Christ, united to him by faith and partakers of his resurrection life, is inevitably consistent with his estimate of Christ. Paul prays here that his readers may appreciate the value which God places on them, his plan to accomplish his eternal purpose through them as the first fruits of the reconciled universe of the future, in order that their lives may be in keeping with this high calling[132] and that they may accept in grateful humility the grace and glory thus lavished on them.

19 Four synonyms are piled up in genitival phrases when Paul prays further that his readers may come to know in experience "the surpassing greatness of the *power* of God in the lives of believers, according to the *operation* of the *strength* of his *might*."[133] If the death of Christ is the supreme demonstration of the love of God, as Paul wholeheartedly believed (Rom. 5:8), the resurrection of Christ is the supreme demonstration of his power. "Christ was raised from the dead by the glory of the Father" (Rom. 6:4)—that is to say, by "the power of God gloriously exercised."[134] And glorious power, in its "surpassing greatness," is at work in the people of Christ: it is "the Spirit of him who raised Jesus from the dead" that dwells in them (Rom. 8:11), energizing the new life within their mortal bodies and so making the hope of resurrection real for them.

Although the words that follow are closely linked with these in grammatical construction, these words effectively conclude the present prayer of intercession.[135] The prayer is, however, resumed in Eph. 3:1 and then (after a long parenthesis) completed in Eph. 3:14-19.

(2) God's Mighty Strength Shown in the Raising of Christ (1:20-23)

20 *(This was the mighty strength) that he exerted*[136] *in Christ, when he*

---

[131]Cf. Phil. 2:9-11.

[132]Cf. Eph. 4:1.

[133]Gk. τὸ ὑπερβάλλον μέγεθος τῆς δυνάμεως αὐτοῦ . . . κατὰ τὴν ἐνέργειαν τοῦ κράτους τῆς ἰσχύος αὐτοῦ. Cf. the rather less elaborate construction of Col. 1:11, ἐν πάσῃ δυνάμει δυναμούμενοι κατὰ τὸ κράτος τῆς δόξης αὐτοῦ ("empowered with all power in accordance with his glorious might").

[134]C. E. B. Cranfield, *The Epistle to the Romans*, ICC, I (Edinburgh, 1975), 304.

[135]See P. T. O'Brien, "Ephesians 1: An Unusual Introduction to a New Testament Letter," *NTS* 25 (1978-79), 505.

[136]For the aorist ἐνήργησεν (the verb is cognate with the antecedent ἐνέργειαν in v. 19) A B Ψ 81 *pc* read the perfect ἐνήργηκεν.

raised him from the dead and seated[137] him at his right hand in the heavenly realm,[138]

21 high above every principality and power, might and dominion, and every name that is named, not only in this present age but also in the coming one.

22 He "subjected all things beneath his feet"[139] and gave him as head supreme[140] to the church,

23 which is his body, (even him who is) the fullness of that which is being constantly and totally filled.[141]

20 This paragraph is syntactically attached to what precedes: it begins as an adjective clause qualifying the antecedent "operation" in v. 19. In the RSV v. 20 follows on in the same sentence as v. 19, without even a comma between them.[142] But while the adjective clause provides the transition, the new paragraph quickly becomes an independent statement of the raising and enthronement of Christ, by way of preparation for the following statement (Eph. 2:4-7) of the raising and enthronement along with Christ of "the church, which is his body."

That Christ was raised from the dead and enthroned at the right hand of God (in accordance with the oracle of Ps. 110:1)[143] was affirmed in the church's primitive confession and preaching (cf. Rom. 8:34; Acts 2:32-35, etc.). With his insistence on believers' union by faith with the living Christ, Paul applied the substance of this confession and proclamation to the practical business of Christian faith and life. Not only was the resurrection of Christ the first fruits of his people's future resurrection (1 Cor. 15:20, 23); it provided the reason for their here and now walking "in newness of life" (Rom. 6:4). The indwelling Spirit, who supplied the hope of their future resurrection (Rom. 8:11), also supplied the power to live day by day as those who had died with Christ and been raised to new

---

[137]ἐγείρας ("having raised") and καθίσας ("having seated"), for which D F G and the majority of cursives read the indicative ἐκάθισεν, are further examples of the "coincident" aorist participle (see p. 265, n. 94). After καθίσας ℵ A 33 81 2464 *pc* insert a further αὐτόν.

[138]Gk. ἐν τοῖς ἐπουρανίοις, for which B 365 629 *pc* read ἐν τοῖς οὐρανοῖς ("in the heavens").

[139]Quoted from Ps. 8:7 LXX: πάντα ὑπέταξας ὑποκάτω τῶν ποδῶν αὐτοῦ.

[140]Gk. κεφαλὴν ὑπὲρ πάντα, lit., "head over all things."

[141]Gk. τὸ πλήρωμα τοῦ τὰ πάντα ἐν πᾶσιν πληρουμένου. On the meaning of πλήρωμα and the voice of πληρουμένου see pp. 275-77 below.

[142]". . . according to the working of his great might which he accomplished in Christ. . . ."

[143]Ps. 109:1 LXX: Κάθου ἐκ δεξιῶν μου, ἕως ἂν θῶ τοὺς ἐχθρούς σου ὑποπόδιον τῶν ποδῶν σου. See p. 132 with nn. 2-4 (on Col. 3:1).

life with him (Rom. 6:6-11; 8:12-14). We have seen the moral driven home in Colossians: "if you died with Christ . . ." (2:20); "if you were raised with Christ . . ." (3:1). It is driven home again, and further elaborated, in Eph. 1:20–2:10.

The power, then, with which God works in the lives of believers is the power by which he raised Christ from death to share his throne. The throne of God is set in "the heavenly realm"—in that realm in which, as has been said above, the people of Christ are endowed with "every spiritual blessing" in him.[144]

21 There is evidently a succession of planes in the heavenly realm.[145] It is, as we are told later, the residence of "principalities and powers" (Eph. 3:10; 6:12). But the throne of God, to which Christ has been exalted, is "high above" all these: Christ has "ascended high above all the heavens" (Eph. 4:10).[146] The language of spatial elevation is used to symbolize transcendence.

Various designations of authority are piled up to emphasize the supremacy of Christ. Whatever grades of authority there may be in the universe, they are all inferior to him. The authorities here listed (not in any technical sense)—"principality and power, might and dominion"[147]— correspond for the most part to those of Col. 1:16—"thrones or dominions, principalities or powers"—although the order is different ("might" in the present list takes the place of "thrones" in Colossians). As for "every name that is named,"[148] it may be recalled that in the Christ-hymn of Phil. 2:6-11 God, in exalting the humiliated Jesus, gives him "the name which is above every name,"[149] ordaining that at Jesus' name universal homage shall be paid. The present passage echoes that affirmation; "every name" here implies not so much the conventional label of personal identity as the designation of rank or honor. Whether the rank or honor be borne by human or superhuman beings, whether it be borne "in this present age" or "in the coming one,"[150] it disappears from view in comparison with the glory which Christ has received from the Father. The mention of the coming age prepares the reader for what is said below in Eph. 2:7 about the

---

[144]Eph. 1:3 (see pp. 253-54, nn. 25-27).

[145]Cf. pp. 25, 406.

[146]Cf. Heb. 4:14, where Jesus has "passed through the heavens" (διεληλυθότα τοὺς οὐρανούς) to be "exalted above the heavens" (Heb. 7:26, ὑψηλότερος τῶν οὐρανῶν γενόμενος).

[147]Gk. πάσης ἀρχῆς καὶ ἐξουσίας καὶ δυνάμεως καὶ κυριότητος.

[148]Gk. παντὸς ὀνόματος ὀνομαζομένου.

[149]Gk. τὸ ὄνομα τὸ ὑπὲρ πᾶν ὄνομα.

[150]Gk. οὐ μόνον ἐν τῷ αἰῶνι τούτῳ ἀλλὰ καὶ ἐν τῷ μέλλοντι.

ages to come. And the emphasis on the supremacy of Christ in this age and in that is reminiscent of the emphasis placed in Col. 1:15-18 on his preeminence in the old creation and in the new alike: the firstborn of all creation is also the firstborn from the dead.

22 "He subjected all things beneath his feet" is a quotation from Ps. 8:6.[151] In the psalm, which repeats the language used of the creation of man in Gen. 1:26-28, wondering adoration is expressed at the contemplation of the honor which the Creator has bestowed on man, giving him dominion over the works of his hands. In the NT the words of the psalm are applied to Christ as the last Adam, notably by Paul in 1 Cor. 15:27 and by the writer to the Hebrews in Heb. 2:6-9. In 1 Cor. 15:24-28 the words of Ps. 8:6 are linked with those of Ps. 110:1, "Sit at my right hand, till I make your enemies your footstool,"[152] the "enemies" being identified as "every principality and every power and might."[153] Here there is no express reference to the subjection of *enemies* beneath the feet of Christ; even so, the mention in v. 20 of his session at the right hand of God makes it probable that the clause immediately following "Sit at my right hand" was not remote from the writer's mind.

Christ, then, exercises universal lordship,[154] and in particular God has given him as "head over all things"—that is, "supreme head"—to the church. If "head" be understood in the sense of origin, then Christ is divinely appointed as source of the church's life, and with the insistence on his universal lordship goes the implication that he is also the church's lord.[155] In Colossians the statements that Christ is "the head of the body, the church" (1:18) and "head of every principality and power" (2:10)[156] appear in separate contexts; here they are brought together.[157] Here indeed

---

[151]Ps. 8:7 LXX (see n. 139 above).

[152]Ps. 109:1 LXX (see n. 143 above).

[153]1 Cor. 15:24, ὅταν καταργήσῃ πᾶσαν ἀρχὴν καὶ πᾶσαν ἐξουσίαν καὶ δύναμιν.

[154]Cf. Matt. 28:18; Acts 10:36.

[155]Cf. Col. 1:18, with exposition and notes *ad loc.*; see also H. Schlier, *TDNT* 3, pp. 679-81 (*s.v.* κεφαλή); F. Mussner, *Christus, das All und die Kirche* (Trier, 1955); P. Benoit, "Body, Head and *Pleroma* in the Epistles of the Captivity" (1956), E.T. in *Jesus and the Gospel*, II (London, 1974), 51-92; I. J. Du Plessis, *Christus as Hoof van Kerk en Kosmos* (Groningen, 1962); R. Yates, "A Re-examination of Ephesians 1:23," *ExT* 83 (1971-72), 146-51; G. Howard, "The Head-Body Metaphor of Ephesians," *NTS* 20 (1973-74), 350-56.

[156]See p. 102, n. 52.

[157]H. Schlier, *Der Brief an die Epheser*, p. 89; he appears to take ὑπὲρ πάντα in κεφαλὴν ὑπὲρ πάντα τῇ ἐκκλησίᾳ as denoting Christ's headship over the universe, comparing the subjection of τὰ πάντα to him in Heb. 2:8 (a christological interpretation of Ps. 8:6).

the word "head" is not explicitly used (as it is in Col. 2:10) to denote his supremacy over principalities and powers or the rest of creation. Moreover, there is a difference in character between his supremacy over the latter and his headship over the church. The principalities and powers, insofar at least as they are hostile, "are subjected, put down by force, and are placed under Christ's feet by victory. On the other hand, the Church is one with him, even if she is subjected to him. Over her he exercises a supremacy only of sanctification and love, and force does not come into it at all."[158]

23 A further sense of the word "head" enters in as soon as the church is said to be "his body."[159] The organic relation between head and body suggests the vital union between Christ and the church, sharers of a common life, which is his own risen life communicated to his people. The church is here the complete or universal church—manifested visibly, no doubt, in local congregations (although local congregations scarcely come into the picture in Ephesians, as they do in all the other Pauline writings). It is going farther than the argument of Ephesians warrants to say, with Heinrich Schlier, that "body" plus "head" equals "Christ."[160] The only Pauline text from which such an inference might be drawn is 1 Cor. 12:12 ("As the body is one and has many members, . . . so also is Christ").

For further comment on "the church, which is his body," reference may be made to what has been said above on Col. 1:18. For the present, attention is demanded by the additional phrase, translated above as "the fullness of that which is being constantly and totally filled." There is no reason for taking "fullness" (Gk. *plērōma*) in a gnostic or other technical sense. It is clearly in apposition to one of the foregoing nouns or else to the total idea of the foregoing phrase. Along with this question of the relation of "fullness" goes a further question about the verb in the following adjective clause: should it be translated "fills" (the Greek form being understood as in the middle voice) or "is filled" (the form being understood as passive)?

It is perhaps most natural to think of "fullness" as in apposition to the immediately preceding noun "body." If the head-body analogy be maintained, the body may be thought of as the complement of the head,

[158]L. Cerfaux, *The Church in the Theology of St. Paul*, E.T. (New York, 1959), pp. 338-39.
[159]Cf. R. H. Gundry, *"Sōma" in Biblical Theology* (Cambridge, 1976), pp. 223-44. See pp. 66-71, nn. 128-49.
[160]*Der Brief an die Epheser*, p. 90.

and this is a perfectly acceptable interpretation of *plērōma*.[161] But *plērōma* may mean either "that which fills" or "that which is filled," and in the latter sense the church may be viewed as that which is filled by Christ with his life, attributes, and powers. This is the interpretation preferred by Ernest Best, who points out that what is here stated as a fact becomes part of a prayer in Eph. 3:19: "that you may be filled up to (the measure of) God's own fullness."[162]

On the other hand, *plērōma* may stand in apposition with "him" in the expression "gave him as head supreme to the church" (in the Greek "him" occupies the position of emphasis at the beginning of the clause, before the verb "gave").[163] This view, for which A. E. N. Hitchcock argued in 1910,[164] has, in C. F. D. Moule's words, "received less than justice."[165] If Christ is the *plērōma,* then he is the *plērōma* of God, in the sense indicated in Col. 1:19; 2:9: God, that is to say, is the one "who fills the universe in all its parts" (NEB margin).

But perhaps the most satisfactory account of the construction is that given by Bengel in his *Gnomon: plērōma,* he says, "is neither predicated of the church, as most think; nor, as others have decided, is it construed with 'gave'; but it is put absolutely in the accusative case (like 'testimony' in 1 Tim. 2:6). It is a finishing touch or summary (*epiphōnēma*) of what has been said from verse 20 onwards."[166] To the same effect H. Chadwick more recently expresses preference for the interpretation which "takes *plērōma* to be in apposition to the whole idea of the preceding phrase, i.e. as Christ transcendent over and immanent within the Church."[167]

As for the participle, which may be understood either as middle voice ("the one who fills") or as passive ("the one that is being filled"), it must be conceded that parallels to its use as middle voice are hard to find. But if God were the subject of the verb of filling—if, as Bengel concludes, "the apostle indicates that in Christ is the 'fullness' of the Father who fills all in all"—then the middle voice would clearly be more

---

[161]Cf. J. A. Robinson, *Ephesians,* pp. 42-44, 255-59. E. K. Simpson (*Ephesians,* p. 43) concedes that the grounds for accepting Robinson's exegesis of πλήρωμα "doubtless preponderate," but he cannot accede to Robinson's further idea of Christ as the one who is being "fulfilled."

[162]E. Best, *One Body in Christ* (London, 1955), pp. 141-44.

[163]Gk. καὶ αὐτὸν ἔδωκεν κεφαλὴν κτλ.

[164]A. E. N. Hitchcock, "Ephesians i.23," *ExT* 22 (1910-11), 91.

[165]C. F. D. Moule, "A Note on Ephesians i.22, 23," *ExT* 60 (1948-49), 53.

[166]J. A. Bengel, *Gnomon Novi Testamenti* (1773) (London: Williams and Norgate, ³1862), p. 699.

[167]H. Chadwick, "Ephesians," p. 983. Cf. his "Die Absicht des Epheserbriefes," *ZNW* 51 (1960), 152.

appropriate: God, it might be said, fills the universe for his own glory.[168] If Christ were the subject, then too, in spite of J. A. Robinson's arguments for the "somewhat startling thought" (as he calls it)[169] that he is described as the one "who all in all is being fulfilled" (passive voice), it would be necessary to translate the participle as "the one who fills,"[170] in much the same sense as Eph. 4:10, where he is said to have "ascended high above all the heavens, in order to fill all things" (where the verb is in the active voice).[171]

But if we follow current usage and treat the participle as a passive in sense as well as in form, it is not necessary to take the subject as being either Christ or God, but rather as being the church. If *plērōma* is in apposition to the general sense of what precedes, the sense may well be that Christ, who is transcendent over the church, his body, is also immanent within it and fills it "as it attains to the maximum of its perfect plenitude"[172]—that is, as it is being totally filled. The fullness of deity resides in him, and out of that fullness his church is being constantly supplied.[173]

[168]The use of the middle voice to denote the doing of something in one's own interest.

[169]J. A. Robinson, *Ephesians*, p. 43; "it is so startling as to be improbable" (E. Best, *One Body in Christ*, p. 143).

[170]E. Best, however, does not find this necessary: "He who fills the Church is himself being filled" with the *plērōma* of deity (*One Body in Christ*, p. 143). Cf. W. L. Knox, *St. Paul and the Church of the Gentiles* (Cambridge, 1939), pp. 164, 186.

[171]Gk. ἵνα πληρώσῃ τὰ πάντα. The Latin versions are unanimous in treating πληρουμένου in Eph. 1:23 as passive (cf. Vulgate: "qui omnia in omnibus adimpletur"), as do the other ancient versions apart from the Syriac Peshitta.

[172]H. Chadwick, "Die Absicht des Epheserbriefes," p. 152; "Ephesians," p. 983: Christ's relation to the church is analogous to God's relation to "the cosmic hierarchy."

[173]Cf. John 1:16, ἐκ τοῦ πληρώματος αὐτοῦ ἡμεῖς πάντες ἐλάβομεν.

EPHESIANS 2

3. THE SAVING GRACE OF GOD (2:1-10)

(1) New Life in Christ (2:1-7)

1 *You too (were raised to life), when you were dead through your trespasses and sins,[1]*

2 *in which you once led your lives according to the "aeon" of this world, according to the ruler of the domain of the air, (the domain) of the spirit which now operates in the disobedient.*

3 *Among them we also,[2] all of us, led our lives at one time, in our fleshly desires, doing the will of the flesh, the will of our minds; by nature, in fact, we were as liable to divine wrath as the rest of mankind.*

4 *But God, who is rich in mercy, because of his[3] great love with which he loved[4] us,*

5 *brought us to life together with Christ[5] even when we were dead through our trespasses[6]—it is by grace[7] that you have been saved—*

6 *and he raised us up with him and seated us with him in the heavenly realm, in Christ Jesus.*

---

[1]For ἁμαρτίαις B reads ἐπιθυμίαις (probably under the influence of v. 3).

[2]For καὶ ἡμεῖς A* D* 81 326 365 *pc* read the discordant καὶ ὑμεῖς ("you also"); cf. p. 263, n. 82.

[3]αὐτοῦ *om* P⁴⁶ D* F G.

[4]For ἦν ἠγάπησεν P⁴⁶, supported by a few Latin witnesses, reads ἠλέησεν ("had mercy on").

[5]P⁴⁶ B 33 with Latin and Coptic witnesses read ἐν τῷ Χριστῷ.

[6]B reads ἐν τοῖς παραπτώμασιν καὶ ταῖς ἐπιθυμίαις (cf. n. 1 above); D* reads ταῖς ἁμαρτίαις, P⁴⁶ τοῖς σώμασιν (!).

[7]Before χάριτι D* F G with Latin and Syriac witnesses insert οὗ ("by whose grace").

7 *This was to show in the ages to come the surpassing wealth[8] of his grace, in his kindness toward us in Christ Jesus.*

1 "You" at the beginning of v. 1 probably means ":you Gentiles," over against "we also"—that is to say, we Jews—in v. 3. "You" stands in the accusative case, but there is no expressed verb to which it forms the object. The verb implied is either "raised" as in Eph. 1:20 (God not only raised Christ from the dead; he raised "you also")[9] or (more probably) "brought to life"[10] in v. 5 below. In the latter case the construction begun in v. 1 is broken off after the succession of adjective clauses, and the sense is resumed with the new sentence "But God . . ." in vv. 4 and 5.

It was necessary that the readers should be raised to life, because they were spiritually dead, severed and alienated from God, the source of true life. Their spiritual death was the result of their "trespasses and sins"[11]—two words which, as we have seen already,[12] are used as synonyms in the Pauline writings. Etymologically they may mean respectively "falling aside" and "missing the mark," but in practice they are interchangeable (in the plural, at least).[13] NT parallels to the use of "dead" in a spiritual sense here and in v. 5 are found in Rom. 11:15; Eph. 5:14; Col. 2:13.

2 In these things[14] (trespasses and sins) you formerly led your lives—lit., "you walked"[15]—these were the things that characterized you. This is a clear echo of Col. 3:7. The two following phrases, "according to the *aiōn* of this world" and "according to the *archōn* of the domain of

---

[8]τὸ ὑπερβάλλον πλοῦτος, the noun being construed as neuter; but D² Ψ and the majority of cursives exhibit the masculine τὸν ὑπερβάλλοντα πλοῦτον.

[9]Gk. καὶ ὑμᾶς (ἤγειρεν).

[10]Gk. καὶ ὑμᾶς (συνεζωοποίησεν).

[11]Calvin takes the dative τοῖς παραπτώμασιν καὶ ταῖς ἁμαρτίαις ὑμῶν as expressing cause: "he says that *they were dead,* and states at the same time the cause of the death, namely, *sins.*" But he goes on to say, "we are all born dead" (*Ephesians,* p. 139).

[12]Cf. p. 259 with n. 62.

[13]The singular ἁμαρτία may mean not only an individual sin but the root principle of sin (cf. Rom. 5:12-13; 7:7ff.); the singular παράπτωμα is not used in this latter sense.

[14]Gk. ἐν αἷς ("in which"), the relative pronoun agreeing in gender with the nearer antecedent ἁμαρτίαις.

[15]Gk. περιεπατήσατε (cf. Col. 3:7, ἐν οἷς καὶ ὑμεῖς περιεπατήσατέ ποτε, ὅτε ἔζητε ἐν τούτοις).

the air,"[16] are naturally taken as parallel to each other. Since, then, *archōn* unquestionably means "ruler," it is natural to conclude that *aiōn*, which normally means "age," is personified here. It is certainly difficult to take it in its usual sense: what would "the age of this world" mean?[17] The traditional rendering, "the course of this world," makes good sense, but it assigns an unnatural meaning to *aiōn*. Paul sometimes uses "this world *(kosmos)*" as a synonym for "this age *(aiōn),*"[18] the present age dominated by the force of evil (cf. "the present evil age" in Gal. 1:4). This force is personified in 2 Cor. 4:4, where the minds of unbelievers are said to be blinded by "the god of this age."[19] (Compare 1 Cor. 2:6-8, where the "rulers [*archontes*] of this age" are said, through their ignorance of the divine wisdom, to have "crucified the Lord of glory.") The suggestion that "the *aiōn* of this world" in our present text is identical with "the god of this age" is attractive, but if so, this is by far the earliest certain Christian instance of *aiōn* in a personal sense.[20] The plural use of the noun in Eph. 3:9 and Col. 1:26, where mention is made of "the mystery hidden from the *aiōnes*," should not be adduced as a parallel,[21] for there the ordinary meaning "ages" makes perfectly good sense (and indeed in Col. 1:26 this sense is demanded by the following words, "and from the generations").[22] The suggestion may be made that the term is here borrowed from the

---

[16]Gk. κατὰ τὸν αἰῶνα τοῦ κόσμου τούτου, κατὰ τὸν ἄρχοντα τῆς ἐξουσίας τοῦ ἀέρος.

[17]The genitive τοῦ κόσμου τούτου might be taken as genitive of definition ("the age consisting of this world") or as a qualifying genitive: "the age of this world" being "the age characterized by this godless world" (in contrast to the age to come, which will bear a different character).

[18]Cf. 1 Cor. 1:20; 2:12; 3:19; 7:31. But αἰών is Paul's preferred term, in keeping with his inherited *schema* of the two ages; John, on the other hand, habitually uses κόσμος of the world-order that is opposed to God (e.g., 1 John 2:15-17; 4:4-6).

[19]Gk. ὁ θεὸς τοῦ αἰῶνος τούτου, no doubt identical with ὁ ἄρχων τοῦ κόσμου (τούτου) in John 12:31; 14:30; 16:11 (cf. 1 John 5:19, ὁ κόσμος ὅλος ἐν τῷ πονηρῷ κεῖται).

[20]In the second century αἰών occurs in Valentinian and other gnostic systems to denote a divine entity or emanation (Irenaeus, *Haer.* 1.1.1, etc.). In Hermeticism it occurs as *(inter alia)* a divine hypostasis (e.g., *C.H.* 11.3, δύναμις δὲ τοῦ θεοῦ ὁ αἰών, ἔργον δὲ τοῦ αἰῶνος ὁ κόσμος).

[21]As it is by R. Reitzenstein, *Das iranische Erlösungsmysterium* (Bonn, 1921), pp. 86 (n. 3), 235-36. The mystery concealed ἀπὸ τῶν αἰώνων was in due course manifested τοῖς αἰῶσιν, says Ignatius (*Eph.* 19.2), with more particular reference to the mystery (or mysteries) of the incarnation.

[22]Cf. Eph. 3:5, ἑτέραις γενεαῖς οὐκ ἐγνωρίσθη ("in other generations it was not made known").

pagan vocabulary formerly familiar to those addressed: there was indeed a mystery cult in honor of a god *Aiōn* (of Iranian origin) at Alexandria around 200 B.C.[23] (attested at Eleusis in the 1st cent. B.C.).[24] But it is quite improbable that anything so specific as this lies behind the use of *aiōn* here. Markus Barth, who translates the phrase "this world-age," suggests the possibility that "Paul thinks of a personified world-age, . . . a personal antagonist of God's good creation and of God himself," and considers that it might be capitalized and written "World-Age," as one of the titles of the devil.[25]

There is little doubt that the devil is the being described as "the ruler of the domain of the air." The question that arises here relates to the word "air." The Greek word *(aēr)* is used of the air which mortals breathe in contrast to the *aithēr*, the sky. But it is unlikely that such a contrast is intended here; for one thing, the noun *aithēr* does not appear in the NT. The domain or dominion *(exousia,* "authority") of the air differs little in meaning from "the dominion of darkness" in Col. 1:13, but it would be hazardous to suppose that we are dealing with a revival of the Homeric and Hesiodic use of *aēr* in the sense of "mist" or "haze." Nor can we think of our own figurative use of the word "air" as when we speak of an idea in the air or of the atmosphere of opinion. The word is used here as it is by Philo, who explains Jacob's ladder as a figure of speech for the air *(aēr),* which extends upward from the earth's surface to the sphere of the moon (the lowest of the heavenly zones). The air, he says, "is the home of incorporeal souls . . ., called 'demons' by the other philosophers but customarily 'angels' by the sacred record."[26] The "domain of the air," in fact, is another way of indicating the "heavenly realm" which, according to Eph. 6:12, is the abode of those principalities and powers, "world-rulers of this darkness" and "spiritual forces of wickedness" against which the people of Christ wage war.[27]

[23]Pseudo-Callisthenes, *Alexander* 30.6; Epiphanius, *Pan.* 51.22.
[24]W. Dittenberger, *SIG*³ 1125.8 (74/73 B.C.). On the Iranian source of this concept cf. W. Bousset, *Hauptprobleme der Gnosis* (Göttingen, 1907), pp. 139-44; S. G. F. Brandon, "Time as God and Devil," *BJRL* 47 (1964-65), 12-31; *History, Time and Deity* (Manchester, 1965), pp. 31-64; A. D. Nock, *Essays on Religion and the Ancient World* (Oxford, 1972), I, 377-96.
[25]M. Barth, *Ephesians*, p. 214. H. Sasse, *TDNT* 1, p. 207 (*s.v.* αἰών), after saying that "the idea of a personal Αἰών . . . is alien to the NT," concedes that "it may perhaps be found only in Eph. 2:2."
[26]Philo, *On Dreams* 1.134-35, 141; cf. *On the Giants* 6, where the "angels of God" (Gen. 6:2 LXX) are said to be "souls that fly in the air" (κατὰ τὸν ἀέρα). Cf. W. Foerster, *TDNT* 1, p. 165 (*s.v.* ἀήρ).
[27]See p. 406.

As for "the spirit which now operates in the disobedient," the noun "spirit" *(pneuma)* is in the genitive case, and is therefore naturally taken as governed by one of the two preceding nouns—"ruler" or "domain." To speak of "the ruler of the spirit which now operates" would be strange; if we translate the clause as "the domain of the spirit which now operates," then either this spirit is identical with the "ruler of the domain of the air," the malign power that blinds the minds of unbelievers, or else "spirit" is in apposition with "air"[28] and could denote (as "air" would not) the atmosphere or climate of thought which influences people's minds against God.[29] The "disobedient" (lit., "sons of disobedience,"[30] as in Eph. 5:6) are rebels against the authority of God, responsive to the prompting of the arch-rebel. The verb rendered "operate" *(energeō)* is the same as is used in Eph. 3:20 of "the power which operates in us"[31] (i.e., in believers); the distinction between the two opposed indwelling powers is pointed in 1 Cor. 2:12, "we have received not the spirit of the world but the Spirit that comes from God."

3 The readers have been reminded of their former pagan existence, before they received new life in Christ, but it is freely conceded that Jews were in no better case: "we also" were included among the disobedient. So, after the detailed exposure of the moral bankruptcy of the pagan world in Rom. 1:18-32, it is shown that Jews are no better off in this respect: "all, both Jews and Greeks, are under the power of sin" (Rom. 3:9) and equally in need of the justifying grace of God if there is to be any hope for them.[32]

"Among them"—that is, most probably, among the disobedient[33]—we Jews also followed our course of life,[34] in conformity with "the desires of our flesh." While the term "flesh" has a variety of meanings in the Pauline writings, its distinctive Pauline usage denotes that self-regarding element in human nature which has been corrupted at the source, characterized by appetites and propensities which, if unchecked, produce "the

---

[28]So H. Schlier, *Der Brief an die Epheser,* p. 104.

[29]The German word *Zeitgeist* would be an especially apt equivalent.

[30]Gk. υἱοὶ τῆς ἀπειθείας.

[31]Gk. κατὰ τὴν δύναμιν τὴν ἐνεργουμένην ἐν ἡμῖν.

[32]Note the emphatic twofold ἡμεῖς in Gal. 2:15-16, "*we* who are by nature Jews . . . , *we* also have believed in Christ Jesus . . ." (i.e., for us as much as for them faith in Christ is the only way to justification before God).

[33]The antecedent to ἐν οἷς is to be found in τοῖς υἱοῖς τῆς ἀπειθείας (contrast ἐν αἷς at the beginning of v. 2, for which see p. 280, n. 14).

[34]Gk. ἀναστρέφομαι, which here has much the same sense as περιπατέω in v. 2 (cf. the related noun ἀναστροφή, "way of life," in Eph. 4:22).

works of the flesh" listed in Gal. 5:19-20.[35] These *fleshy* include not only various forms of bodily impurity and excess but also such things as quarrelsomeness, envy, enmity, uncontrolled rage, and selfish ambition. The "desire of the flesh"[36] which, according to Gal. 5:16, can be countered only by leading one's life in the power of the Spirit embraces everything that is in opposition to the will of God. The "mind of the flesh"[37]—the unregenerate outlook—is in a state of war with God and is incapable of submitting to his law (Rom. 8:7). So, says Paul, our conduct was once in keeping with the desires of this unregenerate outlook; we carried out the dictates of our flesh, of our minds.[38] He adds "of our minds" probably in order to emphasize that the dictates of the flesh are not merely physical urges but include such qualities as pride and self-seeking, qualities which presented a greater temptation to Paul in his younger days, when he strove to outstrip his contemporaries in zeal for the ancestral traditions (Gal. 1:14), than the vices of the pagan world could ever have done.[39]

Paul speaks elsewhere of Peter and himself as Jews "by nature,"[40] which can only mean "by birth" (Gal. 2:15 RSV); here he says that he and his fellow-Jews were "by nature children of wrath" (i.e., worthy to receive divine judgment) as much as the Gentiles were. This common plight of humanity, Jews and Gentiles alike, has been inherited, according to Paul, from that one man through whom "sin came into the world . . . , and so death spread to all human beings inasmuch as all sinned" (Rom. 5:12). If that "one man's trespass led to condemnation for all human beings," as Paul puts it in Rom. 5:18 (because all humanity was encapsulated in that one man), this is tantamount to saying that all human beings

---

[35] See E. Schweizer, *TDNT* 7, pp. 98-151 (*s.v.* σάρξ); A. Sand, *Der Begriff "Sarx" in den paulinischen Hauptbriefen* (Regensburg, 1967); R. Jewett, *Paul's Anthropological Terms* (Leiden, 1971); F. F. Bruce, *Galatians,* pp. 242-50.

[36] The singular ἐπιθυμία σαρκός of Gal. 5:16 comprehends the multiple ἐπιθυμίαι τῆς σαρκὸς ἡμῶν of Eph. 2:3.

[37] Gk. τὸ φρόνημα τῆς σαρκός (Rom. 8:6-7), contrasted with τὸ φρόνημα τοῦ πνεύματος (Rom. 8:27).

[38] Gk. τὰ θελήματα τῆς σαρκὸς καὶ τῶν διανοιῶν. For the plural θελήματα cf. Acts 13:22. For this sense of διάνοια (which normally has the nobler sense of "intelligence") cf. Eph. 4:13; Col. 1:21. The plural of the noun is unusual; cf., however, Num. 15:39 LXX: οὐ διαστραφήσεσθε ὀπίσω τῶν διανοιῶν ὑμῶν, "you shall not turn away after your own impulses" (Heb. *lᵉbabkem*, "your heart"). The θελήματα of the διάνοιαι are not a different set of desires from those of the σάρξ.

[39] Cf. the list of endowments and achievements in which Paul at one time took pride (Phil. 3:4-6), although boasting of such things now, he says, would be "speaking as a fool" (2 Cor. 11:21).

[40] Gk. φύσει, as here (cf. also Rom. 2:14; Gal. 4:8).

are inherently ("by nature") subject to condemnation. With this use of the Hebrew idiom "children of wrath"[41] may be compared King David's denunciation of the rich man who seized his poor neighbor's ewe-lamb: "the man who has done this is a 'son of death,' "[42] that is, he "deserves to die" (2 Sam. 12:5 RSV).

4 When Paul speaks of the results of one man's disobedience, he also tells how humanity can be delivered from the *damnosa hereditas* incurred thereby through the obedience of another man, which brings righteousness and life to those who are united to him (Rom. 5:18-21). Essentially the same thought is expressed here, but in different language. There is a way of release from the hopelessness of existence in alienation from God—an existence which is no better than death—and it is provided by God, because he is "rich in mercy." This characterization of God is frequent in the OT: he "abounds in mercy" (Exod. 34:6; Ps. 103:8; Jon. 4:2, etc.);[43] indeed, he "delights in mercy" (Mic. 7:18). With his mercy is conjoined his love: "the great love with which he loved us"[44]—Gentiles and Jews together. The pronoun "us" here is comprehensive, not exclusive—not "us in distinction from you" but "us together with you," "all of us alike." Men and women owe their salvation to the mercy and love of God. "God shows his love for us in that, while we were yet sinners, Christ died for us" (Rom. 5:8).

5 We were dead through our trespasses, says Paul (Jews and Gentiles alike), but from that state of death God brought us to life with Christ.[45] Paul does teach elsewhere that believers in Christ "have been brought from death to life" with him (e.g., in Rom. 6:13), but there the death from which they have been brought to life is their death with Christ. Through faith-union with him they have died with him to their old existence and come alive with him to a new existence. "If we have died with Christ, we believe that we shall also live with him" (Rom. 6:8). Similarly in Colossians, "you were raised with Christ" (3:1) is the sequel to "you died with Christ" (2:20). But in Ephesians to be raised with Christ is the sequel to

---

[41]Gk. τέκνα . . . ὀργῆς. Cf. υἱοὶ τῆς ἀπειθείας (Eph. 2:2; 5:6); τέκνα φωτός (Eph. 5:8). (In the Pauline writings υἱοί and τέκνα are interchangeable; cf. Rom. 8:14, 16.) Cf. J. Mehlmann, *Natura Filii Irae*, AnBib 6 (Rome, 1957).
[42]Heb. *ben māwet* (LXX υἱὸς θανάτου).
[43]He is *rab ḥesed* (LXX πολυέλεος).
[44]Gk. διὰ τὴν πολλὴν ἀγάπην αὐτοῦ ἣν ἠγάπησεν ἡμᾶς (a good example of the internal accusative; the same construction is used of a very different kind of ἀγάπη in 2 Sam. [LXX 2 Kingdoms] 13:15).
[45]Cf. Col. 2:13, καὶ ὑμᾶς νεκροὺς ὄντας [ἐν] τοῖς παραπτώμασιν . . . συνεζωοποίησεν (p. 108).

being spiritually dead—to death through trespasses rather than to death with Christ.[46] This, of course, is in line with general NT language: "this my son was dead, and is alive again" (Luke 15:24); "he who hears my word and believes him who sent me . . . has passed from death to life" (John 5:24). But it departs from *distinctively* Pauline usage.

The affirmation that salvation is entirely dependent on divine grace is, however, totally in agreement with Paul's thought. Men and women who have no hope or possibility of winning God's approval by effort or merit of their own "are justified freely by his grace, through the redemption which is in Christ Jesus" (Rom. 3:24). Paul prefers to speak of being justified; salvation is a more general term, denoting more particularly deliverance from the adverse judgment of God to be meted out at the end-time. If believers are here and now justified by the blood of Christ, "much more shall we be saved from the (coming) wrath through him" (Rom. 5:9).[47] In Paul's thought, salvation for the most part belongs to the future: it is "nearer to us now than when we first believed" (Rom. 13:11). In one place, indeed, it is spoken of in the past tense, but even there its collocation with hope gives it a future reference: "by hope we were saved"[48] (Rom. 8:24). Here, however, salvation is something accomplished and experienced; it has much the same force as justification has in the capital epistles: "it is by grace that you have been saved"[49] (perfect tense). The statement is parenthetical here: it anticipates the fuller assertion of v. 8. But that people who were dead in sin should be granted a share in Christ's resurrection life is such a demonstration of divine grace that it calls for an immediate tribute to that grace.

6 In Paul's exposition of believers' dying and rising with Christ in Rom. 6:3-11, their rising with Christ is a future experience which (by the Spirit's power) is effectively anticipated in the present. "If we have been united with him in a death like his, we shall certainly be united with him in a resurrection like his" (Rom. 6:5), but the purpose and effect of our being united by faith to a risen Christ is that here and now "we too might walk in newness of life" (Rom. 6:3). In Colossians and Ephesians, however, the emphasis is placed on the "realized" aspect of believers' being raised with Christ: "you were raised with Christ," the Colossians are reminded (Col. 3:1); God "raised us up with him," the readers of Ephesians are told. Indeed, not only has God raised believers up with Christ

---

[46]In Colossians both kinds of death are mentioned (2:13, 20).
[47]Cf. 1 Thess. 1:10; 5:9.
[48]Gk. τῇ γὰρ ἐλπίδι ἐσώθημεν (aorist passive).
[49]Gk. χάριτί ἐστε σεσωσμένοι.

in the sense of raising them from death to life; he has raised them to his throne and seated them there with Christ "in the heavenly realm."[50] This goes farther than Colossians, where believers, raised to new life with Christ, remain on earth at present, but know that their life is secure with Christ, already enthroned at God's right hand, and that they will share his glory on the coming day of his manifestation (3:1-4). Here, however, they are already enthroned with him. Taken by itself, this might express a totally realized eschatology.[51] It is balanced, however, by the thoroughly Pauline doctrine of the Spirit found elsewhere in this epistle: the Spirit is the present guarantee of the future inheritance, sealing the people of God against the coming day of redemption (Eph. 1:13-14; 4:30). That God has already seated his people with Christ in the heavenly realm is an idea unparalleled elsewhere in the Pauline corpus. It can best be understood as a statement of God's purpose for his people—a purpose which is so sure of fulfilment that it can be spoken of as having already taken place: "whom he justified, them he also glorified" (Rom. 8:30).[52]

The added phrase "in Christ Jesus" clarifies the meaning. Enthronement with Christ in the heavenly realm is not yet part of the experience of believers,[53] but that is their proper location because they are incorporated in him. Their true home is where Christ is; their citizenship is in heaven (Phil. 3:20). The community to which they now belong, though "militant here in earth," is heavenly in origin, character, and destiny. H. Schlier, who posits a baptismal setting for Ephesians, quotes Origen: "Those who are regenerated through divine baptism are placed in paradise—that is, in the church."[54]

---

[50]Gk. ἐν τοῖς ἐπουρανίοις, as in Eph. 1:20, etc.

[51]Such a totally realized (or "overrealized") eschatology may have been held by some members of the Corinthian church (1 Cor. 15:12; cf. 2 Tim. 2:17-18), and finds expression in the Valentinian *Epistle to Rheginos on the Resurrection* (one of the Nag Hammadi treatises), which interprets Paul as teaching that "the Savior swallowed up death" and that "we suffered with him, and arose with him, and went to heaven with him" (45.14ff.).

[52]Gk. οὓς δὲ ἐδικαίωσεν, τούτους καὶ ἐδόξασεν. The aorist indicative ἐδόξασεν may have the force of the Hebrew prophetic perfect (cf. Jude 14, ἦλθεν κύριος, quoting 1 Enoch 1:9). That, so far as believers' experience is concerned, their being glorified lies in the future is evident from Rom. 8:17, εἴπερ συμπάσχομεν ἵνα καὶ συνδοξασθῶμεν.

[53]It is held out as a promise to the overcomer in Rev. 3:21 ("I will grant him to sit with me on my throne, as I myself overcame and sat down with my Father on his throne").

[54]οἱ ἀναγεννώμενοι διὰ τοῦ θείου βαπτίσματος ἐν τῷ παραδείσῳ τίθενται— τουτέστιν ἐν τῇ ἐκκλησίᾳ (*Select Notes on Genesis*, 2:13). J. H. Bernard, "The Odes of Solomon," *JTS* 12 (1910-11), 1-31, points out that the eastern fathers

7 In thus lavishing his mercy on sinners, giving them a share in Christ's risen life and in his exaltation, God has a further purpose—namely, that they should serve as a demonstration of his grace to all succeeding ages.[55] "The ages to come" is a more general conception than "the coming age" of Eph. 1:21, which reflects the traditional division of time into two ages (the present age and the resurrection age). It implies one age supervening on another like successive waves of the sea, as far into the future as thought can reach. Throughout time and in eternity the church, this society of pardoned rebels, is designed by God to be the masterpiece of his goodness. When he brings into being the reconciled universe of the future,[56] the church will provide the pattern after which it will be modeled. He is "rich in mercy"—"his compassion is over all that he has made" (Ps. 145:9)—but "the surpassing wealth of his grace"[57] is displayed in "his kindness[58] toward us in Christ Jesus." The "surpassing greatness of his power" exerted in the raising of Christ (Eph. 1:19-20)[59] is matched by the "surpassing wealth of his grace" in his dealings with those who belong to Christ. Because they are "in Christ Jesus," he deals with them as he has dealt with him.[60] The vindication and exaltation that Christ has received are his by right; the share in that vindication and exaltation bestowed on believers in Christ is theirs by divine mercy, grace, and kindness.[61]

(2) God's New Creation (2:8-10)

8 *It is by this grace that you have been saved, through faith,*[62] *and this does not proceed from yourselves; it is God's gift.*

---

frequently express the thought that the baptized have been restored to Paradise and its privileges; he quotes Basil (*Hom.* 13.2) and Gregory of Nyssa (*Sermon on Christ's Baptism*) to this effect, as well as the *Odes of Solomon* (11.14; 20.7), which he takes to be baptismal hymns. Schlier, in addition to quoting Origen, cites the *Odes of Solomon* as evidence that "the conception of baptism as a journey heavenwards is . . . widespread in early Christianity" (*Der Brief an die Epheser*, p. 111).

[55]There is no ground for treating the αἰῶνες here as other than temporal— for translating ἐν τοῖς αἰῶσιν τοῖς ἐπερχομένοις as "among the attacking [hostile] aeons," a rendering which M. Barth quotes but does not accept (*Ephesians*, pp. 222-23). See p. 281 above, with nn. 20-21.

[56]Eph. 1:9-10 (p. 261).

[57]Gk. τὸ ὑπερβάλλον πλοῦτος τῆς χάριτος αὐτοῦ (cf. Eph. 1:7).

[58]Gk. χρηστότης.

[59]See p. 271, n. 133.

[60]Cf. John Bunyan: "Sinner, thou thinkest that because of thy sins and infirmities I cannot save thy soul, but behold my Son is by me, and upon him I look, and not on thee, and will deal with thee according as I am pleased with him" (*Grace Abounding*, § 258).

[61]Gk. ἔλεος (v. 4), χάρις (vv. 5, 7, 8), χρηστότης (v. 7).

[62]Gk. διὰ πίστεως. A D¹ Ψ and the majority of cursives insert τῆς before πίστεως.

9 *It is not based on works, so that no one has room for boasting.*

10 *We are his workmanship, created in Christ Jesus for good works, which God prepared in advance, so that we might lead our lives in them.*

8 It is by this surpassingly rich grace of God, then, that salvation is secured for men and women.[63] As in v. 5, "you have been saved" is equivalent to "you have been justified." What Paul says here about salvation he says elsewhere about justification, which is freely bestowed by God's grace (Rom. 3:24) and received "not on the ground of legal works but through faith in Jesus Christ" (Gal. 2:16). "Through faith" here implies Jesus Christ as the object of that faith, as he is explicitly its object in Gal. 2:16 and Rom. 3:22, 26.[64]

The words "and this does not proceed from yourselves; it is God's gift" are probably to be taken as parenthetical, inserted into the statement that salvation is received "through faith, . . . not on the basis of works." Interpreters have differed on the precise reference of "this." If the Greek pronoun were feminine, agreeing in gender with "faith," then the reference to faith would be plain. The sense would be: even the faith through which you have been saved is not your own doing; you could not have exercised it unless God had given it to you. But the pronoun is neuter,[65] and does not *necessarily* refer to faith. Even so, it may refer generally to faith: "the difference of gender is not fatal to such a view" (J. A. Robinson).[66] That faith is referred to has been the view of many exegetes,[67] including Augustine,[68] C. Hodge (who argues that the passage is tautological on any other understanding),[69] and E. K. Simpson ("Nor is this very faith a product of the soil, but a gift of God imparted from on high conjointly with a change of heart").[70] Among those who take the reference to be to salvation itself (imparted by grace and accepted by faith) is Calvin, in whose

---

[63]The article in τῇ γὰρ χάριτί ἐστε σεσῳσμένοι points back to the χάρις already mentioned in vv. 5 and 7.

[64]That is to say, διὰ πίστεως here has the same force as the fuller διὰ πίστεως Ἰησοῦ Χριστοῦ in Gal. 2:16, where Ἰησοῦ Χριστοῦ is objective genitive (see F. F. Bruce, *Galatians*, pp. 138-39). Cf. p. 322, n. 70.

[65]Gk. καὶ τοῦτο (adverbial accusative), "and at that, and especially" (BDF § 290 (5)); cf. Rom. 13:11; 1 Cor. 6:6, 8; Phil. 1:28.

[66]J. A. Robinson, *Ephesians*, p. 157; "but the context," he adds, "demands the wider reference . . . 'salvation by grace.' "

[67]H. Schlier (who himself prefers the wider reference) cites, as holding that faith is referred to, Chrysostom, Theodoret, Beza, Estius, Bengel, Westcott, Staab (*Der Brief an die Epheser*, p. 115, n. 1).

[68]Augustine, *Enchiridion* 31; *On the Predestination of the Saints* 12.

[69]C. Hodge, *Ephesians*, pp. 119-20.

[70]E. K. Simpson, *Ephesians*, p. 55.

view "not of yourselves" is parallel to "not on the basis of works" (v. 9) and "it is God's gift" is parallel to "by (God's) grace."[71] This particular word for "gift" *(dōron),* common as it is, does not appear elsewhere in the Pauline corpus; other words with much the same meaning are used to denote God's gift of righteousness and life in Christ (Rom. 5:15-17; 6:23).[72] It is probably best to understand "and this" as referring to salvation as a whole, not excluding the faith by which it is received.

9 "It is not based on works"—of course not, for "if it is by grace, it is no longer on the basis of works; otherwise grace would no longer be grace" (Rom. 11:6). If it were based on works, those who received it could claim some credit for it. "If Abraham was justified by works, he has something to boast about"[73] (Rom. 4:2), but it was Abraham's *faith* that was "reckoned to him as righteousness" (Gen. 15:6, quoted in Rom. 4:3; Gal. 3:6). "For this reason it is based on faith, that it might be according to grace" (Rom. 4:16). And where divine grace operates, human merit is excluded, and human boasting too (Rom. 3:27).[74] There is no room for such boasting in God's presence; "therefore, as it is written, 'Let anyone who boasts, boast in the Lord' " (1 Cor. 1:29, 31, quoting Jer. 9:24).

10 The work of grace which has transformed those who were spiritually and morally dead into new men and women, alive with the resurrection life of Christ, is God's work from first to last: "we are his workmanship." The word so translated[75] is used in one other place in the Pauline writings—in Rom. 1:20, where it refers (in the plural) to God's created works.[76] Here, however, it refers to the new creation of which Paul speaks more than once. This new creation (as is emphasized below in v. 15) transcends natural distinctions of the old order: in it "neither circumcision counts for anything, nor uncircumcision, but a new creation" (Gal. 6:15); "if anyone is in Christ, there is a new creation; the old has passed away, behold, the new has come" (2 Cor. 5:17). The new heaven and earth of which an OT prophet spoke (Isa. 65:17; 66:22) have come into existence already in this new order, "created in Christ Jesus." If those

---

[71]J. Calvin, *Ephesians,* p. 144.

[72]Gk. δωρεά (Rom. 5:15, 17), δώρημα (Rom. 5:16), χάρισμα (Rom. 5:15-16; 6:23).

[73]Gk. ἔχει καύχημα, a noun derived from the verb καυχάομαι (used here, ἵνα μή τις καυχήσηται).

[74]ποῦ οὖν ἡ καύχησις; ἐξεκλείσθη.

[75]Gk. ποίημα (whence Eng. "poem"; but this provides no basis for the fanciful rendering "we are his poem").

[76]"His invisible qualities, namely his everlasting power and divinity, are clearly seen, being understood by his works" (τοῖς ποιήμασιν νοούμενα).

who belonged to the old order were dead through their trespasses and sins, those who belong to the new creation are characterized by "good works,"[77] works performed not to secure salvation but as the fruit of salvation. God, we are told, "prepared" these good works "in advance," that they might mark his people's way of life.[78] They are the good works which reflect the character and action of God himself. God gave his people the law that they might be like him: "I am the LORD your God; . . . you shall therefore be holy, for I am holy" (Lev. 11:44-45). Jesus similarly taught his disciples to behave in a manner befitting God's children, to be merciful as their Father is merciful (Luke 6:35-36).[79] But to live like this, to accomplish the good works prepared for his children by God, the empowering gift of his Spirit is necessary. The good works were promulgated long ago, but thanks to the saving act of God "the righteous requirement of the law" is fulfilled in those who "walk not according to the flesh but according to the Spirit" (Rom. 8:4).[80] His new creation "in Christ Jesus" is brought into being by the agency of the Spirit, and by the Spirit's agency the promise of the new covenant is realized when men and women are found "doing the will of God from the heart" (Eph. 6:6).[81]

4. THE INCORPORATION OF THE GENTILES (2:11-22)

(1) Their Former Plight (2:11-12)

11 *Therefore, remember that you were formerly Gentiles by natural descent,[82] called "uncircumcision" by the so-called man-made external[83] circumcision—*

[77]The quotation from Origen on p. 287 (n. 54) continues thus: ". . . in order to produce the spiritual works which are therein" (ἐργάζεσθαι τὰ ἔνδον ὄντα ἔργα πνευματικά).

[78]Cf. Col. 1:10, ἐν παντὶ ἔργῳ ἀγαθῷ καρποφοροῦντες. The plural ἔργα ἀγαθά or ἔργα καλά occurs several times in the Pastorals; cf. 1 Tim. 2:10; 5:10, 25; 6:18; Tit. 2:7, 14; 3:8, 14. Whereas here God has prepared good works for his people to "walk therein," in the Pastorals it is his people who are to be prepared "for every good work" (2 Tim. 2:21; 3:17; Tit. 3:1).

[79]Cf. Matt. 5:45, 48.

[80]Cf. 2 Cor. 3:4-18.

[81]Gk. ἐκ ψυχῆς (see p. 400). The NT application of the new covenant oracle of Jer. 31:31-34 also draws on Ezekiel's prophecy of the new heart and new spirit which God's people will receive in the age of restoration (Ezek. 11:19-20; 36:25-27).

[82]Gk. ἐν σαρκί, "in flesh"; σάρξ may denote here either their bodily flesh, which was uncircumcised, or their unregenerate existence (perhaps both ideas are in view).

[83]Gk. ἐν σαρκὶ χειροποιήτου, here plainly with reference to their bodily flesh. Cf. Rom. 2:28, ἡ ἐν τῷ φανερῷ ἐν σαρκὶ περιτομή. For χειροποιήτου see p. 103, n. 62 (on Col. 2:11).

12 *(remember, I say,) that at that time you were without Christ, aliens*[84] *from the commonwealth of Israel and strangers from the covenants (which embodied) the promise;*[85] *you were bereft of hope and existed in the world without God.*[86]

11 The privileges now enjoyed by Gentile believers in Christ would be appreciated all the more gratefully if they bore in mind the state of life from which they had been delivered. The pious Jew was ever conscious of the privileges which he had inherited: daily he thanked God that he had not been made a Gentile. To him and to his people the true God had revealed himself in a unique manner: he had "not dealt thus with any other nation"; no other nation "knew his ordinances" (Ps. 147:20). The external sign of the Jews' special relationship with God was circumcision, the seal of the covenant which he had made with their ancestor Abraham (Gen. 17:9-14). Although they were not the only nation to practice circumcision,[87] the Jews' practice of it was sufficiently distinctive in the Graeco-Roman world for them to be called comprehensively the "circumcision," while they could refer to non-Jews comprehensively as the "uncircumcision."[88] The Jews' circumcision might be a matter of reproach against them on the lips of their Gentile neighbors,[89] but in the eyes of Jews the uncircumcision of Gentiles was a token of their estrangement from God. It was a religious handicap which could be overcome only if a Gentile became a proselyte to the Jewish faith, accepting circumcision and the attendant obligation to keep the law of Moses. (That only males bore the covenant seal in their bodies gave them greater religious prerogatives than women

---

[84]Gk. ἀπηλλοτριωμένοι, "alienated" (perfect participle passive); but to translate it so might suggest (wrongly) that they had once been members of the πολιτεία τοῦ Ἰσραήλ but had subsequently been separated from it.

[85]Gk. τῶν διαθηκῶν τῆς ἐπαγγελίας, where the genitive τῆς ἐπαγγελίας is epexegetic of διαθηκῶν, having similar force to that which it has in Eph. 1:13 (τῷ πνεύματι τῆς ἐπαγγελίας).

[86]Gk. ἄθεοι ἐν τῷ κόσμῳ. This is the only NT occurrence of ἄθεος (found in literature from Aeschylus onward). The word came to be used by pagans of Christians and by Christians of pagans (*Mart. Pol.* 3:2; 9:2, where αἶρε τοὺς ἀθέους, "Away with the atheists!" is repeated in both senses).

[87]In earlier OT times other Semitic groups and the Egyptians practiced circumcision, while the Philistines notoriously did not and were therefore known distinctively as "the uncircumcised" (e.g., 1 Sam. 31:4; 2 Sam. 1:20).

[88]For ἀκροβυστία ("uncircumcision") and περιτομή ("circumcision") used as collective nouns cf. Rom. 3:30; Gal. 2:7.

[89]Cf. Apion, according to Josephus, *Apion* 2.137 (τὴν τῶν αἰδοίων χλευάζει περιτομήν); Horace, *Sat.* 1.9.70 (*hodie tricesima sabbata; vin tu / curtis Iudaeis oppedere?*); Juvenal, *Sat.* 14.99 (*mox et praeputia ponunt*).

enjoyed: the man who thanked God daily that he had not been made a Gentile thanked him at the same time that he had not been made a woman.)[90] Paul, who before his conversion had taken pride in the fact that he was "circumcised on the eighth day" (Phil. 3:5) and may well have been an ardent proselytizer, inviting Gentiles to submit to circumcision and thus be incorporated in the covenant people (cf. Gal. 5:11), had now learned that circumcision in the flesh was religiously irrelevant.[91] This "man-made external circumcision" he now depreciated; in one place he dismisses it as no better than mutilation (Phil. 3:2).[92] What mattered in the sight of God was the circumcision or cleansing of the heart of which Moses and the prophets spoke (Deut. 10:16; 30:6; Jer. 4:4), the "circumcision not made with hands" or "circumcision of Christ," as it is called in Col. 2:11.[93] This spiritual "circumcision" is equally available to Jews and Gentiles, to men and women. In the new order which the gospel has inaugurated there is no room for mutual disparagement between the circumcised and the uncircumcised.

12 The religious privileges inherited by the Jews were substantial: not only were they "entrusted with the oracles of God" (Rom. 3:2), but, as Paul emphasizes in Rom. 9:4-5, "to them belong the sonship,[94] the glory,[95] the covenants,[96] the giving of the law, the worship,[97] and the promises;[98] to them belong the patriarchs, and of their race, according to the flesh, is the Christ." From all those privileges the Gentiles had been cut off. They were foreigners, not members of the chosen people. The covenants with the patriarchs, which held out the promise of great blessing for them and their posterity, did indeed make mention of "all the nations of the earth" as somehow involved in that blessing;[99] but not until the

---

[90]"In Christ Jesus," according to Paul, both these religious inequalities are removed, together with that between the slave and the free person (Gal. 3:28; cf. F. F. Bruce, *Galatians*, pp. 187-90).

[91]Cf. Gal. 5:6; 1 Cor. 7:19.

[92] βλέπετε τὴν κατατομήν.

[93]See p. 104. Cf. Rom. 2:29, περιτομὴ καρδίας ἐν πνεύματι οὐ γράμματι.

[94]"Israel is my firstborn son" (Exod. 4:22; cf. Hos. 11:1).

[95]That is, the divine glory (the *shekhinah*) dwelling in the sanctuary in the midst of the people (Exod. 40:34-35; 1 Kings 8:11).

[96]Those made with Abraham (Gen. 15:18), with Israel in the wilderness (Exod. 24:8), and with David (Ps. 89:28-37).

[97]Comprising priesthood, sanctuary, and sacrifice, according to the levitical legislation.

[98]Especially those made to the patriarchs (Gen. 12:2-3; 18:18; 22:17-18; 26:3-5; 28:13-14).

[99]Cf. J. Schreiner, "Segen für die Völker in der Verheissung an die Väter," *BZ* 6 (1962), 1-31.

coming of Christ and the free proclamation of the gospel could believing Gentiles, without first becoming Jews, "be blessed with believing Abraham" (Gal. 3:9). Gentiles did not share the hope of Israel,[100] they did not know the God of Israel, nor did it seem possible that the Messiah of Israel should have any significance for them.

There is another place in the Pauline correspondence where those "who do not know God" are described as having "no hope" (1 Thess. 4:5, 13). There the hope which pagans lack is not simply the hope of Israel but the hope of resurrection in the new light given to it for those who "believe that Jesus died and rose again." The absence of hope in the face of death is amply attested in the literature and epigraphy of the Graeco-Roman world of that day.[101] But here the reference is more general: God is "the God of hope" (Rom. 15:13) and to be without him is to be without real hope even in this world, not to speak of that which is to come.

(2) Their Present Access (2:13-18)

13 *But now in Christ Jesus you who once were far off have been brought near by the blood of Christ.*

14 *For he is himself our peace: he has made us both one, and has broken down the intervening wall which formed a barrier between us.*

15 *In his flesh he has abolished the hostility, the law of commandments, ordinances and all,*[102] *in order to create of the two in himself*[103] *one new*[104] *human being, (thus) making peace,*

16 *and to reconcile both to God in one body through the cross, having by its means*[105] *put the hostility to death.*

17 *Then he came and proclaimed peace to you who were far off as well as peace*[106] *to those who were near.*

---

[100]The hope of Israel, as Paul had been brought up to view it, included the hope of resurrection (Acts 24:15; 26:6-8; 28:20).

[101]See F. F. Bruce, *1 and 2 Thessalonians,* WBC (Waco, 1982), p. 96.

[102]Gk. ἐν δόγμασιν (omitted by P⁴⁶ lat^{vg.cod}), translated here like τοῖς δόγμασιν in Col. 2:15, although it might well be rendered "consisting in ordinances" (see p. 106, n. 80). Cf. p. 298, n. 119.

[103]Reading ἐν ἑαυτῷ, with ℵ² D G Ψ and the majority of cursives, or treating the variant αυτω (P⁴⁶ ℵ* A B *al*) as bearing the rough breathing (αὑτῷ).

[104]For καινόν ("new") P⁴⁶ F G read κοινόν ("common"); K reads καὶ μόνον, "(one) and only (human being)."

[105]Reading ἐν αὐτῷ, for which F G *pc* (supported by the Latin versions) read ἐν ἑαυτῷ ("by himself").

[106]The second occurrence of εἰρήνην is omitted by Ψ with the majority of cursives and the Harclean Syriac.

18 *It is through him that we both have our access in one Spirit to the Father.*

13 The new order "in Christ Jesus" has now changed the whole situation. Gentiles, who formerly were "far off" from God (in contrast to the Israelites, who had been accepted into his covenant), have now been "brought near." The designation of Gentiles as "far off" may derive from OT usage (compare the quotation from Isa. 57:19 in v. 17 below);[107] it is found elsewhere in the NT—by implication, for example, in the apostolic message of Acts 2:39 ("the promise is to you and to your children and to all that are far off") and expressly in the Lord's commission to Paul recorded in Acts 22:21 ("I will send you far off to the Gentiles").

The means by which Gentile believers have been "brought near" is stated: it is "by the blood of Christ." The blood of Christ, his sacrificial death, mentioned already as the means of their redemption (Eph. 1:7), is also the means of their reconciliation to God (cf. Col. 1:20-22; Rom. 5:10). There is a noteworthy parallel between the language used here and that of Heb. 10:19-22, where believers are encouraged to "have confidence to enter the [heavenly] sanctuary by the blood of Jesus" and thus "draw near" to God. It may be that in Hebrews Jewish Christians are addressed, whereas in the present context Gentile believers are more directly in view; but "in Christ Jesus" the ground of approach for both groups is the same.

14 "For he is himself our peace"[108] in a twofold sense—not only has he reconciled his people to God through his death but he has reconciled them to each another; in particular, he has reconciled those of Jewish birth to those of Gentile birth. To say that he *is* our peace sets forth the truth more emphatically than to say that he has "made peace" (v. 15) or "proclaimed peace" (v. 17). It is in him, as fellow-members of his body, that his people enjoy their twofold peace. It is he who has brought the formerly hostile groups into a new unity, in which the old distinction between Jew and Gentile has been transcended.[109] Whereas Jews formerly tended to speak of the division of humanity into Jews and Gentiles, Paul makes a

---

[107]Cf. Isa. 5:26, ἀρεῖ σύσσημον ἐν τοῖς ἔθνεσιν τοῖς μακράν.

[108]For attempts to find a hymnic structure in vv. 14-18 see G. Schille, *Frühchristliche Hymnen* (Berlin, 1965), pp. 24-31; J. Gnilka, "Christus unser Friede—ein Friedens-Erlöserlied in Eph 2, 14-17," in *Die Zeit Jesu*, ed. G. Bornkamm and K. Rahner (Freiburg, 1970), pp. 190-207; H. Merklein, "Zur Tradition und Komposition von Eph 2, 14-18," *BZ* 17 (1973), 79-102; cf. J. T. Sanders, *The New Testament Christological Hymns* (Cambridge, 1971), pp. 14-15, 88-92.

[109]"The Pauline teaching on reconciliation gains a fresh dimension by being applied to persons-in-community" (R. P. Martin, *Reconciliation: A Study of Paul's Theology* [London, 1981], p. 198).

threefold classification into Jews, Greeks (Gentiles), and church of God (1 Cor. 10:32), the last embracing former Jews and former Gentiles. No wonder that Christians spoke of themselves as a "third race" or "new race," no longer Jewish, no longer Gentile.[110]

The barrier which formerly separated Jews and Gentiles has been demolished by Christ. This traditional barrier was both religious and sociological: as the following words make plain, it consisted of the Jewish law, more particularly of those features of it which marked Jews off from Gentiles—circumcision and the food restrictions, for example.[111] In the gospel order such features were superseded. No longer did circumcision or uncircumcision have any religious relevance: such matters as the observance of special days or abstention from certain kinds of food belonged henceforth to the realm of personal conscience; with regard to them everyone should be "fully convinced in his own mind," without being condemned or despised by anyone else for his decision (Rom. 14:5-12).

Several commentators have suggested, however, that some actual barrier provided the analogy for this description of the Jewish law. One view, maintained by Heinrich Schlier and others, is that the analogy was provided by the barrier which, in some gnostic and other schemes of thought, separated the world below from the upper world of the plērōma.[112] The gnostic form of this concept is not attested early enough for one to accept with any confidence the idea that it has influenced the language of our present passage.[113] A nongnostic instance comes in the pseu-

---

[110]Cf. *Preaching of Peter,* quoted in Clement of Alexandria, *Strom.* 6.5.41.6: "we who worship God in a new way, as the third race (τρίτῳ γένει), are Christians"; *Ep. Diog.* 1, "this new race" (καινὸν τοῦτο γένος).

[111]The food restrictions would have prevented Peter from accepting Cornelius's hospitality, but for his vision at Joppa (Acts 10:28). Cf. *Letter of Aristeas* 139: "Our lawgiver . . . fenced us round (περιέφραξεν) with impregnable ramparts and walls of iron, that we might not mingle at all with any of the other nations, but remain pure in body and soul."

[112]H. Schlier, *Christus und die Kirche im Epheserbrief* (Tübingen, 1930), pp. 18-26; *Der Brief an die Epheser,* pp. 126-33.

[113]This is particularly so with regard to the passages from Mandaean literature which Schlier adduces from R. Reitzenstein, *Das mandäische Buch des Herrn der Grösse und die Evangelienüberlieferung* (Heidelberg, 1919), p. 32; *Das iranische Erlösungsmysterium* (Bonn, 1921), pp. 60, 267. The surviving Mandaean texts belong to the fifth century and later, even if they attest earlier concepts. Apart from Mandaean texts, Schlier adduces parallels to the heavenly barrier from Valentinianism (*apud* Iren., *Haer.* 1.1.2), in which it was variously called ὅρος and σταυρός, and from the *Acts of Thomas* 32, where the serpent claims to have "entered through the barrier (φραγμός) into Paradise"; cf. G. Bornkamm, *Mythos und Legende in den apokryphen Thomas-Akten* (Göttingen, 1933), p. 29; A. F. J. Klijn, *The Acts of Thomas* (Leiden, 1962), p. 225.

donymous "Acts of Thaddaeus," preserved by Eusebius, according to which the apostle Thaddaeus preached the gospel to Abgar, ruler of Edessa, and told how Jesus, having been crucified, "descended into Hades and rent asunder the barrier which had not been rent from eternity, and raised up the dead: he descended alone, but ascended to his Father with a great multitude."[114] The concept of this horizontal barrier might be relevant to the passage about Christ's descending and ascending in Eph. 4:8-10, but the barrier between Jews and Gentiles was not a horizontal barrier, separating those above from those below, but rather a vertical barrier.

Such a vertical barrier stood in the temple precincts in Jerusalem, preventing Gentiles from proceeding from the outer court ("the court of the Gentiles") into any of the inner courts. Josephus describes how this barrier encircled the higher ground which contained the inner courts and had attached to it at intervals notices in Greek and Latin warning Gentiles not to proceed farther on pain of death.[115] This was indeed a material barrier keeping Jews and Gentiles apart. It cannot be said with certainty that it provided the analogy for the wording of our text, but it would have been a more appropriate analogy than any horizontal barrier. It might indeed be asked if the readers of this epistle would have recognized such an allusion.[116] Perhaps not; but they would have had greater difficulty in recognizing an allusion to the barrier separating the upper from the lower world. Whatever the readers may or may not have recognized, however, it should be remembered that the temple barrier in Jerusalem played an

---

[114]Eusebius, *HE* 1.13.20 (καὶ κατέβη εἰς τὸν ᾅδην, καὶ διέσχισε φραγμὸν τὸν ἐξ αἰῶνος μὴ σχισθέντα, καὶ ἀνήγειρεν νεκρούς, καὶ κατέβη μόνος, ἀνέβη δὲ μετὰ πολλοῦ ὄχλου πρὸς τὸν πατέρα αὐτοῦ). There is a markedly similar passage in the longer (post-Ignatian) recension of the letters of Ignatius (*Trall.* 9:4): καὶ κατῆλθεν εἰς ᾅδην μόνος, ἀνῆλθεν δὲ μετὰ πλήθους· καὶ ἔσχισεν τὸν ἀπ᾽ αἰῶνος φραγμὸν καὶ τὸ μεσότοιχον αὐτοῦ ἔλυσεν ("He went down to Hades alone, but ascended with a multitude; and he rent the barrier which had existed from eternity and broke down its intervening wall"). The occurrence of φραγμός and μεσότοιχον together in Pseudo-Ignatius suggests dependence on our Ephesians passage (τὸ μεσότοιχον τοῦ φραγμοῦ λύσας), although the figure is applied differently.

[115]Josephus, *BJ* 5.194. Two of these Greek notices have been discovered—one in 1871 (now in the Archaeological Museum, Istanbul) and one in 1934 (now in the Rockefeller Museum, Jerusalem). See C. S. Clermont-Ganneau, "Une stèle du Temple de Jérusalem," *RA* 13 (1872), 214-34, 290-96 (cf. *CIJ* 2.1400); J. H. Iliffe, "The *Thanatos* Inscription from Herod's Temple: Fragments of a Second Copy," *QDAP* 6 (1938), 1-3.

[116]The question is asked by M. Dibelius, *An die Kolosser, An die Epheser, An Philemon* (Tübingen, ³1953), p. 69. E. J. Goodspeed sees the Jerusalem temple barrier here, but thinks that its figurative use in this context was suggested by its actual destruction in A.D. 70 (*The Meaning of Ephesians* [Chicago, 1933], p. 37).

important part in the chain of events which led to Paul's becoming the "prisoner of Christ Jesus for the sake of you Gentiles" (as he is called in Eph. 3:1). For, according to Acts 21:27-36, Paul's arrest came about because he was charged with aiding and abetting illegal entry by a Gentile Christian through the temple barrier. The charge could not be sustained when it came to court, as no witnesses were forthcoming, but Paul was not released but kept in custody, first in Caesarea and then in Rome. That literal "middle wall of partition," the outward and visible sign of the ancient cleavage between Jew and Gentile, could have come very readily to mind in this situation.[117]

15 The question arises whether "hostility" should be construed as a second object after "has broken down," in apposition with "wall," or as the first object of "has abolished," in apposition with "law." Since "wall," "hostility," and "law" are so closely associated, the sense is not materially affected by the construction, but the balance of the clauses is better maintained if the second construction is preferred.[118] The barrier between Jews and Gentiles was largely a psychological barrier, the antipathy aroused by the separateness of the Jews, accompanied as it often was by a sense of superiority on their part. But this antipathy, it is affirmed, has been abolished by Christ "in his flesh"—that is, by his death (compare the fuller wording of Col. 1:22, "in the body of his flesh, through death"). How? Because by his death he has done away with that which separated the Jew from the Gentile, "the law of commandments, ordinances and all."[119]

It is not the law as a revelation of the character and will of God that has been done away with in Christ. In that sense of the term the question and answer of Rom. 3:31 remain valid: "Do we then overthrow the law[120] by this faith? By no means! On the contrary, we uphold the law." The righteousness required by the law of God is realized more fully by the inward enabling of the Spirit—in Jew and Gentile alike—than was possible under the old covenant. But the law as a written code, threatening death instead of imparting life, is done away with in Christ, as Paul argues

---

[117]For the wider significance of the removal of the barrier in the argument of the epistle see M. Barth, *The Broken Wall* (London, 1960).

[118]"It is in any case simpler to take τὴν ἔχθραν with καταργήσας, although that verb is chosen by an afterthought as specially applicable to τὸν νόμον κτλ. The sense remains the same whichever construction is adopted" (J. A. Robinson, *Ephesians*, p. 161).

[119]Gk. τὸν νόμον τῶν ἐντολῶν ἐν δόγμασιν καταργήσας. That ἐν δόγμασιν is a later gloss (cf. p. 294, n. 102) is argued by C. J. Roetzel, "Jewish Christian–Gentile Relations: A Discussion of Ephesians 2:15a," *ZNW* 74 (1983), 81-89.

[120]Gk. νόμον οὖν καταργοῦμεν . . .; (the same verb as here).

in 2 Cor. 3:6-15.[121] And when the law in that sense is done away with, the barrier between Jews and Gentiles is removed; Jewish particularism and Gentile exclusion are things of the past. In another place Paul describes how even one commandment of the law, brought to the conscious attention of a man or woman, can constitute an instrument by which sin gains a foothold, so that the result attained is the opposite of what the commandment enjoins (Rom. 7:7-11). In speaking here of the law, "it is as a code of manifold precepts, expressed in definite ordinances, that he declares it to have been annulled" (J. A. Robinson).[122]

The phrase rendered "ordinances and all" might be otherwise translated "consisting of ordinances" or "contained in ordinances"; the rendering given above follows the analogy of Col. 2:14 (although the Greek phrase there is not exactly the same as here).[123]

Now that the barrier has been removed, there is no further need for the communities which it kept apart to remain separate. The purpose of the work of Christ is that they should be brought together into a new unity. In place of the former hostility, he has now made peace. Where two opposed groups once stood over against each other, he has "in himself"— "in Christ Jesus" (v. 13)—created a new humanity, indeed, a new human being.[124]

Since this human being—the people of Christ united in him as fellow-members of his body—is a new creation, it is unnecessary to seek previously existing analogies for it. One such analogy has been found in the heavenly *anthrōpos* of Mandaism and other forms of gnosticism.[125] This has been traced back, at least in part, to the Avestan figure of Gayōmart, the primal man.[126] But the new *anthrōpos* of this passage and

---

[121]In 2 Cor. 3:6-15 καταργέω is used repeatedly (vv. 7, 11, 13, 14) of doing away with the law in this sense.

[122]J. A. Robinson, *Ephesians,* p. 161.

[123]See p. 294, n. 102; also p. 106, n. 80.

[124]Gk. εἰς ἕνα καινὸν ἄνθρωπον.

[125]Cf. H. Schlier, *Christus und die Kirche im Epheserbrief,* pp. 27-37, where parallels are adduced from the *Acts of Philip* 122, from Manichaean texts, and from the Naassene doctrine described by Irenaeus (*Haer.* 1.6.3; 1.28.1) and Hippolytus (*Ref.* 5.7). But all such parallels are derivative from NT teaching.

[126]In the Avesta primal man is called *Yima* (cf. Vedic *Yama*), while *Gaya-maretan* (meaning "mortal life") appears occasionally as the ancestor of the Aryans and the first believer in the teaching of Ahura-mazda. But in the *Bundahišn* and other Zoroastrian texts of the seventh century A.D. and later Gayōmart plays an important part in the cosmic drama as a heavenly being, primal man, the son of Ohrmazd (Avestan *Ahura-Mazda*); he battles with Ahriman (Avestan *Angra-mainyu*), the evil power, for a cycle of 3,000 years, at the end of which he is overcome and killed. From him, after his death, the human race springs up and when, at the end of time, Saošyant ("the savior") appears to raise the dead, Gayōmart will rise first

Eph. 4:24 is a corporate entity, the counterpart in the gospel order of the "old *anthrōpos*" which, according to Rom. 6:6, was "crucified with" Christ. If that old entity died in Christ's death, the new entity has come to life in his resurrection. A more adequate background to this idea than one drawn from any extraneous source is provided by Paul himself when he tells his Galatian converts how he endures birth pangs over them until (as he says) "Christ be formed in you" (Gal. 4:19).

16 The reconciliation of former Jews and Gentiles "in one body" is the result of their reconciliation to God. The instrument of this twofold reconciliation is the cross of Christ. In Col. 1:20 Christ is said to have "made peace through the blood of his cross" in the sense of reconciling an estranged creation to God; here it is through that same cross that those who have by its means been reconciled to God are reconciled one to another. Human hostility to God has to be overcome—"while we were enemies we were reconciled to God by the death of his Son" (Rom. 5:10)—and hostility within the human family (and within creation as a whole) must similarly be overcome. Both forms of hostility have been "put to death" by Christ through his own death on the cross.[127] This is no doubt an ideal not yet fully realized in experience; but the insistence of this epistle is that the ideal will one day be seen as a worldwide reality, thanks to the completeness of Christ's reconciling sacrifice.

17 "The word which God sent to Israel, preaching good news of peace by Jesus Christ (he is Lord of all)," began to be made available to the Gentile world also when Peter spoke those words in the house of Cornelius (Acts 10:36). Here Christ himself is the preacher (acting by his Spirit in his messengers): "he came and proclaimed peace." The language is borrowed from Isa. 57:19, "Peace, peace to the far and to the near, says the LORD,"[128] as he promises healing and restoration to his people, those

---

and be promoted to archangelic rank. This myth had a long career in oral tradition before it received literary form, but it cannot well be dated before the Sassanian era (A.D. 226) and has no bearing on NT teaching. See R. Reitzenstein, *Das iranische Erlösungsmysterium*, pp. 119, 134; J. M. Creed, "The Heavenly Man," *JTS* 26 (1924-25), 113-36.

[127]ἀποκτείνας τὴν ἔχθραν ἐν αὐτῷ. The reading ἐν αὐτῷ means "by means of the cross"; if ἐν ἑαυτῷ be preferred (see p. 294, n. 105), "in himself" would be parallel to "in his flesh" of v. 14. Christ has put the hostility to death by drawing it off onto himself and allowing it to put him on the cross. For the ἔχθρα see W. Rader, *The Church and Racial Hostility: A History of the Interpretation of Ephesians 2:11-22*, BGBE 20 (Tübingen, 1978).

[128]LXX εἰρήνην ἐπ' εἰρήνην τοῖς μακρὰν καὶ τοῖς ἐγγὺς οὖσιν. For οἱ μακράν used in the prophets to denote dispersed Jews cf. Zech. 6:15, καὶ οἱ μακρὰν ἀπ' αὐτῶν ἥξουσιν καὶ οἰκοδομήσουσιν ἐν τῷ οἴκῳ κυρίου.

in distant exile as well as those close at hand. The welcome sound of the Lord's messenger has been celebrated in Isa. 52:7, "How beautiful upon the mountains are the feet of him who brings good tidings, who publishes peace"—words echoed already by Paul in Rom. 10:15 and later in Eph. 6:15. But for Paul and his fellow-preachers those who are "far off" are no longer, or at least not only, Jews of the distant dispersion: they are Gentiles, who "once were far off" but have now "been brought near by the blood of Christ" (v. 13), "brought near" to God himself, and assured of an equal welcome from him with their fellow-believers of Jewish birth, whose ground of approach to him is no different from theirs.

18 For it is through Christ that Jewish and Gentile believers alike have their access to the Father.[129] In Christ they have become members of his family, and when they address him by the family name "Abba! Father!" (the name by which Jesus addressed him), they give evidence of being indwelt by one and the same Spirit,[130] the Spirit of God's Son (Gal. 4:6). Within his family the Father makes no distinction between those children who are Jewish by birth and those who are Gentile. To us the abolition of the barrier separating Jews and Gentiles may not be so revolutionary as it was for Paul and his associates; but there are other divisions within the human family which are equally irrelevant in the sight of God and ought to be irrelevant in his children's sight.

Mention has been made earlier of the parallel between this teaching about free access to God and the teaching of Heb. 10:19-22. Another parallel is found in Jesus' words to the Samaritan woman about the nature of true worship: "The hour is coming when neither on this mountain [Gerizim] nor in Jerusalem will you worship the Father. . . . God is spirit, and those who worship him must worship in spirit and truth" (John 4:21-24).[131]

(3) Their Membership in the House of God (2:19-22)

19 So then,[132] you are no longer strangers and aliens, but you are[133] fellow-citizens of the saints and members of the house of God;

---

[129]For προσαγωγή cf. Eph. 3:12; cf. also Rom. 5:2, where "we have obtained access (προσαγωγή) through Christ into our present state of grace."

[130]Cf. Rom. 8:15-16 (quoted on p. 256). For "one Spirit," as for the "one body" of v. 16, see Eph. 4:4 (p. 336).

[131]See H. Merklein, *Christus und die Kirche: Die theologische Grundstruktur des Epheserbriefes nach Eph 2, 11-18* (Stuttgart, 1973).

[132]Gk. ἄρα οὖν (οὖν *om* P⁴⁶vid F G Ψ 1739 1881 etc.).

[133]In place of ἐστέ (which is omitted in D² Ψ and the majority of cursives) 1739 and 1881 read καί.

20 *you have been built on the foundation of the apostles and prophets,
Christ Jesus himself being the cornerstone,*[134]
21 *for it is in him that the whole structure*[135] *is bonded together and
grows into a holy sanctuary in the Lord;*
22 *it is in him that you too are being built together for God's*[136] *dwelling-place in the Spirit.*

19 The first Gentile believers who were admitted to a church comprising Jewish Christians could well have felt ill at ease; it was desirable that they should be made to feel completely at home. The church had a Jewish base; its members had Jewish presuppositions, and it would have been too easy for Gentile Christians to do or say something which was felt to be out of place. What indeed was their status in such a community? Were they there on sufferance, as visitors, like the God-fearing Gentiles who attended synagogue in cities of the dispersion? Was their position like that of resident aliens in a Greek city, or that of *peregrini* in Rome?[137] In a crisis like that which arose in Antioch when Peter and others abandoned the practice of table-fellowship with Gentile Christians, the latter must have got the impression that they were at best second-rate citizens. Against this apparent demotion of Gentile Christians Paul protested vigorously at Antioch (Gal. 2:11-14), and it is Paul's attitude that finds uncompromising expression here. Gentile Christians are not adherents or visitors or second-rate citizens in the believing community; they are full members. If the community is viewed as a city, they are citizens, not resident aliens. The "saints" with whom they are fellow-citizens are the original "saints"— "we who first placed our hope in Christ," as they are called in Eph. 1:12. Gentile believers are now included among the "saints"—not only among the followers of Jesus but among the people of God of all ages. Once the Gentiles had no place among the people of God, but now a new situation

---

[134]Gk. ἀκρογωνιαίου, to which λίθου (which is in any case implied) is added by D* F G 629 and Origen.

[135]πᾶσα οἰκοδομή (ℵ* B D F G Ψ with the majority of cursives); πᾶσα ἡ οἰκοδομή (ℵ¹ A C P 6 81 326 1739^{r.1.} 1881 *pc*).

[136]For τοῦ θεοῦ B erratically has τοῦ Χριστοῦ.

[137]They are no longer ξένοι and πάροικοι, the latter term denoting resident aliens, like μέτοικοι ("metics") in Attic Greek. In Heb. 11:13 the patriarchs are said to have acknowledged themselves as ξένοι καὶ παρεπίδημοι on earth (an allusion to Abraham's calling himself ξένος καὶ παρεπίδημος in Gen. 23:4); in 1 Pet. 2:11 the "exiles of the dispersion" are addressed as πάροικοι and παρεπίδημοι. But there they are viewed as having been "desocialized" from the attachments of this world; here they are encouraged as those who have been "resocialized" among the burgesses of the city of God (cf. Phil. 3:20). See F. Lyall, "Roman Law in the Writings of Paul—Aliens and Citizens," *EQ* 48 (1976), 3-14.

has come about—a situation to which Paul has already applied words from the book of Hosea:

> "Those who were not my people I will call 'my people,'
> and her who was not beloved I will call 'my beloved.'
> And in the very place where it was said to them, 'You are not my people,'
> they will be called 'sons of the living God' " (Rom. 9:25-26).[138]

If the community is viewed as a house or household, the Gentile believers are full members of the family—not household servants but sons and daughters, with all the rights of inheritance that sons and daughters enjoy. The Father to whom they have access is the same Father as he to whom their brothers and sisters of Jewish origin have access—it is by the same Spirit that his Gentile and Jewish children alike acknowledge him as their Father.

In writing to the Christians of Rome, Paul implies that some of the Gentiles among them were inclined to look down on their Jewish fellow-Christians as poor relations, mercifully rescued from an apostate nation, and he warns them against such an attitude: "remember it is not you that support the root, but the root that supports you" (Rom. 11:18). They had been cut out of the wild olive, the fruitless shoot to which they originally belonged, and grafted into the good olive tree, to share the nutriment and fertility of the true people of God. The credit was not theirs; they were entirely indebted to God's mercy. In our present epistle there is no suggestion that its Gentile recipients stood in need of such a warning; what they are given is full encouragement to magnify the grace of God which has rescued them from their former place as rank outsiders and instated them among his children.

20 If the community is viewed as a building, the Gentile believers are integral parts of the structure. This is one of the figures employed by Paul in writing to the Corinthian church: "you are God's field," he says, and then, changing the metaphor, "you are God's building" (1 Cor. 3:9). There he speaks of himself as the "skilled master builder" who laid the foundation—the foundation being Jesus Christ himself (1 Cor. 3:10-11).

---

[138] Quoted from Hos. 2:23 and 1:10. These passages from Hosea, originally directed to a situation within Israel, are similarly applied to Gentile converts in 1 Pet. 2:10. The principle embodied in Hosea's message was being worked out on a worldwide scale in apostolic days, when people who had no previous claim on God's covenant-mercy were being adopted into his family. See F. F. Bruce, *This is That: The New Testament Development of Some Old Testament Themes* (Exeter/Grand Rapids, 1968), pp. 66-67.

Here the figure of the building is retained, but the figures for certain parts of it are changed: the foundation now consists of the apostles and prophets, and Christ is the cornerstone. These changes in metaphor are no argument in themselves for diversity of authorship: metaphors may be altered to emphasize this or that lesson.

It is possible indeed, with the NEB, to understand "the foundation laid by the apostles and prophets";[139] but it is more natural to understand the foundation as consisting of the apostles and prophets. These prophets, as elsewhere in this epistle where they are conjoined with apostles (Eph. 3:5; 4:11), are Christian prophets. (The fact that the definite article is not repeated before "prophets" does not imply that the prophets and apostles are identical.)[140] Apostles and prophets[141] constitute the foundation ministries in the church, not only in Ephesians but in 1 Corinthians: "God has appointed in the church first apostles, second prophets . . ." (1 Cor. 12:28). Apostles and prophets, then, might well be viewed as the first stones to be laid in the new building.[142] (The probability of Paul's using such language, in the light of his own special apostleship, will be variously assessed.)

But what is meant by the cornerstone? The wording (like that in

[139]By rendering the θεμέλιος τῶν ἀποστόλων καὶ προφητῶν thus, the NEB is able to continue: "and Christ Jesus himself is the foundation-stone" (but "foundation-stone" is an unnatural translation of ἀκρογωνιαῖος, whatever may be said of the OT background of the word).

[140]See p. 315, n. 29.

[141]As in Eph. 3:5 and 4:11, "apostles" is probably used here in the rather broad sense in which Paul habitually employs the word. For Paul, the designation is not confined to those who were sent out by Jesus during his earthly ministry (in that case he could not have used it of himself); it includes others, who received some special commission from the risen Christ, such as (probably) James the Lord's brother (Gal. 1:19). "All the apostles," mentioned along with James in 1 Cor. 15:7 among those to whom the Lord appeared in resurrection, are evidently a larger body than "the twelve" (1 Cor. 15:5). Andronicus and Junia are described in Rom. 16:7 as "of note among the apostles" (ἐπίσημοι ἐν τοῖς ἀποστόλοις) in a way which suggests that they themselves were "apostles." See p. 38 with n. 2 (on Col. 1:1) for further observations and bibliography. For Christian prophets see G. Friedrich, *TDNT* 6, pp. 828-61 (*s.v.* προφήτης); É. Cothenet, *DBSupp.* 8, cols. 1222-1337 ("Prophétisme dans le Nouveau Testament"); T. M. Crone, *Early Christian Prophecy* (Baltimore, 1973); U. B. Müller, *Prophetie und Predigt im Neuen Testament* (Gütersloh, 1975); J. Panagopoulos (ed.), *Prophetic Vocation in the New Testament and Today* (Leiden, 1977); E. E. Ellis, *Prophecy and Hermeneutic in Early Christianity* (Tübingen/Grand Rapids, 1978); D. Hill, *New Testament Prophecy* (London/Richmond, VA, 1979); W. A. Grudem, *The Gift of Prophecy in 1 Corinthians* (Washington, D.C., 1982); D. E. Aune, *Prophecy in Early Christianity and the Ancient Mediterranean World* (Grand Rapids, 1983).

[142]Compare the acclamation of Peter in Matt. 16:18 as the πέτρα on which Jesus planned to build his church.

1 Pet. 2:6) is drawn from Isa. 28:16. The word translated "cornerstone" *(akrogōniaios)* appears in the Septuagint version of that text; it is unknown in classical Greek literature. In the context of Isa. 28:16 the prophet utters a warning about the impending deluge of an Assyrian invasion which will sweep away the "refuge of lies" in which the king and people of Judah have put their trust. While the existing structure of the Judaean nation has become useless for the accomplishment of the divine purpose, there remains a small minority of faithful souls which will form the basis of a new community and ensure the fulfilment of that purpose. The foundation of this community is announced in the oracle:

> *"Behold, I am laying in Zion for a foundation*
> *a stone, a tested stone,*   Isaha 28:16
> *a precious cornerstone, of a sure foundation:*
> *'He who believes will not be in haste.' "*

The Hebrew wording leaves no doubt that the stone being laid is a foundation stone: "Behold, I am founding . . . a founded foundation."[143] Yet this foundation stone is in some sense a cornerstone,[144] bonding the structure together. Not only so: it is a "stone of testing,"[145] which might mean one that is tested and found true but means more probably here one that tests the work to show if it has been carried out to the architect's specifications.

The NT application of the oracle to Christ finds some support in the Septuagint wording;[146] a similar interpretation appears later in the Targum of Jonathan: "Behold, I am setting in Zion a king, a mighty king . . ." (that is, the Messiah). At Qumran the stone, in line with the original intention, was interpreted of the initial nucleus of the covenanted community:[147] "This is the tested wall, the precious cornerstone; its foundations shall not tremble nor be moved from their place."[148]

The Septuagint translator saw that a foundation stone was in view and made this doubly explicit: "Behold, I lay for the foundations of Zion a stone . . . even for its foundations."[149] But, having done this, he used the word *akrogōniaios*, which is an unsuitable designation for a foundation

---

[143]Heb. *hinnᵉnî yissaḏ . . . mûsāḏ mûssāḏ* (for *yissaḏ* read *mᵉyassēḏ* with 1QIsᵃ).
[144]It is called *pinnat yiqrat*, "a precious corner(stone)."
[145]Heb. *'eḇen bōḥan*.
[146]To ὁ πιστεύων ("he who believes") LXX adds ἐπ' αὐτῷ (*om* B), "on it" or (as the NT interprets it in Rom. 9:33; 10:11; 1 Pet. 2:6) "on him" (i.e., on Christ).
[147]The *'ăṣat hayyaḥaḏ*, consisting of twelve laymen and three priests (1QS 8.1); see E. F. Sutcliffe, *The Monks of Qumran* (London, 1960), pp. xi, 152-53; A. R. C. Leaney, *The Rule of Qumran and its Meaning* (London, 1966), pp. 210-12.
[148]1QS 8.7-8.
[149]ἰδοὺ ἐγὼ ἐμβαλῶ εἰς τὰ θεμέλια Σιων λίθον . . . εἰς τὰ θεμέλια αὐτῆς.

stone. For *akrogōniaios*, so far as can be determined, does not mean a cornerstone, but a stone which crowns the building, like the "top stone" of Zerubbabel's temple, the last stone to be placed in position—placed in position by Zerubbabel himself, who had begun the work by laying the foundation stone (Zech. 4:7, 9).[150] While the Septuagint uses *akrogōniaios* only in Isa. 28:16, the later Greek version of Symmachus uses it in 2 Kings (4 Kingdoms) 25:17[151] and again in Ps. 118 (LXX 117):22, where it denotes the stone which has become "head of the corner"[152]—in other words, top of the pediment.

Elsewhere in the NT the cornerstone of Isa. 28:16 is combined with the once rejected stone of Ps. 118 (117):22 (and also with the stone of stumbling of Isa. 8:14-15) to form a composite *testimonium* (cf. 1 Pet. 2:6-8).[153] But here there is no conflation and no risk of confusing the foundation with the cornerstone: the apostles and prophets constitute the foundation, and Christ is the cornerstone.

21 It is in relation to the cornerstone that every other part of the building is allotted its proper place. In the margin of the NEB Christ is here called the "keystone," which holds the entire structure together.[154] Under his direction the whole building "grows up" to form a sanctuary. With the importation of biological language into the architectural figure may be compared the importation of architectural language into the bio-

---

[150]On ἀκρογωνιαῖος (which is an adjective qualifying λίθος, whether that substantive is expressed or not) the *Patristic Greek Lexicon* (ed. G. W. H. Lampe) comments: "*(stone) as topmost angle* or *point* of pyramid, obelisk, etc., which being cut out before being set in position, and being last laid, would not fit if construction were not true." See, however, R. J. McKelvey, "Christ the Cornerstone," *NTS* 8 (1961-62), 352-59, in defense of the meaning *Grundstein*.

[151]Of the "capital" of a column (Heb. *kōteret*), three times in one verse.

[152]Heb. *leʾrōʾš pinnāh* (LXX εἰς κεφαλὴν γωνίας).

[153]Isa. 8:14-15 and 28:16 are conflated in Rom. 9:32-33. In Luke 20:17-18 the rejected stone which became head of the corner (cf. Mark 12:10-11) is conflated not only with the rock of stumbling of Isa. 8:14-15 but also with the stone of Nebuchadnezzar's dream (Dan. 2:34-35). A conflation of Isa. 28:16 with Ps. 118 (LXX 117):22 appears in the Naassene exposition quoted by Hippolytus (*Ref.* 5.7.35-36), where Adamas, the heavenly man (cf. p. 299 with n. 125), is described as "the corner stone which has become head of the corner." H. Schlier (*Christus und die Kirche im Epheserbrief*, pp. 47-48) looked to this exposition for a background to Eph. 2:19-21, but there is no good reason for assigning a pre-Christian date to this exposition or to an earlier stage of gnostic speculation supposed to underlie both it and the Mandaean doctrine of the "secret Adam." If a background be sought for the present application of Isa. 28:16 the application quoted above from 1QS 8.7-8 is a stronger candidate.

[154]A better rendering of ἀκρογωνιαῖος than "foundation-stone." (In the same marginal note "the foundation of the apostles and prophets" is given as an alternative to "the foundation laid by the apostles and prophets.")

logical figure of Eph. 4:16.[155] This passage does not mean that "every building" grows together to form one grand complex edifice, as though the reference were to a multiplicity of local churches making up the church universal.[156] The church universal is viewed as a structure complete in itself, just as in 1 Cor. 3:9-17 the local church is similarly viewed. Moreover, as the local church is God's sanctuary, a dwelling-place for his Spirit (1 Cor. 3:16-17), so is the church universal.

An important background to the conception of the community as a sanctuary is provided at Qumran, where the community constituted "a most holy dwelling for Aaron . . . and a house of perfection and truth in Israel."[157] ("Aaron" denotes the priestly members of the community and "Israel" the lay members: the community, in other words, was regarded as a living sanctuary in which the laity constituted the holy place and the priesthood the holy of holies. Any such distinction between laity and priesthood is foreign to the conception of the church in the NT.)

22 If the apostles and prophets were the foundation members of this living sanctuary and other Jewish believers were among the earliest "stones" built into its fabric, the situation now was that Gentile believers ("you too") were being added to the structure, in constantly increasing numbers.[158] The new community, God's fellowship of reconciliation, transcends all distinctions of race, status, and sex. Properly oriented to the one cornerstone, based on the foundation of the apostles and prophets, Gentile Christians, along with their fellow-believers of Jewish birth, belonged equally to God's holy house. As the God of Israel had once taken up residence in the wilderness tabernacle and later in the Jerusalem temple by his name[159] and his glory,[160] so now by his Spirit he makes the fellowship of believers, Jewish and Gentile alike, his chosen dwelling-place. No privilege is bestowed on the people of God in which Gentiles do not enjoy an equal share.

---

[155]The passive participle of συναρμολογέω ("fitted together"), used in the architectural figure here, is used in the biological figure in Eph. 4:16.

[156]In πᾶσα οἰκοδομή the noun οἰκοδομή may denote the building process rather than the structure itself. See also p. 325, n. 80.

[157]1QS 8.5-6. See R. A. Cole, *The New Temple* (London, 1950); B. Gärtner, *The Temple and the Community in Qumran and the New Testament* (Cambridge, 1965), pp. 60-66; R. J. McKelvey, *The New Temple: The Church in the New Testament* (Oxford, 1969), pp. 108-23.

[158]There is little basis in the context for treating συνοικοδομεῖσθε as imperative ("be built together"); cf. 1 Pet. 2:5, οἰκοδομεῖσθε οἶκος πνευματικός, which some wish to translate: "be built up (as) a spiritual house."

[159]Deut. 12:5; 1 Kings (LXX 3 Kingdoms) 8:29, etc.

[160]Exod. 40:34-35; 1 Kings (LXX 3 Kingdoms) 8:11, etc.

EPHESIANS 3

5. INTERCESSORY PRAYER RESUMED (3:1)

1 *For this reason I Paul, the prisoner of Christ Jesus¹ for the sake of you Gentiles, [bend my knees in prayer].²*

1 The intercessory prayer of Eph. 1:15-19, which passes into a statement of the exaltation of Christ and of his people with him, followed by the celebration of God's grace to the Gentiles, is now resumed. Almost immediately, however, it is broken off to make way for an account of Paul's distinctive ministry. The subject "I Paul" is left without a verb, which is not supplied until the prayer is taken up again in v. 14: "For this reason I bend my knees. . . ."

The locution "I Paul" denotes some special emphasis. In 1 Thess. 2:18 (in a letter of multiple authorship) it introduces a personal statement in a context where Paul and his associates speak in the first person plural; in 2 Cor. 10:1 and Gal. 5:2 it introduces a solemn entreaty or warning; in Philem. 19 it introduces a formal undertaking to pay a debt; in Col. 1:23 it stresses Paul's special call to the gospel ministry,³ and something of the same emphasis is expressed here. It is Paul, preacher to the Gentiles *par excellence,* who prays for the Gentile believers.

As in Philem. 1, 9, he calls himself the "prisoner of Christ Jesus";⁴ here, however, he adds that his imprisonment is "for the sake of you Gentiles." The situation which led to Paul's arrest and subsequent detention in Jerusalem, Caesarea, and Rome arose directly out of his Gentile min-

¹τοῦ Χριστοῦ ᾽Ιησοῦ (᾽Ιησοῦ is omitted by ℵ* D* F G and a few other witnesses).
²The missing verb is supplied from v. 14 (κάμπτω τὰ γόνατά μου). Here πρεσβεύω is supplied by D 104* *pc*, κεκαύχημαι by 2464 *pc*.
³See p. 80.
⁴See pp. 205-06.

istry. It was while he was in Jerusalem with representatives of his Gentile churches who were taking their churches' respective gifts to the mother-church that he was charged with violating the sanctity of the temple by taking one of those representatives within forbidden bounds. This charge, and others associated with it, still hung over him as he waited in Rome for his appeal to come up for hearing in the supreme court. If the record of Acts 21:17-36 be read against the background of Rom. 15:14-32, where some of Paul's thoughts about his mission are disclosed, it can scarcely be doubted that he was indeed a prisoner for the sake of Gentiles. And, if Phil. 1:12-18 refers to the same imprisonment as Eph. 3:1, that impris-onment was being actively overruled for the furtherance of the gospel at the heart of the Gentile world.

Luke tells how Paul, shortly after his arrival in Rome, invited the leaders of the local Jews to visit him, "since," as he said, "it is because of the hope of Israel that I am bound with this chain" (Acts 28:20). It was natural that he should adapt his language to the people addressed, but there is no contradiction between the two representations of the reason for his being bound: in his eyes "the hope of Israel" looked forward to the coming of the Messiah and the resurrection of the dead, which had been fulfilled in the risen Lord whom he proclaimed. But, since he was called specifi-cally to proclaim this risen Lord to the Gentiles, it was directly in con-sequence of his Gentile mission that he was bound.

6. THE MYSTERY OF CHRIST (3:2-13)

(1) Paul's Stewardship (3:2-7)

2 *You have heard—have you not?[5]—of the stewardship of God's grace which was given to me for you:*
3 *that by revelation the mystery was made known to me,[6] as I wrote before in brief.*
4 *(By reference to what I wrote[7] you can discern, as you read, my insight into the mystery of Christ.)*
5 *In other generations this mystery was not made known to the children*

[5]Gk. εἴ γε ἠκούσατε, "if indeed you have heard," "at least if you have heard." (For εἴ γε cf. Eph. 4:21; Col. 1:23.)
[6]Gk. ὅτι κατὰ ἀποκάλυψιν ἐγνωρίσθη μοι (ὅτι is omitted by P[46] B F G *al*, while γάρ is inserted after ἀποκάλυψιν by F G). For ἐγνωρίσθη the majority of cursives read ἐγνώρισε ("he made known").
[7]Gk. πρὸς ὅ ("by reference to which").

of men as it has now been revealed in the Spirit to God's holy apostles[8] and prophets—

6 *namely, that the Gentiles should be fellow-heirs, members of the same body, joint-partakers of the promise[9] (fulfilled) in Christ Jesus through the gospel.*

7 *Of this gospel I have been made a minister according to the gift of God's grace given[10] to me according to the operation of his power.*

2 The parenthesis with which the opening sentence of the renewed intercession is broken off develops into a substantial digression. The words with which the digression begins—"If indeed you have heard . . ." or "On the assumption that you have heard . . ."—imply that the people addressed at least include some who were personally unacquainted with the apostle. To his friends in Ephesus he would more probably have said "You know. . . ."

The digression is designed to explain more fully Paul's description as the Lord's prisoner "for the sake of you Gentiles" (it is immediately after the word "Gentiles" that the construction is broken off). Paul has received, by divine appointment, a special responsibility with regard to the evangelization of the Gentile world. "I have been entrusted with a stewardship,"[11] he says to the Corinthians (1 Cor. 9:17); he speaks to the Gentile believers of Colossae of "the stewardship of God given to me with reference to you" (Col. 1:25). There, as here, the stewardship involves the impartation and disclosure of a "mystery"; similarly, in 1 Cor. 4:1 he refers to himself and other preachers of the gospel as "stewards of the mysteries of God."

In calling his stewardship "the stewardship of God's grace," he is thinking not so much of the grace of apostleship (mentioned below in v. 7) as of the grace of God embodied and proclaimed in the gospel ("the good news of God's grace," as it is called in Acts 20:24). To make this gospel, revealed to him on the Damascus road, known among the Gentiles is Paul's distinctive commission.

3 The "revelation" by which the divine mystery was made known to Paul cannot be divorced from the "revelation of Jesus Christ" granted

---

[8]ἀποστόλοις is omitted by B lat^b Ambst (leaving τοῖς ἁγίοις αὐτοῦ καὶ προφήταις, "to his saints and prophets").

[9]D¹ F G Ψ with the majority of cursives add αὐτοῦ after ἐπαγγελίας ("his promise").

[10]For τῆς δοθείσης (in agreement with χάριτος) Ψ and the majority of cursives read τὴν δοθεῖσαν (in agreement with δωρεάν).

[11]Gk. οἰκονομίαν πεπίστευμαι.

to him on the Damascus road—on the occasion when, as he says, "God . . . was pleased to reveal his Son in me" (Gal. 1:12, 15-16).[12] He did not fully apprehend all that was involved in the revelation there and then: a lifetime of apostolic service was scarcely sufficient for him to plumb its depths. But one thing he appreciated on the spot: henceforth it was his calling to proclaim among the Gentiles the Son of God who had been newly revealed to him. What this calling entailed could be learned only through experience, but the call itself was conveyed in the revelation.

Where did Paul "write before in brief"[13] about the revelation of the mystery? Presumably in some document to which the present readers had access, whether this letter or another. In this letter one might think of the mention of the mystery of the divine purpose in Eph. 1:9-10, or of the creation in Christ of "one new man" described in Eph. 2:14-16.[14] Or, on the view (probable on other grounds) that Ephesians was addressed *(inter alios)* to the Christians of the Lycus valley, one might think of Col. 1:25-27, where Paul's stewardship involves the unfolding to the Gentiles of the contents of that rich mystery "concealed for ages and generations."[15] The statement of Col. 1:25-27 is indeed "in brief" compared with the more ample statement of Eph. 3:2-13. Certainty is unattainable, and no single interpretation of the words "I wrote before in brief" is free from difficulties.

4 Whatever be the precise relevance of the previous brief written account, reference to it will enable the readers to discern Paul's "insight into the mystery of Christ." The phrase "as you read"[16] has been explained by E. J. Goodspeed in terms of his own view of the character and purpose of this letter. If Ephesians was written after the other letters in the Pauline collection, to serve as an introduction to that collection, then everything else in the collection had been written before. Paul had made repeated references in his letters to the revelation he had received and his commis-

---

[12]See G. Bornkamm, "The Revelation of Christ to Paul on the Damascus Road and Paul's Doctrine of Justification and Reconciliation," in *Reconciliation and Hope,* ed. R. J. Banks (Exeter/Grand Rapids, 1974), pp. 90-103; S. Kim, *The Origin of Paul's Gospel* (Tübingen/Grand Rapids, 1981/82), pp. 22-25, etc.

[13]Gk. καθὼς προέγραψα ἐν ὀλίγῳ (a different sense of the verb from that in Gal. 3:1).

[14]So H. Schlier, *Der Brief an die Epheser,* p. 149.

[15]"The only possible explanation on the basis of Pauline authorship seems to be that which applies the word to Colossians, which is thought of as written before Ephesians, but as not likely to reach the recipients of Ephesians until they have read their own epistle" (C. L. Mitton, *The Epistle to the Ephesians* [Oxford, 1951], p. 234).

[16]The participle ἀναγινώσκοντες probably means "reading it" (or hearing it read) aloud in meetings of the church.

sion to make it known, but each of those references was "in brief" in comparison with the exposition of the subject in Ephesians. "The readers of Ephesians are expected to read Paul's letters, and find in them, as the writer of Ephesians has done, the proof of his deep understanding of the Christian faith."[17]

The "mystery of Christ" into which Paul has received such exceptional insight is the content of the "revelation of Jesus Christ" of which he speaks in Gal. 1:12.[18] Christ is himself "the mystery of God" (Col. 2:2; cf. Col. 1:26-27) in the sense that in him the unseen God is fully revealed; "the mystery of Christ" may best be understood as the mystery which consists in Christ, the mystery which is disclosed in him.[19] This mystery is proclaimed in the gospel, which may indeed be called "the mystery of God" in 1 Cor. 2:1.[20] Paul sometimes uses the term "mystery" of one particular element in his message—the transformation of believers into spiritual bodies at the last trumpet (1 Cor. 15:51) or Israel's final restoration as the goal of its temporary relegation in favor of the Gentiles (Rom. 11:25). But his use of the term in Ephesians to denote the gospel in its fullness is in keeping with his general practice.[21] The gospel which he received on the Damascus road by "revelation of Jesus Christ" was the law-free gospel which he proceeded to preach throughout the rest of his life; and precisely because it was law-free it was as applicable to Gentiles as to Jews (the law being the barrier that had formerly kept them apart). The incorporation of Gentiles along with Jews in the new people of God— incorporation by grace through faith—was implicit in that gospel. This incorporation is the aspect of the "mystery of Christ" which is now emphasized.

5 This is a mystery in the sense that it was not made known to

[17]E. J. Goodspeed, *The Meaning of Ephesians* (Chicago, 1933), p. 42.
[18]According to H. Merklein, the μυστήριον here corresponds to the εὐαγγέλιον of Gal. 1:12, 15-16. "The content of the mystery of Eph. 3:6 is the ecclesiological interpretation of the revelation of Jesus Christ in its outworking in salvation history. When the author makes the outworking in salvation history of the ἀποκάλυψις of Jesus Christ (Gal. 1) the subject-matter of the ἀποκάλυψις itself, his mystery acquires ecclesiological content" (*Das kirchliche Amt nach dem Epheserbrief* [Munich, 1973], p. 208).
[19]That is to say, in τῷ μυστηρίῳ τοῦ Χριστοῦ the genitive τοῦ Χριστοῦ is epexegetic (genitive of definition).
[20]In 1 Cor. 2:1 the textual evidence is rather evenly balanced between τὸ μυστήριον τοῦ θεοῦ (i.e., the gospel itself) and τὸ μαρτύριον τοῦ θεοῦ, "the testimony of God" (i.e., the proclamation of the gospel).
[21]Compare "the mystery of his will" (Eph. 1:9); on its relation to the present exposition of the divine mystery see p. 319 below.

human beings in other generations. Similar language is used in the doxology at the end of the letter to the Romans, where Paul's gospel, "the preaching of Jesus Christ," is said to be "the revelation of the mystery which was kept secret for long ages" (Rom. 16:25),[22] and in Col. 1:25-27, where "the word of God" which Paul is commissioned to make known is called "the mystery which has been concealed for ages and generations."[23] In Col. 1:27 this mystery is summed up in Christ, dwelling in the hearts of Gentile believers as their hope of glory.

Elsewhere Paul insists that his gospel is no innovation. It was promised in advance through the prophets in the holy scriptures (Rom. 1:2); it was preached beforehand to Abraham (Gal. 3:8). That faith was the principle by which God would justify men and women, Gentiles as well as Jews, was not a truth concealed in earlier generations. It is a truth attested, according to Paul, in the Law, the Prophets, and the Writings.[24] He adduces evidence from the Law, the Prophets, and the Writings[25] to establish that Christ came not only "to confirm the promises given to the patriarchs" regarding their descendants but also "in order that the Gentiles might glorify God for his mercy" (Rom. 15:8-12), and in this evidence he finds the scriptural basis for his own Gentile mission.

That God would bless the Gentiles, then, was not a new revelation. What then was the new revelation, the mystery hitherto concealed? It was this: that God's blessing of the Gentiles would involve the obliteration of the old line of demarcation which separated them from Jews and the incorporation of Gentile believers together with Jewish believers, without any discrimination, in the new, comprehensive community of God's chosen people.

This had not been foreseen; this was now "revealed in the Spirit to God's holy apostles and prophets." In Rom. 16:26 what had long been kept secret was "now disclosed and through prophetic writings . . . made known to all the nations." In Col. 1:26 the previously hidden mystery was "now made manifest to his saints." It was made known now to all the nations in the worldwide preaching of the gospel; it was made known to

[22]The provenance of the doxology of Rom. 16:25-27 is a matter of debate; see C. E. B. Cranfield, *The Epistle to the Romans* (Edinburgh, 1973-79), pp. 5-11, 808-09; E. Käsemann, *Commentary on Romans,* E.T. (Grand Rapids, 1980), pp. 421-28.
[23]See pp. 84-86.
[24]Cf. his citation of Gen. 15:6 (Rom. 4:3; Gal. 3:6), Hab. 2:4b (Rom. 1:17; Gal. 3:11), and Ps. 32 (LXX 31):1-2 (Rom. 4:7-8).
[25]From the Law: Deut. 32:43; from the Prophets: Isa. 11:10; from the Writings: Pss. 18 (LXX 17):49; 117 (LXX 116):1.

God's holy people because they were the natural recipients of his revelation; it was made known to the apostles and prophets because they were the ministers through whom the truth of God was communicated to their fellow-believers. It emerges almost immediately that among those ministers it is Paul himself who holds the primacy.

But the form of the words—God's "holy apostles and prophets"[26]—gives the reader pause. There is a note of detachment about it which suggests another hand than Paul's. If Paul himself had used the plural here, he would probably have said "to us apostles" (cf. 1 Cor. 4:9); as it is, the form of words, and especially the reverential adjective "holy,"[27] would have come more naturally from one who was not himself an apostle or prophet—not necessarily a later writer, but conceivably a colleague of Paul. "The Church is built upon the twofold foundation of apostles and prophets . . . , the apostles representing the authority of primary witness to the Gospel facts, while prophets represent the living guidance of the Spirit by which the facts were apprehended in ever fuller meaning and scope."[28] Through these two ministries—the apostles empowered by the Spirit of Christ and the prophets inspired by the same Spirit[29]—effect was now being given to the divine purpose which had for so long remained unrevealed.

6 What has now been revealed is the plan of God that human beings without distinction—Gentiles as well as Jews—should on the common ground of faith be his sons and daughters in Christ. "If children, then heirs" (Rom. 8:17). To Abraham God had pledged a noble heritage of blessing, and of that heritage Abraham's descendants were the heirs. Addressing Jews in Jerusalem in the earliest days of the church, Peter had said, "You are the sons of the prophets and of the covenant which God gave to your fathers, saying to Abraham, 'And in your posterity shall all the families of the earth be blessed' " (Acts 3:25).[30] But now the divine plan has been revealed—that "all the families of the earth" should through

---

[26]Gk. τοῖς ἁγίοις ἀποστόλοις αὐτοῦ καὶ προφήταις.

[27]The use of ἅγιος as an adjective has a different nuance from its use as a substantive in the plural to denote the people of God in general, the "saints." The few textual witnesses which omit ἀποστόλοις here make the wording conform to Col. 1:26 (but add "prophets" to "saints"). OT prophets are qualified as "holy" in Luke 1:70; Acts 3:21.

[28]C. H. Dodd, *The Johannine Epistles* (London, 1946), p. 105.

[29]Here and in Eph. 2:20 ἀπόστολοι and προφῆται come under the regimen of a common article, but "Granville Sharpe's first rule" cannot be pressed in this instance to make the apostles and prophets the same persons, since in Eph. 4:11 (cf. 1 Cor. 12:28) they are distinct orders of ministry.

[30]A free quotation of Gen. 22:18 (12:3; 18:18; 26:4).

the gospel not only be blessed in Abraham's posterity but should be reckoned among his posterity, children of Abraham because they share the faith of Abraham, who "is the father of us all" (Rom. 4:16). Gentile believers are therefore with Jewish believers "fellow-heirs" of all the blessings pledged to Abraham and his descendants—"heirs of God," in fact, "and fellow-heirs[31] with Christ," as Paul puts it elsewhere (Rom. 8:17). For, as the readers of this letter have already been told, it is in Christ that believers receive their inheritance and have been sealed with the Spirit as the guarantee of their eventual entry upon it (Eph. 1:13-14).

Gentile believers, moreover, have been incorporated into the same body as Jewish believers; they are fellow-members of the body of Christ. This is the first (and only NT) occurrence of the compound adjective meaning "belonging to the same body";[32] it seems to be used only by Christian writers. It might be regarded as appropriate that a new word should be coined to express so revolutionary a concept as the inclusion of Gentiles in the people of God on the same footing as Jews. Even proselytes from paganism to the Jewish faith were debarred from a few minor privileges which were reserved for Israelites by birth.[33] In the new community there were no such restrictions (indeed, the necessity arose at times of reminding Gentile members that their Jewish fellow-Christians had equal rights with them).

In adding that Gentiles were "joint-partakers[34] of the promise in Christ Jesus through the gospel," Paul emphasizes a truth which he had already expounded at some length in Gal. 3:6-29. The promise was made to Abraham; it was fulfilled in Christ, Abraham's offspring *par excellence,* "that what was promised to faith in Jesus Christ might be given to those who believe" (Gal. 3:22). "If you are Christ's," Paul continues, it makes no difference whether you are Jew or Gentile, slave or free, male or female: "you are Abraham's offspring, heirs according to promise" (Gal. 3:29).[35] Through the gospel, preached beforehand to Abraham and now accomplished in Christ, barriers between separated portions of the human family have been removed.

7 "Of this gospel," says Paul, repeating what he had recently written to the Colossians (Col. 1:23), "I have been made a minister"[36]—and

---

[31]Gk. συγκληρονόμοι, the same compound as is used here. Cf. 1 Pet. 3:7.
[32]Gk. σύσσωμος. See E. Preuschen, "σύνσωμος Eph. 3, 6," *ZNW* 1 (1900), 85-86.
[33]See Mishnah *Bikkurim* 1.4.
[34]Gk. συμμέτοχος, used again in Eph. 5:7.
[35]Cf. F. F. Bruce, *Galatians,* pp. 175-91.
[36]Cf. 1 Tim. 1:12-16; 2 Tim. 1:11-12.

to be commissioned to proclaim such a gospel was in his eyes the highest imaginable honor (all the higher in view of his former record as an opponent of that gospel). If there was a note of detachment about the reference to God's "holy apostles and prophets," the note now is one of full personal commitment.

In calling his commission to preach the gospel "the gift of God's grace,"[37] Paul sees in it one facet of that grace which transformed him from a persecutor into a grateful recipient of "the righteousness of God through faith in Jesus Christ for all who believe" (Rom. 3:22). Repeatedly he speaks of his apostolic ministry as "the grace of God given to me" (1 Cor. 3:10, etc.).[38] Both in God's initial call and in the subsequent enablement which he received throughout his career he experienced "the operation of his power"[39]—"his power which operates mightily within me," as he had said to the Colossians (Col. 1:29).

Paul was both an apostle and a prophet, but it was in the exercise of his apostleship that he gave practical effect to the divine plan made known to him by revelation.

(2) The Eternal Purpose (3:8-13)

8 *To me, the lessermost*[40] *of all saints,*[41] *this grace was given, to bring to the Gentiles the good news*[42] *of Christ's unfathomable wealth,*

9 *and to make everyone understand*[43] *what is the stewardship of the mystery which was hidden from eternity in God, the Creator of all things,*[44]

10 *in order that God's manifold wisdom might now*[45] *be made known through the church to the principalities and the powers in the heavenly realm.*

---

[37]Gk. κατὰ τὴν δωρεὰν τῆς χάριτος τοῦ θεοῦ.

[38]Cf. Rom. 1:5 (where χάριν καὶ ἀποστολήν is probably to be construed as hendiadys, "[the] grace of apostleship"); 12:3; 15:15; Gal. 2:9.

[39]Gk. κατὰ τὴν ἐνέργειαν τῆς δυνάμεως αὐτοῦ. Cf. Eph. 1:19 (p. 271, n. 133).

[40]Gk. ἐλαχιστότερος, a coined combination of the superlative ἐλάχιστος with the comparative suffix -ότερος (the rendering "lessermost" is a similarly coined combination on the analogy of "nethermost").

[41]ἀγίων is omitted after πάντων by P[46] Tert.

[42]τοῖς ἔθνεσιν εὐαγγελίσασθαι. D F G with the majority of cursives and the Latin versions read ἐν before τοῖς ἔθνεσιν ("among the Gentiles").

[43]φωτίσαι πάντας ("to illuminate all"). πάντας *om* ℵ* A 6 1739 1881 *pc* Ambst Aug.

[44]ἐν τῷ θεῷ τῷ τὰ πάντα κτίσαντι. ἐν is omitted by ℵ* 614 Mcion ("hidden by God"); διὰ Ἰησοῦ Χριστοῦ is added after κτίσαντι by D[1] with the majority of cursives and syr[hcl]**.

[45]νῦν *om* F G 629 lat syr[pesh] Tert M.Vict.

317

11 *Such was the eternal purpose*[46] *which he formed*[47] *in Christ Jesus our Lord,*

12 *in whom we have our freedom of access*[48] *with confidence*[49] *through faith in him.*

13 *Therefore I beg you not to lose heart*[50] *at my afflictions on your behalf; they are indeed your glory.*[51]

8 As he contemplates his commission to be Christ's apostle to the Gentiles and the instrument of their incorporation into the "one body," Paul is filled with wondering humility at the honor thus conferred on him of all people. In an earlier letter, considering the risen Lord's appearance to him, he said, "I am the least of the apostles, unfit to be called an apostle, because I persecuted the church of God. But by the grace of God I am what I am, and his grace toward me was not in vain. On the contrary, I worked harder than any of them [the other apostles], though it was not I, but the grace of God which is with me" (1 Cor. 15:9-10).

Some have said that the present phrase "the lessermost of all saints" (to translate a coinage by a coinage) is too exaggerated and indeed artificial a self-denigration to be authentic. This is inevitably a subjective judgment. Even more self-denigrating is Paul's description as "first and foremost of sinners" in 1 Tim. 1:15, regarded by some as the mark of a later hand,[52] while others look on it as a sure token of authenticity (not least in the use of the present tense "I am" rather than "I was").[53] If it be asked if a

---

[46]κατὰ πρόθεσιν τῶν αἰώνων. Clem. Alex. reads πρόγνωσιν for πρόθεσιν.

[47]Gk. ἣν ἐποίησεν, referring to the formation of the purpose rather than to its fulfilment.

[48]Translating παρρησίαν καὶ προσαγωγήν is a hendiadys.

[49]ἐν πεποιθήσει, where ἐν is best treated as comitative; cf. Eph. 1:4 (p. 256, n. 35). For πεποιθήσει D* has the remarkable variant τῷ ἐλευθερωθῆναι ("in being set free").

[50]For ἐγκακεῖν C D¹ F G Ψ with the majority of cursives read the synonymous ἐκκακεῖν.

[51]Gk. ἥτις ἐστὶν δόξα ὑμῶν ("which is your glory"), the relative being attracted into the gender and number of δόξα instead of agreeing with its antecedent θλίψεσιν. In 1175 1881 it is divided ἢ τίς ("or what is your glory?").

[52]Cf. B. S. Easton, *The Pastoral Epistles* (London, 1948), p. 117: " 'I am less than the least of all saints' . . . shows the influence of formalized devotional phrasing and 'I am the chief of sinners' [ἁμαρτωλοὺς . . . ὧν πρῶτός εἰμι ἐγὼ] is purely formalized; in both these cases the post-Pauline writers exalt their hero by exaggerating his humility—with the implication that so humble a man must have been very holy indeed."

[53]Cf. C. Spicq, *Saint Paul: Les Épîtres Pastorales* (Paris, ³1969), p. 344 (he compares the tax-collector in Luke 18:13 and asks, "Would a pseudepigraphist ever have dared to blacken his hero to this extent?").

Paulinist would have used such denigrating language of the apostle, the question cannot be answered with certainty. The authentic Paul did at any rate see a great contrast between his former career as a persecutor and his commissioning to be the herald of the one whom he had persecuted (in the person of his followers), and in this contrast he recognized the amazing grace of God. The special "grace" which was given to him for the discharge of his apostleship was all of a piece with the more comprehensive grace which had made him what he was.[54]

When his commission is said to be "to bring the Gentiles the good news of Christ's unfathomable wealth," this is a more rhetorical wording of his statement in Gal. 1:16, that the purpose of the Damascus-road revelation of the Son of God was "that I might preach him among the Gentiles." But the language of this rhetorical expansion is not un-Pauline. In Rom. 11:32-33 Paul sees in God's consigning all (Jews and Gentiles alike) to disobedience, "that he may have mercy upon all" (Jews and Gentiles alike), evidence of the deep wealth of his wisdom and knowledge.[55] And in the same context the adjective here translated "unfathomable" is used of God's "inscrutable" ways.[56] The wealth of divine grace and glory unfolded in the gospel is summed up in Christ. The proclamation of such a Savior to the world was a service which Paul might well "glorify," as he puts it in Rom. 11:13.[57]

9 Paul's commission also involved the public demonstration of his stewardship—not only the stewardship of God's grace (v. 2) but the stewardship of the long-hidden mystery.[58] Not that these are two distinct stewardships, for the mystery of God is the revelation of his grace. As Paul fulfilled his commission by preaching the gospel to the Gentiles, as through his preaching Gentiles were brought to faith in Christ and found themselves united in church fellowship with fellow-believers of Jewish birth, the long-hidden mystery was being revealed before the eyes of men and women. For the church fellowship in which Gentile and Jewish believers were united was no mere enrollment on a register of membership; it involved their union with Christ by faith and therefore their union with each other as fellow-members of his body. The "third race"[59] was coming

---

[54]See p. 317, n. 38.

[55]In this letter πλοῦτος is used of God's grace (Eph. 1:7; 2:7) and glory (Eph. 1:18[?]; 3:16); cf. πλούσιος ὢν ἐν ἐλέει (Eph. 2:4).

[56]Gk. ἀνεξιχνίαστος (from ἴχνος, "footprint," "track"), not found in the NT apart from these two occurrences.

[57]. . . ἐθνῶν ἀπόστολος, τὴν διακονίαν μου δοξάζω.

[58]Cf. v. 4 (p. 313 with n. 18); also Col. 1:26 (p. 80 with n. 196).

[59]Cf. p. 296, n. 110.

visibly to life: something that had not been seen or imagined before was now a matter of experience. Before all ages God's undisclosed purpose had existed in his own mind; now its accomplishment was evident not only to human beings on earth but also "to the principalities and powers in the heavenly realm."

The designation of God in this context as "the Creator of all things" might be designed to refute gnosticizing modes of thought which made a distinction between the Creator and the Redeemer.[60] The gospel tells how God has procured redemption for his people and reconciled them through the sacrifice of Christ both to himself and to one another.[61] But the God who has acted thus in grace is the God who created all things. Before the world's foundation he chose his people in Christ and destined them in love to be his sons and daughters;[62] before the world's foundation, too, he cherished this plan, to go into effect at the proper time, of bringing into being a community which would bear practical witness on earth to his reconciling work. Creation does not militate against redemption and reconciliation: it subserves their accomplishment, since all alike take place "according to the purpose of him who works all things according to the counsel of his will" (Eph. 1:11).

When he sets his own life and ministry in the setting of the divine purpose and its fulfilment, Paul shows his awareness of his eschatological significance. This awareness finds particular expression in Rom. 11:13-21, where Johannes Munck does not exaggerate in saying that "Paul, as the apostle to the Gentiles, becomes the central figure in the story of salvation."[63] This central significance was not of Paul's seeking: as he realized the unique role which he filled in God's giving effect to his saving plan, he could only marvel at the grace which had selected him for such a ministry.

10 This new, comprehensive community is to serve throughout the universe as an object-lesson of the wisdom of God—his "much-variegated" wisdom. The compound adjective here used is poetic in origin: its first occurrence is in Attic tragedy.[64] The variety of divine wisdom is spelled

---

[60]So H. Schlier, *Der Brief an die Epheser,* pp. 154-55. He compares the gnostic teaching ascribed to Simon Magus (*apud* Iren. *Haer.* 2.8.2, etc.), Menander (*apud* Iren. *Haer.* 1.17), and Satornilos (*apud* Iren. *Haer.* 1.18); but one would like firm evidence that such teaching was known in the circles in which Ephesians was composed and read.

[61]2 Cor. 5:18-19.

[62]Eph. 1:4-5.

[63]J. Munck, *Paul and the Salvation of Mankind,* E.T. (London, 1959), p. 49.

[64]Gk. πολυποίκιλος, first attested in a lyric passage in Euripides, *Iphigeneia in Tauris* 1149 (where it is applied to φάρεα, "many-colored cloaks").

out (without the use of this particular adjective) in Wisdom 7:22-23: "For in her there is a spirit that is intelligent, holy, unique, manifold, subtle, mobile, clear, unpolluted, distinct, invulnerable, loving the good, keen, irresistible, beneficent, humane, steadfast, sure, free from anxiety, all-powerful, overseeing all, and penetrating through all spirits that are intelligent and pure and most subtle."[65] "The being of God," says Schlier, ". . . reveals itself in the economy of grace as the one divine wisdom in various forms and modes, one after another—as the predestined wisdom, as the wisdom shown in creation, in Christ, the personal Wisdom, and lastly in the church as the wisdom which is *multiformi specie* and yet one, in Christ."[66] The "hidden wisdom" of God, decreed before the ages for his people's glory, to which Paul makes brief reference in 1 Cor. 2:6-10, is expounded here for the readers of Ephesians.[67]

There is no need to limit the "principalities and powers" in such a context as this to hostile forces.[68] All created intelligences are in view here. When the foretelling and accomplishment of the Christian salvation are said in 1 Pet. 1:12 to be "things into which angels long to look," something of the same sort is intended as we find here. The wisdom of God revealed in the cross of Christ and in its saving efficacy in the lives of believers upsets all conventional notions of wisdom and demands their reappraisal in the minds of the spiritually mature (1 Cor. 1:18–2:6).

The "principalities and powers" learn from the church that they too have a place in the plan of God. The reconciliation between Jews and Gentiles in this new creation is a token of the reconciliation in which they in their turn are to be embraced. In Col. 1:19-22 the cosmic reconciliation which God has planned is anticipated in the experience of believers in Christ, whom "he has now reconciled"—and the means of reconciliation in the one case as in the other is the saving work of Christ, who has "made peace through the blood of his cross." The church thus appears to be God's pilot scheme for the reconciled universe of the future, the mystery

---

[65]This spelling out of the πολυποικιλία of divine wisdom is adduced by H. Schlier, in a short excursus, 'Η πολυποίκιλος σοφία τοῦ θεοῦ (*Der Brief an die Epheser*, pp. 159-66), where he mentions the possibility that Wisdom 7:22-23 is a riposte to the language of an Isis aretalogy.

[66]*Der Brief an die Epheser*, p. 165. He borrows *multiformi specie* from the Isis aretalogy of Apuleius, *Metamorphoses* 11.5.

[67]So H. Schlier, *Der Brief an die Epheser*, pp. 21, 156.

[68]Cf. H. Schlier, *Der Brief an die Epheser*, p. 155: "The ἀρχαὶ καὶ ἐξουσίαι are not *sancti angeli*, as many expositors assume, but . . . 'evil' powers." They certainly include the *kosmokratores* of Eph. 6:12 (cf. the *archontes* of 1 Cor. 2:8, who were previously ignorant of the divine purpose), but there is no reason why even the angels of the presence should not learn lessons about the ways of God from the working out of his saving purpose.

of God's will "to be administered in the fullness of the times," when "the things in heaven and the things on earth" are to be brought together in Christ (Eph. 1:9-10).[69] There is probably the further implication that the church, the product of God's reconciling work thus far, is designed by him to be his agency (existing as it does "in Christ") for the bringing about of the ultimate reconciliation. If so, then Paul, who is the direct instrument of God in creating the present fellowship of reconciliation, is indirectly his instrument for the universal reconciliation of the future.

11 The divine purpose, to be consummated in Christ, was originally conceived in him. Jewish and Gentile believers who have now been reconciled in him were already chosen in him "before the world's foundation" (Eph. 1:4), and what is true of the church is true of the universe: its final reconciliation in Christ was decreed in Christ according to God's "eternal purpose." And in the outworking of this "purpose of the ages" the people of Christ are given an essential part to play.

12 It is through Christ, the readers have already been assured, that Jewish and Gentile believers alike have their access "in one Spirit to the Father" (Eph. 2:18). This assurance is now repeated. Through faith in Christ[70] they are united with him, and in him they therefore enjoy "freedom of access with confidence." As his place in the presence of God is unchallengable, so is theirs, because they are "in him."

The word translated "freedom" *(parrhēsia)* is used later, in Eph. 6:19, of the freedom of utterance which Paul desires for himself in the proclamation of the gospel—especially, perhaps, at his forthcoming hearing before the imperial tribunal. The attempt has been made to find the same kind of reference here,[71] but the context indicates freedom of another kind—the freedom which is twice expressed by means of the same word in the letter to the Hebrews, where Christians are encouraged to draw near with "confidence" *(parrhēsia)* to the throne of grace (Heb. 4:16) and to enter the heavenly sanctuary with "confidence" *(parrhēsia)* by the blood of Jesus (Heb. 10:19).

13 As the prisoner of Christ Jesus on behalf of the Gentiles, then,

---

[69]See p. 261.

[70]διὰ τῆς πίστεως αὐτοῦ, the genitive αὐτοῦ being taken as objective. See, however, M. Barth (*Ephesians*, p. 347) for the rendering "because of his faithfulness"; the article τῆς before πίστεως, he states, "distinguishes 3:12 from the parallel passages Gal. 2:16; 3:22; Rom. 3:22; Phil. 3:9" (on pp. 224-25 he makes a similar suggestion about διὰ [τῆς] πίστεως in Eph. 2:8).

[71]Cf. W. C. van Unnik, "The Christian's Freedom of Speech in the New Testament," *BJRL* 44 (1961-62), 475, where appeal is made to the emphasis in the preceding verses on Paul's commission to preach the gospel.

Paul sets before them the eternal purpose of God, their place in that purpose, and also his own place in that purpose. To be Christ's prisoner is for him an honorable status.[72] Ever since his call on the Damascus road, he had been Christ's apostle, responsive to his guidance, unreservedly at his disposal. Whether he discharged his commission along the highways of the empire and in its main centers of communication, or (as now) under house arrest in Rome, was not something which he could choose if he was at present in custody, he was where Christ wanted him to be, obedient to his commander's orders, posted there "for the defense of the gospel" (Phil. 1:16). Therefore he was content.

Paul follows Christ—this is his purpose

But many of his friends might not see his imprisonment in that light. Gentile Christians, who recognized him as their apostle, the champion of their liberty, might well be dismayed at the thought of his being in chains, deprived of his freedom to move around for the advancement of the gospel and the strengthening of the churches. But let them not lose heart: he was as completely engaged in their interests under his present restraint as he had been when he was at liberty. Indeed, if they could only see the significance of his arrest and imprisonment, they would understand that, in the providence of God, their interests were promoted and not endangered thereby. Instead of being bewildered and discouraged, they would rejoice. If it was an honor for Paul to be Christ's prisoner on the Gentiles' behalf, it was an honor for the Gentiles themselves. Paul accepted his "afflictions" as a "filling up" of the afflictions of Christ which had yet to be endured, "for the sake of his body, which is the church" (Col. 1:24-25).[73] The members of Christ's body should take encouragement from that. Moreover, Paul knew that his present endurance of affliction was preparing for him "an eternal weight of glory beyond all comparison" (2 Cor. 4:17): that glory, which was a participation in the glory of Christ (Rom. 8:17), would be shared by those on whose behalf the present affliction was endured. Paul's afflictions should therefore call forth from his friends as wholehearted a doxology as they called forth from himself.

7. INTERCESSORY PRAYER CONCLUDED (3:14-19)

14 *For this reason I bend my knees to the Father,*[74]
15 *from whom all fatherhood in heaven*[75] *and on earth takes its name,*

[72]See Philem. 1, 9 (pp. 205-06, 212).
[73]See pp. 81-84.
[74]πρὸς τὸν πατέρα, after which τοῦ κυρίου ἡμῶν Ἰησοῦ Χριστοῦ is added by ℵ[2] D F G Ψ and the majority of cursives with the Latin and Syriac versions.
[75]For οὐρανοῖς P 81 104 365 945 1175 and a few other cursives read the singular οὐρανῷ.

16 *(praying) him to grant that you, according to the wealth of his glory, may be strengthened with power through his Spirit in your inner being,*

17 *so that Christ may dwell in your hearts through faith, while you, being rooted and well founded in love,*

18 *may prevail to comprehend with all the saints what is the breadth and length and height and depth,*[76]

19 *and to know the love of Christ, which surpasses knowledge, so that you may be filled up to all the fullness of God.*[77]

14 The prayer of intercession, already begun, is now resumed and this time carried to its conclusion. It is a prayer that knowledge may be granted to the readers—not the kind of knowledge that was cultivated in many gnosticizing schools of thought, but knowledge that finds its consummation in knowing the love of Christ. To know the love of Christ involves the personal knowledge of Christ himself, that personal knowledge whose attainment was Paul's own high ambition (Phil. 3:8, 10). Paul prays that his readers may be endowed with all the resources of spiritual strength necessary to attain this knowledge, and he addresses his prayer to the Father. The people of Christ, he has said already, have access through him "in one Spirit to the Father" (Eph. 2:18); and Paul avails himself of this access to make intercession for his friends.

15 The Father to whom Jesus directed his prayers, and in whom he taught his disciples to trust with the implicit confidence of children, is presented as the archetypal Father: all other fatherhood in the universe is derived from his. In its two other NT occurrences, the noun here translated "fatherhood" is rendered "family"—a group sharing a common father (Luke 2:4; Acts 3:25).[78] Here too the word is commonly rendered "family"—"every family in heaven and on earth" (RSV)—but in what sense, the English reader might ask, is every family "named" from him? The Greek noun *(patria)* is self-evidently related to the word meaning "father" *(patēr),* and it makes immediate sense to say that every *patria* is named after the heavenly *patēr.* Likewise it makes immediate sense to say that

---

[76]ὕψος and βάθος are placed in the reverse order by ℵ A Ψ and the majority of cursives.

[77]For πληρωθῆτε εἰς P^{46} B 33 1175 and a few cursives read πληρωθῇ ("that all the fullness of God may be filled"); after πᾶν τὸ πλήρωμα τοῦ θεοῦ 33 adds εἰς ὑμᾶς ("for you").

[78]Gk. πατριά. In Luke 2:4 Joseph is said to belong to the πατριά of David (those who claimed David as their ancestor); in Acts 3:25 all the πατριαί of the earth are to be blessed in Abraham's posterity (see p. 315, n. 30).

every *fatherhood* is named after the heavenly *Father*.[79] True, if the rendering "family" is used, it can be said that "family" implies "fatherhood"; but the relation between the two Greek words is best preserved if "Father" and "fatherhood" are used in English.[80]

In rabbinical thought the angels constitute the "family above," and men and women on earth—whether the people of Israel particularly or the human race as such—constitute the "family below."[81] As in the reference to God as "the Creator of all things" in v. 9, so here every gnosticizing idea of an inferior deity or demiurge who has to do with the earth as opposed to the heavenly realm is excluded.

To this Father, then, Paul directs his prayer on behalf of those who have become members of his family in Christ—those whose reception of "the Spirit of his Son" is made evident by their calling him "Abba! Father!" (Gal. 4:6).

16 He prays that they may receive an inward endowment of spiritual strength, and that in no niggardly measure, but "according to the wealth of God's glory," or perhaps "according to his glorious wealth."[82]

---

[79]The Vulgate renders happily: *ad patrem . . . ex quo omnis paternitas . . . nominatur.* Cf. Tyndale, Coverdale, Great Bible: "the father . . . which is father over all that is called father in heaven and in earth." See G. Schrenk, *TDNT* 5, pp. 1016-19 (*s.v.* πατριά).

[80]"The whole family" (KJV) is a mistranslation of πᾶσα πατριά. It is unlikely that "every πατριά" means "every family, whether Jewish or Gentile": Jews and Gentiles, by faith, have already become fellow-members of one household (Eph. 2:19, οἰκεῖοι τοῦ θεοῦ). C. L. Mitton, following E. J. Goodspeed (*The Meaning of Ephesians,* pp. 48-49), suggests that the reference is to "every local church." Since ἐκκλησία in this letter is used of the universal church only, another word had to do duty for the local church, and πατριά was pressed into service for this purpose (*The Epistle to the Ephesians,* pp. 237-38; similarly, it is proposed, the ναὸς ἅγιος of Eph. 2:21 is the universal church, while πᾶσα οἰκοδομή is every local church).

[81]The *pᵉmîlyâ šel maʿālāh* and the *pᵉmîlyâ šel maṭṭāh* (TB *Bᵉrākôt* 16b, etc.). But *pᵉmîlyâ* is a loanword from Latin *(familia),* comprising not children but household servants, in relation to whom God is not father *('āb)* but master *(baʿal habbayiṭ,* οἰκοδεσπότης). See H. Odeberg, *The View of the Universe in the Epistle to the Ephesians,* AUL, NF 1, 29, 6 (1934), p. 20. E. Percy (*Probleme,* p. 277, n. 30) argues that there is no specific allusion to the heavenly family as against the earthly family, the point simply being that "there is absolutely no fatherly relation in existence that does not have its prototype in God."

[82]Gk. κατὰ τὸ πλοῦτος τῆς δόξης αὐτοῦ. The question is whether the genitive τῆς δόξης has substantive force or is to be taken as adjectival, after the Hebrew idiom (cf. p. 258, n. 46). It is, however, an academic question here, since the infinite resources of God's wisdom, power, and love may be spoken of as his "wealth" or his "glory." (Cf. Phil. 4:19, κατὰ τὸ πλοῦτος αὐτοῦ ἐν δόξῃ ἐν Χριστῷ Ἰησοῦ.)

In the intercessory prayer which accompanied the introductory thanksgiving of this letter, God was asked so to enlighten the readers' spiritual eyesight that they might know "the glorious wealth of his inheritance in the saints" (Eph. 1:18).[83] That was one aspect of his "glorious wealth" (or "the wealth of his glory"). The glory of God may be viewed as the sum-total of all his attibutes. Because God himself is infinite and eternal, his glory is inexhaustible, and provides the measure of his generosity when he bestows his gifts. Because his resources are inexhaustible, he cannot be impoverished by sharing them with his children.

To try to comprehend the being of God is a mind-stretching exercise; an endowment of special spiritual power[84] is necessary even to make the attempt. Paul prays that through the Spirit, the vehicle of the impartation of divine power to human beings, this endowment may be theirs. The "inner being"[85] is the new creation inwardly begotten by the Spirit in those who are united by faith to Christ. It is in tune with the mind of God and delights in his law (Rom. 7:22); it is renewed from day to day even when the "outer," mortal nature wastes away (2 Cor. 4:16).[86] It is the immortal personality which constitutes here and now the seed of that fuller immortality to be manifested in the resurrection age. Gnostic speculation about the "inner man" does not help us to understand Paul's use of the phrase;[87] Paul is his own best interpreter.

17 The "inner being" may be viewed as the locus of the indwelling Spirit. But the ministry of the Spirit is devoted to making the presence and power of the risen Christ real to those whom he indwells: hence the experience of the indwelling Spirit and of the indwelling Christ is the same experience. The prayer that Christ may dwell in their hearts through faith

---

[83] See p. 270.

[84] Gk. δυνάμει κραταιωθῆναι (for κραταιόω cf. 1 Cor. 16:13, γρηγορεῖτε, στήκετε . . . , ἀνδρίζεσθε, κραταιοῦσθε).

[85] Gk. εἰς τὸν ἔσω ἄνθρωπον, taking εἰς in the sense of ἐν. M. Barth renders " 'to grow' toward the Inner Man," the "Inner Man" being the ἀνὴρ τέλειος of Eph. 4:13. But the other Pauline occurrences of ὁ ἔσω ἄνθρωπος are against this interpretation (Rom. 7:22; 2 Cor. 4:16).

[86] Cf. 1 Pet. 3:4, "the hidden man of the heart" (ὁ κρυπτὸς τῆς καρδίας ἄνθρωπος).

[87] H. Schlier (Christus und die Kirche im Epheserbrief, p. 32) compares the Naassene teaching quoted by Hippolytus, Ref. 5.7.35-36), where the "stone" of Isa. 28:16 and Dan. 2:45 (cf. p. 306, n. 153 above) is said to be the "inner man" who has fallen from Adamas, the archetypal man above, to be imprisoned in the human body, within the ἔρκος ὀδόντων ("enclosure of the teeth") of which Homer speaks. When R. Reitzenstein remarks that the "inner man," like the "new man," is mentioned repeatedly in the Manichaean fragments from Turfan (Das iranische Erlösungsmysterium, p. 153, n. 2), he throws no light on the origin of the Pauline phrases.

is parallel to the prayer that they may be inwardly strengthened by the Spirit of God. The aorist tense of the verb might suggest the rendering: "that Christ may take up residence in your hearts."[88] This would be appropriate in an exhortation addressed to new Christians, whose faith was of recent origin. But the initial act of faith, by which the believer is united to Christ, is followed by the life of faith, in which that union is maintained, or in which, to change the form of words, Christ continues to dwell in his people's hearts,[89] supplying spiritual strength for the present and the hope of glory hereafter. "If Christ is in you, although your bodies are dead because of sin, your spirits are alive because of righteousness" and "he who raised Christ Jesus from the dead will give life to your mortal bodies through his Spirit who dwells in you" (Rom. 8:10-11). If this note of hope does not find expression in the present intercessory prayer (as it does in the prayer-report of Eph. 1:18), it is implicit in the thought of the indwelling Christ.[90]

Those in whose hearts Christ has made his abode are "rooted and well founded in love."[91] Here we have a further instance of the combining of biological and architectural figures, comparable to the admonition in Col. 2:7 to be "rooted and built up" in Christ.[92] To be "rooted and built up" in Christ is to be "rooted and well founded in love." This love is the love of God revealed in Christ and poured into his people's hearts by the Spirit,[93] so that they in turn may show it to one another and to all.[94]

18 The outcome of the spiritual strengthening for which the apostle prays, together with the experience of the indwelling Christ, will be their prevailing to grasp God's revelation in its totality—its "breadth and length and height and depth." The exact reference of this dimensional language has been a subject of diverse and unending debate;[95] it would be pointless to examine all the interpretations that have been offered.[96] The best analogy

---

[88]Gk. κατοικῆσαι τὸν Χριστόν, where the aorist infinitive could be ingressive (cf. possibly Col. 1:19; see p. 72 with n. 159); though this is not necessarily so.
[89]Cf. Gal. 2:20, ζῇ δὲ ἐν ἐμοὶ Χριστός.
[90]Cf. Col. 1:27 (p. 86).
[91]Gk. ἐν ἀγάπῃ ἐρριζωμένοι καὶ τεθεμελιωμένοι.
[92]See p. 94. Cf. Eph. 2:21; 4:16.
[93]Cf. Rom. 5:5.
[94]Cf. 1 Thess. 3:12; 5:15.
[95]See the summary of interpretations in M. Barth, *Ephesians,* pp. 395-97.
[96]In evaluating gnostic and similar analogies one should bear in mind that dimensional language is liable to be used for a variety of unconnected subjects; cf. the invocation of Light in K. Preisendanz, *Papyri Graecae Magicae,* I (Leipzig, 1928), 4.978-79, "I adjure thee, holy light, holy beam, breadth, depth, length, height (πλάτος, βάθος, μῆκος, ὕψος). . . ." Where literally measurable dimensions are not in view, the expression is another way of saying "fullness."

is found in passages of the wisdom literature where the infinite scope of divine wisdom is emphasized. Of this wisdom (equated with "the deep things of God") Zophar the Naamathite said (Job 11:8-9):

> "It is higher than heaven—what can you do?
> Deeper than Sheol—what can you know?
> Its measure is longer than the earth,
> and broader than the sea."[97]

The divine "wisdom in a mystery"[98] which is unfathomable to mortal intelligence has been made incarnate in Christ and revealed to his servants—not least to Paul, whose mission is to make known to all "the mystery which was hidden from eternity in God" (v. 9). To grasp this revelation in its totality is not the achievement of a moment—Paul himself, toward the end of his apostolic career, did not suppose that he had fully comprehended it—but to grasp it was his personal ambition, and he prayed that his Christian friends might share and attain that ambition.[99] Here was a spiritual exercise that would make demands on them all their lives.

Nor is it only the immediate circle of his own converts and friends that he has in view: he prays that his readers may have strength to grasp the eternal mystery in common with "all the saints."[100] The disclosure of this mystery is the heritage of all the people of God: it is fitting that they should have an intelligent appreciation of it.[101] There may be the further thought that the deep things of God are more likely to be apprehended by his children in fellowship one with another than in isolation. The idea that spiritual illumination is most likely to be received by followers of the solitary life has been widely held: Paul does not appear to have favored it either for himself or for his Christian friends.[102]

19 The NEB rendering of v. 18b—"what is the breadth and length

---

[97]Cf. Job 28:12-14, 21-22; Sir. 1:3; also Deut. 30:11-14, quoted in Rom. 10:6-8. Paul includes ὕψωμα and βάθος in a list of created forces in Rom. 8:38-39.

[98]1 Cor. 2:7 (see p. 321 with n. 67).

[99]Cf. Phil. 3:12-16.

[100]Gk. ἵνα ἐξισχύσητε καταλαβέσθαι σὺν πᾶσιν τοῖς ἁγίοις . . . (this is the only NT occurrence of the compound ἐξισχύω). The phrase "with all the saints" effectively excludes the notion of a revelation of higher truth for a privileged elite (cf. Col. 1:28, with the repeated πάντα ἄνθρωπον).

[101]"The 'breadth, length, height and depth' can . . . refer to nothing other than that which is above all the object of Christian knowledge—the whole divine plan of salvation, which forms the subject-matter of the apostle's presentation up to this point" (E. Percy, *Probleme*, p. 310).

[102]M. Barth observes that the principle applies to the biblical commentator, who should not ignore what his predecessors have thought and said on the same texts (*Ephesians*, p. 395, n. 112).

and height and depth of the love of Christ"—represents a popular interpretation, attested as early as Origen,[103] but it is not precisely what the
text says. Yet it is not a misrepresentation of the general sense, for it is
impossible to grasp the divine purpose in all its dimensions without knowing the love of Christ—and this cannot be other than an experimental
knowledge. The disclosure of the eternal mystery is no object of merely
intellectual comprehension, although it calls for all the intellectual power
at one's command; it requires personal acquaintance with the revealer,
whose nature is perfect love. "If one loves God, one is known by him"
(1 Cor. 8:3)—and to be known by him is the antecedent to knowing him.
If Paul was prepared to sacrifice everything for "the surpassing worth of
knowing Christ Jesus my Lord" (Phil. 3:8), the one to whom he thus refers
is the one whom he describes elsewhere as "the Son of God, who loved
me and gave himself for me" (Gal. 2:20). Both the knowledge and the
love are mutual, and in both it is God in Christ who takes the initiative.
To know[104] the love of Christ is to know Christ himself, in ever widening
experience, and to have his outgoing and self-denying love reproduced in
oneself. It could not be otherwise, if he dwells in his people and they in
him.

To speak of knowing something that "surpasses knowledge" is to
be deliberately paradoxical; but however much one comes to know of the
love of Christ, there is always more to know: it is inexhaustible.

By knowing the love of Christ, and only so, is it possible to be
filled up to the measure of God's own fullness.[105] This, one may say, is
the language of hyperbole: how can the finite reach the infinite? But the
Christ whose love is to be known is the Christ in whom "all the fullness
of deity resides" and in whom his people have found their fullness (Col.
2:9-10).[106] By the knowledge of his love, and only so, m they hope to
attain to the divine fullness—insofar as that attainment is possible for
created beings. In "the summit of this flight . . . Paul has accumulated

---

[103]Origen, *Catenae* 6.162; cf. Thomas Aquinas, *Commentary on Ephesians*, 3.5;
J. Calvin, *Ephesians*, p. 168 ("By these dimensions Paul means nothing other
than the love of Christ, of which he speaks afterwards").

[104]If κατοικῆσαι (v. 17) is ingressive aorist, the same might be said of γνῶναι
(in γνῶναί τε τὴν ὑπερβάλλουσαν τῆς γνώσεως ἀγάπην τοῦ Χριστοῦ), but
it is not ingressive in Paul's statement of his ambition: τοῦ γνῶναι αὐτόν (Phil.
3:10).

[105]ἵνα πληρωθῆτε εἰς πᾶν τὸ πλήρωμα τοῦ θεοῦ. To render εἰς by "with" (as
in the RSV: "that you may be filled with all the fulness of God") is unsatisfactory.
(The NEB is better: "So may you attain to fullness of being, the fullness of God
himself.")

[106]See pp. 100-101.

329

everything that is strongest, most intense and most 'cosmic' in his vocabulary," says P. Benoit. God, who is the source and goal of all things, is the source and goal of the work of Christ; it is in God, "in his total Fullness, that salvation is achieved: this is the final term to which the saved come, loaded with a fullness which integrates them into the whole Fullness of God."[107] Could apostolic intercession reach farther than this?

8. DOXOLOGY (3:20-21)

20 *Now to him who can do far more abundantly than all[108] we ask or think, according to the power that operates in us—*
21 *to him be the glory in the church and[109] in Christ Jesus to all the generations of eternity. Amen.*

20 Has Paul sought too much from God for his fellow-believers—praying that they may be filled up to the level of the divine fullness? They might think so as they heard this letter read aloud, but Paul reassures them: it is impossible to ask God for too much. His capacity for giving far exceeds his people's capacity for asking—or even imagining.

The contemplation of God's eternal purpose and its fulfilment in the gospel calls forth a doxology. A doxology takes the basic form, "To God be the glory," but it may be variously expanded as the immediate occasion for ascribing glory to God is elaborated.[110] Other doxologies of this pattern in the Pauline writings are found in Rom. 11:36; 16:25-27; Gal. 1:5; Phil. 4:20; 1 Tim. 1:17; 2 Tim. 4:18. Such ascriptions, together with such utterances as "Praise God!"[111] or "Blessed be God!" were common in temple and synagogue worship and were taken over into the liturgy of the church.[112]

Here, in the light of the far-reaching prayer which has just been

[107]P. Benoit, "Body, Head and *Pleroma* in the Epistles of the Captivity," E.T. in *Jesus and the Gospel,* II (London, 1974), 91.
[108]ὑπὲρ πάντα ποιῆσαι ὑπερεκπερισσοῦ (ὑπέρ is omitted by P[46] D F G lat—the ascription then being "to him who can do in exceeding abundance all we ask or think").
[109]ἐν τῇ ἐκκλησίᾳ καὶ ἐν Χριστῷ Ἰησοῦ (καί is omitted by D[2] Ψ with the majority of cursives and several versions, the resultant sense being probably "in the church by Christ Jesus," as the KJV has it).
[110]A good OT example is Ps. 29: cf. 1 Chron. 29:11; Prayer of Manasseh 15; 4 Macc. 18:24. In the NT see Rev. 1:6; 5:13; 7:12; 19:1.
[111]Cf. the Hallelujah psalms (Pss. 146–150, etc.).
[112]Cf. the benedictions which conclude the first four books of the Psalter (Pss. 41:13; 72:18-19; 89:52; 106:48) or the *'Amidah* (the Eighteen Benedictions) in the Jewish synagogue service; also the *Benedicite* (Dan. 3:52-90 Gk.) and the exordium of the *Benedictus* (Luke 1:68). Pauline instances, apart from Eph. 1:3, are Rom. 1:25; 9:5; 2 Cor. 1:3; 11:31.

offered, God is described as the one "who can do far more abundantly than all we ask or think." The power by which he can do this is the power which he has implanted in his people[113]—"the surpassing greatness of his power in us who believe" which, as has been said in Eph. 1:19-20, is nothing less than "the operation of his mighty strength" exerted in the resurrection of Christ. By the Spirit who imparts this power to believers the full realization of God's gracious purpose for them and in them becomes possible.

21 The wording "to him be the glory in the church and in Christ Jesus" is unusual. It does not imply that "the church" and "Christ Jesus" are placed on a level with each other. God is to be glorified in the church because the church, comprising Jews and Gentiles, is his masterpiece of grace. It is through the church that his wisdom is made known to the spiritual forces of the heavenly realm. "The heavens declare the glory of God" but even greater glory is shown by his handiwork in the community of reconciliation. This community, moreover, consists of human beings who are united in Christ, members of his body, in whom Christ dwells: the glory of God "in the church" cannot be divorced from his glory "in Christ Jesus." The "glory of God in the face of Christ" has illuminated the hearts of his people (2 Cor. 4:6) and is reflected in the glory which, in life as well as in word, they ascribe to God through Christ.

This ascription of glory will have no end: not only now but "in the ages to come the surpassing wealth of his grace" continues to be shown "in his kindness toward us in Christ Jesus" (Eph. 2:7), and provides occasion for eternal praise.[114]

The "Amen" which follows the doxology would be the congregation's response as it was read in their hearing.[115] It is through Christ, as Paul says in another letter, that his people "utter the Amen . . . to the glory of God" (2 Cor. 1:20). With this loud "Amen" the first half of the present letter is concluded.

---

[113]Gk. κατὰ τὴν δύναμιν τὴν ἐνεργουμένην ἐν ἡμῖν. As in Col. 1:29, the question whether ἐνεργουμένην should be understood as middle voice ("operates") or passive ("is inwrought") is probably to be answered, in accordance with Pauline usage, in favor of the middle (see p. 88, n. 224).

[114]The expression εἰς πάσας τὰς γενεὰς τοῦ αἰῶνος τῶν αἰώνων ("to all the generations of the age of the ages"), in the characteristic style of Ephesians, is unparalleled in the NT; more common is the reduplicated εἰς τοὺς αἰῶνας τῶν αἰώνων (Rom. 16:27; Gal. 1:5; Phil. 4:20; 1 Tim. 1:17; 2 Tim. 4:18; and especially frequent in Revelation). The present use of γενεά in such a locution reflects the similar use of Heb. *dôr*, as in Ps. 145:13, *bᵉḵol dôr wādôr*, LXX (144:13) ἐν πάσῃ γενεᾷ καὶ γενεᾷ.

[115]On the responsive ἀμήν see 1 Cor. 14:16.

EPHESIANS 4

III. THE NEW HUMANITY IN EARTHLY LIFE
(4:1 – 6:20)

1. EXHORTATION TO UNITY (4:1-3)

1 *Therefore, prisoner in the Lord as I am, I beseech you to lead lives worthy of the calling with which you were called,*
2 *with all humility and gentleness, with patience, bearing with one another in love.*
3 *Make every effort to preserve the unity of the Spirit in the bond of peace.*

1 As in other Pauline letters, the doctrine expounded in the earlier part is to be worked out according to the practical guidance given in the later part, the transition from the one to the other being marked by the adverb "therefore."[1] As members of the new humanity, the readers have already been reminded of the purpose to which God has called them: the hope of their calling (Eph. 1:18) requires lives which are in keeping with their high destiny. Paul, as "the prisoner in the Lord,"[2] appeals to them to conduct themselves accordingly.

In calling himself "the prisoner in the Lord," he associates himself with them in a rather different way from that implied in Eph. 3:1, where he is Christ's prisoner for their sake. He addresses them as one who belongs to the same fellowship as they: being "in the Lord" currently involves his being a prisoner; what should being "in the Lord" involve for them?[3]

---

[1]Eph. 4:1 opens, like Rom. 12:1, with παρακαλῶ οὖν ὑμᾶς (cf. 1 Cor. 4:16). For οὖν in this position in a letter cf. Col. 3:5. On παρακαλῶ see C. J. Bjerkelund, *Parakalô: Form, Funktion und Sinn der Parakalô-Sätze in den paulinischen Briefen* (Oslo, 1967).
[2]Gk. ὁ δέσμιος ἐν κυρίῳ.
[3]See p. 164, n. 178 (on Col. 3:18).

There is nothing unworthy of the Christian calling in Paul's being at present in custody, if that is where the Lord desires him to be; he is still the Lord's ambassador, even if, for the time being, he is an "ambassador in chains" (Eph. 6:20).

Similar language about fitting behavior is used in Col. 1:10, where the Colossian Christians are told of Paul and Timothy's prayer that they may conduct themselves "in a manner worthy of the Lord, to please him in everything."[4] An admonition of this kind is more far-reaching than a list of detailed rules; it affects areas of life for which it might be difficult to frame rules. As members of a reputable family will have the family's good name in mind as they order their public conduct, so members of the Christian society will have in mind not only the society's reputation in the world but the character of him who called it into being and the purpose for which he so called it.

2 Some guidelines are drawn to show what is meant by the injunction to lead worthy lives: mutual relations among members of the society are uppermost in the writer's mind. Hence they are urged, like the Colossians in Col. 3:12-13, to show humility and gentleness in their dealings one with another, along with patience and mutual forbearance and tolerance.[5] They are urged, in short, to let the fruit of the Spirit be seen in their lives. It is possible to construe "in love" as an adverbial phrase with the following imperative "Make every effort," but it is more consistent with the idiom of Ephesians to attach it to the preceding words.[6]

3 "In one Spirit," the Corinthians were told, "we were all baptized into one body, whether Jews or Greeks, whether slaves or free persons" (1 Cor. 12:13); certain practical consequences followed from this, not only for the Christians of Corinth but for members of other churches too. The unity of the Spirit, which is to be preserved, is not the fact that there is one Spirit: that fact cannot be affected by anything that human beings do. But the one Spirit, in whom believers are baptized into one body, imparts unity to those who are thus baptized: as fellow-members of the one body, they should live in unity one with another. To the same effect the Colossians are reminded that it was to the "peace of Christ" that they "were called in one body" (Col. 3:15). It is this peace that is in view in the present exhortation to "preserve the unity of the Spirit in the bond of peace"; if they live at peace with one another the unity of the Spirit will

[4]See p. 47 with nn. 33-35.
[5]See comments and notes on these qualities (ταπεινοφϱοσύνη, πϱαΰτης, μαϰϱοθυμία, ἀνεχόμενοι ἀλλήλων) in the exposition of Col. 3:12-13 (pp. 153-55 with nn. 125-34).
[6]ἐν ἀγάπῃ may either be properly adverbial ("bearing with one another lovingly") or ἐν may be comitative (see p. 43, n. 17).

be preserved. Indeed, since Christ is himself their peace (Eph. 2:14),[7] it would be unnatural for them to live otherwise than at peace with one another. If "the bond of peace" is spoken of here, love is "the perfect bond" in Col. 3:14; but there is no dissonance between the two: love and peace alike are the fruit of the Spirit (Gal. 5:22). "The mind of the Spirit is life and peace" (Rom. 8:6).

2. CONFESSION OF FAITH (4:4-6)

4 *There is one body and one Spirit (as indeed you were called[8] in one hope of your calling);*
5 *one Lord, one faith, one baptism;*
6 *one God and[9] Father of all, who is over all and through all and in all.*[10]

4 This section has the nature of an early Christian *credo*, not unprecedented in the Pauline writings, but more elaborate than its predecessors. "To us," says Paul in 1 Cor. 8:6, "there is one God, the Father, from whom are all things and for whom we exist; and one Lord, Jesus Christ, through whom are all things and through whom we exist." This binary *credo* is followed, later in the same letter, by a triadic pattern of words, framing "the same Spirit . . . the same Lord . . . the same God" (1 Cor. 12:4-6). So also the wording of Eph. 4:4-6 is built up around "one Spirit . . . one Lord . . . one God." Here we have the prototype of the Eastern creeds, with their emphatic repetition of the numeral "one";[11] thus, over against the old Roman creed,[12] "I believe in God, the Father almighty . . . ," we have the creed of Nicaea (following the pattern of earlier Eastern creeds): "We believe in one God, the Father almighty . . . and in one Lord Jesus Christ . . ." (later expansions add ". . . one holy catholic and apostolic church . . . one baptism for the forgiveness of sins . . .").[13]

---

[7]Especially as the one who has made peace between Jews and Gentiles; in the present section, too, unity and peace between Jewish and Gentile believers may be especially implied (as it receives explicit mention in 1 Cor. 12:13).

[8]Gk. καθὼς καὶ ἐκλήθητε (καί is omitted by B and a few other witnesses).

[9]Gk. εἷς θεὸς καὶ πατὴρ πάντων (καί is omitted by a handful of witnesses).

[10]Gk. ἐν πᾶσιν, after which ἡμῖν ("us") is added in D F G Ψ with the majority of cursives and the Latin and Syriac versions. A few other witnesses, followed by TR, add ὑμῖν (whence KJV "and in you all").

[11]See R. R. Williams, "Logic *versus* Experience in the Order of Credal Formulae," *NTS* 1 (1954-55), 42-44.

[12]If the Roman creed was not the ancestor of the Apostles' Creed, as was argued (e.g.) by A. E. Burn (*The Apostles' Creed* [London, 1914]), it was an earlier representative of the same Western tradition (see J. N. D. Kelly, *Early Christian Creeds* [London, 1950], pp. 404-34).

[13]See J. N. D. Kelly, *Early Christian Creeds*, pp. 215-16, 297-98.

In the present confession, "one Spirit," "one Lord," and "one God" are successively amplified. "One body and one Spirit" echo 1 Cor. 12:13 (quoted above), which affirms the association between these two: in the one Spirit the people of Christ have been baptized into the one body, the Spirit being the animating principle of the corporate body of Christ. The unity of the Spirit is maintained as the members of the body function together harmoniously for the well-being of the whole. This is taught in 1 Cor. 12:12-26 in relation to the local church; here the principle is applied more generally. It was, in any case, never envisaged as applicable to one local church only: wherever the people of Christ were found, there was his body,[14] of which they were individually members.[15]

The parenthetical clause, "as indeed you were called in one hope of your calling," may be attached to "one body and one Spirit" because those whom God "has called, not from the Jews only but also from the Gentiles" (Rom. 9:24), have been called "in one body" (Col. 3:15)—that is, as fellow-members of one body. The "one hope" which they share in virtue of that calling (Eph. 1:18) is variously called "the hope of the gospel" (Col. 1:23) because it is held forth in the saving message, and "the hope of glory" (Col. 1:27) because it will be realized in the attainment of coming glory. And of that coming glory the "one Spirit" is here and now the guarantor (Eph. 1:13-14).

5 It is not difficult to understand why "one faith" and "one baptism" are attached to "one Lord": he is the object of his people's faith (Eph. 3:12) and it is into him that they have been baptized (Rom. 6:3; Gal. 3:27). The "one faith" is not their common body of belief (even if it is mentioned in a credal context); it is their common belief in Christ.[16] The God of the Jews and of the Gentiles, as Paul reminded the Roman Christians, is one, "and he will justify the circumcised on the ground of their faith and the uncircumcised through their faith" (Rom. 3:29-30)— one faith, placed in one Lord.

As for the "one baptism," it is beside the point to ask whether it

---

[14]Cf. Ignatius, *Smyrnaeans* 8:2 ("wherever Jesus Christ is, there is the catholic church"). Elsewhere Ignatius insists on "the unity of the church" (*Philadelphians* 3:2), which is identical with "the unity of Jesus Christ" (*Philadelphians* 5:2). "In Eph. and Hb. unity and uniqueness, unity and absoluteness, and unity and perfection are all interwoven into close patterns of thought. Hence the theology of ἑνότης (Eph. 4:4-5) is closely linked with that of ἐφάπαξ (Hb. 9:12) in the NT" (O. Michel, *TDNT* 3, p. 624, n. 2, *s.v.* καταντάω).

[15]Cf. 1 Cor. 12:27.

[16]It is doubtful whether πίστις is ever used in the NT (apart from Jude 3, 20) in the sense of a creed or body of belief, although a few occurrences of the word in the Pastorals may have this force.

is baptism in water or the baptism of the Spirit: it is Christian baptism—baptism "into the name of the Lord Jesus" (Acts 8:16; 19:5; cf. 1 Cor. 1:13-15)—which indeed involved the application of water, as John's baptism had done, but (as its inauguration on the day of Pentecost indicates) was closely associated with the gift of the Spirit.[17]

6 The third article in this *credo,* "one God and Father of all," is expanded not by the addition of other aspects of Christian experience but by an adjective clause, as in the *credo* of 1 Cor. 8:6.

As for the genitive "of all," this probably means more specifically "of all—both Jews and Gentiles." "Have we not all one Father?" asked a Hebrew prophet: "Has not one God created us?" (Mal. 2:10). That question was directed to a situation within Israel, in which the covenant-bond which united the people of God was being violated. Here the same principle is applied in a wider context: the people of God are now "elect from every nation."

Whereas the adjective clause appended to "one God, the Father," in 1 Cor. 8:6 acknowledges him as creator of all and goal of all, the present adjective clause describes him as transcendent, pervasive, and immanent. But how is one to understand the "all" over whom (or which) he is transcendent, through whom (or which) he is pervasive, in whom (or which) he is immanent? So far as the grammatical forms are concerned, the gender might be either masculine or neuter, but the word is most probably to be understood as personal, as in the preceding phrase: "one God and Father *of all.*"[18] That he is transcendent over all his children needs no emphasizing. He exists "through" them perhaps in the sense that they are instruments or agents through whom he works.[19] "There are varieties of working,

---

[17]No more than this need be said on the relation of water-baptism to the Spirit, so far as the exegesis of Ephesians requires. (If baptismal candidates were especially in view, there would be a special point in the inclusion of "one baptism" in the sevenfold unity.) Even J. D. G. Dunn, who minimizes the relation of water-baptism and Spirit-baptism to the point of saying that they "remain distinct and even antithetical," agrees that water-baptism "symbolizes the spiritual cleansing which the Spirit brings" (*Baptism in the Holy Spirit* [London, 1970], pp. 227-28). In Acts Christian baptism is regularly followed (2:38; 8:14-17; 19:5-6) or even preceded (10:44-48) by the gift of the Spirit: the time-lag between the Samaritan converts' baptism and their reception of the Spirit (Acts 8:14-17) is anomalous and calls for a special explanation. See G. W. H. Lampe, *The Seal of the Spirit* (London, 1951), pp. 70-72 *et passim.*

[18]The personal force is made explicit in those later textual witnesses which read "in us all" or "in you all" (cf. p. 335, n. 10).

[19]Cf. H. Schlier, *Der Brief an die Epheser,* p. 189.

337

but it is the same God who works them all in everyone"[20] (1 Cor. 12:6). As for his being "in" them,[21] this might be taken in much the same sense, but more probably it should be related to the statement of Eph. 2:22, that the people of God constitute his "dwelling-place in the Spirit." When divine immanence in the hearts of individuals is in view, the Spirit or the indwelling Christ is regularly the subject: here "in all" may denote the people of God collectively. The presence of God in their midst is a reality of which others than themselves can be conscious, as when an unbeliever finds his way into a meeting of the church and, hearing the mind of God declared in the power of the Spirit, falls down and confesses, "God is really among you!" (1 Cor. 14:24-25).

If it be asked why the unusual order "one Spirit . . . one Lord . . . one God" is followed here, the answer no doubt is (as in 1 Cor. 12:4-6) that the Spirit has been mentioned in the immediately preceding sentence (v. 3; cf. 1 Cor. 12:3), so that there is a natural transition to "one Spirit" before "one Lord" and "one God." The confession of faith in vv. 4-6 interrupts the paraenetic section begun in vv. 1-3, which is not resumed until v. 17. This confession, it has been further suggested, replaces the "order of logic, of metaphysics, and of apologetics" (Father–Son–Spirit) by the "order based on experience." As in 1 Cor. 12:4-6 Paul "works 'upwards' . . . from the present obvious fact of the gifts of the Spirit, to the service of Christ which such gifts make possible, and to the ultimate origin of all divine activity, the creative power of God," so in Eph. 4:4-6 "the unity of the Spirit" is shown to spring "from the deep, underlying unities of the Christian faith." Even today, it is concluded, "catechumens and converts should be led up this *scala sancta* whenever possible. It holds out more hope than the metaphysical order, which derives its power from a previous *experiential* contact with the realities it tries to explain."[22]

3. PROVISION FOR SPIRITUAL HEALTH AND GROWTH (4:7-16)

7 *But to each one of us grace[23] has been given according to the measure of Christ's gift.*

[20]Gk. διαιρέσεις ἐνεργημάτων εἰσίν, ὁ δὲ αὐτὸς θεὸς ὁ ἐνεργῶν τὰ πάντα ἐν πᾶσιν (cf. ἐν πᾶσιν here at the end of v. 6).
[21]It is unlikely that the present text expresses the hymn-writer's thought: "In all life thou livest, the true life of all" (the correlative of the words quoted in Acts 17:28, ἐν αὐτῷ γὰρ ζῶμεν καὶ κινούμεθα καὶ ἐσμέν).
[22]R. R. Williams, "Logic *versus* Experience in the Order of Credal Formulae," pp. 43-44.
[23]ἡ χάρις (ἡ is omitted by B D* F G L P* 082 6 326 1739 1881).

8 *Therefore it is said:*
  "When he ascended on high he led captivity captive;
  he gave gifts to mankind." [24]

9 *Now what does "he ascended" mean, if not that he also descended[25]*
  into the lower parts of the earth?[26]

10 *He who descended is the same who also "ascended" high above all*
  the heavens, in order to fill the universe.

11 *It is he also who "gave"[27] some as apostles and some as prophets,*
  some as evangelists and some as pastors and teachers.

12 *He gave them to equip the saints for the work of ministry, for the*
  building up of the body of Christ,

13 *until we all attain the unity of faith and knowledge of the Son[28] of*
  God, reaching the dimensions of a fully mature man, the measure
  of the stature of Christ's fullness.

14 *Let us no longer be infants,[29] tossed about and carried around by*
  every wind of teaching, through human craftiness and trickery which
  schemes to lead people astray;[30]

15 *but let us speak the truth[31] with love and grow up in all things to*
  him who is the[32] head—that is, Christ.[33]

16 *It is from him that the whole body, fitted and held together through*
  every supporting ligament, grows effectively[34] according to the due
  measure of each separate part,[35] so that it is built up[36] in love.

7 Within the unity of the body each member has a distinctive part
to play, a distinctive service to perform, for the effective functioning of the

---

[24]ἔδωκεν δόματα τοῖς ἀνθρώποις (καί is read before ἔδωκεν by א² B C* D²
Ψ and the majority of cursives). Τo τοῖς ἀνθρώποις the preposition ἐν is prefaced
by F G 614 630 2464 *pc* (cf. Ps. 67:19 LXX: ἐν ἀνθρώπῳ).

[25]κατέβη, after which πρῶτον is read by א² B C³ Ψ and the majority of cursives
with lat^vg syr^pesh (expressing what is in any case implied).

[26]εἰς τὰ κατώτερα μέρη τῆς γῆς (μέρη is omitted by P⁴⁶ D* F G and several
Latin witnesses).

[27]ἔδωκεν (aorist), for which P⁴⁶ reads δέδωκεν (perfect).

[28]τοῦ υἱοῦ *om* F G lat^b (the resultant reading being "the knowledge of God").

[29]Gk. ἵνα μηκέτι ὦμεν νήπιοι, "in order that we should no longer be infants."

[30]πρὸς τὴν μεθοδείαν τῆς πλάνης ("for the scheming of error"), to which A
adds τοῦ διαβόλου ("of the devil").

[31]ἀληθεύοντες δέ, paraphrased in F G as ἀλήθειαν δὲ ποιοῦντες (cf. lat^vg
ueritatem autem facientes).

[32]ἡ κεφαλή (ἡ is omitted by D* F G 6 1739 1881 *pc*).

[33]Χριστός, to which א² D F G Ψ and the majority of cursives preface ὁ (P⁴⁶ reads
τοῦ Χριστοῦ).

[34]κατ' ἐνέργειαν, omitted by F G lat^vet (P⁴⁶ reads καὶ ἐνεργείας).

[35]μέρους, for which A C Ψ 365 *pc* read μέλους ("member," "limb").

[36]εἰς οἰκοδομὴν ἑαυτοῦ, "for the building up of itself" (for ἑαυτοῦ א D* F G
pc read αὐτοῦ).

whole. The ability to perform this service is here called the "grace" given to each. Paul has referred above to the special "grace" granted to him— the grace of apostleship (Eph. 3:7-8),[37] to be exercised not in any one local church but throughout the Gentile world. But other members of the body had their respective varieties of "grace"; since "we, though many, are one body in Christ," says Paul to the Romans, therefore, "having gifts[38] that differ according to the grace given to us, let us use them" (Rom. 12:5-6).[39]

Whereas in 1 Cor. 12:7-11 it is through the Spirit that the various "manifestations" are given "for the common good," together with the power to exercise them, they are given here "according to the measure of Christ's gift."[40] Since Christ is the one who baptizes his people with the Spirit,[41] it is not inconsistent to credit him with bestowing the gifts of the Spirit also: this is one of the differences in emphasis and wording between the treatment of this subject elsewhere in the Pauline writings and its treatment in Ephesians.[42] The proportionate allocation of the gifts is consistently stressed, but while in 1 Cor. 12:11 it is the Spirit who "apportions to each one individually as he wills," here the apportioning, like the general giving, is the work of the ascended Christ.

8 This is confirmed by the application of an OT text, introduced by the formula "Therefore it is said" (lit., "Therefore it says,"[43] i.e., "scripture says" or "God says"). This precise formula occurs once again in this letter (in Eph. 5:14, introducing what is not recognizably a quotation from scripture) but nowhere else in the Pauline corpus;[44] no particular significance attaches to this, however ("it says" or "he says" is common

---

[37]See p. 317 with n. 38.

[38]Gk. χαρίσματα (used thus also in 1 Cor. 12:4, 9, 28, 30-31), a word not found in the present letter, where the word for "gift" in this sense is δωρεά (Eph. 3:7; 4:7) or δόμα (in the OT citation in v. 8).

[39]Cf. 1 Pet. 4:10, "as each has received a gift (χάρισμα), employ it for one another, as good stewards of God's manifold grace" (ὡς καλοὶ οἰκονόμοι ποικίλης χάριτος θεοῦ).

[40]Gk. κατὰ τὸ μέτρον τῆς δωρεᾶς τοῦ Χριστοῦ. Cf. Rom. 12:3, "according to the measure of faith that God has assigned to each" (ἑκάστῳ ὡς ὁ θεὸς ἐμέρισεν μέτρον πίστεως).

[41]Mark 1:8; John 1:33, etc. In Luke 24:49; John 15:7, 26; 16:7 Christ is said to "send" the Spirit.

[42]Another is the designation of those who receive and exercise the gifts of the Spirit as themselves "gifts" (v. 11 below).

[43]Gk. διὸ λέγει.

[44]It occurs in Jas. 4:6 (introducing Prov. 3:34).

enough in Paul when scripture is being quoted, whatever the accompanying adverb or conjunction may be).[45]

The text quoted is Ps. 68:18 (MT 19). A rather literal rendering of the Hebrew wording is:

"Thou hast ascended on high;
thou hast led captivity captive;
thou hast received gifts among mankind—
yes, even the rebels, that Yah may dwell (there as) God."

The enigmatic reference to the "rebels" (who perhaps resent Yahweh's choice of Zion as his dwelling-place) need not detain us; it is not included in the quotation. The first three clauses of the verse are translated word for word in the LXX (Ps. 67:19) into unidiomatic Greek.[46]

The psalm as a whole, or at least this section of it, is, as Calvin called it, an *epinikion*, a victory ode.[47] One may picture a military leader returning to Jerusalem at the head of his followers, after routing an enemy army and taking many prisoners. The victorious procession, with the captives in its train, makes its way up to the temple mount, preceded by the sacred ark, which symbolizes the invisible presence of the God of Israel. To him a sacrifice of thanksgiving will be offered when the procession reaches the temple precincts, and the tribute received by the victor from the vanquished foe will be dedicated to him. This tribute is referred to as "gifts" which the victor has received "among men"—perhaps the NEB and NIV translators have rightly rendered the phrase "from men."[48]

---

[45]See E. E. Ellis, *Paul's Use of the Old Testament* (Grand Rapids, ²1981), p. 23: " 'The Scripture says,' 'God says,' and 'Isaiah says' are for Paul only different ways of expressing the same thing" (for λέγει without a subject when an OT quotation is being introduced cf. Rom. 9:25; 10:21; 15:10; Gal. 3:16). See also B. B. Warfield, *The Inspiration and Authority of the Bible* (Philadelphia, 1948), pp. 299-348.

[46]Thus εἰς ὕψος represents *lammārôm* (RSV "the high mount"), ἠχμαλώτευσας αἰχμαλωσίαν represents *šābîtā šebî* (where the abstract noun "captivity" does duty as a collective in the sense of "captives," like ἀκροβυστία and περιτομή in the sense of ἀπερίτμητοι and περιτετμημένοι in Eph. 2:11), and ἐν ἀνθρώπῳ represents *bā'ādām* (where Heb. *'ādām* has a collective force alien to the Gk. singular ἄνθρωπος).

[47]Calvin, *Ephesians*, p. 174.

[48]If Heb. *bᵉ* can be taken here to have the sense of Ugaritic *bᵉ*, "from." M. Dahood goes farther and reads here *bᵉ'ādēm*, "from their hands" (*Psalms* II, AB [Garden City, NY, 1968], 143; cf. *Psalms* I, AB [Garden City, NY, 1966], 95); he was anticipated by T. H. Gaster, *Thespis* (New York, 1950), p. 458. But note J. Barr's *caveat* in *Comparative Philology and the Text of the Old Testament* (Oxford, 1968), pp. 175-77.

341

In the present quotation the second person singular of the original (addressed either to Yahweh or to his anointed king) is changed to the third person so as to adapt the construction to the contextual argument. That is a minor deviation: the major deviation is the replacement of the verb "received" by its antonym "gave." This is supported neither by the Hebrew nor by the Greek wording (so far as extant copies go); it does occur, however, as a targumic rendering.[49] An early targumic rendering is found in the Peshitta:[50]

> *"Thou hast ascended on high;*
> *thou hast led captivity captive;*
> *thou hast given gifts to men."*

A later amplification appears in the traditional Targum on the Psalter, which provides the text with a life-setting far removed from Jerusalem under the monarchy:

> *"Thou hast ascended to the firmament, prophet Moses;*
> *thou hast led captivity captive;*
> *thou hast taught the words of the law;*
> *thou hast given gifts to men."*

Paul and other NT writers occasionally give evidence of using targumic renderings (or renderings known to us nowadays only from the Targums), especially where such renderings are better suited to the argument to which they are applied than the Hebrew or Septuagint wording would be.[51] Even when a written Targum is quite late,[52] the renderings it presents often had a long oral prehistory. However far "thou hast given gifts to men" deviates from "thou hast received gifts among (from) men,"

[49]Calvin, not knowing the Aramaic and Syriac readings, concluded that "Paul purposely changed the word" (from "received" to "gave") to enhance the glory of Christ's ascension, "because it is more excellent for a conqueror to dispense all his bounty freely to all, than to gather spoils from the vanquished" (*Ephesians*, pp. 175-76).

[50]See E. Nestle, "Zum Zitat in Eph 4, 8," *ZNW* 4 (1903), 344-45. P. E. Kahle thought of the OT Peshitta as an Eastern Aramaic Targum prepared in the first instance for the proselytes of Adiabene in the first century A.D. (*The Cairo Geniza* [Oxford, ²1959], pp. 270-73).

[51]Cf. the targumic rendering of Deut. 32:35 ("Vengeance is mine; I will repay") in Rom. 12:19 (and Heb. 10:30); of Isa. 6:10 ("and be forgiven") in Mark 4:12; of Isa. 6:1 ("I saw the glory of the Lord") in John 12:41.

[52]The Targum on the Psalms appears to be not later than A.D. 476, since it knows both the western and eastern divisions of the Roman Empire.

it circulated as an acceptable interpretation in the first century A.D.[53] (It might be said that a conqueror, having received "gifts" from the defeated enemy, bestows them as largesse on the spectators lining the processional route; we have no means of knowing if this harmonizing consideration was used to bridge the gap between original text and interpretation.)

9 The targumic rendering is explained as a reference to the ascension of Christ and his bestowal of gifts on the church. The mode of explanation is that which is commonly called *pesher,* because of its regular employment (under that Hebrew word) in the biblical commentaries from Qumran.[54] A section of biblical text is quoted, and its explanation *(pesher)* is then given, word by word or phrase by phrase, in terms not of its original life-setting but of the new life-setting to which it is now being applied. Two verbs are here selected from the OT passage as quoted to receive their appropriate explanation: "he ascended" and "he gave."

As for "he ascended," this is applied to Christ's return from earth to the highest heaven, mentioned already in Eph. 1:20-21. In Eph. 1:20-21 God was the subject: he raised Christ from the dead and "seated him . . . in the heavenly realm." Here Christ is the subject: it is he who ascended. The expression "he ascended" is seen to imply that he first "descended." The same sequence "ascended/descended" appears in the Fourth Gospel. "No one has ascended into heaven but he who descended from heaven" (John 3:13; cf. John 6:38, 62, where the one who claims to "have come down from heaven, not to do my own will, but the will of him who sent me," asks his scandalized hearers, "Then what if you were to see the Son of man ascending where he was before?"). In the Fourth Gospel the ascent is from earth to heaven and the preceding descent correspondingly from heaven to earth; and so it is here. That is to say, "the lower parts of the earth" should be understood as meaning "the earth below."[55]

But this phrase, "the lower parts of the earth," has traditionally

---

[53]Presumably in a Greek form; the quotation in v. 8 seems to be a deliberate deviation from the LXX wording.

[54]Cf. F. F. Bruce, *Biblical Exegesis in the Qumran Texts* (London, 1960), pp. 7-19. In OT Heb. *pēšer* occurs in Eccl. 8:1; the Aramaic equivalent *pᵉšar* occurs in Dan. 2:4ff.; 4:6ff. (MT 3ff.); 5:7ff.; 7:16.

[55]In τὰ κατώτερα τῆς γῆς the genitive τῆς γῆς is epexegetic after τὰ κατώτερα (genitive of definition). The phrase means much the same as τὰ κατώτατα τῆς γῆς in Ps. 138:15 LXX (MT 139:15). "A comparison is drawn, not between one part of the earth and another, but between the whole earth and heaven; as if he had said, 'From that lofty habitation He descended into our deep gulf' " (J. Calvin, *Ephesians,* p. 176).

343

been interpreted as the abode of the dead,[56] and the passage has served as one of the few biblical proof-texts for the harrowing of hell—the idea that between his death and resurrection Christ invaded the abode of the dead and released the men and women of God who, from Adam onward, had been held fast there, thus "leading captivity captive."[57] No explanation is offered in this *pesher* of the multitude of captives taken by the conqueror in Ps. 68:18; but the words would refer more naturally to prisoners-of-war from the enemy army than to the conqueror's rightful subjects who had been released from the enemy leader's unwelcome control. (If the multitude of captives had been given a christological interpretation, the vanquished principalities and powers of Col. 2:15 would have been more suitable for the purpose.)[58]

10 Having descended to the earth below in incarnation, Christ then "ascended" to heaven above—"high above all the heavens," in fact. Similarly in the letter to the Hebrews he is said to have "passed through the heavens" in order to be "exalted above the heavens" (Heb. 4:14; 7:26). He ascended there, we are now told, to "fill all things"—to pervade the universe with his presence. This is in keeping with a possible interpretation of Eph. 1:23, that he is the one who "fills the universe in all its parts." There his relation to "the church, which is his body," is especially in view: so here, the "filling" of the universe inaugurated in his ascension is now

---

[56]This interpretation is not extinct; cf. F. Büchsel, *TDNT* 3, pp. 641-42 (*s.v.* κάτω κτλ), whose arguments that there is a reference here to "the sphere of the underworld, the place of the dead," proved so powerful that they persuaded J. Schneider to weaken in his view that the reference is "to the earthly journey of the Redeemer, not to His descent into Hades," which he had maintained in *TDNT* 1, p. 523 (*s.v.* καταβαίνω), and concede that either interpretation is tenable (*TDNT* 4, pp. 597-98, *s.v.* μέρος). But his first thoughts were right.

[57]Another proof-text for this tradition is 1 Pet. 3:19-20, where, however, τὰ ἐν φυλακῇ πνεύματα are probably the errant angels of Gen. 6:1-4 (cf. Jude 6; 2 Pet. 2:4). (Similarly, the καταχθόνιοι of Phil. 2:10 are probably spirits or demons rather than dead human beings.)

[58]This was the view of Irenaeus: "by *captivity* he means the destruction of the rule of the apostate angels" (*Epideixis* 83). Cf. H. Traub, *TDNT* 5, pp. 525-26 (*s.v.* οὐρανός): Christ's journey to earth and return to heaven broke the power of the hostile forces which controlled the heavenly zones and prevented men and women's access to God. H. Schlier supposed that the language, if not the thought, of this passage was influenced by the gnostic account of the descent and ascent of the redeemed redeemer, his ascent being at the same time the regeneration (ἀναγέννησις) of the "perfect man" (*Christus und die Kirche im Epheserbrief*, p. 33); but, as has been said before, evidence for the pre-Christian circulation of this account is hard to come by. On the passage in general see G. B. Caird, "The Descent of Christ in Ephesians 4, 7-11," *SE* 2 = *TU* 87 (Berlin, 1964), 535-45.

being put into effect more particularly as he supplies the church with everything necessary to promote the growth of the body until it matches his own fullness.

In the OT and other literature derived from it the filling of the universe is a divine property: " 'Do I not fill heaven and earth?' says the LORD" (Jer. 23:24).[59] Now, part of the exaltation conferred by the Father on the Son is the sharing by the Son in the Father's ubiquity.

11 As for the statement in the OT text, "he gave gifts to mankind," it is emphasized that the one who gave the gifts is the one who ascended: it is because he ascended that he has given them.[60] Something comparable is said in Acts 2:33 of his bestowal of the Spirit: "Being therefore exalted by the right hand of God, and having received from the Father the promise of the Holy Spirit, he has poured out this which you see and hear" (i.e., the gift of the Spirit with attendant manifestations). If it had been thought necessary to make allowance in the interpretation for the original as for the targumic reading (a proceeding well attested in the Qumran commentaries), it could have been said of the gifts of the Spirit, as of the gift of the Spirit himself, that Christ "received" them from the Father and then bestowed them on men. Some such idea may have lain behind the use of the preposition "for" in the Coverdale and KJV renderings of Ps. 68:18: "thou hast received gifts for men." But it is not even hinted at here.[61]

Whereas in 1 Cor. 12:4-11 the "varieties of gifts"[62] are the diverse ministries allocated by the Spirit to individual members of the church, together with the ability to exercise those ministries, here the "gifts" are the persons who exercise those ministries and who are said to be "given" by the ascended Christ to his people to enable them to function and develop as they should. It is not suggested that such "gifts" are restricted to those that are specifically named; those that are named exercise their ministries in such a way as to help other members of the church to exercise their

---

[59]H. Schlier (*Der Brief an die Epheser*, pp. 193-94) points out how this OT thought is reproduced repeatedly in Philo in stoicizing language; cf. *Leg. Alleg.* 3.4 ("God has filled and penetrated all things, and has left nothing void or empty of himself"); *On Dreams* 2.221; *Life of Moses* 2.238.

[60]Cf. Justin, *Dialogue* 39.2-4, where a summary of 1 Cor. 12:8-10, being challenged by Trypho, is defended by an appeal to Ps. 68:18: "it was prophesied that, after Christ's ascension into heaven, he should take us captive from the (grip of) error and give us gifts."

[61]According to Calvin, "the exposition of some, that Christ received from the Father what He would distribute to us, is forced, and utterly foreign to the argument" (*Ephesians*, p. 176).

[62]Gk. διαιρέσεις . . . χαρισμάτων (neither word is used in Ephesians).

345

own respective ministries (no member is left without some kind of service to perform).

Of the "gifts" that are named, three are mentioned in order of precedence in 1 Cor. 12:28, where God is said to have set in the church "first apostles, second prophets, third teachers." Here evangelists are placed between prophets and teachers, and teachers are given the twofold designation "pastors and teachers."

Both lists agree in placing apostles first and prophets after them. Apostles and prophets, as was indicated in Eph. 2:20, are viewed as the foundation "gifts" in the church, and what was said about them in the exposition and notes above need not be repeated here.[63]

As for evangelists, they do not appear in the catalogue of ministries in 1 Cor. 12:4-11; indeed, they are not mentioned elsewhere in the Pauline corpus apart from 2 Tim. 4:5, where Timothy is enjoined to "do the work of an evangelist." The one other NT occurrence of the noun is in Acts 21:8, where Philip (further identified as "one of the seven" of Acts 6:3-6) is called "Philip the evangelist."[64] Too much should not be made of the infrequency of the noun in the NT (it may indeed be a Christian coinage);[65] the verb meaning "evangelize" or "preach the gospel," from which it is derived, appears frequently, especially in the writings of Paul and Luke.[66]

One of the principal functions—indeed, the primary function—of an apostle (in the special Christian use of the word) was the preaching of the gospel.[67] The apostles, as an order of ministry in the church, were not

---

[63]See pp. 303-06 with n. 141.

[64]In expounding the present text, Chrysostom thinks of evangelists contemporary with Paul, but instead of Philip he mentions Priscilla and Aquila, "who did not go about everywhere, but only preached the gospel" (*Homilies on Ephesians* 11 [*PG* 62, 82D]). (No doubt they did preach the gospel, but among the various forms of Christian service which Paul and Luke record them as rendering in Corinth, Ephesus, or Rome, this finds no explicit mention.) Elsewhere, alongside the masculine εὐαγγελιστής Chrysostom uses a feminine form, εὐαγγελίστρια, by which he designates the Canaanite woman of Matt. 15:21-28 (*On the Dismissal of the Canaanite Woman* 4 [*PG* 52, 452A]) and the Samaritan woman of John 4:7-42 (*Diverse Homilies* 7.1 [*PG* 63, 493C]).

[65]Its non-Christian occurrence on an inscription of Rhodes (*IG* XII.1.675.6), of a deliverer of oracles, has been assigned a Christian origin by H. Achelis, "Spuren des Urchristentums auf den griechischen Inseln?" *ZNW* 1 (1900), 87-100; arguments to the contrary are given by A. Dieterich, "εὐαγγελιστής," *ZNW* 1 (1900), 336-38.

[66]εὐαγγελίζομαι (in the NT the active εὐαγγελίζω is found only in Revelation). On the εὐαγγέλιον word-group see H. Schniewind, *Euangelion* I-II (Gütersloh, 1927-31).

[67]Cf. Gal. 2:7, etc.

perpetuated beyond the apostolic age,[68] but the various functions which they discharged did not lapse with their departure, but continued to be performed by others—notably by the evangelists and the pastors and teachers listed here.

It is conceivable that evangelists are not included among the ministries set by God "in the church" in 1 Cor. 12:28 because, strictly speaking, they do not exercise their special ministry in the church but outside, in the world. The church is the community of those who have heard the preaching of the gospel and responded to it in faith; they do not need to be evangelized further. The gospel is preached to unbelievers, in order that they may be brought to faith in Christ and so be incorporated in the believing community. If the ministry of the evangelist is not exercised "in the church" it is certainly exercised *for* the church; but for the evangelist's ministry, the church would speedily die out. The apostles preached the gospel before they planted churches and gave their converts further teaching; they were in effect evangelists (as well as pastors and teachers) though they are not specifically called so. The evangelists given by the ascended Christ continued to exercise the gospel-preaching aspect of the apostolic ministry, so that the church might grow in succeeding generations by the adhesion of new believers.

When new believers are incorporated in the church, they require further ministry (as indeed do older believers): they need to be "shepherded" and taught. The noun "pastor" (i.e., "shepherd")[69] does not occur elsewhere in the NT in reference to a ministry in the church, but the derivative verb "to shepherd"[70] is used several times in this sense, and the noun "flock" (also derived from the noun meaning "shepherd")[71] is used of the church. The verb "to shepherd" and the noun "flock" are not found

---

[68]Insofar as ἀπόστολος corresponds to Heb. šālîaḥ, it is apposite to recall that the authority of the šālîaḥ ended with the completion of the work entrusted to him and could not be transferred to another; T. W. Manson compares the maxim of English law: *delegatus non potest delegare* (*The Church's Ministry* [London, 1948], p. 37). The authority of the apostle (in the sense of 1 Cor. 15:3-9) was bound up with a special appearance and commissioning of the risen Christ, but while that authority could not be transmitted, the apostle's various activities could be continued by others.

[69]Gk. ποιμήν (used of Christ in Mark 14:27 par. [quotation from Zech. 13:7]; John 10:11, 14, 16; Heb. 13:20; 1 Pet. 2:25).

[70]Gk. ποιμαίνω, used by Paul in the literal sense in 1 Cor. 9:7, τίς ποιμαίνει ποίμνην . . .;

[71]Gk. ποίμνη, as in 1 Cor. 9:7, quoted in the preceding note; in John 10:16 (μία ποίμνη) it is used of the flock of Christ as the good shepherd. In Acts 20:28-29; 1 Pet. 5:2-3, the synonymous ποίμνιον is used.

347

in this sense in the Pauline letters, but in Acts 20:28 Paul at Miletus enjoins the elders of the Ephesian church to "take heed to . . . all the flock, in which the Holy Spirit has made you guardians, to shepherd the church of God. . . ." "Pastors" may readily be identified with the ministers who are elsewhere called "elders" *(presbyteroi)* or "bishops" *(episkopoi,* rendered "guardians" in our preceding citation of Acts 20:28: "shepherd the flock of God that is in your charge" is the injunction given to "elders" by a "fellow elder" in 1 Pet. 5:2). (It is fitting that this injunction should be ascribed to the apostle whose final commission from the Lord, according to John 21:15-17, was "Feed my sheep.")[72]

A bishop, according to 1 Tim. 3:2, should be "an apt teacher."[73] Teaching is an essential part of the pastoral ministry; it is appropriate, therefore, that the two terms, "pastors and teachers,"[74] should be joined together to denote one order of ministry. The risen Christ is depicted in Matt. 28:19-20 as commanding the eleven to "make disciples of all the nations" by "teaching them to observe all that I have commanded you." The distinction between *kērygma* and *didachē,* made familiar in the 1930s by C. H. Dodd[75] and other leaders of the biblical theology movement, is not such a mutually exclusive distinction as has sometimes been implied, but in general the *kērygma* was proclaimed by the evangelist, whereas *didachē* was imparted by the teacher (indeed, since *didachē* is simply "teaching," the latter statement would be tautologous). The content of the teaching was wide-ranging: it included the teaching of Jesus with its implications for Christian belief and conduct. In Acts 2:42 it is called "the apostles' teaching," to which the primitive church of Jerusalem is said to have devoted itself. In Acts 13:1 five named leaders of the church in Syrian Antioch (including Barnabas and Paul) are described as "prophets and teachers." As the number of new churches increased, there would have been a call for more teachers to give young converts the basic instruction they needed. Paul assumes, in writing to Rome, that the "form of teaching"[76] which the Christians of that city had received was sufficiently clear

---

[72]βόσκε τὰ ἀρνία μου . . . ποίμαινε τὰ πρόβατά μου . . . βόσκε τὰ πρόβατά μου.

[73]Gk. διδακτικός.

[74]Gk. ποιμένες καὶ διδάσκαλοι.

[75]C. H. Dodd, *The Apostolic Preaching and its Developments* (London, [1936] 1944), pp. 1-2; J. I. H. MacDonald, *Kerygma and Didache* (Cambridge, 1980). But διδαχή is used occasionally in a wider sense that includes κήρυγμα. The "teaching (διδαχή) of the Lord" that so impressed Sergius Paulus (Acts 13:12) included the preaching of the gospel.

[76]Gk. εἰς ὃν παρεδόθητε τύπον διδαχῆς (Rom. 6:17).

and comprehensive to enable them to detect and reject propaganda which was incompatible with it (Rom. 6:17; 16:17). Timothy is directed not only to pursue a teaching ministry himself but also to entrust what he has learned "to faithful men who will be able to teach others also" (1 Tim. 4:13, 16; 2 Tim. 2:2); provision would thus be made for the continuity of the teaching in the next generations.

12 These various forms of ministry were given to the people of God to equip them for the diversity of service which they were to render in the community, so that the community as a whole—"the body of Christ"—would be built up. The three prepositional phrases in this verse are not coordinate one with another, as might be suggested by the RSV rendering ("for the equipment of the saints, for the work of ministry, for building up the body of Christ");[77] the second and third phrases are dependent on the first, as is indicated by their being introduced by a different preposition from the first.[78]

13 The "building up" of the body (a term borrowed perhaps from the architectural figure of Eph. 2:21-22) involves its growth to full maturity, to the dimensions of a "perfect man." This mention of a "perfect man" has reminded some students of the "perfect man" envisaged in Naassene gnosticism, the primal man who fell from his heavenly environment but will be redeemed and restored to his original perfection.[79] In the light of this analogy it has been argued that Christ, having himself ascended as the heavenly man, has from heaven given the various ministries mentioned to build up his body until its members collectively attain his

---

[77]The first phrase is introduced by πρός (πρὸς τὸν καταρτισμὸν τῶν ἁγίων), the second and third by εἰς (εἰς ἔργον διακονίας, εἰς οἰκοδομὴν τοῦ σώματος τοῦ Χριστοῦ). In such a construction these two prepositions are interchangeable, but the variation suggests that the three phrases are not coordinate, and this is borne out by the sense of the sentence.

[78]On ministry in the early church see (in addition to works listed on p. 38, n. 2, and p. 304, n. 141) J. B. Lightfoot, "The Christian Ministry," in *St. Paul's Epistle to the Philippians* (London, 1868), pp. 181-269 = *Dissertations on the Apostolic Age* (London, 1892), pp. 137-246; T. M. Lindsay, *The Church and the Ministry in the Early Centuries* (London, 1902); H. B. Swete (ed.), *The Early History of the Church and the Ministry* (London, ²1921); B. H. Streeter, *The Primitive Church* (London, 1929); C. Gore (ed.), *The Church and the Ministry* (London, ²1936); J. V. Bartlet, *Church-Life and Church-Order during the First Four Centuries* (Oxford, 1943); K. E. Kirk (ed.), *The Apostolic Ministry* (London, 1946); T. W. Manson, *The Church's Ministry* (London, 1948); A. Ehrhardt, *The Apostolic Ministry* (Edinburgh, 1958); E. Schweizer, *Church Order in the New Testament,* E.T. (London, 1961); K. Kertelge, *Gemeinde und Amt im Neuen Testament* (München, 1972); H. Merklein, *Das kirchliche Amt nach dem Epheserbrief* (München, 1973).

[79]Cf. Hippolytus, *Ref.* 5.8.10. See p. 299, nn. 125-26.

level in the heavenly world.⁸⁰ But the analogy is farfetched: indeed, the expression rendered "perfect man" here is not identical with that quoted by Hippolytus from the Naassene "mystery" (although this would not be important if a material relationship could be established between the two).⁸¹ The new humanity on earth, it is here emphasized, must grow up to adult maturity in order to resist all the adverse forces that threaten its health and effectiveness.

This maturity is marked by "the unity of faith and knowledge of the Son of God"; these are attained through accepting the various ministries provided. The unity of the faith is effectively the same as the unity of the Spirit which the readers have earlier been exhorted to preserve; it is the unity which binds together those who share the common faith in Christ. (As in v. 5 above, where "one faith" anticipates the present "unity of the faith," it is unlikely that a body of belief is intended.) It is by faith that the people of Christ are united to him, and in being united to him they realize their own unity one with another. The "knowledge of the Son of God" is that personal knowledge of him which comes through experience. It is not to be distinguished from knowing "the love of Christ, which surpasses knowledge," mentioned above in Paul's prayer for them, when he desires that by such knowledge they may be "filled up to all the fullness of God" (Eph. 3:19). As the personal knowledge of Christ was the attainment which he most earnestly sought for himself (Phil. 3:10), so he seeks it for all his fellow-believers.

The full spiritual maturity that is to be attained is more specifically defined as "the measure of the stature of Christ's fullness."⁸² The glorified Christ provides the standard at which his people are to aim: the corporate

---

⁸⁰Cf. H. Schlier, *Christus und die Kirche im Epheserbrief*, pp. 28-37 (see p. 344, n. 58 above). See also J. Schneider, *TDNT* 2, pp. 942-43 (*s.v.* ἡλικία); G. Bornkamm, *TDNT* 4, pp. 811-13 (*s.v.* μυστήριον); E. Percy, *Probleme*, pp. 316-27.

⁸¹The Naassene "perfect man" is τέλειος ἄνθρωπος, whereas the expression in Eph. 4:13 is εἰς ἄνδρα τέλειον (ἀνήρ is used instead of ἄνθρωπος, perhaps because it is Christ who is the "perfect man").

⁸²The same thought is expressed in the two phrases εἰς ἄνδρα τέλειον and εἰς μέτρον ἡλικίας τοῦ πληρώματος τοῦ Χριστοῦ, but it is expressed in fuller detail in the second phrase, a genitival structure typical of the style of Ephesians. The πλήρωμα of Christ is not to be understood in any technical sense (gnostic or otherwise); it denotes his full manhood. Indeed, the genitive τοῦ πληρώματος might be taken as an adjectival genitive after ἡλικίας, so that "the measure of the stature of Christ's fullness" means "the measure of Christ's full stature." It is probable that ἡλικία has the meaning "stature" here (cf. Luke 19:3) rather than its earlier sense "time of life" (cf. John 9:21, 23, ἡλικίαν ἔχει, "he is of age"), but either would be appropriate.

Christ cannot be content to fall short of the perfection of the personal Christ.

14 While the maturity of the body of Christ as such has been in view, an obligation is placed on the individual members of the body, "that we be no longer infants." More than once the NT writers use the term "infants"[83] to denote spiritual immaturity—an immaturity which is culpable when sufficient time has passed for those so described to have grown out of infancy. Paul tells the Corinthian Christians that, for all their cultivation of "knowledge," he could not address them as spiritual men and women but as "infants" in Christ," still needing to be fed with milk rather than solid food (1 Cor. 3:1-2). Similarly, the writer to the Hebrews tells his readers that "everyone who lives on milk is unskilled in the word of righteousness, for he is an infant" (Heb. 5:13). No blame is attached to the people addressed in 1 Peter for being "newborn babes,"[84] because they are recent converts; but they are urged to develop an appetite for "the pure spiritual milk" and thus "grow up to salvation" (1 Pet. 2:2). It may be that the people addressed in Ephesians have been "infants" in this sense thus far, but they must not be content to remain at this stage. Infants are defenseless, unable to protect themselves; in the spiritual life they are an easy prey for false teachers and others who would like to lead them astray from the true path. Like ships at sea without adequate means of steering, they are tossed about by the waves and carried this way and that according to the prevailing wind.[85] Maturity brings with it the capacity to evaluate various forms of teaching, to accept what is true and reject what is false. The mature "have their faculties trained by practice to distinguish good from evil" (Heb. 5:14).

The "winds of teaching" that threaten to drive the immature from the right course proceed from no pure motives: false teaching is promoted by "craftiness and trickery which schemes to lead people astray."[86] There

---

[83]Gk. νήπιοι. For natural infancy as a parable of spiritual infancy see Gal. 4:1, 3. See W. Grundmann, "Die νήπιοι in der urchristlichen Paränese," *NTS* 5 (1958-59), 188-205.

[84]Not νήπιοι but ἀρτιγέννητα βρέφη. It may be that the people addressed in 1 Peter were younger in the faith than those addressed in Ephesians.

[85]Gk. κλυδωνιζόμενοι (from κλύδων, "wave," "rough water"); cf. Jas. 1:6, κλύδωνι θαλάσσης ἀνεμιζομένῳ καὶ ῥιπιζομένῳ ("a wave of the sea that is driven and tossed by the wind").

[86]Gk. ἐν τῇ κυβείᾳ τῶν ἀνθρώπων ἐν πανουργίᾳ πρὸς τὴν μεθοδείαν τῆς πλάνης, "by the sleight of men, in craftiness, after the wiles of error" (ASV), where "sleight" represents κυβεία ("playing with dice"), "craftiness" represents πανουργία ("rascality"), and "wiles" represents μεθοδεία ("scheming")—a further piling up of synonyms. For πλάνη ("error," "straying") as the antithesis to ἀλήθεια ("truth") cf. 2 Thess. 2:11-12; 1 John 4:6.

may be a link here with Paul's warning to the elders of the Ephesian church in Acts 20:30 that from their own ranks, in days to come, "men will arise speaking perverse things, to draw away the disciples after them." More generally, Paul's severe words about "deceitful workmen" who infiltrated the church of Corinth and preached "another Jesus" and a "different gospel" from his own provide a parallel: it was plain to him that those interlopers at Corinth were moved by the ambition to gain followers for themselves (2 Cor. 11:4, 13, 20).

15 Over against such false teaching, let them embrace and follow the truth. Some Western witnesses to the text exhibit a reading which means "doing truth,"[87] and possibly "doing truth" as well as telling it is included in the sense of the injunction. "Doing truth" (or "acting truly") is an OT expression used especially when fidelity between two parties is the subject.[88] Whether spoken or expressed in action, the truth is never to be dissociated from love. The confession of the Christian faith can be cold and indeed unattractive if it is not accompanied by the spirit of Christian love. It may not be irrelevant to recall the testimony of the Fourth Evangelist, that "grace and truth[89] came through Jesus Christ" (John 1:17).

In truth and love together, then, the readers are exhorted to grow up in all parts of their being so that the body of Christ may be properly proportioned in relation to the head. This idea of the growth of the body of Christ until it matches the head has been compared to the normal development of the human body: in infancy the body is small in comparison with the head, but it grows until it attains the proportions which the body bears to the head in a fully grown human being.[90] This analogy may be helpful up to a point, but the language used here about the interrelation of body and head is conditioned by the relation existing between Christ and his people. They grow up to the measure of his full stature, but at the same time it is from him that they draw the resources necessary for growth. Christ is the head, but the full man comprises both head and body, so Christ the head is also, from another point of view, Christ corporate.[91]

16 It is from him that the body, in all its parts, derives its life. By his power it is "fitted together"[92]—a participle used in Eph. 2:21 of the building which is growing into "a holy sanctuary in the Lord"—so that

[87]See p. 339, n. 31.
[88]E.g., Gen. 47:29; Josh. 2:14; Judg. 9:16, 19.
[89]χάρις καὶ ἀλήθεια, derived perhaps from the revelation of the divine name in Exod. 34:6. (Cf. Col. 1:6, τὴν χάριν τοῦ θεοῦ ἐν ἀληθείᾳ.)
[90]Cf. R. A. Knox, *Saint Paul's Gospel* (London, 1953), p. 84.
[91]Cf. H. Schlier, *Christus und die Kirche im Epheserbrief*, pp. 38-39.
[92]Gk. συναρμολογούμενον.

through all its joints or ligaments the means necessary for its development flow from the head into every limb and organ. The thought is identical with that of Col. 2:19 (the wording of which indeed is closely followed): from the head, Paul says there, "the whole body, supplied and fitted together through the joints and ligaments,[93] grows with the growth that comes from God." It is not from the head, important as it is, that the natural body receives all the supplies requisite for health and development; but it is indeed from the living Christ that his people receive (through the Spirit) all that they need to make them effectively his people.

This is true of his people as a whole, and it is true of each individual believer. The body "grows effectively"[94]—grows by the inner strength that he supplies—"according to the due measure of each separate part."[95] Each one functions best in union with him and with the others. The bond that unites the members one with another is the bond of love—the love of Christ constraining them (2 Cor. 5:14)[96]—so that only by love can the body be built up to his stature.

4. CHRISTIAN CONDUCT (4:17–5:20)

(1) The Old Man and the New (4:17-24)

17 *This, then, is what I say and affirm in the Lord: you must no longer lead your lives as the*[97] *Gentiles do, in the futility of their minds,*

---

[93]Gk. πᾶν τὸ σῶμα διὰ τῶν ἁφῶν καὶ συνδέσμων ἐπιχορηγούμενον καὶ συμβιβαζόμενον. Of these words or phrases πᾶν τὸ σῶμα and ἁφή occur in both passages; to the participle ἐπιχορηγούμενον in Col. 2:19 corresponds the noun ἐπιχορηγία here (in the translation above the genitive τῆς ἐπιχορηγίας is treated adjectivally after διὰ πάσης ἁφῆς, "through every supporting joint"). As for συμβιβαζόμενον, which is also common to both passages, in Col. 2:19 it has much the same force as συναρμολογούμενον here ("put together"); by analogy it may be regarded here as a doublet of συναρμολογούμενον.

[94]Gk. κατ' ἐνέργειαν (for ἐνέργεια of divine power cf. Eph. 1:19; 3:7). Instead of the verb αὐξάνει or αὔξει ("grows" intransitively, as in Col. 2:19; the accusative τὴν αὔξησιν there is internal), the periphrasis τὴν αὔξησιν . . . ποιεῖται ("makes the growing," i.e., "causes to grow," active) is used: "the body" is both the subject and the object of the clause ("from whom the whole body . . . causes the body to grow").

[95]While μέρους rather than μέλους is to be read (see p. 339, n. 35), μέρος here has the sense of μέλος. The two words are linked as doublets from Plato onward (cf. J. Horst, *TDNT* 4, pp. 555, 566 n. 81, *s.v.* μέλος).

[96]ἡ γὰρ ἀγάπη τοῦ Χριστοῦ συνέχει ἡμᾶς.

[97]τὰ ἔθνη. ℵ² D¹ Ψ and the majority of cursives with the Syriac versions insert λοιπά between the article and the noun ("the other Gentiles," KJV)

18 *darkened⁹⁸ in their understanding, alienated from the life of God because of their deep-rooted ignorance,⁹⁹ because of the hardening of their hearts.*

19 *Having lost all moral sensitivity,¹⁰⁰ they have given themselves over to debauchery, to the practice of all sorts of impurity with covetousness.¹⁰¹*

20 *But as for you, that was not the lesson you learned in the school of Christ¹⁰²—*

21 *for I take it that you heard of him¹⁰³ and were taught in him the way of truth as it is in Jesus.¹⁰⁴*

22 *This means that you must put off your former way of life,¹⁰⁵ the "old man" who is corrupted by deceitful desires,¹⁰⁶*

23 *and must be renewed¹⁰⁷ in the spirit¹⁰⁸ of your mind*

24 *and put on¹⁰⁹ the "new man," who has been created according to God in righteousness and true holiness.¹¹⁰*

17 The ethical paraenesis, begun in v. 1 and broken off after v. 3 by the digression on the one body, is now resumed and carried on to Eph. 5:20 (if not indeed to 6:20).

⁹⁸ἐσκοτωμένοι (from σκοτόω); D F G and the majority of cursives read ἐσκοτισμένοι (the corresponding form from σκοτίζω).

⁹⁹διὰ τὴν ἄγνοιαν τὴν οὖσαν ἐν αὐτοῖς ("because of the ignorance that is in them").

¹⁰⁰ἀπηλγηκότες, for which D F G P and a few cursives, with the Latin versions *(desperantes)* and syrᵖᵉˢʰ, read ἀπηλπικότες.

¹⁰¹For ἐν πλεονεξίᾳ (comitative ἐν) D F G and a few cursives read καὶ πλεονεξίας.

¹⁰²ὑμεῖς δὲ οὐχ οὕτως ἐμάθετε τὸν Χριστόν ("but you did not thus learn Christ").

¹⁰³εἴ γε . . . ἠκούσατε, "if at least you heard," "assuming that you heard" (εἴ γε as in Eph. 3:2).

¹⁰⁴καὶ ἐν αὐτῷ ἐδιδάχθητε, καθώς ἐστιν ἀλήθεια ἐν τῷ Ἰησοῦ ("and were taught in him, as truth is in Jesus"). Since the earliest manuscripts rarely mark iota subscript or adscript, it is possible to read the dative ἀληθείᾳ instead of the nominative ἀλήθεια, and some commentators do so ("as he is in truth, in Jesus").

¹⁰⁵κατὰ τὴν προτέραν ἀναστροφήν ("according to your former way of life").

¹⁰⁶κατὰ τὰς ἐπιθυμίας τῆς ἀπάτης ("according to the desires of deceitfulness"); for the plural τὰς ἐπιθυμίας D reads the singular τὴν ἐπιθυμίαν.

¹⁰⁷For the infinitive ἀνανεοῦσθαι P⁴⁶ D¹ K 33 and a few cursives read the imperative ἀνανεοῦσθε.

¹⁰⁸τῷ πνεύματι. P⁴⁹ B 33 and a few cursives read ἐν τῷ πνεύματι.

¹⁰⁹For the infinitive ἐνδύσασθαι P⁴⁶ ℵ B* D² K and several cursives read the imperative ἐνδύσασθε.

¹¹⁰For ὁσιότητι τῆς ἀληθείας ("holiness of truth") D* F G and some other witnesses read ὁσιότητι καὶ ἀληθείᾳ ("holiness and truth"); cf. καὶ πλεονεξίας for ἐν πλεονεξίᾳ in v. 19 (n. 101).

The readers are Gentile converts to the Christian faith. They were brought up in the pagan way of life; that must now be abandoned. The darker side of that way of life is depicted in the following clauses, which repeat, but more concisely, the picture of the ethical bankruptcy of contemporary paganism presented in Rom. 1:18-32. "They became futile in their thinking and their senseless minds were darkened" (Rom. 1:21). The terms "futile" and "futility" are sometimes used in the NT to denote idolatry,[111] and although the "futility" of the pagan mind in the present context cannot be restricted to idolatry, it is the result of the idolatrous conditioning of that mind (as is argued at length in Rom. 1:18-32, wrong lines of conduct follow from wrong ideas about God). Even in the ethical field, it is implied, the most strenuous efforts of pagans are vain, because they lack the inner power to enable them to live up to their highest ideals.

18 Because they are "darkened in their understanding," as was said above in Eph. 2:3, doing the "will of their minds" leads them into courses which can only incur divine retribution. Their "deep-rooted ignorance" is the result of their not "seeing fit to acknowledge God" (Rom. 1:28). They were accordingly "estranged and hostile in mind" (Col. 1:21), alienated from the life of God, which is the source of all life that is worth living, and therefore, as they have been told already, "dead through . . . trespasses and sins" (Eph. 2:1, 5). The "hardening[112] of their hearts" is the progressive inability of conscience to convict them of wrongdoing. Conscience, as Paul has said in Rom. 2:15, serves as a witness to the law of God implanted within, but habitual ignoring of the warning signals it sends out incapacitates it from fulfilling its proper function; such a conscience is "seared," in the vivid figure of 1 Tim. 4:2.[113]

19 This idea of the "hardening of their hearts" is carried on in the statement that they have "lost all moral sensitivity"—a classical term which means primarily that one's skin has become callous and no longer

---

[111]The Gentiles walk, it is said, ἐν ματαιότητι τοῦ νοὸς αὐτῶν. (This is a more specific ματαιότης than that to which, according to Rom. 8:20, creation as a whole was made subject.) In 1 Pet. 1:18 (in a similar paraenesis to this) converted pagans are said to have been redeemed from the futile way of life which they had inherited (ἐκ τῆς ματαίας ὑμῶν ἀναστροφῆς πατροπαραδότου); both there and here μάταιος/ματαιότης may have much the same force as in Acts 14:15, where the pagans of Lystra are urged to turn "from these futilities" (ἀπὸ τούτων τῶν ματαίων) to serve the living God (cf. 1 Thess. 1:9-10).

[112]Gk. πώρωσις, as in Mark 3:5; Rom. 11:25 (the verb πωρόω is similarly used in Mark 6:42; 8:17; John 12:40; Rom. 11:7; 2 Cor. 3:14). The noun πῶρος is used of a light kind of stone, and then of various stony formations in the joints, bladder, or other parts of the body.

[113]Gk. κεκαυστηριασμένων τὴν ἰδίαν συνείδησιν.

feels pain.[114] The debauchery, impurity, and covetousness to which they have accordingly abandoned themselves sum up the moral delinquency which is described in greater detail in the letter to the Romans—although there the element of divine retribution is emphasized in that God is said to have abandoned them to this way of life because of their refusal to accept his self-revelation (Rom. 1:24, 26, 28).[115]

"Debauchery"[116] is wantonness—vice that throws off all restraint and flaunts itself, "unawed by shame or fear," without regard for self-respect, for the rights and feelings of others, or for public decency. "Impurity" has a wide range of meaning: it includes sexual misconduct, but is applicable to various forms of moral evil, as is noted in the comment on Col. 3:5, where it is included in the list of practices that believers must "put off."[117] As for "covetousness," it appears as the climax of that list; a further warning against it comes in Eph. 5:5 (where it forms the climax of a similar list).[118] It is possible to take the word here as qualifying the practice of the previously mentioned vices: "greedy to practice every kind of uncleanness" (RSV).[119] But more probably it is listed as a third vice in itself, alongside debauchery and impurity.

20 "This is not how you learned Christ,"[120] says Paul, succinctly: this is not the kind of lesson that you learned in the school of Christ. When writing to people who were personally acquainted with him, he reminded them of his own example: he himself had been a diligent pupil in the school of Christ and saw to it that he shared with others the lessons he had learned there, by practice as well as by precept. Thus he tells the Corinthian Christians that he is sending Timothy to visit them, "to remind you of my ways in Christ, as I teach them everywhere in every church" (1 Cor. 4:17). Or the meaning may be that, since Christ is the truth, they "learned Christ" in learning the truth—the truth embracing right conduct

[114]Gk. ἀπηλγηκότες, perfect participle of ἀπαλγέω, which means, in classical usage, "put away sorrow" but also "be despondent" (cf. the variant ἀπηλπικότες here, mentioned in n. 100 above). For the present force of the word cf. ἀπάλγησις, "ceasing to feel pain," in Heliodorus Eroticus 6.5 (3rd cent. A.D.).

[115]With ἑαυτοὺς παρέδωκαν here cf. παρέδωκεν αὐτοὺς ὁ θεός in Rom. 1:24, 26, 28.

[116]Gk. ἀσέλγεια, one of "the works of the flesh" in Gal. 5:19.

[117]See p. 143, nn. 62, 63.

[118]See p. 143, n. 66.

[119]This translation takes ἐν πλεονεξίᾳ at the end of the verse as an adverbial phrase modifying παρέδωκαν, but it is better to treat ἐν as comitative (cf. p. 256, n. 35).

[120]The expression "implies full acceptance of Christ and His work, even in respect of the direction of life" (K. H. Rengstorf, *TDNT* 4, p. 410, *s.v.* μανθάνω).

as well as right belief. So, in Col. 2:6, those who have had the Christian tradition of faith and practice delivered to them are said to have "received Christ Jesus the Lord."[121]

21 If Paul were writing to his own converts, he would not say, "I take it that you heard of Christ and were taught in him . . ."—any more than he would say that he assumed they had heard of his own special apostolic commission (Eph. 3:2). He does not express doubt about the instruction they have received; he takes it for granted that they have learned something of the Christian way of life. Even if these words are addressed to recent believers on the occasion of their baptism, they appear to have had some preliminary instruction. Christ was the subject-matter of that instruction, together with the ethical implications of being "in Christ"; to be taught in Christ is to be taught in the context of the Christian fellowship. It is difficult to discern any distinction in emphasis between "in Christ" and "in Jesus"; the point may be that the truth imparted to new converts was the truth once heard on the lips of the historical Jesus, preserved in the apostolic "tradition" and delivered to those who, one after another, were added to the community of faith.[122] It was from Epaphras that the Colossian Christians "came to know the grace of God in truth" (Col. 1:6-7); whether from him or from others, the recipients of the present letter had embraced the same saving knowledge. Let it not be said (this may be implied) that the instruction received by Gentile Christians was one whit less genuinely "truth as it is in Jesus" than the instruction received by those "who first hoped in Christ" (Eph. 1:12).

22 The instruction took the same catechetical form as that which is evident in the companion letter to the Colossians: its ethical directives were expressed in terms of "putting off" and "putting on." They were taught to "put off" their pagan way of life—that is to say, "the old man," the person they formerly were. The same expression occurs in Col. 3:9, but with a difference.[123] There the Colossian believers are reminded that they have put him off; here the readers are taught to put him off. This tension between the indicative and the imperative, between the "already" and the "not yet," is common in the Pauline letters; it is summed up in the admonition: "Be what you are!"—Be in practice what the calling of God has made you.[124] Because the people of God are holy by calling, they

---

[121]See pp. 92-94 with nn. 21-23.
[122]H. Schlier discerns a reaction against the gnostic tendency to make a cleavage between "Christ and Jesus" (cf. 1 John 4:2-3; 5:1, 6): to be in [the ascended] Christ means to be "in [the historical] Jesus" (*Der Brief an die Epheser*, p. 217).
[123]See p. 146 with n. 77 for the παλαιὸς ἄνθρωπος.
[124]See pp. 142, 221, n. 96.

are to be holy in life. But the change from indicative to imperative as between Colossians and Ephesians may have a further explanation. Colossians was sent to established Christians, whose baptism had signified the putting off of their old ways; if Ephesians is addressed to new Christians on the occasion of their baptism, the imperative "put off ... put on" would be very much in order. The "old man" is the sum-total of their former practices, propensities, and attitudes; he is a prey to harmful desires which beguile people into sin and error. Corruption and destruction are consequently working themselves out in him; they must bid him a long and final farewell.

23 If the old ways are to be abandoned, renewal is called for, and this must be an inward renewal. The new life is not to be regulated by conformity to some external standard; its wellspring lies within, "in the spirit of your mind." So Paul exhorts the Roman Christians: "Do not be conformed to this world but be transformed by the renewal of your mind" (Rom. 12:2). This inward renewal is the work of the Holy Spirit, progressively transforming believers into the image of Christ, "from one degree of glory to another" (2 Cor. 3:18).[125] It is by the Spirit's power, too, that "the inner being is being renewed every day," no matter to what attrition the body may be exposed (2 Cor. 4:16), until what is mortal is "swallowed up by life"—a consummation of which the Spirit is the present guarantee (2 Cor. 5:4-5).

24 In the parallel text in Col. 3:10, it is the "new man" himself who is "being renewed after his Creator's image."[126] Here the injunction to be "renewed in the spirit of the mind" is repeated in different terms by the injunction to "put on the new man." Again, the imperative replaces the indicative of Col. 3:10;[127] but such a use of the imperative is no

---

[125]In 2 Cor. 3:18 as in Rom. 12:2 to be "transformed" is μεταμορφοῦσθαι.

[126]In Col. 3:10 the new (νέος) man is being renewed (ἀνακαινοῦται, with which cf. ἀνακαίνωσις in Rom. 12:2 and ἀνακαινοῦται in 2 Cor. 4:16); here "be renewed" is ἀνανεοῦσθαι and "the new man" is ὁ καινὸς ἄνθρωπος. In this instance, at any rate, no distinction can be pressed between καινός and νέος.

[127]The infinitives ἀποθέσθαι, ἀνανεοῦσθαι, and ἐνδύσασθαι in vv. 22, 23, and 24 are to be treated as complementary to ἐδιδάχθησαν and as virtually indirect commands: what they were taught was "Put off ... be renewed ... put on. ..." They have occasionally been treated, however, as indirect statements; cf. J. N. Darby, *The New Testament: A New Translation* (London, ²1871): "ye have ... been instructed in him ...; [namely] your having put off ...; and being renewed ...; and [your] having put on. ..." Similarly J. Eadie (*Commentary on the Greek Text of Ephesians* [London, 1861]) and T. W. Peile (*Annotations on the Apostolical Epistles* [London, 1848-52]), whose rendering "that ye have put off ... and have put on ..." is mentioned by W. Kelly. For all his devotion to Darby,

innovation in Pauline usage, even when established Christians are being addressed: the ethical paraenesis of Rom. 12:1–13:14 is summed up in the injunction: "Put on the Lord Jesus Christ." For the "new man" is essentially the Lord Jesus Christ—or at least the Lord Jesus Christ as his life is lived out in his people, who by the new creation have been incorporated into that new humanity of which he is the head. It is this new creation that is referred to when the "new man" is said to have been "created according to God in righteousness and true holiness."[128] The phrase "according to God" means "in the image of God"; so, in Col. 3:10, the "new man" is "renewed after his Creator's image so as to attain true knowledge." Christ, the Son of God, is the uncreated one; but the reproduction of his likeness in his people is an act of divine creation. If, in Colossians, the goal of this divine renewal is said to be the attainment of "true knowledge," here the qualities manifested in the new creation are "righteousness and true holiness" (or "true righteousness and holiness"). The knowledge of God is never divorced from walking in his ways: to know him is to be like him, righteous as he is righteous, holy as he is holy.

(2) Negative and Positive Precepts (4:25-32)

25 Therefore,[129] put off falsehood. "Each of you must speak truth with his neighbor," because we are members of one another.
26 "Be angry but do not sin"; do not let the sun set on your anger,
27 and give no opportunity to the devil.
28 Let the thief give up stealing; rather, let him labor, doing an honest

---

Kelly's feeling for Greek usage was too sensitive for him to accept Darby's rendering: he refers to it with respect but prefers to translate "that ye should put off . . . and be renewed . . . and put on . . . ," commenting accordingly (*The Epistle to the Ephesians* [London, 1870], pp. viii, 223-24). The infinitives ἀποθέσθαι and ἐνδύσασθαι are aorist, because an action (baptismal?) is in view; ἀνανεοῦσθαι is present, because a continuous way of life is meant.
[128]Lit., "holiness of truth" (ὁσιότητι τῆς ἀληθείας); ὁσιότης is not found elsewhere in the Pauline corpus. The adjective ὅσιος comes in 1 Tim. 2:8 (ὁσίους χεῖρας) and Tit. 1:8 (where it appears between δίκαιος and ἐγκρατής in a list of qualifications in a church elder), and the adverb ὁσίως in 1 Thess. 2:10 (ὁσίως καὶ δικαίως καὶ ἀμέμπτως, in relation to the conduct of Paul and his companions). As for the collocation of δικαιοσύνη with ὁσιότης here, cf. (in addition to 1 Thess. 2:10 and Tit. 1:8 just cited) Luke 1:75, ἐν ὁσιότητι καὶ δικαιοσύνη. In classical Greek the difference between ὅσιος and δίκαιος is that the former belongs to one's attitude to God and the latter to one's attitude to other human beings. In the LXX ὅσιος renders Heb. *ḥāsîd* ("loyal," "pious") whereas ἅγιος renders Heb. *qāḏôš* ("set apart [to God]").
[129]διό *om* P[46] *al.*

359

job with his own hands,[130] *so that he may having something to share
with the one who is in need.*

29 *Let no corrupt speech proceed from your mouth, but rather speech
that is good for building one another up, as the need may arise,*[131]
so that it may minister grace to the hearers.

30 *Do not grieve the Holy Spirit of God, by whom you were sealed
against the day of redemption.*

31 *Let all harshness, wrath, anger, clamor, and slander be put away
from you; with malice of every sort;*

32 *but*[132] *be kind and tenderhearted to one another, forgiving one another, just as God in Christ forgave you.*[133]

Instead of a list of vices to be discarded and another list of virtues to be
cultivated, this paragraph counterbalances each vice that is mentioned with
a virtue: falsehood is to be replaced by truth, unrestrained anger by timely
reconciliation, stealing of others' property by the generous sharing of one's
own, foul language by helpful speech, animosity by kindness.

25 Falsehood was a characteristic of the "old man"; the people of
Christ should be men and women of truth. "Each of you must speak truth
with his neighbor" is a straight quotation from Zech. 8:16,[134] where members of the postexilic community of Judah are urged to keep covenant one
with another. So here openhearted candor within the fellowship is especially enjoined, "because we are members of one another";[135] but it is
plain that in their relations with the world in general Christians should
have a reputation for truthfulness, men and women whose word is their
bond. This is part of the wise conduct toward outsiders which the Colossians are urged to practice (Col. 4:5): "tell no lies to one another" (Col.
3:9) is as valid in the wider context as in the narrower. The ethical implications for Christians of their being "members of one another" have been
drawn out in earlier Pauline letters (Rom. 12:4-5; 1 Cor. 12:14-26); they
are reinforced in Colossians and Ephesians by the consideration that the
body of which they are fellow-members is the body of Christ:[136] his grace
and truth should be exhibited in them.

26 Anger figures in both Colossians and Ephesians in lists of vices

---

[130]ταῖς ἰδίαις χερσίν (cf. 1 Cor. 4:12); ἰδίαις *om* $P^{46, \ 49}$ $\aleph^2$ B L P Ψ and the
majority of cursives.

[131]Gk. χρείας, for which D* F G *pc* lat^{vet} read πίστεως.

[132]δέ *om* P^{46} B 6 1739* 1881; for δέ D* F G 1175 read οὖν.

[133]ὑμῖν, for which P^{49} B D Ψ and the majority of cursives read ἡμῖν ("us").

[134]LXX λαλεῖτε ἀλήθειαν ἕκαστος πρὸς τὸν πλησίον αὐτοῦ.

[135]Cf. Rom. 12:5, τὸ δὲ καθ᾽ εἷς ἀλλήλων μέλη.

[136]Cf. Eph. 5:30 (p. 392 with n. 126).

which the Christian must put away.[137] Our Lord himself warned his disciples that "everyone who is angry with his brother shall be liable to judgment" (Matt. 5:22). Where God is concerned, the noun commonly rendered "anger" has the sense of "retribution,"[138] but that is irrelevant in the immediate context. How is it possible to "be angry without sinning" (as the readers are directed in words drawn from Ps. 4:4)?[139] There is no doubt a proper place for righteous indignation; but there is a subtle temptation to regard my anger as righteous indignation and other people's anger as sheer bad temper. Here it is suggested that anger can be prevented from degenerating into sin if a strict time limit is placed on it: "do not let the sun set on your anger." Let reconciliation be effected before nightfall, if possible.[140] If that is not possible—if the person with whom one is angry is not accessible, or refuses to be reconciled—then at least the heart should be unburdened of its animosity by the committal of the matter to God. In a not dissimilar situation Paul deprecates anything in the nature of private vengeance: "leave it to the wrath of God" (Rom. 12:19).[141] If retribution is called for, let God take care of it: his retribution will be just, and free from self-regarding motives.

27 "Nursing one's wrath to keep it warm" is not recommended as a wise policy, and least of all for Christians: it magnifies the grievance, makes reconciliation more difficult, and destroys friendly relations. "Pressing anger produces strife" (Prov. 30:33) is a sentiment repeated in various forms in Israel's wisdom literature. One who "sows discord among brothers" (or sisters) is an abomination in the sight of God (Prov. 6:19), and the prime promoter and exploiter of such discord is the devil. It i͏ ͏e of his wiles against which the readers of this letter are later urged to be armed

---

[137]Cf. Col. 3:8; Eph. 4:31.

[138]Cf. Col. 3:6; Eph. 2:3; 5:6.

[139]LXX (4:5) ὀργίζεσθε καὶ μὴ ἁμαρτάνετε. The NEB renders the MT *(rigᵉzû wᵉʾal tehᵉṭāʾû)* "However angry your hearts, do not do wrong"; cf. G. Stählin, *TDNT* 5, p. 421 (*s.v.* ὀργή), who translates Eph. 4:26, "If you are angry, be careful not to sin," and adds: "Anger is not called sin here, but there lies in the background the thought that when one is angry sin couches at the door."

[140]A. D. Nock, "Early Gentile Christianity and its Hellenistic Background," *Essays on Religion and the Ancient World,* ed. Z. Stewart, I (Oxford, 1972), 127, compares Plutarch's description of the Pythagoreans who, "if ever moved by anger to abusive words, joined hands, embraced and were reconciled before the sun set" (*On Brotherly Love* 17, 448B). Cf. more generally Josephus's statement that the Essenes were ὀργῆς ταμίαι δίκαιοι, θυμοῦ καθεκτικοί, "righteous stewards of anger, holding their temper in restraint" (*BJ* 2.135).

[141]δότε τόπον τῇ ὀργῇ (for this sense of ὀργή cf. n. 137 above); one might contrast this injunction with μηδὲ δίδοτε τόπον τῷ διαβόλῳ in Eph. 4:27.

(Eph. 6:11). Paul himself was on his guard against providing him with a loophole when relations were strained between himself and his converts, or among his converts. In encouraging the Corinthian church to forgive and reinstate one of their number who had been guilty of some offense, apparently against Paul in particular, he says, "Anyone whom you forgive, I also forgive. What I have forgiven, if I have had anything to forgive, has been for your sake in the presence of Christ, to keep Satan from gaining the advantage over us; for we are not ignorant of his designs" (2 Cor. 2:10-11).

In the Pauline corpus the word "devil" *(diabolos)* occurs only in Ephesians and the Pastorals;[142] in the other letters he is always referred to as "Satan" (as also in 1 Tim. 1:20; 5:15).[143]

28 If a thief is converted to faith in Christ, it goes without saying that he should abandon the practice of theft. The commandment "Thou shalt not steal" (Exod. 20:15; Deut. 5:19) expresses one of the most elementary of ethical principles; it is repeated in NT summaries of the Decalogue (Mark 10:19 and parallels; Rom. 13:9), and Paul includes thieves among various other wrongdoers who cannot "inherit the kingdom of God" (1 Cor. 6:10). But when the thief becomes a Christian, he will not only give up stealing: he will do what he can to earn an honest livelihood and have something to give to those who are in need. Instead of regarding *tuum* as *suum,* he will treat *suum* as *tuum.* The grace of generosity is part and parcel of the Christian way of life (Luke 6:29-36; 2 Cor. 8:1-15; 9:6-12), but when it is practiced by a former thief it stands in total contrast to his previous course of life. To "work with one's own hands" is a favorite expression of Paul (cf. 1 Cor. 4:12; 1 Thess. 4:11); in recommending such activity to others, he set an example himself (cf. Acts 20:34).[144]

29 It is not only from lying that Christians should keep their lips free: foul language of any kind is inappropriate on lips that confess Christ as Lord. The Colossians were told to put such language "right out of their mouths" (Col. 3:8); the same admonition is now given in the sister-letter. By foul language[145] may be understood in this context not only obscene

---

[142]Cf. Eph. 6:11; 1 Tim. 3:6-7, 11; 2 Tim. 2:26; 3:3; Tit. 2:3; also Acts 13:10, where Paul addresses Elymas the sorcerer as υἱὲ διαβόλου.

[143]Gk. Σατανᾶς (cf., in addition to 2 Cor. 2:11, Rom. 16:20; 1 Cor. 5:5; 7:5; 2 Cor. 11:14; 12:7; 1 Thess. 2:18; 2 Thess. 2:9). Heb. *śāṭān* means "adversary" or, in a forensic setting, "accuser," "prosecutor"; in the latter sense Gk. διάβολος, "calumniator," is its equivalent.

[144]See R. F. Hock, *The Social Context of Paul's Ministry: Tentmaking and Apostleship* (Philadelphia, 1980).

[145]Gk. λόγος σαπρός, " 'rotten' language"; cf. αἰσχρολογία, Col. 3:8 (and αἰσχρότης in Eph. 5:4).

vulgarity but slanderous and contemptuous talk, any talk that works to the detriment of the persons addressed or of those who are spoken about. In a remarkably sobering utterance our Lord declared that people would have to render account on the day of judgment for every careless word they speak (Matt. 12:36); the Christian's words should be well chosen, uttered "always with grace, seasoned with salt" (Col. 4:6), helping to build up the common life in Christ and serving as means of grace to those who hear.[146] The conversation of some Christians is a benediction in itself; this should be true of the conversation of all Christians. The subject is important enough to be taken up again in Eph. 5:4.

30 Conversation that helps to build up the common life in Christ is a congenial instrument for the Holy Spirit to use to this end. On the other hand, conversation (or any other activity) that endangers the unity of the body of Christ "grieves" the Holy Spirit.[147] The corporate reference of this clause was appreciated by Marius Victorinus: " 'do not grieve him'—either in yourselves, when you utter bad language, or in those who hear you."[148] Another Latin father, of uncertain date and identity, knows the *logion* as part of a couplet:

> *Do not grieve the Holy Spirit who is in you,*
> *and do not extinguish the light which has been lit in you.*[149]

Similar language is found in Isa. 63:10, where the people of Israel are said to have "rebelled and grieved his holy Spirit"[150]—but there the commandment of God given through his prophets has been disobeyed. In the same way the Damascus document speaks of Israelites who "defiled their holy spirit" through disregard of the covenant ordinances.[151] That believers, whether Gentile or Jewish, have been "sealed" with the Spirit "against the day of redemption" has been stated above in Eph. 1:14, where the

---

[146]See p. 175 with n. 21. The phrase πρὸς οἰκοδομὴν τῆς χρείας is rendered "such as will build up where it is necessary" in BAG (*s.v.* χρεία), τῆς χρείας being treated as objective genitive. J. A. Findlay suggested that χρεία should be taken here in its rhetorical sense of "pointed saying" or "good story," and rendered the verse: "Let no unclean speech issue from your lips, but such witty talk as is useful for edification, that a pleasant impression may be left on those who listen to it" ("Ephesians iv.29," *ExT* 46 [1934-35], 429).

[147]"Grieving" the Holy Spirit is different from "quenching" him (1 Thess. 5:19), which implies the suppression of the gift of prophecy.

[148]Victorinus, *In Epistulam ad Ephesios, ad loc.* (*PL* 8.1282A).

[149]Pseudo-Cyprian, *De Aleatoribus (On Gamblers)* 3.

[150]LXX αὐτοὶ δὲ ἠπείθησαν καὶ παρώξυναν τὸ πνεῦμα τὸ ἅγιον αὐτοῦ (the verb in Eph. 4:30 is λυπεῖτε, which could have served equally well as a rendering of Heb. *'iṣṣēb*).

[151]CD 5.12; 7.4.

"redemption" is said more explicitly to be God's redemption of his own possession—that is, of his people.[152] The reminder of what they are "sealed" for should be an incentive to right living and right speaking, together with the fact that the Spirit with whom they have been sealed is God's *holy* Spirit.[153]

31 It is clear that unworthy speech is especially in view when the grieving of the Holy Spirit is mentioned: what such unworthy speech might consist of is spelled out in greater detail. It is speech which has some quality of "malice"[154] about it—speech marked by "harshness, wrath, anger, clamor, and slander."[155] Together with "malice" itself, wrath, anger, and slander are listed in Col. 3:8 as things to be put away.[156] This mention of anger as something that is bad without qualification, so soon after v. 26, suggests that to be angry without sinning is as rare as it is difficult. Harshness or bitterness is an attitude which husbands are forbidden to adopt to their wives in Col. 3:19;[157] here Christians in general are forbidden to adopt it one to another. The word translated "clamor"[158] is used to indicate all kinds of shouting; the context here shows that quarrelsome shouting or brawling is meant. In the version of Isa. 42:1-4 followed by the First Evangelist, it is said that the Servant of the Lord "will not strive or shout"[159] (Matt. 12:19); the proximity to striving suggests that quarrelsome or contentious shouting is intended, as it plainly is here.

There is a strong resemblance between this verse and 1 Pet. 2:1— "put away all malice and all guile and insincerity and envy and all slander"—although the only term strictly common to the two passages is "malice."[160] Similarly there is a strong resemblance between the positive exhortation of v. 32 and 1 Pet. 3:8—"have unity of spirit, sympathy, love of the brethren, a tender heart, and a humble mind"—although, again, there is only one term ("tenderhearted") in common.[161]

32 The converse to the unlovely attitudes of v. 31 is now recommended: a kind, tenderhearted, and forgiving spirit. All these graces, with

---

[152]See p. 266.
[153]Cf. the emphasis on τὸ ἅγιον in 1 Thess. 4:8 (τὸν καὶ διδόντα τὸ πνεῦμα αὐτοῦ τὸ ἅγιον εἰς ὑμᾶς); cf. also 1 Cor. 6:19.
[154]Gk. κακία.
[155]Gk. πικρία καὶ θυμὸς καὶ ὀργὴ καὶ κραυγὴ καὶ βλασφημία.
[156]See pp. 145-46, nn. 72-75.
[157]Gk. μὴ πικραίνεσθε πρὸς αὐτάς (see p. 164 with n. 181).
[158]Gk. κραυγή, only here in the Pauline corpus.
[159]οὐκ ἐρίσει οὐδὲ κραυγάσει (see P. E. Kahle, *The Cairo Geniza* [Oxford, ²1959], pp. 250-51); cf. LXX οὐ κεκράξεται οὐδὲ ἀνήσει.
[160]In 1 Pet. 2:1 "slander" is καταλαλιά ("backbiting"), not βλασφημία.
[161]Gk. εὔσπλαγχνοι.

others closely related, the readers of Col. 3:12-13 are urged to "put on."[162] "As the Lord forgave you," says Paul to the Colossians, "so do you also forgive." It may be asked whether "the Lord" in Col. 3:13 is God the Father or Christ, although Pauline usage suggests that Christ is meant. In practice it does not matter: in the whole work of redemption the Father and the Son act as one. But here the situation is stated unambiguously: "God in Christ forgave you."[163] It is in Christ that God has given his people their "redemption through his blood, the forgiveness of their sins" (Eph. 1:7),[164] just as it is in Christ that God was "reconciling the world to himself" (2 Cor. 5:19). The KJV rendering, "even as God for Christ's sake hath forgiven you," goes back to Tyndale, from whom it was taken over successively by Coverdale and the Geneva and Bishops' Bibles; it expresses a most important part of the apostolic meaning, but not quite all of it.

As so constantly in the teaching of Jesus, the free grace of the Father's forgiving love is the pattern for his children in their forgiveness of one another.[165]

---

[162]See pp. 153-55 with nn. 121-34. To the adjective χρηστός here corresponds the noun χρηστότης in Col. 3:12; to εὔσπλαγχνος corresponds σπλάγχνα οἰκτιρμοῦ.

[163]The verb is χαρίζομαι, as in Col. 3:13, and also in Col. 2:13 (see pp. 108-09 with nn. 87, 90). Paul uses it of his own forgiving in 2 Cor. 2:10 (quoted above, p. 362).

[164]See p. 259.

[165]See Matt. 6:12, 14-15; 18:23-35; Mark 11:25; Luke 7:41-47; 11:4.

EPHESIANS 5

(3) The Imitation of God (5:1-2)

1 *Therefore, become imitators of God, as (his) dear children,*
2 *and lead your lives in love, as Christ for his part loved us[1] and gave himself up for us,[2] an offering and sacrifice to God, yielding a fragrant odor.*

1 The readers, then, are urged to imitate their heavenly Father by showing the same large-hearted forgiveness to others as he has shown to them; by this it will be evident that they are his children, reproducing the family likeness.

The theme of imitation is a recurrent one in Paul. More than once he recommends his own example to his converts for their imitation—only because he was so careful to be an imitator of Christ (especially where it was a matter of considering the interests of others before his own, as in 1 Cor. 10:33–11:1).[3] His converts for the most part had seen no example of Christian living before he and his companions came among them and evangelized them; in teaching them how Christians ought to live he made use of practice as well as precept (the verbal precept would in any case have been worthless if it had been contradicted by apostolic practice). To those whom he had not evangelized directly and with whom he enjoyed no face-to-face acquaintance he could not recommend his personal example in the same way. But in believing the gospel they had experienced the forgiving grace of God. No higher example of the grace of forgiveness

---

[1]ὑμᾶς ("you") is read for ἡμᾶς by ℵ* A B P *al* lat^vet co.
[2]ὑμῶν is read for ἡμῶν by B *pc* lat^b.m* co.
[3]Cf. (with μιμέομαι, μιμητής, or συμμιμητής) 1 Cor. 4:16; Phil. 3:17; 1 Thess. 1:6; 2 Thess. 3:7, 9; also (in other terms) Phil. 4:9. See W. P. DeBoer, *The Imitation of Paul* (Kampen, 1962).

367

was possible: let them imitate God in this regard, the more so as they had now been adopted into his family.[4]

Jesus had taken the same line in teaching his disciples: if they showed love to their enemies and did them good, then, he said, "you will be sons of the Most High; for he is kind to the ungrateful and the selfish. Be merciful, even as your Father is merciful" (Luke 6:35-36; cf. Matt. 5:44-48).[5]

2 The example of Christ is appealed to alongside the example of God: their way of life must be marked by love, as Christ's was. He showed his love by giving himself up to death on their behalf; the practical implication is clear, even if Paul does not spell it out expressly here as John does: "by this we know love, that he laid down his life for us; and we ought to lay down our lives for the brethren" (1 John 3:16).[6]

In an earlier letter Paul manifests his personal appreciation of this love when he speaks of "the Son of God, who loved me and gave himself up for me" (Gal. 2:20). It is open to every believer to use the same language: Christ loved each one of them individually and gave himself up for them, just as he loved the whole church collectively and gave himself up for it (Eph. 5:25). Paul can speak of Christ as giving himself up (cf. Gal. 1:4)[7] and of the Father as giving him up (cf. Rom. 8:32); in the whole *ordo salutis* the Father and the Son act as one. When the Son's giving himself up is spoken of, the language of sacrifice lies ready to hand. The lifelong obedience of Christ was an acceptable sacrifice to God: willing obedience is the only kind of sacrifice that God desires.[8] His crowning act of obedience in saying "Not my will, but thine, be done" (Mark 14:36

---

[4]Imitation is not divorced from the recognition of authority: the imitation of God is the children's imitation of their Father; the imitation of Christ is the disciples' imitation of their Lord; the imitation of Paul is the converts' imitation of their apostle. See W. Michaelis, *TDNT* 4, pp. 666-73 (*s.v.* μιμέομαι κτλ); E. Schweizer, *Lordship and Discipleship*, E.T. (London, 1960); H. D. Betz, *Nachfolge und Nachahmung Jesu Christi im Neuen Testament* (Tübingen, 1967).

[5]Cf. Targ. Ps.–Jon. Lev. 22:28, "As our Father is compassionate in heaven, so you must be compassionate on earth," and, more generally, the recurrent theme of the "holiness code" in Leviticus: "You shall be holy, for I the LORD your God am holy" (Lev. 19:2, etc.).

[6]Following Christ's example is a theme that pervades the NT; cf. Matt. 10:24 par. Luke 6:40; Mark 8:34 and parallels; John 15:12; Heb. 12:2; 1 Pet. 2:21; 1 John 2:6; Rev. 14:4.

[7]The verb commonly used is the compound παραδίδωμι (as here). In Gal. 1:4 the simple verb is used: τοῦ δόντος ἑαυτὸν ὑπὲρ τῶν ἁμαρτιῶν ἡμῶν.

[8]Compare the treatment of Ps. 40:6-8 in Heb. 10:5-10, where animal sacrifices are set aside and the sacrifice of Christ is the fulfilment of his undertaking: "Lo, I have come to do thy will, O God."

and parallels), and in embracing the cross in that spirit, was preeminently acceptable. The writer to the Hebrews consistently speaks of the work of Christ in terms of sacrifice: Paul does so occasionally.[9] The "fragrant odor" of all the main types of sacrifice in the levitical ritual betokened their acceptance by God;[10] in the NT the language, like the idea of sacrifice in its totality, is transferred to the spiritual and personal realm. It is used of the perfect self-offering of Christ and of his people's dedication of themselves and their means. The one other place in the Pauline writings where this phrase—"a fragrant odor"—occurs is in Phil. 4:18, where Paul uses it of the gift which his friends in Philippi had sent him: "a fragrant odor, an acceptable sacrifice, well pleasing to God."

(4) From Darkness to Light (5:3-14)

3 *As for fornication and every form of impurity or covetousness, let such things not even be named among you: such (reticence) is fitting for holy people.*

4 *Have nothing to do with shameful talk and foolish speech or levity: such things are not fitting. (Let your conversation be marked) rather by thanksgiving.*

5 *Of this you are well aware: no fornicator or impure or covetous person (that is, an idolater)[11] has any inheritance in the kingdom which is Christ's and God's.[12]*

6 *Let no one beguile you with empty arguments: it is because of these things that the wrath of God is coming on the disobedient.*

7 *Therefore, do not become partakers with them.*

8 *Once you were darkness, but now you are light in the Lord: lead your lives as children of light—*

9 *for the fruit of light[13] (consists) in all goodness and righteousness and truth—*

[9]Cf. Rom. 3:25, where he is set forth by God as an atonement (ἱλαστήριον); Rom. 8:3, where he is sent as a sin-offering (περὶ ἁμαρτίας); 1 Cor. 5:7, where "Christ, our paschal lamb, has been sacrificed" (ἐτύθη). For the doublet προσφορὰ καὶ θυσία ("offering and sacrifice") cf. Ps. 40:6 (LXX 39:7), quoted in Heb. 10:5 (θυσίαν καὶ προσφορὰν οὐκ ἠθέλησας).

[10]Gk. ὀσμὴ εὐωδίας (representing Heb. *rêaḥ nîḥōaḥ*, first found in Gen. 8:21); it is used of the burnt-offering (Lev. 1:9, etc.), the meal-offering (Lev. 2:2, etc.), the peace-offering (Lev. 3:5, etc.), and the sin-offering (Lev. 4:31).

[11]ὅ ἐστιν εἰδωλολάτρης. For ὅ A D and the majority of cursives read ὅς, "who (is an idolater)."

[12]ἐν τῇ βασιλείᾳ τοῦ Χριστοῦ καὶ θεοῦ. For τοῦ Χριστοῦ καὶ θεοῦ P[46] and Tertullian read simply τοῦ θεοῦ, F G Ambst read τοῦ θεοῦ καὶ Χριστοῦ, 1739* reads τοῦ Χριστοῦ τοῦ θεοῦ ("of God's Christ").

[13]For φωτός P[46] D[2] Ψ and the majority of cursives, with syr[hcl], read πνεύματος (under the influence of Gal. 5:22).

10 *and approve what is well pleasing to the Lord.*[14]
11 *Have no fellowship with the unfruitful works of darkness, but rather
    expose them;*
12 *for their secret actions are shameful even to mention,*
13 *but they are all exposed when they are revealed by the light.
    For "everything that is revealed is light."*
14 *Therefore, as it is said,*
    Wake up, O thou that sleepest,
    And from the dead arouse thee,
    And Christ will shine upon thee.[15]

3 Now comes a further list of vices to be avoided, partly overlapping those already mentioned, although here it is not simply their practice, but the very mention of them, that is deprecated. The injunction, "let such things not even be named among you," does not imply a mealy-mouthed refusal to call a spade a spade,[16] after the fashion of some modern Bible versions[17] (else the vices would not be named so plainly as they are in this and similar lists); it means rather that such unholy things should not be acceptable subjects of conversation among people whom God has called to be holy. Fornication, impurity, and covetousness are included in the fivefold catalogue of vices in Col. 3:5.

4 If subjects of conversation are in view, further direction in this area of life is provided. "Shameful talk"[18] might be foul language, or it might be talk about shameful things (as v. 12 may indicate). "Foolish speech"[19] is at best a waste of time, but it can lead to grave trouble. Life is a serious matter, and provides ample material for serious and profitable discussion. The term rendered "levity" is defined by Aristotle as "cultured insolence"; he regards it as a quality characteristic of the young, who are "fond of laughter."[20] But here it is a quality not appropriate for the people of God. The Colossians have been urged to be known as thankful people

---

[14]For κυρίῳ D* F G 81* *pc* lat read θεῷ.

[15]ἐπιφαύσει σοι ὁ Χριστός, for which D* lat[b] with Marius Victorinus, Ambrosiaster, and Jerome read ἐπιψαύσεις τοῦ Χριστοῦ ("thou wilt touch Christ"). See p. 376, n. 43.

[16]The attitude recommended is not that which obtained in Roman society, which looked on such a word as *crux* ("cross") as unmentionable to ears polite (Cicero, *Pro C. Rabirio* 16).

[17]Those, for example, which persist in rendering the quite explicit term πορνεία vaguely as "immorality" or "unchastity."

[18]Gk. αἰσχρότης, with which cf. αἰσχρολογία in Col. 3:8.

[19]Gk. μωρολογία (here only in the NT).

[20]Aristotle, *Rhetoric* 2.12.1389b.11; εὐτραπελία, he says, is πεπαιδευμένη ὕβρις. In *Nicomachean Ethics* 2.7.1108a.24 it is called the mean between buffoonery (βωμολοχία) and boorishness (ἀγροιότης).

(Col. 3:15); believers have received so many blessings from God, in grace as well as in nature, that thanksgiving should be a dominant note in their speech as well as in their thought.[21]

5 As for the practitioners of the vices mentioned in v. 3, they have no part or lot in the heavenly kingdom. They are not, indeed, left without hope; the gate of repentance stands open. But those who persist in such practices—even if, by some mischance, they bear the Christian name—show thereby that they are excluded from eternal life. Paul found it necessary to warn his converts repeatedly about this. He reminds the Corinthians that "the unrighteous will not inherit the kingdom of God," and spells out what is meant by "the unrighteous" by listing practitioners of ten vices (including the three mentioned in Eph. 5:3, 5) whose way of life debars them from the kingdom.[22] He adds a note of hope, however: "And such were some of you," he says; "but you were washed, you were sanctified, you were justified in the name of the Lord Jesus Christ and in the Spirit of our God" (1 Cor. 6:9-11). But the fact that they still have to be warned against such vices shows how strong, in a pagan environment, was the temptation to indulge in them even after conversion. The warning here is made the more emphatic by the double verb with which it is introduced: "Be well assured of this," or, more probably, "you know very well."[23]

---

[21]Origen *(Commentary, ad loc.)* interpreted εὐχαριστία here as εὐχαριτία (a coinage meaning something like "the mark of fine training"); cf. O. Casel, "Εὐχαριστία–εὐχαριτία (Eph. 5, 3 f)," *BZ* 18 (1929), 84-85. J. A. Robinson *(Ephesians,* p. 198) has a valuable note in which he demonstrates that Jerome's comment *ad loc. (PL* 26, 552D-53B) is dependent on Origen.

[22]N. A. Dahl ("Der Epheserbrief und der erste Korintherbrief," in *Abraham unser Vater,* ed. O. Betz, M. Hengel, and P. Schmidt [Leiden/Köln, 1963], pp. 65-77) compares Eph. 5:5-11 with what we learn from 1 Cor. 5:9-11 about Paul's "previous" letter to Corinth, and concludes that both passages reproduce, in one form or another (as do also 1 Cor. 6:9-10; 2 Cor. 6:14–7:1), pieces of Pauline catechesis, including the warning that those who practice the vices mentioned forfeit all share in the kingdom of God; cf. further Gal. 5:21. (According to Mishnah, *Sanhedrin* 10.1-4, "all Israelites have a share in the age to come" with certain specified exceptions, including those who deny the resurrection of the dead or the heavenly origin of the Torah.)

[23]Gk. ἴστε γινώσκοντες, "(you) know, knowing." With ἴστε, second plural indicative or imperative of οἶδα, cf. ἴσασιν, third plural indicative, in Acts 26:4; the common Hellenistic replacements for these classical forms are οἴδατε, οἴδασιν. The problem whether ἴστε is to be taken as indicative or imperative here may be solved by comparing ἢ οὐκ οἴδατε . . .; (1 Cor. 6:9) and προλέγω ὑμῖν, καθὼς προεῖπον (Gal. 5:21), where the warning about failure to inherit the kingdom of God is preceded by a reminder that the readers have been told this already. So here ἴστε γινώσκοντες may be rendered "you know very well."

If, as Col. 3:5 affirms, covetousness or avarice is idolatry, it follows that the covetous or avaricious person is an idolater, as is said here: he worships the created thing (whatever the object of his covetousness may be) instead of the Creator.

The kingdom in which such persons have no inheritance is described, more fully than elsewhere, as "the kingdom which is Christ's and God's." There is a tendency in Paul's letters to reserve the phrase "the kingdom of God" for the future and eternal phase of the heavenly kingdom and to consider the kingdom of Christ as the present phase, which is destined to merge with the future phase.[24] But those whose lives are marred by the vices mentioned cannot be in any sense joint-heirs with the Christ who is at present reigning until all his enemies are subjugated, just as they cannot hope for admission to the eternal kingdom: they are self-excluded from the kingdom in all its phases—the kingdom which is both Christ's and God's.

6 Then, as now, sophistries encouraging ethical permissiveness were current; the readers are warned not to be misled by them, for they are "empty arguments," having no more substance than the "empty illusion" of another kind against which the Colossian Christians are put on their guard (Col. 2:8).[25] Those sophistries fail to reckon with God, and ignore the fact that he has set his canon against the practices and attitudes referred to—not by the imposition of an arbitrary ban but by implanting his law within the human constitution, in such a way that those who defy it reap a harvest of retribution. Whether the ongoing process of retribution is uppermost in the apostle's mind (as in Rom. 1:18-32) or the "wrath to come" at the end-time (as in 1 Thess. 1:10; 5:9), it remains true (as was said in Col. 3:6) that these are the things that incur the wrath of God. Those on whom it falls are "the disobedient" (lit., "the sons of disobedience"), as they have been called already in Eph. 2:2.[26] They are disobedient to the law of God, whether they know it in codified form or as "written on their hearts" and confirmed by the voice of conscience (Rom. 2:15).

7 "Do not become partakers with such people," the readers are warned. It is not merely associating with them that is forbidden (as the RSV has it); those who associate with them run the risk of sharing their inheritance, which is at the farthest remove possible from "the inheritance of the saints in light" in which the people of Christ have a share (Col.

---

[24]Cf. 1 Cor. 15:24, 28; Col. 1:13 (p. 52 with n. 61).
[25]With the χενοὶ λόγοι here cf. the χενὴ ἀπάτη of Col. 2:8.
[26]See p. 144 with nn. 67, 68.

1:12). The word "partakers" is literally "joint-partakers";[27] it is the word used in Eph. 3:6 to emphasize Gentile believers' full participation in the promises of God held out to faith. These two forms of "joint-partaking" are mutually exclusive.

8 "What fellowship has light with darkness?" asks Paul in another letter (2 Cor. 6:14)—the answer obviously implied being "None!"[28] For believers to be joint-partakers with the "sons of disobedience" would be for the children of light to have fellowship with the children of darkness— a moral impossibility.

The Colossian Christians were reminded that God had rescued them from the dominion of darkness and transferred them to the kingdom of his Son. This was equally true of the recipients of this companion-letter. They too had once been under the dominion of darkness but now they had become "light in the Lord." However characteristic the light–darkness vocabulary is of the thought and literature of the Qumran community,[29] there is no need to conclude that the use of this vocabulary here implies anything like direct Qumran influence.[30] In the NT the light–darkness vocabulary is a special mark of the Johannine writings, but it is not absent from Paul. "You are all sons of light and sons of the day," the Thessalonian Christians are told; "we are not of the night or of darkness" (1 Thess. 5:5); the Philippian Christians are said to "shine as lights in the world" (Phil. 2:15).[31]

The Qumran use of the light–darkness vocabulary has this in common with the NT use: it has a thoroughly ethical content. There is nothing here of the substantial dualism which the antithesis between light and darkness regularly expresses in gnostic teaching. In the NT, as at Qumran, the antithesis is between doing right and doing wrong. The children of light do the will of God; that is what is meant by the direction: "lead your lives as children of light."

9 The lives of children of light will yield the "fruit of light"—that

---

[27]Gk. συμμέτοχοι.

[28]This is one of a series of rhetorical questions introduced by the admonition: "Do not be mismated (ἑτεροζυγοῦντες) with unbelievers."

[29]Cf. 1QS 3.18-25, where the human race is divided between the lots of the prince of light and the angel of darkness, so that the "sons of light" practice truth and righteousness while the "sons of darkness" practice falsehood and iniquity; also 1QM, which lays down the "rule" for the end-time war between the sons of light and the sons of darkness.

[30]Still less is there any need to detect the influence of Zoroastrian dualism here (cf. R. Reitzenstein, *Das iranische Erlösungsmysterium*, pp. 6, 55 [n. 1], 112, 135-39).

[31]With "now you are light in the Lord" cf. Matt. 5:14-16.

is, "all goodness and righteousness and truth." The fruit of light, in fact, is identical with the "fruit of the Spirit" in Gal. 5:22-23; it is not surprising that the latter reading has found its way into the text of Eph. 5:9 in many manuscripts (including the oldest extant Pauline manuscript). This ethical sense of "fruit" seems to be unknown to the Qumran writers.

Goodness, righteousness, and truth are basic moral qualities. Goodness belongs to the "fruit of the Spirit" in Gal. 5:22 where, as a specific virtue among others, it may mean something like "generosity"; but its range of meaning is as wide as that of the adjective "good." One may think of the "good works" for which, according to Eph. 2:10, God has created his people in Christ Jesus; similarly Paul prays that the Colossians may "bear fruit in every good work" (Col. 1:10). As for righteousness, the "new man" has been described above as "created according to God in righteousness" (Eph. 4:24). Paul prays that his Philippian friends may be "filled with the fruit of righteousness" (Phil. 1:11), and the writer to the Hebrews speaks of discipline as yielding "the peaceful fruit of righteousness to those who have been trained by it" (Heb. 12:11). Truth is the antithesis of falsehood, which the readers have already been urged to "put off"; the truth of speech which they are exhorted to practice one with another (Eph. 4:25) should be the expression of that "truth in the inward being" which is divinely implanted in the children of light.

10 The followers of Christ will naturally desire to do what pleases him. This was Paul's own ambition, and he cherished the same ambition for his Christian friends (1 Cor. 4:4; 2 Cor. 5:9).[32] They should not only "try to learn what is pleasing to the Lord" (RSV) but have their minds so attuned to his that, when they have learned what pleases him, they may approve it. The same verb,[33] which is capable of both shades of meaning, is used in Rom. 12:2, where the renewing of believers' minds leads them to "prove—and thereby also to approve—what is the will of God, all that is good and acceptable and perfect." Paul similarly prays that the church of Philippi may be given spiritual discernment to "approve what is excellent" (Phil. 1:9-10).[34]

11 The "works of darkness" are called "unfruitful" because, unlike the deeds that mark out the children of light, they are dead and sterile. We may compare the antithesis between "the *works* of the flesh" and "the *fruit* of the Spirit" in Gal. 5:19, 22. (In other contexts the figure of "fruit" may be used differently, as in Rom. 6:21, where it refers to the outcome

---

[32]Cf. Col. 1:10, εἰς πᾶσαν ἀρέσκειαν. See also p. 379, n. 54.
[33]Gk. δοκιμάζω.
[34]δοκιμάζειν τὰ διαφέροντα (cf. Rom. 2:18).

of a sinful life.) There is no difference in practice between being joint-partakers with the children of darkness and sharing in their works.[35] Such works must not be condoned or excused, but exposed for what they are.

It is not necessary to go along with K. G. Kuhn and recognize here a "continuity" of Essene tradition, but he does helpfully illustrate the duty of exposing the works of darkness from Qumran literature. It is laid down as the duty of each member of the community "who sees another member breaking God's commandment . . . to rebuke the person concerned, i.e. to say to him, What you have done or are doing is not just in the eyes of God. He must not express this reprimand angrily or with pride or with hatred, but rather 'with real faithfulness, humility and merciful love.' But he must make the other aware of his sin on the same day and may not postpone the matter until the next day, otherwise he is held responsible before God for any further sinning on the part of the other."[36] The same procedure, it may be recalled, is laid down for the community of Jesus' disciples in Matt. 18:15.[37] But not only the sins of fellow-members of the community are to be rebuked: Kuhn adds that "when, according to Mark 6:18, John the Baptist comes before Herod and tells him, '. . . it is not lawful for thee to have thy brother's wife', we have an instance of the Essene practice of 'correction'."[38] (But John stood in the authentic prophetic tradition of Israel in thus pointing out to a ruler the error of his ways.)

12 If "their secret actions are shameful even to mention," why expose them to the light of day? Perhaps because exposure to the light is the best way to make them wither and die. Schlier suggests that Paul may allude to the libertine rites of many mystery cults:[39] if they were made public, they might lose their glamor (just as the spells of the Ephesian specialists in magic lost their potency when they were openly divulged, according to Acts 19:18). This could be so, but nothing in the context requires a reference to mystery cults. However, it is not by accident that the term *orgia*, used of mystery rites, has developed semantically into our word "orgies," which, in the sense which it bears for us, may be very much what is intended here: such things are "unspeakably shameful."[40]

[35] μὴ συγκοινωνεῖτε . . . (Paul uses the verb in a good sense in Phil. 4:14).
[36] K. G. Kuhn, "The Epistle to the Ephesians in the Light of the Qumran Texts," in *Paul and Qumran*, ed. J. Murphy-O'Connor (London, 1968), pp. 122-25.
[37] "If your brother commits a sin . . ." (εἰς σέ, "against you," is probably not part of the original text).
[38] K. G. Kuhn, "The Epistle to the Ephesians," p. 124, n. 8.
[39] H. Schlier, *Der Brief an die Epheser*, p. 239.
[40] J. A. Robinson, *Ephesians*, p. 201.

13 That all things are "exposed when they are revealed by the light" takes up a proverbial saying, along the lines of Luke 8:17, "For nothing is hid that shall not be made manifest, nor anything secret that shall not be known and come to light." The words of John 3:20-21 are also apposite: "For everyone who does evil hates the light, and does not come to the light, lest his deeds should be exposed; but he who does what is true comes to the light, that it may be clearly seen that his deeds have been wrought in God."

For the collocation of the verbs to be "exposed" and "revealed by the light" K. G. Kuhn compares a passage in the Damascus document, concerning an errant member of the Qumran community: "when his deeds are revealed by the light, he shall be sent away from the congregation like one whose lot has not fallen in the midst of those 'taught by God.' According to his sin shall men of discernment expose (correct) him, until the day when he shall stand again in the conclave of the men of perfect holiness."[41] But it does not appear to be fellow-Christians or their unworthy actions that are primarily in view in Eph. 5:13. If they do commit things that bring the Christian name into disrepute, then indeed their conduct calls for reproof; but the reference here is wider.

14 The paraenesis on light and darkness is clinched by a quotation, introduced by the same formula[42] as the quotation from Ps. 68:18 in Eph. 4:8, but not identifiable as a biblical text. The words quoted do indeed echo one or two OT passages—Isa. 26:19 ("O dwellers in the dust, awake and sing for joy!") and Isa. 60:1 ("Arise, shine; for your light has come, and the glory of the LORD has risen upon you"), and perhaps even Jon. 1:6 ("What do you mean, you sleeper? Arise . . .!")—but the echo, especially in Greek, is a distant one. The quotation is a tristich, best interpreted as a primitive baptismal hymn, in which the congregation greets the new convert as he or she emerges sacramentally from the sleep of spiritual death into the light of life.[43] The ethical admonition is reinforced by a call

---

[41]K. G. Kuhn, "The Epistle to the Ephesians," p. 125, in reference to CD 20.3-5 (the Hebrew verbs are the Hiph'il of *yāpa'*, "cause to shine," and the Hiph'il of *yākaḥ*, "convict," "reprove").

[42]διὸ λέγει.

[43]See, however, B. Noack, "Das Zitat in Ephes. 5:14," *ST* 5 (1951), 52-64, for its being primarily a resurrection hymn (although applicable secondarily to baptism), with comment by R. P. Martin, "Aspects of Worship in the New Testament Church," *VE* 2 (1963), 30. Noack refers to Jerome (*Commentary on Ephesians, ad loc.* [*PL* 26, 559A]), who interprets the words as addressed by Christ to Adam when releasing him from Hades (the third line of the tristich having the form *et continges Christum*, "and thou shalt touch Christ"; see p. 370, n. 15). Jerome,

to the readers to remember their baptism and its significance, just as in Rom. 6:3-4 Paul refutes the suggestion that one should "continue in sin that grace may abound" by appealing to the Roman Christians' baptismal experience: "Do you not know that all of us who have been baptized into Christ Jesus were baptized into his death? We were buried therefore with him by baptism into death, so that as Christ was raised from the dead by the glory of the Father, we too might walk in newness of life." If ever the readers of the present letter were tempted to forget that, while once they had been children of darkness, they were now children of light, let them remember their baptism and the words they heard then: they would be left in no doubt about their present status and its moral implications.

Attempts have been made to strengthen the identification of the tristich as a baptismal hymn by the argument that its rhythm is that found in the initiation formulae of various Hellenistic cults. The formula most commonly adduced is one quoted by Firmicus Maternus as uttered by the person newly initiated into the Attis mystery.[44] Such formal parallels are difficult to establish, and throw no light on the meaning of what is, in context and content, an explicitly Christian composition. Clement of Alexandria quotes this tristich and accompanies it with another tristich amplifying the reference to Christ in its third clause:

The sun of resurrection,

---

like Epiphanius (*Pan.* 1.3.46.5 [*PG* 41, 843D-45B]), says that Adam was held prisoner directly beneath the place where Christ was crucified, the name Golgotha being derived from Adam's skull, which was held to be buried there.

[44]Firmicus Maternus, *On the Error of Profane Religions* 18.1:

ἐκ τυμπάνου βέβρωκα,
ἐκ κυμβάλου πέπωκα,
γέγονα μύστης Ἄττεως

("I have eaten from the drum, I have drunk from the cymbal, I have become an initiate of Attis"). See E. Peterson, ΕΙΣ ΘΕΟΣ (Göttingen, 1926), p. 132; F. Cumont, *Les religions orientales dans le paganisme romain* (Paris, ⁴1929), p. 226, n. 46. Firmicus quotes other rhythmical formulae from a variety of mystery cults, but in different meters from this. H. Schlier mentions similar calls to wake up from sleep, drunkenness, or death in *Odes of Solomon* 8.3-5; *Acts of Thomas* 110.43-48; *Corpus Hermeticum* 1.27. They are too late to have much relevance; still later are the Mandaean analogies which he adduces (*Der Brief an die Epheser*, pp. 240-41). The same applies to Manichaean parallels quoted from Turfan texts by R. Reitzenstein, *Das iranische Erlösungsmysterium*, pp. 3, 11-12; H. Jonas, *The Gnostic Religion* (Boston, ²1963), p. 83.

Begotten before the day-star,
Who has given life with his own beams.[45]

(5) "Be Filled with the Spirit" (5:15-20)

15 *So then, be careful about your conduct:*[46] *do not live unwisely but as wise persons,*

16 *buying up the present opportunity, because the days are evil.*

17 *Therefore, do not be foolish, but discern*[47] *what the Lord's will*[48] *is.*

18 *Do not be intoxicated with wine—for with that comes dissipation—but be filled with the Spirit,*

19 *addressing one another in psalms, hymns, and Spirit-inspired songs, singing*[49] *and making melody in your hearts*[50] *to the Lord,*

20 *giving thanks at all times for everything to our God and Father*[51] *in the name of our Lord Jesus Christ.*

15 A further paraenetic paragraph now opens, setting out more general principles for Christian living. Like the Colossians, the recipients of this letter are admonished to conduct themselves wisely in the world (Col. 4:5). They form a small minority, and because of their distinctive ways their lives will be scrutinized by others: the reputation of the gospel is bound up with their public behavior. Hence the need for care and wisdom, lest the Christian cause should be inadvertently jeopardized by thoughtless speech or action on the part of Christians.

16 The injunction to "buy up the present opportunity"[52] is repeated

---

[45]Clement, *Protrepticus* 9.84.2:

ὁ τῆς ἀναστάσεως ἥλιος,
ὁ πρὸ ἑωσφόρου γεννώμενος,
ὁ ζωὴν χαρισάμενος ἀκτῖσιν ἰδίαις.

(With the second line cf. Ps. 110 [LXX 109]:3.)

[46]βλέπετε οὖν ἀκριβῶς πῶς περιπατεῖτε. The words ἀκριβῶς πῶς are transposed to πῶς ἀκριβῶς in D F G Ψ and the majority of cursives (whence KJV "See then that ye walk circumspectly"), also in ℵ² A 629 *pc* lat^vg co^bo, which insert ἀδελφοί before πῶς ἀκριβῶς.

[47]For the imperative συνίετε Ψ and the majority of cursives read the participle συνιέντες.

[48]τὸ θέλημα τοῦ κυρίου. ℵ* reads φρόνημα for θέλημα, A 81 and several cursives read θεοῦ for κυρίου, while P^46 reads Χριστοῦ.

[49]Before "singing" (ᾄδοντες) A inserts ἐν χάριτι (cf. Col. 3:16).

[50]The codices vary between τῇ καρδίᾳ (P^46 ℵ* B 1739 1881), ἐν τῇ καρδίᾳ (Ψ and the majority of cursives), and ἐν ταῖς καρδίαις (ℵ² A D F G P *al*); this last reading is influenced by Col. 3:16.

[51]For τῷ θεῷ καὶ πατρί P^46 D F G *pc* lat^vet read τῷ πατρὶ καὶ θεῷ.

[52]ἐξαγοραζόμενοι τὸν καιρόν (see p. 174, n. 17).

from Col. 4:5; in both places it has special reference to Christian witness in the world. The statement that "the days are evil" may imply that, whatever difficulties lie in the way of Christian witness now, they will increase as time goes on. It must be borne in mind not only that the present time remains an "evil age" (Gal. 1:4) even if it has been invaded by the powers of the age to come but also that, as the Corinthians were warned, "the appointed time has grown very short" (1 Cor. 7:29), so that opportunities must be exploited while they last.[53] The perspective on the end-time has not changed radically since Paul's earlier letters; moreover, from Rome to Judaea there were signs that the relative freedom from molestation currently enjoyed by Christians was liable shortly to be curtailed.

17 It is always incumbent on the people of Christ to know and to do his will—the readers have already been told to "approve what is well pleasing to the Lord" (v. 10)[54]—but it is doubly necessary in the present situation. The doing of his will is not a matter of irrational impulse but of intelligent reflection and action.

18 "Do not be intoxicated with wine" is yet another OT quotation—from Prov. 23:31 (LXX).[55] It is introduced here not so much for its own sake (although such a warning is never untimely) as for the sake of its antithesis: "be filled with the Spirit." Overindulgence in wine leads to dissipation, which is good neither for the winebibber nor for others; the fullness of the Spirit is helpful both for those who are filled with him and for those with whom they associate. The noun rendered "dissipation" appears also in Tit. 1:6 (where the children of church elders must not be chargeable with dissipation) and 1 Pet. 4:4 (in reference to the profligacy which marked the former lives of people recently converted from paganism to Christianity); the corresponding adverb is used of the "riotous living" in which the prodigal son wasted his substance (Luke 15:13).[56]

"Be filled with the Spirit" is literally "Be filled in spirit";[57] this

---

[53]Cf. Eph. 6:13, ἐν τῇ ἡμέρᾳ τῇ πονηρᾷ (in Gal. 1:4 and here in Eph. 5:16 the adjective is likewise πονηρός).

[54]With τί τὸ θέλημα τοῦ κυρίου here and τί ἐστιν εὐάρεστον in v. 10 cf. Rom. 12:2, τί τὸ θέλημα τοῦ θεοῦ, τὸ . . . εὐάρεστον.

[55]μὴ μεθύσκεσθε οἴνῳ, a paraphrase of Heb. 'al tēre' yayin ("do not look at wine . . .").

[56]ἀσωτία (ἀσώτως in Luke 15:13).

[57]πληροῦσθε ἐν πνεύματι. The Holy Spirit is "at once the Inspirer and the Inspiration," says J. A. Robinson (*Ephesians*, pp. 203-04); he discusses the force of the preposition ἐν (whether it denotes the instrumentality or the sphere) and finds support for taking it to denote instrumentality (or agency) in 1 Cor. 12:3, 13; Rom. 15:16. He takes the interpretation to be "Let your fulness be that which

has given rise to the question whether the human spirit of the believer or the Spirit of God is meant. The same phrase, "in spirit," occurs in three other places in this letter—in Eph. 2:22, with regard to the new community of believers as the dwelling-place of God; in 3:5, with regard to the revelation of the "mystery" of the new community to God's "holy apostles and prophets"; and in 6:18, with regard to the prayer life of Christians. In those three places the Holy Spirit is certainly intended, and equally certainly it is he that is intended here. The Holy Spirit is given to believers to fill them with his presence and power. The choice of drunkenness as an antithesis to the fullness of the Spirit is not unparalleled: when the disciples were all filled with the Holy Spirit on the day of Pentecost the resultant phenomena moved some of the spectators to say in derision that they were "filled with new wine" (Acts 2:13),[58] and Paul had to warn the Corinthians that a stranger, coming into their company when they were all exercising the spiritual gift of tongues, would conclude that they were mad (1 Cor. 14:23). But the Spirit given by God to his children is the Spirit "of power and love and self-control" (2 Tim. 1:7);[59] the normal exercise of intelligence is not eclipsed but enhanced when he is in control.

The antithesis between wine and the Spirit does not suggest that the Spirit is a sort of fluid with which one may be filled, any more than the collocation of baptism in water with baptism in the Spirit suggests that the Spirit is a sort of fluid in which one may be dipped.[60] Whatever grammatical constructions are used, the Spirit operates as a personal subject—"the Lord who is the Spirit" (2 Cor. 3:18).

19 If the Spirit is the source of their fullness, then, instead of songs which celebrate the joys of Bacchus, their mouths will be filled with words which build up the lives of others and bring glory to the living and true God. The reference to "psalms, hymns, and Spirit-inspired songs" is reproduced from Col. 3:16.[61] The construction of the clauses is rather different, but the general tenor is the same. The meetings of those early Christians must have been musical occasions, as they not only sang and made melody to the Lord, in their hearts as well as with their tongues,

---

comes through the Holy Spirit," but concludes that the rendering "Be filled with the Spirit," while "not strictly accurate, suffices to bring out the general sense of the passage."

[58]Gk. γλεύκους μεμεστωμένοι εἰσίν.

[59]Gk. πνεῦμα . . . δυνάμεως καὶ ἀγάπης καὶ σωφρονισμοῦ.

[60]Or which may be poured out on one, as in Acts 2:17-18, 33; Tit. 3:6 (ἐκχέω); cf. 1 Cor. 12:13b (ποτίζω). The verbs which are used primarily in reference to liquids have figurative force when they are used of the Spirit.

[61]See pp. 158-59 with nn. 149-58 for fuller discussion.

but addressed one another for mutual help and blessing in compositions already known to the community or in songs improvised under immediate inspiration. Testimonies to the prevalence of music in their fellowship and worship have been cited in the exposition and notes on Col. 3:16. One of these testimonies—Pliny's report of antiphonal singing "to Christ as God"[62]—has a bearing on both clauses in this verse, where the singing is antiphonal ("addressing one another") and is offered "to the Lord." The hymn quoted in v. 14 could serve as one example of their "addressing one another." If "singing and making melody in your hearts *to the Lord*" in the present context has as its parallel in Col. 3:16 "singing with thanksgiving in your hearts *to God*," it reminds us that in the church, from the earliest days, praise has been offered alike to God and to Christ. Thus in the Apocalypse, where the worship presented by the holy ones before the heavenly throne is echoed by the church on earth, "Worthy art thou, our Lord and God, . . . for thou didst create all things" (Rev. 4:11) has as its counterpart the "new song": "Worthy art thou, . . . for thou wast slain and by thy blood didst accomplish redemption" (Rev. 5:9), while both God and Christ are conjoined in the doxology: "To him who sits upon the throne and to the Lamb be blessing and honor and glory and might forever and ever!" (Rev. 5:13).

20 The call for thanksgiving is made again (cf. the end of v. 4) in the most comprehensive terms, in language echoing Col. 3:17.[63] The words "at all times for everything" sum up "whatever you do, in word or in action, do it all" in the Colossians passage, while ". . . in the name of the Lord Jesus, giving thanks through him to God the Father" there has as its counterpart here: "giving thanks . . . to our God and Father in the name of our Lord Jesus Christ."[64] A life filled with such thanksgiving will find spontaneous expression in psalms and hymns and spiritual songs.

5. "BE SUBJECT" (5:21–6:9)

(1) Mutual Submission (5:21)

21 *Be subject one to another in the fear of Christ.*[65]

---

[62]Pliny, *Epistles* 10.96.7, *carmenque Christo quasi deo dicere secum inuicem* ("and that they recited one to another in turns a hymn to Christ as to God"). See p. 158, n. 153.

[63]See p. 160 with nn. 159-61.

[64]It is through Christ (Eph. 2:18) or in his name that his people have access to God for all purposes, including (as here) thanksgiving.

[65]Many cursives (including 6 81 614 630 1881) read θεοῦ for Χριστοῦ (cf. KJV "in the fear of God").

21 The household code which follows (Eph. 5:22–6:9) is a special application of the Christian grace of submission;[66] it is introduced by this general exhortation to mutual submissiveness. Christians should not be self-assertive, each insisting on getting his or her own way. As the Philippian believers are told, they should be humble enough to count others better than themselves and put the interests of others before their own, following the example of Christ, who "emptied himself," "humbled himself," and "became obedient," even when the path of obedience led to death on the cross (Phil. 2:3-8). Out of reverence for their Lord, who set such a precedent, his followers should place themselves at one another's disposal, living so that their forbearance is a matter of public knowledge (Phil. 4:7), even when others are encouraged on this account to take advantage of them (1 Cor. 6:7). Even those who fill positions of responsibility and honor in the Christian community, to whom their fellow-believers are urged to render submission and loving respect (1 Cor. 16:16; 1 Thess. 5:12-13), earn such recognition by being servants, not lords (cf. 1 Pet. 5:3). For all his exercise of apostolic authority when the situation called for it, Paul invites his converts to regard him and his colleagues as "your *slaves* for Jesus' sake" (2 Cor. 4:5).[67]

(2) Wives and Husbands (5:22-33)

22 *Wives, (be subject)[68] to your own husbands as to the Lord,*
23 *for a husband is head of his wife, as also Christ is head of the church, being himself [69] savior of the body.*
24 *But as[70] the church is subject to Christ, so also let wives be to their husbands in everything.*
25 *Husbands, love your wives,[71] as also Christ loved the church and gave himself up for it,*
26 *in order to sanctify it, purifying it by the washing of water with (the) word,*

---

[66]On household codes see pp. 160-63.
[67]Cf. Rom. 12:10, τῇ τιμῇ ἀλλήλους προηγούμενοι. Christians are repeatedly reminded that in this regard they have a supreme exemplar in their Lord (cf. Mark 10:45; Luke 22:27; John 13:12-17).
[68]The unexpressed verb in this clause is supplied by ℵ A I P Ψ and many cursives (ὑποτασσέσθωσαν, "let [the wives] be subject") and by D F G and the majority of cursives (ὑποτάσσεσθε, "be subject").
[69]αὐτός is expanded to καὶ αὐτός ἐστιν in ℵ² D² Ψ and the majority of cursives.
[70]ὡς is omitted in B Ψ and a few other witnesses.
[71]ἀγαπᾶτε τὰς γυναῖκας, to which ὑμῶν is added in F G and ἑαυτῶν ("your own wives") in D Ψ and the majority of cursives.

27 *in order to present the church to himself invested with glory, free from spot, wrinkle, or anything of the sort, but holy and blameless.*

28 *So indeed*[72] *husbands ought to love their own wives as their own bodies. He who loves his own wife loves himself.*

29 *No one ever hated his own flesh but nourishes and cherishes it, as Christ*[73] *does the church,*

30 *for we are members of his body.*[74]

31 *"This is why a man will leave his father and mother*[75] *and be joined to his wife,*[76] *and the two will become one flesh."*

32 *This mystery is a deep one: I am quoting it in reference to Christ and to the church.*[77]

33 *But as for you, individually, let each man love his own wife as he loves himself, and let the wife reverence her husband.*

While the household code is introduced by a plea for mutual submissiveness,[78] the submissiveness enjoined in the code itself is not mutual. As in the parallel code in Col. 3:18–4:1, wives are directed to be subject to their husbands, children to be obedient to their parents, and slaves to their masters, but the submissiveness is not reciprocated: husbands are told to love their wives, parents to bring up their children wisely, and masters to treat their slaves considerately. As for the section dealing with wives and husbands, its distinctive feature in Ephesians is that the relationship between husband and wife is treated as analogical to that between Christ and the church.

22 No verb is expressed in v. 22, the imperative "be subject" (a

---

[72]οὕτως ὀφείλουσιν καὶ οἱ ἄνδρες (א Ψ and the majority of cursives omit καί).

[73]For ὁ Χριστός D² and the majority of cursives read ὁ κύριος.

[74]א² D F G Ψ and the majority of cursives add ἐκ τῆς σαρκὸς αὐτοῦ καὶ ἐκ τῶν ὀστέων αὐτοῦ, based apparently on Gen. 2:23 (cf. KJV).

[75]τὸν πατέρα καὶ τὴν μητέρα (the article is omitted before both πατέρα and μητέρα by B D* F G).

[76]πρὸς τὴν γυναῖκα αὐτοῦ, for which א A P 33 81 and a number of witnesses read the dative τῇ γυναικὶ αὐτοῦ.

[77]εἰς Χριστὸν καὶ εἰς τὴν ἐκκλησίαν (B K and a few witnesses omit the preposition before τὴν ἐκκλησίαν).

[78]It can indeed be argued that the plea for mutual submissiveness (v. 21) is attached to the preceding paragraph, the participle ὑποτασσόμενοι being coordinate with λαλοῦντες . . . ᾄδοντες καὶ ψάλλοντες (v. 19) and εὐχαριστοῦντες (v. 20). But it is more closely attached to what follows, supplying the unexpressed verb in v. 22. On the imperatival participle ὑποτασσόμενοι see D. Daube, "Participle and Imperative in 1 Peter," in E. G. Selwyn, *The First Epistle of St. Peter* (London, 1946), pp. 467-88. On the literary unity of vv. 21-33 see J. P. Sampley, *"And the Two shall become One Flesh": A Study of Traditions in Ephesians 5:21-33* (Cambridge, 1971), pp. 104, 109-47.

participle in the Greek text) being understood from v. 21.[79] There is no special emphasis on the pronoun "own" in "your own husbands" (as though a contrast were pointed between their own husbands and other women's husbands); it might be said that we have here an instance of the "exhausted" use of this pronoun, but it seems to have been a feature of household codes.[80]

Whereas in Col. 3:18 wives are told to be subject to their husbands "as is fitting in the Lord," the phrase here, "as to the Lord,"[81] has a rather different force. "The Lord" is certainly Christ and not the husband (despite the analogy of 1 Pet. 3:6); the singular noun does not stand in apposition to the plural "husbands." The implication rather is that Christian wives' submission to their husbands is one aspect of their obedience to the Lord. This is found to be the more appropriate when their submission to their husbands is seen to have a counterpart in the church's submission to Christ.

23 That "a husband is head of his wife" has been stated as part of the ordinance of creation in 1 Cor. 11:3, although there the sense is probably "woman's head is man" (NEB), "head" meaning "source" or "origin."[82] The reference is to the narrative of Gen. 2:21-24, where the woman is made from the man (a narrative which has influenced the thought and language of the present passage too). As Adam was the source of his wife's existence, so the husband is "head" of the wife. But in this context the word "head" has the idea of authority attached to it after the analogy of Christ's headship over the church. As in 1 Cor. 11:3-15 the argument depends on an oscillation between the literal and figurative senses of "head,"[83] so in the present argument from analogy different senses of the word are involved. For when Christ is said to be "head of the church,"

---

[79]ὑποτασσόμεναι (feminine, in agreement with γυναῖκες) is understood from ὑποτασσόμενοι in v. 21. While the ὑποταγή is reciprocal in v. 21 and unilateral in v. 22, it would be precarious to regard v. 21 "as the author's critique of the basic stance of the Haustafel form wherein one group is ordered to be submissive to another group vested with authority over it" (Sampley, "And the Two," p. 117); reciprocal submission is a basic element in Christian ethical tradition, whereas the skeleton at least of the "Haustafel form" is not exclusively Christian.

[80]On "exhausted" ἴδιος see G. A. Deissmann, Bible Studies, E.T. (Edinburgh, ²1909), pp. 123-24; MHT I, 87-90. The characteristic ἴδιος of the household codes has left traces in 1 Tim. 6:1; Tit. 2:5, 9; 1 Pet. 3:1, 5.

[81]ὡς τῷ κυρίῳ (as against ὡς ἀνῆκεν ἐν κυρίῳ in Col. 3:18).

[82]In the same context every man's head is said to be Christ, and Christ's head is God. For the sense "origin" or "source" see S. Bedale, "The Meaning of κεφαλή in the Pauline Epistles," JTS n.s. 5 (1954), 211-15.

[83]Thus in 1 Cor. 11:3-15 the dishonoring of the man's literal head implies the dishonoring of Christ; the dishonoring of the woman's literal head implies the dishonoring of her husband.

that involves the correlative figure of the church as his body (Eph. 1:22-23; 4:15-16; cf. Col. 1:18; 2:19)—a correlative which is absent from the husband-wife relationship.[84] (This is not the force of "their own bodies" in v. 28 or "his own flesh" in v. 29.)

The relevance of the appended statement that Christ is himself "savior of the body"[85] is not obvious. That Christ is the Savior of his people is the essence of the gospel, but is it implied that in some sense the husband is "savior" of the wife? An analogy has been found in Tob. 6:18 (17) where Raphael, speaking to Tobias about his cousin Sarah, who is to be his wife, says, "you will save her"—but there it is Sarah's deliverance from the disastrous attentions of the demon Asmodaeus that is in view. According to W. Foerster, Christ's being "savior of the body" is elucidated in vv. 25-27, in the sense that by his self-sacrifice he has purified the church for himself in order to present it to himself in glory at the consummation, and the conduct of husbands to their wives is to be "in some sense" parallel to this conduct on Christ's part.[86] But, it may be asked, in what sense? A reference to the husband's role as his wife's protector may be implied, but anything more detailed is difficult to discern. At the other extreme J. P. Sampley thinks that in this particular respect there is a contrast between Christ and the earthly husband: "Christ, unlike the husband, is the savior of his own body."[87] The adversative particle "but" at the beginning of v. 24 is taken to indicate that a contrast is being pointed; but even if this is so, it is not clear that this is the contrast.

24 Referring to "many commentators" who give full adversative force to the conjunction "but" at the beginning of this verse by interpreting the preceding words "as intended to enhance the headship of Christ, as being vastly superior to that of the husband" (the conjunction then meaning "but notwithstanding this difference"), J. A. Robinson points out that the conjunction need not have adversative force. It is used here rather "to fix the attention on the special point of immediate interest." The apostle, having made the general point that "it is the function of the head to plan for the safety of the body, to secure it from danger and to provide for its welfare," checks himself from a fuller exposition of this and resumes his main line of thought: "*but*—for this is the matter in hand—*as the church*

---

[84]When the husband is said to be head of the wife, it is not implied that the wife is his body. Even v. 29 does not say this.

[85]αὐτὸς σωτὴρ τοῦ σώματος (see n. 69 above).

[86]W. Foerster, *TDNT* 7, p. 1016 (*s.v.* σωτήρ); he points out rightly that the emphatic pronoun αὐτός before σωτὴρ τοῦ σώματος "shows that the author is not expounding κεφαλὴ τῆς ἐκκλησίας but wants to make a new point."

[87]Sampley, *"And the Two,"* p. 125.

is subject unto Christ, so let *the wives* be *to their husbands in everything.*"[88] This is the most satisfactory account of the connection between vv. 23 and 24, since v. 24 is largely resumptive of v. 22, adding a reference to the church's submission to Christ as the pattern for the wife's submission to her husband. That wives should be submissive to their husbands "in everything"[89] follows from the undoubted fact—too undoubted to call for specific mention—that the church is submissive to Christ in everything.[90]

25 As in Col. 3:19, husbands are exhorted to love their wives, but here the self-sacrificing love of Christ for the church is set forth as the pattern for the husband's love for his wife. This does not imply a nobler view of the institution of marriage than that expressed in the earlier Pauline letters: even there Paul shows himself to be a "philogamist,"[91] regarding matrimony as the norm for the majority of Christians and commending it as a way of life sanctified by God (1 Cor. 7:3-14). In 2 Cor. 11:2-3 he has already used the marriage relationship as a figure for the union between Christ and the church; in the present household code this figure is worked out in greater detail. It is sometimes pointed out that the Greek word for "bride" appears neither here nor in 2 Cor. 11:2-3[92]—as though its appearance were necessary when bridal language is so plainly used. In both places the bridal language is used by way of a simile; there is no reason to give ontological status to a figure of speech. The believing community is here compared to a maiden for whom Christ laid down his life that she might become his bride. In v. 2 of this chapter Paul has said that "Christ loved us and gave himself up for us";[93] now he repeats the statement,

---

[88]J. A. Robinson, *Ephesians*, pp. 124, 205. With this use of ἀλλά in v. 24 he compares that of πλήν in v. 33 below.

[89]Gk. ἐν παντί. For similar phrases used in reference to Christ cf. Eph. 1:22 (ὑπὲρ πάντα), 23 (ἐν πᾶσιν, for which see also Col. 1:18); 4:15 (τὰ πάντα). When submission ἐν παντί is enjoined on the wife, the possibility is not mentioned that obedience to her husband might sometimes clash with obedience "to the Lord."

[90]For wives' ὑποταγή to their husbands see also Tit. 2:5; 1 Pet. 3:1, 5; similarly the embryonic church orders in the NT lay down woman's ὑποταγή in teaching and other exercises ἐν ἐκκλησίᾳ (1 Cor. 14:34; 1 Tim. 2:11). It is not easy to reconcile such ὑποταγή with the ἐξουσία with which she is invested in 1 Cor. 11:10 or, in general, with the freedom with which Christ has set her free (Gal. 5:1).

[91]The term is J. M. Ford's; cf. her "St. Paul, the Philogamist," *NTS* 11 (1964-65), 326-48.

[92]Gk. νύμφη does not occur in the Pauline writings. In 2 Cor. 11:2 the RSV translates παρθένος ("virgin") as "bride" ("I betrothed you to Christ to present you as a pure bride to her one husband").

[93]Cf. also Gal. 2:20 (see p. 368 above).

except that instead of "us" the object is "the church," referred to by the feminine form of the third person singular pronoun ("her"). Christ's love for the church is a self-sacrificing love, and the same, it is implied, should be true of husbands' love for their wives. The idea of self-sacrifice inheres not in the verb "love" as such, but in its context.[94]

26 Before the bride was presented to the bridegroom she received a cleansing bath and was then dressed in her bridal array. This provides part of the imagery in Yahweh's account of his treatment of the foundling in Ezek. 16:6-14, where he reminds her that, when she reached marriageable age, "I bathed you with water . . . I clothed you also with embroidered cloth . . . and I decked you with ornaments."[95] So here, the purpose of Christ's giving himself up for the church is said to be her sanctification and cleansing with water. It is pointed out that the Hebrew verb "to sanctify" is used, in appropriate contexts, in the sense of betrothal ("to take someone apart for oneself as a wife"), so that the present passage might mean: "he gave himself up for her in order to betroth her to himself."[96] But it is unnecessary to see this special meaning here: the verb "sanctify" anticipates the adjective "holy" toward the end of v. 27.

The sanctification takes places by means of cleansing "by the washing of water with the word." The verb "cleanse" or "purify" occurs in 2 Cor. 7:1, in the exhortation: "let us cleanse ourselves[97] from every defilement of body and spirit, and make holiness perfect in the fear of God." But here it is not the believers who cleanse themselves, but Christ who cleanses them, as also in Tit. 2:14 (the only other instance of the verb in the Pauline corpus), where he is said to have given himself "for us to redeem us from all iniquity and to purify for himself a people of his own who are zealous for good deeds."[98] When believers are exhorted to purify themselves, something in the nature of ethical discipline is suggested; but

---

[94]There is much uninformed opinion on the allegedly superior quality of ἀγαπάω and ἀγάπη as such over other kinds of love (cf. p. 164, n. 180; p. 285, n. 44).

[95]The foundling is Jerusalem. Bridal language is similarly used of Yahweh and Israel in Jer. 2:2; Hos. 2:14-15. In Isa. 62:4-5 it is the land rather than the people that is married *(bᵉ'ûlāh)* to Yahweh.

[96]For this use of the pi'el of *q-d-š* see M. Jastrow, *Dictionary of the Targumim, the Talmud,* etc. (London, 1926), pp. 1319-20; K. G. Kuhn, *TDNT* 1, pp. 97-98 *(s.v.* ἅγιος); J. P. Sampley, *"And the Two,"* pp. 42-43.

[97]καθαρίσωμεν ἑαυτούς. On the critical problems of 2 Cor. 6:14–7:1 see F. F. Bruce, *1 & 2 Corinthians,* NCB (London, 1971), pp. 213-16. See also p. 371, n. 22.

[98]ἵνα . . . καθαρίσῃ (in Eph. 5:26 the aorist participle καθαρίσας is used, epexegetic of ἵνα . . . ἁγιάσῃ).

when Christ is said to purify them (as in our present passage and in Tit. 2:14), the reference is probably to his activity as baptizer.[99]

The noun translated "washing" occurs in only one other place in the NT—in Tit. 3:5, where Christ is said to have saved his people "by the washing of regeneration[100] and renewal in the Holy Spirit." The reference is to Christian initiation, in which the bestowal of the Spirit and baptism in water play a central part—the baptism involving not only the external washing but the inward and spiritual grace which it signifies. When Ananias of Damascus said to Paul, "Rise and be baptized, and wash away[101] your sins, calling on his name" (Acts 22:16), he implied that the external washing symbolized the more important inward cleansing from sin. And the participial clause, "calling on his name"[102] (that is, the name of Christ), throws light on the phrase "with the word" or "with a word" in our present text: the "word" or "utterance" is the convert's confession of the name of Christ as baptism is administered.[103] A similar emphasis, in slightly different language, is found in 1 Pet. 3:21: "baptism . . . now saves you, not as a removal of dirt from the body but as a pledge to God proceeding from a good conscience [a conscience cleansed from sin], through the resurrection of Jesus Christ." The "pledge"[104] in which the convert's pur-

[99]So also in 1 Cor. 6:11, ἀλλὰ ἀπελούσασθε, ἀλλὰ ἡγιάσθητε, ἀλλὰ ἐδικαιώθητε . . . (where ἀπολούω is used in the sense of καθαρίζω). In the fourth-century Roman church Tit. 2:14 was quoted in the eucharistic prayer of oblation: "purify for thyself a people of thine own (curiously rendered in Latin *populum circumuitalem*), zealous for good deeds" (Marius Victorinus, *Adversus Arium* 1.30; 2.8 [*PL* 8, 1063B, 1094D]).

[100]διὰ λουτροῦ παλιγγενεσίας. The noun λουτρόν occurs three times in the LXX: in Cant. 4:2; 6:6, of sheep that have "come up from the washing" (ἀπὸ τοῦ λουτροῦ), and in Sir. 34:25, where a man who contracts defilement after washing himself has gained nothing "by his washing" (τῷ λουτρῷ αὐτοῦ). It is attested as early as Homer, who uses the uncontracted form λοετρόν, always in the plural (e.g., θερμὰ λοετρά, "a hot bath," *Iliad* 22.444).

[101]Both imperatives are in the middle voice, βάπτισαι καὶ ἀπόλουσαι, where βάπτισαι might mean "get yourself baptized" or (as with verbs of washing) "baptize yourself."

[102]Gk. ἐπικαλεσάμενος τὸ ὄνομα αὐτοῦ, a locution (with Joel 2:32 as a precedent) common in Acts and Paul (Acts 2:21; 9:14, 21; Rom. 10:13; 1 Cor. 1:2).

[103]Gk. ἐν ῥήματι (ἐν being comitative). Another possibility is that the ῥῆμα was the invocation of the name of Christ by the baptizer on the person being baptized (cf. Acts 15:17 [quoting Amos 9:12]; Jas. 2:7); so H. Schlier, *Der Brief an die Epheser*, p. 257.

[104]Gk. ἐπερώτημα. For the meaning "pledge" see LSJ; cf. also G. C. Richards, "I Peter iii.21," *JTS* 32 (1931), 77; E. G. Selwyn, *The First Epistle of St. Peter*, pp. 205-06. The meaning "prayer to God for a good conscience" is defended by H. Greeven, *TDNT* 2, pp. 688-89 (*s.v.* ἐπερώτημα).

ified conscience makes its response to the saving act of God in Christ is the "word" which here accompanies the "washing of water."

If "baptism is a sacrament, wherein the washing with water in the name of the Father, and of the Son, and of the Holy Ghost, doth signify and seal our ingrafting into Christ . . . and our engagement to be the Lord's,"[105] the engagement, which is made in the heart but expressed with the lips, is the "word" of Ephesians and the "pledge" of 1 Peter. "Each individual member of the Church had become dedicated to God at the time of his symbolic purification from sin; and what happened to each separate individual is said to have happened to the entire New Society";[106] the whole church, personified as a bride, is said in effect to have been "washed, . . . sanctified, . . . justified in the name of the Lord Jesus Christ and in the Spirit of our God" (1 Cor. 6:11).[107]

27 In his earlier bridal analogy (2 Cor. 11:2) Paul speaks of himself as the *paranymphios* whose role it is to "present" the church to Christ "as a pure virgin."[108] He may have been acquainted with the Jewish conception of Moses as fulfilling a similar role in presenting Israel as a bride to Yahweh (although this is not attested in literature until later).[109] Without the bridal imagery he speaks in Col. 1:28 of his purpose "to present everyone perfect in Christ."[110] There, as in 2 Cor. 11:2, the time of the presentation is probably the *parousia* of Christ; and here it is evidently at his *parousia* that Christ plans "to present the church to himself."[111] But here Christ is his own *paranymphios*, just as he has already done all that is necessary to make the church fit to be presented to him as his bride—sanctified and purified and now (at the *parousia*) "invested with glory."[112] So John in the Apocalypse sees the bride, the holy Jerusalem, "having the glory of God" (Rev. 21:9-11). The royal bride in Ps. 45:13 is described as "all-glorious within, clothed in gold embroidery"; the adornment of the glorified church is the perfection of character with which her Lord has endowed her, so that she is "free from spot, wrinkle, or

---

[105]*Westminster Shorter Catechism,* answer to Q. 94.
[106]A. Borland, "Baptism in Ephesians," *The Believer's Magazine* 64 (1954), 174.
[107]See n. 99 above.
[108]See n. 92 above. The noun παρανύμφιος (or παράνυμφος) does not occur in the NT; it is synonymous with the phrase φίλος τοῦ νυμφίου used of John the Baptist's relation to Christ in John 3:29.
[109]*Mekhilta* on Exod. 19:17; *ExR* 46.1 on Exod. 34:1. The Hebrew term is šôšᵉbîn.
[110]Cf. Col. 1:22 (see pp. 78-79). The verb is παρίστημι/παριστάνω, on which see B. Reicke, *TDNT* 5, pp. 840-41.
[111]See J. Jeremias, *TDNT* 4, pp. 1104-05 (*s.v.* νύμφη).
[112]ἵνα παραστήσῃ αὐτὸς ἑαυτῷ ἔνδοξον τὴν ἐκκλησίαν.

anything of the sort."[113] The OT law envisaged a situation in which a husband, having married a wife, might find "something unseemly"[114] in her (Deut. 24:1); no such possibility exists for the glorified church, whom her Lord has fitted for himself and graced with all the "seemliness" that he could desire to find in her. Spots, wrinkles,[115] and the like are physical blemishes which might make an earthly bride distasteful to her bridegroom; here they are spiritual and ethical defects, which have been removed by the Lord's sanctifying and cleansing act.

Thus the purpose of his sanctifying and cleansing act has been achieved: that the church should be "holy and blameless." In Eph. 1:4 the purpose for which God chose his people in Christ "before the world's foundation" is said to be that they should be "holy and blameless before him."[116] Similarly, in Col. 1:22, believers are told that Christ has reconciled them to God by his death "in order to present you holy, blameless, and irreproachable in his presence"—and there, be it noted (as in Eph. 5:27), it is Christ who presents them. The adjectives which are used in the plural in those two passages to describe individual believers are used here in the singular to describe the church.[117]

To this picture of the church's being presented to Christ as his bride analogies have been found in the "sacred marriage"[118] of ancient ritual and in the "heavenly syzygy"[119] of some gnostic schemes. But such analogies are fortuitous; they are certainly not conscious. The sacred marriage of the fertility cults was designed to ensure the production of fruit; no such idea is present here. The gnostic "syzygy" probably owes something

[113]The fine linen in which the bride of the Apocalypse is arrayed symbolizes "the righteous deeds of the saints" (Rev. 19:8).

[114]Heb. 'erwaṭ dāḇār (LXX ἀσχημον πρᾶγμα), on the interpretation of which the rabbinical schools differed.

[115]The Gk. words are σπίλος (cf. 2 Pet. 2:13, σπίλοι καὶ μῶμοι, the only other NT occurrence) and ῥυτίς (here only in the Greek Bible).

[116]See p. 255.

[117]Gk. ἁγία καὶ ἄμωμος. For μῶμος ("blemish") cf. Cant. 4:7, ὅλη καλὴ εἶ, ἡ πλησίον μου, καὶ μῶμος οὐκ ἔστιν ἐν σοί.

[118]On the ἱερὸς γάμος see H. Schlier, *Der Brief an die Epheser*, pp. 264-76; also R. A. Batey, "Jewish Gnosticism and the 'Hieros Gamos' of Eph. v.21-33," *NTS* 10 (1963-64), 121-27; "The μία σάρξ Union of Christ and the Church," *NTS* 13 (1966-67), 270-81.

[119]"Die himmlische Syzygie" is the title of ch. 6 of H. Schlier's *Christus und die Kirche im Epheserbrief* (pp. 60-75). One may compare the "mystery of the bridal chamber" in the *Gospel of Philip* (68, etc.) and other Nag Hammadi treatises; this was apparently a sacramental reunification of the original androgyne. A similar sacrament seems to have been celebrated by the Marcosians (Irenaeus, *Haer.* 1.14.2) and the Simonians (Hippolytus, *Ref.* 6.18.2–19.5).

to the bridal terminology of the present passage and related NT texts. If a background for this terminology is sought, the OT portrayal of Israel as the bride of Yahweh provides all the background necessary.[120]

28 The statement that "husbands ought to love their own wives as their own bodies" applies to this special relationship the more general commandment of Lev. 19:18, "you shall love your neighbor as yourself."[121] There is a reason for the use of "their own bodies" in place of "themselves," but the echo of the second of the two great commandments is scarcely to be missed. In more than one place in the Talmud this commandment is quoted as a reason for the husband's behaving toward his wife with propriety, "lest he find something repulsive in her."[122] And the same word translated "neighbor," in its feminine form, is used repeatedly by the lover in the Song of Songs when addressing his beloved or speaking about her to others (Cant. 1:9, 15; 2:2, 10, 13; 4:1, 7; 5:2; 6:4).[123]

The locution "as their own bodies" instead of "as themselves" is due to the influence of Gen. 2:24, the text quoted in v. 31 below. Since husband and wife are "one flesh" or one body, to love one's wife is not merely a matter of loving someone else *as* oneself; it is in effect loving oneself. Adam recognized Eve as "bone of my bones and flesh of my flesh" (Gen. 2:23); to love her therefore was to love part of himself. Hence, "he who loves his own wife loves himself."

29 That it is natural to love oneself is evident from the way in which most people care for themselves, and especially for their bodies. They feed their bodies, clothe their bodies, and do what they can for their comfort. To the statement that "no one ever hated his own flesh" it might be replied that some people have practiced severity to their bodies, starving them, subjecting them to all sorts of discomfort, flagellating them, and so forth. But such "severity to the body" is unnatural; it is deprecated in Col. 2:23 as powerless to promote true humility. It is natural conduct that is in view in the present context: just as a man provides for his own comfort and well-being, so he should provide for his wife's. Again, Christ is invoked as the perfect exemplar: he makes every provision for the church.

---

[120]See p. 387 with n. 95. On the church as the bride of Christ see C. Chavasse, *The Bride of Christ* (London, 1940), pp. 72-85; P. S. Minear, *Images of the Church in the New Testament* (Philadelphia, 1960), pp. 54-56, 218-20; E. Best, *One Body in Christ* (London, 1955), pp. 169-83.

[121]The simple reflexive (ὡς ἑαυτόν) is used in v. 33 below.

[122]E.g., TB *Qiddušin* 41a; *Niddāh* 17a (in both places "something repulsive" is *dᵉḇar mᵉḡînāh*).

[123]He calls her *ra'yātî* (LXX ἡ πλησίον μου, as in the quotation in n. 117 above); correspondingly, she calls him *rē'î* (LXX πλησίον μου) in Cant. 5:16.

It is hardly necessary to say that the expression "his own flesh" has nothing to do with the distinctive Pauline use of "flesh" in the sense of that basically perverted element in human nature which puts self in the place of God;[124] it is simply a synonym of "his own body" (under the influence of "one flesh" in Gen. 2:24).[125]

30 Because "we are members of his body," and collectively "his body," Christ "nourishes and cherishes" us. The church as the body of Christ and the church as the bride of Christ are two concepts with distinct origins, but a link between the two is found in Gen. 2:24, where husband and wife become "one flesh." The fact that "no one ever hated his own flesh" underlies the maxim that one should love one's neighbor—and preeminently one's wife—*as oneself.* Christ's love for his "neighbor," and preeminently for the church, is the paradigm for a husband's love of his wife; the paradigm is made the more effective by importing into it the thought of the church as the body of Christ, already expounded in this letter, together with the thought of individual believers as members of his body.[126]

The phrase "of his body" was later amplified by the epexegetic "of his flesh and of his bones" (as in the KJV). These additional words are self-evidently derived from Gen. 2:23. H. Schlier may be right in detecting an antignostic tendency in their insertion here; he points out that Irenaeus uses them as an antignostic argument.[127]

31 What has been said thus far about the unity of husband and wife is now reinforced by an OT quotation. In Gen. 2:24, after describing how woman was taken from the side of man to be his companion, the narrator adds the comment: "This is why a man[128] will leave his father and mother and be joined to his wife, and the two will become one flesh."

---

[124]See Eph. 2:3 (pp. 283-84).

[125]Cf. 1 Cor. 6:16, where εἰς μίαν σάρκα is quoted from Gen. 2:24 LXX (as in v. 31 below), but in the application of the text ἓν σῶμα is used instead of μία σάρξ. See R. H. Gundry, *"Sōma" in Biblical Theology,* pp. 64-65.

[126]See J. Horst, *TDNT* 4, pp. 561-67, especially p. 566 (*s.v.* μέλος). Paul tells the Corinthians similarly that their bodies are τὰ μέλη τοῦ Χριστοῦ (1 Cor. 6:15). A purely verbal parallel is Seneca's expression of a Stoic tenet: "omne . . . quo diuina et humana conclusa sunt, unum est: membra sumus corporis magni" (*Epistulae Morales* 15.95.52).

[127]H. Schlier, *Der Brief an die Epheser,* p. 261, n. 1, citing Irenaeus, *Haer.* 5.2.3 (and Tertullian, *De anima* 11). Cf. Luke 24:39, where the risen Christ says, "a spirit has not flesh and bones, as you see that I have."

[128]Gk. ἄνθρωπος, following the LXX, where ἀνήρ (rendering Heb. *'îš*) would have been more appropriate, now that the original ἄνθρωπος (*'ādām*) had been differentiated into ἀνήρ (*'îš*) and γυνή (*'iššāh*).

392

In Jesus' response to a question about divorce in Mark 10:6-8 this comment is attached to the statement that "from the beginning of creation 'God made them male and female' " (Gen. 1:27);[129] the two texts together constitute an argument against divorce: "What therefore God has joined together, let not man put asunder" (Mark 10:9). (In the parallel passage in Matt. 19:4-5 the comment of Gen. 2:24 is quoted as an utterance of God: "he who made them from the beginning made them male and female, *and said,* 'This is why a man will leave his father and mother. . . .' ")[130]

It is evidently by sexual union that husband and wife are viewed as becoming "one flesh"; indeed, in 1 Cor. 6:16 Paul applies Gen. 2:24 to the most casual intercourse with a prostitute: "Do you not know that he who joins himself to a harlot becomes one body with her?" (In taking this line, it has been said, Paul "displays a psychological insight into human sexuality which is altogether exceptional by first-century standards," insisting that the sexual act is one "which, by reason of its very nature, engages and expresses the whole personality in such a way as to constitute a unique mode of self-disclosure and self-commitment.")[131] In 1 Cor. 6:17, by analogy (and contrast) with the "one flesh" or "one body" union of man and woman, the union of the believer and Christ is said to be one of spirit: "whoever is joined to the Lord is one spirit." But the body language of Ephesians makes it natural for the union both of husband and wife and of Christ and the church to be equally expressed in terms of "one body."

Referring to the use of Gen. 2:24 in rabbinical *halakhah* as providing a basis for divorce, J. P. Sampley asks, "Could the author of Ephesians be confronted with a need to reclaim Gen. 2:24 as . . . grounds for marriage, not divorce?"[132]

32 "This mystery is great" apparently refers to the scripture just quoted (Gen. 2:24). Attempts have been made to understand "mystery" here in a sense similar to that which it has earlier in Ephesians,[133] but this is not easy. The "mystery" of Eph. 3:3-4, made known to Paul and man-

---

[129]In CD 4.21–5.1 these words from Gen. 1:27 (described as $y^e s\hat{o}d\ habb^e r\hat{\imath}' \bar{a}h$, corresponding to ἀρχὴ κτίσεως of Mark 10:6) are combined with Gen. 7:9 to form an argument against plurality of wives.

[130]Cf. J. W. Wenham, *Christ and the Bible* (London, 1972), p. 28.

[131]D. S. Bailey, *Sexual Relation in Christian Thought* (New York, 1959), pp. 9-10. The introduction of the question in 1 Cor. 6:16 by ἢ οὐκ οἴδατε; may imply that the Corinthian Christians had already received oral instruction on this matter.

[132]"And the Two," p. 57, n. 2; he refers to M. R. Lehmann, "Gen 2,24 as the Basis for Divorce in Halakhah and New Testament," *ZAW* 31 (1960), 263-67.

[133]As by J. P. Sampley, *"And the Two,"* pp. 86-96.

ifested by his ministry, relates more particularly to the incorporation of believing Gentiles along with believing Jews as fellow-members of the one body of Christ. While the conception of the church as the body of Christ finds expression in the present context, it is incidental to the portrayal of the church as his bride, and the inclusion of Gentiles as well as Jews in the body receives no mention here. Here it is not God's eternal plan of salvation in Christ that is in view so much as the relationship of life and love between Christ and the church, of which the husband-wife relationship is treated as a parable.[134] It has, indeed, been suggested that "mystery" in this verse has much the same sense as "parable"; but it is better to take it as a reference to the OT text reproduced in the previous sentence.[135]

We have, in fact, an example here of the principle of exegesis found regularly in the Qumran commentaries and not unknown in the NT. To the Qumran commentators a text of scripture was a mystery, a *rāz*, as they called it in Hebrew.[136] They treated all OT scripture as prophetic, and believed that, when God made known his purpose to the prophets, he revealed so much, but withheld part (especially the part relating to the time of its fulfilment).[137] Thus the text of scripture, while it embodied a divine revelation, remained a mystery until God made known the interpretation to someone else. (In the belief of the Qumran community, this "someone else" was the Teacher of Righteousness, "to whom God disclosed all the mysteries of the words of his servants the prophets,"[138] enabling him thus "to show to the last generations what God was about to do to the last generation.")[139] So here, Gen. 2:24, which on the surface explains why a man will leave his parents' home and live with his wife, is taken to convey a deeper, hidden meaning, a "mystery," which could not be understood until Christ, who loved his people from eternity, gave himself up for them in the fullness of time. In the light of his saving work,

[134]Cf. W. Munro, *Authority in Paul and Peter*, p. 34.
[135]See also G. Bornkamm, *TDNT* 4, p. 823 (*s.v.* μυστήριον); R. E. Brown, "The Semitic Background of the New Testament *Mysterion*, II," *Biblica* 40 (1959), 70-87, especially 83-84.
[136]See F. F. Bruce, *Biblical Exegesis in the Qumran Texts* (Grand Rapids/London, 1960), pp. 7-11. The word *rāz* is of Persian origin; in the OT it occurs only in the Aramaic section of Daniel (2:18-19, 27-30, 47; 4:9), where the Greek versions render it by μυστήριον.
[137]1QpHab 7.1-2 (on Hab. 2:2). So, in 1 Pet. 1:10-11 the OT prophets were not told "what person or time" was indicated in the oracles which they uttered under inspiration; not until their fulfilment was it understood that the person was Jesus and the time was now (cf. Peter in Acts 2:16).
[138]1QpHab 7.4-5 (on Hab. 2:2, "so he may run who reads it").
[139]CD 1.11-12.

the hidden meaning of Gen. 2:24 now begins to appear: his people constitute his bride, united to him in "one body." The formation of Eve to be Adam's companion is seen to prefigure the creation of the church to be the bride of Christ. This seems to be the deep "mystery" contained in the text, which remains a mystery no longer to those who have received its interpretation.[140]

The following words, "but *I* am speaking with reference to Christ and to the church," seem to contrast the writer's preferred interpretation with other interpretations: the pronoun "I" is emphatic.[141] But it is difficult to discover what the rival interpretations of the text might be, or who might have propounded them. "It is possible," says J. P. Sampley, "that it is the recipients of Ephesians who have chosen Gen. 2:24 and have drawn conclusions about the relationship between a husband and a wife or perhaps about the relationship between Christ and the church"—conclusions which were deemed "dangerous and worthy of refutation"[142]—but on this there can be no certainty. What does seem to be certain is that Gen. 2:24 is being applied here to the relationship between Christ and the church.

33 The paragraph about the mutual duties and responsibilities of husband and wife, which has launched out into the realm where Christology embraces ecclesiology, is now concluded with an admonitory summing up in which these mutual duties and responsibilities are briefly recapitulated. "Do you at least grasp this"[143]—the practical lesson to be learned from the excursus on Christ and the church—that the husband is to love his wife as himself (a further echo of the commandment about neighborly love in Lev. 19:18), and that the wife is to reverence her husband.[144] The verb "to reverence" is the ordinary verb meaning "to fear"; the character of the "fear" is suggested by v. 21: "Be subject one to another in the fear of Christ."[145] "Fear" in the sense of terror is not in the picture here: "there

---

[140]Cf. J. Coppens, " 'Mystery' in the Theology of St. Paul and its Parallels at Qumran," E.T. in *Paul and Qumran*, ed. J. Murphy-O'Connor (London, 1968), pp. 132-58, especially pp. 146-50.

[141]ἐγὼ δὲ λέγω εἰς Χριστὸν καὶ εἰς τὴν ἐκκλησίαν. M. Smith (*Tannaitic Parallels to the Gospels* [Philadelphia, 1951], p. 28) points out that the repeated ἐγὼ δὲ λέγω of Matt. 5:22-44 has parallels in rabbinical sayings of the tannaitic period where "a legal opinion contradicting that generally accepted" is introduced.

[142]*"And the Two,"* p. 100, n. 2.

[143]So J. A. Robinson, *Ephesians*, p. 209; he regards the use of πλήν in πλὴν καὶ ὑμεῖς here as "closely parallel" to that of ἀλλά in v. 24 above (see p. 386 with n. 88).

[144]The conjunction ἵνα in ἵνα φοβῆται τὸν ἄνδρα has imperatival force.

[145]ἐν φόβῳ Χριστοῦ.

is no fear in love" (1 John 4:18).[146] It is fear in the sense of terror that is excluded in the exhortation to Christian wives in 1 Pet. 3:6, where they are assured that they are true daughters of Sarah "if you do right and are not made afraid by any intimidation."[147] (Sarah, as 1 Pet. 3:6 has recalled, showed her husband reverence by calling him "my lord,"[148] but the patriarchal narrative nowhere implies that she lived in fear of him: her record is marked by laughter[149] rather than terror.)

[146]φόβος οὐκ ἔστιν ἐν τῇ ἀγάπῃ.
[147]. . . καὶ μὴ φοβούμεναι μηδεμίαν πτόησιν.
[148]Gen. 18:12, where she calls Abraham 'ăḏōnî (ὁ . . . κύριός μου).
[149]Gen. 18:12; 21:6.

EPHESIANS 6

(3) Children and Parents (6:1-4)

1 Children, obey your parents in the Lord;[1] for this is right.
2 "Honor your father and mother" —that is[2] the first commandment accompanied by a promise—
3 "so that it may go well with you and you may live a long time on earth."
4 Fathers, do not make your children angry, but bring them up in the training and instruction of the Lord.

1 The directions to children and parents are quite similar to those in Col. 3:20-21, although that to children is reinforced by an OT quotation.

The phrase "in the Lord" is of doubtful authenticity. It is in any case a Christian household that is envisaged; there is no question here of Christian children's being told to obey their (possibly non-Christian) parents except where such obedience would conflict with their duty "in the Lord."[3] Attempts to establish dependence of the Ephesians passage on its counterpart in Colossians, or *vice versa*, are totally inconclusive.[4]

2-3 This direction is undergirded by the quotation of the fifth com-

---

[1] ἐν κυρίῳ *om* B D* F G lat[b] Marcion Clem.-Alex. Cypr. Ambst.
[2] ἥτις ἐστίν (B omits ἐστίν).
[3] See exposition of Col. 3:20 (p. 165).
[4] C. L. Mitton (*The Epistle to the Ephesians*, pp. 70-71) argues that the "twofold adaptation" of Col. 3:25—the change of the "warning note of severity" ("he who does wrong . . .") to a "sentence of encouragement" ("whatever good thing each one does . . .") and the transferring of the statement about "no favoritism" from the direction to slaves to the direction to masters—"is best explained as a later modification by the writer of Ephesians." On the other hand, W. Munro (*Authority in Paul and Peter*, p. 31) argues that Col. 3:18–4:1 is later than Ephesians as a whole and Eph. 5:21–6:9 in particular, since (among other things) Col. 3:20 "has the appearance of a conflation combining Eph. 5:10 with 6:1."

mandment of the Decalogue, quoted according to Deut. 5:16 rather than Exod. 20:12, from which the clause "so that it may go well with you" is absent (on the other hand, part of Deut. 5:16 is missing from this quotation).[5] The "promise" which accompanies this commandment[6] is the promise of prosperity and long life; no such promise is attached to any of the four preceding commandments. In the original form of the commandment (both in Exod. 20:12 and in Deut. 5:16) the long life is to be enjoyed "in the land which the LORD your God gives you," that is, in the land of Israel; such a limitation would be inappropriate in a Gentile-Christian context, so the final adjective clause is omitted and "in the land" understood as "on the earth."[7] Verse 3 may be designed mainly to state what the attached promise is; in what sense prosperity and long life might be assured to Christians in the Roman Empire in the second half of the first century A.D. is uncertain. The chief point of the quotation of the fifth commandment may be to confirm that obedience to parents is "right"[8] because it is enjoined in the law of God.

The fifth commandment was cited by Jesus as an example of a divine ordinance which was nullified in practice by a rabbinical ruling, current in his day, regarding the law of vows (Mark 7:9-13).[9]

4 As in Col. 3:21, fathers (or parents) are urged not to assert their authority over children in a manner more calculated to provoke resentment than ready obedience. The verb expressing such unreasonable parental conduct is different from that in the parallel passage, but the general sense is the same.[10] Where Col. 3:21 adds the clause "lest they be disheartened," the Ephesians injunction recommends a better course of action: "bring them up in the training and instruction of the Lord."[11] The "training and instruction of the Lord" would involve following Christ's example, with due regard to his "meekness and gentleness" (2 Cor. 10:1), as well as putting into practice his precepts. And the children will the more readily

---

[5]In Deut. 5:16 the main imperative clause is followed by "as the LORD your God commanded you" (presumably a reference back to Exod. 20:12). In the LXX (followed here) the MT clauses "that your days may be prolonged" and "that it may go well with you" are transposed.

[6]ἐν ἐπαγγελίᾳ, with comitative ἐν.

[7]Gk. ἐπὶ τῆς γῆς (omitting ἧς κύριος ὁ θεός σου δίδωσίν σοι).

[8]Gk. τοῦτο γὰρ ἐστιν δίκαιον (whereas in Col. 3:20 such obedience is εὐάρεστον . . . ἐν κυρίῳ).

[9]The ruling criticized by Jesus, according to which money which might have been used to help one's parents must not be used for that purpose if it had already been devoted to God (qorbān), was effectively annulled before the end of the first century A.D. by Eliezer ben Hyrcanus and his colleagues (Mishnah, Nᵉdārîm 9.1).

[10]Here μὴ παροργίζετε, as compared with Col. 3:21 μὴ ἐρεθίζετε.

[11]Gk. ἐν παιδείᾳ καὶ νουθεσίᾳ κυρίου.

learn these lessons if the parents themselves show the way—by following Christ's example and practicing his precepts. The only other occurrence of the word "training" in the Pauline corpus is in 2 Tim. 3:16, where inspired scripture is said to be "profitable" (among other things) "for training in righteousness."[12] In Heb. 12:5-11 it appears four times in the sense of "discipline" or even "chastisement." The word "instruction" is also used in relation to OT scripture—in 1 Cor. 10:11, where the record of Israel's rebellion in the wilderness is said to have been "written for our instruction."[13] It carries with it the sense of admonition and sometimes of warning, as in Tit. 3:10, where a factious man is to have no more time wasted over him "after a first and second warning."[14]

J. A. Robinson compares the injunction to a parent in *Didache* 4.9: "You shall not withhold your hand from your son or daughter, but teach them the fear of God from their youth up."[15] Only, in the NT household codes nothing is said (explicitly, at any rate) about corporal punishment.

(4) Slaves and Masters (6:5-9)

5 *Slaves, obey your earthly masters with fear and trembling, in the sincerity of your heart,[16] as (you obey) Christ,*

6 *not by way of eye-service, as men-pleasers, but as slaves of Christ, doing the will of God heartily,*

7 *rendering service with goodwill, as to the Lord[17] and not to human beings.*

8 *You should know that, whatever good thing each one does, this is what he will receive from the Lord, whether he is a slave or a free person.*

9 *As for you masters, do the same to them; give up threatening, for you know that both their master and yours is in heaven, and there is no favoritism with him.*

5 The directions to slaves and masters follow those in Col. 3:22–4:1 quite closely, and the exposition of those verses will for the most part be

---

[12]πρὸς παιδείαν τὴν ἐν δικαιοσύνῃ.

[13]ἐγράφη δὲ πρὸς νουθεσίαν ἡμῶν.

[14]αἱρετικὸν ἄνθρωπον μετὰ μίαν καὶ δευτέραν νουθεσίαν παραιτοῦ.

[15]Gk. ἀπὸ νεότητος, with which cf. ἐκ νεότητος, Mark 10:20 par. Luke 18:21; Acts 26:4; also 2 Tim. 3:15, ἀπὸ βρέφους. This passage in the *Didache* belongs to a truncated household code, of which only the directions to parents, masters, and slaves are reproduced (4.9-11). See nn. 20, 33 below.

[16]ἐν ἁπλότητι τῆς καρδίας (τῆς *om* ℵ 1739 1881 *al*, in conformity with Col. 3:22).

[17]ὡς τῷ κυρίῳ (ὡς *om* K L Ψ *al*, perhaps in conformity with Col. 3:24, τῷ κυρίῳ Χριστῷ δουλεύετε).

applicable here too. The phrase "with fear and trembling" is a recurring one in Paul (cf. 1 Cor. 2:3; 2 Cor. 7:15; Phil. 2:12); it appears a number of times in the Septuagint.[18] Here it probably catches up the phrase "in the fear of Christ" in Eph. 5:21.[19] It is Christ rather than their earthly masters that slaves should fear, although the fear of Christ will teach them to show due reverence and respect to their earthly masters (lit., their "masters according to the flesh," as in Col. 3:22). In serving their earthly masters they will bear in mind that they are primarily serving Christ.[20]

The words "in sincerity of heart" are used by David of himself in the Septuagint version of 1 Chron. 29:17, where the Hebrew text means "in the uprightness of my heart."[21] J. B. Lightfoot suggests the translation here and in Col. 3:22: "with undivided service";[22] he compares the exordium of the book of Wisdom, where the rulers of the earth are called upon to seek the Lord "with sincerity of heart."[23]

6 "Not by way of eye-service, as men-pleasers" practically repeats Col. 3:22: "not with eye-service, as men-pleasers." J. B. Lightfoot regarded "eye-service" as a "happy expression" and thought that it might be Paul's own coinage.[24] The contrast between being a slave of Christ and a pleaser of men is pointed by Paul, with reference to his own policy, in Gal. 1:10.[25] There is indeed one place in his letters where he speaks of himself as "pleasing everybody in everything," but there he means putting other people's preferences before his own for the gospel's sake, "not seeking my own advantage but that of the many, that they may be saved" (1 Cor. 10:33).

Doing the will of God "heartily"—from the heart or from the

---

[18]Gk. μετὰ φόβου καὶ τρόμου, used here, as in Phil. 2:12, of a proper spirit of Christian reverence.

[19]Cf. Col. 3:22, φοβούμενοι τὸν κύριον.

[20]In *Didache* 4.11 slaves are directed to be subject to their masters "as to the representative of God" (ὡς τύπῳ θεοῦ).

[21]Heb. *bᵉyōšer lᵉbābî.*

[22]J. B. Lightfoot, *Colossians and Philemon,* p. 228.

[23]Wisdom 1:1, ἐν ἁπλότητι καρδίας.

[24]"At least there are no traces of it earlier"; he compares ὀφθαλμόδουλος in *Apostolic Constitutions* 4.12 (*Colossians and Philemon,* p. 228). See p. 168, n. 206. There is probably no significance in the prepositional variation between κατ' ὀφθαλμοδουλίαν here and ἐν ὀφθαλμοδουλίᾳ in Col. 3:22 (cf. W. Munro, *Authority in Paul and Peter,* p. 32).

[25]W. Munro concludes that the present passage is a conflation of Gal. 1:10 with Eph. 1:18 (πεφωτισμένους τοὺς ὀφθαλμοὺς τῆς καρδίας ὑμῶν), Col. 3:22 being then dependent on Eph. 6:6 (*Authority in Paul and Peter,* pp. 28-29). This is quite improbable.

soul²⁶—is set in contrast (as in Col. 3:23, "whatever you do, do it heartily") with eye-service.

7 Eye-service may pass muster for a time when one is working for an earthly master, but the Lord judges by the heart and not by outward appearance. Even if the work to be done for an earthly master were tedious and burdensome, if the Christian slave looked on it as a service rendered "to the Lord and not to human beings" that would transform his attitude to it and enable him to do it with "the ready good will, which does not wait to be compelled" (J. A. Robinson).²⁷

8 "You should know,"²⁸ the apostle adds—implying that what he is about to say is a piece of common Christian catechesis—that each person will receive from the Lord a recompense for what he or she has done; and it makes no difference whether one is enslaved or free.²⁹ The time when the recompense will be awarded appears from other Pauline references to be the advent of Christ, when his people will be manifested before his tribunal.³⁰ In Col. 3:25 the one who does wrong will be requited for that wrongdoing; here it is the good deed that is fittingly rewarded. The Pauline teaching echoes the dominical logion of Matt. 16:27, which declares that when the Son of Man comes in glory, "then he will render to everyone according to what he has done."³¹

9 When masters are told to "do the same" to their slaves,³² the sense is that they are to treat their slaves with Christian consideration, the spirit with which Christian slaves are to obey their masters. They should make it easy for their slaves to work for them with goodwill. Threatening with punishment, or harsh language and behavior in general, may ensure outward obedience, but hardly that obedience which comes "from the heart." There is no word of abolishing the institution of slavery, but where masters and slaves are fellow-members of a Christian household their re-

---

²⁶Gk. ἐκ ψυχῆς, as in Col. 3:23. It might be pressing too much out of the phrase here to say that doing God's will ἐκ ψυχῆς is the result of having his law written on the heart, in the sense of Jer. 31:33.

²⁷J. A. Robinson, *Ephesians*, p. 211.

²⁸εἰδότες, as at the beginning of Col. 3:24 (see p. 169, n. 209).

²⁹In εἴτε δοῦλος εἴτε ἐλεύθερος W. A. Meeks discerns "an allusion to the baptismal reunification of opposites," as in Gal. 3:28; Col. 3:11 (see p. 149, n. 95); cf. 1 Cor. 7:13; 12:13 ("The Image of the Androgyne: Some Uses of a Symbol in Earliest Christianity," *History of Religions* 13 [1973-74], 205).

³⁰Cf. 2 Cor. 5:10, where good deeds and bad alike (εἴτε ἀγαθὸν εἴτε φαῦλον) receive appropriate requital at the tribunal of Christ.

³¹Cf. Rom. 2:6, where God "will render to everyone according to his works" (ἀποδώσει ἑκάστῳ κατὰ τὰ ἔργα αὐτοῦ).

³²τὰ αὐτὰ ποιεῖτε πρὸς αὐτούς.

lationship should be mutually helpful. As in Col. 4:1, Christian masters are reminded that they themselves serve a Master in heaven: their treatment of their slaves is a matter for which he will hold them responsible to him. The statement that "there is no favoritism with him" is appended to the direction to slaves in the Colossians household code (Col. 3:25).[33]

6. "BE STRONG IN THE LORD" (6:10-17)

10 *For the rest,*[34] *be strong*[35] *in the Lord and in his mighty power.*[36]

11 *Put on the panoply of God so that you may be able to stand against the wiles of the devil;*

12 *because it is not against flesh and blood that we wrestle,*[37] *but against the principalities, against the powers, against the world-rulers of this dark domain,*[38] *against the spiritual forces of evil in the heavenly realm.*[39]

[33]See p. 170, n. 215. In *Didache* 4.10 masters are called on to have the fear of God before them in their treatment of their slaves, "for he does not come to call people with partiality" (κατὰ πρόσωπον). C. L. Mitton calls the transference of this statement from its context in Colossians to the place it occupies here "a wise adjustment, for in a general letter such as Ephesians emphasis on God's impartiality is more relevant to masters than to slaves; for it is masters of high social standing, rather than slaves, who normally need more to be reminded that special favours on grounds of worldly importance are not to be looked for from God" (*The Epistle to the Ephesians*, pp. 70-71).

[34]Gk. τοῦ λοιποῦ (as in Gal. 6:17); ℵ² D F G Ψ and the majority of cursives read τὸ λοιπόν (as in Phil. 3:1; 4:8; 2 Thess. 3:1). The phrase is followed by ἀδελφοί (μου) in ℵ² A F G Ψ and the majority of cursives with the Latin and Syriac versions (possibly under the influence of Phil. 3:1). Apart from this doubtful reading, the characteristic Pauline use of the vocative ἀδελφοί is absent from both Colossians and Ephesians (contrast the singular ἀδελφέ in Philem. 7, 20). The implications of this for the authorship of Colossians and Ephesians are discussed by E. Schweizer, "Zur Frage der Echtheit des Kolosser- und des Epheserbriefes," *ZNW* 47 (1956), 287.

[35]ἐνδυναμοῦσθε (δυναμοῦσθε P⁴⁶ B 33).

[36]Lit., "in the power of his might" (ἐν τῷ κράτει τῆς ἰσχύος αὐτοῦ, as in Eph. 1:19).

[37]"Flesh and blood" is literally "blood and flesh" (αἷμα καὶ σάρξ); cf. Heb. 2:14 (for the commoner σάρξ καὶ αἷμα cf. 1 Cor. 15:50; Gal. 1:16). There is no significance in the word order; the phrase (in either form) means "human beings," "(mortal) humanity." "We wrestle" is literally "our wrestling is" (ἔστιν ἡμῖν ἡ πάλη, where P⁴⁶ B D* F G Ψ 81 *al* lat^vet syr^pesh read ὑμῖν instead of ἡμῖν).

[38]τοῦ σκότους τούτου, amplified to τοῦ σκότους τοῦ αἰῶνος τούτου in ℵ² D² Ψ and the majority of cursives.

[39]P⁴⁶ omits ἐν τοῖς ἐπουρανίοις—probably an editorial emendation arising from unwillingness to associate evil with the heavenly realm.

13 *Therefore, take up the panoply of God, so that you may be able to withstand them in the evil day and, having done everything, to stand your ground.*

14 *Stand therefore, with the girdle of truth round your waist, having put on the breastplate of righteousness*

15 *and having shod your feet with the preparation of the gospel of peace.*

16 *Take up, in addition to all these,*[40] *the shield of faith, with which you will be able to quench all the fire-tipped darts of the evil one;*

17 *and take*[41] *the helmet of salvation, and the sword of the Spirit, which is God's word.*

10 "Be strong in the Lord" might be rendered more literally "Strengthen yourselves in the Lord." This form of words has OT precedent. In a critical situation in the life of David, he is said to have "strengthened himself in the LORD his God" (1 Sam. 30:6). At a later date the God of Israel says of his people gathered home from exile, "I will make them strong in the LORD" (Zech. 10:12).[42] But the idea of divinely imparted strength finds frequent expression without the explicit addition of the phrase "in the LORD"; the exhortation to Joshua, "be strong and very courageous" (Josh. 1:7),[43] is given to many others in the OT, and is taken up in the NT. "Be watchful, stand firm in your faith, be courageous, be strong," says Paul to the Corinthians (1 Cor. 16:13),[44] and these words are echoed here.

The "mighty power" of God by which his children are to be strengthened—literally, "the power of his might"—has been mentioned already in this letter. It is "the surpassing greatness of his power in us who believe"; it is the "operation of his mighty strength" by which he raised Christ from the dead (Eph. 1:19-20); it is the power with which Paul has prayed that his readers may be strengthened by the Spirit of God in their inner being (Eph. 3:16).[45] Here they are told one way in which this power can be effective in their lives—in enabling them to resist those forces in the world that are hostile to their well-being and opposed to the gospel.

11 To resist those forces their natural strength and resolution will

[40]ἐν πᾶσιν (comitative ἐν), for which A D F G Ψ and the majority of cursives read ἐπὶ πᾶσιν.

[41]δέξασθε (*om* D* F G lat^b ^m*).

[42]In 1 Sam. 30:6 (LXX 1 Kingdoms 30:6) the Greek verb is κραταιόω (ἐκραταιώθη); in Zech. 10:12 it is κατισχύω.

[43]LXX ἴσχυε καὶ ἀνδρίζου (cf. Deut. 31:6-7, 23).

[44]γρηγορεῖτε, στήκετε ἐν τῇ πίστει, ἀνδρίζεσθε, κραταιοῦσθε.

[45]See pp. 271-73, 325-26.

not suffice. The "panoply of God," spiritual armor, is necessary. The word "panoply," which occurs several times in the Septuagint, is found once only in the NT outside our present passage—in the parable of the strong man armed in Luke 11:21-22, where one who is even stronger comes and strips him of his "panoply"—"his armor in which he trusted." It denotes a complete outfit of personal armor, for defense and for attack.[46]

"Though we live in the world," says Paul to the Corinthians, "we are not carrying on a worldly war, for the weapons of our warfare are not worldly but have divine power to destroy strongholds" (2 Cor. 10:3-4). But there it is not body armor that Paul has in mind, but siege engines, with which he intends to "demolish arguments and every lofty structure that is raised against the knowledge of God," with the aim of "taking every design prisoner and subjecting it to the obedience of Christ" (2 Cor. 10:5).

Here it is the "wiles"[47] of the devil that have to be resisted. These may be even more subtle than the "human craftiness and trickery which schemes to lead people astray" against which a warning has been sounded in Eph. 4:14. One of the devil's wiles has already been mentioned in this letter: it is his readiness to exploit strained relations and angry feelings between believers so as to damage their personal or corporate welfare and witness (Eph. 4:27). To be forewarned about the nature of his wiles is to be forearmed against them.

12 Nor do believers need to be on their guard only against the wiles of the devil. The whole climate of opinion in the Graeco-Roman world of apostolic days was inimical to the principles of the gospel. "The god of this age" who "has blinded the minds of the unbelievers, to keep them from seeing the light of the gospel of the glory of Christ" (2 Cor. 4:4), has a host of allies, principalities and powers, here described as "the world-rulers of this dark domain" (lit., "this darkness") and "the spiritual forces of evil in the heavenly realm."

The former references to principalities and powers in this letter have been neutral, nothing being said expressly about their character. In Eph. 1:21 Christ has been exalted above them; in Eph. 3:10 they are meant to learn through the church something of God's "manifold wisdom." It is

---

[46]Polybius (*History* 6.23) lists the various parts of the Roman legionary's πανοπλία, including the shield (θυρεός, *scutum*), breastplate (θώραξ, *lorica*), greaves (προκνημῖδες, *ocreae*), helmet (περικεφαλαία, *galea* or *cassis*), sword (μάχαιρα, *gladius*), and two javelins (ὑσσοί, *pila*). See A. Oepke, *TDNT* 5, pp. 295-315 (*s.v.* πανοπλία).

[47]Gk. μεθοδεία, as in Eph. 4:14 (see p. 351, n. 86). By a curious slip, P^{46} substitutes μεθοδείας for ἀρχάς immediately below, in v. 12.

404

not necessary to infer from the present reference that all principalities and powers are viewed as evil, or hostile to the cause of Christ. But those mentioned here certainly are viewed as hostile,[48] and the question arises whether they are to be identified with the principalities and powers disarmed by Christ in the vivid picture of Col. 2:15. If they are identical, how can disarmed powers still constitute a threat? The answer is that they constitute no threat to those who are united by faith to the victorious Christ and avail themselves of his resources, the resources which are here described metaphorically as "the panoply of God." But to those who neglect those resources, and especially to those who are disposed to give them some room in their lives, they continue to present a threat.

The term "world-rulers"[49] appears here only in the NT, but it is difficult to dissociate them from the "rulers of this age" who, according to 1 Cor. 2:6, 8, are on the way out because their failure to discern God's eternal wisdom led them to "crucify the Lord of glory." In the Fourth Gospel the singular form, "the ruler of this world," is found three times (John 12:31; 14:30; 16:11); this "ruler" (*archōn*) endeavors to take advantage of Christ as his passion draws near, but finds no means of doing so: on the contrary, he himself is judged and cast out. The same malign figure is mentioned as "the ruler of the domain of the air" in Eph. 2:2.[50]

The original application of the term "world-rulers" (*kosmokratores*) appears to have been to the planets,[51] but it is used also of a variety of dominant deities and later of the Roman emperor, who on the human level was indeed the "world-ruler."[52] It was taken over as a loanword in rabbinical Hebrew, with reference to the Roman emperor and other human potentates and also to spiritual powers like the angel of death.[53] In the *Testament of Solomon* (2nd or 3rd cent. A.D.) demons who come to Solomon introduce themselves as *stoicheia*,[54] "the world-rulers of this dark

---

[48]W. Carr, concluding that only here in the Pauline corpus are they hostile, argues that this verse is a mid-second-century interpolation (*Angels and Principalities* [Cambridge, 1981], pp. 104-10).

[49]Gk. κοσμοκράτορες. See W. Michaelis, *TDNT* 3, pp. 913-14 (*s.v.* κοσμοκράτωρ). Cf. the ἄρχοντες τοῦ αἰῶνος τούτου in 1 Cor. 2:6, 8.

[50]See p. 282. Cf. R. Reitzenstein, *Das iranische Erlösungsmysterium*, p. 235.

[51]Especially in astrological writers, such as Vettius Valens (171.6; 360.7, etc.).

[52]The first Roman emperor to be so designated appears to be Caracalla (A.D. 211-17); cf. *Archiv für Papyrusforschung*, ed. U. Wilcken, 2 (1903), p. 449, no. 83.

[53]Heb. *qôzmôqrātôr*, used (e.g.) of Joseph as governor of all Egypt in *Pesiqta Rabbati* 3.

[54]See p. 98, n. 40 (on Col. 2:8).

domain" (18:2)⁵⁵—but these words are probably dependent on the present text.

When they are called rulers of "this dark domain," they are associated with the "dominion of darkness" from which, according to Col. 1:13, the people of Christ have been rescued.⁵⁶ They will do their best to reclaim the people of Christ for their own dominion, but their attempts will be fruitless if the people of Christ resist them with the spiritual resources which are now placed at their disposal. Only spiritual resources can prevail against them, for they themselves are "spiritual forces," and forces of evil at that.⁵⁷ The heavenly realm⁵⁸ in which they are located has been mentioned already as the realm in which "principalities and powers" learn lessons in divine wisdom (Eph. 3:10); it is also the realm in which Christ sits enthroned at God's right hand, high above every principality and power (Eph. 1:20-21) and in which his people have been made to sit along with him (Eph. 2:6). The heavenly realm may be envisaged as comprising a succession of levels, with the throne of God on the highest of these and the hostile forces occupying the lowest.⁵⁹ The level which they occupy is probably identical with "the domain of the air," ruled (according to Eph. 2:2) by "the spirit which now operates in the disobedient."⁶⁰ At any rate, these are real forces of evil which are encountered in the spiritual sphere, and they have to be withstood. The spirit of the age—any age—is rarely found in alliance with the Spirit of Christ.

13 The panoply of God, then, is available for his children to take up and use. The "evil day" (like the "evil age" of Gal. 1:4) is the period that is dominated by the forces of evil,⁶¹ with special emphasis, perhaps, on those occasions when the hostility of evil is experienced in exceptional power, and the temptation to yield is strong. It is then that the panoply of divine grace and strength is indispensable, enabling the believer to resist the pressure and stand firm. A Roman centurion, according to Polybius, had to be the kind of man who could be relied upon, when hard-pressed, to stand fast and not give way;⁶² and the same quality is necessary in the

---

⁵⁵οἱ κοσμοκράτορες τοῦ σκότους τοῦ αἰῶνος τούτου, following the fuller reading of Eph. 6:12 (see p. 402, n. 38). In *Test. Sol.* 8:2 seven demons (as opposed to the thirty-six of 18:2) quote more concisely: ἡμεῖς ἐσμεν στοιχεῖα, κοσμοκράτορες τοῦ σκότους.
⁵⁶ἡ ἐξουσία τοῦ σκότους (see p. 51 with nn. 54-56). Cf. Eph. 5:8.
⁵⁷Gk. τὰ πνευματικὰ τῆς πονηρίας.
⁵⁸See pp. 253-54 with nn. 25-27.
⁵⁹See p. 25 with nn. 103-06.
⁶⁰See H. Traub, *TDNT* 5, p. 540, n. 14 (*s.v.* ἐπουράνιος).
⁶¹See G. Harder, *TDNT* 6, pp. 554, 566 (*s.v.* πονηρός, πονηρία).
⁶²Polybius, *History* 6.24.

spiritual warfare. "Having done everything" is explained by J. A. Robinson as "having accomplished all that your duty requires."[63] When all that has been accomplished, the one thing needful is to stand one's ground.

14 "Stand therefore," comes the command; and then the panoply of God is described in detail, each piece of armor being identified with some divine gift or virtue.

There are literary antecedents for this metaphorical use of armor. In Isa. 59:17 the God of Israel, displeased because no one has shown himself willing to stand up for justice, arms himself for the defense of the cause of truth:

> *He put on righteousness as a breastplate,*
> *and a helmet of salvation upon his head;*
> *he put on garments of vengeance for clothing,*
> *and wrapped himself in fury as a mantle.*

In partial dependence on this passage the author of the book of Wisdom describes God as acting in defense of the righteous when they are oppressed (5:17-20):

> *The Lord will take his zeal as his panoply,*
> *and will arm all creation to repel his enemies;*
> *he will put on righteousness as a breastplate,*
> *and wear impartial justice as a helmet;*
> *he will take holiness as an invincible shield,*
> *and sharpen stern wrath for a sword,*
> *and creation will join with him*
> *to fight against his frenzied foes.*

Paul uses military language from time to time to describe his own ministry.[64] A closer parallel to the present passage is found in the exhortation to "put on the breastplate of faith and love, and for a helmet the hope of salvation" (1 Thess. 5:8). But what we have here is more elaborate. Truth is to be their belt or girdle (lit., "having girt[65] your loins with truth"); this may be an echo of Isa. 11:5, where it is said of the coming "shoot from the stump of Jesse" that "righteousness shall be the girdle of his waist, and faithfulness (LXX "truth") the girdle of his loins." Here truth

[63]J. A. Robinson, *Ephesians*, p. 214.
[64]As in 1 Cor. 9:7; 2 Cor. 6:7; 10:3-4; cf. the ὅπλα φωτός of Rom. 13:12 (which might be regarded as a more summary statement of the πανοπλία of the present passage). See A. Harnack, *Militia Christi* (Tübingen, 1905).
[65]περιζωσάμενοι (cf. Isa. 11:5, ἐζωσμένος). See A. Oepke, *TDNT* 5, pp. 304-08 (*s.v.* ζώννυμι, ζώνη).

remains the girdle[66] but righteousness becomes the breastplate, as in Isa. 59:17 and Wisdom 5:18. It is truth and righteousness as ethical qualities that are meant, rather than truth of doctrine and justification by faith; though the latter are not unrelated to the ethical qualities.[67]

15 The designation of the military footwear (the *caligae*, if we use the Roman term) as "the preparation of the gospel of peace" is patently borrowed from Isa. 52:7: "How beautiful upon the mountains are the feet of him who brings good tidings, who publishes peace"—words applied by Paul, in an abridged form, to those who are sent to preach the Christian message (Rom. 10:15). Here he "means to express the readiness which belongs to the bearer of good tidings," says J. A. Robinson,[68] who points out that the Greek noun meaning "preparation" is used in the Septuagint for a stand or base.[69] Those who must at all costs stand their ground need to have a secure footing; in the spiritual conflict, this is supplied by the gospel, appropriated and proclaimed.

16 In addition to the defensive equipment actually worn on the body comes the shield, carried on the left arm and maneuvered so as to repel attacks of various kinds, including "fire-tipped darts"[70] or other flaming missiles designed to cause personal or material damage. Even when such a missile was caught by the shield and did not penetrate to the body, says Livy, it caused panic, because it was thrown when well alight and its motion through the air made it blaze more fiercely, so that the soldier was tempted to get rid of his burning shield and expose himself to the enemy's spear-thrusts.[71] But the "shield of faith" not only catches the incendiary devices but extinguishes them. The "fire-tipped darts of the evil one" are the "wiles of the devil" already mentioned; the best defense against them is faith in God. Here too a question arises: is it faith in God or faithfulness to God that is meant? In 1 Pet. 5:8-9, where the assaults of the devil are described by means of a different figure of speech (he "prowls around like a roaring lion, seeking someone to devour"), faith again is recommended as the best means of defense against him: "resist him, firm in your faith." There, as E. G. Selwyn says, "a flint-like resolution" is what is called for;[72] such a resolution is the product of an unshakable faith in God.

[66]The actual word for "girdle" (ζώνη, Lat. *cingulum*) is not here used.
[67]Cf. C. Hodge, *Ephesians*, pp. 383-84; E. K. Simpson, *Ephesians*, pp. 147-48.
[68]J. A. Robinson, *Ephesians*, p. 215.
[69]Gk. ἑτοιμασία (cf. Ezra [LXX 2 Esdr.] 2:68; 3:3; Zech. 5:11).
[70]Gk. βέλη . . . πεπυρωμένα.
[71]Livy, *History* 21:8. The flaming missile would penetrate the skin and linen covers of the shield and stick in its wooden core, setting it alight.
[72]E. G. Selwyn, *The First Epistle of St. Peter*, p. 238.

There is a figurative reference to fiery missiles in the Qumran *Hymns of Thanksgiving*, where the speaker says of the mighty men who surround him with their weapons of war:

"They have let fly arrows
 against which there is no cure,
and the flame of (their) javelins
 is like a consuming fire among trees."

But his loyalty to God's covenant protects him; his "foot remains upon level ground."[73]

17 The "helmet of salvation" is taken from Isa. 59:17, where Yahweh wears it.[74] In such a context it might well be the helmet of victory (cf. GNB: "He will wear . . . victory like a helmet"), for the God of Israel does not receive salvation; he bestows it. Here too the "helmet of salvation" recommended to the believer might be called the helmet of victory, for God's victory is his people's salvation. In 1 Thess. 5:8 "the hope of salvation" serves as a helmet, for in that letter salvation is something which believers are "destined . . . to obtain . . . through our Lord Jesus Christ"— at his *parousia*. In this letter, however, salvation is viewed as already accomplished—"it is by grace that you have been saved" (Eph. 2:5)—so "the helmet of salvation" is available for the protection of believers.

The only weapon of attack that is included in the equipment is the sword. It is the "sword of the Spirit," the sword of the breath of God. Of the expected prince of the house of David it is said in Isa. 11:4 that "he shall smite the earth with the rod of his mouth, and with the breath of his lips he shall slay the wicked." This prophecy is taken up in the vivid picture of the conquering Word of God in Rev. 19:15: "from his mouth issues a sharp sword with which to smite the nations."[75] But now the sword is used not to smite the earth or slay the wicked, but to repel the spiritual foes of the people of God. "God's word" is his utterance— "every word that proceeds from the mouth of God" (Deut. 8:3 LXX). It is through his Spirit that his word is both uttered and received on earth. Perhaps the best example of the use of his word to repel spiritual foes is seen in Jesus' employment of the text just quoted (Deut. 8:3) to repel the tempter in the wilderness.[76] The divine utterance, the product of the Spirit, lends itself

---

[73] 1QH 2.25-26, 29 (G. Vermes, *The Dead Sea Scrolls in English* [Harmondsworth, 1962], pp. 155-56).

[74] LXX περιέθετο περικεφαλαίαν σωτηρίου ἐπὶ τῆς κεφαλῆς (Heb. *kôḇaʿ yᵉšûʿāh bᵉrōʾšô*); here τὴν περικεφαλαίαν τοῦ σωτηρίου δέξασθε.

[75] But in Rev. 19:15 the sword is an eastern ῥομφαία (scimitar), not a Roman μαχαίρα, as here.

[76] Matt. 4:4 (the quotation is shorter in Luke 4:4).

409

readily to the believer who has laid it up in his heart[77] for effective use in the moment of danger against any attempt to seduce him from allegiance to Christ.

The pieces of armor listed cover most of those which might have been seen on a Roman soldier at the time. The most obvious omission would be the greaves, which were worn to protect the front of the legs.[78] When John Bunyan described the equipment which Christian received in the armory of the House Beautiful and used to good effect against Apollyon on the next stage of his journey, he drew on this passage in Ephesians, and noted that no armor was provided for the back, so that at the approach of Apollyon Christian had no option but "to venture and stand his ground."[79]

This account of the spiritual conflict and the panoply of God has inspired others to develop the theme—notably Bunyan in *The Holy War* (*The Holy War made by Shaddai upon Diabolus for the Regaining of the Metropolis of the World or the Losing and Taking Again of the Town of Mansoul*, 1682)—a work which, had the same author not written *The Pilgrim's Progress*, would have been acclaimed as the greatest allegory in the English language. Twenty to twenty-seven years before *The Holy War* was published, another Puritan, William Gurnall, minister of Lavenham, Suffolk, produced his encyclopaedic exposition of these verses (Eph. 6:10-20), *The Christian in Complete Armour* (1655-62), which in its twentieth-century reprint (London: The Banner of Truth Trust, 1964) runs to some 1200 double-column pages—an exhaustive body of practical divinity.[80]

7. "WATCH AND PRAY" (6:18-20)

18 *Pray in the Spirit at all times with all prayer and supplication, and keep awake for this very purpose with all perseverance and supplication for all the saints,*

19 *and also for me: pray that I may be given utterance as I open my mouth, to make known the mystery of the gospel[81] with liberty of speech.*

20 *It is for the sake of the gospel that I am an ambassador—an am-*

[77]Cf. Ps. 119:11; also Col. 3:16a.
[78]More particularly, the right leg. In later (imperial) times the *ocreae* were perhaps worn by centurions only.
[79]*The Pilgrim's Progress*, Part 1.
[80]For a modern (and superior) counterpart see D. M. Lloyd-Jones, *The Christian Warfare* (Edinburgh, 1976) and *The Christian Soldier* (Edinburgh, 1977), two in a series of expository volumes on Ephesians.
[81]τοῦ εὐαγγελίου *om* B F G lat[h m] M.Vict Ambst.

bassador in chains! Pray that I may enjoy liberty in this matter,[82]
and speak as I ought.

18 This paragraph is closely similar to its counterpart in Col.
4:2-5, but neither passage can be shown to be dependent on the other.
Both reflect a common situation, existing at the time and place of writing.

There is no obvious separation in the Greek text between this exhortation to prayer and the immediately preceding encouragement to resist
spiritual foes.[83] The imperative "pray" (in our rendering above) renders
the participle "praying" in the Greek.[84] This might be a further instance
of the imperatival use of the participle;[85] but, so far as the construction
goes, "praying" (with the following "keeping awake") seems to belong to
the series of participles dependent on the imperative "stand" at the beginning of v. 14 ("having girt," "having shod," "having taken up").[86]

Praying "in the Spirit" means praying under the Spirit's influence
and with his assistance. "I will pray with the spirit[87] and I will pray with
the mind also," says Paul (1 Cor. 14:15), by way of response, it appears,
to some who believed that to pray in a "tongue" unintelligible to speaker
and hearers alike was to pray "in the Spirit." It is no criterion of the power
of the Spirit that the person praying does not understand his own prayer.
On the other hand, there are prayers and aspirations of the heart that cannot
well be articulated; these can be offered in the Spirit, who, as Paul says,
"himself intercedes for us with sighs too deep for words" (Rom. 8:26).

Both in his own practice and in that of his converts and others,
Paul insists on the necessity of constant prayer—praying "at every time"
(as the literal rendering is here).[88] "Pray without ceasing," the Thessalonian Christians are exhorted (1 Thess. 5:17), while Paul himself repeatedly

---

[82] ἐν αὐτῷ, for which P^{46} B 1739 1881 read αὐτό.

[83] Hence Bunyan's Christian, beset in the valley of the shadow of death by forces
against which his other armor was useless, "was forced to put up his sword, and
betake himself to another weapon, called 'All-prayer' " (*The Pilgrim's Progress,*
Part 1).

[84] προσευχόμενοι.

[85] See p. 383, n. 78 (on Eph. 5:21, ὑποτασσόμενοι).

[86] περιζωσάμενοι . . . ἐνδυσάμενοι . . . ὑποδησάμενοι. For a similar series of
participles, concluding with a possibly imperatival participle, cf. Eph. 5:19-21
(p. 383, n. 78).

[87] Gk. προσεύξομαι τῷ πνεύματι, where πνεῦμα is ambiguous: τὸ πνεῦμά μου
in the preceding verse might suggest Paul's own spirit, but his emphasis throughout
the chapter is that such devotional exercises are effective only if performed through
the Spirit of God (cf. 1 Cor. 12:7-11).

[88] Gk. ἐν παντὶ καιρῷ, perhaps "at every opportunity."

411

assures his readers of his unremitting prayer for them (cf. Col. 1:3). Here the general word for prayer is used, together with "supplication," the word emphasizing the element of petition or entreaty in prayer.[89]

As in Col. 4:2, the importance of watchfulness, keeping spiritually alert, is stressed. A different word for keeping awake is used here[90]—the same word as appears in a similar exhortation in Luke 21:36, where Jesus, warning his disciples of the impending crisis, urges them to "keep awake at all times, praying that you may prevail . . . to stand before the Son of Man."[91] The eschatological note is not explicitly prominent in Colossians and Ephesians, but it can be discerned wherever watchfulness and perseverance[92] are enjoined.

The readers have already been commended for their love "to all the saints" (Eph. 1:15); one way of continuing to show this love is to persevere in making supplication for them.

19 With the exhortation to pray "for all the saints" comes a special request to pray for Paul in particular, in language closely akin to that in Col. 4:3-4. If the life-setting of the letter was Paul's detention in Rome, where he looked forward to his appearance before the supreme tribunal, then he might well ask for prayer as he tried to exploit every opportunity for gospel witness in his present restricted situation, and especially when the time came (as he hoped) to bear witness before Caesar himself.[93] Much might depend on what Paul said on that occasion, and on the manner in which he said it—not so much for his own safety (a matter of minor importance in his eyes) as for the progress of the gospel in the Roman world. He had made known in the eastern provinces the "mystery"[94] with which he had been entrusted on the Damascus road; the impending opportunity of making it known at the very heart of the imperial administration carried great responsibility with it, wholeheartedly as he welcomed

[89]Gk. διὰ πάσης προσευχῆς καὶ δεήσεως (for the collocation of the two nouns see Phil. 4:6).
[90]ἀγρυπνοῦντες, over against γρηγοροῦντες in Col. 4:2 (see p. 172, n. 9). For ἀγρυπνέω cf. also Heb. 13:17.
[91]Cf. Mark 13:33, βλέπετε, ἀγρυπνεῖτε.
[92]Perseverance is emphasized here in ἐν πάσῃ προσκαρτερήσει. Cf. Col. 4:2, τῇ προσευχῇ προσκαρτερεῖτε (also Rom. 12:12). See p. 172, n. 8.
[93]Paul could not be sure that the emperor would hear his appeal in person; he might appoint a deputy. See F. F. Bruce, *Paul: Apostle of the Free Spirit* (Exeter, 1977), pp. 366-67.
[94]In Col. 4:3, it is called "the mystery of Christ." Here τοῦ εὐαγγελίου (see n. 81 above) is epexegetic genitive after τὸ μυστήριον—the mystery *is* the gospel. See pp. 173, 311-15.

it. Hence he besought the prayers of his fellow-Christians, that he might say the right thing in the right way,[95] and do so without inhibitions.

20 Twice in this prayer request he expresses the desire that he may be granted liberty of speech as he makes the gospel known.[96] This liberty of speech cannot be divorced from the inward liberty of spirit which enables one to speak from the heart. His sense of liberty was the greater because he knew that what he had to make known was not his own message but the Lord's. He was but the ambassador; Christ was the sovereign on whose behalf he was to speak. He had no uncertainty about his commission: as he put it to Philemon, if he was the prisoner of Christ Jesus, he was at the same time the ambassador of Christ Jesus[97]—none the less an ambassador even if he was, as he says here, "an ambassador in chains."[98]

If it is to the hearing of his appeal that 2 Tim. 4:17 looks back, then the answer to the prayer requested here is recorded there: "the Lord stood by me and gave me strength to proclaim the message fully, so that all the Gentiles might hear it." "All the Gentiles" could not be present in court while Paul made his defense, but this is an instance of Paul's "representative universalism";[99] what was said in public at the center of the empire would reverberate as far as the distant frontiers.

IV. LETTER-CLOSING (6:21-24)

1. PERSONAL NOTES (6:21-22)

21 *So that you also may know my affairs, how I am getting on, you will learn everything from Tychicus, my dear brother and a trusty servant in the Lord.*

22 *I am sending him to you for this very purpose, that you may learn our news and that he may encourage your hearts.*

---

[95] ὡς δεῖ με λαλῆσαι, as in Col. 4:4.

[96] ἐν παρρησίᾳ γνωρίσαι . . . (v. 19), ἵνα ἐν αὐτῷ παρρησιάσωμαι (v. 20). For παρρησία cf. Eph. 3:12 (with p. 322, n. 71); Phil. 1:20 (ἐν πάσῃ παρρησίᾳ); for παρρησιάζομαι cf. 1 Thess. 2:2 (ἐπαρρησιασάμεθα . . . λαλῆσαι . . . τὸ εὐαγγέλιον τοῦ θεοῦ).

[97] See p. 212 with nn. 53-55.

[98] ὑπὲρ οὖ πρεσβεύω ἐν ἁλύσει. The antecedent to οὖ is τοῦ εὐαγγελίου (if it be retained in the text), otherwise τὸ μυστήριον. Cf. Col. 4:3, δι' ὃ καὶ δέδεμαι (the antecedent to ὃ being τὸ μυστήριον).

[99] See J. Munck, *Paul and the Salvation of Mankind*, E.T. (London, 1959), pp. 330-34.

21-22 This note about Tychicus follows Col. 4:7-8 almost word for word. The implication is that Tychicus was entrusted with this letter together with that to the church of Colossae, and would deliver it on his journey to the Lycus valley—perhaps in the Lycus valley itself. The words at the beginning of v. 21—"so that *you also* may know my affairs"—most probably mean "so that you, in addition to others who are receiving news of me, may know my affairs."[100] This would be natural if Colossians and Ephesians were written and sent at the same time.

Tychicus, who was evidently in Paul's company at the time of writing, would be able to convey further information about him by word of mouth.

If this letter is pseudonymous, then the reference to Tychicus is a literary borrowing from Col. 4:7-8, and it might be asked why a reference to Tychicus in particular was thought apposite here. An answer to this question must necessarily be speculative.[101]

2. FINAL BENEDICTION (6:23-24)

23 *Peace to the brothers,[102] and love[103] with faith, from God the Father and the Lord Jesus Christ.*
24 *Grace and immortality be with all who love our Lord Jesus Christ.[104]*

23 The grace and peace which figured in the initial greeting are repeated here in the final blessing, but in reverse order and less closely tied together. "Peace" is mentioned similarly in the letter-closing of Galatians (Gal. 6:16);[105] more fully, the presence of "the God of peace" is

---

[100]Gk. ἵνα δὲ εἰδῆτε καὶ ὑμεῖς τὰ κατ᾽ ἐμέ. Another possible meaning of καὶ ὑμεῖς would be "you for your part"—"so that you for your part may know my affairs, as I for my part have heard about you" (cf. Eph. 1:15). See J. A. Robinson, *Ephesians*, p. 217.

[101]W. L. Knox (*St. Paul and the Church of the Gentiles* [Cambridge, 1939], p. 203) discerned a hint here that Tychicus was the real author of Ephesians. C. L. Mitton (*The Epistle to the Ephesians*, p. 268) suggests that the proposal to write the letter in Paul's name was submitted to Tychicus ("still living as an old man in the neighbourhood of Ephesus") and approved by him as conveying the Pauline message. G. H. P. Thompson (*Ephesians, Colossians, Philemon*, CBC [Cambridge, 1967], pp. 18-19) suggests that Ephesians is a "manifesto" composed by Tychicus with Paul's authorization.

[102]For ἀδελφοῖς P⁴⁶ reads ἁγίοις.

[103]For ἀγάπη A reads ἔλεος.

[104]At the end of the letter ℵ² D Ψ and the majority of cursives add ἀμήν.

[105]Cf. 1 Pet. 5:14; 3 John 15.

the substance of the benedictions of Rom. 15:33 (cf. 16:20); Phil. 4:9; 1 Thess. 5:23,[106] of "the Lord of peace" in 2 Thess. 3:16, and of "the God of love and peace" in 2 Cor. 13:11.

"Love with faith" is love accompanied by faith. "Love" in a final blessing is not surprising, whether it be the love of God (as in 2 Cor. 13:14) or Paul's own love (as in 1 Cor. 16:24). But what is the force of "faith"? Most probably its present collocation with love takes up the thanksgiving of Eph. 1:15, in which the apostle expresses his pleasure at news of the readers' faith or fidelity as members of the Christian fellowship and their love shown to "all the saints."[107] At the end of the letter he prays that these qualities may continue to characterize them. Such qualities would be their response to the peace and grace bestowed by God; like all the Christian virtues, they have their source in God—"God the Father and the Lord Jesus Christ" (cf. Eph. 1:2).

24 "Grace be with you," as in Col. 4:18, is Paul's basic benediction at the end of a letter; it is generally expanded in various forms. Here it is cast in the third person (like "to the brothers" in v. 23).[108] "This," says J. A. Robinson, "is in harmony with the circular nature of this epistle"—possibly so, but its circular nature has not inhibited the use of the second person in vv. 21-22.

The present expansion bespeaks grace on "all who love our Lord Jesus Christ." This is a positive counterpart to the negative "if anyone has no love for the Lord" of 1 Cor. 16:22[109] (which perhaps takes up a word of eucharistic admonition).[110] The construction of the last two words in the Greek text of the letter—"in immortality" or "with immortality"[111]— is uncertain. Their position would suggest that they be taken as an adver-

---

[106]Cf. Heb. 13:20.

[107]See pp. 267-68 with n. 110 for the possibility that "your love toward all the saints" has found its way into the text of Eph. 1:15 under the influence of Col. 1:4.

[108]For the possibility that "the brothers" are a particular group within the wider community of "all who love our Lord Jesus Christ" see E. E. Ellis, "Paul and his Co-Workers," *NTS* 17 (1970-71), 445-51: he argues that "the brothers" are Paul's colleagues or fellow-preachers (cf. 1 Cor. 16:20; Gal. 1:2; Phil. 4:21; Col. 4:15). He suggests (p. 446, n. 3) that the added grace-benediction of v. 24 is "Paul's greeting in his own hand" (cf. p. 186 above with n. 79).

[109]εἴ τις οὐ φιλεῖ τὸν κύριον. There is no material distinction between φιλέω and ἀγαπάω in such expressions, but ἀγαπάω, not φιλέω, is Paul's word; the implication is that the if-clause of 1 Cor. 16:22 is quoted from a current form of words.

[110]See J. A. T. Robinson, "The Earliest Christian Liturgical Sequence?" in *Twelve New Testament Studies* (London, 1962), pp. 154-57.

[111]ἐν ἀφθαρσίᾳ.

bial phrase modifying the verb "love": hence RSV "all who love our Lord Jesus Christ with love undying" (similarly ASV, NAB, NIV, GNB).[112] The KJV took the Greek word *aphtharsia* in a moral sense, translating ". . . that love our Lord Jesus Christ in sincerity" (RV, with excessive literalness, "in uncorruptness"). But J. A. Robinson found it impossible to "point to any passage in the writers of the second century" in which the word was "used of moral incorruptness, though . . . common enough in the usual sense of immortality." He further considered that "the disposition of the sentence" was "fatal" to the rendering adopted above, in which the word is attached to "grace."[113] The justification for adopting this rendering lies mainly in the prevalence throughout this letter of the preposition "in" with a "comitative" sense, attaching the following word to one or more preceding words so as to complete a series.[114] Cf. NEB ("God's grace be with all who love our Lord Jesus Christ, grace and immortality"); Jerusalem Bible ("May grace and eternal life be with all who love our Lord Jesus Christ").

---

[112]Cf. Ignatius, *Rom.* 7.3, where the blood of Christ is described as ἀγάπη ἄφθαρτος, "incorruptible love."

[113]J. A. Robinson, *Ephesians*, pp. 219-20.

[114]For comitative ἐν see p. 256 with n. 35. Cf. Eph. 1:4, 8; 3:12; 4:19; 6:2, 16.

INDEX OF PRINCIPAL SUBJECTS

417

INDEX OF AUTHORS

INDEX OF SCRIPTURE REFERENCES